FUNDAMENTALS OF JAVA

AP* Computer Science Essentials for the A and AB Exams

Lambert and Osborne

THOMSON
COURSE TECHNOLOGY

Australia • Canada • Mexico • Singapore • Spain • United Kingdom • United States

THOMSON
™
COURSE TECHNOLOGY

**Fundamentals of Java: AP* Computer Science Essentials
for the A and AB Exams, Third Edition**

by Kenneth Lambert, Martin Osborne

Sr. Acquistions Editor:
Jane Mazares

Sr. Marketing Manager:
Kim Ryttel

Product Managers:
David Rivera
Jodi Anderson

Developmental Editors
Rose Marie Kuebbing,
Rita Rebholz
Custom Editorial Productions, Inc.

Editorial Assistant:
Jeannine Lawless

Associate Production Manager:
Jennifer Goguen

Production Editor
GEX Publishing Services

Sr. Manufacturing Coordinator:
Justin Palmeiro

**Manuscript Quality
Assurance Lead:**
Burt LaFountain

Cover Design:
Deborah Van Rooyen

Cover Image:
Paul Vismara

Compositor
GEX Publishing Services

Printer:
TransContinental Interglobe
Printing

Thomson Course Technology is proud to release *AP* Computer Science Review Companion for Fundamentals of Java*

Our new Java textbooks wouldn't be complete without a proper review companion. We know that studying isn't easy. This review companion can make studying for programming a snap.

Chapter Summary and Outline—helpful synopsis reviews the order of the chapter and highlights.

Vocabulary—a list of key terms and their definitions are conveniently listed in each appropriate lesson for quick review.

Relevance to the AP* Exam—more than a mapping of each key requirement for the A and AB exams, this section makes concrete connections between key requirements and the textbook's tables, figures, and specific paragraphs.

CHAPTER 3   SYNTAX, ERRORS, AND DEBUGGING

CHAPTER SUMMARY

Programming languages, like natural languages such as English, have vocabulary, syntax, and semantics. In order to write Java programs, you must be familiar with the rules of the language. The rules for a programming language are generally more strict and rigid than the rules for a natural language, but the vocabulary is much smaller. This chapter discusses the syntax and semantics of several Java language elements, including the following:

- **Data Types:** There are two categories of data types – primitive and reference. Primitive data types include numeric data types, boolean data types, and character data types. Reference types are defined by classes. Every class is a distinct data type.
- **Literals:** Values that do not change in a program.

OUTLINE

3.1 Language Elements
3.2 Basic Java Syntax and Semantics
3.3 Terminal I/O for Different Data Types
3.4 Comments
      Case Study 1: Income Tax Calculator

VOCABULARY

Arithmetic expression: A statement involving numerical operands and arithmetic operators that evaluates to a specific numerical result.
Comments: Explanatory sentences inserted into a program in such a manner that the compiler ignores them. Single line comments begin with the characters `//`. Multi-line comments are contained within the characters `/*` and `*/`.

RELEVANCE TO AP EXAM – COMPUTER SCIENCE A AND AB

The following sections describe the relevance of the contents of this chapter to specific goals of the Computer Science AP Exam. Unless otherwise noted, the AP goals listed apply to both the Computer Science A and the Computer Science AB exams.

AP Goal: Object-Oriented Program Design > Program Design > Read and understand a problem description, purpose, and goals: The two cases studied in this chapter illustrate the processes involved in analyzing and designing a program based on a problem description. In case study 2, a thorough analysis of a complicated problem is examined. This case study illustrates the types of questions that must be posed when attempting to understand the problem.

AP Goal: Object-Oriented Program Design > Class Design > Choose appropriate data representation and algorithms: Section 3.2 introduces most of the primitive data types. When analyzing, designing, and implementing a program you must be aware of the constraints placed on various data types and when each data type should be used. For instance, it is inappropriate for a variable that stores a monetary amount to be typed as an `int`.

Exercises—gives students an opportunity to reinforce programming concepts by answering *Fill In the Blank, True and False, Multiple Choice,* and *Written Questions*.

FILL IN THE BLANK

Complete the following sentences by writing the correct word or words in the blanks provided.

1. The Java programming language has a total of _____ numeric data types.

2. An item in a program whose value can change during program execution is called a(n) _____.

TRUE/FALSE

Circle T if the statement is true or F if the statement is false.

T F 1. Java's syntax consists of the rules for combining words and symbols into a program statement.

T F 2. When defining a variable in Java, you must always declare the variable's data type.

MULTIPLE CHOICE

Select the best response for the following statements.

1. What is the maximum positive value that can be stored in a Java variable of type `int`?
   a. 32,755
   b. 1,073,741,824
   c. 2,147,483,647
   d. 4,294,967,294

2. Which of the following statements shows the correct syntax for declaring a variable named alpha, of data type double?
   a. `alpha = double;`
   b. `alpha(double);`
   c. `double(alpha);`
   d. `double alpha;`

WRITTEN QUESTIONS

Write a brief answer to each of the following questions.

1. What are the two categories of data types in the Java programming language? Give an example of a data type in each of the two categories.

Case Projects—gives students an opportunity to reinforce programming concepts through hands-on activities. These activities also encourage critical thinking once a student completes the hands-on activity.

CASE PROJECT

Now you will gain some experience writing and using methods. Assume that the requirements for the problem now state that there will be three types of debt to process. **For each debt amount, only the minimum payment will be made**. The final balance, interest paid, and principle paid will be displayed for each debt amount. In addition, once all of the payments have been calculated, the program should display how much of the disposable income was left over. You will be writing a `main` method and one additional method – `processDebt`. The `processDebt` method should take the disposable income as a parameter, gather the information for a single debt amount, calculate the amount to be applied to the debt, and return the disposable income minus the amount applied to the debt. Use the following program shell to get you started. The comments indicate the tasks that you must complete. All variables declarations are provided. Copy this "shell" into your text editor, save it as a *.java* file, and fill in the appropriate program statements to yield the correct program behavior.

So make studying programming a snap!

AP* Computer Essentials Review Companion for Fundamentals of Java by Adelman and Nagin, 1-4239-0381-1 Softcover, reviews all requirements for the AP* Computer Science for the A & AB Exams

PREFACE

This text is intended for a complete course in programming and problem solving. The book covers the material of typical Computer Science 1 and Computer Science 2 courses at the undergraduate level, but it is intended for the high school audience. The book is Advanced Placement (AP)-compliant for the A and AB levels, covering all of the required subset of Java™ for both levels. The AP A-level material is covered in the first 12 chapters of the book. The AB-only material is covered in Chapters 13 through 19.

We present six major aspects of computing, some in stand-alone chapters and others spread across several chapters:

1. **Programming Basics.** This deals with the basic ideas of problem solving with computers, including primitive data types, control structures, methods, algorithm development, and complexity analysis.

2. **Object-Oriented Programming.** OOP is today's dominant programming paradigm. All the essentials of this subject are covered.

3. **Data and Information Processing.** Fundamental data structures are discussed. These include strings, arrays, files, lists, stacks, queues, trees, sets, and maps. The general concept of abstract data types is introduced, and the difference between abstraction and implementation is illustrated. Complexity analysis is used to evaluate space/time tradeoffs of different implementations of ADTs.

4. **Software Development Life Cycle.** Rather than isolate software development techniques in one or two chapters, the book deals with them throughout in the context of numerous case studies.

5. **Graphical User Interfaces and Event-Driven Programming.** Many books at this level restrict themselves to character-based terminal I/O. The reason is simple. Graphical user interfaces and event-driven programming usually are considered too complex for beginning students. In this book, we circumvent the complexity barrier and show how to develop programs with graphical user interfaces with almost the same ease as their terminal-based counterparts.

6. **Web Basics.** The programming of Web pages with HTML and applets is introduced.

Focus on Fundamental Computer Science Topics

There seem to be two types of introductory Java textbooks. The first emphasizes basic problem solving and programming techniques, and the second emphasizes language features. This book takes the former approach and introduces Java features as they are needed to support programming concepts. In this way, all the AP-required syntax is covered without allowing the book to be syntax driven. Some additional and more advanced Java features, not part of the AP requirement, are covered in end-of-chapter sections and in the appendices.

Methods and Objects, Early or Late?

Occasionally, people argue about whether methods and objects should be introduced early or late in the first course. In Java, even the simplest program involves both, so the problem really becomes one of how to introduce these concepts in a clear and meaningful manner from the outset. Starting with the first program, we show how to instantiate and send messages to objects. The book's early chapters (2 through 4) focus on the use of objects, arithmetic expressions, control constructs, and algorithms in the context of short, simple programs. As programs become more complex, it becomes advantageous to decompose them into cooperating components. With this end in mind, Chapter 5 shows how to develop systems of cooperating classes and methods. Thus, we take a pragmatic rather than an ideological approach to the question of when to introduce methods and objects with complete confidence that students will master both by the end of the course.

Revisiting Control Structures, Classes, and Arrays

Years of teaching experience have demonstrated that beginning programming students have the most difficulty with control structures, classes, and arrays. In this text, we have sought to soften the blow by introducing these ideas in two steps. First, a chapter gives an initial overview of a topic using the most basic features in simple but realistic applications. A follow-up chapter then revisits the topic to fill in and refine the details.

Two Approaches to Data Structures

There are two approaches usually taken to data structures, that of the client who uses them and that of the implementer who writes their code. Courses that emphasize the first approach tend to be application oriented. Modern languages such as Java tend to support this approach well by providing a large set of classes for such data structures as lists and sets. However, some data structures, for example, heaps and binary search trees, are not provided, so instructors must provide add-ons or require students to implement them.

Courses that emphasize data structure implementation tend to use it as a vehicle for discussing space/time complexity tradeoffs and as an entry point for examining broad concepts such as memory management and algorithm design. Unfortunately, students who are expected to implement a list interface with arrays, linked structures, and iterators are likely to get bogged down in hundreds of lines of code and never see an application.

This text straddles both of these approaches to data structures. We provide introductory chapters on the interfaces and applications of each data structure and then follow-up chapters on implementations. Moreover, each implementation is presented as a prototype or trimmed-down version that allows students to explore its essential features and the space/time trade-offs without getting bogged down in details.

New in This Edition

The Advanced Placement test now requires an understanding of certain new features available in Java 5.0. From the AP perspective, the most important new feature in Java 5.0 is the generic collection. A generic collection requires the programmer to specify the collection's element type. AP A level students must know how to use the generic array list collection. They must also know how to use an enhanced `for` loop with arrays and array lists. The material on arrays, array lists and `for` loops has been updated to reflect these changes in requirements.

The AP AB level students must also know how to use the generic versions of lists, sets, maps, stacks, queues, priority queues, and iterators. The material in Chapters 13 through 19, which covers the AP AB requirements, has been thoroughly revised to adhere to the new standard. We also show how to define new classes that implement generic collections, such as stacks, queues, binary search trees, and heaps.

As in previous years, the AP test requires an understanding of simple standard terminal output but no input. A realistic first course will need some form of input, if only from the keyboard. Java 5.0 includes a delightful new Scanner class for input from the keyboard and from text files. Also included are methods for formatting data for output. The new edition of the book now uses these new features instead of an open source toolkit for text I/O.

In response to the suggestions of some instructors, we have moved the material on graphics and GUIs, which is not required for the AP test, to end-of-chapter sections. The introduction of this extra material is gradual enough that we have been able to dispense with the use of an open source toolkit and rely on the standard Java toolkits in the new edition. Instructors are now free to view graphics and GUIs as extra material to challenge students, and will not have to install or teach non-standard toolkits to accomplish this.

However, one non-standard toolkit, a `TurtleGraphics` package, has proven to be so popular with instructors and students that we have retained it in a late chapter to illustrate some advanced concepts. As usual, this toolkit is available on the instructor resource CD and from the Web site *http://www.wlu.edu/~lambertk/hsjava/*. The Web site is the preferred source because it contains the latest release of `TurtleGraphics` together with online documentation and other related materials. An online tutorial that introduces the use of `TurtleGraphics` is also available from the Web site.

Because of these changes, there is now no need to retain the extra unit of chapters on material such as graphics, file processing, the Web, and GUIs from the previous edition. The chapter on the Web and applets has been move up so it can be examined earlier in the course; the material on file processing has been moved to an appendix.

Case Studies, the Software Life Cycle, and Comments

The book contains numerous case studies. These are complete Java programs ranging from the simple to the substantial. To emphasize the importance and usefulness of the software development life cycle, case studies are presented in the framework of a user request followed by analysis, design, and implementation, with well-defined tasks performed at each stage. Some case studies are carried through several chapters or extended in end-of-chapter programming projects.

Programming consists of more than just writing code, so we encourage students to submit an analysis and design as part of major programming assignments. We also believe that code should be properly commented, and for purposes of illustration, we include comments in selected examples of the code in the book.

Exercises

The book contains several different types of exercises. Most sections end with exercise questions that reinforce the reading by asking basic questions about the material in the section. Each chapter ends with a set of review exercises. All chapters except the first one include programming projects of varying degrees of difficulty. Finally, each chapter has a critical thinking activity that allows the student to reflect on a major topic covered in the chapter.

Special Features

Scattered throughout the book are short essays called Notes of Interest. These present historical and social aspects of computing, including computer ethics and security.

We Appreciate Your Feedback

We have greatly appreciated all of the helpful suggestions and comments from the many instructors who have used the previous edition of this book. As always, we have tried to produce a high-quality text, but should you encounter any errors, please report them to *klambert@wlu.edu*. A listing of errata, should they exist, and other information about the book will be posted on the Web site *http://www.wlu.edu/~lambertk/hsjava/*.

Acknowledgments

We would like to thank several people whose work made this book possible:

Rose Marie Kuebbing
Developmental Editor
Custom Editorial Productions Inc.

Rita Rebholz
Developmental Editor
Custom Editorial Productions Inc.

Kelly Murphy
Production Editor
GEX Publishing Services

Jane Mazares
Senior Acquisitions Editor
Thomson Course Technology

David Rivera and Jodi Anderson
Product Managers
Thomson Course Technology

Kim Ryttel
Senior Marketing Manager
Thomson Course Technology

Jennifer Goguen
Associate Product Manager
Thomson Course Technology

Burt LaFountain
Manuscript Quality Assurance Lead
Thomson Course Technology

Justin Palmeiro
Senior Manufacturing Coordinator
Thomson Course Technology

Deborah Van Rooyen
Design Director
Thomson Course Technology

In addition, several individuals contributed material to the Instructor Resource Kit:

Jeannine Lawless
Editorial Assistant
Thomson Course Technology

Jan Clavey
Assistant Product Manager
Custom Editorial Production, Inc.

Dedication

To Carolyn and Smokey

Kenneth A. Lambert
Lexington, Virginia

Martin Osborne
Bellingham, Washington

TABLE OF CONTENTS

UNIT 2 THE NEXT STEP WITH JAVA

UNIT 3 ARRAYS, RECURSION, AND COMPLEXITY

UNIT 4 USING ABSTRACT DATA TYPES

UNIT 5   IMPLEMENTING ABSTRACT DATA TYPES

GETTING STARTED WITH JAVA

Unit 1

Estimated Time for Unit: 13 hours

BACKGROUND

This is the only chapter in the book that is not about the details of writing Java programs. This chapter discusses computing in general, hardware and software, the representation of information in binary (i.e., as 0s and 1s), and general concepts of object-oriented programming. All this material will give you a broad understanding of computing and a foundation for your study of programming.

1.1 History of Computers

ENIAC, or Electronic Numerical Integrator and Computer, built in the late 1940s, was one of the world's first digital electronic computers. It was a large standalone machine that filled a room and used more electricity than all the houses on an average city block. ENIAC contained hundreds of miles of wire and thousands of heat-producing vacuum tubes. The mean time between failures was less than an hour, yet because of its fantastic speed when compared to hand-operated electromechanical calculators, it was immensely useful.

In the early 1950s, IBM sold its first business computer. At the time, it was estimated that the world would never need more than 10 such machines. By comparison, however, its awesome computational power was a mere 1/2000 of the typical 2-gigahertz Pentium personal computer purchased for about $1000 in 2006. Today, there are hundreds of millions of computers in the world, most of which are PCs. There are also billions of computers embedded in everyday products such as handheld calculators, microwave ovens, cell phones, cars, refrigerators, and clothing.

The first computers could perform only a single task at a time, and input and output were handled by such primitive means as punch cards and paper tape.

In the 1960s, time-sharing computers, costing hundreds of thousands and even millions of dollars, became popular at organizations large enough to afford them. These computers were powerful enough for 30 people to work on them simultaneously—and each felt as if he or she were the sole user. Each person sat at a teletype connected by wire to the computer. By making a connection through the telephone system, teletypes could even be placed at a great distance from the computer. The teletype was a primitive device by today's standards. It looked like an electric typewriter with a large roll of paper attached. Keystrokes entered at the keyboard were transmitted to the computer, which then echoed them back on the roll of paper. In addition, output from the computer's programs was printed on this roll.

In the 1970s, people began to see the advantage of connecting computers in networks, and the wonders of e-mail and file transfers were born.

In the 1980s, PCs appeared in great numbers, and soon after, local area networks of interconnected PCs became popular. These networks allowed a local group of PCs to communicate and share such resources as disk drives and printers with each other and with large centralized multiuser computers.

The 1990s saw an explosion in computer use. Hundreds of millions of computers appeared on many desktops and in many homes. Most of them are connected through the Internet (Figure 1-1).

FIGURE 1-1
An interconnected world of computers

During the first decade of the 21st century, computing has become *ubiquitous* (meaning anywhere and everywhere). Tiny computer chips play the role of brains in cell phones, digital cameras, portable music players, and PDAs (portable digital assistants). Many of these devices now connect to the Internet via wireless technology, giving users unprecedented mobility.

And the common language of many of these computers is Java.

1.2 Computer Hardware and Software

Computers can be viewed as machines that process information. They consist of two primary components: hardware and software. *Hardware* consists of the physical devices that you see on your desktop, and *software* consists of the programs that give the hardware useful functionality. The main business of this book, which is programming, concerns software. But before diving into programming, let us take a moment to consider some of the major hardware and software components of a typical PC.

Bits and Bytes

It is difficult to discuss computers without referring to bits and bytes. A *bit*, or *binary digit*, is the smallest unit of information processed by a computer and consists of a single 0 or 1. A *byte* consists of eight adjacent bits. The capacity of computer memory and storage devices is usually expressed in bytes. Some commonly used quantities of bytes are shown in Table 1-1.

TABLE 1-1
Some commonly used quantities of information storage

UNIT OF BYTES	NUMBER OF BYTES	TYPE OF STORAGE
Kilobyte	1000 bytes	A single file
Megabyte	1 million bytes	Large files, RAM, flash memory, CDs
Gigabyte	1 billion bytes	RAM, hard disk drives, DVDs
Terabyte	1000 gigabytes	File server disks

Computer Hardware

As illustrated in Figure 1-2, a PC consists of six major subsystems.

FIGURE 1-2
A PC's six major subsystems

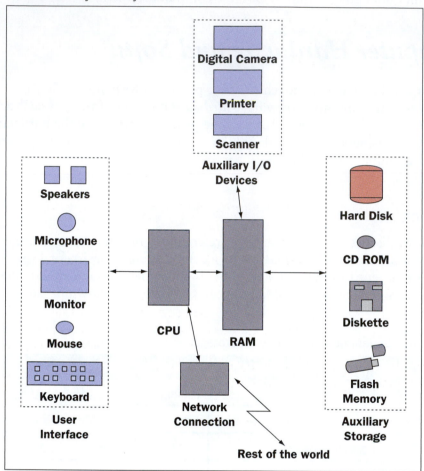

Listed in order from outside and most visible to inside and most hidden, the six major subsystems are as follows:

- The user interface, which supports moment-to-moment communication between a user and the computer

- Auxiliary input/output (I/O) devices such as printers and scanners

- Auxiliary storage devices for long-term storage of data and programs

- A network connection for connecting to the Internet and thus the rest of the world

- Internal memory, or RAM, for momentary storage of data and programs

- The all important CPU, or central processing unit

Now we explore each of these subsystems in greater detail.

User Interface

The user interface consists of several devices familiar to everyone who has used a PC. In this book, we assume that our readers have already acquired basic computer literacy and have performed common tasks such as using a word processor or surfing the Internet. The keyboard and mouse are a computer's most frequently used input devices, and the monitor or screen is the principal output device. Also useful, and almost as common, are a microphone for input and speakers for output.

Auxiliary I/O Devices

Computers have not yet produced a paper-free world, so we frequently rely on the output from printers. Scanners are most commonly used to enter images, but in conjunction with appropriate software they can also be used to enter text. Digital cameras can record static images and video for transfer to a computer. Numerous other I/O devices are available for special applications, such as joysticks for games.

Auxiliary Storage Devices

The computer's operating system, the applications we buy, and the documents we write are all stored on devices collectively referred to as auxiliary storage or *secondary memory*. The current capacity of these devices is incredibly large and continues to increase rapidly. In 2006, as these words are being written, *hard disks* typically store tens of billions of bytes of information, or gigabytes (GB) as they are commonly called. In addition to hard disks, which are permanently encased within computers, there are several *portable storage media*. Most computer software is now purchased on *CD-ROMs*. CD stands for compact disk and ROM stands for read-only memory. The term *ROM* is becoming somewhat misleading in this context as PCs are increasingly being equipped with CD devices that can read and write. Most CDs have a capacity of about 700 million bytes (megabytes or MB), enough for a little over an hour of music or a small PC software package. Currently, CDs are being supplanted by *DVDs*, which have about 10 times a CD's capacity. *Flash memory* sticks with a capacity of 100MB to 2GB are the most convenient portable storage devices. They support input and output and are used primarily for transporting data between computers that are not interconnected and for making backup copies of crucial computer files.

Network Connection

A network connection is now an essential part of every PC, connecting it to all the resources of the Internet. For home computer users, a modem has long been the most widely used connection device. *Modem* stands for modulator–demodulator and refers to the fact that the device converts the digital information (0s and 1s) of the computer to an analog form suitable for transmission on phone lines and vice versa. Of course, as phone technology becomes increasingly digital, the term *modem* is fast becoming a misnomer. Other devices for connecting to the Internet include cable modems, which use a TV cable or a satellite dish rather than a phone connection; Ethernet cards, which attach directly to local area networks and from there to the Internet; and wireless cards, which transmit digital information through the air and many other objects.

Internal Memory

Although auxiliary storage devices have great capacity, access to their information is relatively slow in comparison to the speed of a computer's central processing unit. For this reason, computers include high-speed internal memory, also called *random access memory (RAM)* or *primary memory*. The contents of RAM are lost every time the computer is turned off, but when the computer is running, RAM is loaded from auxiliary storage with needed programs and data.

Because a byte of RAM costs about 100 times as much as a byte of hard disk storage, PCs usually contain only about 512MB to 1GB of RAM. Consequently, RAM is often unable to simultaneously hold all the programs and data a person might be using during a computer session. To deal with this situation, the computer swaps programs and data backward and forward between RAM and the hard disk as necessary. Swapping takes time and slows down the apparent speed of the computer from the user's perspective. Often the cheapest way to improve a computer's performance is to install more RAM.

Another smaller piece of internal memory is called *ROM*—short for *read-only memory*. This memory is usually reserved for critical system programs that are used when the computer starts up and that are retained when the computer is shut down.

Finally, most computers have 64MB or 128MB of specialized *video RAM* for storing images for graphics and video applications.

Central Processing Unit

The *central processing unit (CPU)* does the work of the computer. Given the amazing range of complex tasks performed by computers, one might imagine that the CPU is intrinsically very complex, but such is not the case. In fact, the basic functions performed by the CPU consist of the everyday arithmetic operations of addition, subtraction, multiplication, and division together with some comparison and I/O operations. The complexity lies in the programs that direct the CPU's operations rather than in the CPU itself, and it is the programmer's job to determine how to translate a complex task into an enormous series of simple operations, which the computer then executes at blinding speed. One of the authors of this book uses a computer that operates at 1 billion cycles per second (1 GHz), and during each cycle, the CPU executes all or part of a basic operation.

Perhaps we have gone too far in downplaying the complexity of the CPU. To be fair, it too is highly complex—not in terms of the basic operations it performs, but rather in terms of how it achieves its incredible speed. This speed is achieved by packing several million transistors onto a silicon chip roughly the size of a postage stamp. Since 1955, when transistors were first used in computers, hardware engineers have been doubling the speed of computers about every 18 months, principally by increasing the number of transistors on computer chips. This phenomenon is commonly known as *Moore's Law*. However, basic laws of physics guarantee that the process of miniaturization that allows ever greater numbers of transistors to be packed onto a single chip will soon end. How soon this will be, no one knows.

The *transistor*, the basic building block of the CPU and RAM, is a simple device that can be in one of two states—ON, conducting electricity, or OFF, not conducting electricity. All the information in a computer—programs and data—is expressed in terms of these ONs and OFFs, or 1s and 0s, as they are more conveniently called. From this perspective, RAM is merely a large array of 1s and 0s, and the CPU is merely a device for transforming patterns of 1s and 0s into other patterns of 1s and 0s.

To complete our discussion of the CPU, we describe a typical sequence of events that occurs when a program is executed, or run:

1. The program and data are loaded from disk into separate regions of RAM.

2. The CPU copies the program's first instruction from RAM into a decoding unit.

3. The CPU decodes the instruction and sends it to the Arithmetic and Logic Unit (ALU) for execution; for instance, it may add a number at one location in RAM to one at another location and store the result at a third location.

4. The CPU determines the location of the next instruction and repeats the process of copy, decode, and execute until the end of the program is reached.

5. After the program has finished executing, the data portion of RAM contains the results of the computation performed by the program.

Needless to say, this description has been greatly simplified. We have, for instance, ignored the use of separate processors for graphics and all issues related to input and output; however, the description provides a view of the computational process that will help you understand what follows.

Computer Software

Computer hardware processes complex patterns of electronic states or 0s and 1s. Computer software transforms these patterns, allowing them to be viewed as text, images, and so forth. Software is generally divided into two broad categories—*system software* and *application software*.

System Software

System software supports the basic operations of a computer and allows human users to transfer information to and from the computer. This software includes

- The operating system, especially the file system for transferring information to and from disk and schedulers for running multiple programs concurrently

- Communications software for connecting to other computers and the Internet

- Compilers for translating user programs into executable form

- The user interface subsystem, which manages the look and feel of the computer, including the operation of the keyboard, the mouse, and a screen full of overlapping windows

Application Software

Application software allows human users to accomplish specialized tasks. Examples of types of application software include

- Word processors

- Spreadsheets

- Database systems

- Multimedia software for digital music, photography, and video

- Other programs we write

*E*XERCISE 1.2

1. What is the difference between a bit and a byte?

2. Name two input devices and two output devices.

3. What is the purpose of auxiliary storage devices?

4. What is RAM and how is it used?

5. Discuss the differences between hardware and software.

1.3 Binary Representation of Information and Computer Memory

As we saw in the previous section, computer memory stores patterns of electronic signals, which the CPU manipulates and transforms into other patterns. These patterns in turn can be viewed as strings of binary digits or bits. Programs and data are both stored in memory, and there is no discernible difference between program instructions and data; they are both just sequences of 0s and 1s. To determine what a sequence of bits represents, we must know the context. We now examine how different types of information are represented in binary notation.

Integers

We normally represent numbers in decimal (base 10) notation, whereas the computer uses binary (base 2) notation. Our addiction to base 10 is a physiological accident (10 fingers rather than 8, 12, or some other number). The computer's dependence on base 2 is due to the on/off nature of electric current.

To understand base 2, we begin by taking a closer look at the more familiar base 10. What do we really mean when we write a number such as 5403? We are saying that the number consists of 5 thousands, 4 hundreds, 0 tens, and 3 ones, or expressed differently:

$$(5 * 10^3) + (4 * 10^2) + (0 * 10^1) + (3 * 10^0)$$

In this expression, each term consists of a power of 10 times a coefficient between 0 and 9. In a similar manner, we can write expressions involving powers of 2 and coefficients between 0 and 1. For instance, let us analyze the meaning of 10011_2, where the subscript 2 indicates that we are using a base of 2:

$$
\begin{aligned}
10011_2 &= (1 * 2^4) + (0 * 2^3) + (0 * 2^2) + (1 * 2^1) + (1 * 2^0) \\
&= 16 + 0 + 0 + 2 + 1 = 19 \\
&= (1 * 10^1) + (9 * 10^0)
\end{aligned}
$$

The inclusion of the base as a subscript at the end of a number helps us avoid possible confusion. Here are four numbers that contain the same digits but have different bases and thus different values:

$$1101101_{16}$$
$$1101101_{10}$$
$$1101101_{8}$$
$$1101101_{2}$$

Computer scientists use bases 2 (*binary*), 8 (*octal*), and 16 (*hexadecimal*) extensively. Base 16 presents the dilemma of how to represent digits beyond 9. The accepted convention is to use the letters A through F, corresponding to 10 through 15. For example:

$$
\begin{aligned}
3BC4_{16} &= (3 * 16^3) + (11 * 16^2) + (12 * 16^1) + (4 * 16^0) \\
&= (3 * 4096) + (11 * 256) + (12 * 16) + 4 \\
&= 15300_{10}
\end{aligned}
$$

As you can see from these examples, the next time you are negotiating your salary with an employer, you might allow the employer to choose the digits as long as she allows you to pick the base. Table 1-2 shows some base 10 numbers and their equivalents in base 2. An important fact of the base 2 system is that 2^N distinct values can be represented using N bits. For example, four bits represent 2^4 or 16 values 0000, 0001, 0010, ..., 1110, 1111. A more extended discussion of number systems appears in Appendix E of this book.

TABLE 1-2
Some base 10 numbers and their base 2 equivalents

BASE 10	BASE 2
0	0
1	1
2	10
3	11
4	100
5	101
6	110
7	111
43	101011

Floating-Point Numbers

Numbers with a fractional part, such as 354.98, are called *floating-point numbers*. They are a bit trickier to represent in binary than integers. One way is to use the *mantissa/exponent notation* in which the number is rewritten as a value between 0 and 1, inclusive ($0 \le x < 1$), times a power of 10. For example:

$$354.98_{10} = 0.35498_{10} * 10^3$$

where the mantissa is 35498, and the exponent is 3, or the number of places the decimal has moved. Similarly, in base 2

$$10001.001_2 = 0.10001001_2 * 2^5$$

with a mantissa of 10001001 and exponent of $5_{10} = 101_2$. In this way we can represent any floating-point number by two separate sequences of bits, with one sequence for the mantissa and the other for the exponent.

Many computers follow the slightly different IEEE standard in which the mantissa contains one digit before the decimal or binary point. In binary, the mantissa's leading 1 is then suppressed. Originally, this was a 7-bit code, but it has been extended in various ways to 8 bits.

Characters and Strings

To process text, computers must represent characters such as letters, digits, and other symbols on a keyboard. There are many encoding schemes for characters. One popular scheme is called *ASCII* (*American Standard Code for Information Interchange*). In this scheme, each character is represented as a pattern of 8 bits or a byte.

In binary notation, byte values can range from 0000 0000 to 1111 1111, allowing for 256 possibilities. These are more than enough for the characters

- A...Z

- a...z

- 0...9

- +, -, *, /, etc.

- And various unprintable characters such as carriage return, line feed, a ringing bell, and command characters

Table 1-3 shows some characters and their corresponding ASCII bit patterns.

TABLE 1-3
Some characters and their corresponding ASCII bit patterns

CHARACTER	BIT PATTERN	CHARACTER	BIT PATTERN	CHARACTER	BIT PATTERN
A	0100 0001	a	0110 0001	0	0011 0000
B	0100 0010	b	0110 0010	1	0011 0001
. . .	. . .	. . .	. . .	. . .	. .
Z	0101 1010	z	0111 1010	9	0011 1001

Java, however, uses a scheme called *Unicode* rather than ASCII. In this scheme, each character is represented by a pattern of 16 bits, ranging from 0000 0000 0000 0000 to 1111 1111 1111 1111. Unicode allows for 65,536 possibilities and can represent many alphabets simultaneously. Within Unicode, the patterns 0000 0000 0000 0000 to 0000 0000 1111 1111 duplicate the ASCII encoding scheme.

Strings are another type of data used in text processing. Strings are sequences of characters, such as "The cat sat on the mat." The computer encodes each character in ASCII or Unicode and strings them together.

Sound

The information contained in sound is *analog*. Unlike integers and text, which on a computer have a finite range of discrete values, analog information has a continuous range of infinitely many values. The analog information in sound can be plotted as a periodic waveform such as the one shown in Figure 1-3. The amplitude or height of a waveform measures the volume of the sound. The time that a waveform takes to make one complete cycle is called its period. The frequency or number of cycles per second of a sound's waveform measures its pitch. Thus, the higher a wave is, the louder the sound's volume, and the closer together the cycles are, the higher the sound's pitch.

FIGURE 1-3
A sound waveform

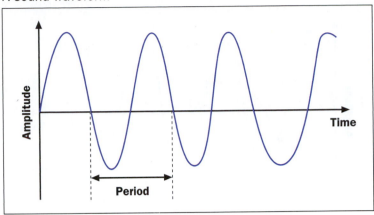

An input device for sound must translate this continuous analog information into discrete, digital values. A technique known as sampling takes a reading of the amplitude values on a waveform at regular intervals, as shown in Figure 1-4a. If the intervals are short enough, the digital information can be used to reconstruct a waveform that approximates a sound that most human beings cannot distinguish from the original. Figure 1-4b shows the waveform generated for output from the waveform sampled in Figure 1-4a. The original waveform is shown as a dotted line, whereas the regenerated waveform is shown as a solid line. As you can see, if the sampling rate is too low, some of the measured amplitudes (the heights and depths of the peaks and valleys in the waves) will be inaccurate. The sampling rate must also be high enough to capture the range of frequencies (the waves and valleys themselves), from the lowest to the highest, that most humans can hear. Psychologists and audiophiles agree that this range is from 20 to 22,000 Hertz (cycles per second). Because a sample must capture both the peak and the valley of a cycle, the sampling rate must be double the frequency. Therefore, a standard rate of 44,000 samples per second has been established for sound input. Amplitude is usually measured on a scale from 0 to 65,535.

FIGURE 1-4a
Sampling a waveform

FIGURE 1-4b
Regenerating the sound from the samples

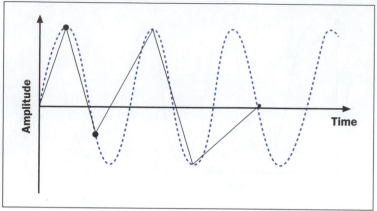

Because of the high sampling rate, the memory requirements for storing sound are much greater than those of text. For example, to digitize an hour of stereo music, the computer must perform the following steps:

■ For each stereo channel, every 1/44,000 of a second, measure the amplitude of the sound on a scale of 0 to 65,535.

■ Convert this number to binary using 16 bits.

Thus, 1 hour of stereo music requires

```
                1 hour    60 minutes   60 seconds    44,000 samples    16 bits
2 channels *  ——— *  ————— *  ———— *  —————— *  ———
                channel   hour          minute        second            sample

= 5,068,800,000 bits
= 633,600,000 bytes
```

which is the capacity of a standard CD.

The sampling rate of 44,000 times a second is not arbitrary, but corresponds to the number of samples required to reproduce accurate sounds with a frequency of up to 22,000 cycles per second. Sounds above that frequency are of more interest to dogs, bats, and dolphins than to people.

Many popular sound-encoding schemes, such as MP3, use data compression techniques to reduce the size of a digitized sound file while minimizing the loss of fidelity.

Images

Representing photographic images on a computer poses similar problems to those encountered with sound. Once again, analog information is involved, but in this case we have an infinite set of color and intensity values spread across a two-dimensional space. And once again, the solution involves the sampling of enough of these values so that the digital information can reproduce an image that is more or less indistinguishable from the original.

Sampling devices for images are flatbed scanners and digital cameras. These devices measure discrete values at distinct points or *pixels* in a two-dimensional grid. In theory, the more pixels that are taken, the more continuous and realistic the resulting image will appear. In practice, however, the human eye cannot discern objects that are closer together than 0.1 mm, so a sampling rate of 10 pixels per linear millimeter (250 pixels per inch and 62,500 pixels per square inch) would be plenty accurate. Thus, a 3-by-5-inch image would need

```
3 * 5 * 62,500 pixels/inch² = 937,500 pixels
```

For most purposes, however, we can settle for a much lower sampling rate and thus fewer pixels per square inch.

The values sampled are of course color values, and there are an infinite number of these on the spectrum. If we want a straight black-and-white image, we need only two possible values, or one bit of information, per pixel. For grayscale images, 3 bits allow for 8 shades of gray, while 8 bits allow for 256 shades of gray. A true-color scheme called RGB is based on the fact that the human retina is sensitive to red, green, and blue components. This scheme uses 8 bits for each of the three color components, for a total of 24 bits or 16,777,216 (the number of possible sequences of 24 bits) color values per pixel. No matter which color scheme is used, the sampling device selects a discrete value that is closest to the color and intensity of the image at a given point in space.

The file size of a true-color digitized image can be quite large. For example, the 3-by-5-inch image discussed earlier would need 937,500 pixels * 24 bits/pixel or about 2.5MB of storage. As with sound files, image files can be saved in a compressed format, such as GIF or JPEG, without much loss of realism.

Video

Video consists of a soundtrack and a set of images called *frames*. The sound for a soundtrack is recorded, digitized, and processed in the manner discussed earlier. The frames are snapshots or images recorded in sequence during a given time interval. If the time intervals between frames are short enough, the human eye will perceive motion in the images when they are replayed. The rate of display required for realistic motion is between 16 and 24 frames per second.

The primary challenge in digitizing video is achieving a suitable data compression scheme. Let's assume that you want to display each frame on a 15-inch laptop monitor. Each frame will then cover about 120 square inches, so even with a conservative memory allocation of 10 kilobytes (KB) of storage per square inch of image, we're looking at 1.2MB/frame * 16 frames/second = 19MB/second of storage. A 2-hour feature film would need 432,000 seconds * 19MB/second = 8,208,000MB without the soundtrack! A typical DVD has space for several gigabytes of data, so our uncompressed video would obviously not fit on a DVD. Needless to say, very sophisticated data compression schemes, such as MPEG, have been developed that allow 3-hour films to be placed on a DVD and shorter, smaller-framed video clips to be downloaded and played from the Internet.

Program Instructions

Program instructions are represented as a sequence of bits in RAM. For instance, on some hypothetical computer, the instruction to add two numbers already located in RAM and store their sum at some third location in RAM might be represented as follows:

```
0000 1001 / 0100 0000 / 0100 0010 / 0100 0100
```

where

- The first group of 8 bits represents the ADD command and is called the *operation code*, or *opcode* for short

- The second group of 8 bits represents the location (64_{10}) in memory of the first operand

- The third group of 8 bits represents the location (66_{10}) in memory of the second operand

- The fourth group of 8 bits represents the location (68_{10}) at which to store the sum

In other words, add the number at location 64 to the number at location 66 and store the sum at location 68.

Computer Memory

We can envision a computer's memory as a gigantic sequence of bytes. A byte's location in memory is called its *address*. Addresses are numbered from 0 to 1 less than the number of bytes of memory installed on that computer, say, 32M – 1, where *M* stands for *megabyte*.

A group of contiguous bytes can represent a number, a string, a picture, a chunk of sound, a program instruction, or whatever, as determined by context. For example, let us consider the meaning of the two bytes starting at location 3 in Figure 1-5.

FIGURE 1-5
A 32MB RAM

Address	Memory
0	
1	
2	
3	0100 1000
4	0110 1001
	.
	.
	.
	.
32M ± 2	
32M ± 1	

The several possible meanings include these:

■ If it is a string, then the meaning is "Hi".

■ If it is a binary encoded integer, then the meaning is 18537_{10}.

■ If it is a program instruction, then it might mean ADD, depending on the type of computer.

EXERCISE 1.3

1. Translate 11100011_2 to a base 10 number.

2. Translate $45B_{16}$ to a base 10 number.

3. What is the difference between Unicode and ASCII?

4. Assume that 4 bits are used to represent the intensities of red, green, and blue. How many total colors are possible in this scheme?

5. An old-fashioned computer has just 16 bits available to represent an address of a memory location. How many total memory locations can be addressed in this machine?

Computer Ethics

THE ACM CODE OF ETHICS

The Association for Computing Machinery (ACM) is the flagship organization for computing professionals. The ACM supports publications of research results and new trends in computer science, sponsors conferences and professional meetings, and provides standards for computer scientists as professionals. The standards concerning the conduct and professional responsibility of computer scientists have been published in the ACM Code of Ethics. The code is intended as a basis for ethical decision making and for judging the merits of complaints about violations of professional ethical standards.

The code lists several general moral imperatives for computer professionals:

- Contribute to society and human well-being.

- Avoid harm to others.

- Be honest and trustworthy.

- Be fair and take action not to discriminate.

- Honor property rights including copyrights and patents.

- Give proper credit for intellectual property.

- Respect the privacy of others.

- Honor confidentiality.

The code also lists several more specific professional responsibilities:

- Strive to achieve the highest quality, effectiveness, and dignity in both the process and products of professional work.

- Acquire and maintain professional competence.

- Know and respect existing laws pertaining to professional work.

- Accept and provide appropriate professional review.

- Give comprehensive and thorough evaluations of computer systems and their impacts, including analysis of possible risks.

- Honor contracts, agreements, and assigned responsibilities.

- Improve public understanding of computing and its consequences.

- Access computing and communication resources only when authorized to do so.

In addition to these principles, the code offers a set of guidelines to provide professionals with explanations of various issues contained in the principles. The complete text of the ACM Code of Ethics is available at the ACM's Web site, http://www.acm.org.

1.4 Programming Languages

Question: "If a program is just some very long pattern of electronic states in a computer's memory, then what is the best way to write a program?" The history of computing provides several answers to this question in the form of generations of programming languages.

Generation 1 (Late 1940s to Early 1950s)—Machine Languages

Early on, when computers were new, they were very expensive, and programs were very short. Programmers toggled switches on the front of the computer to enter programs and data directly into RAM in the form of 0s and 1s. Later, devices were developed to read the 0s and 1s into memory from punched cards and paper tape. There were several problems with this machine language-coding technique:

■ Coding was error prone (entering just a single 0 or 1 incorrectly was enough to make a program run improperly or not at all).

■ Coding was tedious and slow.

■ It was extremely difficult to modify programs.

■ It was nearly impossible for one person to decipher another's program.

■ A program was not portable to a different type of computer because each type had its own unique machine language.

Needless to say, this technique is no longer used!

Generation 2 (Early 1950s to Present)—Assembly Languages

Instead of the binary notation of machine language, assembly language uses mnemonic symbols to represent instructions and data. For instance, here is a machine language instruction followed by its assembly language equivalent:

```
0011 1001 / 1111 0110 / 1111 1000 / 1111 1010
ADD         A,          B,          C
```

meaning

1. Add the number at memory location 246, which we refer to as A

2. To the number at memory location 248, which we refer to as B

3. And store the result at memory location 250, which we refer to as C

Each *assembly language* instruction corresponds exactly to one machine language instruction. The standard procedure for using assembly language consists of several steps:

1. Write the program in assembly language.

2. Translate the program into a machine language program—this is done by a computer program called an *assembler*.

3. Load and run the machine language program—this is done by another program called a *loader*.

When compared to machine language, assembly language is

- More programmer friendly
- Still unacceptably (by today's standards) tedious to use, difficult to modify, and so forth
- No more portable because each type of computer still has its own unique assembly language

Assembly language is used as little as possible by programmers today, although sometimes it is used when memory or processing speed are at a premium. Thus, every student of computer science probably learns at least one assembly language.

Generation 3 (Mid-1950s to Present)—High-Level Languages

Early examples of *high-level languages* are FORTRAN and COBOL, which are still in widespread use. Later examples are BASIC, C, and Pascal. Recent examples include Smalltalk, C++, and Java. All these languages are designed to be human friendly—easy to write, easy to read, and easy to understand—at least when compared to assembly language. For example, all high-level languages support the use of algebraic notation, such as the expression $x + (y * z)$.

Each instruction in a high-level language corresponds to many instructions in machine language. Translation to machine language is done by a program called a *compiler*. Generally, a program written in a high-level language is portable, but it must be recompiled for each different type of computer on which it is going to run. Java is a notable exception because it is a high-level language that does not need to be recompiled for each type of computer. We learn more about this in Chapter 2. The vast majority of software written today is written in high-level languages.

*E*XERCISE 1.4

1. State two of the difficulties of programming with machine language.

2. State two features of assembly language.

3. What is a loader, and what is it used for?

4. State one difference between a high-level language and assembly language.

1.5 The Software Development Process

High-level programming languages help programmers write high-quality software in much the same sense as good tools help carpenters build high-quality houses, but there is much more to programming than writing lines of code, just as there is more to building houses than pounding nails. The "more" consists of organization and planning and various diagrammatic conventions for expressing those plans. To this end, computer scientists have developed a view of the software development process known as the *software development life cycle (SDLC)*. We now present a particular version of this life cycle called the *waterfall model*.

The waterfall model consists of several phases:

1. *Customer request*—In this phase, the programmers receive a broad statement of a problem that is potentially amenable to a computerized solution. This step is also called the *user requirements phase*.

2. *Analysis*—The programmers determine what the program will do. This is sometimes viewed as a process of clarifying the specifications for the problem.

3. *Design*—The programmers determine how the program will do its task.

4. *Implementation*—The programmers write the program. This step is also called the *coding phase*.

5. *Integration*—Large programs have many parts. In the integration phase, these parts are brought together into a smoothly functioning whole, usually not an easy task.

6. *Maintenance*—Programs usually have a long life; a life span of 5 to 15 years is common for software. During this time, requirements change and minor or major modifications must be made.

The interaction between the phases is shown in Figure 1-6. Note that the figure resembles a waterfall, in which the results of each phase flow down to the next. A mistake detected in one phase often requires the developer to back up and redo some of the work in the previous phase. Modifications made during maintenance also require backing up to earlier phases.

FIGURE 1-6
The waterfall model of the software development life cycle

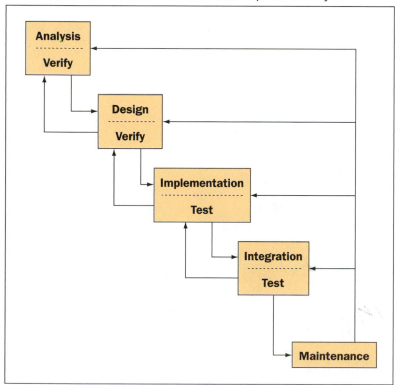

Programs rarely work as hoped the first time they are run; hence, they should be subjected to extensive and careful testing. Many people think that testing is an activity that applies only to the implementation and integration phases; however, the outputs of each phase should be scrutinized carefully. In fact mistakes found early are much less expensive to correct than those found late. Figure 1-7 illustrates some relative costs of repairing mistakes when found in different phases.

FIGURE 1-7
Relative costs of repairing mistakes when found in different phases

Finally, the cost of developing software is not spread equally over the phases. The percentages shown in Figure 1-8 are typical.

FIGURE 1-8
Percentage of total cost incurred in each phase of the development process

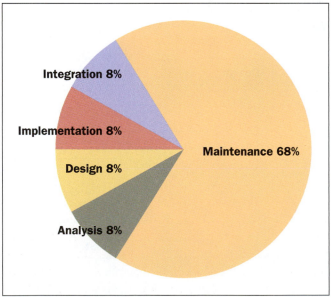

Most people probably think that implementation takes the most time and therefore costs the most. However, maintenance is, in fact, the most expensive aspect of software development. The cost of maintenance can be reduced by careful analysis, design, and implementation.

As you read this book and begin to sharpen your programming skills, you should remember two points:

1. There is more to software development than hacking out code.

2. If you want to reduce the overall cost of software development, write programs that are easy to maintain. This requires thorough analysis, careful design, and good coding style. We have more to say about coding style throughout the book.

*E*XERCISE 1.5

1. What happens during the analysis and design phases of the software development process?

2. Which phase of the software development process incurs the highest cost to developers?

3. How does the waterfall model of software development work?

4. In which phase of the software development process is the detection and correction of errors the least expensive?

For a thorough discussion of the software development process and software engineering in general, see Stephen R. Schach, *Software Engineering with Java* (Chicago: Irwin, 1997).

1.6 Basic Concepts of Object-Oriented Programming

The high-level programming languages mentioned earlier fall into two major groups, and these two groups utilize two different approaches to programming. The first group, consisting of the older languages (COBOL, FORTRAN, BASIC, C, and Pascal), uses what is called a *procedural approach*. Inadequacies in the procedural approach led to the development of the *object-oriented approach* and to several newer languages (Smalltalk, C++, and Java). There is little point in trying to explain the differences between these approaches in an introductory programming text, but suffice it to say that everyone considers the object-oriented approach to be the superior of the two. There are also several other approaches to programming, but that too is a topic for a more advanced text.

Most programs in the real world contain hundreds of thousands of lines of code. Writing such programs is a highly complex task that can only be accomplished by breaking the code into communicating components. This is an application of the well-known principle of "divide and conquer" that has been applied successfully to many human endeavors. There are various strategies for subdividing a program, and these depend on the type of programming language used. We now give an overview of the process in the context of *object-oriented programming* (OOP)—that is, programming with objects. Along the way, we introduce fundamental OOP concepts, such as class, inheritance, and polymorphism. Each of these concepts is also discussed in greater detail later in the book. For best results, reread this section as you encounter each concept for a second time.

We proceed by way of an extended analogy in an attempt to associate something already familiar with something new. Like all analogies, this one is imperfect but ideally useful. Imagine that it is your task to plan an expedition in search of the lost treasure of Balbor. How familiar can this be, you ask? Well, that depends on your taste in books, movies, and video games. Your overall approach might consist of the following steps:

1. *Planning*—You determine the different types of team members needed, including leaders, pathfinders, porters, and trail engineers. You then define the responsibilities of each member in terms of

   ■ A list of the resources used—these include the materials and knowledge needed by each member

   ■ The rules of behavior followed—these define how the team member behaves and responds in various situations

   Finally, you decide how many of each type will be needed.

2. *Execution*—You recruit the team members and assemble them at the starting point, send the team on its way, and sit back and wait for the outcome. (There is no sense in endangering your own life, too.)

3. *Outcome*—If the planning was done well, you will be rich; otherwise, prepare for disappointment.

How does this analogy relate to OOP? We give the answer in Table 1-4. On the left side of the table we describe various aspects of the expedition, and on the right side are listed corresponding aspects of OOP. Do not expect to understand all the new terms now. We explore them with many other examples in the rest of this book.

TABLE 1-4
Expedition analogy to OOP

THE WORLD OF THE EXPEDITION	THE WORLD OF OOP
The trip must be planned.	Computer software is created in a process called **programming**.
The team is composed of different types of team members, and each type is characterized by its list of resources and rules of behavior.	A program is comprised of different types of software components called **classes**. A class defines or describes a list of data resources called *instance variables* and rules of behavior called **methods**. Combining the description of resources and behaviors into a single software entity is called **encapsulation**.
First the trip must be planned. Then it must be set in motion.	First a program must be written. Then it must be run, or executed.
When the expedition is in progress, the team is composed of individual members and not types. Each member is, of course, an instance of a particular type.	An executing program is composed of interacting objects, and each object's resources (instance variables) and rules of behavior (methods) are described in a particular class. An object is said to be an instance of the class that describes its resources and behavior.
At the beginning of the expedition, team members must be recruited.	While a program is executing, it creates, or instantiates, objects as needed.

TABLE 1-4 Continued
Expedition analogy to OOP

THE WORLD OF THE EXPEDITION	THE WORLD OF OOP
Team members working together accomplish the mission of the expedition. They do this by asking each other for services.	Objects working together accomplish the mission of the program. They do this by asking each other for services or, in the language of OOP, by sending messages to each other.
When a team member receives a request for service, she follows the instructions in a corresponding rule of behavior.	When an object receives a message, it refers to its class to find a corresponding rule or method to execute.
If someone who is not a pathfinder wants to know where north is, she does not need to know anything about compasses. She merely asks one of the pathfinders, who are well-known providers of this service. Even if she did ask a pathfinder for his compass, he would refuse. Thus, team members tell others about the services they provide but never anything about the resources they use to provide these services.	If an object A needs a service that it cannot provide for itself, then A requests the service from some well-known provider B. However, A knows nothing of B's data resources and never asks for access to them. This principle of providing access to services but not to data resources is called ***information hiding***.
The expedition includes general-purpose trail engineers plus two specialized subtypes. All trail engineers share common skills, but some specialize in bridge building and others in clearing landslides. Thus, there is a hierarchy of engineers.	Classes are organized into a hierarchy also. The class at the root, or base, of the hierarchy defines methods and instance variables that are shared by its subclasses, those below it in the hierarchy. Each subclass then defines additional methods and instance variables. This process of sharing is called *inheritance*.
At the end of the day, the leader tells each member to set up camp. All members understand this request, but their responses depend on their types. Each type responds in a manner consistent with its specific responsibilities.	Different types of objects can understand the same message. This is referred to as *polymorphism*. However, an object's response depends on the class to which it belongs.

TABLE 1-4 Continued
Expedition analogy to OOP

THE WORLD OF THE EXPEDITION	THE WORLD OF OOP
During the trip, everyone is careful not to ask an individual to do something for which he is not trained—that is, for which he does not have a rule of behavior.	When writing a program, we never send a message to an object unless its class has a corresponding method.
One can rely on team members to improvise and resolve ambiguities and contradictions in rules.	In contrast, a computer does exactly what the program specifies—neither more nor less. Thus, programming errors and oversights, no matter how small, are usually disastrous. Therefore, programmers need to be excruciatingly thorough and exact when writing programs.

*E*XERCISE 1.6

1. In what way is programming like planning?

2. An object-oriented program is a set of objects that interact by sending messages to each other. Explain.

3. What is a class, and how does it relate to objects in an object-oriented program?

4. Explain the concept of inheritance with an example.

5. Explain the concept of information hiding with an example.

Computer Ethics

COPYRIGHT, INTELLECTUAL PROPERTY, AND DIGITAL INFORMATION

For hundreds of years, copyright law has existed to regulate the use of intellectual property. At stake are the rights of authors and publishers to a return on their investment in works of the intellect, which include printed matter (books, articles, etc.), recorded music, film, and video. More recently, copyright law has been extended to include software and other forms of digital information. For example, copyright law protects the software used with this book. This prohibits the purchaser from reproducing the software for sale or free distribution to others. If the software is stolen or "pirated" in this way, the perpetrator can be prosecuted and punished by law. However, copyright law also allows for "fair use"—the purchaser may make backup copies of the software for personal use. When the purchaser sells the software to another user, the seller thereby relinquishes the right to use it, and the new purchaser acquires this right.

When governments design copyright legislation, governments try to balance the rights of authors and publishers to a return on their work against the rights of the public to fair use. In the case of printed matter and other works that have a physical embodiment, the meaning of fair use is usually clear. Without fair use, borrowing a book from a library or playing a CD at a high school dance would be unlawful.

With the rapid rise of digital information and its easy transmission on networks, different interest groups—authors, publishers, users, and computer professionals—are beginning to question the traditional balance of ownership rights and fair use. For example, is browsing a copyrighted manuscript on a network service an instance of fair use? Or does it involve a reproduction of the manuscript that violates the rights of the author or publisher? Is the manuscript a physical piece of intellectual property when browsed or just a temporary pattern of bits in a computer's memory? When you listen to an audio clip on a network are you violating copyright, or only when you download the clip to your hard drive? Users and technical experts tend to favor free access to any information placed on a network. Publishers and to a lesser extent authors tend to worry that their work, when placed on a network, will be resold for profit.

Legislators struggling with the adjustment of copyright law to a digital environment face many of these questions and concerns. Providers and users of digital information should also be aware of the issues. For more information about these topics, visit the Creative Commons Web site at http://creativecommons.org/.

SUMMARY

In this chapter, you learned:

■ The modern computer age began in the late 1940s with the development of ENIAC. Business computing became practical in the 1950s, and time-sharing computers advanced computing in large organizations in the 1960s and 1970s. The 1980s saw the development and first widespread sales of personal computers, and the 1990s saw personal computers connected in networks.

■ Modern computers consist of two primary components: hardware and software. Computer hardware is the physical component of the system. Computer software consists of programs that enable us to use the hardware.

■ All information used by a computer is represented in binary form. This information includes numbers, text, images, sound, and program instructions.

■ Programming languages have been developed in the course of three generations: generation 1 is machine language, generation 2 is assembly language, and generation 3 is high-level language.

■ The software development process consists of several standard phases: customer request, analysis, design, implementation, integration, and maintenance.

■ Object-oriented programming is a style of programming that can lead to better quality software. Breaking code into easily handled components simplifies the job of writing a large program.

VOCABULARY *Review*

Define the following terms:

Application software	Information hiding	Software development life
Bit	Object-oriented programming	cycle (SDLC)
Byte	Primary memory	System software
Central processing unit (CPU)	Secondary memory	Ubiquitous computing
Hardware	Software	Waterfall model

REVIEW *Questions*

WRITTEN QUESTIONS

Write a brief answer to each of the following questions.

1. What are the three major hardware components of a computer?

2. Name three input devices.

3. Name two output devices.

4. What is the difference between application software and system software?

5. Name a first-generation programming language, a second-generation programming language, and a third-generation programming language.

FILL IN THE BLANK

Complete the following sentences by writing the correct word or words in the blanks provided.

1. All information used by a computer is represented using _____ notation.

2. The _____ phase of the software life cycle is also called the *coding phase*.

3. More than half of the cost of developing software goes to the _____ phase of the software life cycle.

4. ACM stands for _____.

5. Copyright law is designed to give fair use to the public and to protect the rights of _____ and _____.

PROJECTS

PROJECT 1-1

Take some time to become familiar with the architecture of the computer you will use for this course. Describe your hardware and software using the following guidelines:

- What hardware components make up your system?

- How much memory does your system have?

- What are the specifications of your CPU? (Do you know its speed and what kind of micro-processor it has?)

- What operating system are you using? What version of that operating system is your computer currently running?

- What major software applications are loaded on your system?

CRITICAL *Thinking*

You have just written some software that you would like to sell. Your friend suggests that you copyright your software. Discuss why this might be a good idea.

CHAPTER 2

FIRST JAVA PROGRAMS

OBJECTIVES

Upon completion of this chapter, you should be able to:

- Discuss why Java is an important programming language.

- Explain the Java virtual machine and byte code.

- Choose a user interface style.

- Describe the structure of a simple Java program.

- Write a simple program.

- Edit, compile, and run a program using a Java development environment.

- Format a program to give a pleasing, consistent appearance.

- Understand compile-time errors.

- Write a simple graphics program.

Estimated Time: 3.5 hours

VOCABULARY

Applet

Assignment operator

Byte code

DOS development environment

Graphical user interface (GUI)

Hacking

Integrated development environment (IDE)

Java virtual machine (JVM)

Just-in-time compilation (JIT)

Parameter

Source code

Statement

Terminal I/O user interface

Variable

Programs are written in programming languages, and the language used in this book is Java. This chapter gets you up and running with a couple of simple Java programs. We show how to write these first programs, compile them, and run them. In the process, you will become acquainted with a Java programming environment, the structure of a simple Java program, and the basic ideas of variables, input and output (I/O) statements, and sending messages to objects.

2.1 Why Java?

Java is the fastest growing programming language in the world. Companies such as IBM and Sun have adopted Java as their major application development language. There are several reasons for this.

First, Java is a modern object-oriented programming language. The designers of Java spent much time studying the features of classical object-oriented languages such as Smalltalk and C++ and made a successful effort to incorporate the good features of these languages and omit the less desirable ones.

Second, Java is secure, robust, and portable. That is, the Java language

- Enables the construction of virus-free, tamper-free systems (secure)
- Supports the development of programs that do not overwrite memory (robust)
- Yields programs that can be run on different types of computers without change (portable)

These features make Java ideally suited to develop distributed, network-based applications, which is an area of ever-increasing importance.

Third, Java supports the use of advanced programming concepts such as threads. A *thread* is a process that can run concurrently with other processes. For example, a single Java application might consist of two threads. One thread transfers an image from one machine to another across a network, while the other thread simultaneously interacts with the user.

Fourth and finally, Java bears a superficial resemblance to C++, which is currently the world's most popular industrial-strength programming language. Thus, it is easy for a C++ programmer to learn Java and for a Java programmer to learn C++. Compared to C++, however, Java is easier to use and learn, less error prone, more portable, and better suited to the Internet.

On the negative side, Java runs more slowly than most modern programming languages because it is interpreted. To understand this last point we must now turn our attention to the Java virtual machine and byte code.

*E*XERCISE 2.1

1. What is a portable program?

2. Describe two features of Java that make it a better language than C++.

3. What is a thread? Describe how threads might be used in a program.

2.2 *The Java Virtual Machine and Byte Code*

Compilers usually translate a higher-level language into the machine language of a particular type of computer. However, the Java compiler translates Java not into machine language, but into a pseudomachine language called Java *byte code*. Byte code is the machine language for an imaginary Java computer. To run Java byte code on a particular computer, you must install a *Java virtual machine* (JVM) on that computer, unless you use a computer such as Apple's Macintosh, in which the JVM comes with the operating system.

A JVM is a program that behaves like a computer. Such a program is called an *interpreter*. An interpreter has several advantages as well as some disadvantages. The main disadvantage of an interpreter is that a program pretending to be a computer runs programs more slowly than an actual computer. JVMs are getting faster every day, however. For instance, some JVMs translate byte code instructions into machine language when they are first encountered—called *just-in-time compilation* (JIT)—so that the next time the instruction is encountered it is executed as fast machine code rather than being interpreted as slow byte code. Also, new computer chips are being developed that implement a JVM directly in hardware, thus avoiding the performance penalty.

The main advantage of an interpreter is that any computer can run it. Thus, Java byte code is highly portable. For instance, many of the pages you download on the Web contain small Java programs already translated into byte code. These are called *applets*, and they are run in a JVM that is incorporated into your Web browser. These applets range from the decorative (displaying a comical animated character on a Web page) to the practical (displaying a continuous stream of stock market quotes).

Because Java programs run inside a virtual machine, it is possible to limit their capabilities. Thus, ideally, you never have to worry about a Java applet infecting your computer with a virus, erasing the files on your hard drive, or stealing sensitive information and sending it across the Internet to a competitor. In practice, however, computer hackers have successfully penetrated Java's security mechanisms in the past and may succeed again in the future. But all things considered, Java applets really are very secure, and security weaknesses are repaired as soon as they become known.

*E*XERCISE 2.2

1. What does JVM stand for?

2. What is byte code? Describe how the JVM uses byte code.

3. What is an applet? Describe how applets are used.

2.3 Choosing a User Interface Style

Before writing our first program, we must make a difficult decision. What type of user interface do we want to use? There are two choices: the *graphical user interface* (GUI), familiar to all PC users, and the less common *terminal I/O user interface*. Figure 2-1 illustrates both in the context of a program that converts degrees Fahrenheit to degrees Celsius. The graphical user interface on the left is familiar and comfortable. The user enters a number in the first box, clicks the command button, and the program displays the answer in the second box. The terminal-based interface on the right begins by displaying the prompt "Enter degrees Fahrenheit: ". The user then enters a number and presses the Enter key. The program responds by displaying the answer.

FIGURE 2-1
Two user interfaces for a temperature conversion program

We use terminal I/O user interface in most of the program examples in this book. Beginning with this chapter, an optional end-of-chapter section introduces various aspects of graphics and GUI programming. In the long run, you will discover that this book's core material is independent of interface issues. There are three reasons for using terminal I/O. First, in Java and many other languages, a terminal user interface is easier to implement than a GUI, although in other languages, such as Visual BASIC, the opposite is true. Second, there are programming situations that require terminal I/O rather than a GUI, so familiarity with the techniques of terminal-oriented programming is important. Third, terminal-oriented programs are similar in structure to programs that process files of sequentially organized data, and what we learn here will be transferable to that setting.

2.4 *Hello World*

In conformance with a long and honorable tradition dating back to the early days of the language C, a textbook's first program often does nothing more than display the words "Hello World" in a terminal window. Actually, as you can see in Figure 2-2, we could not resist adding a few embellishments. In case you have not guessed, the imagery is the words "Hello World" rising like steam from the cup of hot Java.

FIGURE 2-2
Hello World

The Source Code

Just as a recipe is a sequence of instructions for a chef, a program is a sequence of instructions for a computer. And just as a recipe does nothing until executed by a chef, so a program does nothing until executed by a computer. With that in mind, the following is the bulk of the instructions, or *source code*, for our HelloWorld program:

```
System.out.println("                d           ");
System.out.println("          o     l           ");
System.out.println("        l    r              ");
System.out.println("         l       o          ");
System.out.println("          e     W           ");
System.out.println("         H                  ");
System.out.println("     xxxxxxxxxxxxxxxx        ");
System.out.println("     x          x   x        ");
System.out.println("     x    Java   x   x       ");
System.out.println("     x             xxxx      ");
System.out.println("     x  is hot!  x           ");
System.out.println("     x          x            ");
System.out.println("     x          x            ");
System.out.println("     xxxxxxxxxxxxx           ");
```

The Explanation

In this code

- `System.out` is the name of an object that knows how to display or print characters in a terminal window.

- `println` is the name of the message being sent to the `System.out` object.

- The strings enclosed in quotation marks contain the characters to be printed.

- Semicolons (;) mark the end of each *statement* or sentence in the program.

As mentioned at the end of Chapter 1, an object-oriented program accomplishes its tasks by sending messages to objects. In this program, a `System.out` object responds to a `println` message by printing a string of characters in the terminal window. The string of characters that appears between the parentheses following the message is called a *parameter*. Some messages require several parameters, separated from each other by commas, whereas other messages have no parameters. The "ln" in the message `println` stands for "line" and indicates that the `System.out` object should advance to the beginning of the next line after printing a string.

Sending messages to objects always takes the form

```
<name of object>.<name of message>(<parameters>)
```

The period (.) between the object's name and the message's name is called a *method selector operator*. The period between the words `System` and `out` is not a method selector operator. For now you can just think of it as part of the object's name.

The Larger Framework

The program as presented so far is not complete. It must be embedded in a larger framework defined by several additional lines of code. No attempt will be made to explain this code until a later chapter, but, fortunately, it can be reused with little change from one program to the next. Following then is the complete program with the new lines shown in color:

```java
// Example 2.1: Our first program

public class HelloWorld{

    public static void main(String [] args) {
        System.out.println("                    d           ");
        System.out.println("              o      l           ");
        System.out.println("            l      r             ");
        System.out.println("            l      o             ");
        System.out.println("          e      W               ");
        System.out.println("        H                         ");
        System.out.println("      xxxxxxxxxxxxxxxxx           ");
        System.out.println("      x              x   x        ");
        System.out.println("      x     Java     x   x        ");
        System.out.println("      x              xxxx         ");
        System.out.println("      x   is hot!   x            ");
        System.out.println("      x              x            ");
        System.out.println("      x              x            ");
        System.out.println("      xxxxxxxxxxxxx              ");
    }
}
```

To reuse the framework, replace `HelloWorld` with the name of another program:

```java
public class <name of program> {
    public static void main(String [] args) {
        . . . put the source code here . . .
    }
}
```

In this text, we write program comments in green, reserved words in blue, and the rest of the program code in black. Program comments and reserved words will be explained in Chapter 3.

EXERCISE 2.4

1. Give a short definition of "program."

2. What is the effect of the message `println`?

3. Describe how to use the `System.out` object.

4. Write a sequence of statements to display your name, address, and phone number in the terminal window.

2.5 Edit, Compile, and Execute

In the preceding section, we presented the source code for our first program. Now we discuss how to enter it into a computer and run it. There are three steps:

1. *Edit*. In the first step, the programmer uses a word processor or editor to enter the source code into the computer and save it in a text file. The name of the text file must match the name of the program with the extension .java added, as in HelloWorld.java.

2. *Compile*. In the second step, the programmer invokes the Java language compiler to translate the source code into Java byte code. In this example, the compiler translates source code in the file HelloWorld.java to byte code in the file HelloWorld.class. The extension for a byte code file is always .class.

3. *Execute*. In the third step, the programmer instructs the JVM to load the byte code into memory and execute it. At this point the user and the program can interact, with the user entering data and the program displaying instructions and results.

Figure 2-3 illustrates the steps. The ovals represent the processes edit, compile, and execute. The names of the files HelloWorld.java and HelloWorld.class are shown between parallel lines.

FIGURE 2-3
Editing, compiling, and running a program

Development Environments

The details involved in editing, compiling, and running a program vary with the development environment being used. Some common development environments available to Java programmers include the following:

- UNIX or Linux using a standard text editor with command-line activation of the compiler and the JVM. UNIX is available on any Macintosh computer that runs MacOS X.

- Various versions of Microsoft Windows using Notepad for the editor with command-line activation of the compiler and the JVM from inside a command or DOS window. We call this the *DOS development environment.*

- Windows or MacOS using an *integrated development environment* (IDE) such as Metrowerks' Code Warrior, Microsoft's Visual J++, Borland's Jbuilder, or free educational-use-only IDEs such as BlueJ and JGrasp.

The first two options are free and may require you to download and install the Java software development kit (SDK) as described in Appendix A. The third option, an integrated development environment, may cost money, but it has the advantage of combining an editor, a Java compiler, a debugger, and a JVM in a manner intended to increase programmer productivity. IDEs take time to master, however, and they can obscure fundamental details of the edit, compile, and run sequence.

Because we cannot possibly discuss all of these environments simultaneously, we give our instructions in terms of the DOS development environment that has the most widespread use. Macintosh users can use the UNIX command prompt and TextEdit. The installation and use of some of the major alternatives are presented in our supplemental materials on the book's Web site (the URL is in Appendix A).

Preparing Your Development Environment

Before writing your first program, you must install a Java development environment on your computer. Guidelines for doing this are presented in Appendix A.

Step-by-Step Instructions

We are now ready to present step-by-step instructions for editing, compiling, and running the `HelloWorld` program. These instructions apply to users of the Windows XP system. After reading what follows, read the supplemental material for an explanation that matches the development environment on your computer.

Step 1. Use Windows Explorer to create the directory in which you intend to work (for instance, C:\Javafiles). Open a terminal window by selecting **Command Prompt** (or something similar) on the **Start/All Programs/Accessories** menu. In the terminal window, use the **cd** command to move to the working directory as illustrated in Figure 2-4.

FIGURE 2-4
Using the **cd** command to move to the working directory

Step 2. Open the Notepad editor and create the file `HelloWorld.java` by typing the text as shown in Figure 2-5.

FIGURE 2-5
Activating Notepad to edit the program

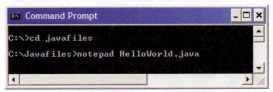

Once Notepad opens, type in the lines of code for the program. Figure 2-6 shows the Notepad window after the program has been entered.

FIGURE 2-6
The program as typed into Notepad

Step 3. Save the file and switch back to the terminal window. Compile the program by typing `javac HelloWorld.java`. The DOS prompt returns when the compilation is complete.

Step 4. Run the program by typing `java HelloWorld`. Figure 2-7 illustrates this step as well as the previous step.

FIGURE 2-7
Compiling and running the program

Compile-Time Errors

It is inevitable that we will make typographical errors when we edit programs, and the compiler will nearly always detect them. Mistakes detected by the compiler are called *syntax errors* or *compile-time errors*. To illustrate these, we modify the program so that it includes a syntax error. After reading this subsection, read the supplemental material that matches your development environment.

On line 6 of the program we misspell `println` as `prinrln`. Figure 2-8 shows the program with the error as it appears in Notepad.

FIGURE 2-8
The program with a compile-time error on line 6

When the program is compiled, the compiler prints a list of errors in the terminal window as shown in Figure 2-9. The error message is not difficult to understand. It refers to line 6 of the source program and says that a symbol cannot be found. More specifically, the symbol for method `prinrln` within the class `java.io.PrintStream` cannot be found. In fact, the object `System.out` is a member of this class, and the program has attempted to send a message that the class does not recognize. A caret symbol (^) points to the location of the error in the code. Unfortunately, some error messages may be difficult to decipher, but at least they indicate where the compiler encountered text it could not translate into byte code.

FIGURE 2-9
The compiler's error message

Readability

Programs typically have a long life and are usually maintained by many people other than their original authors. For this reason, if for no other, it is extremely important to write programs that are highly readable. The main factor affecting a program's readability is its layout. Indentation, the inclusion of blank lines and spaces, and other typographical considerations make the difference between an intelligible program and an incomprehensible mess. Interestingly, the compiler completely ignores a program's format, provided that there are no line breaks in the middle of words or quoted strings. Throughout the book, we attempt to format our programs in a pleasing and consistent manner, and you should strive to do the same. For your enjoyment the following example is a very unreadable but completely functional rendering of the `HelloWorld` program:

```
public class
     HelloWorld
{public static void main (String [] args) {System.out.println(
"                d             ");System.out.println
     ("         o    l         ");
System.out.println("         l    r         ");
 System.   out
.println("         l    o        ")
; System.out.println("         e     W          ");System.out
.println("        H                 ");System.out.println
("     xxxxxxxxxxxxxxxxx        ");System.out.println(
"    x            x   x     ")
;System.out.println("    x     Java    x   x     ");
     System.out.println("      x              xxxx       ");
          System.out.println("     x   is hot!  x          ");
System.out.println("     x           x           ");
     System.out.println("      x           x         ");
          System.out.println("     xxxxxxxxxxxxx              ");  }  }
```

 Computer Ethics

INTRUSIVE HACKING

Hacking is a term whose use goes back to the early days of computing. In its original sense, a "hack" is a programmer who exhibits rare problem-solving ability and commands the respect of other programmers. The culture of hackers began in the late 1950s at the MIT computer science labs. These programmers, many of them students and later professionals and teachers in the field, regarded hacking as an accomplishment along the lines of Olympic gymnastics. These programmers even advocated a "hacker ethic," which stated, among other things, that hackers should respect the privacy of others and distribute their software for free. For a narrative of the early tradition of hacking, see Steven Levy, *Hackers: Heroes of the Computer Revolution* (Garden City, New York: Anchor Press/Doubleday, 1984).

Unfortunately, the practice of hacking has changed over the years, and the term has acquired darker connotations. Programmers who break into computer systems in an unauthorized way are called hackers, whether their intent is just to impress their peers or to cause actual harm. Students and professionals who lack a disciplined approach to programming are also called hackers. An excellent account of the most famous case of intrusive hacking can be found in Clifford Stoll, *The Cuckoo's Egg: Tracking Through the Maze of Computer Espionage* (New York: Doubleday, 1989).

*E*XERCISE 2.5

1. Name the three steps in writing and running a program.

2. What are compile-time errors?

3. Find the compile-time errors in the following statements:

a. System.out.println("Here is an error);

b. System.out.println("Here is another error";

4. Why is readability a desirable characteristic of a program?

2.6 Temperature Conversion

We now present code for the temperature conversion program illustrated earlier in the chapter. To refresh your memory, we show the user interface again in Figure 2-10. This program is fundamentally more interesting than the `HelloWorld` program because it reads user inputs and performs computations. Despite its brevity and simplicity, the program demonstrates several important concepts.

FIGURE 2-10
The user interface for the temperature conversion program

The Source Code

The program's source code is

```
// Example 2.2: inputs degrees Fahrenheit
// from the keyboard and outputs degrees Celsius

import java.util.Scanner;

public class Convert{

    public static void main(String [] args){
        Scanner reader = new Scanner(System.in);
        double fahrenheit;
        double celsius;

        System.out.print("Enter degrees Fahrenheit: ");
        fahrenheit = reader.nextDouble();

        celsius = (fahrenheit - 32.0) * 5.0 / 9.0;
```

```
            System.out.print("The equivalent in Celsius is ");
            System.out.println(celsius);
        }
    }
```

The Explanation

Following is a line-by-line explanation of the most significant portions of the program.

```
import java.util.Scanner;
```

The program's first line of code is an *import statement*. The program must read inputs entered at the keyboard, and this functionality is provided by something called a scanner object. Such objects are instances of the class `Scanner`. In this line of code, we are telling the compiler where to find complete specifications for the class. The periods that appear in this statement are NOT method selectors.

```
Scanner reader = new Scanner(System.in);
```

In this statement, we instantiate or create a `Scanner` object. We have arbitrarily decided to call the object `reader`. The name suggests what the object does, so it is a good choice. As mentioned in Chapter 1, an object is always an instance of a class and must be created, or instantiated, before being used. In general, instantiation is done like this:

```
SomeClass someObject = new SomeClass(some parameters);
```

The code `System.in` names a variable in the `System` class that refers to the keyboard. This object is passed as a parameter to the code that instantiates the `Scanner` object in order to connect the two objects. Parameters are used to share information between objects.

```
double fahrenheit;
double celsius;
```

In these statements, we declare that the program will use two numeric variables called `fahrenheit` and `celsius`. A numeric *variable* names a location in RAM in which a number can be stored. The number is usually referred to as the variable's *value*. During the course of a program, a variable's value can change, but its name remains constant. The variables in this program are of type `double`, which means they will contain only floating-point numbers. It is customary, though not required, to begin variable names with a lowercase letter, thus `fahrenheit` rather than `Fahrenheit`. We are allowed to declare as many variables as we want in a program, and we can name them pretty much as we please. Restrictions are explained in Chapter 3.

```
System.out.print("Enter degrees Fahrenheit: ");
```

This statement is similar to those we saw in the `HelloWorld` program, but there is a minor difference. The message here is `print` rather than `println`. A `print` message positions the cursor immediately after the last character printed rather than moving it to the beginning of the next line.

```
fahrenheit = reader.nextDouble();
```

In this statement, the `reader` object responds to the message `nextDouble` by waiting for the user to type a number and then press Enter, at which point the `reader` object returns the number to the program. The number is then assigned to the variable `fahrenheit` by means of the *assignment operator* (=). The number entered by the user is now stored in the variable. Note that although the `nextDouble` message has no parameters, the parentheses are still required. As the user types at the keyboard, the characters are automatically echoed in the terminal window, but not until the user presses Enter does this input become available to the program.

```
celsius = (fahrenheit - 32.0) * 5.0 / 9.0;
```

In this statement, the expression to the right of the assignment operator (=) is evaluated, and then the resulting value is stored in memory at location `celsius`. Statements utilizing an assignment operator are called *assignment statements*. When the computer evaluates the expression, it uses the value stored in the variable `fahrenheit`. Notice that all the numbers (32.0, 5.0, and 9.0) contain a decimal point. In Java, some unexpected rules govern what happens when integers and floating-point numbers are mixed in an expression, so until we discuss the rules in Chapter 3, we will not mix integers and floating-point numbers. In the expression, as in algebra, the following symbols are used:

*	indicates the multiplication operator
/	indicates the division operator
-	indicates the subtraction operator

Of course, there is another common operator, namely + for *addition*. Notice the use of parentheses in the previous expression. In Java, as in algebra, multiplication and division are done before addition and subtraction unless parentheses are used to change the order of the computations; in other words, multiplication and division have higher precedence than addition and subtraction.

```
System.out.print("The equivalent in Celsius is ");
```

Here the `System.out` object prints the string "The equivalent in Celsius is ". The cursor is positioned after the last character in preparation for the next line of code.

```
System.out.println(celsius);
```

Here the `System.out` object prints the value of the variable `celsius`. The parameter for a `print` or `println` message can be a string in quotation marks, a variable, or even an expression. When a variable is used, the variable's value is printed, not its name. When an expression is used, the expression is evaluated before its value is printed.

Variables and Objects

Figure 2-11 depicts four of the variables and objects used in the program. All of these exist in the computer's memory while the program is running. The variables `fahrenheit` and `celsius` each hold a single floating-point number. At any given instant, the value stored in a variable depends on the effect of the preceding lines of code. The variables `reader` and `System.out` are very different from the variables `fahrenheit` and `celsius`. Instead of holding numbers, they hold references to objects. The arrows in the figure are intended to suggest this fact. During the course of the program, we think of the `reader` variable as being the name of an object. As the figure indicates, we know nothing about what lies inside the `reader` object (information hiding), but we do know that it responds to the message `nextDouble`. `System.out` also names an object, but one that is never declared in our programs. How this can be so is explained in a later chapter. The `System.out` object responds to the messages `print` and `println`. One of the really significant facts about object-oriented programming is that we can use objects without having the least idea of their internal workings. Likewise, we can design objects for others to use without telling them anything about the implementation details.

FIGURE 2-11
Variables and objects used in the conversion program

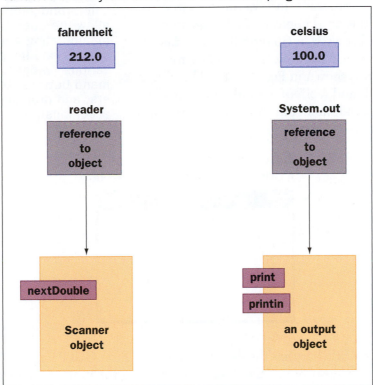

*E*XERCISE 2.6

1. What is a variable in a program and how is it used?

2. Describe the role of the assignment (=) operator in a program.

3. What is a `Scanner` object?

4. Explain the difference between a variable of type `double` and a variable of type `Scanner`.

5. Describe the difference between `print` and `println`, and give an appropriate example of the use of each.

2.7 Graphics and GUIs: Windows and Panels

Java comes with a large array of classes that support graphics and GUI programming. In this section, we examine how to set up and manipulate an application window, explore the use of colors, and lay out regions within the window.

A Simple Application Window

Graphics and GUI programs in Java can run either as standalone applications or as applets. We discuss applets, which run in a Web browser, in Chapter 8. A standalone GUI application runs in a window. The window for our first GUI application is shown in Figure 2-12. The visual appearance or "look and feel" of a window might vary from computer to computer, but several features are constant.

FIGURE 2-12
A GUI program with an empty window

The window has a title bar that displays the message "First GUI Program." The user can drag the window to another position on the desktop by moving the mouse cursor to the title bar and then clicking and dragging.

The title bar contains some controls that allow the user to minimize the window (moving it to the desktop tray or dock), zoom it to full screen size, or close it (which usually quits the application).

The window has an initial width and height that the user can modify by selecting its lower-right corner and dragging appropriately.

Other than exhibiting the basic features and common behavior of all GUI applications, our first GUI application displays no other GUI components and does nothing. Here is the code for the application, followed by an explanation.

```
// Example 2.3: an empty frame

import javax.swing.*;       // Access JFrame

public class GUIWindow{

    public static void main(String[] args){
        JFrame theGUI = new JFrame();
        theGUI.setTitle("First GUI Program");
        theGUI.setSize(300, 200);
        theGUI.setDefaultCloseOperation(JFrame.EXIT_ON_CLOSE);
        theGUI.setVisible(true);
    }
}
```

The code for application windows in Java is located in the class `JFrame`, which is imported from the package `javax.swing`. The `main` method simply creates an instance of `JFrame` and sends it messages to set up and display the window. Unlike a terminal I/O application, the program does not quit when the end of the `main` method is reached but stays alive until the user selects the window's close box.

A `JFrame` object responds to many messages, among them messages to set its title to a given string, set its initial size to a width and height in pixels, set the operation that will be performed when it closes (exits the application), and set its visibility (true/visible or false/invisible). A set of commonly used `JFrame` methods is listed in Table 2-1.

TABLE 2-1
Some commonly used `JFrame` methods

JFRAME METHOD	WHAT IT DOES
`Container getContentPane()`	Returns the frame's container to which components can be added
`void setResizable(boolean b)`	If b is `false`, the user cannot resize the window; if b is `true`, the user can resize the window. The default is that the window is resizable.
`void setDefaultCloseIndicator(int i)`	Sets the operation to be performed when the user closes the frame
`void setSize(int width, int height)`	Sets the size of the frame to the width and height in pixels
`void setTitle(String title)`	Displays the title in the frame's title bar
`void setVisible(boolean b)`	Displays the frame if b is `true` or hides it if b is `false`

Panels and Colors

An application window is really just an empty container that we can fill with other objects. One such object is called a *panel*. A panel is a flat, rectangular area suitable for displaying other objects such as geometric shapes and images. Windows are often organized into multiple panels or *panes*, each of which contains related objects such as images and widgets. Panels themselves have fairly simple features, including a width, height, and background color. The class `JPanel`, also in `javax.swing`, represents panels in Java.

As we mentioned in Chapter 1, colors in most computer systems use the RGB scheme, which encodes 16,777,216 distinct colors. The `Color` class, which appears in the package `java.awt`, can be used to create any of these color values, as follows:

```
Color aColor = new Color(redValue, greenValue, blueValue)
```

where the red, green, and blue values are integers ranging from 0 to 255. Recall that 255 indicates the maximum intensity of a color component, whereas 0 indicates the absence of that component. Thus, the code `new Color(0, 0, 0)` would create an object representing the color black. For convenience, the `Color` class also includes constants for several commonly used colors, which are listed with their RGB values in Table 2-2.

TABLE 2-2
Some `Color` constants

COLOR CONSTANT	RGB VALUE
Color.red	new Color(255, 0, 0)
Color.green	new Color(0, 255, 0)
Color.blue	new Color(0, 0, 255)
Color.yellow	new Color(255, 255, 0)
Color.cyan	new Color(0, 255, 255)
Color.magenta	new Color(255, 0, 255)
Color.orange	new Color(255, 200, 0)
Color.pink	new Color(255, 175, 175)
Color.black	new Color(0, 0, 0)
Color.white	new Color(255, 255, 255)
Color.gray	new Color(128, 128, 128)
Color.lightGray	new Color(192, 192, 192)
Color.darkGray	new Color(64, 64, 64)

Our next example program creates a panel, sets its background color to pink, and adds the panel to the application window.

```java
// Example 2.4: a frame with an empty, pink panel

import javax.swing.*;      // For JFrame and JPanel
import java.awt.*;         // For Color and Container

public class GUIWindow{

    public static void main(String[] args){
        JFrame theGUI = new JFrame();
        theGUI.setTitle("Second GUI Program");
        theGUI.setSize(300, 200);
        theGUI.setDefaultCloseOperation(JFrame.EXIT_ON_CLOSE);
        JPanel panel = new JPanel();
        panel.setBackground(Color.pink);
        Container pane = theGUI.getContentPane();
        pane.add(panel);
        theGUI.setVisible(true);
    }
}
```

When this program is run, its window looks just like that of the first program, except that the area below the title bar is pink. Note the procedure for adding the panel to the window. We must first obtain the window's container object by running the method `getContentPane()`. We then add the panel to this container.

Layout Managers and Multiple Panels

The previous example displayed a single panel in an application window. When we have more than one panel or other objects to display in a window, we have to be concerned about how they are organized or laid out. In Java, each container object, such as a frame or a panel, uses an object called a *layout manager* to accomplish this. Thus, when a program adds an object to a container, the container's layout manager actually influences its placement. Each type of container has a default layout manager, which we can reset to a different type of layout manager if the default does not suit our needs.

The default layout manager for frames is an instance of the class `BorderLayout`. A border layout allows us to arrange up to five objects in positions that correspond to the directions north (top), east (right), south (bottom), west (left), and center. If we add fewer than five objects, the layout manager stretches some of them to fill the unoccupied areas. To see what these areas look like when they are all occupied, we modify our second program to add five colored panels to the window. The north and south panels are red, the east and west panels are blue, and the center panel is white. The result is displayed in Figure 2-13.

```java
// Example 2.5: a frame with 5 colored panels
// that show the border layout

import javax.swing.*;      // For JFrame and JPanel
import java.awt.*;         // For Color and Container

public class GUIWindow{

    public static void main(String[] args){
        JFrame theGUI = new JFrame();
        theGUI.setTitle("Third GUI Program");
        theGUI.setSize(300, 200);
        theGUI.setDefaultCloseOperation(JFrame.EXIT_ON_CLOSE);
        JPanel northPanel = new JPanel();
        northPanel.setBackground(Color.red);
        JPanel eastPanel = new JPanel();
        eastPanel.setBackground(Color.blue);
        JPanel southPanel = new JPanel();
        southPanel.setBackground(Color.red);
        JPanel westPanel = new JPanel();
        westPanel.setBackground(Color.blue);
        JPanel centerPanel = new JPanel();
        centerPanel.setBackground(Color.white);
        Container pane = theGUI.getContentPane();
        pane.add(northPanel, BorderLayout.NORTH);
        pane.add(eastPanel, BorderLayout.EAST);
        pane.add(southPanel, BorderLayout.SOUTH);
        pane.add(westPanel, BorderLayout.WEST);
        pane.add(centerPanel, BorderLayout.CENTER);
        theGUI.setVisible(true);
    }
}
```

FIGURE 2-13
A border layout with five panels

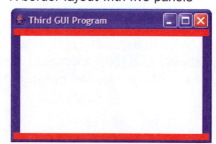

Note the use of the `BorderLayout` constants to specify the area of the container to which an object is added. When the constant is omitted, as it was in our previous program, a border layout places the object in the center area.

Suppose we want to organize the colored areas in a grid to make a checkerboard. A border layout will not do. Fortunately, the package `java.awt` includes the class `GridLayout` for this purpose. When it's created, a grid layout is given a number of rows and columns. The areas of the cells in the resulting grid are the same size. The objects are placed in cells from left to right, starting with the first row and moving down. Our final program example resets the container's layout to a 2-by-2 grid layout and then places four panels colored white, black, gray, and white in it. The result is shown in Figure 2-14.

```java
// Example 2.6: a frame with a 2 by 2 grid of colored panels

import javax.swing.*;      // For JFrame and JPanel
import java.awt.*;         // For Color, Container, and GridLayout

public class GUIWindow{

    public static void main(String[] args){
        JFrame theGUI = new JFrame();
        theGUI.setTitle("Fourth GUI Program");
        theGUI.setSize(300, 200);
        theGUI.setDefaultCloseOperation(JFrame.EXIT_ON_CLOSE);
        JPanel panel1 = new JPanel();
        panel1.setBackground(Color.white);
        JPanel panel2 = new JPanel();
        panel2.setBackground(Color.black);
        JPanel panel3 = new JPanel();
        panel3.setBackground(Color.gray);
        JPanel panel4 = new JPanel();
        panel4.setBackground(Color.white);
        Container pane = theGUI.getContentPane();
        pane.setLayout(new GridLayout(2, 2));
        pane.add(panel1);
        pane.add(panel2);
        pane.add(panel3);
        pane.add(panel4);
        theGUI.setVisible(true);
    }
}
```

FIGURE 2-14
A 2-by-2 grid layout with four panels

EXERCISE 2.7

1. Write the integer values of red, green, and blue for the following RGB colors:
   a. white
   b. black
   c. highest intensity blue
   d. medium gray

2. Describe the roles and responsibilities of a frame, a panel, and a layout manager in a GUI application.

3. Where are panels displayed when a border layout is used to control their placement in a window?

4. Write a code segment that would be used to set the layout for adding panels to a 5-by-5 grid in a window. You may assume that the panel's content pane is named pane.

SUMMARY

In this chapter, you learned:

- Java is the fastest growing programming language in the world. It is secure, robust, and portable. It is also similar to C++, the world's most popular programming language.

- The Java compiler translates Java into a pseudomachine language called Java byte code. Byte code can be run on any computer that has a Java virtual machine installed. The Java virtual machine (JVM) is a program that behaves like a computer—an interpreter.

- Java programs include variables, arithmetic expressions, statements, objects, messages, and methods.

- Three basic steps in the coding process are editing, compiling, and running a program using a Java development environment. Programmers should pay attention to a program's format to ensure readability.

- Java programs accomplish many tasks by sending messages to objects. Examples are sending text to the terminal window for output and receiving input data from the keyboard.

- There are several user interface styles, among them terminal based and graphical based.

VOCABULARY *Review*

Define the following terms:

Applet	Hacking	Parameter
Assignment operator	Integrated development	Source code
Byte code	environment (IDE)	Statement
DOS development	Java virtual machine (JVM)	Terminal I/O interface
environment	Just-in-time compilation (JIT)	Variable
Graphical user interface (GUI)		

REVIEW *Questions*

WRITTEN QUESTIONS

Write a brief answer to each of the following questions.

1. List three reasons why Java is an important programming language.

2. What is byte code?

3. What is the JVM?

4. List two objects that are used for terminal input and output in Java programs.

5. Give examples of two compile-time errors.

6. What steps must be followed to run a Java program?

7. What is the purpose of an import statement in a Java program?

FILL IN THE BLANK

Complete the following sentences by writing the correct word or words in the blanks provided.

1. Two user interface styles are _____ and _____.

2. The message _____ is used to output data to the terminal window.

3. The message _____ is used to input a number from the keyboard.

4. A(n) _____ names a place where data can be stored in a Java program.

5. A(n) _____ stores the value of the expression in the variable.

6. Programs manipulate objects by sending them _____.

PROJECTS

Beginning with this chapter, we conclude each chapter with a set of programming problems and activities. We want to emphasize that programming is not just coding. Thus, a complete solution to each exercise in this section would include not just a set of .java and .class files for the program but also a report that covers the analysis, design, and results of testing the program. Ideally, you would do analysis and design before coding, and perhaps turn in this work for review before coding proceeds. How this is done depends on the size of the class and the time available to the instructor. In any case, when you see the words "write a program that . . .", you should at least pause to reflect on the nature of the problem before coding the solution. For example, your analysis might consist of a description of how the program would be used.

PROJECT 2-1

Write a program that displays your name, address, and telephone number.

PROJECT 2-2

A yield sign encloses the word YIELD within a triangle. Write a program that displays a yield sign. (Use stars to represent the sides of the triangle.)

PROJECT 2-3

Write a program that takes as input a number of kilometers and prints the corresponding number of nautical miles. You may rely on the following items of information:

- A kilometer represents 1/10,000 of the distance between the North Pole and the equator.

- There are 90 degrees, containing 60 minutes of arc each, between the North Pole and the equator.

- A nautical mile is 1 minute of an arc.

PROJECT 2-4

Write a program that calculates and prints the number of minutes in a year.

PROJECT 2-5

An object's momentum is its mass multiplied by its velocity. Write a program that expects an object's mass (in kilograms) and velocity (in meters per second) as inputs and prints its momentum.

PROJECT 2-6

National flags are displayed on various Web sites, such as http://flagspot.net/flags/. The flags of France, Mauritius, and Bulgaria consist of flat, colored areas. Write separate programs that display these flags.

PROJECT 2-7

Write a program that displays a 3-by-3 grid of black and white rectangles. The rectangles should be positioned so that no two rectangles of the same color are adjacent to each other.

CRITICAL *Thinking*

You have an idea for a program that will help the local pizza shop handle takeout orders. Your friend suggests an interview with the shop's owner to discuss her user requirements before you get started on the program. Explain why this is a good suggestion, and list the questions you would ask the owner to help you determine the user requirements.

CHAPTER 3

SYNTAX, ERRORS, AND DEBUGGING

OBJECTIVES

Upon completion of this chapter, you should be able to:

- Construct and use numeric and string literals.

- Name and use variables and constants.

- Create arithmetic expressions.

- Understand the precedence of different arithmetic operators.

- Concatenate two strings or a number and a string.

- Know how and when to use comments in a program.

- Tell the difference between syntax errors, run-time errors, and logic errors.

- Insert output statements to debug a program.

- Understand the difference between Cartesian coordinates and screen coordinates.

- Work with color and text properties.

Estimated Time: 4.0 hours

VOCABULARY

Arithmetic expression

Comments

Coordinate system

Exception

Graphics context

Literal

Logic error

Origin

Package

Pseudocode

Reserved words

Run-time error

Screen coordinate system

Semantics

Syntax

Virus

To use a programming language, one must become familiar with its vocabulary and the rules for forming grammatically correct statements. You must also know how to construct meaningful statements and statements that express the programmer's intent. Errors of form, meaning, and intent are possible, so finally one must know how to detect these errors and correct them. This chapter discusses the basic elements of the Java language in detail and explores how to find and correct errors in programs.

3.1 Language Elements

Before writing code in any programming language, we need to be aware of some basic language elements. Every natural language, such as English, Japanese, and German, has its own vocabulary, syntax, and semantics. Programming languages also have these three elements.

Vocabulary is the set of all of the words and symbols in the language. Table 3-1 illustrates some examples taken from Java.

TABLE 3-1
Some Java vocabulary

TYPE OF ELEMENT	EXAMPLES
arithmetic operators	`+ - * /`
assignment operator	`=`
numeric literals	`5.73    9`
programmer defined variable names	`fahrenheit celsius`

Syntax consists of the rules for combining words into sentences, or *statements*, as they are more usually called in programming languages. Following are two typical syntax rules in Java:

1. In an expression, the arithmetic operators for multiply and divide must not be adjacent. Thus,

   `(f - 32) * / 9`

   is invalid.

2. In an expression, left and right parentheses must occur in matching pairs. Thus,

   `)f - 32( * 5 / 9`

   and

   `f - 32) * 5 / 9`

   are both invalid.

Semantics define the rules for interpreting the meaning of statements. For example, the expression

   `(f - 32.0) * 5.0 / 9.0`

means "go into the parentheses first, subtract `32.0` from the variable quantity indicated by `f`, then multiply the result by `5.0`, and finally divide the whole thing by `9.0`."

Programming versus Natural Languages

Despite their similarities, programming languages and natural languages differ in three important ways: size, rigidity, and literalness.

Size

Programming languages have small vocabularies and simple syntax and semantics compared to natural languages. Thus, their basic elements are not hard to learn.

Rigidity

In a programming language one must get the syntax absolutely correct, whereas a grammatically incorrect English sentence is usually comprehensible. This strict requirement of correctness often makes writing programs difficult for beginners, though no more difficult than writing grammatically correct sentences in English or any other natural language.

Literalness

When we give a friend instructions in English, we can be a little vague, relying on the friend to fill in the details. In a programming language, we must be exhaustively thorough. Computers follow instructions in a very literal manner. They do exactly what they are told—no more and no less. When people blame problems on computer errors, they should more accurately blame sloppy programming. This last difference is the one that makes programming difficult even for experienced programmers.

Although programming languages are simpler than human languages, the task of writing programs is challenging. It is difficult to express complex ideas using the limited syntax and semantics of a programming language.

EXERCISE 3.1

1. What is the vocabulary of a language? Give an example of an item in the vocabulary of Java.

2. Give an example of a syntax rule in Java.

3. What does the expression (x + y) * z mean?

4. Describe two differences between programming languages and natural languages.

3.2 Basic Java Syntax and Semantics

Having seen several Java programs in Chapter 2, we are ready for a more formal presentation of the language's basic elements. Some points have already been touched on in Chapter 2, but others are new.

Data Types

In Chapter 1, we showed that many types of information can be represented in computer memory as patterns of 0s and 1s, and as far as we know, so can information of every type. In this book, however, we are less ambitious and restrict our attention to just a few types of data. These fall into two main categories. The first category consists of what Java calls *primitive data types* and includes numbers (both integer and floating-point), characters (such as *A*, *B*, and *C*), and Booleans (restricted to the logical values `true` and `false`). The second category consists of objects, for instance, scanners. Strings are also in this second category.

Syntax

Java's syntax for manipulating primitive data types differs distinctly from the syntax for manipulating objects. Primitive data types are combined in expressions involving operators, such as addition and multiplication. Objects, on the other hand, are sent messages. In addition, objects must be instantiated before use, and there is no comparable requirement for primitive data types. For more information about data types, see Appendix B.

Actually, this concise picture is confused slightly by strings, which on the one hand are objects and are sent messages, but on the other hand do not need to be instantiated and can be combined using something called the *concatenation operator*.

Numbers

We close this subsection with a few details concerning the primitive data types for representing numbers, or *numeric data types*, as they are called for short. Java includes six numeric data types, but we restrict ourselves to just two. These are int (for integer) and double (for floating-point numbers—numbers with decimals). The range of values available with these two data types is shown in Table 3-2.

TABLE 3-2
Some Java numeric data types

TYPE	STORAGE REQUIREMENTS	RANGE
int	4 bytes	–2,147,483,648 to 2,147,483,647
double	8 bytes	–1.79769313486231570E+308 to 1.79769313486231570E+308

The other numeric data types are *short* (2 bytes for small integers), *long* (4 bytes for large integers), *byte*, and *float* (4 bytes for smaller, less precise floating-point numbers). The data types for Booleans and characters will be discussed in Chapters 6 and 7, respectively. A complete table of the storage requirements and range of each type appears in Appendix B.

Numeric calculations are a central part of most, though not all, programs, so we will become very familiar with the numeric data types. Programs that manipulate numeric data types often share a common format: input numeric data, perform calculations, output numeric results. The temperature conversion program in Chapter 2 adhered to this format.

EXERCISE 3.2

1. What is the difference between double and int data types?

2. How does the syntax for manipulating numeric data types and objects differ?

Literals

Literals are items in a program whose values do not change. They are restricted to the primitive data types and strings. Examples from the temperature conversion program in Chapter 2 included the numbers 5.0 and 9.0 and the string "Enter degrees Fahrenheit: ". Table 3-3 gives other examples of numeric literals (note that numeric literals never contain commas).

TABLE 3-3
Examples of numeric literals

EXAMPLE	DATA TYPE
51	an integer
–31444843	a negative integer
3.14	a floating-point number (double)
5.301E5	a floating-point number equivalent to $5.301 * 10^5$, or 530,100
5.301E–5	a floating-point number equivalent to $5.301 * 10^{-5}$, or 0.00005301 (double)

The last two examples in Table 3-3 are written in what is called *exponential* or *scientific notation* and are expressed as a decimal number followed by a power of 10. The letter *E* can be written in upper- or lowercase.

<u>EXERCISE 3.2 Continued</u>

3. Convert the following floating-point numbers to exponential notation:

    a. 23.5

    b. 0.046

4. Convert the following numbers from exponential notation to floating-point notation:

    a. 32.21E4

    b. 55.6E–3

5. Give two examples of string literals.

Variables and Their Declarations

A variable is an item whose value can change during the execution of a program. A variable can be thought of as a named location or cell in the computer's memory. Changing the value of a variable is equivalent to replacing the value that was in the cell with another value (Figure 3-1). For instance, at one point in a program we might set the value of the variable `fahrenheit` to 78.5. Later in the program, we could set the variable to another value such as –23.7. When we do this, the new value replaces the old one.

FIGURE 3-1
Changing the value of a variable

Although the value of a variable can change, the type of data it contains cannot; in other words, during the course of a program a specific variable can hold only one type of data. For instance, if it initially holds an integer, then it can never hold a floating-point number, and if it initially holds a reference to a pen, it can never hold a reference to a scanner.

Declarations

Before using a variable for the first time, the program must declare its type. This is done in a *variable declaration statement*, as illustrated in the following code:

```
int age;
double celsius;
String name;
Scanner reader;
```

The type appears on the left and the variable's name on the right. Frequently, we will speak of a *variable's type*, meaning the type indicator that appears on the left. Thus, we will say that celsius is a double.

It is permitted to declare several variables in a single declaration and simultaneously to assign them initial values. For instance, the following code segment initializes the variables z, q, pi, name, and reader:

```
int x, y, z = 7;
double p, q = 1.41, pi = 3.14, t;
String name = "Bill Jones";
Scanner reader = new Scanner(System.in);
```

The last statement declares the object variable reader, instantiates or creates a Scanner object that is attached to the keyboard input stream, System.in, and finally assigns the object to the variable. Instantiation takes the form

```
new <name of class>(<zero or more parameters>)
```

Object instantiation will be explained in detail in Chapter 5.

Constants

When initializing a variable, we occasionally want to specify that its value cannot change thereafter. This seems somewhat contradictory but is useful, as we shall see later. The next example illustrates how to do this:

```
final double SALES_TAX_RATE = .0785;
```

The keyword here is final, and a variable declared in this way is called a *constant*. It is customary to write the names of constants in uppercase. Any attempt to change the value of a constant after it is initialized is flagged by the compiler as an error.

EXERCISE 3.2 Continued

6. Why is a variable called a variable?

7. Return to the programs in Chapter 2 and find an example of each of the different types of variables. Which of the types listed in this subsection are not included?

EXERCISE 3.2 Continued

8. Declare a floating-point variable called `payRate` and simultaneously initialize it to $35.67.

9. Declare three integer variables (a, b, c) in a single declaration and simultaneously initialize b to `4`.

10. Give two examples of data that cannot be stored in a variable of type `int`.

11. There are approximately 2.2 pounds in a kilogram. Name and declare a constant to represent this value.

Assignment Statements

An assignment statement has the following form:

```
<variable> = <expression>;
```

where the value of the expression on the right is assigned to the variable on the left. For instance,

```
double celsius, fahrenheit;
String name;
Scanner reader;
. . .
fahrenheit = reader.nextDouble();
celsius = (fahrenheit - 32.0) * 5.0 / 9.0;
name = "Bill Smith";
reader = new Scanner(System.in);
```

Arithmetic Expressions

An *arithmetic expression* consists of operands and operators combined in a manner familiar from algebra. The usual rules apply:

- Multiplication and division are evaluated before addition and subtraction; that is, multiplication and division have higher precedence than addition and subtraction.

- Operators of equal precedence are evaluated from left to right.

- Parentheses can be used to change the order of evaluation.

Unlike in algebra, multiplication must be indicated explicitly: thus, a * b cannot be written as ab. Binary operators are placed between their operands (a * b, for example), whereas unary operators are placed before their operands (-a, for example). Table 3-4 shows several operands from the conversion program in Chapter 2, and Table 3-5 shows some common operators and their precedence.

TABLE 3-4
Examples of operands

TYPE	EXAMPLE
Literals	32.0 5.0 9.0
Variables	fahrenheit celsius
Parenthesized expressions	(fahrenheit - 32.0)

TABLE 3-5
Common operators and their precedence

OPERATOR	SYMBOL	PRECEDENCE (FROM HIGHEST TO LOWEST)	ASSOCIATION
Grouping	( )	1	Not applicable
Method selector	.	2	Left to right
Unary plus	+	3	Not applicable
Unary minus	–	3	Not applicable
Instantiation	new	3	Right to left
Cast	(double) (int)	3	Right to left
Multiplication	*	4	Left to right
Division	/	4	Left to right
Remainder or modulus	%	4	Left to right
Addition	+	5	Left to right
Subtraction	–	5	Left to right
Assignment	=	10	Right to left

Division

Several points concerning operators need explanation. The semantics of division are different for integer and floating-point operands. Thus,

```
5.0 / 2.0   yields   2.5
5 / 2 yields 2 (a quotient in which the fractional portion of the answer is
   simply dropped)
```

Modulus

The operator % yields the remainder obtained when one number is divided by another. Thus,

```
9 % 5 yields 4
9.3 % 5.1 yields 4.2
```

Precedence

When evaluating an expression, Java applies operators of higher precedence before those of lower precedence, unless overridden by parentheses. The highest precedence is 1.

```
3 + 5 * 3   yields 18
-3 + 5 * 3   yields 12
```

```
+3 + 5 * 3   yields 18 (use of unary + is uncommon)
3 + 5 * -3   yields -12
3 + 5 * +3   yields 18 (use of unary + is uncommon)
(3 + 5) * 3  yields 24
3 + 5 % 3    yields 5
(3 + 5) % 3  yields 2
```

Association

The column labeled "Association" in Table 3-5 indicates the order in which to perform operations of equal precedence. Thus,

```
18 - 3 - 4   yields 11
18 / 3 * 4   yields 24
18 % 3 * 4   yields 0
a = b = 7;   assigns 7 to b and then b to a
```

More Examples

Some more examples of expressions and their values are shown in Table 3-6. In this table, we see the application of two fairly obvious rules governing the use of parentheses:

1. Parentheses must occur in matching pairs.

2. Parenthetical expressions may be nested but must not overlap.

TABLE 3-6
Examples of expressions and their values

EXPRESSION	SAME AS	VALUE
3 + 4 – 5	7 – 5	2
3 + (4 – 5)	3 + (–1)	2
3 + 4 * 5	3 + 20	23
(3 + 4) * 5	7 * 5	35
8 / 2 + 6	4 + 6	10
8 / (2 + 6)	8 / 8	1
10 – 3 – 4 – 1	7 – 4 – 1	2
10 – (3 – 4 – 1)	10 – (–2)	12
(15 + 9) / (3 + 1)	24 / 4	6
15 + 9 / 3 + 1	15 + 3 + 1	19
(15 + 9) / ((3 + 1) * 2)	24 / (4 * 2) 24 / 8	3
(15 + 9) / (3 + 1) * 2	24 / 4 * 2 6 * 2	12

EXERCISE 3.2 Continued

12. Assume that the integer variable x is 5 and the integer variable y is 10. Give the values of the following expressions:

a. x + y * 2

b. x – y + 2

c. (x + y) * 2

d. y % x

13. Find the syntax errors in the following expressions:

a. a – * b + c

b. – (a + b) * c)

c. ()

Maximum, Minimum, and Arithmetic Overflow

Numeric data types in any programming language support a finite range of values. For example, values of type int in Java range from a minimum of –2,147,483,648 to a maximum of 2,147,483,647. Instead of having to remember these numbers, the programmer can refer to them with the constants Integer.MIN_VALUE and Integer.MAX_VALUE, respectively. The same constants are included in the Double class for the bounds of double values.

It is natural to ask what would happen if a program tried to add 1 to the maximum integer value. This would result in a condition known as arithmetic overflow. Subtracting 1 from the minimum value would produce the same error. Programs written in some languages would halt with a run-time error, whereas others would continue after ruining part of the computer's operating system. The JVM simply inverts the sign of the number and allows the program to continue. Thus, adding 1 to Integer.MAX_VALUE would produce Integer.MIN_VALUE. So, if you see large negative integers in your program's output, you might have this type of error.

Mixed-Mode Arithmetic

When working with a handheld calculator, we do not give much thought to the fact that we intermix integers and floating-point numbers. This is called *mixed-mode arithmetic*. For instance, if a circle has radius 3, we compute the area as follows:

```
3.14 * 3 * 3
```

In Java, when there is a binary operation on operands of different numeric types, the less inclusive type (int) is temporarily and automatically converted to the more inclusive type (double) before the operation is performed. Thus, in

```
double d;
d = 5.0 / 2;
```

the value of d is computed as 5.0/2.0, yielding 2.5. However, problems can arise when using mixed-mode arithmetic. For instance

```
3 / 2 * 5.0 yields   1 * 5.0   yields   5.0
```

whereas

```
3 / 2.0 * 5 yields   1.5 * 5   yields   7.5
```

Mixed-mode assignments are also allowed, provided the variable on the left is of a more inclusive type than the expression on the right. Otherwise, a syntax error occurs, as shown in the following code segment:

```
double d;
int i;
i = 45;   ← OK, because we assign an int to an int.
d = i;    ← OK, because d is more inclusive than i. The value 45.0 is stored in d.
i = d;    ← Syntax error because i is less inclusive than d.
```

EXERCISE 3.2 Continued

14. Assume that x is 4.5 and y is 2. Write the values of the following expressions:

a. x / y

b. y / x

c. x % y

15. Assume that x and y are of type `double` and z is of type `int`. For each of the following assignment statements, state which are valid and which produce syntax errors:

a. x = z

b. x = y * z

c. z = x + y

Casting to `int` and `double`

The difficulties associated with mixed-mode arithmetic can be circumvented using a technique called *casting*, which allows one data type to be explicitly converted to another. For instance, consider the following example:

```
int i;
double d;

i = (int)3.14;        ← i equals 3, truncation toward 0
d = (double)5 / 4;    ← d equals 1.25
```

The cast operator, either `(int)` or `(double)`, appears immediately before the expression it is supposed to convert. The `(int)` cast simply throws away the digits after the decimal point, which has the effect of truncation toward 0.

Precedence

The cast operator has high precedence (see Table 3-5) and must be used with care, as illustrated in the following code:

```
double x, y;

x = (double)5 / 4;     ← x equals 5.0 / 4 equals 1.25
y = (double)(5 / 4);   ← y equals (double)(1) equals 1.0
```

Rounding

The cast operator is useful for rounding floating-point numbers to the nearest integer:

```
int m, n;
double x, y;

x = . . . ;              ← some positive value is assigned to x
m = (int)(x + 0.5);

y = - . . .;             ← some negative value is assigned to y
n = (int)(x - 0.5);
```

Other numeric casts such as (char) and (float) are discussed in Appendix B.

EXERCISE 3.2 Continued

16. Assume that x is of type double and y is of type int. Also assume that x is 4.5 and y is 2. Write the values of the following expressions:

a. (int) x * y

b. (int) (x * y)

17. Assume that x is of type double and y is of type int. Write a statement that assigns the value contained in x to y after rounding this value to the nearest whole number.

String Expressions and Methods

Strings are used in programs in a variety of ways. As already seen, they can be used as literals or assigned to variables. Now we see that they can be combined in expressions using the concatenation operator, and they also can be sent messages.

Simple Concatenation

The concatenation operator uses the plus symbol (+). The following is an example:

```
String firstName,                              // declare four string
        lastName,                              // variables
        fullName,
        lastThenFirst;

firstName = "Bill";                            // initialize firstName
lastName = "Smith";                            // initialize lastName

fullName = firstName + " " + lastName;         // yields "Bill Smith"
lastThenFirst = lastName + ", " + firstName    // yields "Smith, Bill"
```

Concatenating Strings and Numbers

Strings also can be concatenated to numbers. When this occurs, the number is automatically converted to a string before the concatenation operator is applied:

```
String message;
int x = 20, y = 35;
```

```
message = "Bill sold " + x + " and Sylvia sold " + y + " subscriptions.";
// yields "Bill sold 20 and Sylvia sold 35 subscriptions."
```

Precedence of Concatenation

The concatenation operator has the same precedence as addition, which can lead to unexpected results:

```
"number " + 3 + 4        →  "number 3" + 4    →  "number 34"
"number " + (3 + 4)      →  "number " + 7     →  "number 7"
"number " + 3 * 4        →  "number " + 12    →  "number 12"
3 + 4 + "number"         →  7 + "number"      →  "7 number"
```

Escape Character

String literals are delimited by quotation marks ("..."), which presents a dilemma when quotation marks are supposed to appear inside a string. Placing a special character before the quotation mark, indicating the quotation mark is to be taken literally and not as a delimiter, solves the problem. This special character, also called the *escape character*, is a back slash (\).

```
message = "As the train left the station, " +
          "the conductor yelled, \"All aboard.\"";
```

Other Uses for the Escape Character

The escape character also is used when including other special characters in string literals. The sequence backslash-t (\t) indicates a tab character, and backslash-n (\n) indicates a newline character. These special sequences involving the backslash character are called **escape sequences**. The following code gives an example of the use of escape sequences followed by the output generated by the code:

Code

```
System.out.print ("The room was full of animals: \n" +
                  "\tdogs,\n\tcats, and\n\tchimpanzees.\n";
```

Output

```
The room was full of animals:
      dogs,
      cats, and
      chimpanzees.
```

Escaping the Escape Character

In solving one problem, we have introduced another. The backslash is the designated escape character, but sometimes a string must contain a backslash. This is accomplished by placing two backslashes in sequence:

```
path = "C:\\Java\\Ch3.doc";        • yields the string C:\Java\Ch3.doc
```

There are several other escape sequences, but we omit them from this discussion (see Appendix B for further details).

The `length` Method

Strings are objects and implement several methods. In this chapter, we consider only the `length` method and defer discussions of others until Chapters 6 and 11 (for users of the Introductory and Comprehensive texts). A string returns its length in response to a `length` message:

```
String theString;
int theLength;

theString = "The cat sat on the mat.";
theLength = theString.length();          ← yields 23
```

EXERCISE 3.2 Continued

18. Assume that x refers to the string "`Wizard`" and y refers to the string "`Java`". Write the values of the following expressions:

a. `y + x`

b. `y + y.length() + x`

c. `y + "\n" + x + "\n"`

19. Declare a variable of type `String` called `myInfo` and initialize it to your name, address, and telephone number. Each item of information in this string should be followed by a newline character.

Methods, Messages, and Signatures

Classes implement methods, and objects are instances of classes. An object can respond to a message only if its class implements a corresponding method. To correspond, the method must have the same name as the message. Thus a pen object responds to the `move` message because the `StandardPen` class defines a `move` method.

Messages are sometimes accompanied by parameters and sometimes not:

```
double x = reader .nextDouble();   // No parameters expected
System.out.println(50.5);          // One parameter expected
```

The parameters included when a message is sent must match exactly in number and type the parameters expected by the method. For instance, the `Math.sqrt` method expects a single parameter of type `double`.

```
double d = 24.6;

Math.sqrt(d)           // Perfect! A parameter of type double is expected.
Math.sqrt(2.0 * d)     // Perfect! The expression yields a double.
Math.sqrt(4)           // Fine! Integers can stand in for doubles.
Math.sqrt();           // Error! A parameter is needed.
Math.sqrt(6.7, 3.4);   // Error! One parameter only please.
Math.sqrt("far");      // Error! A string parameter is NOT acceptable.
```

Some methods return a value and others do not. The `println` method does not return a value; however, the method `nextDouble` in class `Scanner` does:

```
Scanner reader = new Scanner();
double x;

x = reader.nextDouble();        // Returns the number entered by the user.
```

To use a method successfully we must know

- What type of value it returns

- Its name

- The number and type of the parameters it expects

A method's name and the types and number of its parameters are called the method's *signature*. From now on, when we introduce a new class, we will make a point of listing method signatures together with brief descriptions of what the methods do. Following are two examples, the first from the `Scanner` class and the second from the `PrintStream` class:

```
double nextDouble()      Returns a double entered by the user at the
                         keyboard.
void   println (double n)   Writes n to the print stream.
```

The word `void` indicates that the method does not return a value.

EXERCISE 3.2 Continued

20. What is the difference between a message and a method?

21. Describe the purpose of each item of information that appears in a method's signature.

User-Defined Symbols

Variable and program names are examples of user-defined symbols. You will see other examples later in the book. We now explain the rules for forming or naming user-defined symbols. These names must consist of a letter followed by a sequence of letters and/or digits. Letters are defined to be

- A ... Z

- a ... z

- _ and $

- Symbols that denote letters in several languages other than English

Digits are the characters 0 ... 9. Names are case-sensitive; thus, `celsius` and `Celsius` are different names.

Some words cannot be employed as user-defined symbols. These words are called *keywords* or **reserved words** because they have special meaning in Java. Table 3-7 shows a list of Java's reserved words. You will encounter most of them by the end of the book. They appear in blue in program code examples. These words are case-sensitive also, thus "import" is a reserved word but "Import" and "IMPORT" are not.

TABLE 3-7
Java's reserved words

abstract	double	int	static
assert	false	strictfp	true
boolean	else	interface	super
break	extends	long	switch
byte	final	native	synchronized
case	finally	new	this
catch	float	null	throw
char	for	package	throws
class	goto	private	transient
const	if	protected	try
continue	implements	public	void
default	import	return	volatile
do	instanceof	short	while

Here are examples of valid and invalid variable names:

Valid Names   `surfaceArea3`   `_$_$$$`

Invalid Names   `3rdPayment`   `pay.rate`   `abstract`

The first invalid name begins with a digit. The second invalid name contains a period. The third invalid name is a reserved word.

Well-chosen variable names greatly increase a program's readability and maintainability; consequently, it is considered good programming practice to use meaningful names such as

`radius`   rather than   `r`

`taxableIncome`   rather than   `ti`

When forming a compound variable name, programmers usually capitalize the first letter of each word except the first. For instance,

`taxableIncome`   rather than

`taxableincome`   or

`TAXABLEINCOME`   or

`TaxableIncome`

On the other hand, all the words in a program's name typically begin with a capital letter, for instance, `ComputeEmployeePayroll`. Finally, constant names usually are all uppercase. The goal of these rules and of all stylistic conventions is to produce programs that are easier to understand and maintain.

EXERCISE 3.2 Continued

22. State whether each of the following are valid or invalid user-defined symbols in Java:

   a. pricePerSquareInch

   b. student2

   c. 2GuysFromLexington

   d. PI

   e. allDone?

23. Write names for the following items that follow good programming practice:

   a. A variable that represents the diameter of a circle

   b. A constant that represents the standard deduction for an income tax return

   c. A method that draws a rectangle

Packages and the `import` statement

Programmers seldom write programs from scratch. Instead, they rely heavily on code written by many other programmers, most of whom they will never meet. Fortunately, Java provides a mechanism called a *package* that makes it easy for programmers to share code. Having written a class or group of classes that provide some generally useful service, a programmer can collect the classes together in a package. Other programmers who want to use the service can then import classes from the package. The programs in Chapter 2 illustrated the use of a package called `java.util`. The Java programming environment typically includes a large number of standard packages, some of which we use in subsequent chapters. These packages are standard because we expect to find them in every Java programming environment. Some packages are nonstandard and are created by their authors to support various applications.

When using a package, a programmer imports the desired class or classes. The general form of an `import` statement is

```
import x.y.z;
```

where

■ `x` is the overall name of the package.

■ `y` is the name of a subsection within the package.

■ `z` is the name of a particular class in the subsection.

It is possible to import all the classes within a subsection at once; however, we do not usually do so. The statement to import all the classes with a subsection looks like this:

```
import x.y.*;
```

In general, a package can have any number of subsections, including zero, which is the case for several packages used in this book, and each subsection can in turn have any number of subsubsections, and so on. When used, an asterisk (*) can appear only at the lowest level. The asterisk is used to make available all of the classes in a package.

24. Describe the role of the items x, y, and z in the statement import x.y.Z;.

25. What happens when the computer executes the statement import x.y.*;?

3.3 Terminal I/O for Different Data Types

Objects support terminal input and output (I/O). An instance of the class Scanner supports input and the object System.out supports output. The latter object is an instance of the class PrintStream. This class, together with a number of others, is available to Java programmers without specifying their names in import statements. Although System.out is an instance of the class PrintStream, do not try to instantiate this class until you become familiar with working in Java files.

Table 3-8 summarizes some of the methods in the class Scanner. The object System.out understands two messages, print and println. Both messages expect a single parameter, which can be of any type, including an object; however, we postpone using an object as a parameter until Chapter 5.

TABLE 3-8
Methods in class Scanner

METHOD	DESCRIPTION
double nextDouble()	Returns the first double in the input line. Leading and trailing spaces are ignored.
int nextInt()	Returns the first integer in the input line. Leading and trailing spaces are ignored.
String nextLine()	Returns the input line, including leading and trailing spaces. *Warning*: A leading newline is returned as an empty string.

The following program illustrates the major features of terminal I/O:

```java
// Example 3.1: tests 3 types of input data

import java.util.Scanner;

public class TestTerminalIO {

    public static void main (String [] args) {
        Scanner reader = new Scanner(System.in);

        String name;
        int age;
        double weight;
```

```
      System.out.print ("Enter your name (a string): ");
      name = reader.nextLine();

      System.out.print ("Enter your age (an integer): ");
      age = reader.nextInt();

      System.out.print ("Enter your weight (a double): ");
      weight = reader.nextDouble();

      System.out.println ("Greetings " + name +
                           ". You are " + age +
                           " years old and you weigh " + weight +
                           " pounds.");

   }
}
```

When the program encounters an input statement—for instance, `reader.nextInt();`—it pauses and waits for the user to press Enter, at which point the `reader` object processes the user's input. The interaction with the user looks something like this, where the user's input is shown in boldface and the use of the Enter key is shown in italics:

```
Enter your name (a string): Carole JonesEnter
Enter your age (an integer): 45Enter
Enter your weight (a double): 130.6Enter
Greetings Carole Jones. You are 45 years old and you weigh 130.6 pounds.
```

The example program in this section reads a line of text followed by two numbers. Let's consider a code segment that reads numbers followed by a line of text, as follows:

```
System.out.print("Enter your age (an integer): ");
age = reader.nextInt();

System.out.print("Enter your weight (a double): ");
weight = reader.nextDouble();

System.out.print("Enter your name (a string): ");
name = reader.nextLine();
```

The program will receive the numbers as entered, but unfortunately the string input on the last line of code will be empty (""). The reason for this is that the method `nextDouble`, which input the last number two steps earlier, ignored but did not consume the newline that the user entered following the number. Therefore, this newline character was waiting to be consumed by the next call of `nextLine`, which was expecting more data! To avoid this problem, you should either input all the lines of text before the numbers or, when that is not feasible, run an extra call of `nextLine` after numeric input to eliminate the trailing newline character. Here is code that uses the second alternative:

```
System.out.print("Enter your age (an integer): ");
age = reader.nextInt();

System.out.print("Enter your weight (a double): ");
weight = reader.nextDouble();
```

```
reader.nextLine();    // Consume the newline character

System.out.print("Enter your name (a string): ");
name = reader.nextLine();
```

EXERCISE 3.3

1. Write code segments that perform the following tasks:

   a. Prompt the user for an hourly wage and read the wage into a `double` variable `wage`.

   b. Prompt the user for a Social Security number and read this value into the `String` variable `ssn`.

2. What is the purpose of the method `nextInt()`?

3. Explain what happens when a program reads a number from the keyboard and then attempts to read a line of text from the keyboard.

 Programming Skills

THE JAVA API AND javadoc

Most programming languages are defined in language reference manuals. These manuals show the syntax, the semantics, and how to use the basic features of the language. For Java, this documentation can be found in the Java Application Programming Interface (API). You can browse the Java API online at Sun's Web site or download the API for your particular version of Java to browse locally on your own computer.

You can browse for a given class's information by selecting the name of the class from a master list of classes or by selecting its package from a master list of packages. You can quickly drill down from there to a list of the class's methods and finally to the information for an individual method. The screen shots in Figure 3-2 show part of the method list in the `Scanner` class and the detailed information for the method `hasNext()`, respectively. The API for Java is enormous, with dozens of packages, hundreds of classes, and thousands of methods. However, the browser allows you to locate most information on a given item with a few mouse clicks, and links provide helpful cross-references to related items.

In addition to the `javac` and `java` commands for compiling and running programs, Sun provides a `javadoc` command that allows you to create browsable documentation for your own code. We explore how to create this documentation when we examine interfaces for user-defined classes in Chapter 10.

FIGURE 3-2

A portion of Sun's documentation for the Java API

3.4 Comments

When we first write a program, we are completely familiar with all its nuances; however, six months later, when we or someone else has to modify it, the code that was once so clear often seems confusing and mysterious. There is, however, a technique for dealing with this situation. The remedy is to include comments in the code. *Comments* are explanatory sentences inserted in a program in such a manner that the compiler ignores them. There are two styles for indicating comments:

- End of line comments: these include all of the text following a double slash (//) on any given line; in other words, this style is best for just one line of comment.

- Multiline comments: these include all of the text between an opening /* and a closing */.

Comments appear in green in this book. The following code segment illustrates the use of both kinds of comments:

```
/* This code segment illustrates the
use of assignment statements and comments */

a = 3;              // assign 3 to variable a
b = 4;              // assign 4 to variable b
c = a + b;          // add the number in variable a
                    //     to the number in variable b
                    //     and assign the result, 7, to variable c
c = c * 3;          // multiply the number in variable c by 3
                    //     and assign the result, 21, to variable c
```

Although this code segment illustrates the mechanics of how to include comments in a program, it gives a misleading idea of when to use them. The main purpose of comments is to make a program more readable and thus easier to maintain. With this end in mind, we usually

■ Begin a program with a statement of its purpose and other information that would help orient a programmer called on to modify the program at some future date.

■ Accompany a variable declaration with a comment that explains the variable's purpose.

■ Precede major segments of code with brief comments that explain their purpose.

■ Include comments to explain the workings of complex or tricky sections of code.

The case study in the next section follows these guidelines and illustrates a reasonable and helpful level of comments. Because the programs in this book usually are accompanied by an extensive discussion of what they do, we sometimes include few or no comments; however, the programs you write should always be well commented.

Too many comments are as harmful as too few because, over time, the burden of maintaining the comments becomes excessive. No matter how many comments are included in a program, future programmers must still read and understand the region of code they intend to modify. Common sense usually leads to a reasonable balance. We should always avoid comments that do nothing more than restate the obvious. For instance, the next comment is completely pointless:

```
a = 3;      // assign 3 to variable a. Duh!
```

The best-written programs are self-documenting; that is, the reader can understand the code from the symbols used and from the structure and overall organization of the program.

EXERCISE 3.4

1. Describe the difference between an end-of-line comment and a multiline comment.

2. State two rules of thumb for writing appropriate comments in a program.

Case Study 1: Income Tax Calculator

It is now time to write a program that illustrates some of the concepts we have been presenting. We do this in the context of a case study that adheres to the software development life cycle discussed in Chapter 1. This life cycle approach may seem overly elaborate for small programs, but it scales up well when programs become larger.

Each year nearly everyone with an income faces the unpleasant task of computing his or her income tax return. If only it could be done as easily as suggested in this case study.

Request

Write a program that computes a person's income tax.

Analysis

Here is the relevant tax law (mythical in nature):

- There is a flat tax rate of 20 percent.

- There is a $10,000 standard deduction.

- There is a $2000 additional deduction for each dependent.

- Gross income must be entered to the nearest penny.

- The income tax is expressed as a decimal number.

The user inputs are the gross income and number of dependents. The program calculates the income tax based on the inputs and the tax law and then displays the income tax. Figure 3-3 shows the proposed terminal user interface. Characters in boldface indicate user inputs. The program prints the rest. The inclusion of a user interface at this point is a good idea because it allows the customer and the programmer to discuss the intended program's behavior in a context understandable to both.

FIGURE 3-3
The user Interface for the income tax calculator

```
Enter the gross income: 50000.50
Enter the number of dependents: 4
The income tax is $6400.1
```

Design

During analysis, we specify what a program is going to do, and during design we describe how it is going to do it. This involves writing the algorithm used by the program. *Webster's New Collegiate Dictionary* defines an *algorithm* as "a step-by-step procedure for solving a problem or accomplishing some end." A recipe in a cookbook is a good example of an algorithm. Program algorithms are often written in a somewhat stylized version of English called **pseudocode**. The following is the pseudocode for our income tax program:

```
read grossIncome
read numDependents
compute taxableIncome = grossIncome - 10000 - 2000 * numDependents
compute incomeTax = taxableIncome * 0.20
print incomeTax
```

Although there are no precise rules governing the syntax of pseudocode, you should strive to describe the essential elements of the program in a clear and concise manner. Over time, you will develop a style that suits you.

Implementation

Given the preceding pseudocode, an experienced programmer now would find it easy to write the corresponding Java program. For a beginner, on the other hand, writing the code is the most difficult part of the process. The following is the program:

```java
/*Case study 3.1: an income tax calculator
Compute a person's income tax
1. Significant constants
      tax rate
      standard deduction
      deduction per dependent
2. The inputs are
      gross income
      number of dependents
3. Computations:
      net income = gross income - the standard deduction -
                   a deduction for each dependent
      income tax = is a fixed percentage of the net income
4. The outputs are
      the income tax
*/

import java.util.Scanner;

public class IncomeTaxCalculator{

    public static void main(String [] args){

        // Constants
        final double TAX_RATE = 0.20;
        final double STANDARD_DEDUCTION = 10000.0;
        final double DEPENDENT_DEDUCTION = 2000.0;

        Scanner reader = new Scanner(System.in);

        double grossIncome;         // the gross income (input)
        int   numDependents;        // the number of dependents (input)
        double taxableIncome;       // the taxable income (calculated)
        double incomeTax;           // the income tax (calculated and
                                    // output)

        // Request the inputs
        System.out.print("Enter the gross income: ");
        grossIncome = reader.nextDouble();
        System.out.print("Enter the number of dependents: ");
        numDependents = reader.nextInt();
```

```
    // Compute the income tax
    taxableIncome = grossIncome - STANDARD_DEDUCTION -
                    DEPENDENT_DEDUCTION * numDependents;
    incomeTax = taxableIncome * TAX_RATE;

    // Display the income tax
    System.out.println("The income tax is $" + incomeTax);
  }
}
```

Notice that we have used mixed-mode arithmetic, but in a manner that does not produce any undesired effects.

 Computer Ethics

COMPUTER VIRUSES

A *virus* is a computer program that can replicate itself and move from computer to computer. Some programmers of viruses intend no harm; they just want to demonstrate their prowess by creating viruses that go undetected. Other programmers of viruses intend harm by causing system crashes, corruption of data, or hardware failures.

Viruses migrate by attaching themselves to normal programs, and then become active again when these programs are launched. Early viruses were easily detected if one had detection software. This software examined portions of each program on the suspect computer and could repair infected programs.

Viruses and virus detectors have coevolved through the years, however, and both kinds of software have become very sophisticated. Viruses now hide themselves better than they used to; virus detectors can no longer just examine pieces of data stored in memory to reveal the presence or absence of a virus. Researchers have recently developed a method of running a program that might contain a virus to see whether or not the virus becomes active. The suspect program runs in a "safe" environment that protects the computer from any potential harm. As you can imagine, this process takes time and costs money. For an overview of the history of viruses and the new detection technology, see Carey Nactenberg, "Computer Virus-Antivirus Coevolution," *Communications of the ACM*, Volume 40, No. 1 (January 1997): 46–51.

3.5 *Programming Errors*

According to an old saying, we learn from our mistakes, which is fortunate because most people find it almost impossible to write even simple programs without making numerous mistakes. These mistakes, or errors, are of three types: syntax errors, run-time errors, and logic errors.

The Three Types of Errors

Syntax errors, as we learned in Chapter 2, occur when we violate a syntax rule, no matter how minor. These errors are detected at compile time. For instance, if a semicolon is missing at the end of a statement or if a variable is used before it is declared, the compiler is unable to translate the program into byte code. The good news is that when the Java compiler finds a syntax error, it prints an error message, and we can make the needed correction. The bad news, as we saw previously, is that the error messages are often quite cryptic. Knowing that there is a syntax error at a particular point in a program, however, is usually a sufficient clue for finding the error.

Run-time errors occur when we ask the computer to do something that it considers illegal, such as dividing by 0. For example, suppose that the symbols x and y are variables. Then the expression x/y is syntactically correct, so the compiler does not complain. However, when the expression is evaluated during execution of the program, the meaning of the expression depends on the values contained in the variables. If the variable y has the value 0, then the expression cannot be evaluated. The good news is that the Java runtime environment will print a message telling us the nature of the error and where it was encountered. Once again, the bad news is that the error message might be hard to understand.

Logic errors (also called *design errors* or *bugs*) occur when we fail to express ourselves accurately. For instance, in everyday life, we might give someone the instruction to turn left when what we really meant to say is to turn right. In this example,

- The instruction is phrased properly, and thus the syntax is correct.

- The instruction is meaningful, and thus the semantics are valid.

- But the instruction does not do what we intended, and thus is logically incorrect.

The bad news is that programming environments do not detect logic errors automatically. The good news is that this text offers useful tips on how to prevent logic errors and how to detect them when they occur.

Now let's look at examples of each of these types of errors.

Illustration of Syntax Errors

We have already seen examples of syntax errors in Chapter 2; however, seeing a few more will be helpful. The following is a listing of the income tax calculator program with the addition of two syntax errors. See if you can spot them. The line numbers are not part of the program but are intended to facilitate the discussion that follows the listing.

```
1    import java.util.Scanner;
2
3    public class IncomeTaxCalculator{
4      public static void main(String [] args){
5
6          final double TAX_RATE = 0.20;
7          final double STANDARD_DEDUCTION = 10000.0;
```

```
 8         final double DEPENDENT_DEDUCTION = 2000.0;
 9
10         Scanner reader = new Scanner(System.in);
11
12         double grossIncome;
13         int numDependents;
14         double taxableIncome;
15         double incomeTax;
16
17         System.out.print("Enter the gross income: ");
18         grossIncome = reader.readDouble();
19         System.out.print("Enter the number of dependents: ");
20         numDependents = reader.nextInt();
21
22         taxableIncome = grossincome - STANDARD_DEDUCTION -
23                         DEPENDENT_DEDUCTION * numDependents;
24         incomeTax = taxableIncome * TAX_RATE
25
26         System.out.println("The income tax is $" + incomeTax);
27    }
28 }
```

Just in case you could not spot them, the errors in the code are

- In line 22, where `grossIncome` has been misspelled as `grossincome` (remember Java is case-sensitive)

- In line 24, where the semicolon is missing at the end of the line

When the program is compiled, the terminal window contains the following error message (we could show a snapshot of the window, but we think the following plain text is more readable):

```
IncomeTaxCalculator.java:25: ';' expected
^
1 error-
```

Although the compiler says that the error occurs on line 25, the semicolon is actually missing on the previous line. The corrective action is to go back into the editor, fix this error, save the file, and compile again. Then you will see a message to the effect that the symbol `grossincome` cannot be found. You may need to repeat this process a number of times until the compiler stops finding syntax errors.

Turn to the supplemental materials and read any additional instructions that apply to your development environment.

Illustration of Run-time Errors

There are a variety of run-time errors. We now present several of the most basic. We encounter others later in the book.

Division by Integer Zero

For our first run-time error, we write a small program that attempts to perform division by 0. As is well known, division by 0 is not a well-defined operation and should be avoided. Nonetheless, we must ask what happens if we accidentally write a program that tries it. The following is a trivial program that illustrates the situation:

```java
// Example 3.2: attempt to divide an int by zero

public class DivideByIntegerZero{
   public static void main(String [] args){
      int i, j = 0;
      i = 3 / j;
      System.out.println("The value of i is " + i);
   }
}
```

When we attempt to run this program, execution stops prematurely, and the following error message is displayed:

```
Exception in thread "main" java.lang.ArithmeticException: / by zero
        at DivideByIntegerZero.main(DivideByIntegerZero.java:4)
```

In this circumstance, we say that the JVM has thrown an *exception*. The message indicates the nature of the problem, "ArithmeticException: / by zero," and its location, in line 4 of method `main`.

Division by Floating-Point Zero

Interestingly, the JVM responds rather differently when the division involves a floating-point rather than an integer 0. Consider the following nearly identical program:

```java
// Example 3.3: attempt to divide a double by zero

public class DivideByFloatingPointZero {
   public static void main(String [] args) {
      double i, j = 0.0;
      i = 3.0 / j;
      System.out.println ("The value of i is " + i);
      System.out.println ("10 / i equals " + 10 / i);
   }
}
```

The program now runs to completion, and the output is

```
The value of i is Infinity
10 / i equals 0.0
```

In other words, the value of the variable `i` is considered to be `Infinity`, which is to say it falls outside the range of a `double`, and if we now divide another number by `i`, we obtain 0.

Null Pointer Exception

Not all run-time errors involve arithmetic. Variables frequently represent objects. Sending a message to such a variable before the corresponding object has been instantiated causes a null pointer exception. Fortunately, many compilers detect the possibility of this error before it arises; however, later in this book the problem occurs in situations that the compiler cannot detect. The following is an example program with the accompanying compiler error message:

The Program

```java
import java.util.Scanner;

public class Test{
   public static void main(String [] args){
      Scanner reader;
      int age;
      age = reader.nextInt();
   }
}
```

The Compiler Error Message

```
C:\Test.java:7: Variable reader may not have been initialized.
     age = reader.nextInt();
                 ^

1 error
```

In this code, the compiler says that the variable `reader` may not have been initialized. If that's true (and in this case, it is), the attempt to send a message to it at runtime will cause an error. The reason the variable is not initialized is that no value has been assigned to it with an assignment statement.

No Such Method Error

The following is a final, and rather puzzling, example of a run-time error. You might not notice it, even after you examine the program and the error message.

The Program

```java
// Example 3.4: a puzzling run-time error

public class PuzzlingRuntimeError{
   public static void Main(String [] args){
      System.out.println ("Hello World!");
   }
}
```

The Run-time Error Message

```
Exception in thread "main" java.lang.NoSuchMethodError: main
```

Have you spotted the problem? The word `main` has been misspelled as `Main`. Remember that Java is case-sensitive, and computers are exasperatingly literal minded. They never try to guess what you meant to say, so every mistake, no matter how small, is significant.

Illustration of Logic Errors

Incorrect output is the most obvious indication that there is a logic error in a program. For instance, suppose our temperature conversion program converts 212.0 degrees Fahrenheit to 100.06 instead of 100.0 degrees Celsius. The error is small, but we notice it. And if we do not, our customers, for whom we have written the program, surely will. We caused the problem by incorrectly using 31.9 instead of 32 in the following statement:

```
celsius = (fahrenheit - 31.9) * 5.0 / 9.0;
```

Test Data

Errors of this sort are usually found by running a program with test data for which we already know the correct output. We then compare the program's output with the expected results. If there is a difference, we reexamine the program's logic to determine why the program is not behaving as expected.

But how many tests must we perform on a program before we can feel confident that it contains no more logic errors? Sometimes the fundamental nature of a program provides an answer. Perhaps your mathematical skills are sufficiently fresh to recognize that the statement

```
celsius = (fahrenheit  - 32.0) * 5.0 / 9.0;
```

is actually the equation of a line. Because two points determine a line, if the program works correctly for two temperatures, it should work correctly for all. In general, however, it is difficult to determine how many tests are enough. But we often can break down the data into categories and test one number in each, the assumption being that if the program works correctly for one number in a category, it will work correctly for all the other numbers in the same category. Careful choice of categories then becomes crucial.

Desk Checking

We can also reduce the number of logic errors in a program by rereading the code carefully after we have written it. This is called *desk checking* and is best done when the mind is fresh. It is even possible to use mathematical techniques to prove that a program or segment of a program is free of logic errors. Because programming requires exhausting and excruciating attention to detail, avoid programming for long stretches of time or when tired, a rule you will break frequently unless you manage your time well.

Usually, we never can be certain that a program is error free, and after making a reasonable but large number of tests, we release the program for distribution and wait anxiously for the complaints. If we release too soon, the number of errors will be so high that we will lose credibility and customers, but if we wait too long, the competition will beat us to the market.

E XERCISE 3.5

1. At what point in the program development process are syntax errors, run-time errors, and logic errors detected?

2. Give an example of a run-time error and explain why the computer cannot catch it earlier in the program development process.

EXERCISE 3.5 Continued

3. State the type of error (compile-time, run-time, or logic) that occurs in each of the following pieces of code:

a. x = y / 0

b. x + y = z

c. area = length + width

3.6 Debugging

After we have established that a program contains a logic error, or *bug* as it is more affectionately called, we still have the problem of finding it. Sometimes the nature of a bug suggests its general location in a program. We then can reread this section of the program carefully with the hope of spotting the error. Unfortunately, the bug often is not located where we expect to find it, and even if it is, we probably miss it. After all, we thought we were writing the program correctly in the first place, so when we reread it, we tend to see what we were trying to say rather than what we actually said.

Programmers, as a consequence, are frequently forced to resort to a rather tedious, but powerful, technique for finding bugs. We add to the program extra lines of code that print the values of selected variables in the terminal window. Of course, we add these lines where we anticipate they will do the most good—that is, preceding and perhaps following the places in the program where we think the bug is most likely located. We then run the program again, and from the extra output, we can determine if any of the variables deviate from their expected values. If one of them does, then we know the bug is close by, but if none do, we must try again at a different point in the program. A variable's value is printed in the terminal window as follows:

```
System.out.println ("<some message>" + <variable name>);
```

Now let us try to find a bug that has been secretly inserted into the temperature conversion program. Suppose the program behaves as shown in Figure 3-4. Something is seriously wrong. The program claims that 212 degrees Fahrenheit converts to 41.1 degrees Celsius instead of the expected 100.

FIGURE 3-4
Incorrect output from the temperature conversion program

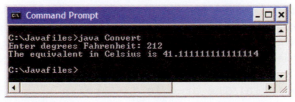

Perhaps we can find the problem by checking the value of fahrenheit just before celsius is calculated. The needed code looks like this:

```
System.out.println ("fahrenheit = " + fahrenheit);   ← This is the
                                                          debugging code

celsius = (fahrenheit - 32.0) * 5.0 / 9.0;
```

When we run the program again with the debugging code included, we get the following output:

```
Enter degrees Fahrenheit: 212
Fahrenheit = 106.0
The equivalent in Celsius is 41.111111111111114
```

We entered 212, but for some reason, the program says the value of `fahrenheit` is 106. Perhaps we should look at the surrounding code and see if we can spot the error. Here is the relevant code:

```
. . .
System.out.print ("Enter degrees Fahrenheit: ");
fahrenheit = reader.nextDouble() / 2.0;
System.out.println ("fahrenheit = " + fahrenheit);
celsius = (fahrenheit - 32.0) * 5.0 / 9.0;
. . .
```

Ah, there is the error. It looks as if the value entered by the user is divided by 2 just before it is assigned to the variable `fahrenheit`. Devious, but we cannot be deceived for long.

*E*XERCISE 3.6

1. Describe how one can modify code so that the cause of a logic error can be discovered.

2. The following program contains a logic error. Describe where to insert the appropriate debugging statements to help locate the error:

```
import java.util.Scanner;

public class AreaTriangle{

    public static void main(String [] args){

        double base, height, area;
        Scanner reader = new Scanner(System.in);

        System.out.print("Enter the base of the triangle: ");
        base = reader.nextDouble();
        System.out.print("Enter the height of the triangle: ");
        height = reader.nextDouble();
        area = base + height / 2;
        System.out.println("The area is " + area);

    }
}
```

Case Study 2: Count the Angels

Computers have been applied to many complex problems, from predicting the weather, to controlling nuclear power plants, to playing the best chess in the world. Now this case study extends computing into the realm of metaphysics. Although this case study is fanciful and humorous, it illustrates important issues regarding analysis and design. During analysis and design we deliberately introduce several subtle errors, which during implementation we incorporate into the program, yet the program runs perfectly and gives no hint that there are underlying problems. As you read the case study, see if you can spot the errors. At the end we will point out what they are and make some general comments about the software development process.

Request

Write a program that determines how many angels can dance on the head of a pin.

Analysis

To solve this problem, we first consulted several prominent theologians. We learned that the pertinent factors are the size of the pinhead, the space occupied by a single angel, and the overlap between adjacent angels. Although angels are incorporeal beings, there are limits to the amount of overlap they can tolerate. Also, no region of space is ever occupied by three angels simultaneously. This seems somewhat confusing. On further questioning, the experts explained that angels have what one might call an overlap factor. If, for instance, this factor is 30 percent, then

■ An angel can share at most 30 percent of its space with other angels.

■ 70 percent of its space cannot be shared.

■ Within any shared region, only two angels can overlap.

The inputs to the program are now fairly obvious: the radius of the pinhead, the space occupied by an angel, and the overlap factor. Based on these inputs, the program will calculate

■ The area of pinhead = πr^2.

■ Nonoverlapping space required by an angel = space occupied by an angel * (1 - overlap factor).

■ Number of angels on pinhead = area of pinhead / nonoverlapping space required by an angel.

The proposed user interface is shown in Figure 3-5.

FIGURE 3-5
Proposed interface for the count angels program

```
Enter the radius in millimeters: 10
Enter the space occupied by an angel in square micrometers: 0.0001
Enter the overlap factor: 0.75
The number of angels = 1.256E7
```

Design

Our rather crude estimate for π is 3.14. Obviously, more accurate estimates yield more accurate calculations of the area. Later we see how Java itself can provide an excellent estimate. Following is the pseudocode for the count angels program:

```
read radius
read angelSpace
read overlapFactor
area = 3.14 * radius * radius
nonOverlapSpace = angelSpace * (1.0 - overlapFactor)
numberAngels = area / nonOverlapSpace
print numberAngels
```

Implementation

The following code is a straightforward translation of the pseudocode into Java. Comments are included.

```java
/*Case study 2: count the angels
Count the number of angels that can dance on the head of a pin.
1. The user inputs are
        The radius of the pinhead
        The space occupied by an angel
        The allowed overlap between angels subject to the restriction
        that no space can simultaneously be occupied by more than two
2. The program computes
        The area of the pinhead based on its radius
        The amount of nonoverlapping space required by an angel
        The number of angels based on the preceding two values
3. The program ends by printing the number of angels.
*/

import java.util.Scanner;

public class CountAngels {
   public static void main(String [] args){

        Scanner reader = new Scanner(System.in);

        double radius;            //Radius of the pinhead in millimeters

        double angelSpace;        //Space occupied by an angel
                                  //in square micrometers
        double overlapFactor;     //Allowed overlap between angels from 0 to 1
        double area;              //Area of the pinhead in square millimeters
        double nonOverlapSpace;   //Nonoverlapping space required by an angel
        double numberAngels;      //Number of angels that can dance on the
                                  //pinhead

        //Get user inputs
        System.out.print ("Enter the radius in millimeters: ");
        radius = reader.nextDouble();
        System.out.print
```

```
                ("Enter the space occupied by an angel in square micrometers: ");
        angelSpace = reader.nextDouble();
        System.out.print ("Enter the overlap factor: ");
        overlapFactor = reader.nextDouble();

        //Perform calculations
        area = 3.14 * radius * radius;
        nonOverlapSpace = angelSpace * (1.0 - overlapFactor);
        numberAngels = area / nonOverlapSpace;

        //Print results
        System.out.print ("The number of angels = " + numberAngels);
    }
}
```

Discussion

So what were the mysterious errors we mentioned and what is their general significance? There were three errors, two during analysis and one during design.

First Analysis Error

During analysis we did not consider the shape of the region occupied by an angel, overlapping or otherwise. To appreciate the significance of our oversight, consider the problem of placing as many pennies as possible on a plate without overlap. Because there are gaps between the pennies, the answer is not obtained by dividing the area of the plate by the area of a penny. Even if two pennies are allowed to overlap by some amount, there are still gaps. Thus our solution is correct only if angels can mold their shapes to eliminate all empty spaces. Unfortunately, we did not think of asking the theologians about this.

Second Analysis Error

Let us now simplify the problem and suppose that angels pack onto the pinhead without leaving empty spaces. Now the space occupied by two overlapping angels equals the space each would occupy alone minus the amount by which they overlap or

```
space for two overlapping angels
    = 2 * space occupied by an angel -
        space occupied by an angel * overlap factor
    = 2 * space occupied by an angel * (1.0 - overlap factor / 2)
```

Thus,

```
    space for one angel with overlap = space occupied by an angel *
      (1.0 - overlap factor / 2)
```

and

```
    number of angels on pinhead = area of pinhead / space for one
      angel with overlap
```

Well, we certainly got that wrong the first time.

Design Error

The radius of the pin is given in millimeters and the space requirements of an angel are given in square micrometers. Our calculations need to take this difference in units into account. We leave the actual correction as an exercise.

Conclusions

There are three lessons to draw from all this. First, the people who write programs usually are not the ones most familiar with the problem domain. Consequently, many programs fail to solve problems correctly either because they completely ignore important factors or because they treat factors incorrectly. Second, careful analysis and design are essential and demand careful thought. As you can see, the errors had nothing to do with programming per se, and they would have occurred even if we were solving the problem with paper and pencil. And by the way, before writing a program to solve a problem, we definitely need to know how to do it correctly by hand. We are not going to make a practice of making analysis and design errors, and we did so just this once in order to make a point. Third, just because computers perform complex calculations at lightning speed does not mean we should have unquestioning confidence in their outputs.

3.7 Graphics and GUIs: Drawing Shapes and Text

The GUI programs in Section 2.7 displayed one or more flat-colored rectangular areas. Now it is time to learn how to fill these areas with other objects, such as geometric shapes and text.

Extra Challenge

This Graphics and GUIs section gives you the opportunity to explore concepts and programming techniques required to develop modern graphics applications and graphical user interfaces. This material is not required in order to proceed with the other chapters of the book.

Defining a Specialized Panel Class

An application window in GUI programs has a clearly defined set of responsibilities. A window establishes its initial size, decides what it will do when the user resizes or closes it, and creates and lays out the panels that appear within it. Before we create and display other objects within a panel, we have to ask which will be responsible for them, the application window or the panel in which they appear? Because there might be many panels and many objects in each panel, it would be a good idea to assign at least some of the responsibilities for managing these objects to the panels themselves. We use two principles of any good organization: Divide the labor and Delegate responsibility.

A window does just what it did before: create a panel with a given background color. But a panel now has the additional responsibility of setting its own background color and displaying geometric shapes and text. To provide a panel with these additional capabilities, we define a new type of panel by extending the `JPanel` class. Our new class, called `ColorPanel`, has all of the behavior of a `JPanel`. But a `ColorPanel` also knows how to draw specific shapes and instantiate itself with a given background color. For example, instead of the code

```
JPanel panel = new JPanel();
panel.setBackround(Color.white);
```

an application window now uses the code

```
ColorPanel panel = new ColorPanel(Color.white);
```

to create a panel with a given background color. The following program sets up an application window for all of the examples discussed in this section.

```java
// Main application window for Chapter 3 graphics examples

import javax.swing.*;
import java.awt.*;

public class GUIWindow {

    public static void main(String[] args){
        JFrame theGUI = new JFrame();
        theGUI.setTitle("GUI Program");
        theGUI.setSize(300, 200);
        theGUI.setDefaultCloseOperation(JFrame.EXIT_ON_CLOSE);
        ColorPanel panel = new ColorPanel(Color.white);
        Container pane = theGUI.getContentPane();
        pane.add(panel);
        theGUI.setVisible(true);
    }
}
```

The class `ColorPanel` in each example extends `JPanel` and includes a constructor that expects a `Color` parameter. The constructor runs when the panel is instantiated and sets its background color. Here is the code for this minimal behavior:

```java
// Example 3.5: an empty colored panel

import javax.swing.*;
import java.awt.*;

public class ColorPanel extends JPanel{

    public ColorPanel(Color backColor){
        setBackground(backColor);
    }
}
```

All we have done thus far is substitute a new class, `ColorPanel`, for the `JPanel` class used in the examples of Section 2.7. Those example programs would have the same behavior if they used the new class. The only difference is that the code for the application windows would be slightly simplified.

When you're working with more than one programmer-defined class, the source code for the classes is usually maintained in separate files and edited and compiled separately. An easy way to compile all of the classes in your current working directory is to use the command `javac *.java` at the command line prompt. The `java` command to run a program is used as before, with the byte code file that contains the `main` method.

Coordinate Systems

Underlying every graphics application is a ***coordinate system***. Positions in this system are specified in terms of points. Points in a two-dimensional system have x and y coordinates. For example, the point (10, 30) has an x coordinate of 10 and a y coordinate of 30.

The x and y coordinates of a point express its position relative to the system's ***origin*** at (0, 0). Figure 3-6 presents some examples of points in the familiar Cartesian coordinate system. In this system, two perpendicular lines define an x axis and a y axis. The point of intersection is labeled (0, 0). Increasing values of x are to the right and increasing values of y are upward.

FIGURE 3-6
A Cartesian coordinate system

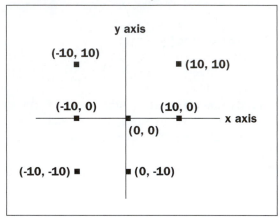

In Java and most other programming languages, the coordinate system is oriented as shown in Figure 3-7. Note that the only quadrant shown is the one that defines the coordinates of the computer's screen. In the positive direction, it extends downward and to the right from the point (0, 0) in the upper-left corner. The other three quadrants exist, but the points in them never appear on the screen. This is called a ***screen coordinate system***.

FIGURE 3-7
Orientation of Java's coordinate system

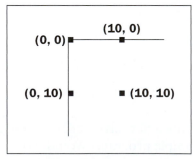

In a window-based application, each window has a coordinate system whose origin is located at the upper-left outside corner of the window. Each integer point in this coordinate system, extending from the origin to the window's lower-right corner, locates the position of a pixel, or picture element, in the window. By an integer point, we mean a point both of whose coordinates are integers. Each panel also has its own coordinate system that is similar in form to the window's coordinate system. In the discussion that follows, we assume that we are drawing geometric shapes and text in panels.

The Graphics Class

The package `java.awt` provides a `Graphics` class for drawing in a panel. A panel maintains an instance of this class, called a *graphics context*, so that the program can access and modify the panel's bitmap. The program sends messages to the graphics context to perform all graphics operations. Hereafter, we refer to the graphics context using the variable name g. Some commonly used `Graphics` drawing methods are listed in Table 3-9. The table also shows the results of running these methods in a window that has a single panel.

TABLE 3-9
Common methods in the `Graphics` class

GRAPHICS METHOD	EXAMPLE CALL AND OUTPUT	WHAT IT DOES

`drawLine(`
`    int x1,`
`    int y1,`
`    int x2,`
`    int y2)`
	`g.drawLine(10, 25, 40, 55)`	Draws a line from point (x1, y1) to (x2, y2).

`drawRect(`
`    int x,`
`    int y,`
`    int width,`
`    int height)`
	`g.drawRect(10, 25, 40, 30)`	Draws a rectangle whose upper-left corner is (x, y) and whose dimensions are the specified width and height.

`drawOval(`
`    int x,`
`    int y,`
`    int width,`
`    int height)`
	`g.drawOval(10, 25, 50, 25)`	Draws an oval that fits within a rectangle whose origin (upper-left corner) is (x, y) and whose dimensions are the specified width and height. To draw a circle, make the width and height equal.

TABLE 3-9 Continued
Common methods in the `Graphics` class

GRAPHICS METHOD	EXAMPLE CALL AND OUTPUT	WHAT IT DOES

`drawArc(`
 	
`    int x,`
`    int y,`
`    int width,`
`    int height,`
`    int startAngle,`
`    int arcAngle)`
	`g.drawArc(10, 25, 50, 50, 0, 90)`	Draws an arc that fits within a rectangle whose upper-left corner is (x, y) and whose dimensions are the specified width and height. The arc is drawn from `startAngle` to `startAngle + arcAngle`. The angles are expressed in degrees. A start angle of 0 indicates the 3 o'clock position. A positive arc indicates a counterclockwise rotation, and a negative arc indicates a clockwise rotation from 3 o'clock.

`drawRoundRect(`
`    int x,`
`    int y,`
`    int width,`
`    int height,`
`    int arcWidth,`
`    int arcHeight)`
	`g.drawRoundRect(10, 25, 40, 30, 20, 20)`	Draws a rounded rectangle.

`drawString(`
`    String str,`
`    int x,`
`    int y)`
	`g.drawString("Java rules!", 10, 50)`	Draws a string. The point (x, y) indicates the position of the base line of the first character.

In addition, there are the methods `fillArc`, `fillRect`, and `fillOval`, which draw filled shapes.

Each shape is drawn in a graphics context with a foreground color, which by default is black. This color can be changed using the method `setColor(aColor)`, which affects the color of all images drawn subsequently but not earlier. In general, if you want to draw a shape in a given color, it's a good idea to set the color of the graphics object immediately before drawing the shape. The following code draws a filled red circle in the graphics context g:

```
g.setColor(Color.red);
g.fillOval(100, 100, 50, 50);
```

You can erase a shape by setting the foreground color to the same color as the panel's background color and redrawing the shape. The methods `getColor()` and `getBackground()` return the colors of a graphics context and a panel's background, respectively.

Drawing Shapes with the Method `paintComponent`

The responsibilities of a panel class are to draw images in response to messages from an application and also to redraw images whenever the window is refreshed. We discuss the refresh process in this section and examine how a panel receives messages from an application in later chapters.

When a window opens, the JVM sends the message `paintComponent` to each object contained in the window. If an object has any images to draw, its `paintComponent` method accomplishes this. Thus, for example, when a window containing a button opens at program startup, the button's `paintComponent` method draws the image of the button on the screen. This process also occurs whenever the window is refreshed—for instance, after it is minimized and restored. The important point here is that the application never calls `paintComponent` directly; it is triggered automatically by the JVM in response to certain events. `paintComponent` receives the panel's graphics context as a parameter, so this object is accessible for drawing. The method also is implemented in a superclass of the class `ColorPanel`, so the programmer can override it to draw the appropriate images.

Our next program example uses a modified version of the code for the `ColorPanel` class. We have added a `paintComponent` method that draws a blue rectangle containing a red text message when the window opens and whenever it is refreshed. The resulting window is shown in Figure 3-8.

```
// Example 3.6: A colored panel containing a red text
// message in a blue rectangle

import javax.swing.*;
import java.awt.*;

public class ColorPanel extends JPanel{

    public ColorPanel(Color backColor){
        setBackground(backColor);
    }

    public void paintComponent(Graphics g){
        super.paintComponent(g);
        g.setColor(Color.blue);
        g.drawRect(10, 5, 120, 20);
        g.setColor(Color.red);
        g.drawString("Hello world!", 20, 20);
    }
}
```

FIGURE 3-8
Displaying a shape and text in a panel

Note that the `paintComponent` method first calls the same method in the superclass, using the reserved word `super`. The reason is that the method in the superclass paints the background of the panel. This effectively clears any images in the panel before they are redrawn.

Finding the Width and Height of a Panel

Occasionally, it is useful to know the width and height of a panel. For instance, one might want to center an image in a panel and keep the image centered when the user resizes the window. The methods `getWidth()` and `getHeight()` return the current width and height of a panel, respectively. If these methods are called before the window is opened, they return a default value of 0. Our next `ColorPanel` example maintains the shapes of the previous example near the center of the panel:

```java
// Example 3.7: A colored panel containing a red text
// message in a blue rectangle, centered in the panel

import javax.swing.*;
import java.awt.*;

public class ColorPanel extends JPanel{

    public ColorPanel(Color backColor){
        setBackground(backColor);
    }

    public void paintComponent(Graphics g){
        super.paintComponent(g);
        int x = getWidth() / 2 - 60;
        int y = getHeight() / 2;
        g.setColor(Color.blue);
        g.drawRect(x, y, 120, 20);
        g.setColor(Color.red);
        g.drawString("Hello world!", x + 10, y + 15);
    }
}
```

Text Properties and the `Font` Class

In the context of a bitmapped display, text is drawn like any other image. A text image has several properties, as shown in Table 3-10. These are set by adjusting the color and font properties of the graphics context in which the text is drawn.

TABLE 3-10
Text properties

TEXT PROPERTY	EXAMPLE
Color	Red, green, blue, white, black, etc.
Font style	Plain, **bold**, *italic*
Font size	10 point, 12 point, etc.
Font name	Courier, Times New Roman, etc.

An object of class `Font` has three basic properties: a name, a style, and a size. The following code creates one `Font` object with the properties **Courier bold 12** and another with the properties *Arial bold italic 10*:

```
Font courierBold12     = new Font("Courier", Font.BOLD, 12);

Font arialBoldItalic10 = new Font("Arial", Font.BOLD + Font.ITALIC, 10);
```

The `Font` constants PLAIN, BOLD, and ITALIC define the font styles. The font size is an integer representing the number of points, where one point equals 1/72 of an inch. The available font names depend on your particular computer platform.

Our final program example modifies the previous one so that the text message is displayed in Courier bold 14 font.

```
// Example 3.8: A colored panel containing a red text
// message in a blue rectangle
// Text font is Courier bold 14

import javax.swing.*;
import java.awt.*;

public class ColorPanel extends JPanel{

    public ColorPanel(Color backColor){
        setBackground(backColor);
    }

    public void paintComponent(Graphics g){
        super.paintComponent(g);
        int x = getWidth() / 2 - 60;
        int y = getHeight() / 2;
        g.setColor(Color.blue);
        g.drawRect(x, y, 120, 20);
        g.setColor(Color.red);
        Font font = new Font("Courier", Font.BOLD, 14);
        g.setFont(font);
        g.drawString("Hello world!", x + 10, y + 15);
    }
}
```

EXERCISE 3.7

1. Write the code segments that would draw the following objects in the graphics context `g`:

  a. A filled rectangle with corner point (45, 20) and size 100 by 50

  b. A line segment with end points (20, 20) and (100, 100)

  c. A circle with center point (100, 100) and radius 50

  d. A triangle with vertices (100, 100), (50, 50), and (200, 200)

2. Describe the design of a program that displays a filled blue rectangle on a red background.

3. How does one compute the center point of a panel?

4. List the three properties of a text font.

SUMMARY

In this chapter, you learned:

■ Java programs use the `int` data type for whole numbers (integers) and `double` for floating-point numbers (numbers with decimals).

■ Java variable and method names consist of a letter followed by additional letters or digits. Java keywords cannot be used as names.

■ Final variables behave as constants; their values cannot change after they are declared.

■ Arithmetic expressions are evaluated according to precedence. Some expressions yield different results for integer and floating-point operands.

■ Strings may be concatenated to form a new string.

■ The compiler catches syntax errors. The JVM catches run-time errors. Logic errors, if they are caught, are detected by the programmer or user of the program at runtime.

■ A useful way to find and remove logic errors is to insert debugging output statements to view the values of variables.

■ Java uses a screen coordinate system to locate the positions of pixels in a window or panel. The origin of this system is in the upper-left corner or the drawing area, and the *x* and *y* axes increase to the right and downward, respectively.

■ The programmer can modify the color with which images are drawn and the properties of text fonts for a given graphics object.

VOCABULARY *Review*

Define the following terms:

Arithmetic expression	Logic error	Screen coordinate system
Comments	Origin	Semantics
Coordinate system	Package	Syntax
Exception	Pseudocode	Virus
Graphics context	Reserved words	
Literal	Run-time error	

REVIEW *Questions*

WRITTEN QUESTIONS

Write a brief answer to the following questions.

1. Write a pseudocode algorithm that determines the batting average of a baseball player. *Hint*: To compute a batting average, divide number of hits by number of at-bats. Batting averages have three decimal places.

2. Give examples of an integer literal, a floating-point literal, and a string literal.

3. Declare variables to represent a person's name, age, and hourly wage.

4. Why must care be taken to order the operators in an arithmetic expression?

5. Is it possible to assign a value of type `int` to a variable of type `double`? Why or why not?

6. State which of the following are valid Java identifiers. For those that are not valid, explain why.
   A. length

   B. import

   C. 6months

   D. hello-and-goodbye

   E. HERE_AND_THERE

FILL IN THE BLANK

Complete the following sentences by writing the correct word or words in the blanks provided.

1. In mixed-mode arithmetic with operand types `int` and `double`, the result type is always _____.

2. A method's name, parameters, and return type are also known as its _____.

3. The operation that joins two strings together is called _____.

4. End-of-line comments begin with the symbol _____.

5. A quotient results when the _____ operator is used with two operands of type _____.

PROJECTS

PROJECT 3-1

The surface area of a cube can be known if we know the length of an edge. Write a program that takes the length of an edge (an integer) as input and prints the cube's surface area as output. (*Remember*: analyze, design, implement, and test.)

PROJECT 3-2

Write a program that takes the radius of a sphere (a double) as input and outputs the sphere's diameter, circumference, surface area, and volume.

PROJECT 3-3

The kinetic energy of a moving object is given by the formula $KE=(1/2)mv^2$, where m is the object's mass and v is its velocity. Modify the program of Chapter 2, Project 2-5, so that it prints the object's kinetic energy as well as its momentum.

PROJECT 3-4

An employee's total weekly pay equals the hourly wage multiplied by the total number of regular hours plus any overtime pay. Overtime pay equals the total overtime hours multiplied by 1.5 times the hourly wage. Write a program that takes as inputs the hourly wage, total regular hours, and total overtime hours and displays an employee's total weekly pay.

PROJECT 3-5

Modify the program of Project 3-4 so that it prompts the user for the regular and overtime hours of each of five working days.

PROJECT 3-6

The Müller-Lyer illusion is caused by an image that consists of two parallel line segments. One line segment looks like an arrow with two heads, and the other line segment looks like an arrow with two tails. Although the line segments are of exactly the same length, they appear to be unequal (see Figure 3-9). Write a graphics program that illustrates this illusion.

FIGURE 3-9
The Müller-Lyer Illusion

PROJECT 3-7

Write a graphics program that displays the coordinates of the center point of a panel in the form (x, y). This information should be displayed at the panel's center point and be automatically updated when the panel is resized.

CRITICAL *Thinking*

During the summer before the academic year, the registrar's office must enter new data for incoming freshmen. Design and implement a program that prompts the user for the following inputs:

Last name

First name

Class year (an integer)

Campus phone

After all the inputs are taken, the program should echo them as output.

INTRODUCTION TO CONTROL STATEMENTS

All the programs to this point have consisted of short sequences of instructions that are executed one after the other. Such a scheme, even if we allowed the sequence of instructions to become extremely long, would not be very useful. In computer programs, as in real life, instructions must express repetition and selection. Expressing these notions in Java is the major topic of this chapter, but before doing so we present a couple of topics that we use throughout the rest of the chapter.

4.1 Additional Operators

Strange to say, the operators presented in this section are completely unnecessary, and we could easily manage without them; however, Java programmers use them frequently, and we cannot ignore them. Fortunately, they are convenient and easy to use.

Extended Assignment Operators

The assignment operator can be combined with the arithmetic and concatenation operators to provide extended assignment operators. Following are several examples:

```java
int a = 17;
String s = "hi";

a += 3;              // Equivalent to a = a + 3;
a -= 3;              // Equivalent to a = a - 3;
a *= 3;              // Equivalent to a = a * 3;
a /= 3;              // Equivalent to a = a / 3;
a %= 3;              // Equivalent to a = a % 3;
s += " there";       // Equivalent to s = s + " there";
```

All of these examples have the format

```java
variable op= expression;
```

which is equivalent to

```java
variable = variable op expression;
```

Note that there is no space between op and =. The extended assignment operators and the standard assignment operator have the same precedence. For more information about these additional operators, see Appendix C.

Increment and Decrement

Java includes increment (++) and decrement (--) operators that increase or decrease a variable's value by one:

```java
int m = 7;
double x = 6.4;

m++;        // Equivalent to m = m + 1;
x--;        // Equivalent to x = x - 1.0;
```

Here and throughout the book we use these operators only in the manner just illustrated; however, they can also appear in the middle of expressions. The rules for doing so are tricky and involve complexities that lead to programming errors and confusion. We encourage you to restrict yourself to the simplest uses of these operators. The precedence of the increment and decrement operators is the same as unary plus, unary minus, and cast.

*E*XERCISE 4.1

1. Translate the following statements to equivalent statements that use extended assignment operators:

  a. x = x * 2;

  b. y = y % 2;

2. Translate the following statements to equivalent statements that do not use the extended assignment operators:

a. `x += 5;`

b. `x *= x;`

4.2 Standard Classes and Methods

The standard Java library includes two classes that are frequently useful. These are the `Math` and the `Random` classes. The `Math` class provides a range of common mathematical methods, whereas the `Random` class supports programs that incorporate random numbers.

The Math Class

The `Math` class is quite extensive; however, we limit our attention to the methods listed in Table 4-1. Notice that two methods in the table are called `abs`. They are distinguished from each other by the fact that one takes an integer and the other takes a double parameter. Using the same name for two different methods is called *overloading*.

TABLE 4-1
Seven methods in the Math class

METHOD	WHAT IT DOES
`static int abs(int x)`	Returns the absolute value of an integer x
`static double abs(double x)`	Returns the absolute value of a double x
`static double pow(double base, double exponent)`	Returns the base raised to the exponent
`static long round(double x)`	Returns x rounded to the nearest whole number (Note: Returned value must be cast to an `int` before assignment to an `int` variable.)
`static int max(int a, int b)`	Returns the greater of a and b
`static int min(int a, int b)`	Returns the lesser of a and b
`static double sqrt(double x)`	Returns the square root of x

The sqrt Method

The next code segment illustrates the use of the `sqrt` method:

```
// Given the area of a circle, compute its radius.
// Use the formula a = pr², where a is the area and r is the radius.

double area = 10.0, radius;
radius = Math.sqrt(area / Math.PI);
```

To understand this code we must consider two points. First, messages are usually sent to objects; however, if a method's signature is labeled `static`, the message is sent to the method's class. Thus, to invoke the `sqrt` method, we send the `sqrt` message to the `Math` class. Second, in addition to methods, the `Math` class includes good approximations to several important constants. Here we use `Math.PI`, which is an approximation for π accurate to about 17 decimal places.

The Remaining Methods

The remaining methods described in Table 4-1 are illustrated in the following program code:

```java
int m;
double x;

m = Math.abs(-7);          // m equals 7
x = Math.abs(-7.5);        // x equals 7.5

x = Math.pow(3.0, 2.0);    // x equals 3.0^2.0 equals 9.0
x = Math.pow(16.0, 0.25);  // x equals 16.0^0.25 equals 2.0

m = Math.max(20, 40);      // m equals 40
m = Math.min(20, 40);      // m equals 20
m = (int) Math.round(3.14); // m equals 3
m = (int) Math.round(3.5);  // m equals 4
```

The methods `pow` and `sqrt` both expect parameters of type `double`. If an `int` is used instead, it is automatically converted to a double before the message is sent. The methods `max` and `min` also have versions that work with doubles. Other useful methods, including trigonometric methods, are described in Appendix B.

The Random Class

Programs are often used to simulate random events such as the flip of a coin, the arrival times of customers at a bank, the moment-to-moment fluctuations of the stock market, and so forth. At the heart of all such programs is a mechanism called a *random number generator* that returns numbers chosen at random from a predesignated interval. Java's random number generator is implemented in the `Random` class and utilizes the methods `nextInt`, and `nextDouble`, as described in Table 4-2.

TABLE 4-2
Methods in the Random class

METHOD	WHAT IT DOES
`int nextInt(int n)`	Returns an integer chosen at random from among 0, 1, 2, ..., $n-1$
`double nextDouble()`	Returns a double chosen at random between 0.0, inclusive, and 1.0, exclusive

A program that uses the `Random` class first must import `java.util.Random`. Following is a segment of code that illustrates the importing of `java.util.Random` and the use of the `nextInt` method:

```
import java.util.Random;
. . .

// Generate an integer chosen at random from among 0, 1, 2

Random generator = new Random();
System.out.print(generator.nextInt(3));
```

The output from this segment of code is different every time it is executed. Following are the results from three executions:

```
2
0
1
```

The method `nextDouble` behaves in a similar fashion but returns a `double` greater than or equal to 0.0 and less than 1.0.

EXERCISE 4.2

1. Assume that x has the value 3.6 and y has the value 4. State the value of the variable z after the following statements:

a. `z = Math.sqrt(y);`

b. `z = Math.round(x);`

c. `z = Math.pow(y, 3);`

d. `z = Math.round(Math.sqrt(x));`

2. Write code segments to print the following values in a terminal window:

a. A random integer between 1 and 20, inclusive

b. A random double between 1 and 10, inclusive

4.3 A Visit to the Farm

To introduce the main topic of this chapter, control statements, we begin with a "real world" example. Once upon a time in a faraway land, Jack visited his cousin Jill in the country and offered to milk the cow. Jill gave him a list of instructions:

```
fetch the cow from the field;
tie her in the stall;
milk her into the bucket;
pour the milk into the bottles;
drive her back into the field;
clean the bucket;
```

Although Jack was a little taken aback by Jill's liberal use of semicolons, he had no trouble following the instructions. A year later, Jack visited again. In the meantime, Jill had acquired a herd of cows, some red and some black. This time, when Jack offered to help, Jill gave him a more complex list of instructions:

```
herd the cows from the field into the west paddock;
while (there are any cows left in the west paddock){
   fetch a cow from the west paddock;
   tie her in the stall;
   if (she is red){
      milk her into the red bucket;
      pour the milk into red bottles;
   }else{
      milk her into the black bucket;
      pour the milk into black bottles;
   }
   put her into the east paddock;
}
herd the cows from the east paddock back into the field;
clean the buckets;
```

These instructions threw Jack for a loop (pun intended) until Jill explained that

```
while (some condition){
   do stuff;
}
```

means "do the stuff repeatedly as long as the condition holds true," and

```
if (some condition){
   do stuff 1;
}else{
   do stuff 2;
}
```

means "if some condition is true, do stuff 1, and if it is false, do stuff 2."

"And what about all the semicolons and braces?" asked Jack.

"Those," said Jill, "are just a habit I picked up from programming in Java, where while and if-else are called *control statements*."

EXERCISE 4.3

1. Why does Jill use a while statement in her instructions to Jack?

2. Why does Jill use an if-else statement in her instructions to Jack? Write pseudocode control statements that are similar in style to the farm example for the following situations:

   a. If a checker piece is red, then put it on a red square; otherwise, put it on a black square.

   b. If your shoes are muddy, then take them off and leave them outside the door.

   c. Pick up all the marbles on the floor and put them into a bag.

3. Describe in English what the following code segments do:

a.

```
if (x is larger than y){
    temp = x;
    x = y;
    y = temp;
}else{
    temp = y;
    y = x;
    x = temp;
}
```

b.

```
sum = 0;
count = 1;
read an integer into total;
while (count is less than or equal to total){
    read an integer into x;
    sum = sum + Math.abs(x);
    count++;
}
if (total is greater than 0)
    print (sum / total)
```

4.4 The `if` and `if-else` Statements

We now explore in greater detail the `if-else` statement and the slightly simpler but related `if` statement. The meanings of `if` and `else` in Java sensibly adhere to our everyday usage of these words. Java and other third-generation programming languages achieve their programmer–friendly qualities by combining bits and pieces of English phrasing with some of the notational conventions of elementary algebra.

Principal Forms

To repeat, in Java, the `if` and `if-else` statements allow for the conditional execution of statements. For instance,

```
if (condition){
    statement;        //Execute these statements if the
    statement;        //condition is true.
}

if (condition){
    statement;        //Execute these statements if the
    statement;        //condition is true.
}else{
    statement;        //Execute these statements if the
    statement;        //condition is false.
}
```

The indicated semicolons and braces are required; however, the exact format of the text depends on the aesthetic sensibilities of the programmer, who should be guided by a desire to make the program as readable as possible. Notice that braces always occur in pairs and that no semicolon immediately follows a closing brace.

Additional Forms

The braces can be dropped if only a single statement follows the word `if` or `else`; for instance,

```
if (condition)
    statement;

if (condition)
    statement;
else
    statement;

if (condition){
    statement;
        ...
    statement;
}else
    statement;

if (condition)
    statement;
else{
    statement;
        ...
    statement;
}
```

Braces

In general, it is better to overuse braces than to under use them. Likewise, in expressions it is better to overuse parentheses. The extra braces or parentheses can never do any harm, and their presence helps to eliminate logic errors.

Boolean Expressions

The condition in an `if` statement must be a *Boolean expression*. This type of expression returns the value `true` or `false`.

Flowchart

Figure 4-1 shows a diagram called a *flowchart* that illustrates the behavior of if and if-else statements. When the statements are executed, either the left or the right branch is executed depending on whether the condition is true or false.

FIGURE 4-1
Flowcharts for the if and if-else statements

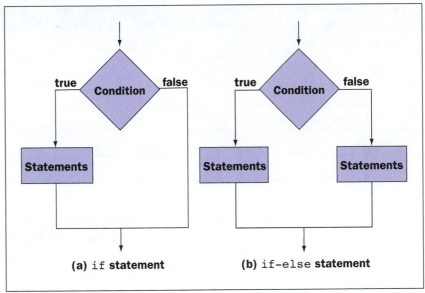

(a) if **statement**   (b) if-else **statement**

Examples

Following are some examples of if statements:

```
// Increase a salesman's commission by 10% if his sales are over $5000
if (sales > 5000)
   commission *= 1.1;

// Pay a worker $14.5 per hour plus time and a half for overtime
pay = hoursWorked * 14.5;
if (hoursWorked > 40){
   overtime = hoursWorked - 40;
   pay += overtime * 21.75;
}

// Let c equal the larger of a and b
if (a > b)
   c = a;
else
   c = b;
```

Relational Operators

The previous examples all use the relational operator for greater than (>); however, there are five other relational operators. Table 4-3 shows the complete list of relational operators available for use in Java.

TABLE 4-3
Relational operators

OPERATOR	WHAT IT MEANS
>	greater than
>=	greater than or equal to
<	less than
<=	less than or equal to
==	equal to
!=	not equal to

The notation for the last two relational operators is rather peculiar at first glance, but it is necessary. The double equal signs (==) distinguish the equal-to operator from the assignment operator (=). In the not-equal-to operator, the exclamation mark (!) is read as *not*. When these expressions are evaluated, their values will be either true or false, depending on the values of the operands involved. For example, suppose

```
a = 3          c = 10
b = 7          d = -20
```

then

```
a < b              is true
a <= b             is true
a == b             is false
a != b             is true
a - b > c + d      is true (the precedence of > is lower than + and -)
a < b < c          is invalid (syntactically incorrect)
a == b == c        is invalid
```

Checking Input for Validity

if-else statements are commonly used to check user inputs before processing them. For example, consider an admittedly trivial program that inputs the radius of a circle and outputs its area. If the user enters a negative number, the program should not go ahead and use it to compute an area that would be meaningless. Instead, the program should detect this problem and output an error message. Our next program example does this.

```java
// Example 4.1: Computes the area of a circle if the
// radius >= 0, or displays an error message otherwise

import java.util.Scanner;

public class CircleArea{

    public static void main(String[] args){
        Scanner reader = new Scanner(System.in);
        System.out.print("Enter the radius: ");
        double radius = reader.nextDouble();
        if (radius < 0)
            System.out.println("Error: Radius must be >= 0");
        else{
            double area = Math.PI * Math.pow(radius, 2);
            System.out.println("The area is " + area);
        }
    }
}
```

EXERCISE 4.4

1. What type of expression must the condition of an `if` statement contain?

2. Describe the role of the curly braces (`{}`) in an `if` statement.

3. What is the difference between an `if` statement and an `if-else` statement?

4. Assume that x is 5 and y is 10. Write the values of the following expressions:

   a. `x <= 10`
   b. `x - 2 != 0`
   c. `x > y`

5. Given the following mini-specifications, write expressions involving relational operators:

   a. Determine if an input value x is greater than 0.
   b. Determine if a given number of seconds equals a minute.
   c. If a, b, and c are the lengths of the sides of a triangle and c is the largest side, determine if the triangle is a right triangle. (*Hint*: Use the Pythagorean equation and round the operand before comparing.)

6. Write the outputs of the following code segments:

   a.

```java
int x = 20, y = 15, z;

if (x < y)
    z = 10;
else
    z = 5;
System.out.println(z);
```

EXERCISE 4.4 Continued

b.

```
int x = 2;

if (Math.round(Math.sqrt(x)) == 1)
    System.out.println("Equal");
else
    System.out.println("Not equal");
```

7. Given the following mini-specifications, write expressions involving `if-else` statements and output statements:

a. Print the larger of two numbers.

b. Prompt the user for two whole numbers and input them. Then print the numbers in numeric order.

4.5 The while Statement

The `while` statement provides a looping mechanism that executes statements repeatedly for as long as some condition remains true. Following is the `while` statement's format:

```
while (condition)        // loop test
    statement;               // one statement inside the loop body


while (condition){       // loop test
    statement;               // many statements
    statement;               // inside the
    ...                      // loop body
}
```

If the condition is false from the outset, the statement or statements inside the loop never execute. Figure 4-2 uses a flowchart to illustrate the behavior of a `while` statement.

FIGURE 4-2
Flowchart for a `while` statement

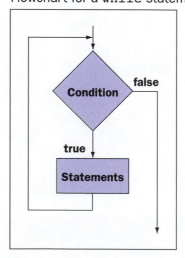

To help you become familiar with `while` statements, several short examples follow.

Compute 1 + 2 + ... + 100

The first example computes and displays the sum of the integers between 1 and 100, inclusive:

```
// Compute 1 + 2 + … + 100

int sum = 0, cntr = 1;
while (cntr <= 100){
    sum += cntr;    // point p (we refer to this location in Table 4-4)
    cntr++;         // point q (we refer to this location in Table 4-4)
}
System.out.println (sum);
```

The behavior of this portion of code is clear. The variable `cntr` acts as a counter that controls how many times the loop executes. The counter starts at 1. Each time around the loop, it is compared to 100 and incremented by 1. Clearly the code inside the loop is executed exactly 100 times, and each time through the loop, `sum` is incremented by increasing values of `cntr`.

Count-Controlled Loops

This is an example of what is called a *count-controlled loop*. The variable `cntr` is called the *counter*.

Tracing the Variables

To fully understand the loop, we must analyze the way in which the variables change on each pass or *iteration* through the loop. Table 4-4 helps in this endeavor. On the 100th iteration, `cntr` is increased to 101, so there is never a 101st iteration, and we are confident that the `sum` is computed correctly.

TABLE 4-4
Trace of how variables change on each iteration through a loop

ITERATION NUMBER	VALUE OF CNTR AT POINT P	VALUE OF SUM AT POINT P	VALUE OF CNTR AT POINT Q
1	1	1	2
2	2	1 + 2	3
...	...	...	...
100	100	1 + 2 +...+ 100	101

Adding Flexibility

In the next example, we again add a sequence of integers, but vary the counter's starting value, ending value, and increment:

```java
// Display the sum of the integers between a startingValue
// and an endingValue, using a designated increment.

int cntr, sum, startingValue, endingValue, increment;

startingValue = 10;
endingValue = 100;
increment = 7;

sum = 0;
cntr = startingValue;
while (cntr <= endingValue){
   sum += cntr;
   cntr += increment;
}
System.out.println (sum);
```

This portion of code computes the value of 10 + 17 + 24 + ... + 94. For greater flexibility the code could be modified to ask the user for the starting value, the ending value, and the increment.

Counting Backward

We can also run the counter backward as in the next example, which displays the square roots of the numbers 25, 20, 15, and 10. Here the counter variable is called number:

```java
// Display the square roots of 25, 20, 15, and 10

int number = 25;
while (number >= 10){
   System.out.println ("The square root of " + number +
                       " is " + Math.sqrt (number));
   number -= 5;
}
```

The output is

```
The square root of 25 is 5.0
The square root of 20 is 4.47213595499958
The square root of 15 is 3.872983346207417
The square root of 10 is 3.1622776601683795
```

Task-Controlled Loop

Sometimes loops are structured so that they continue to execute until some task is accomplished. These are called *task-controlled loops*. To illustrate, we write code that finds the first integer for which the sum 1 + 2 + ... + n is over 1 million:

```java
// Display the first value n for which 1 + 2 + . . . + n
// is greater than 1 million

int sum = 0;
int number = 0;
while (sum <= 1000000){
   number++;
   sum += number;              // point p
}

System.out.println (number);
```

To verify that the code works as intended, we can reason as follows:

- The first time we reach point p, number = 1, sum = 1, and sum <= 1,000,000.

- The second time we reach point p, number = 2, sum = 1 + 2, and sum <= 1,000,000.

- Etc. ...

- The last time we reach point p, number = n, sum = 1 + 2 + ... + n, and sum > 1,000,000.

- After that we will not enter the loop again, and number contains the first value to force the sum over a million.

Common Structure

All the preceding examples share a common structure:

```
initialize variables                              // initialize
while (condition){                                //   test
   perform calculations and                       //   loop body
   change variables involved in the condition
}
```

For the loop to terminate, each iteration through the loop must move the variables involved in the condition significantly closer to satisfying the condition.

Computing Factorial

The factorial of a given number n is the product of the numbers between 1 and n, inclusive (1 * 2 * 3 * ... * n). The following program prompts the user for n and displays its factorial:

```java
// Example 4.2: Compute and display the factorial of n

import java.util.Scanner;

public class Factorial{

   public static void main(String[] args){
      Scanner reader = new Scanner(System.in);
      System.out.print("Enter a number greater than 0: ");
      int number = reader.nextInt();
      int product = 1;
      int count = 1;
      while (count <= number){
         product = product * count;
         System.out.println(product);
         count++;
      }
      System.out.println("The factorial of " + number +
                     " is " + product);
   }
}
```

*E*XERCISE 4.5

1. When does a while loop terminate execution?

2. List the three components of a while loop.

3. What happens if the condition of a while loop is false from the outset?

4. Describe in English what the following code segments do:

a.

```
int expo = 1, limit = 10;

while (expo <= limit){
    System.out.println(expo + " " + Math.pow(2, expo));
 expo++;
    }
```

b.

```
Scanner reader = new Scanner(System.in);
int product = 1;
System.out.print("Enter a positive number or -999 to halt");
int x = reader.nextInt();

while (x != -999){
    product *= x;
    System.out.print("Enter a positive number or -999 to halt");
    x = reader.nextInt();
}
```

5. Write code segments to perform the following tasks:

   a. Print the squares and cubes of the first 10 positive integers.

   b. Print 10 random integers between 1 and 10 inclusive.

   c. Input names and ages of people until a person's age is 100.

4.6 The for *Statement*

Count-controlled loops are used so frequently that many programming languages (including Java) include a special statement to make them easy to write. It is called *the* for *statement*, and it combines counter initialization, condition test, and update into a single expression. Following is its form:

```
for (initialize counter; test counter; update counter)
    statement;     // one statement inside the loop body

for (initialize counter; test counter; update counter){
    statement;    // many statements
    statement;    // inside the
    . . .;        // loop body
}
```

When the statement is executed, the counter is initialized. Then, as long as the test yields `true`, the statements in the loop body are executed, and the counter is updated. It is essential to understand that the counter is updated at the bottom of the loop, after the statements in the body have been executed. Even though the update appears at the top of the loop, it is executed at the bottom.

To demonstrate how the `for` statement works, we have rewritten the count-controlled loops presented in the previous sections:

```java
// Compute 1 + 2 + … + 100

int sum = 0, cntr;
for (cntr = 1; cntr <= 100; cntr++)
    sum += cntr;
System.out.println (sum);
```

```java
// Display the sum of the integers between a startingValue
// and an endingValue, using a designated increment.

int cntr, sum, startingValue, endingValue, increment;

startingValue = 10;
endingValue = 100;
increment = 7;

sum = 0;
for (cntr = startingValue; cntr <= endingValue; cntr += increment)
    sum += cntr;
System.out.println (sum);
```

```java
// Display the square roots of 25, 20, 15, and 10

int number;
for (number = 25; number >= 10; number -= 5)
    System.out.println ("The square root of " + number +
                        " is " + Math.sqrt (number));
```

Count-Controlled Input

Programs often need to read and process repeating inputs. For instance, consider a program that computes the average of a list of numbers. Here the repeating input is a single number. As each number is read into the program, it is added to a sum. When all the numbers have been read, the program computes and prints the average. For maximum flexibility the program must process a list of any length, but this requirement seemingly creates a dilemma. When we write the program, we have no way of knowing how many numbers will be in the list. So how can we write the program? There are two approaches. We illustrate one method in this section and the other in Section 4.8.

In the first method, we begin by asking the user for the length of the list and then we read exactly that many additional values:

```java
Scanner reader = new Scanner(System.in);
double number, sum = 0;
int i, count;

System.out.print("How long is the list? ");
count = reader.nextInt();
for (i = 1; i <= count; i++){
   System.out.print("Enter a positive number: ");
   number = reader.nextDouble();
   sum += number;
}

if (count == 0)
   System.out.println ("You entered no numbers.");
else
   System.out.println ("The average is " + sum / count);
```

Following is a sample run:

```
How long is the list? 3
Enter a positive number: 1.1
Enter a positive number: 2.2
Enter a positive number: 3.3
The average is 2.1999999999999997
```

Declaring the Loop Control Variable in a `for` Loop

The loop control variables in the examples shown thus far have been declared outside of and above the loop structure. However, the `for` loop allows the programmer to declare the loop control variable inside of the loop header. Following are equivalent loops that show these two alternatives:

```java
int i;                            // Declare control variable above loop

for (i = 1; i <= 10; i++)
   System.out.println(i);


for (int i = 1; i <= 10; i++)     // Declare control variable in loop header
   System.out.println(i);
```

Although both loops are equivalent in function, the second alternative is considered preferable on most occasions for two reasons:

1. The loop control variable is visible only within the body of the loop where it is intended to be used.

2. The same name can be declared again in other `for` loops in the same program.

    We discuss this important property of variable names, called *scope*, in more detail in Chapter 5.

Choosing a while Loop or a for Loop

Because while loops and for loops are quite similar, the following question arises: Which type of loop is more appropriate in a given situation? Both for loops and while loops are *entry-controlled loops*. This means that a continuation condition is tested at the top of the loop on each pass, before the loop's body of code is executed. If this condition is true, the loop continues. If it is false, the loop terminates. This also means that the loop's body of code might not execute at all (when its continuation condition is initially false). Thus, both types of loops can be used in exactly the same situations.

The choice between a while loop and a for loop is often a matter of programmer style or taste. However, some programmers argue that there are two minor advantages in using a for loop:

1. All of the loop control information, including the initial setting of the loop control variable, its update, and the test of the continuation condition, appears within the for loop's header. By contrast, only the test appears in the header of a while loop. Some programmers argue that you are more likely to forget the update in a while loop, which can cause a logic error.

2. The loop control variable of a for loop can be declared in its header. This restricts the variable's visibility to the body of the loop, where it is relevant. Although there are exceptions to this practice, restricting the visibility of variables in a program can make it more likely to be free of logic errors. We discuss this idea in more detail in Chapter 5.

*E*XERCISE 4.6

1. Describe in English what the following code segments do:

   a.
   ```
   for (int expo = 1; expo <= limit; expo++)
                 System.out.println(expo + " " + Math.pow(2, expo));
   ```

   b.
   ```
          int base = 2;

          for (int count = expo; count > 1; count-)
       base = base * base;
   ```

2. Write code segments that use for loops to perform the following tasks:
   a. Print the squares and cubes of the first 10 positive integers.
   b. Build a string consisting of the first 10 positive digits in descending order.

3. Translate the following for loops to equivalent while loops:

   a.
   ```
      Scanner reader new Scanner(System.in);

      for (int i = 1; i <= 5; i++){
         System.out.print("Enter an integer: ");
         int number = reader.nextInt();
         System.out.println(Math.pow(number, 2));
      }
   ```

b.

```
int base = 2;

for (int count = expo; count > 1; count-)
    base = base * base;
```

4.7 Nested Control Statements and the break Statement

Control statements can be nested inside each other in any combination that proves useful. We now present several illustrative examples and also demonstrate a mechanism for breaking out of a loop early, that is, before the loop condition is false. All the examples use for loops, but similar examples can be constructed using while loops.

Print the Divisors

As a first example, we write a code segment that asks the user for a positive integer n, and then prints all its proper divisors, that is, all divisors except 1 and the number itself. For instance, the proper divisors of 12 are 2, 3, 4, and 6. A positive integer d is a divisor of n if d is less than n and n % d is zero. Thus, to find n's proper divisors, we must try all values of d between 2 and n / 2. Here is the code:

```
// Display the proper divisors of a number

System.out.print("Enter a positive integer: ");
int n = reader.nextInt();

int limit = n / 2;

for (int d = 2; d <= limit; d++){
   if (n % d == 0)
       System.out.print (d + " ");
}
```

Is a Number Prime?

A number is prime if it has no proper divisors. We can modify the previous code segment to determine if a number is prime simply by counting its proper divisors. If there are none, the number is prime. Following is code that implements this plan:

```
// Determine if a number is prime

System.out.print(("Enter an integer greater than 2: ");
int n = reader.nextInt();

int count = 0;
int limit = n/2;
```

```
for (int d = 2; d <= limit; d++){
   if (n % d == 0)

      count++;
}

if (count != 0)
   System.out.println ("Not prime.");
else
   System.out.println ("Prime.");
```

The break Statement

Most programmers, including the authors of this text, enjoy the challenge of trying to write efficient programs. You can do two things to improve the efficiency of the previous segment of code. First, the limit does not need to be as large as n / 2. If a*b equals n, then either a or b must be less than or equal to the square root of n. Second, as soon as we find the first divisor of n, we know n is not prime, so there is no point in going around the loop again. To get out of a loop prematurely, that is, before the loop condition is false, we can use a break statement. A loop, either for or while, terminates immediately when a break statement is executed.

In the following segment of code, we check d after the for loop terminates. If n has a divisor, the break statement executes, the loop terminates early, and d is less than or equal to the limit. Following is the code:

```
// Determine if a number is prime

System.out.print("Enter an integer greater than 2: ");
int n = reader.nextInt();

int limit = (int)Math.sqrt (n);

int d;                                  // Declare control variable here

for (d = 2; d <= limit; d++){
   if (n % d == 0)
      break;
}

if (d <= limit)                         // So it's visible here
   System.out.println ("Not prime.");
else
   System.out.println ("Prime.");
```

Note that the loop control variable d must now be declared above the loop so that it will be visible below it.

Sentinel-Controlled Input

In addition to the count-controlled input mentioned in the previous section, there is a second method for handling repeating user inputs. We again use the example of finding the average of a list of numbers. Now we read numbers repeatedly until we encounter a special value called a *sentinel* that marks the end of the list. For instance, if all the numbers in the list are positive, then the sentinel could be –1, as shown in the following code:

```java
Scanner reader = new Scanner(System.in);
double number, sum = 0;
int count = 0;

while (true){
   System.out.print("Enter a positive number or -1 to quit: ");
   number = reader.nextDouble();
   if (number == -1) break;
   sum += number;
   count++;
}

if (count == 0)
   System.out.println ("The list is empty.");
else
   System.out.println ("The average is " + sum / count);
```

Following is a sample run:

```
Enter a positive number or -1 to quit: 1.1
Enter a positive number or -1 to quit: 2.2
Enter a positive number or -1 to quit: 3.3
Enter a positive number or -1 to quit: -1
The average is 2.1999999999999997
```

Like any other high-level language, Java is rich in control statements. For example, the switch statement, the do-while statement, and the continue statement allow the programmer to express selection and repetition in a different manner than the control statements in this chapter. For details on these statements, see Appendix B.

*E*XERCISE 4.7

1. Describe in English what the following code segments do:

a.

```java
for (int i = 1; i <= limit; i++)
   if (i % 2 == 0)
      System.out.println(i);
```

b.

```java
Random gen = new Random();
int myNumber = gen.nextInt(10);
int x = 0;
int yourNumber;

while (x == 0){
   System.out.println("I'm guessing a number between 1 and 10.");
   System.out.print("Which number is it? ");
   yourNumber = reader.nextInt();
```

```
    if (myNumber == yourNumber){
        System.out.println("That's it!");
        break;
    }else System.out.println("Sorry, try again");
}
```

2. Write code segments that use loops to perform the following tasks:

   a. Print the squares and cubes of the first 10 positive, odd integers.

   b. Build a string consisting of the first 10 positive, even digits in descending order.

4.8 *Using Loops with Text Files*

Thus far in this book, we have seen examples of programs that have taken input data from human users at the keyboard. Most of these programs can receive their input data from text files as well. A text file is a software object that stores data on a permanent medium such as a disk, CD, or flash memory. When compared to keyboard input from a human user, the main advantages of taking input data from a file are as follows:

- The data set can be much larger.

- The data can be input much more quickly and with less chance of error.

- The data can be used repeatedly with the same program or with different programs.

Text Files and Their Format

The data in a text file can be created, saved, and viewed with a text editor, such as Notepad. Alternatively, a program can output the data to a file, a procedure that we discuss shortly. The data in a text file can be viewed as characters, words, numbers, or lines of text, depending on the text file's format and on the purposes for which the data is used. When the data are treated as numbers (either integers or floating-points), they must be separated by whitespace characters. These are the space, tab, and newline characters. For example, a text file containing six floating-point numbers might look like

```
34.6 22.33 66.75
77.12 21.44 99.01
```

when examined with a text editor.

Any text file, including the special case of an empty file, must contain at least one special character that marks the end of the file. This character can serve as a sentinel for a program loop that reads each datum until the end-of-file condition is encountered. When a program opens a file, an input pointer is set to the first character in it. Assuming that the end-of-file condition has not yet been reached, when each datum is read, the pointer moves to the next datum.

The Scanner and File Classes

Fortunately, we can use the same `Scanner` class for text file input that we use for keyboard input. The first step is to create a scanner object by opening it on a file object rather than the keyboard object. File objects are instances of the class `File`, which appears in the package `java.io`. We obtain a file object by running the code new `File(aFileName)`, where `afileName` is a pathname or the name of a file in the current working directory. For example, let's assume that we have a text file of floating-point numbers named `"numbers.txt"`. The following code opens a scanner on this file:

```java
Scanner reader = new Scanner(new File("numbers.txt"));
```

A sentinel-controlled loop can then be used to read all of the data from the file. Before each datum is read, we must check to see if the end of the file condition has been reached. The `Scanner` method `hasNext()` returns `true` if the end of file is not yet present. Now let's assume that we want to compute the average of the numbers in the file. A slight modification of the sentinel-controlled loop from section 4.7 accomplishes this:

```java
Scanner reader = new Scanner(new File("numbers.txt"));
double number, sum = 0;
int count = 0;

while (reader.hasNext()){
    number = reader.nextDouble();
    sum += number;
    count++;
}
```

Note that we test for the sentinel before reading the data and we omit the output of the prompt to the user.

Files and Exceptions

When a Java program encounters an operation that it cannot perform at runtime, the JVM throws an exception. We have seen examples of exceptions thrown in earlier chapters when a program commits run-time errors, such as an attempt to divide an integer by zero. When working with files, a program may encounter errors that it cannot handle. For example, the file could be missing when the program tries to open it, or the file's data may be corrupted on the storage medium. In these cases, an I/O exception is thrown. I/O exceptions are generally so serious that they belong to a category called *checked exceptions*. This means that a program must at least acknowledge they might be thrown, if not do something to recover from them. We see how to recover from an exception in Chapter 10. For now, to meet the minimal requirement, we can place the simple phrase `throws IOException` after the header of the `main` method of any program that does text file input. If the program encounters an `IOException`, the JVM will halt execution with an error message.

The following program uses our sentinel-controlled loop to compute and display the average of the numbers in a text file:

```java
// Example 4.3: Computes and displays the average of
// a file of floating-point numbers

import java.io.*;                // For File and IOException
import java.util.Scanner;
```

```
public class ComputeAverage{
  public static void main(String[] args) throws IOException {
    Scanner reader = new Scanner(new File("numbers.txt"));
    double number, sum = 0;
    int count = 0;

    while (reader.hasNext()){
      number = reader.nextDouble();
      sum += number;
      count++;
    }
    if (count == 0)
      System.out.println("The file had no numbers");
    else
      System.out.println("The average of " + count + " numbers is " +
                         sum / count);
  }
}
```

Output to Text Files

Data can be output to a text file using the class `PrintWriter`. This class includes the methods `print` and `println` that you have already used for terminal output, so there is not much new to be learned. A `PrintWriter` is opened like scanner, using the form

```
PrintWriter writer = new PrintWriter(new File(aFileName));
```

After the outputs have been completed, you must close the `PrintWriter` with the statement

```
writer.close();
```

Failure to close the output file may result in no data being saved to it. Because an `IOException` might be thrown during these operations, the `main` method must use a `throws IOException` clause to keep the compiler happy.

Our next example program filters a set of integers by removing all of the zeroes and retaining the other values. The inputs are in a text file named numbers.txt, whereas the outputs go to a file named newnumbers.txt. Here is the code:

```
// Example 4.4: Inputs a text file of integers and writes these
// to an output file without the zeroes

import java.io.*;             // For File, IOException, and PrintWriter
import java.util.Scanner;

public class FilterZeroes{

  public static void main(String[] args) throws IOException {

    // Open the scanner and print writer
    Scanner reader = new Scanner(new File("numbers.txt"));
    PrintWriter writer = new PrintWriter(new File("newnumbers.txt"));
```

```
        // Read the numbers and write all but the zeroes
        while (reader.hasNext()){
            int number = reader.nextInt();
            if (number != 0)
                writer.println(number);
        }

        // Remember to close the output file
        writer.close();
    }
}
```

Note that this program also runs correctly with an empty input file or one that contains no zeroes.

EXERCISE 4.8

1. Describe in English what the following code segment does:

```
Scanner reader = new Scanner(new File("myfile.txt"));
```

2. Write code segments that use loops to perform the following tasks:
   a. Read integers from a file and display them in the terminal window.
   b. Assume that there are an even number of integers in a file. Read them in pairs from the file and display the larger value of each pair in the terminal window.

Case Study: The Folly of Gambling

It is said, with some justification, that only the mathematically challenged gamble. Lotteries, slot machines, and gambling games in general are designed to take in more money than they pay out. Even if gamblers get lucky and win a few times, in the long run they lose. For this case study we have invented a game of chance called Lucky Sevens that seems like an attractive proposition, but which is, as usual, a sure loser for the gambler. The rules of the game are simple:

■ Roll a pair of dice.

■ If the sum of the spots equals 7, the player wins $4; else the player loses $1.

To entice the gullible, the casino tells players that there are lots of ways to win: (1, 6), (2, 5), etc. A little mathematical analysis reveals that there are not enough ways to win to make the game worthwhile; however, many people's eyes glaze over at the first mention of mathematics, so the challenge is to write a program that demonstrates the futility of playing the game.

Request

Write a program that demonstrates the futility of playing Lucky Sevens.

Analysis

We use the random number generator to write a program that simulates the game. The program asks the user how many dollars he has, plays the game repeatedly until the money is gone, and displays the number of rolls taken. The program also displays the maximum amount of money held by the player, thus demonstrating that getting ahead at some point does not avoid the inevitable outcome. Figure 4-3 shows the proposed interface.

FIGURE 4-3

Interface for the lucky sevens simulator

```
How many dollars do you have? 100
You are broke after 543 rolls.
You should have quit after 47 rolls when you had $113
```

Design

The design is captured in the following pseudocode:

```
read the initial amount the gambler has to wager
initialize to zero a counter representing the number of rolls

the maximum amount equals the initial amount
the count at the maximum equals zero

while (there is any money left){
   increment the rolls counter
   roll the dice

   if (the dice add to seven)
      add $4 to the gambler's amount
   else
      subtract $1 from the gambler's amount

   if (the amount is now greater than ever before){
      remember this maximum amount
      remember the current value of the rolls counter
   }
}
display the rolls counter
display the maximum amount
display the count at the maximum amount
```

Implementation

Following is a program based on the pseudocode:

```
/*LuckySevens.java
Simulate the game of lucky sevens until all funds are depleted.
1) Rules:
        roll two dice
        if the sum equals 7, win $4, else lose $1
2) The inputs are:
        the amount of money the user is prepared to lose
3) Computations:
        use the random number generator to simulate rolling the dice
        loop until the funds are depleted
        count the number of rolls
        keep track of the maximum amount
4) The outputs are:
        the number of rolls it takes to deplete the funds
        the maximum amount
*/

import java.util.Scanner;
import java.util.Random;

public class LuckySevens {
   public static void main (String [] args) {

      Scanner reader = new Scanner(System.in);
      Random generator = new Random();

      int die1, die2,        // two dice
          dollars,           // initial number of dollars (input)
          count,             // number of rolls to reach depletion
          maxDollars,        // maximum amount held by the gambler
          countAtMax;        // count when the maximum is achieved

      // Request the input
      System.out.print("How many dollars do you have? ");
      dollars = reader.nextInt();

      // Initialize variables
      maxDollars = dollars;
      countAtMax = 0;
      count = 0;

      // Loop until the money is gone
      while (dollars > 0){
         count++;

         // Roll the dice.
         die1 = generator.nextInt (6) + 1; // 1-6
         die2 = generator.nextInt (6) + 1; // 1-6
```

```
        // Calculate the winnings or losses
        if (die1 + die2 == 7)
            dollars += 4;
        else
            dollars -= 1;

        // If this is a new maximum, remember it
        if (dollars > maxDollars){
            maxDollars = dollars;
            countAtMax = count;
        }
    }

    // Display the results
    System.out.println
        ("You are broke after " + count + " rolls.\n" +
         "You should have quit after " + countAtMax +
         " rolls when you had $" + maxDollars + ".");
    }
}
```

Output

Running this program is just about as exciting (in our opinion) as going to Las Vegas, and it's a lot cheaper. (Perhaps we should translate it into a Java applet as shown in Chapter 8 of this book, make it part of a Web page, and charge people 10 cents each to run it.) Following are the results from several trial runs:

```
How many dollars do you have? 100
You are broke after 255 rolls.
You should have quit after 35 rolls when you had $110.

How many dollars do you have? 100
You are broke after 500 rolls.
You should have quit after 179 rolls when you had $136.

How many dollars do you have? 1000000
You are broke after 6029535 rolls.
You should have quit after 97 rolls when you had $1000008.
```

These results show that there is very little money to be gained in this game of chance—regardless of how much you have available to gamble.

4.9 Errors in Loops

We can easily make logic errors when coding loops, but we can avoid many of these errors if we have a proper understanding of a loop's typical structure. A loop usually has four component parts:

1. *Initializing statements*. These statements initialize variables used within the loop.

2. *Terminating condition*. This condition is tested before each pass through the loop to determine if another iteration is needed.

3. *Body statements*. These statements execute with each iteration and implement the calculation in question.

4. *Update statements.* These statements, which usually are executed at the bottom of the loop, change the values of the variables tested in the terminating condition.

A careless programmer can introduce logic errors into any one of these components. To demonstrate, we first present a simple but correct `while` loop and then show several revised versions, each with a different logic error. The correct version is

```
//Compute the product of the odd integers from 1 to 100
//Outcome - product will equal 3*5*...*99
int product = 1;
int i = 3;
while (i <= 100){
    product = product * i;
    i = i + 2;
}
System.out.println (product);
```

Initialization Error

We first introduce an error into the initializing statements. Because we forget to initialize the variable `product`, it retains its default value of zero.

```
//Error - failure to initialize the variable product
//Outcome - zero is printed
int product;
int i = 3;
while (i <= 100){
    product = product * i;
    i = i + 2;
}
System.out.println (product);
```

Off-by-One Error

The next error involves the terminating condition:

```
//Error - use of "< 99" rather than "<= 100" in the
//    terminating condition
//Outcome - product will equal 3*5...*97
int product = 1;
int i = 3;
while (i < 99){
    product = product * i;
    i = i + 2;
}
System.out.println (product);
```

This is called an *off-by-one error,* and it occurs whenever a loop goes around one too many or one too few times. This is one of the most common types of looping errors and is often difficult to detect. Do not be fooled by the fact that, in this example, the error is glaringly obvious.

Infinite Loop

Following is another error in the terminating condition:

```
//Error - use of "!= 100" rather than "<= 100" in the terminating condition
//Outcome - the program will never stop
int product = 1;
int i = 3;

while (i != 100){
    product = product * i;
    i = i + 2;
}
System.out.println (product);
```

The variable i takes on the values 3, 5, ..., 99, 101, ... and never equals 100. This is called an *infinite loop*. Anytime a program responds more slowly than expected, it is reasonable to assume that it is stuck in an infinite loop. Do not pull the plug. Instead, on a PC, select the terminal window and press Ctrl+C; that is, press the Control and "C" keys simultaneously. This will stop the program.

Error in Loop Body

Following is an error in the body of the loop. Again, the error is comically obvious because we are pointing it out, but these kinds of errors often can be difficult to detect—particularly for the person who wrote the program.

```
//Error - use of + rather than * when computing product
//Outcome - product will equal 3+5+...+99
int product = 1;
int i = 3;
while (i <= 100){
    product = product + i;
    i = i + 2;
}
System.out.println (product);
```

Update Error

If the update statement is in the wrong place, the calculations can be thrown off even if the loop iterates the correct number of times:

```
//Error - placement of the update statement in the wrong place
//Outcome - product will equal 5*7*...*99*101
int product = 1;
int i = 3;
while (i <= 100){
    i = i + 2;              //this update statement should follow the calculation
    product = product * i;
}
System.out.println (product);
```

Effects of Limited Floating-Point Precision

Numbers that are declared as `double` have about 18 decimal digits of precision. This is very good, but it is not perfect and can lead to unexpected errors. Consider the following lines of code, which seem to be free of logic errors, yet produce an infinite loop:

```
double x;
for (x = 0.0; x != 1.0; x += 0.1)
   System.out.print (x + " ");
```

When this code runs, the expected output is

```
0.0   0.1   0.2   0.3   0.4   0.5   0.6   0.7   0.8   0.9   1.0
```

However, the actual output is

```
0.0   0.1   0.2   0.30000000000000004   0.4   0.5   0.6   0.7   0.7999999999999999
0.8999999999999999   0.9999999999999999   1.0999999999999999   1.2   1.3
1.4000000000000001   1.5000000000000002   ... etc ...
```

To understand what went wrong, consider the decimal representation of ⅓. It is 0.33333... The 3s go on forever, and consequently no finite representation is exact. The same sort of thing happens when 1/5 is represented in binary as a `double`. Consequently, in the previous code, x never exactly equals 1.0 and the loop never terminates. To fix the code, we rewrite it as

```
double x, delta;
delta = 0.01;
for (x = 0.0; x <= 1.0 + delta; x += 0.1)
   System.out.print (x + " ");
```

The code now works correctly, provided `delta` is less than the increment 0.1. The new output is

```
0.0   0.1   0.2   0.30000000000000004   0.4   0.5   0.6   0.7   0.7999999999999999
0.8999999999999999   0.9999999999999999
```

Debugging Loops

If you suspect that you have written a loop that contains a logic error, inspect the code and make sure the following items are true:

- Variables are initialized correctly before entering the loop.

- The terminating condition stops the iterations when the test variables have reached the intended limit.

- The statements in the body are correct.

- The update statements are positioned correctly and modify the test variables in such a manner that they eventually pass the limits tested in the terminating condition.

In addition, when writing terminating conditions, it is usually safer to use one of the operators

<   <=   >   >=

than either of the operators

==   !=

as demonstrated earlier.

Also, if you cannot find an error by inspection, then use `System.out.println` statements to "dump" key variables to the terminal window. Good places for these statements are

- Immediately after the initialization statements

- Inside the loop at the top

- Inside the loop at the bottom

You will then discover that some of the variables have values different than expected, and this will provide clues that reveal the exact nature and location of the logic error.

*E*XERCISE 4.9

1. Describe the logic errors in the following loops:

a.

```
// Print the odd numbers between 1 and limit, inclusive
for (int i = 1; i < limit; i++)
   if (i % 2 == 1)
      System.out.println(i);
```

b.

```
// Print the first ten positive odd numbers
int number = 1;
while (number != 10)
   System.out.println(number);
   number += 2;
}
```

4.10 Graphics and GUIs: I/O Dialog Boxes and Loops

Our graphics and GUI programs in earlier chapters displayed images but were not interactive, in that they did not accept user input. In this section we explore the use of dialog boxes for I/O. We also examine the use of loops and selection statements in graphics and GUI-based programs.

Extra Challenge

This Graphics and GUIs section gives you the opportunity to explore concepts and programming techniques required to develop modern graphics applications and graphical user interfaces. This material is not required in order to proceed with the other chapters of the book.

I/O Dialogs

A very convenient way to accept input from a user is to pop up an *input dialog box*. A typical input dialog box is a small window that contains a message asking for information, a text field for entering it, and command buttons labeled OK and Cancel. The text field can either be empty or contain a default data value, such as a number, when the dialog box pops up. The user places her mouse cursor in the text field and edits the data. She then clicks **OK** to accept the data or **Cancel** to back out of the interaction.

The class `JOptionPane` in the package `javax.swing` includes several versions of the method `showInputDialog` for input dialog boxes. One such version expects two strings as parameters. The first string is the message to be displayed in the dialog box. The second string is the default data value to be displayed in the input text field. If you want the field to be empty, you can pass the empty string ("") in this position. The following code segment pops up the input dialog box shown in Figure 4-4, which asks for the user's age:

```
String inputStr = JOptionPane.showInputDialog("Enter your age", "");
```

FIGURE 4-4
An input dialog

If the user clicks **OK**, the dialog box closes and returns the string that happens to be in the text input field. In our example, the code assigns this string to the variable `inputStr`. If the user clicks **Cancel** to back out, the dialog box closes and returns the value `null`, which our code also assigns to `inputStr`. Clearly, the program code must then check for `null` before passing the input datum on to the next step. The simplest way to handle the `null` value is shown in the next code segment:

```
if (inputStr == null)
    return;
```

The `return` statement in this code quits the method if the input string is `null`.

If the expected input is a number, one other thing must be done before it can be processed. The dialog box returns a string of digits, which must be converted to an `int` or a `double`. The methods `Integer.parseInt(aString)` and `Double.parseDouble(aString)` accomplish this for integers and floating-point numbers, respectively.

To output a message, we can use a *message dialog box*. The method `JOptionPane.showMessageDialog(anObserver, aString)` pops up a small window that displays the second parameter and waits for the user to click the OK button. For now, the first parameter is `null`.

The next program example incorporates dialog box I/O into the `CircleArea` program of Section 4.4. Shots of the dialog boxes from an interaction are shown in Figure 45.

```java
// Example 4.5: CircleARea with dialog I/O

import javax.swing.JOptionPane;

public class CircleArea{

    public static void main(String[] args){
        String inputStr = JOptionPane.showInputDialog("Enter the radius", "0");
        if (inputStr == null)
            return;
        double radius = Double.parseDouble(inputStr);
        if (radius < 0)
            JOptionPane.showMessageDialog(null, "Error: Radius must be >= 0");
        else{
            double area = Math.PI * Math.pow(radius, 2);
            JOptionPane.showMessageDialog(null, "The area is " + area);
        }
    }
}
```

FIGURE 4-5

Dialog I/O user interface for the circle area program

Unlike the graphics and GUI programs shown earlier, this one runs in the terminal window and does not pop up a main program window. Note also that if the user cancels the input dialog box, the program simply quits by returning from the main method.

Setting Up Lots of Panels

Some of our early graphics programs used multiple panels. Occasionally, many panels are called for. For example, a program might display a regular pattern such as those seen on quilts. In these situations, a loop can be used to initialize and install the panels. Consider the following fanciful program, which prompts the user for the dimensions of a grid of randomly colored panels and then displays them:

```java
// Example 4.6: Display random colors in a grid
// whose dimensions are input by the user

import javax.swing.*;
import java.awt.*;
import java.util.Random;

public class GUIWindow{

    public static void main(String[] args){
        JFrame theGUI = new JFrame();
        theGUI.setTitle("GUI Example");
        String inputStr = JOptionPane.showInputDialog("Number of rows", "5");
```

```
    if (inputStr == null) return;
    int rows = Integer.parseInt(inputStr);
    inputStr = JOptionPane.showInputDialog("Number of columns", "5");
    if (inputStr == null) return;
    int cols = Integer.parseInt(inputStr);
    theGUI.setSize(cols  * 50, rows * 50);
    theGUI.setDefaultCloseOperation(JFrame.EXIT_ON_CLOSE);
    Container pane = theGUI.getContentPane();
    pane.setLayout(new GridLayout(rows, cols));
    Random gen = new Random();
    for (int i = 1; i <= rows * cols; i++){
        int red = gen.nextInt(256);
        int green = gen.nextInt(256);
        int blue = gen.nextInt(256);
        Color backColor = new Color(red, green, blue);
        ColorPanel panel = new ColorPanel(backColor);
        pane.add(panel);
    }
    theGUI.setVisible(true);
  }
}
```

The user's inputs not only determine the number of rows and columns in the grid, but also the initial size of the application window. The loop works correctly, whether these values are the defaults (5 by 5), or 1 by 1, or 50 by 50 (a pretty big window).

Setting the Preferred Size of a Panel

In the graphics program we have seen thus far, the main window class sets its dimensions at program startup. The dimensions of any panels that appear within the main window are then adjusted to fit within the window when it is displayed. Another way to arrange things is to give each panel a preferred size and ask the window to shrink-wrap its dimensions to accommodate all of the panels. This alternative is useful when we want to fix the exact size of each panel before it is displayed. For instance, if we want the size of each panel to be exactly 50 by 50, the code in the previous example will not do because the window's title bar and borders occupy some of its "real estate."

To solve this problem, we drop the call of the method setSize from the main window class and add a call of the method pack(). This method asks the window to wrap itself around the minimal area necessary to display all of its components (panels or other widgets) at their preferred sizes. Here is the code for the main method of that program with the needed changes:

```
public static void main(String[] args){
    JFrame theGUI = new JFrame();
    theGUI.setTitle("GUI Example");
    String inputStr = JOptionPane.showInputDialog("Number of rows", "5");
    if (inputStr == null) return;
    int rows = Integer.parseInt(inputStr);
    inputStr = JOptionPane.showInputDialog("Number of columns", "5");
    if (inputStr == null) return;
    int cols = Integer.parseInt(inputStr);
    //theGUI.setSize(cols  * 50, rows * 50);   Dropped!!!
    theGUI.setDefaultCloseOperation(JFrame.EXIT_ON_CLOSE);
    Container pane = theGUI.getContentPane();
```

```
pane.setLayout(new GridLayout(rows, cols));
Random gen = new Random();
for (int i = 1; i <= rows * cols; i++){
    int red = gen.nextInt(256);
    int green = gen.nextInt(256);
    int blue = gen.nextInt(256);
    Color backColor = new Color(red, green, blue);
    //Use new constructor to specify the preferred size of the panel
    ColorPanel panel = new ColorPanel(backColor, 50, 50);
    pane.add(panel);
}
theGUI.pack();                                    //Added!!
theGUI.setVisible(true);
}
```

If a panel does not set its own preferred size, its default size is 0 by 0. We add a second constructor to the `ColorPanel` class that receives a preferred width and height from the client. This constructor calls the method `setPreferredSize`, which expects an object of class `Dimension` as a parameter. This object, in turn, is created with the width and height received from the client. Here is the modified code for the `ColorPanel` class:

```
// Example 4.7: A color panel whose background is
// a color provided by the client
// A client-specified preferred size is optional

import javax.swing.*;
import java.awt.*;

public class ColorPanel extends JPanel{

    // Client provides color and preferred width and height
    public ColorPanel(Color backColor, int width, int height){
        setBackground(backColor);
        setPreferredSize(new Dimension(width, height));
    }

    // Client provides color
    // Preferred width and height are 0, 0 by default
    public ColorPanel(Color backColor){
        setBackground(backColor);
    }
}
```

Drawing Multiple Shapes

Consider the problem of displaying a bull's-eye, as shown in Figure 4-6. This particular bull's-eye is a pattern of five concentric filled ovals, whose colors alternate. Each oval is centered in the panel. The outermost oval's width and height are the width and height of the panel minus 1. Each oval's radius is a constant amount (called the thickness) larger than the next smaller oval's radius. One can create this pattern by drawing the largest oval first and then drawing the other ovals on top, layering them in descending order of size. The algorithm starts with a thickness of the panel's width divided by 10, an initial corner point of (0, 0), a size of the panel's width − 1 and height − 1, and the color red. The algorithm then runs a loop that per-forms the following steps five times:

1. Draw the oval with the current color, corner point, and size.

2. Adjust the corner point by subtracting the thickness from each coordinate.

3. Adjust the size by subtracting twice the thickness from each dimension.

4. Adjust the color (to white if red, or to red otherwise).

FIGURE 4-6
A bull's eye

This algorithm is implemented in the `paintComponent` method of the following `ColorPanel` class:

```
// Example 4.8: A color panel containing
// a red and white bull's eye

import javax.swing.*;
import java.awt.*;

public class ColorPanel extends JPanel{

   // Client provides color and preferred width and height
   public ColorPanel(Color backColor, int width, int height){
      setBackground(backColor);
      setPreferredSize(new Dimension(width, height));
   }

   // Client provides color
   // Preferred width and height are 0, 0 by default
   public ColorPanel(Color backColor){
      setBackground(backColor);
   }

   public void paintComponent(Graphics g){
      super.paintComponent(g);

       //Set the attributes of the outermost oval
      int thickness = getWidth() / 10;
      int x = 0;
      int y = 0;
      int width = getWidth() - 1;
      int height = getHeight() - 1;
      Color ringColor = Color.red;
```

```
      for (int count = 1; count <= 5; count++){
         g.setColor(ringColor);
         g.fillOval(x, y, width, height);

          //Adjust corner point for next oval
         x = x + thickness;
         y = y + thickness;

         //Adjust width and height for next oval
         width = width - thickness * 2;
         height = height - thickness * 2;

         //Change the color for the next oval
         if (ringColor == Color.red)
            ringColor = Color.white;
         else
            ringColor = Color.red;
      }
   }
}
```

As you can see, it would be easy to modify the appearance of the bull's-eye by changing the number of ovals drawn, their thickness, and the colors.

EXERCISE 4.10

1. Write a code segment that uses an I/O dialog box to prompt the user for her name.

2. Write a code segment that displays your name and address in a message box. Your name and address should be formatted on separate lines by using the "\n" character.

3. Explain why we need to use the methods `Integer.parseInt` and `Double.parseDouble` when receiving numeric input from an I/O dialog box.

4. Give an example of a situation where you would want a panel to set its preferred size, rather than allow the size of the main window to determine that.

Design, Testing, and Debugging Hints

■ Most errors involving selection statements and loops are not syntax errors caught at compile time. Thus, you will detect these errors only after running the program, and perhaps then only with extensive testing.

■ The presence or absence of the {} symbols can seriously affect the logic of a selection statement or loop. For example, the following selection statements have a similar look but a very different logic:

```
if (x > 0){
   y = x;
   z = 1 / x;
}
```

```
if (x > 0)
    y = x;
    z = 1 / x;
```

The first selection statement guards against division by 0; the second statement only guards against assigning x to y. The next pair of code segments shows a similar problem with a loop:

```
while (x > 0){
    y = x;
    x = x - 1;
}

while (x > 0)
    y = x;
    x = x - 1;
```

The first loop terminates because the value of x decreases within the body of the loop; the second loop is infinite because the value of x decreases below the body of the loop.

- When testing programs that use `if` or `if-else` statements, be sure to use test data that forces the program to exercise all of the logical branches.

- Use an `if-else` statement rather than two `if` statements when the alternative courses of action are mutually exclusive.

- When testing a loop, be sure to use limit values as well as typical values. For example, if a loop should terminate when the control variable equals 0, run it with the values 0, −1, and 1.

- Be sure to check entry conditions and exit conditions for each loop.

- For a loop with errors, use debugging output statements to verify the values of the control variable on each pass through the loop. Check this value before the loop is initially entered, after each update, and after the loop is exited.

- Text files are convenient to use when the data set is large, when the same data set must be used repeatedly with different programs, and when these data must be saved permanently.

SUMMARY

In this chapter, you learned:

- Java has some useful operators for extended assignment, such as +=, and for increment and decrement.

- The `Math` class provides several useful methods, such as `sqrt` and `abs`.

- The `Random` class allows you to generate random integers and floating-point numbers.

- `if` and `if-else` statements are used to make one-way and two-way decisions.

- The comparison operators, such as ==, <=, and >=, return Boolean values that serve as conditions of control statements.

- The `while` loop allows the program to run a set of statements repeatedly until a condition becomes false.

- The `for` loop is a more concise version of the `while` loop.

- Other control statements, such as an `if` statement, can be nested within loops. A `break` statement can be used in conjunction with an `if` statement to terminate a loop early.

- There are many kinds of logic errors that can occur in loops. Examples are the off-by-one error and the infinite loop.

VOCABULARY *Review*

Define the following terms:

Control statements	Flowchart	Overloading
Counter	Infinite loop	Sentinel
Count-controlled loop	Iteration	Task-controlled loop
Entry-controlled loop	Off-by-one error	

REVIEW *Questions*

WRITTEN QUESTIONS

Write a brief answer to the following questions.

1. Assume that the variables x and y contain the values 19 and 2, respectively. Indicate if the Boolean expressions below are true, false, or syntactically incorrect.
   A. `x <= y`
   B. `x * 2 > y`
   C. `x - 1 == y * 9`
   D. `x < y < 25`
   E. `x * 2 != y`

2. For each of the following items, write a valid Java statement.
   A. Display "greater" if the value of variable x is greater than the value of variable y. Otherwise, display "less" if the value of variable x is less than the value of variable y. Otherwise, display "equal."
   B. Add 10 to the value of x and display this value if the variable y is negative.
   C. Display the string A if x is greater than 90, B if x is greater than 80 and less than or equal to 90, or C otherwise.

3. Indicate whether or not each of the following loop headings is syntactically correct. If incorrect, explain why.
   A. `while (x > 0)`
   B. `while (y = 10)`
   C. `while x != 0`

4. Write a valid Java statement for each of the following items.
   A. Output the positive numbers from `x` up to `y`.
   B. Output the product of the squares of the numbers from `x` up to `y`.
   C. Output the numbers from `y` down to 0.

5. Assume that the variables `x` and `y` contain integers. Write code to perform the following tasks.
   A. Output the largest value, using an `if` statement.
   B. Output the largest value, using the method `Math.max`.

PROJECTS

PROJECT 4-1

When you first learned to divide, you expressed answers using a quotient and a remainder rather than a fraction or decimal quotient. For example, if you divided 9 by 2, you gave the answer as 4r. 1. Write a program that takes two integers as inputs and displays their quotient and remainder as outputs. Do not assume that the integers are entered in any order, but be sure to divide the larger integer by the smaller integer.

PROJECT 4-2

Write a program that takes the lengths of three sides of a triangle as inputs. The program should display whether or not the triangle is a right triangle.

PROJECT 4-3

A 2-minute telephone call to Lexington, Virginia, costs $1.15. Each additional minute costs $0.50. Write a program that takes the total length of a call in minutes as input and calculates and displays the cost.

PROJECT 4-4

Run the `Factorial` program of Section 4.5 with inputs of 5, 10, and 20. Notice that the number for the last output is large but negative. Place an output statement in the loop so that you can view the value of `count` and `number` on each pass. Can you explain what the problem is? Now change the type of `product` from `int` to `long`, recompile the program, and run it again with the same inputs. Explain what happens. How large does the input have to be before you encounter the same problem again?

PROJECT 4-5

The German mathematician Gottfried Leibniz developed the following method to approximate the value of π:

$$\pi/4 = 1 - 1/3 + 1/5 - 1/7 + \ldots$$

Write a program that allows the user to specify the number of iterations used in this approximation and displays the resulting value.

PROJECT 4-6

A local biologist needs a program to predict population growth. The inputs would be the initial number of organisms, the rate of growth (a real number greater than 0), the number of hours it takes to achieve this rate, and a number of hours during which the population grows. For example, one might start with a population of 500 organisms, a growth rate of 2, and a growth period to achieve this rate of 6 hours. Assuming that none of the organisms die, this would imply that this population would double in size every 6 hours. Thus, after allowing 6 hours for growth, we would have 1000 organisms, and after 12 hours, we would have 2000 organisms. Write a program that takes these inputs and displays a prediction of the total population.

PROJECT 4-7

Computers use the binary system, which is based on powers of 2. Write a program that displays the positive powers of 2. When the user enters the exponent at a prompt, the program displays 2 to that power. The program halts when the user enters –1.

PROJECT 4-8

Modify the program of Project 4-7 so that the user can specify the base (2 or higher) as well. The first line of the output should display which base was entered.

PROJECT 4-9

Modify the program of Project 4-8 so that it processes a file of inputs. Each line of the file contains a base and an exponent. The program should read the data from each line, compute the result, and display each set of inputs and their result on an output line in the terminal window.

PROJECT 4-10

Teachers in most school districts are paid on a schedule that provides a salary based on their number of years of teaching experience. For example, a beginning teacher in the Bellingham School District might be paid $20,000 the first year. For each year of experience after this up to 10 years, a 2 percent increase over the preceding value is received. Write a program that displays a salary schedule for teachers in a school district. The inputs are the starting salary, the percentage increase, and the number of years in the schedule. Each row in the schedule should contain the year number and the salary for that year.

PROJECT 4-11

A checkerboard consists of an 8-by-8 grid of black and red squares in which no two squares of the same color are adjacent. Write a graphics program that displays a checkerboard.

PROJECT 4-12

Modify the program of Project 4-11 so that it prompts the user for the number of rows and columns of the board before displaying them. Use I/O dialog boxes to accept the inputs.

PROJECT 4-13

An interesting optical illusion is caused by a phenomenon known as *induced contrast*. This illusion occurs when two images of the same shade are placed on backgrounds of sharply contrasting shades, as shown in Figure 4-7. One image appears darker than the other, even though they are exactly the same shade. Write a graphics program that generates such an illusion. (*Hint*: Use two panels that draw the same shape.)

FIGURE 4-7
The phenomenon of induced contrast

CRITICAL *Thinking*

Do the mathematical analysis needed to show that the Lucky Sevens game is not so lucky for the gambler. (*Hint*: The answer involves comparing the number of possible combinations of all totals and the number of possible combinations of 7.)

GETTING STARTED WITH JAVA

REVIEW *Questions*

TRUE/FALSE

Circle T if the statement is true or F if it is false.

T F **1.** The first generation of programming language is assembly language.

T F **2.** Java is an example of a high-level language.

T F **3.** Mistakes found early in the coding process are much more expensive to fix than mistakes found later in the process.

T F **4.** Byte code is a program that behaves like a computer.

T F **5.** An arithmetic expression consists of operands and binary operators combined, as in algebra.

T F **6.** Programs manipulate objects by sending them methods.

T F **7.** An integer is a positive or negative whole number.

T F **8.** Strings are objects, not primitive data types.

T F **9.** A relational operator is used to compare data items.

T F **10.** Most, but not all, information in a computer is represented in binary form.

FILL IN THE BLANK

Complete the following sentences by writing the correct word or words in the blanks provided.

1. OOP stands for _____.

2. The software responsible for translating a program in a high-level language to machine code is called a(n) _____.

3. JVM stands for _____.

4. When an object receives a message, the object responds by running a block of code called a(n) _____.

5. Numbers with a fractional part are called _____.

6. When evaluating an expression, Java performs operations of higher _____ first unless overridden by _____.

7. Use the _____ operator to create a new string out of existing strings.

8. The `while` statement implements a(n) _____.

9. A(n) _____ error occurs when a loop goes around one too many or one too few times.

10. A(n) _____ error occurs when a loop never stops.

WRITTEN QUESTIONS

Write a brief answer to each of the following questions or problems.

1. What is the purpose of a variable in a program?

2. What are the three types of programming errors? Give a brief example of each.

3. Describe the differences between the data types `double` and `int`.

4. Assume that the variables `x` and `y` contain the values 8 and 4, respectively. What are the values of the expressions listed below?
   A. `x + y * 2`
   B. `(x + y) / 3`
   C. `x - y * 3`
   D. `x + y * 1.5`

5. Write a valid Java statement that adds 5 to the value of variable `x` if the value of variable `y` is greater than 10.

6. A program has the following loop heading: `while (3 < x < 10)`. Is the heading syntactically correct? If incorrect, explain why.

7. Write a loop that outputs the first 10 positive powers of 2.

PROJECTS

PROJECT 1

The surface area of a cube is the sum of the areas of its faces. Write a program that expects the length of a cube's edge as input and displays its surface area.

PROJECT 2

Write a program that expects the length and width of a rectangle as inputs. The program should calculate and display the rectangle's area and perimeter.

PROJECT 3

Top-pick videos rent for $3.00 per night, whereas oldies rent for $2.00. Write a program that prompts the user for the number of each type of video to rent and outputs the total cost for that night.

PROJECT 4

The local bookstore has a markup of 10 percent on each book sold. Write a program that takes the sales price of a book as input and displays the following outputs:

- The markup amount of the book just sold
- The wholesale amount (to go to the publisher) of the book just sold
- The total sales prices of all of the books sold thus far
- The total markup amount of all of the books sold thus far

CRITICAL*Thinking*

Modify the program of Project 4 so that it continues to prompt the user for the price of books. The prompts should end when the user enters a negative number for the price. The program should then display the total sales price and total markup of the books sold.

THE NEXT STEP WITH JAVA

Unit 2

Estimated Time for Unit: 15.50 hours

INTRODUCTION TO DEFINING CLASSES

OBJECTIVES

Upon completion of this chapter, you should be able to:

- Design and implement a simple class from user requirements.

- Organize a program in terms of a view class and a model class.

- Use visibility modifiers to make methods visible to clients and restrict access to data within a class.

- Write appropriate mutator methods, accessor methods, and constructors for a class.

- Understand how parameters transmit data to methods.

- Use instance variables, local variables, and parameters appropriately.

- Organize a complex task in terms of helper methods.

Estimated Time: 3.5 hours

VOCABULARY

Accessor

Actual parameter

Behavior

Constructor

Encapsulation

Formal parameter

Helper method

Identity

Instantiation

Lifetime

Mutator

Scope

State

Visibility modifier

We introduced basic object-oriented terminology in Chapter 1 and have used it repeatedly since then. Until now, we have focused on choosing among predefined classes to solve problems. We have shown how to declare variables of different classes, assign objects to these variables, and send them messages. In this chapter, we explore the internal workings of objects. We introduce the basic structure of class definitions so that you will be able to read and modify classes and create classes of your own. We restrict our focus to a few simple concepts and add more detail in later chapters.

5.1 The Internal Structure of Classes and Objects

As we stated in Chapter 1, an object is a runtime entity that contains data and responds to messages. A class is a software package or template that describes the characteristics of similar objects. These characteristics are of two sorts: variable declarations that define an object's data requirements (instance variables) and methods that define its behavior in response to messages.

The combining of data and behavior into a single software package is called *encapsulation*. An object is an instance of its class, and the process of creating a new object is called *instantiation*.

Classes, Objects, and Computer Memory

We begin our discussion of classes and objects by considering how the Java virtual machine (JVM) handles them. When a Java program is executing, the computer's memory must hold

- All class templates in their compiled form
- Variables that refer to objects
- Objects as needed

Each method's compiled byte code is stored in memory as part of its class's template. Memory for data, on the other hand, is allocated within objects. Although all class templates are in memory at all times, individual objects come and go. An object first appears and occupies memory when it is instantiated, and it disappears automatically when no longer needed. The JVM knows if an object is in use by keeping track of whether or not there are any variables referencing it. Because unreferenced objects cannot be used, Java assumes that it is okay to delete them from memory. Java does this during a process called *garbage collection*. In contrast, C++ programmers have the onerous responsibility of deleting objects explicitly. Forgetting to delete unneeded objects wastes scarce memory resources, and accidentally deleting an object too soon or more than once can cause programs to crash. In large programs, these mistakes are easy to make and difficult to find. Fortunately, Java programmers do not have to worry about this problem.

Three Characteristics of an Object

Three characteristics of objects must be emphasized. First, an object has *behavior* as defined by the methods of its class. Second, an object has *state*, which is another way of saying that at any particular moment its instance variables have particular values. Typically, the state changes over time in response to messages sent to the object. Third, an object has its own unique *identity*, which distinguishes it from all other objects in the computer's memory, even those that might momentarily have the same state. An object's identity is handled behind the scenes by the JVM and should not be confused with the variables that might refer to the object. Of the variables, there can be none, one, or several. When there are none, the garbage collector purges the object from memory. Shortly, we will see an example in which two variables refer to the same object.

Clients, Servers, and Interfaces

When messages are sent, two objects are involved—the sender and the receiver, also called the *client* and the *server*, respectively. A client's interactions with a server are limited to sending it messages, so consequently a client needs to know nothing about the internal workings of a server. A client needs to know only a server's *interface*, that is, the list of the methods supported by the server. The server's data requirements and the implementation of its methods are hidden from the client, an approach we referred to as *information hiding* in Chapter 1. Only the person who writes a class needs to understand its internal workings. In fact, a class's implementation details can be changed radically without affecting any of its clients, provided its interface remains the same.

EXERCISE 5.1

1. What is the difference between a class and an object?

2. What happens to an object's memory storage when it is no longer referenced by a variable?

3. List the three important characteristics of an object.

4. Describe the client–server relationship.

5. What is the interface of a class?

5.2 A Student Class

The first class we develop in this chapter is called student. We begin by considering the class from a client's perspective. Later we show its implementation. From a client's perspective, it is enough to know that a student object stores a name and three test scores and responds to the messages shown in Table 5-1.

TABLE 5-1
The interface for the Student class

METHODS	DESCRIPTIONS
void setName(aString)	Example: stu.setName ("Bill"); sets the name of stu to Bill
String getName()	Example: str = stu.getName(); returns the name of stu
void setScore (whichTest, testScore)	Example: stu.setScore (3, 95); sets the score on test 3 to 95 if whichTest is not 1, 2, or 3, then 3 is substituted automatically
int getScore(whichTest)	Example: score = stu.getScore (3); returns the score on test 3 if whichTest is not 1, 2, or 3, then 3 is substituted automatically
int getAverage()	Example : average = stu.getAverage(); returns the average of the test scores
int getHighScore()	Example: highScore = stu.getHighScore(); returns the highest test score
String toString()	Example: str = stu.toString(); returns a string containing the student's name and test scores

Using Student Objects

Some portions of code illustrate how a client instantiates and manipulates student objects. First, we declare several variables, including two variables of type student.

```
Student s1, s2;        // Declare the variables
String str;
int i;
```

As usual, we do not use variables until we have assigned them initial values. We assign a new Student object to s1 using the operator new:

```
s1 = new Student();    // Instantiate a student and associate it with the
                       // variable s1
```

It is important to emphasize that the variable s1 is a reference to a student object and is *not* a student object itself.

A student object keeps track of the name and test scores of an actual student. Thus, for a brand new student object, what are the values of these data attributes? That depends on the class's internal implementation details, but we can find out easily by sending messages to the student object via its associated variable s1:

```
str = s1.getName();
System.out.println (str);    // yields ""

i = s1.getHighScore();
System.out.println (i);      // yields 0
```

Apparently, the name was initialized to an empty string and the test scores to zero. Now we set the object's data attributes by sending it some messages:

```
s1.setName ("Bill");    // Set the student's name to "Bill"
s1.setScore (1,84);     // Set the score on test 1 to 84
s1.setScore (2,86);     //                 on test 2 to 86
s1.setScore (3,88);     //                 on test 3 to 88
```

Messages that change an object's state are called *mutators*. To see if the mutators worked correctly, we use other messages to access the object's state (called *accessors*):

```
str = s1.getName();     // str equals "Bill"
i = s1.getScore (1);    // i equals 84
i = s1.getHighScore();  // i equals 88
i = s1.getAverage();    // i equals 86
```

The object's string representation is obtained by sending the toString message to the object:

```
str = s1.toString();
  // str  now equals
  // "Name:    Bill\nTest 1:  84\nTest2:  86\nTest3:  88\nAverage: 86"
```

When displayed in a terminal window (Figure 5-1), the string is broken into several lines as determined by the placement of the newline characters (`'\n'`). In addition to the explicit use of the `toString` method, there are other situations in which the method is called automatically. For instance, `toString` is called implicitly when a `Student` object is concatenated with a string or is an argument to the method `println`:

```
str = "The best student is: \n" + s1;
   // Equivalent to: str = "The best student is: \n" + s1.toString();
System.out.println (s1);
   // Equivalent to: System.out.println (s1.toString());
```

FIGURE 5-1
Implicit use of `toString` when a `Student` object is sent to a terminal window

Because of these valuable implicit uses of the `toString` method, we frequently include this method in the classes we write. If we forget, however, Java provides a very simple version of the method through the mechanism of inheritance (mentioned in Chapter 1). The simplified version does little more than return the name of the class to which the object belongs.

Objects, Assignment, and Aliasing

We close this demonstration by associating a `Student` object with the variable `s2`. Rather than instantiating a new student, we assign `s1` to `s2`:

```
s2 = s1;              // s1 and s2 now refer to the same student
```

The variables `s1` and `s2` now refer to the *same* `Student` object. This might come as a surprise because we might reasonably expect the assignment statement to create a second `Student` object equal to the first, but that is not how Java works. To demonstrate that `s1` and `s2` now refer to the same object, we change the student's name using `s2` and retrieve the same name using `s1`:

```
s2.setName ("Ann");   // Set the name
str = s1.getName();   // str equals "Ann". Therefore, s1 and s2 refer
                      // to the same object.
```

Table 5-2 shows code and diagrams that clarify the manner in which variables are affected by assignment statements. At any time, it is possible to break the connection between a variable and the object it references. Simply assign the value `null` to the variable:

```
Student s1;
s1 = new Student();       // s1 references the newly instantiated student
...                       // Do stuff with the student
s1 = null;                // s1 no longer references anything
```

TABLE 5-2
How variables are affected by assignment statements

CODE	DIAGRAM	COMMENTS
`int i, j;`	i ??? j ???	i and j are memory locations that have not yet been initialized, but which will hold integers.
`i = 3;` `j = i;`	i 3 j 3	i holds the integer 3. j holds the integer 3.
`Student s, t;`	s ??? t ???	s and t are memory locations that have not yet been initialized, but which will hold references to Student objects.
`s = new Student();` `t = s;`	s t → student object	s holds a reference to a Student object. t holds a reference to the same Student object.

Table 5-2 demonstrates that assignment to variables of numeric types such as `int` produces genuine copies, whereas assignment to variables of object types does not.

Primitive Types, Reference Types, and the `null` Value

We mentioned earlier that two or more variables can refer to the same object. To better understand why this is possible we need to consider how Java classifies types. In Java, all types fall into two fundamental categories:

1. *Primitive types*: `int`, `double`, `boolean`, `char`, and the shorter and longer versions of these

2. *Reference types*: all classes, for instance, `String`, `Student`, `Scanner`, and so on

As we first pointed out in Chapter 2, variables in these two categories are represented differently in memory. A variable of a primitive type is best viewed as a box that contains a value of that primitive type. In contrast, a variable of a reference type is thought of as a box that contains a pointer to an object. Thus, the state of memory after the following code is executed is shown in Figure 5-2.

```
int number = 45;
String word = "Hi";
```

FIGURE 5-2
The difference between primitive and reference variables

As previously mentioned, reference variables can be assigned the value `null`. If a reference variable previously pointed to an object, and no other variable currently points to that object, the computer reclaims the object's memory during garbage collection. This situation is illustrated in the following code segment and in Figure 5-3:

```
Student student = new Student("Mary", 70, 80, 90);
student = null;
```

FIGURE 5-3
The `Student` variable before and after it has been assigned the value `null`

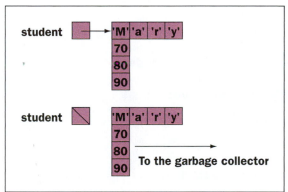

A reference variable can be compared to the `null` value, as follows:

```
if (student == null)
    …                   // Don't try to run a method with that student!
else
    …                   // Process the student

while (student != null){
    …                   // Process the student
                        // Obtain the next student from whatever source
}
```

As we already know from Chapter 3, when a program attempts to run a method with an object that is null, Java throws a *null pointer exception*, as in the following example:

```
String str = null;

System.out.println (str.length());   // OOPS! str is null, so Java throws a
                                     // null pointer exception
```

The Structure of a Class Template

Having explored the Student class from a client's perspective, we now address the question of how to implement it. All classes have a similar structure consisting of four parts:

1. The class's name and some modifying phrases

2. A description of the instance variables

3. One or more methods that indicate how to initialize a new object (called **constructor** methods)

4. One or more methods that specify how an object responds to messages

The order of these parts can be varied arbitrarily provided part 1 (the class's name) comes first; however, for the sake of consistency, we will usually adhere to the order listed, which yields the following class template:

```
public class <name of class> extends <some other class>{

    // Declaration of instance variables
    private <type> <name>;
    ...

    // Code for the constructor methods
    public <name of class>() {
    // Initialize the instance variables
        ...
    }
    ...

    // Code for the other methods
    public <return type> <name of method> (<parameter list>){
        ...
    }
    ...
}
```

Some of the phrases used in the template need to be explained:

```
public class
```

Class definitions usually begin with the keyword public, indicating that the class is accessible to all potential clients. There are some alternatives to public that we ignore for now.

```
<name of class>
```

Class names are user-defined symbols, and thus they must adhere to the rules for naming variables and methods. It is common to start class names with a capital letter and variable and method names with a lowercase letter. There is one exception. Names of final variables are usually completely capitalized.

```
extends <some other class>
```

Java organizes its classes in a hierarchy (see Chapter 1). At the root, or base, of this hierarchy is a class called `Object`. In the hierarchy, if class A is immediately above another class B, we say that A is the *superclass* or *parent* of B and B is a *subclass* or *child* of A (Figure 5-4). Each class, except `Object`, has exactly one parent and can have any number of children.

FIGURE 5-4
Relationship between superclass and subclass

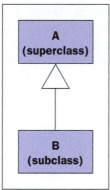

When a new class is created, it is incorporated into the hierarchy by extending an existing class. The new class's exact placement in the hierarchy is important because a new class inherits the characteristics of its superclass through a process called *inheritance* (Chapter 1). The new class then adds to and modifies these inherited characteristics, or in other words, the new class *extends* the superclass. If the clause `extends <some other class>` is omitted from the new class's definition, then by default the new class is assumed to be a subclass of `Object`.

```
private <type> <name>
```

Instance variables are nearly always declared to be `private`. This prevents clients from referring to the instance variables directly. Making instance variables `private` is an important aspect of information hiding.

```
public <return type> <name of method>
```

Methods are usually declared to be `public`, which allows clients to refer to them.

`private` and `public` are *visibility modifiers*. If both `private` and `public` are omitted, the consequences vary with the circumstances. Without explaining why, suffice it to say that in most situations, omitting the visibility modifier is equivalent to using `public`. In most situations, we use `private` for instance variables unless there is some compelling reason to declare them `public`.

To illustrate the difference between `private` and `public`, suppose the class `Student` has a private instance variable `name` and a public method `setName`. Then

```
Student s;
s = new Student();
s.name = "Bill";      // Rejected by compiler because name is private
s.setName ("Bill")    // Accepted by compiler because setName is public
```

As a final note concerning our class template, notice that the constructor does not have a return type, that is, the name of the type of the value that it returns. All other methods do.

Implementation of the `Student` Class

Adhering to the format of our class template, we now implement the `Student` class. It is important to realize that other implementations are acceptable provided they adhere to the interface standards already established for student classes. Following is the code:

```java
/* Student.java
Manage a student's name and three test scores.
*/
public class Student {

    // Instance variables
    // Each student object has a name and three test scores
    private String name;        // Student name
    private int test1;          // Score on test 1
    private int test2;          // Score on test 2
    private int test3;          // Score on test 3

    // Constructor method

    public Student(){
    // Initialize a new student's name to the empty string and the test
    // scores to zero.
        name = "";
        test1 = 0;
        test2 = 0;
        test3 = 0;
    }

    // Other methods

    public void setName (String nm){
    // Set a student's name
        name = nm;
    }
    public String getName (){
    // Get a student's name
        return name;
    }

    public void setScore (int i, int score){
    // Set test i to score
```

```
         if      (i == 1) test1 = score;
         else if (i == 2) test2 = score;
         else             test3 = score;
      }

      public int getScore (int i){
      // Retrieve score i
         if      (i == 1) return test1;
         else if (i == 2) return test2;
         else             return test3;
      }

      public int getAverage(){
      // Compute and return the average
         int average;
         average = (int) Math.round((test1 + test2 + test3) / 3.0);
         return average;
      }

      public int getHighScore(){
      // Determine and return the highest score
         int highScore;
         highScore = test1;
         if (test2 > highScore) highScore = test2;
         if (test3 > highScore) highScore = test3;
         return highScore;
      }

      public String toString(){
      // Construct and return a string representation of the student
         String str;
         str = "Name:    " + name  + "\n" +    // "\n" denotes a newline
               "Test 1:  " + test1 + "\n" +
               "Test 2:  " + test2 + "\n" +
               "Test 3:  " + test3 + "\n" +
               "Average: " + getAverage();
         return str;
      }
   }
```

We explore the structure and behavior of methods in more detail later in this chapter. For now, the meaning of the code is fairly obvious. All the methods, except the constructor method, have a return type, although the return type may be void, indicating that the method in fact returns nothing. To summarize: When an object receives a message, the object activates the corresponding method. The method then manipulates the object's data as represented by the instance variables.

Constructors

The principal purpose of a constructor is to initialize the instance variables of a newly instantiated object. Constructors are activated when the keyword new is used and at no other time. A constructor is never used to reset instance variables of an existing object.

A class template can include more than one constructor, provided each has a unique parameter list; however, all the constructors must have the same name—that is, the name of the class. The constructors we have seen so far have had empty parameter lists and are called *default constructors*.

If a class template contains no constructors, the JVM provides a primitive default constructor behind the scenes. This constructor initializes numeric variables to zero and object variables to null, thus indicating that the object variables currently reference no objects. If a class contains even one constructor, however, the JVM no longer provides a default constructor automatically.

To illustrate these ideas, we add several constructors to the Student class. The following code lists the original default constructor and two additional ones:

```java
// Default constructor -- initialize name to the empty string and
// the test scores to zero.
public Student(){
    name = "";
    test1 = 0;
    test2 = 0;
    test3 = 0;
}

// Additional constructor -- initialize the name and test scores
// to the values provided.
public Student(String nm, int t1, int t2, int t3){
    name = nm;
    test1 = t1;
    test2 = t2;
    test3 = t3;
}

// Additional constructor -- initialize the name and test scores
// to match those in the parameter s.
public Student(Student s){
    name = s.name;
    test1 = s.test1;
    test2 = s.test2;
    test3 = s.test3;
}
```

A class is easier to use when it has a variety of constructors. Following is some code that shows how to use the different Student constructors. In a program, we would use the constructor that best suited our immediate purpose:

```java
Student s1, s2, s3;
s1 = new Student();                   // First student object has
                                      // name "" and scores 0,0,0

s2 = new Student ("Bill",70,80,90);   // Second student object has
                                      // name "Bill" and scores 70,80,90

s3 = new Student (s2);                // Third student object also has
                                      // name "Bill" and scores 70,80,90
```

```
s3.setName ("Ann");                   // Third student object now has
s3.setScore (1,75);                   // name "Ann" and scores 75,80,90
```

There are now three completely separate student objects. For a moment, two of them had the same state—that is, the same values for their instance variables—but that changed in the last two lines of code.

Chaining Constructors

When a class includes several constructors, the code for them can be simplified by *chaining* them. For example, the three constructors in the Student class each do the same thing—initialize the instance variables. We can simplify the code for the first and third constructors by calling the second constructor. To call one constructor from another constructor, we use the notation

```
this(<parameters>);
```

Thus, the code for the constructors shown earlier becomes

```
// Default constructor -- initialize name to the empty string and
// the test scores to zero.
public Student(){
   this("", 0, 0, 0);
}

// Additional constructor -- initialize the name and test scores
// to the values provided.
public Student(String nm, int t1, int t2, int t3){
   name = nm;
   test1 = t1;
   test2 = t2;
   test3 = t3;
}

// Additional constructor -- initialize the name and test scores
// to match those in the parameter s.
public Student(Student s){
   this(s.name, s.test1, s.test2, s.test3);
}
```

*E*XERCISE 5.2

1. What are mutators and accessors? Give examples.

2. List two visibility modifiers and describe when they are used.

3. What is a constructor?

4. Why do we include a toString method with a new user-defined class?

5. How can two variables refer to the same object? Give an example.

EXERCISE 5.2 Continued

6. Explain the difference between a primitive type and a reference type, and give an example of each.

7. What is the `null` value?

8. What is a null pointer exception? Give an example.

9. How does a default constructor differ from other constructors?

10. How does Java handle the initialization of instance variables if no constructors are provided?

11. What is the purpose of a constructor that expects another object of the same class?

5.3 Editing, Compiling, and Testing the Student Class

To use the `Student` class, we must save it in a file called `Student.java` and compile it by typing

```
javac Student.java
```

in a terminal window. If there are no compile-time errors, the compiler creates the byte code file `Student.class`. Once the `Student` class is compiled, applications can declare and manipulate `Student` objects provided that one of the following is true:

- The code for the application and `Student.class` are in the same directory.

- The `Student.class` is part of a package (see Appendix G).

Following is a small program that uses and tests the `Student` class. Figure 5-5 shows the results of running such a program.

```java
// Example 5.1: Tester program for Student class

public class TestStudent{

    public static void main (String[] args){
        Student s1, s2;

        s1 = new Student();       // Instantiate a student object
        s1.setName("Bill");       // Set the student's name to "Bill"
        s1.setScore(1,84);        // Set the score on test 1 to 84
        s1.setScore(2,86);        //              on test 2 to 86
        s1.setScore(3,88);        //              on test 3 to 88
        System.out.println("\nHere is student s1\n" + s1);

            s2 = s1;              // s1 and s2 now refer to the same object
        s2.setName("Ann");        // Set the name through s2
        System.out.println("\nName of s1 is now: " + s1.getName());
    }
}
```

FIGURE 5-5
Output from the `TestStudent` program

Finding the Location of Run-time Errors

Finding run-time errors in programs is no more difficult when there are several classes instead of just one. To illustrate, we introduce a run-time error into the `Student` class and then run the `TestStudent` program again. Following is a listing of the modified and erroneous lines of code. Figure 5-6 shows the error messages generated when the program runs.

```java
public int getAverage(){
    int average = 0;
    average = (int) Math.round((test1 + test2 + test3) / average);
    return average;
}
```

FIGURE 5-6
Divide by zero run-time error message

```
C:\Javafiles>java TestStudent
Exception in thread "main" java.lang.ArithmeticException: / by zero
        at Student.getAverage(Student.java:53)
        at Student.toString(Student.java:69)
        at java.lang.String.valueOf(String.java:2577)
        at java.lang.StringBuilder.append(StringBuilder.java:116)
        at TestStudent.main(TestStudent.java:13)
```

The messages indicate that

■ An attempt was made to divide by zero in the `Student` class's `getAverage` method (line 53),

■ Which had been called from the `Student` class's `toString` method (line 69),

■ Which had been called by some methods we did not write,

■ Which, finally, had been called from the `TestStudent` class's `main` method (line 13).

Following are the lines of code mentioned:

```
Student getAverage line 53 :
            average = (int) Math.round ((test1 + test2 + test3) / average);
Student toString line 69   :
            "Average: " + getAverage();
TestStudent main line 13       :
            System.out.println ("\nHere is student s1\n" + s1);
```

We can now unravel the error

■ In line 13 of main, the concatenation (+) of s1 makes an implicit call s1.toString().

■ In line 69 of toString, the getAverage method is called.

■ In line 53 of getAverage, a division by zero occurs.

Case Study 1: Student Test Scores

Request

Write a program that allows the user to compare test scores of two students. Each student has three scores.

Analysis

A user's interaction with the program is shown in Figure 5-7.

FIGURE 5-7
The user interface for the student test scores program

As you can see, the program

1. Prompts the user for the data for the two students

2. Displays the information for each student, followed by the names of the students with the highest score and the highest average score

As a standard part of analysis, we determine which classes are needed to support the application, and we delineate each class's overall responsibilities. The nature of the current problem suggests the use of two classes:

1. `Student`: Not surprisingly, the `Student` class presented earlier exactly fits the needs of this program.

2. `StudentApp`: This class supports the user interface and declares and manipulates two `Student` objects.

In general, it is a good idea to divide the code for most interactive applications into at least two sets of classes. One set of classes, which we call the *view*, handles the interactions with the human users, such as input and output operations. The other set of classes, called the *model*, represents the data used by the application. One of the benefits of this separation of responsibilities is that one can write different views for the same data model, such as a terminal-based view and a graphical-based view, without changing a line of code in the data model. Alternatively, one can write different representations of the data model without altering a line of code in the views. In most of the case studies that follow, we apply this framework, called the *model/view pattern*, to structure the code.

Design

During analysis, we decided to base the implementation on two classes: `Student` and `StudentApp`. Now, during design, we specify the characteristics of these classes in detail. This involves determining the data requirements of each class and the methods that will be needed by the clients of the classes. This process is usually straightforward. To illustrate, let us pretend for the moment that we have not already written the `Student` class.

Designing the `Student` Class

We know from the work completed during analysis that a `Student` object must keep track of a name and three test scores. The high score and the average can be calculated when needed. Thus, the data requirements are clear. The `Student` class must declare four instance variables:

```java
private String name;
private int test1;
private int test2;
private int test3;
```

To determine the `Student` class's methods, we look at the class from the perspective of the clients who will be sending messages to `Student` objects. In this application, the user interface is the only client. There are some clues that help us pick the appropriate methods:

The user interface needs to instantiate two `Student` objects. This indicates the need for a constructor method, which we always include anyway.

When the user enters input data, the view needs to tell each `Student` object its name and three test scores. This can be handled by two mutator methods: `setName(theName)` and `setScore(whichTest, testScore)`.

The view needs to ask the `Student` objects for their complete information, the highest score, and the average score. This suggests four accessor methods: `toString()`, `getScore(whichTest)`, `getHighScore()`, and `getAverage()`.

We summarize our findings in a *class summary* box:

```
Class:
   Student
Private Instance Variables:
   String name
   int test1
   int test2
   int test3
Public Methods:
   constructors
   void setName (theName)
   String getName()
   void setScore (whichTest, testScore)
   int getScore (whichTest)
   int getAverage()
   int getHighScore()
     String toString()
```

Normally, we would complete a class's design by writing pseudocode for methods whose implementation is not obvious, so we skip this step here.

Designing the `StudentApp` Class

The following is the class summary box for the `StudentApp` class:

```
Class:
   StudentApp
Public Methods:
   static void main (args)
```

Implementation

The code for the `Student` class has already been presented. Code for the `StudentApp` class follows:

```java
import java.util.Scanner;

public class StudentApp{

    public static void main (String[] args){
        // Instantiate the students and the keyboard object
        Student student1 = new Student();
```

```java
        Student student2 = new Student();
        Scanner reader = new Scanner(System.in);

        String name;
        int score;

        // Input the first student's data
        System.out.print("Enter the first student's name: ");
        name = reader.nextLine();
        student1.setName(name);
        for (int i = 1; i <= 3; i++){
            System.out.print("Enter the student's score: ");
            score = reader.nextInt();
            student1.setScore(i, score);
        }
        // Consume the trailing newline character
        reader.nextLine();

        // Input the second student's data
        System.out.print("Enter the second student's name: ");
        name = reader.nextLine();
        student2.setName(name);
        for (int i = 1; i <= 3; i++){
            System.out.print("Enter the student's score: ");
            score = reader.nextInt();
            student2.setScore(i, score);
        }

        // Output the two students' information
        System.out.println(student1);
        System.out.println(student2);

        // Output the student with the highest score
        if (student1.getHighScore() > student2.getHighScore()){
            name = student1.getName();

            score = student1.getHighScore();
        }else{
            name = student2.getName();
            score = student2.getHighScore();
        }
        System.out.println(name + " has the highest score: " + score);

        // Output the student with the highest average score
        if (student1.getAverage() > student2.getAverage()){
            name = student1.getName();
            score = student1.getAverage();
        }else{
            name = student2.getName();
            score = student2.getAverage();
        }
        System.out.println(name + " has the highest average score: " +
                        score);
    }

}
```

5.4 The Structure and Behavior of Methods

As mentioned in earlier chapters, a method is a description of a task that is performed in response to a message. The purpose of this section is to examine more closely some related concepts such as parameters, return types, and local variables.

The Structure of a Method Definition

Methods generally have the following form:

```
<visibility modifier> <return type> <method name> (<parameter list>){

    <implementing code>
}
```

Note the following points:

- The visibility modifier `public` is used when the method should be available to clients of the defining class. The visibility modifier `private` should be used when the method is merely a "helper" used by other methods within the class. We say more about helper methods shortly.

- The return type should be `void` when the method returns no value. A `void` method often is a mutator, that is, a method that modifies an object's variables. If not `void`, the return type can be any primitive or reference type. Methods that return a value often are accessors, that is, methods that allow clients to examine the values of instance variables.

- Method names have the same syntax as other Java identifiers. The programmer should be careful to use names that describe the tasks that the methods perform, however; the names of verbs or verb phrases, such as `getName`, are usually appropriate for methods.

- As mentioned earlier in this book, parentheses are required whether or not parameters are present. The parameter list, if present, consists of one or more pairs of type names and parameter names, separated by commas.

A method's implementing code can be omitted. In that case, the method is called a *stub*. Stubs are used to set up skeletal, incomplete, but running programs during program development. For example, here is a class that contains only variable declarations and method stubs:

```java
public class SomeClass{

    private int someVariable1, someVariable2;

    public void mutator1(int valueIn){}

    public void mutator2(int valueIn){}

    public int accessor1(){
        return 0;
    }
}
```

Return Statements

If a method has a return type, its implementing code must have at least one `return` statement that returns a value of that type. There can be more than one `return` statement in a method; however, the first one executed ends the method. Following is an example of a method that has two `return` statements but executes just one of them:

```
boolean odd(int i){
    if (i % 2 == 0)
        return false;
    else
        return true;
}
```

A `return` statement in a `void` method quits the method and returns nothing

Formal and Actual Parameters

Parameters listed in a method's definition are called *formal parameters*. Values passed to a method when it is invoked are called *arguments* or *actual parameters*. As an example, consider the following two code segments:

```
// Client code

Student s = new Student();
Scanner reader = new Scanner(System.in);
System.out.print("Enter a test score:");
int testScore = reader.nextInt();
s.setScore(1, testScore);
```

```
// Server code

public void setScore (int i, int score){
    if      (i == 1) test1 = score;
    else if (i == 2) test2 = score;
    else             test3 = score;
}
```

In our example, the literal 1 and the variable `testScore` are the actual parameters and the names `i` and `score` are the formal parameters. When a method is called, the value of the actual parameter is automatically transferred to the corresponding formal parameter immediately before the method is activated. Thus, the number 1 and value of `testScore` are transferred to `i` and `score` immediately before `setScore` is activated (see Figure 5-8). It is important to understand that the variable `testScore` and the parameter `score` are otherwise completely independent of each other. For instance, changing the value of `score` would have no effect on the value of `testScore`.

FIGURE 5-8
Parameter passing

```
// Actual parameters in class StudentInterface


s.setScore(1, testScore);



public void setScore (int i, int score){

// Formal parameters in class Student
```

As mentioned in Chapter 3, when a method has multiple parameters, the caller must provide the right number and types of values. That is, the actual parameters must match the formal parameters in position and type. The rules for matching the types of a formal and an actual parameter are similar to those for assignment statements. The actual parameter's type must be either the same as or less inclusive than the type of the corresponding formal parameter. For example, the method `Math.sqrt`, which has a single formal parameter of type `double`, can receive either a `double` or an `int` as an actual parameter from the caller.

Parameters and Instance Variables

The purpose of a parameter is to pass information to a method. The purpose of an instance variable is to maintain information in an object. These roles are clearly shown in the method `setScore`. This method receives the score in the formal parameter `score`. This value is then transferred to one of the instance variables `test1`, `test2`, or `test3`.

Local Variables

Occasionally, it is convenient to have temporary working storage for data in a method. The programmer can declare *local variables* for this purpose. A good example occurs in the method `getAverage`. This method declares a variable `average`, assigns it the result of computing the average of the integer instance variables, and returns its value:

```java
public int getAverage(){
    int average;
    average = (int) Math.round((test1 + test2 + test3) / 3.0);
    return average;
}
```

Note that there is no need for the method to receive data from the client, so we do not use a parameter. Likewise, there is no need for the object to remember the average, so we do not use an instance variable for that.

Helper Methods

Occasionally, a task performed by a method becomes so complex that it helps to break it into subtasks to be solved by several other methods. To accomplish this, a class can define one or more methods to serve as *helper methods*. These methods are usually private because only methods already defined within the class need to use them. For example, it is helpful to define a debug method when testing a class. This method expects a string and a double as parameters and displays these values in the terminal window. Following is the code:

```java
private void debug(String message, double value){
    System.out.println(message + " " + value);
}
```

This method can be called from any other method in the class to display information about the state of an integer or double variable. For example, the Student method getAverage might use this method as follows:

```java
public int getAverage(){
    int average;
    average = (int) Math.round((test1 + test2 + test3) / 3.0);
    debug("Average:", average);
    return average;
}
```

The advantage to this approach is that debugging statements throughout the class can be turned on or off by commenting out a single line of code:

```java
private void debug(String message, double value){
    // System.out.println(message + " " + value);
}
```

We see other examples of helper methods in later chapters.

EXERCISE 5.4

1. Explain the difference between formal parameters and actual parameters.

2. How does Java transmit data by means of parameters?

3. Define a method sum. This method expects two integers as parameters and returns the sum of the numbers ranging from the first integer to the second one.

4. What is the purpose of local variables?

5.5 Scope and Lifetime of Variables

As we have seen repeatedly, a class definition consists of two principal parts: a list of instance variables and a list of methods. When an object is instantiated, it receives its own complete copy of the instance variables, and when it is sent a message, it activates the corresponding method in its class. Thus, it is the role of objects to contain data and to respond to messages, and it is the role of classes to provide a template for creating objects and to store the code for methods. When a method is executing, it does so on behalf of a particular object, and the method has complete access to the object's instance variables. From the perspective of the methods, the instance variables form a common pool of variables accessible to all of the class's methods. For this reason, we sometimes refer to them as *global variables*, in contrast to the variables declared within a method, which we call *local variables*.

Scope of Variables

The *scope* of a variable is that region of the program within which it can validly appear in lines of code. The scope of a parameter or a local variable is restricted to the body of the method that declares it, whereas the scope of a global or instance variable is all the methods in the defining class. Fortunately, the compiler flags as an error any attempt to use variables outside of their scope. Following is an example that illustrates the difference between local and global scope:

```java
public class ScopeDemo {

    private int iAmGlobal;

    public void clientMethod (int parm){

        int iAmLocal;
        ...
    }

    private int helperMethod (int parm1, int parm2){

        int iAmLocalToo;
        ...
    }
    ...
}
```

Table 5-3 shows where each of the variables and parameters can be used (i.e., its scope):

TABLE 5-3
Variables and their scope

VARIABLE	helperMethod	clientMethod
iAmGlobal	Yes	Yes
parm	No	Yes
iAmLocal	No	Yes
parm1 and parm2	Yes	No
iAmLocalToo	Yes	No

Notice that formal parameters are also local in scope; that is, their visibility is limited to the body of the method in which they are declared.

Block Scope

Within the code of a method, there can also be nested scopes. Variables declared within any compound statement enclosed in braces are said to have *block scope*. They are visible only within the code enclosed by braces. For example, consider the following `for` loop to sum 10 input numbers. The accumulator variable `sum` is declared above the loop so the program can access it after the loop terminates. The loop declares its control variable `i` within its header and a local variable `number` to accept input within its body. The variables `i` and `number` thus have block scope, which is appropriate because they are needed only within the loop, and not outside it:

```java
int sum = 0;
Scanner reader = new Scanner(System.in);
for (int i = 1; i <= 10; i++){
    System.out.print("Enter a number: ");
    int number = reader.nextInt();
    sum += number;
}
System.out.println("The sum is " + sum);
```

Lifetime of Variables

The *lifetime* of a variable is the period during which it can be used. Local variables and formal parameters exist during a single execution of a method. Each time a method is called, it gets a fresh set of formal parameters and local variables, and once the method stops executing, the formal parameters and local variables are no longer accessible. Instance variables, on the other hand, last for the lifetime of an object. When an object is instantiated, it gets a complete set of fresh instance variables. These variables are available every time a message is sent to the object, and they, in some sense, serve as the object's memory. When the object stops existing, the instance variables disappear as well.

Duplicating Variable Names

Because the scope of a formal parameter or local variable is restricted to a single method, the same name can be used within several different methods without causing a conflict. Whether or not we use the same name in several different methods is merely a matter of taste. When the programmer reuses the same local name in different methods, the name refers to a different area of storage in each method. In the next example, the names `iAmLocal` and `parm1` are used in two methods in this way:

```java
public class ScopeDemo {

    private int iAmGlobal;

    public void clientMethod (int parm1){

        int iAmLocal;
        ...
    }

    private int helperMethod (int parm1, int parm2){

        int iAmLocal;
        ...
    }
    ...
}
```

A local name and a global variable name can also be the same, as shown in the following code segment:

```java
public class ScopeDemo {

    private int iAmAVariable;

    public void someMethod (int parm){

        int iAmAVariable;
        ...
        iAmAVariable = 3;          // Refers to the local variable
        this.iAmAVariable = 4;     // Refers to the global variable
        ...
    }

    public void someOtherMethod(int iAmAVariable){
        ...
        this.iAmAVariable = iAmAVariable;     // Assign the value of the
// parameter
        ...
// to the global variable
    }
        ...
    }
}
```

In this example, the local variable `iAmAVariable` is said to *shadow* the global variable with the same name. Shadowing is considered a dangerous programming practice because it greatly increases the likelihood of making a coding error. When the variable name is used in the method, it refers to the local variable, and the global variable can be referenced only by prefixing `this.` to the name. The programmer uses the symbol `this` to refer to the current instance of a class within that class's definition.

When to Use Instance Variables, Parameters, and Local Variables

The only reason to use an instance variable is to remember information within an object. The only reason to use a parameter is to transmit information to a method. The only reason to use a local variable is for temporary working storage within a method. A very common mistake is to misuse one kind of variable for another. Following are the most common examples of these types of mistakes.

MISTAKE 1: GLOBAL VARIABLE USED FOR TEMPORARY WORKING STORAGE

This is perhaps the most common mistake programmers make with variables. As we have seen, a global variable is in fact not temporary, but survives the execution of the method. No harm may be done. If more than one method (or the same method on different calls) uses the same variable for its temporary storage, however, these methods might share information in ways that cause subtle bugs. For instance, suppose we decide to include an instance variable `sum` to compute the average score in the `Student` class. We also decide to compute the sum with a loop that uses the method `getScore` as follows:

```
private int sum;
...

public int getAverage(){
    for (int i = 1; i <= 3; i++)
        sum += getScore(i);
    return (int) Math.round(sum / 3.0);
}
```

The method is quite elegant but contains an awful bug. It runs correctly only the first time. The next time the method is called, it adds scores to the `sum` of the previous call, thus producing a much higher average than expected.

MISTAKE 2: LOCAL VARIABLE USED TO REMEMBER INFORMATION IN AN OBJECT

As we have seen, this intent cannot be realized because a local variable disappears from memory after its method has executed. This mistake can lead to errors in cases in which the programmer uses the same name for a local variable and a global variable and believes that the reference to the local variable is really a reference to the global variable (see our earlier discussion of shadowing). All that is required to cause this error is the use of a type name before the first assignment to the variable when it is used in a method. Following is an example from the `Student` class:

```
public void setName (String nm){
// Set a student's name
    String name = nm;     // Whoops! we have just declared name local.
}
```

In this case, the variable name has been accidentally "localized" by prefixing it with a type name. Thus, the value of the parameter `nm` is transferred to the local variable instead of the instance variable, and the student object does not remember this change.

MISTAKE 3: METHOD ACCESSES DATA BY DIRECTLY REFERENCING GLOBAL VARIABLE WHEN IT COULD USE PARAMETER INSTEAD

Methods can communicate by sharing a common pool of variables or by the more explicit means of parameters and return values. Years of software development experience have convinced computer scientists that the second approach is better even though it seems to require more programming effort. There are three reasons to prefer the use of parameters:

1. Suppose that several methods share a pool of variables and that one method misuses a variable. Then other methods can be affected, and the resulting error can be difficult to find. For example, as the following code segment shows, if method `m1` mistakenly sets the variable `x` to 0 and if method `m2` uses `x` as a divisor, then when the program is run, the computer will signal an error in `m2`, even though the source of the error is in `m1`.

```
// Server class

public class ServerClass{

  private int x;

  public void m1(){

      ...
      x = 0;                // The real source of the error
  }

  public void m2(){
      int y = 10 / x;   // Exact spot of run-time error
  }

  ...

}
// Client class


public class ClientClass{
   private s = new ServerClass();
   public void m3(){
      s.m1();             // Misuse of x occurs, but is hidden from client
      s.m2();             // Run-time error occurs
   }
   ...
}
```

2.   It is easier to understand methods and the relationships between them when communications are explicitly defined in terms of parameters and return values.

3.   Methods that access a pool of shared variables can be used only in their original context, whereas methods that are passed parameters can be reused in many different situations. Reuse of code boosts productivity, so programmers try to create software components (in this case, methods) that are as reusable as possible. The method `Math.sqrt` is a good example of a context-independent method.

To summarize, it is a good idea to keep the use of global variables to a minimum, using them only when necessary to track the state of objects, and to use local variables and parameters wherever possible.

*E*XERCISE 5.5

1. What are the lifetimes of an instance variable, a local variable, and a parameter?

2. What is shadowing? Give an example and describe the bad things that shadowing might cause in a program.

EXERCISE 5.5 Continued

3. Consider the following code segment:

```
public class SomeClass{

    private int a, b;

    public void aMutator(int x, y){
        int c, d;
        <lots of code goes here>
    }
}
```

a. List the instance variables, parameters, and local variables in this code.

b. Describe the scope of each variable or parameter.

c. Describe the lifetime of each variable or parameter.

5.6 Graphics and GUIs: Images, a `Circle` Class, and Mouse Events

Realistic graphics applications display many kinds of images, including those that are created under program control and those that are simply loaded from existing image files. As the program-constructed images grow in number and complexity, it becomes useful to delegate responsibility for managing some of their attributes and behavior to the images themselves. This section discusses how to use image files, how to define classes that represent geometric shapes, and how to make graphics programs respond to a user's mouse manipulations.

> **Extra Challenge**
>
> This Graphics and GUIs section gives you the opportunity to explore concepts and programming techniques required to develop modern graphics applications and graphical user interfaces. This material is not required in order to proceed with the other chapters of the book.

Loading Images from Files and Displaying Them

Images are commonly stored in files in JPEG, GIF, or PNG format. You can obtain them from a variety of sources including a digital camera, a flatbed scanner, a screen capture program, or a Web site (but be careful of copyright laws, as discussed in Chapter 1). Once an image file is available, a Java application can load the image into RAM for program use by running the following code:

```
ImageIcon image = new ImageIcon(fileName);
```

where `fileName` is the name of an image file or its pathname. This code creates an `ImageIcon` object with a bitmap for the data in the image. Any images that come from files are typically loaded at program startup and passed to panels when they are instantiated. The panels are then responsible for displaying the images.

Our first example program has a main application class that loads an image of a cat named "Smokey" and passes the image to a new `ColorPanel`. The main window is shown in Figure 5-9. Here is the code for the application class:

```java
// Example 5.2: Loading an image from a file

import javax.swing.*;
import java.awt.*;

public class GUIWindow{

    public static void main(String[] args){
        JFrame theGUI = new JFrame();
        theGUI.setTitle("GUI Program");
        theGUI.setSize(300, 300);
        theGUI.setDefaultCloseOperation(JFrame.EXIT_ON_CLOSE);
        ImageIcon image = new ImageIcon("smokey.jpg");
        ColorPanel panel = new ColorPanel(Color.black, image);
        Container pane = theGUI.getContentPane();
        pane.add(panel);
        theGUI.setVisible(true);
    }
}
```

FIGURE 5-9
Displaying an image

The `ColorPanel` receives the image icon at instantiation and saves a reference to it in an instance variable. When the panel paints itself, it paints the image icon. The code for painting the image appears in the panel's `paintComponent` method and has the following form:

```java
anImageIcon.paintIcon(this, g, x, y)
```

where `this` refers to the panel itself, `g` is the panel's graphics context, and `x` and `y` are the panel coordinates of the image's upper-left corner.

The methods `getIconWidth()` and `getIconHeight()` return the width and height, respectively, of an image in pixels. These methods can be used with the `getWidth()` and `getHeight()`

methods of the panel class to compute the position of the image relative to the center of the panel. Here is the code for a `ColorPanel` class that displays a centered image:

```java
// Displays an image centered in the panel

import javax.swing.*;
import java.awt.*;

public class ColorPanel extends JPanel{

    private ImageIcon image;

    public ColorPanel(Color backColor, ImageIcon i){
        setBackground(backColor);
        image = i;
    }

    public void paintComponent(Graphics g){
        super.paintComponent(g);
        int x = (getWidth() - image.getIconWidth()) / 2;
        int y = (getHeight() - image.getIconHeight()) / 2;
        image.paintIcon(this, g, x, y);
    }
}
```

This `ColorPanel` is different from panels discussed in earlier chapters in that it maintains another object, an image, as part of its state. Another difference is that this panel displays the image by asking an object to paint itself. We see this pattern repeated in the examples that follow.

Geometric Shapes

Graphics examples in earlier chapters displayed geometric shapes such as rectangles and ovals by running the corresponding drawing or filling methods of the `Graphics` class. There are several reasons why it will now be useful to view each shape as a distinct object with its own methods:

1. A shape has its own attributes, such as a color, a position, and a size. Defining a class for a shape allows a user to manipulate it by changing its color, position, or size.

2. Defining shape classes allows us to program with more specific shapes than those implied by the drawing methods of the `Graphics` class. For example, a circle is a specific type of oval, but we usually think of a circle in terms of its center point and radius rather than a corner point, width, and height. This also holds true for triangles and other more complex shapes.

3. If a shape already knows about its own attributes, it just needs a graphics context in order to display itself. Users can then more easily display shapes by asking them to display themselves, using a single `draw(aGraphicsObject)` or `fill(aGraphicsObject)` method.

4. Programs that use multiple shapes in complex arrangements can more easily compose these and manipulate them by using instances of shape classes.

Defining a `Circle` Class

Circles have a color, a center point, and a radius. In addition to modifying any of these attributes, a user can ask a circle to draw itself (just the circumference) or fill itself (like a solid disk) in its current color. Finally, a user can determine whether or not a circle contains a given point (x,y). The methods of our `Circle` class are listed in Table 5-4.

Methods in class `Circle`

METHOD	WHAT IT DOES
`Circle(int x, int y, int r, Color c)`	Constructor; creates a circle with center point (x, y), radius r, and color c
`int getX()`	Returns the x coordinate of the center
`int getY()`	Returns the y coordinate of the center
`int getRadius()`	Returns the radius
`Color getColor()`	Returns the color
`void setX(int x)`	Modifies the x coordinate of the center
`void setY(int y)`	Modifies the y coordinate of the center
`void setRadius(int r)`	Modifies the radius
`Color setColor(Color c)`	Modifies the color
`void draw(Graphics g)`	Draws an outline of the circle in the graphics context
`void fill(Graphics g)`	Draws a filled circle in the graphics context
`boolean containsPoint(int x, int y)`	Returns true if the point (x, y) lies in the circle or false otherwise
`void move(int xAmount, int yAmount)`	Moves the circle by xAmount horizontally to the right and yAmount vertically downward; Negative amounts move to the left and up.

Implementation of the `Circle` Class

For the most part, the implementation of the `Circle` class is trivial. The constructor receives the coordinates of the center point, the radius, and the color from the user and assigns these values to instance variables. We focus on just two methods: `draw` and `containsPoint`. The `draw` method uses `drawOval` to draw the circle. The `drawOval` method expects the position and extent of the circle's bounding rectangle, which can be derived from the circle's center and radius as shown in the following code:

```java
public void draw (Graphics g){
   // Save the current color of the graphics context
   // and set color to the circle's color.
   Color oldColor = g.getColor();
   g.setColor(color);
```

```
      // Translate the circle's position and radius
      // to the bounding rectangle's top left corner, width, and height.
      g.drawOval(centerX - radius, centerY - radius, radius * 2, radius * 2);

      // Restore the color of the graphics context.
      g.setColor(oldColor);
   }
```

To determine if a point is in a circle, we consider the familiar equation for all points on the circumference of a circle:

$$(x - xc)^2 + (y - yc)^2 = r^2 \qquad \text{(Eq. 1)}$$

or

$$(x - xc)^2 + (y - yc)^2 - r^2 = 0 \qquad \text{(Eq. 2)}$$

where (xc, yc) is the circle's center and r is its radius. A point (x, y) is then in the circle if the left side of Equation 2 is less than or equal to 0. For example, given a circle of radius 2 and center $(0, 0)$, the point $(1, 1)$ produces the result

$$1^2 + 1^2 - 2^2 = -2$$

implying that the point is in the circle.

The following method results from this design:

```
public boolean containsPoint (int x, int y){
    int xSquared = (x - centerX) * (x - centerX);
    int ySquared = (y - centerY) * (y - centerY);
    int radiusSquared = radius * radius;
    return xSquared + ySquared - radiusSquared <= 0;
}
```

Here is a partial listing of the Circle class:

```
// Circle.java: Represents a circle

import java.awt.*;

public class Circle{

    private int centerX, centerY, radius;
    private Color color;

    public Circle(int x, int y, int r, Color c){
        centerX = x;
        centerY = y;
        radius = r;
        color = c;
    }
```

```java
public void draw(Graphics g){
   Color oldColor = g.getColor();
   g.setColor(color);
   // Translates circle's center to rectangle's origin for drawing.
   g.drawOval(centerX - radius, centerY - radius,
              radius * 2, radius * 2);
   g.setColor(oldColor);
}

public void fill(Graphics g){
   Color oldColor = g.getColor();
   g.setColor(color);
   // Translates circle's center to rectangle's origin for drawing.
   g.fillOval(centerX - radius, centerY - radius,
              radius * 2, radius * 2);
   g.setColor(oldColor);
}

public boolean containsPoint(int x, int y){
   int xSquared = (x - centerX) * (x - centerX);
   int ySquared = (y - centerY) * (y - centerY);
   int radiusSquared = radius * radius;
   return xSquared + ySquared - radiusSquared <= 0;
}

public void move(int xAmount, int yAmount){
   centerX = centerX + xAmount;
   centerY = centerY + yAmount;
}
}
```

Using the `Circle` Class

Our next example program creates and displays two `Circle` objects (see Figure 5-10). The main window class just creates a `ColorPanel` with a background color and adds it to the window. The `ColorPanel`'s constructor sets two instance variables to different `Circle` objects. When the window is refreshed, the `ColorPanel`'s `paintComponent` method draws one circle and fills the other. Here is the code for `ColorPanel`:

```java
// Example 5.3: Displays a circle and a filled circle

import javax.swing.*;
import java.awt.*;

public class ColorPanel extends JPanel{

   private Circle c1, c2;

   public ColorPanel(Color backColor){
      setBackground(backColor);
      c1 = new Circle(200, 100, 25, Color.red);
      c2 = new Circle(100, 100, 50, Color.blue);
   }
```

```
public void paintComponent(Graphics g){
    super.paintComponent(g);
    c1.fill(g);
    c2.draw(g);
}
}
```

FIGURE 5-10
Displaying two `Circle` objects

The Method `repaint`

Suppose we want to move a shape or image to a new position in a panel in response to a mouse click. Let's assume we have the coordinates of the new position (we see how to get these in the next subsection). There are then just two steps remaining:

1. Set the shape's position to the new position.

2. Refresh the panel, which has the effect of clearing the panel and redrawing the shape at its new position.

The method `repaint` is used to force a refresh of any GUI component, such as a panel. The method essentially invokes that object's `paintComponent` method. Thus, there are two kinds of situations in which `paintComponent` is called:

1. Automatically, by the JVM, at startup; or whenever the main window is altered

2. Under program control, by a call of `repaint`, when the program has made a change to the objects to be displayed

The code that calls `repaint` typically appears in a panel method that has modified one or more shapes in the panel. This method might have the following form:

```
public void modifySomeShapes(someParameters){
    // modify the attributes of one or more shapes
    repaint();
}
```

Responses to Mouse Events

Until now, we have limited our use of the mouse to clicking on command buttons and editing data in I/O dialog boxes. Everyone who has used a drawing program knows that much more can be done with the mouse. Drawing applications usually detect and respond to the following mouse events: button presses and releases, mouse movement, and dragging the mouse (i.e., moving the mouse while a button is depressed). In addition, a program can respond to the mouse's entry into and exit from a given region.

A program can detect and respond to mouse events by attaching *listener objects* to a panel. When a particular type of mouse event occurs in a panel, its listeners are informed. If a listener has a method whose parameter matches that type of event, the JVM automatically runs this method and passes the event object to it as a parameter. The event object contains the mouse's current panel coordinates. The code in the method carries out the program's response to that mouse event.

For example, let's say that a panel should display the coordinates of the mouse whenever its button is pressed in a panel. The panel's constructor sets some instance variables to default coordinates, say, (100,100), and attaches a new listener object to the panel. The class for this listener object, also defined within the panel class, implements the method `mousePressed`, which will be triggered whenever a mouse-pressed event occurs in that panel. This method receives an event object as a parameter from the JVM. The method resets the coordinates to the ones contained in the event object and calls `repaint` to refresh the panel. The panel's `paintComponent` method simply draws the coordinates.

Our next example program shows a `ColorPanel` class that responds to mouse presses by displaying the mouse's coordinates. The class includes a nested listener class, `PanelListener`, which we explain following the listing.

```java
// Example 5.4: Tracks mouse presses by displaying
// the current mouse position

import javax.swing.*;
import java.awt.*;
import java.awt.event.*;    //For the mouse events

public class ColorPanel extends JPanel{

    int x, y;    // Used to track mouse coordinates

    public ColorPanel(Color backColor){
        setBackground(backColor);
        // Establish the default coordinates
        x = 100;
        y = 100;
        // Instantiate and attach the panel's listener
        addMouseListener(new PanelListener());
    }

    public void paintComponent(Graphics g){
        super.paintComponent(g);
        // Draw the current coordinates
        g.drawString("(" + x + ", " + y + ")", x, y);
    }

    private class PanelListener extends MouseAdapter{

        public void mousePressed(MouseEvent e){
        // Obtain the current mouse coordinates and refresh
```

```
        x = e.getX();
        y = e.getY();
        repaint();
      }
    }
  }
```

The `ColorPanel` class imports the package `java.awt.event`, which includes the classes `MouseEvent` and `MouseAdapter`. The panel's constructor uses the method `addMouseListener` to attach a `PanelListener`. This class is defined internally within the `ColorPanel` class, so its methods will have access to all of the panel's instance variables and methods.

The `PanelListener` class extends the class `MouseAdapter`. `MouseAdapter` includes several methods that respond to mouse events by doing nothing (very simple default behavior). One of these methods is `mousePressed`. `PanelListener` overrides the default definition of `mousePressed` by redefining it. The method extracts the coordinates of the mouse from the `MouseEvent` parameter using the methods `getX()` and `getY()`. It resets the panel's instance variables `x` and `y` to these values and then repaints the panel. Note that the visibility modifier of the `PanelListener` class is `private` because the enclosing panel class is its only user.

When you want the panel to respond to other types of mouse events, you just include code for the corresponding method in your listener class. At runtime, the JVM takes care of feeding the event object to the appropriate method.

The `MouseAdapter` class includes methods for all but two mouse events, mouse motion and mouse dragging. The methods for these two events are included in the `MouseMotionAdapter` class. Thus, you will have to define a separate class that extends `MouseMotionAdapter` and include either or both of its methods if you want your program to respond to mouse motion events. The method `addMouseMotionListener` is used to add listeners of this type to a panel. Table 5-5 lists the methods and the corresponding mouse events in the `MouseAdapter` and `MouseMotionAdapter` classes.

TABLE 5-5
Methods for responding to mouse events

CLASS	METHOD	TYPE OF EVENT
MouseAdapter	public void mouseEntered(MouseEvent e) public void mouseExited(MouseEvent e) public void mousePressed(MouseEvent e) public void mouseReleased(MouseEvent e) public void mouseClicked(MouseEvent e)	Enter Exit Press Release Click
MouseMotionAdapter	public void mouseMoved(MouseEvent e) public void mouseDragged(MouseEvent e)	Move Drag

Dragging Circles

Our final program example puts together our ideas about shape objects and mouse events to create a simple program for dragging circles around in a window. The user selects a circle by pressing the mouse within it and then moves it by dragging it to a desired position.

The `ColorPanel` class has the same two instance variables for circles as in the previous version (see Example 5.2). To these we add instance variables for saving the mouse coordinates and for saving a reference to the selected circle. This last variable is `null` at startup and after a circle has been deselected.

Here are the types of mouse events and the associated responses of the program:

1. *Mouse press.* Save the current coordinates of the mouse. If one of the shapes contains those coordinates, save a reference to that shape (thereby selecting it).

2. *Mouse release.* Deselect the selected shape, if there is one, by setting the saved reference to `null`.

3. *Mouse drag.* Compute the x and y distances by using the current mouse coordinates and the saved mouse coordinates. If a shape is currently selected, move it using the distances and repaint. Finally, set the saved coordinates to the current mouse coordinates.

Here is a complete listing of the `ColorPanel` class for dragging shapes:

```java
// Example 5.5: Displays a circle and a filled circle
// Allows the user to drag a circle to another position

import javax.swing.*;
import java.awt.*;
import java.awt.event.*;            //For the mouse events

public class ColorPanel extends JPanel{

    private Circle c1, c2;
    private Circle selectedCircle;    // Used to track selected shape
    private int x, y;                 // Used to track mouse coordinates

    public ColorPanel(Color backColor){
        setBackground(backColor);
        c1 = new Circle(200, 100, 25, Color.red);
        c2 = new Circle(100, 100, 50, Color.blue);
        selectedCircle = null;
        addMouseListener(new PanelListener());
        addMouseMotionListener(new PanelMotionListener());
    }

    public void paintComponent(Graphics g){
        super.paintComponent(g);
        c1.fill(g);
        c2.draw(g);
    }

    private class PanelListener extends MouseAdapter{
```

```
    public void mousePressed(MouseEvent e){
        // Select a circle if it contains the mouse coordinates
        x = e.getX();
        y = e.getY();
        if (c1.containsPoint(x, y))
            selectedCircle = c1;
        else if (c2.containsPoint(x, y))
            selectedCircle = c2;
    }

    public void mouseReleased(MouseEvent e){
        // Deselect the selected circle
        x = e.getX();
        y = e.getY();
        selectedCircle = null;
    }
}

private class PanelMotionListener extends MouseMotionAdapter{

    public void mouseDragged(MouseEvent e){
        // Compute the distance and move the selected circle
        int newX = e.getX();
        int newY = e.getY();
        int dx = newX - x;
        int dy = newY - y;
        if (selectedCircle != null)
            selectedCircle.move(dx, dy);
        x = newX;
        y = newY;
        repaint();
    }
}
}
```

In later chapters, we explore how to write programs that manipulate an arbitrary number of graphical objects.

*E*XERCISE 5.6

1. The program example that displayed an image in this section has a problem. If the image size is larger than that of the window, the user must resize the window to view the entire image. Describe how to fix the program so that the window size exactly fits the image size at startup.

2. Geometric shapes can be scaled up or down in size. For example, scaling by a factor of 3 triples the size of a shape, whereas scaling by a factor of 0.5 reduces the size of a shape by one-half. Write a method scale that expects a parameter of type `double` and scales a circle by that factor.

3. Explain how a program can detect and respond to the user's pressing of a mouse button.

SUMMARY

In this chapter, you learned:

- Java class definitions consist of instance variables, constructors, and methods.

- Constructors initialize an object's instance variables when the object is created. A default constructor expects no parameters and sets the variables to reasonable default values. Other constructors expect parameters that allow clients to set up objects with specified data.

- Mutator methods modify an object's instance variables, whereas accessor methods merely allow clients to observe the values of these variables.

- The visibility modifier `public` is used to make methods visible to clients, whereas the visibility modifier `private` is used to encapsulate or restrict access to variables and methods.

- Helper methods are methods that are called from other methods in a class definition. They are usually declared to be private.

- Variables within a class definition can be instance variables, local variables, or parameters. Instance variables are used to track the state of an object. Local variables are used for temporary working storage within a method. Parameters are used to transmit data to a method.

- A formal parameter appears in a method's signature and is referenced in its code. An actual parameter is a value passed to a method when it is called. A method's actual parameters must match its formal parameters in number, position, and type.

- The scope of a variable is the area of program text within which it is visible. The scope of an instance variable is the entire class within which it is declared. The scope of a local variable or a parameter is the body of the method within which it is declared.

- The lifetime of a variable is the period of program execution during which its storage can be accessed. The lifetime of an instance variable is the same as the lifetime of a particular object. The lifetime of a local variable and a parameter is the time during which a particular call of a method is active.

VOCABULARY *Review*

Define the following terms:

Accessor	Formal parameter	Mutator
Actual parameter	Helper method	Scope
Behavior	Identity	State
Constructor	Instantiation	Visibility modifier
Encapsulation	Lifetime	

REVIEW *Questions*

WRITTEN QUESTIONS

Write a brief answer to the following questions.

1. Explain the difference between a class and an instance of a class.

2. Explain the difference between the visibility modifiers `public` and `private`.

3. What are accessor and mutator methods?

4. Develop a design for a new class called `BaseballPlayer`. The variables of this class are

   name (a `String`)

   team (a `String`)

   home runs (an `int`)

   batting average (a `double`)

   Express your design in terms of a class summary box. The class should have a constructor and methods for accessing and modifying all of the variables.

5. Explain how a parameter transmits data to a method.

6. What are local variables and how should they be used in a program?

PROJECTS

PROJECT 5-1

Add the extra constructors to the `Student` class of this chapter's first case study (Student Test Scores), and test these methods thoroughly with a `Tester` program.

PROJECT 5-2

A `Student` object should validate its own data. The client runs this method, called `validateData()`, with a `Student` object, as follows:

```
String result = student.validateData();
if (result == null)
   <use the student>
else
   System.out.println(result);
```

If the student's data are valid, the method returns the value `null`; otherwise, the method returns a string representing an error message that describes the error in the data. The client can then examine this result and take the appropriate action.

A student's name is invalid if it is an empty string. A student's test score is invalid if it lies outside the range from `0` to `100`. Thus, sample error messages might be

```
"SORRY: name required"
```

and

```
"SORRY: must have 0 <= test score <= 100".
```

Implement and test this method.

PROJECT 5-3

Develop a new class for representing fractions. The numerator and denominator of a fraction are integers. The constructor expects these values as parameters. Define accessor methods to obtain the numerator and the denominator. Use the rules of fraction arithmetic to define methods to add, subtract, multiply, and divide fractions. Each of these methods expects a fraction object as a parameter. This object is considered to be the right operand of the operation. The left operand is the receiver object, that is, the one containing the instance variables for the numerator and denominator. Each arithmetic method builds a new instance of the fraction class with the results of its calculation and returns it as the method's value. Finally, include a `toString()`

method that returns a string of the form <numerator>/<denominator>. Write a tester program that exercises all of the methods. Here are the rules for fraction arithmetic:

$$\frac{n_1}{d_1} + \frac{n_2}{d_2} = \frac{n_1 d_2 + n_2 d_1}{d_1 d_2}$$

$$\frac{n_1}{d_1} - \frac{n_2}{d_2} = \frac{n_1 d_2 - n_2 d_1}{d_1 d_2}$$

$$\frac{n_1}{d_1} \times \frac{n_2}{d_2} = \frac{n_1 n_2}{d_1 d_2}$$

$$\frac{n_1/d_1}{n_2/d_2} = \frac{n_1 d_2}{d_1 n_2}$$

PROJECT 5-4

Redo the Lucky Sevens dice-playing program from Chapter 4 so that it uses dice objects. That is, design and implement a `Dice` class. Each instance of this class should contain the die's current side. There should be an accessor method for a die's current value. The method `roll` is the only mutator method. Be sure to test the `Dice` class in a simple tester program before incorporating it into the application.

PROJECT 5-5

Develop a new class called `BankAccount`. A bank account has an owner's name and a balance. Be sure to include a constructor that allows a client to supply the owner's name and an initial balance. A bank account needs accessors for the name and balance, mutators for making deposits and withdrawals, and a `toString` method. Test-drive your new class with a program similar to the one used to test the `Student` class in Section 5.3.

PROJECT 5-6

Patrons of a library can borrow up to three books. A patron, therefore, has a name and up to three books. A book has an author and a title. Design and implement two classes, `Patron` and `Book`, to represent these objects and the following behavior:

- The client can instantiate a book with a title and author.
- The client can examine but not modify a book's title or author.
- The client can ask a patron whether it has borrowed a given book (identified by title).
- The client can tell a patron to return a given book (identified by title).
- The client can tell a patron to borrow a given book.

The `Patron` class should use a separate instance variable for each book (a total of three). Each of these variables is initially `null`. When a book is borrowed, the patron looks for a variable that is not `null`. If no such variable is found, the method returns `false`. If a `null` variable is found, it is reset to the new book and the method returns `true`. Similar considerations apply to the other methods. Use the method `aString.equals(aString)` to compare two strings for equality. Be sure to include appropriate `toString` methods for your classes and test them with a tester program.

PROJECT 5-7

Write a program that allows the user to display 1, 2, or 4 images in a grid of panels. At program startup, the user is prompted for the number of images. If the input number is not 1, 2, or 4, the program quits with an error message. Otherwise, the program prompts the user for the name of each image file, loads the image, installs it in a `ColorPanel`, and adds the panel to a grid.

PROJECT 5-8

Define a `Rectangle` class to represent rectangles. Modify the program of Section 5.6 so that it uses two rectangles instead of two circles.

PROJECT 5-9

Write a program that displays an 8-by-8 grid of panels, all of which are initially colored white. When the user presses the mouse within a panel, its color should change to a randomly generated color.

CRITICAL *Thinking*

Explain how you could modify the fraction class created in Project 5-3 to display a fraction in a form that is reduced to lowest terms.

CONTROL STATEMENTS CONTINUED

OBJECTIVES

Upon completion of this chapter, you should be able to:

- Construct complex Boolean expressions using the logical operators && (AND), || (OR), and ! (NOT).

- Construct truth tables for Boolean expressions.

- Understand the logic of nested if statements and extended if statements.

- Test if statements in a comprehensive manner.

- Construct nested loops.

- Create appropriate test cases for `if` statements and loops.

- Understand the purpose of assertions, invariants, and loop verification.

Estimated Time: 5 hours

VOCABULARY

Arithmetic overflow

Boundary condition

Combinatorial explosion

Complete code coverage

Equivalence class

Extended if statement

Extreme condition

Input assertion

Logical operator

Loop invariant

Loop variant

Nested if statement

Nested loop

Output assertion

Quality assurance

Robust

Truth table

This chapter explores more advanced aspects of the control statements introduced in Chapter 4. Topics include logical operators, nested `if` statements, and nested loops. The chapter also describes strategies for testing programs that contain control statements. Programmers try to write programs that are free of logic errors, but they seldom succeed. Consequently, they must test their programs thoroughly before releasing them—and even so, errors will still slip through. Notice that we say "will" instead of "might." Software is so incredibly complex that no significant software product has ever been released free of errors; however, the situation would be much worse if we stopped emphasizing the importance of testing.

6.1 Logical Operators

Java includes three logical operators equivalent in meaning to the English words AND, OR, and NOT. These operators are used in the Boolean expressions that control the behavior of `if`, `while`, and `for` statements. Before we examine how these operators are used in Java, we review their usage in English. For instance, consider the following sentences:

1. If the sun is shining AND it is 8 a.m. then let's go for a walk else let's stay home.

2. If the sun is shining OR it is 8 a.m. then let's go for a walk else let's stay home.

3. If NOT the sun is shining then let's go for a walk else let's stay home.

The structure of all three sentences is similar, but their meanings are very different. For clarity we have emphasized key words. In these sentences, the phrases "the sun is shining" and "it is 8 a.m." are operands and the words AND, OR, and NOT are operators. At any particular moment, the value of a condition (true or false) depends on the values of the operands (also true or false) and the operator's meaning. For instance,

- In the first sentence, the operator is AND. Consequently, if both operands are true, the condition as a whole is true. If either or both are false, the condition is false.

- In the second sentence, which uses OR, the condition is false only if both operands are false; otherwise, it is true.

- In the third sentence, the operator NOT has been placed before the operand, as it would be in Java. This looks a little strange in English but is still understandable. If the operand is true, then the NOT operator makes the condition as a whole false.

We summarize these observations in the three parts of Table 6-1. Each part is called a truth table, and it shows how the value of the overall condition depends on the values of the operands. All combinations of values are considered. When there is one operand, there are two possibilities. For two operands, there are four; and for three operands, there are eight possibilities. In general there are 2^n combinations of true and false for n operands.

TABLE 6-1
Truth tables for three example sentences

THE SUN IS SHINING	IT IS 8 A.M.	THE SUN IS SHINING AND IT IS 8 A.M.	ACTION TAKEN
true	true	true	go for a walk
true	false	false	stay at home
false	true	false	stay at home
false	false	false	stay at home
THE SUN IS SHINING	IT IS 8 A.M.	THE SUN IS SHINING OR IT IS 8 A.M.	ACTION TAKEN
true	true	true	go for a walk
true	false	true	go for a walk
false	true	true	go for a walk
false	false	false	stay at home
THE SUN IS SHINING	NOT THE SUN IS SHINING	ACTION TAKEN	
true	false	stay at home	
false	true	go for a walk	

Dropping the column labeled "action taken," we can combine the information in the three truth tables in Table 6-1 into one table of general rules, as illustrated in Table 6-2. The letters P and Q represent the operands.

TABLE 6-2
General rules for AND, OR, and NOT

P	Q	P AND Q	P OR Q	NOT P
true	true	true	true	false
true	false	false	true	
false	true	false	true	true
false	false	false	false	

Three Operators at Once

Now that we know the rules, it is easy to construct and understand more complex conditions. Consider the following sentences:

A. If (the sun is shining AND it is 8 a.m.) OR (NOT your brother is visiting) then let's go for a walk else let's stay at home.

We have added parentheses to remove ambiguity. As usual, expressions inside parentheses are evaluated before those that are not. So now when do we go for a walk? The answer is at 8 a.m. on sunny days or when your brother does not visit; however, rearranging the parentheses changes the meaning of the sentence:

B. If the sun is shining AND (it is 8 a.m. OR (NOT your brother is visiting)) then let's go for a walk else let's stay at home.

Now before we go for a walk, the sun must be shining. In addition, one of two things must be true. Either it is 8 a.m. or your brother is not visiting. It does get a little confusing. Making truth tables for these sentences would make their meanings completely clear.

Java's Logical Operators and Their Precedence

In Java the operators AND, OR, and NOT are represented by &&, ||, and !, respectively. Before writing code that uses these operators, we must consider their precedence as shown in Table 6-3. Observe that NOT (!) has the same high precedence as other unary operators, whereas AND (&&) and OR (||) have low precedence, with OR below AND.

TABLE 6-3
Positions of the logical and relational operators in the precedence scheme

OPERATION	SYMBOL	PRECEDENCE (FROM HIGHEST TO LOWEST)	ASSOCIATION
Grouping	( )	1	Not applicable
Method selector	.	2	Left to right
Unary plus	+	3	Not applicable
Unary minus	–	3	Not applicable
Not	!	3	Not applicable
Multiplication	*	4	Left to right
Division	/	4	Left to right
Remainder or modulus	%	4	Left to right
Addition	+	5	Left to right
Subtraction	–	5	Left to right
Relational operators	< <= > >= == !=	6	Not applicable
And	&&	8	Left to right
Or	||	9	Left to right
Assignment operators	= *= /= %= += –=	10	Right to left

A complete table of operator precedence can be found in Appendix C.

Examples Using Logical Operators

Following are some illustrative examples based on the employment practices at ABC Company. The company screens all new employees by making them take two written tests. A program then analyzes the scores and prints a list of jobs for which the applicant is qualified. Following is the relevant code:

```
Scanner reader = new Scanner(System.in);
int score1, score2;
System.out.print("Enter the first test score: ");
score1 = reader.nextInt();
System.out.print("Enter the second test score: ");
score2 = reader.nextInt();
```

```java
// Managers must score well (90 or above) on both tests.
if (score1 >= 90 && score2 >= 90)
    System.out.println("Qualified to be a manager");

// Supervisors must score well (90 or above) on just one test
if (score1 >= 90 || score2 >= 90)
    System.out.println("Qualified to be a supervisor");

// Clerical workers must score moderately well on one test

// (70 or above), but not badly (below 50) on either.
if ((score1 >= 70 || score2 >= 70) &&
    !(score1 < 50 || score2 < 50))
    System.out.println("Qualified to be a clerk");
```

Boolean Variables

The complex Boolean expressions in the preceding examples can be simplified by using Boolean variables. A Boolean variable can be true or false and is declared to be of type `boolean`. Now we rewrite the previous examples using Boolean variables:

```java
Scanner reader = new Scanner(System.in);
int score1, score2;
boolean bothHigh, atLeastOneHigh, atLeastOneModerate, noLow;
System.out.print("Enter the first test score: ");
score1 = reader.nextInt();
System.out.print("Enter the second test score: ");
score2 = reader.nextInt();

bothHigh           =  (score1 >= 90 && score2 >= 90); // parentheses
atLeastOneHigh     =  (score1 >= 90 || score2 >= 90); // optional
atLeastOneModerate =  (score1 >= 70 || score2 >= 70); // here
noLow              = !(score1 <  50 || score2 <  50);
if (bothHigh)
    System.out.println("Qualified to be a manager");
if (atLeastOneHigh)
    System.out.println("Qualified to be a supervisor");
if (atLeastOneModerate && noLow)
    System.out.println("Qualified to be a clerk");
```

Rewriting Complex Boolean Expressions

A complex `if` statement is sometimes so confusing that it is better rewritten as a series of simpler ones. Here is an example in a mixture of English and Java that we call Javish:

```java
if (the sun shines && (you have the time || it is Sunday))
    let's go for a walk;
else
    let's stay home;
```

To rewrite the previous code, we first create a truth table for the complex if statement, as shown in Table 6-4.

TABLE 6-4
Truth table for complex if statement

P: THE SUN SHINES	Q: YOU HAVE TIME	R: IT IS SUNDAY	P && (Q || R)	ACTION TAKEN
true	true	true	true	walk
true	true	false	true	walk
true	false	true	true	walk
true	false	false	false	stay home
false	true	true	false	stay home
false	true	false	false	stay home
false	false	true	false	stay home
false	false	false	false	stay home

Then implement each line of the truth table with a separate `if` statement involving only && (AND) and ! (NOT). Applying the technique here yields

```
if ( the sun shines &&  you have time &&  it is Sunday) walk;
if ( the sun shines &&  you have time && !it is Sunday) walk;
if ( the sun shines && !you have time &&  it is Sunday) walk;
if ( the sun shines && !you have time && !it is Sunday) stay home;
if (!the sun shines &&  you have time &&  it is Sunday) stay home;
if (!the sun shines &&  you have time && !it is Sunday) stay home;
if (!the sun shines && !you have time &&  it is Sunday) stay home;
if (!the sun shines && !you have time && !it is Sunday) stay home;
```

In this particular example, the verbosity can be reduced without reintroducing complexity by noticing that the first two `if` statements are equivalent to

```
if ( the sun shines &&  you have time) walk;
```

and the last four are equivalent to

```
if (!the sun shines) stay home;
```

Putting all this together yields

```
if ( the sun shines &&  you have time) walk;
if ( the sun shines && !you have time &&  it is Sunday) walk;
if (the sun shines && !you have time  && !it is Sunday) stay home
if (!the sun shines) stay home;
```

Of course, it is also possible to go in the other direction: that is, combine several if statements into a single more complex one, but no matter how we choose to represent complex conditions, truth tables are an essential tool for verifying the accuracy of the result. We can use them anytime we are uncertain about the meaning of the if statements we write.

Some Useful Boolean Equivalences

There is often more than one way to write a Boolean expression. For instance, the following pairs of Boolean expressions are equivalent, as truth tables readily confirm:

!(p || q)	equivalent to	!p && !q
!(p && q)	equivalent to	!p || !q
p || (q && r)	equivalent to	(p || q) && (p || r)
p && (q || r)	equivalent to	(p && q) || (p && r)

Using these equivalences sometimes enables us to rewrite a condition in a more easily understood form. Following is an example in which we display the word "reject" if x is not in the interval [3, 5], or alternatively, if x is less than 3 or greater than 5:

```
if (!(3 <= x && x <= 5))    System.out.println("reject");
if (!(3 <= x) || !(x <= 5)) System.out.println("reject");
if (x < 3 || x > 5)         System.out.println("reject");
```

Short-circuit Evaluation

The Java virtual machine sometimes knows the value of a Boolean expression before it has evaluated all of its parts. For instance, in the expression (p && q), if p is false, then so is the expression, and there is no need to evaluate q. Likewise, in the expression (p || q), if p is true, then so is the expression, and again there is no need to evaluate q. This approach, in which evaluation stops as soon as possible, is called short-circuit evaluation. In contrast, some programming languages use complete evaluation, in which all parts of a Boolean expression are always evaluated. These two methods nearly always produce the same results; however, there are times when short-circuit evaluation is advantageous. Consider the following example:

```
Scanner reader = new Scanner(System.in);
int count, sum;
System.out.print("Enter the count: ");
count = reader.nextInt;
System.out.print("Enter the sum: ");
sum = reader.nextInt();

if (count > 0 && sum / count > 10)
    System.out.println("average > 10");
else
    System.out.println("count = 0 or average <= 10");
```

If the user enters 0 for the count, the condition (count > 0 && sum / count > 10) contains a potential division by zero; however, because of short-circuit evaluation the division by zero is avoided.

EXERCISE 6.1

1. Fill in the truth values in the following truth table:

P	Q	! ((P || Q) && (P && Q))

2. Assume that A is true and B is false. Write the values of the following expressions:

a. A \|\| B

b. A && B

c. A && ! B

d. ! (A \|\| B)

3. Construct truth tables for the expressions listed under the heading "Some Useful Boolean Equivalences" in this section to show that they are equivalent.

4. List the logical operators in the order in which each one would be evaluated at run time.

5. Construct a Boolean expression that tests whether the value of variable x is within the range specified by the variables min (the smallest) and max (the largest).

Case Study 1: Compute Weekly Pay

We illustrate the use of logical operators by writing a program to compute weekly pay.

Request

Write a program to compute the weekly pay of hourly employees.

Analysis

Employees are paid at a base rate for the first 40 hours they work each week. Hours over 40 are paid at an overtime rate equal to twice the base rate. An exception is made for part-time employees, who are always paid at the regular rate, no matter how many hours they work. The hourly rate is in the range $6.75 to $30.50 and hours worked in the range 1 to 60. We use a type attribute to distinguish between full-time (type 1) and part-time (type 2) employees. Figure 6-1 shows the user interface.

We would also like the program to be **robust**, that is, to handle invalid inputs without crashing or producing meaningless results. The easiest and best way to achieve this end is to check data values as soon as they are entered and reject those that are invalid. The user is then given another opportunity to enter a correct value, as shown in Figure 6-2.

FIGURE 6-1
Interface for the compute weekly pay program

```
    Enter employee data
      Name (or blank to quit): Susan Jones
      Type (1 or 2): 1
      Hourly rate (between 6.75 and 30.50, inclusive): 10.50
      Hours worked (between 1 and 60, inclusive): 50
      The weekly pay for Susan Jones is $630.0
    Enter employee data
      Name (or blank to quit): Bill Smith
      Type (1 or 2): 2
      Hourly rate (between 6.75 and 30.50, inclusive): 15.00
      Hours worked (between 1 and 60, inclusive): 60
      The weekly pay for Bill Smith is $900.0
    Enter employee data
      Name (or blank to quit):
```

FIGURE 6-2
How the program responds to invalid inputs

```
    Enter employee data
      Name (or blank to quit): Patricia Nelson
      Type (1 or 2): 3
      Type (1 or 2): 0
      Type (1 or 2): 1
      Hourly rate (between 6.75 and 30.50, inclusive): 99.00
      Hourly rate (between 6.75 and 30.50, inclusive): 3.75
      Hourly rate (between 6.75 and 30.50, inclusive): 20.89
      Hours worked (between 1 and 60, inclusive): 100
      Hours worked (between 1 and 60, inclusive): 25
      The weekly pay for Patricia Nelson is $522.25
```

Following the approach introduced in Chapter 5, we divide the work of the application into two classes: a user interface class (`PayrollSystemApp`) and an employee class (`Employee`). The `Employee` class has four instance variables:

■ Name

■ Type

■ Rate

■ Hours

and three responsibilities:

■ Provide information about data validation rules (`getNameRules`, `getTypeRules`, etc).

■ Set instance variables provided the values are valid (return `true` if valid and `false` otherwise).

■ Get the name and weekly pay.

Figure 6-3 summarizes these points. The user interface class has the usual structure and has the single method main, so we omit a class summary.

FIGURE 6-3
Summary of the `Employee` class

```
Class:
    Employee
Private Instance Variables:
    String name
    int type
    double rate
    int hours
Public Methods:
    constructor
    String getNameRules()
    String getTypeRules()
    String getRateRules()
    String getHoursRules()
    boolean setName(String nm)
    boolean setType(int tp)
    boolean setRate(double rt)
    boolean setHours(int hrs)
    String getName()
    double getPay()
```

Design

Following is the pseudocode for the user interface:

```
while (true){
    read name, break if blank else set the employee name
    read type until valid and set the employee type
    read rate until valid and set the employee rate
    read hours until valid and set the employee hours
    ask the employee for name and pay and print these
}
```

An employee object computes pay as follows:

```
if (hours <= 40 || type == 2)
    pay = rate * hours;
else
    pay = rate * 40 +  rate * 2 * (hours - 40);
```

Implementation

The implementation uses two new `string` methods, `trim` and `equals`. When a `trim()` message is sent to a string, a new string that contains no leading or trailing spaces is returned:

```
String inputName, trimmedName;
System.out.print("Enter the name: ")
inputName = reader.nextLine;
trimmedName = inputName.trim();
```

The `equals` method is used to determine if two string objects contain equal strings. This is in contrast to the `==` operator, which determines if two string variables refer to the same object. Following is an illustration:

```java
String a, b;
a = "cat";
System.out.print("What do you call a small domestic feline? ");
b = reader.nextLine;

if (a == b)
    System.out.println("a and b reference the same object.");
else
    System.out.println("a and b reference different objects.");

if (a.equals(b))
    System.out.println
    ("a and b reference objects that contain equal strings.");
else
    System.out.println
    ("a and b reference objects that contain unequal strings");
```

If the user enters "cat" when this code is run, the output is

```
a and b reference different objects.
a and b reference objects that contain equal strings.
```

We now return to the case study program and present the implementation, which is complicated by all the error checking we have decided to do. The user interface class restricts itself to interacting with the user, and the `Employee` class controls data validation and computation of pay:

```java
/* Case Study 6.1: PayrollSystemApp.java
1. Request employee name, type, pay rate, and hours.
2. Print employee name and pay.
3. Repeat until the name is blank.*/

import java.util.Scanner;

public class PayrollSystemApp{

    public static void main (String [] args) {
        Scanner reader = new Scanner(System.in);
        Employee emp;      // employee
        String name;       //    name
        int    type;       //    type
        double rate;       //    hourly pay rate
        int    hours;      //    hours worked
        String prompt;     // user prompt;

        while (true){

            // Get the name and break if blank
            System.out.println("Enter employee data");
            System.out.print("  Name (or blank to quit): ");
            name = reader.nextLine();
```

```java
        name = name.trim(); // Trim off leading and trailing spaces
        if (name.length() == 0) break;
        emp = new Employee();
        emp.setName(name);

        // Get the type until valid
        while (true){
            prompt = "  Type (" + emp.getTypeRules() + "): ";
            System.out.print(prompt);
            type = reader.nextInt();
            if (emp.setType(type)) break;
        }

        // Get the hourly pay rate until valid
        while (true){
            prompt = "  Hourly rate (" + emp.getRateRules() + "): ";
            System.out.print(prompt);
            rate = reader.nextDouble();
            if (emp.setRate(rate)) break;
        }

        // Get the hours worked until valid
        //   To illustrate the possibilities we compress
        //   into a hard-to-read set of statements.
        System.out.print("Hours worked (" +
                         emp.getHoursRules() + "): ");
        while (!emp.setHours(reader.nextInt()))
             System.out.print("Hours worked (" +
                              emp.getHoursRules() + "): ");

        // Consume the trailing newline
        reader.nextLine();

        // Print the name and pay
        System.out.println("  The weekly pay for " + emp.getName() +
                           " is $" + emp.getPay());
      }
    }
  }



/*  Employee.java
1. Instance variables: name, type, rate, hours
2. Methods to
   get data validation rules
   set instance variables if data are valid
   get name and pay */

public class Employee{

   // Private Instance Variables:
   private String name;
```

```java
private int type;
private double rate;
private int hours;

// Public Methods:
public Employee(){
   name = "";
   type = 0;
   rate = 0;
   hours = 0;
}

  public String getNameRules(){
   return "nonblank";
}

  public String getTypeRules(){
   return "1 or 2";
}

  public String getRateRules(){
   return "between 6.75 and 30.50, inclusive";
}

public String getHoursRules(){
   return "between 1 and 60, inclusive";
}

  public boolean setName(String nm){
   if (nm.equals(""))
      return false;
   else{
      name = nm;
      return true;
   }
}

public boolean setType(int tp){
   if (tp != 1 && tp != 2)
      return false;
   else{
      type = tp;
      return true;
   }
}

public boolean setRate(double rt){
   if (!(6.75 <= rt && rt <= 30.50))
      return false;
   else{
      rate = rt;
      return true;
   }
}
```

```java
public boolean setHours(int hrs){
    if (!(1 <= hrs && hrs <= 60))
        return false;
    else{
        hours = hrs;
        return true;
    }
}

public String getName(){
    return name;
}

public double getPay(){
    double pay;
    if (hours <= 40 || type == 2)
        pay = rate * hours;
    else
        pay = rate * 40 +  rate * 2 * (hours - 40);
    return pay;
}
}
```

6.2 Testing `if` Statements

Q*uality assurance* is the ongoing process of making sure that a software product is developed to the highest standards possible subject to the ever-present constraints of time and money. As we learned in Chapter 1, faults are fixed most inexpensively early in the development life cycle; however, no matter how much care is taken at every stage during a program's development, eventually the program must be run against well-designed test data. Such data should exercise a program as thoroughly as possible. At a minimum, the test data should try to achieve *complete code coverage*, which means that every line in a program is executed at least once. Unfortunately, this is not the same thing as testing all possible logical paths through a program, which would provide a more thorough test, but also might require considerably more test data.

We now design test data for the preceding case study. Because the program is so simple, the test data will provide complete code coverage and test all possible logical paths through the program. Varying the hourly rate has no particular significance in this problem, so we use an hourly rate of $10 for all the tests.

First, we test with an employee type of 1 and hours worked equal to 30 and 50 hours. Because we must compare the program's output with the expected results, we have chosen numbers for which it is easy to perform the calculations by hand. Having tested the program for the input 30 hours, we feel no need to test it for 29 or 31 hours because we realize that exactly the same code is executed in all three cases. Likewise, we do not feel compelled to test the program for 49 and 51 hours. All the sets of test data that exercise a program in the same manner are said to belong to the same *equivalence class*, which means they are equivalent from the perspective of testing the same paths through the program. When the employee type is 1, test data for the payroll program fall into just two equivalence classes: hours between 0 and 40 and hours greater than 40.

The test data should also include cases that assess a program's behavior under *boundary conditions*—that is, on or near the boundaries between equivalence classes. It is common for programs to fail at these points. For the payroll program, this requirement means testing with hours equal to 39, 40, and 41.

We should test under *extreme conditions*—that is, with data at the limits of validity. For this we choose hours worked equal to 0 and 168 hours.

Testing with an employee type of 2 is much simpler because the number of hours does not matter, but just to be on the safe side, we test with the hours equal to 30 and 50.

Finally, we must test the data validation rules. We need to enter values that are valid and invalid, and we must test the boundary values between the two. This suggests that we test using

- Type equal to 0, 1, 2, and 3

- Hourly rate equal to 6.74, 6.75, 10, 30.50, and 30.51

- Hours worked equal to 0, 1, 30, 60, and 61

Table 6-5 summarizes our planned tests. If from this discussion you draw the conclusion that testing is a lot of work, you are correct. Many software companies spend as much money on testing as they do on analysis, design, and implementation combined. The programs in this book, however, are fairly short and simple, and testing takes only a moderate amount of time.

For a discussion of an approach that puts testing at the center of software development, see Kent Beck, Extreme Programming Explained: Embrace Change (Boston: Addison-Wesley, 2000).

TABLE 6-5
Test data for the payroll program

TYPE OF TEST	DATA USED
Code coverage	employee type: 1 hourly rate: 10 hours worked: 30 and 50
Boundary conditions	employee type: 1 hourly rate: 10 hours worked: 39, 40, and 41
Extreme conditions	employee type: 1 hourly rate: 10 hours worked: 0 and 168
Tests when the employee type is 2	employee type: 2 hourly rate: 10 hours worked: 30 and 50
Data validation rules	type: 0, 1, 2, and 3 hourly rate: 6.74, 6.75, 10, 30.50, and 30.51 hours worked: 0, 1, 30, 60, and 61

EXERCISE 6.2

1. Describe appropriate test data for the following code segments:

a.

```
if (number > 0)
    <action 1>
else
    <action 2>
```

b.

```
  if (0 < number && 100 > number)
    <action 1>
else
    <action 2>
```

2. What happens when we provide complete code coverage of a program?

3. What is an equivalence class? Give an example.

4. What are boundary conditions? Give an example.

5. What are extreme conditions? Give an example.

6. Suppose a teacher uses grades from 0 to 100 and wants to discount all grades below 60 in her records. Discuss the equivalence classes, boundary conditions, and extreme conditions used to test a program that processes this information.

6.3 Nested `if` Statements

A program's logic is often complex. Logical operators (`&&`, `||`, and `!`) provide one mechanism for dealing with this complexity. Nested `if` statements offer an alternative. Following is an everyday example of nested ifs written in Javish:

```
if (the time is after 7 PM){
   if (you have a book)
      read the book;
   else
      watch TV;
}else
   go for a walk;
```

Technology Careers

ARTIFICIAL INTELLIGENCE, ROBOTS, AND SOFTBOTS

You have seen in this chapter that a computer not only calculates results but also responds to conditions in its environment and takes the appropriate actions. This additional capability forms the basis of a branch of computer science known as artificial intelligence, or AI. AI programmers attempt to construct computational models of intelligent human behavior. These tasks involve, among many others, interacting in English or other natural languages, recognizing objects in the environment, reasoning, creating and carrying out plans of action, and pruning irrelevant information from a sea of detail.

There are many ways to construct AI models. One way is to view intelligent behavior as patterns of production rules. Each rule contains a set of conditions and a set of actions. In this model, an intelligent agent, either a computer or a human being, compares conditions in its environment to the conditions of all of its rules. Those rules with matching conditions are scheduled to fire—meaning that their actions are triggered—according to a higher-level scheme of rules. The set of rules is either hand-coded by the AI programmer or "learned" by using a special program known as a neural net.

Among other things, AI systems have been used to control *robots*. Although not quite up to the performance of Data in the TV series *Star Trek: The Next Generation*, these robots do perform mundane tasks such as assembling cars.

AI systems also are embedded in software agents known as *softbots*. For example, softbots exist to filter information from electronic mail systems, to schedule appointments, and to search the World Wide Web for information.

For a detailed discussion of robots and softbots, see Rodney Brooks, "Intelligence Without Representation," in *Mind Design II*, ed. John Haugeland (Cambridge, MA: MIT Press, 1997), and Patti Maes, "Agents That Reduce Work and Information Overload," *Communications of the ACM*, Volume 37, No. 7 (July 1994): 30–40.

Although this code is not complicated, it is a little difficult to determine exactly what it means without the aid of the truth table illustrated in Table 6-6.

TABLE 6-6
Truth table for reading a book, watching TV, or going for a walk

AFTER 7 P.M.	HAVE A BOOK	ACTION TAKEN
true	true	read book
true	false	watch TV
false	true	walk
false	false	walk

Having made the table, we are certain that we understand the code correctly. Of course, it is better to make the table first and then write code to match. As a substitute for a truth table, we can draw a flowchart as shown in Figure 6-4. Again, it is better to draw the flowchart before writing the code. Truth tables and flowcharts are useful design tools whenever we must deal with complex logic.

FIGURE 6-4
Flowchart for reading a book, watching TV, or going for a walk

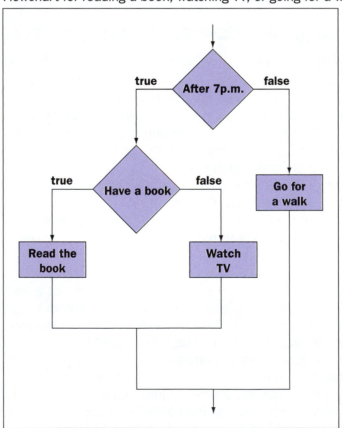

Determine a Student's Grade

Following is a second example of nested `if` statements. The code determines a student's grade based on his test average:

```java
System.out.print("Enter the test average: ");
testAverage = reader.nextInt();
if (testAverage >= 90)
   System.out.println("grade is A");
else{
   if (testAverage >= 80)
      System.out.println("grade is B");
   else{
      if (testAverage >= 70)
         System.out.println("grade is C");
      else{
         if (testAverage >= 60)
            System.out.println("grade is D");
         else{
            System.out.println("grade is F");
         }
      }
   }
}
```

Because in the absence of braces an else is associated with the immediately preceding `if`, we can drop the braces and rewrite the code as follows:

```java
System.out.print("Enter the test average: ");
testAverage = reader.nextInt();
if (testAverage >= 90)
   System.out.println("grade is A");
else
   if (testAverage >= 80)
      System.out.println("grade is B");
   else
      if (testAverage >= 70)
         System.out.println("grade is C");
      else
         if (testAverage >= 60)
            System.out.println("grade is D");
         else
            System.out.println("grade is F");
```

or after changing the indentation slightly as follows:

```java
System.out.print("Enter the test average: ");
testAverage = reader.nextInt();
if (testAverage >= 90)
   System.out.println("grade is A");
else if (testAverage >= 80)
   System.out.println("grade is B");
else if (testAverage >= 70)
```

```
      System.out.println("grade is C");
   else if (testAverage >= 60)
      System.out.println("grade is D");
   else
      System.out.println("grade is F");
```

This last format is very common and is used whenever a variable is compared to a sequence of threshold values. This form of the `if` statement is sometimes called an extended `if` statement or a multiway `if` statement, as compared to the two-way and one-way `if` statements we have seen earlier.

In Java, the `switch` statement provides an alternative to the extended if statement. See Appendix B for details.

*E*XERCISE 6.3

1. Construct a truth table that shows all the possible paths through the following nested if statement:

```
if (the time is before noon)
   if (the day is Monday)
      take the computer science quiz
   else
      go to gym class
else
   throw a Frisbee in the quad
```

2. What is the difference between a nested if statement and a multiway if statement?

6.4 *Logical Errors in Nested* `if` *statements*

It is easy to make logical errors when writing nested `if` statements. In this section we illustrate several fairly typical mistakes.

Misplaced Braces

One of the most common mistakes involves misplaced braces. Consider how repositioning a brace affects the following code:

```
// Version 1
if (the weather is wet){
   if (you have an umbrella)
      walk;
   else
      run;
}

// Version 2
if (the weather is wet){
   if (you have an umbrella)
      walk;
}else
   run;
```

To demonstrate the differences between the two versions, we construct a truth table—as shown in Table 6-7.

TABLE 6-7
Truth table for version 1 and version 2

THE WEATHER IS WET	YOU HAVE AN UMBRELLA	VERSION 1 OUTCOME	VERSION 2 OUTCOME
true	true	walk	walk
true	false	run	none
false	true	none	run
false	false	none	run

The truth table shows exactly how different the two versions are.

Removing the Braces

This example raises an interesting question. What happens if the braces are removed? In such situations, Java pairs the `else` with the closest preceding `if`. Thus

```
if (the weather is wet)
   if (you have an umbrella)
      walk;
   else
      run;
```

Remember that indentation is just a stylistic convention intended to improve the readability of code and means nothing to the computer. Consequently, reformatting the above code as follows does not change its meaning but will almost certainly mislead the unwary programmer.

```
if (the weather is wet)
   if (you have an umbrella)
      walk;
else
   run;
```

Introducing a Syntax Error

Now we consider a final variation:

```
if (the weather is wet)
   if (you have an umbrella)
      open umbrella;
      walk;
   else
      run;
```

Oops, this contains a compile-time error. Can you spot it? The second `if` is followed by more than one statement, so braces are required:

```java
if (the weather is wet)
    if (you have an umbrella){
        open umbrella;
        walk;
    }else
        run;
```

Remembering that it is better to overuse than to underuse braces, we could rewrite the code as follows:

```java
if (the weather is wet){
    if (you have an umbrella){
        open umbrella;
        walk;
    }else{
        run;
    }
}
```

Computation of Sales Commissions

We now attempt to compute a salesperson's commission and introduce a logical error in the process. Commissions are supposed to be computed as follows:

- 10% if sales are greater than or equal to $5000

- 20% if sales are greater than or equal to $10,000

Following is our first attempt at writing the corresponding code:

```java
if (sales >= 5000)
    commission = sales * 0.1;        // line a
else if (sales >= 10000)
    commission = sales * 0.2;        // line b
```

To determine if the code works correctly, we check it against representative values for the sales, namely, sales that are less than $5000, equal to $5000, between $5000 and $10,000, equal to $10,000, and greater than $10,000. As we can see from Table 6-8, the code is not working correctly.

TABLE 6-8
Calculation of commissions for various sales levels

VALUE OF SALES	LINES EXECUTED	VALIDITY
1,000	neither line a nor line b	correct
5,000	line a	correct
7,000	line a	correct
10,000	line a	incorrect
12,000	line a	incorrect

Corrected Computation of Sales Commissions

After a little reflection, we realize that the conditions are in the wrong order. Here is the corrected code:

```
if (sales >= 10000)
    commission = sales * 0.2;        // line b
else if (sales >= 5000)
    commission = sales * 0.1;        // line a
```

Table 6-9 confirms that the code now works correctly.

TABLE 6-9
Corrected calculation of commissions for various sales levels

VALUE OF SALES	LINES EXECUTED	VALIDITY
1,000	neither line a nor line b	correct
5,000	line a	correct
7,000	line a	correct
10,000	line b	correct
12,000	line b	correct

Avoiding Nested `if` statements

Sometimes getting rid of nested `if`s is the best way to avoid logical errors. This is easily done by rewriting nested `if`s as a sequence of independent `if` statements. For example, consider the following code for computing sales commissions:

```
if (5000 <= sales && sales < 10000)
    commission = sales * 0.1;
if (10000 <= sales)
    commission = sales * 0.2;
```

And here is another example involving the calculation of student grades:

```
if (90 <= average                ) grade is A;
if (80 <= average && average < 90) grade is B;
if (70 <= average && average < 80) grade is C;
if (60 <= average && average < 70) grade is D;
if (              average < 60) grade is F;
```

The first question people usually ask when confronted with these alternatives is, "Which is faster?", by which they mean, "Which will execute most rapidly?" In nearly all situations the difference in speed is negligible, so a much better question is, "Which is easier to write and maintain correctly?" There is no hard-and-fast answer to this question, but you should always consider it when writing complex code.

EXERCISE 6.4

1. A tax table provides rates for computing tax based on incomes up to and including a given amount. For example, income above $20,000 up to and including $50,000 is taxed at 18%. Find the logic errors in the following code that determines the tax rate for a given income:

```java
if (income > 10000)
    rate = 0.10;
else if (income > 20000)
    rate = 0.18;
else if (income > 50000)
    rate = 0.40;
else
    rate = 0.0;
```

2. Write a correct code segment for the problem in Question 1.

6.5 Nested Loops

There are many programming situations in which a loop is placed within another loop—this is called a *nested loop*. The first case study in this chapter provided an example of this. We now consider another. In Chapter 4, we showed how to determine if a number is prime. The code involved a `for` loop, and by nesting this `for` loop inside another, we can compute all the primes between two limits. The outside loop feeds a sequence of numbers to the inside loop. Following is the code:

```java
System.out.print("Enter the lower limit: ");
lower = reader.nextInt();
System.out.print("Enter the upper limit: ");
upper = reader.nextInt();
for (n = lower; n <= upper; n++){
   innerLimit = (int)Math.sqrt (n);
   for (d = 2; d <= innerLimit; d++){
      if (n % d == 0)
         break;
   }
   if (d > innerLimit)
      System.out.println (n + " is prime");
}
```

Following is the output when the user enters 55 and 75:

```
59 is prime
61 is prime
67 is prime
71 is prime
73 is prime
```

If the user wants to enter repeated pairs of limits, we enclose the code in yet another loop:

```java
System.out.print("Enter the lower limit or -1 to quit: ");
lower = reader.nextInt();
```

```java
while (lower != -1){
    System.out.print("Enter the upper limit: ");
    upper = reader.nextInt();
    for (n = lower; n <= upper; n++){
        innerLimit = (int)Math.sqrt (n);
        for (d = 2; d <= innerLimit; d++){
            if (n % d == 0)
                break;
        }
        if (d > innerLimit)
            System.out.println (n + " is prime");
    }
    System.out.print("Enter the lower limit or -1 to quit: ");
    lower = reader.nextInt();
}
```

 Note of Interest

RELIABILITY OF COMPUTER SYSTEMS

The next time you step onto an airliner or lie down beneath an x-ray machine, you might ask yourself about the quality of the software system that helps to run them. There are several measures of software quality, such as readability, maintainability, correctness, and robustness. But perhaps the most important measure is *reliability*. Reliability should not be confused with correctness. Software is correct if its design and implementation are consistent with its specifications. That means that the software actually does what it is supposed to do, as described in what we have called analysis. However, software can be correct in this sense yet still be unreliable.

During the analysis phase of software development, we construct a model of what the user wants the software to do, and from this model we build a model of what the software will do. Our design and implementation may reflect this second model correctly, but the software may still be unreliable. It is unreliable if we have built the wrong models during analysis—that is, if we have misunderstood the user's request (have the wrong model of the user) or we have built a model of the software that does not do what we correctly have understood the user to require.

For example, several decades ago, the Navy contracted with a software firm to build a software system to detect the movements of missiles. The software worked just fine in detecting missiles but was thrown off by the presence of the moon in certain cases.

There have been many reports of software unreliability in commercial software installations as well. One of the more tragic cases is that of the x-ray machine Therac-25, which killed several patients a few years ago.

A classic discussion of software reliability in military applications can be found in Alan Borning, "Computer System Reliability and Nuclear War," *Communications of the ACM*, Volume 30, Number 2 (February 1987):112–131. Almost every textbook on computer ethics has case studies on computer reliability in commercial applications. A good place to start is Sara Baase, *A Gift of Fire, Second Edition* (Upper Saddle River, NJ: Prentice Hall, 2002), Chapter 4.

EXERCISE 6.5

1. Write the outputs of the following code segments:

a.

```
for (int i = 1; i <= 3; i++)
    for (int j = 1; j <= 3; j++)
        System.out.print(j + " ");
```

b.

```
for (int i = 1; i <= 3; i++){
    for (int j = 1; j <= 3; j++)
        System.out.print(j + " ");
    System.out.println("");
}
```

2. Write code segments that solve the following problems:

a. Output the numbers 1 to 25 in consecutive order, using five rows of five numbers each.

b. Output five rows of five numbers. Each number is the sum of its row position and column position. The position of the first number is (1, 1).

6.6 Testing Loops

The presence of looping statements in a program increases the challenge of designing good test data. Frequently, loops do not iterate some fixed number of times, but instead iterate zero, one, or more than one time depending on a program's inputs. When designing test data, we want to cover all three possibilities. To illustrate, we develop test data for the print divisors program presented in Chapter 4. First, let's look at the code again:

```
// Display the proper divisors of a number
System.out.print("Enter a positive integer: ");
int n = reader.nextInt();
int limit = n / 2;
for (int d = 2; d <= limit; d++){
    if (n % d == 0)
        System.out.print (d + " ");
}
```

By analyzing the code, we conclude that if n equals 0, 1, 2, or 3, the limit is less than 2, and the loop is never entered. If n equals 4 or 5, the loop is entered once. If n is greater than 5, the loop is entered multiple times. All this suggests the test data shown in Table 6-10. After testing the program with this data, we feel reasonably confident that it works correctly.

TABLE 6-10
Test data for the count divisors program

TYPE OF TEST	DATA USED
No iterations	0, 1, 2, and 3
One iteration	4 and 5
Multiple iterations for a number with divisors	24
Multiple iterations for a number without divisors	29

Combinatorial Explosion

The surprisingly large amount of testing needed to validate even a small program suggests an interesting question. Suppose a program is composed of three parts and that it takes five tests to verify each part independently. Then how many tests does it take to verify the program as a whole? In the unlikely event that the three parts are independent of each other and utilize the same five sets of test data, then five tests suffice. However, it is far more likely that the behavior of each part affects the other two and also that the parts have differing test requirements. Then all possible combinations of tests should be tried, that is 5*5*5 or 125. We call this multiplicative growth in test cases a combinatorial explosion, and it pretty much guarantees the impossibility of exhaustively testing large complex programs; however, programmers still must do their best to test their programs intelligently and well.

Robust Programs

So far, we have focused on showing that a program that uses loops produces correct results when provided with valid inputs, but, surprisingly, that is not good enough. As we learned when we were testing programs with `if` statements earlier in this chapter, we also should consider how a program behaves when confronted with invalid data. After all, users frequently make mistakes or do not fully understand a program's data entry requirements. As we have learned, a program that tolerates errors in user inputs and recovers gracefully is robust. The best and easiest way to write robust programs is to check user inputs immediately on entry and reject those that are invalid. We illustrate this technique in the next case study. At this stage, there are limits to how thoroughly we can check inputs, so in the case study, we merely make sure that inputs fall in the range specified by the prompt.

EXERCISE 6.6

1. Describe appropriate test data for the following code segments:

a.
```
while (number > 0)
   <action>
```

b.
```
while (0 < number && 100 > number)
   <action>
```

EXERCISE 6.6 Continued

2. Design test data for Project 4-6 (in Chapter 4).

3. What would be reasonable test data for a loop that does not execute a fixed number of times?

4. What is a robust program? Give an example.

Case Study 2: Fibonacci Numbers

There is a famous sequence of numbers that occurs frequently in nature. In 1202, the Italian mathematician Leonardo Fibonacci presented the following problem concerning the breeding of rabbits. He assumed somewhat unrealistically that

1. Each pair of rabbits in a population produces a new pair of rabbits each month.

2. Rabbits become fertile one month after birth.

3. Rabbits do not die.

He then considered how rapidly the rabbit population would grow on a monthly basis when starting with a single pair of newborn rabbits.

To answer the question, we proceed one month at a time:

- At the beginning of month 1, there is one pair of rabbits (total = 1 pair).

- At the beginning of month 2, our initial pair of rabbits, A, will have just reached sexual maturity, so there will be no offspring (total = 1 pair).

- At the beginning of month 3, pair A will have given birth to pair B (total = 2 pair).

- At the beginning of month 4, pair A will have given birth to pair C and pair B will be sexually mature (total = 3 pair).

- At the beginning of month 5, pairs A and B will have given birth to pairs D and E, while pair C will have reached sexual maturity (total = 5 pair).

- And so on.

If we continue in this way, we obtain the following sequence of numbers
1   1   2   3   5   8   13   21   34   55   89   144   233   ...

called the *Fibonacci numbers*. Notice that each number, after the first two, is the sum of its two predecessors. Referring back to the rabbits, see if you can demonstrate why this should be the case. Although the sequence of numbers is easy to construct, there is no known formula for calculating the nth Fibonacci number, which gives rise to the following program request.

Request

Write a program that can compute the nth Fibonacci number on demand, where n is a positive integer.

Analysis, Design, and Implementation

The user input should be a positive integer or -1 to quit. Other integer inputs are rejected. The proposed user interface is shown in Figure 6-5.

FIGURE 6-5
Interface for the Fibonacci program

```
Enter a positive integer or -1 to quit: 8
Fibonacci of 8 is 21
```

Here is the code:

```java
// Case Study 6.2: Display the nth Fibonacci number

import java.util.Scanner;

public class Fibonacci {

    public static void main (String [] args) {
        Scanner reader = new Scanner(System.in);
        int n;           // The number entered by the user
        int fib;         // The nth Fibonacci number
        int a,b,count;   // Variables that facilitate the computation

        while (true){

            // Ask the user for the next input
            System.out.print("Enter a positive integer or -1 to quit: ");
            n = reader.nextInt();
            if (n == -1) break;
            else if (n >= 1){

                // Calculate the nth Fibonacci number
                fib = 1;              // Takes care of case n = 1 or 2
                a = 1;
                b = 1;
                count = 3;
                while (count <= n){  // Takes care of case n >= 3
                    fib = a + b;       // Point p. Referred to later.
                    a = b;
                    b = fib;
                    count = count + 1;
                }

                // Print the nth Fibonacci number
                System.out.println ("Fibonacci of " + n + " is " + fib);
            } // end else
        }     // end while
    }         // end main
}
```

Loop Analysis

The loop in the Fibonacci program is not obvious at first glance, so to clarify what is happening, we construct Table 6-11. This table traces the changes to key variables on each pass through the loop.

TABLE 6-11
Changes to Key Variables on Each Pass Through the Loop

COUNT AT POINT P	A AT POINT P	B AT POINT P	FIBONACCI NUMBER AT POINT P
3	1	1	2
4	1	2	3
5	2	3	5
6	3	5	8
...	...	...	...
n	$(n-2)$th Fibonacci number	$(n-1)$th Fibonacci number	nth Fibonacci number

Test Data

We complete the case study by developing suitable test data:

■ To make sure the program is robust, we try the following sequence of inputs for n: -3, 0, 1, 2, –1.

■ To make sure the computation is correct when the second inner loop is not entered, we try n equal to 1 and 2.

■ To make sure the computation is correct when the second inner loop is entered one or more times, we let n equal 3 and 6.

Because all these tests were successful, we can hardly be blamed for thinking that our program works perfectly; however, it contains a completely unexpected problem. When n equals 80, the program returns the value –285,007,387. The problem is due to **arithmetic overflow**. In Java and most programming languages, integers have a limited range (see Chapter 3) and exceeding that range leads to strange results. Adding one to the most positive integer in the range yields the most negative integer, whereas subtracting one from the most negative yields the most positive. Welcome to the strange world of computer arithmetic, where bizarre behavior is always lurking to trip the unwary. To detect the problem automatically, we could include extra lines of code that test for an unexpected switch to a negative value. A somewhat similar problem cost the French space program half a billion dollars and a great deal of embarrassment when a computer guided rocket and its payload exploded shortly after takeoff.

6.7 Loop Verification

Loop verification is the process of guaranteeing that a loop performs its intended task, independently of testing. Some work has been done on constructing formal proofs to determine if loops are "correct." We now examine a modified version of loop verification; a complete treatment of the issue will be the topic of subsequent course work.

The `assert` Statement

Java includes an `assert` statement that allows the programmer to evaluate a Boolean expression and halt the program with an error message if the expression's value is false. If its value is true, the program continues execution. Here are some examples of `assert` statements:

```
assert x != 0;              // Halt if x is 0
assert x >= 0 && x <= MAX;  // Halt if x is not in this range
assert x % 2 == 0;          // Halt if x is not even
```

The general form is `assert <Boolean expression>`. Note that parentheses are omitted. At run time, if the Boolean expression evaluates to false, the JVM will halt with an error message. To enable this mechanism when running the program, use the command line

```
java -enableassertions AJavaProgram
```

Figure 6-6 shows the output of the following short program that includes an `assert` statement:

```
// Example 6.1: Assert that x != 0

public class TestAssert{

   public static void main(String[] args){
      int x = 0;
      assert x != 0;
   }
}
```

FIGURE 6-6
The failure of an `assert` statement

Running a program with `assert` enabled will slow it down, but we do this only during development and testing.

Assertions with Loops

Input assertions state what can be expected to be true before a loop is entered. *Output assertions* state what can be expected to be true when the loop is exited.

To illustrate input and output assertions, we consider the mathematical problem of summing the proper divisors of a positive integer. For example, suppose we have the integers shown in Table 6-12.

TABLE 6-12
The sums of the proper divisors of some integers

INTEGER	PROPER DIVISORS	SUM
6	1, 2, 3	6
9	1, 3	4
12	1, 2, 3, 4, 6	16

The following loop performs this task:

```
divisorSum = 0;
for (trialDivisor = 1; trialDivisor <= num / 2; ++trialDivisor)
    if (num % trialDivisor == 0)
        divisorSum = divisorSum + trialDivisor;
```

Input assertions for this loop are

```
1. num is a positive integer.
2. divisorSum == 0.
```

An output assertion is

```
divisorSum is the sum of all proper divisors of num.
```

When these are placed with the previous code, we have

```
divisorSum = 0;
assert num > 0 && divisorSum == 0;
for (trialDivisor = 1; trialDivisor <= num / 2; ++trialDivisor)
    if (num % trialDivisor == 0)
        divisorSum = divisorSum + trialDivisor;
// Output assertion: divisorSum is the sum of all proper divisors of num.
```

Note that we pass the Boolean expression to the `assert` mechanism of Java so that the JVM actually establishes the truth of that assertion. However, we cannot do this with the output assertion because the sum of all the proper divisors of a number is just what we are computing in the loop!

Invariant and Variant Assertions

A *loop invariant* is an assertion that expresses a relationship between variables that remains constant throughout all iterations of the loop. In other words, it is a statement that is true both before the loop is entered and after each pass through the loop. An invariant assertion for the preceding code segment could be

```
divisorSum is the sum of proper divisors of num that are less than or equal
    to trialDivisor.
```

A *loop variant* is an assertion whose truth changes between the first and final execution of the loop. The loop variant expression should be stated in such a way that it guarantees the loop is exited. Thus, it contains some statement about the loop variable being incremented (or decremented) during execution of the loop. In the preceding code, we could have

```
trialDivisor is incremented by 1 each time through the loop.
It eventually exceeds the value num / 2, at which point the loop is exited.
```

Variant and invariant assertions usually occur in pairs.

We now use four kinds of assertions—input, output, variant, and invariant—to produce the formally verified loop that follows:

```
divisorSum = 0;

// 1. num is a positive integer.                  (input assertion)
// 2. divisorSum == 0.

assert num > 0 && divisorsum == 0;

for (trialDivisor = 1; trialDivisor <= num / 2; ++trialDivisor)

// trialDivisor is incremented by 1 each time     (variant assertion)
// through the loop. It eventually exceeds the
// value (num / 2), at which point the loop is exited.

    if (num % trialDivisor == 0)
        divisorsum = divisorSum + trialDivisor;

// divisorSum is the sum of proper divisors of     (invariant assertion)
// num that are less than or equal to trialDivisor.

// divisorSum is the sum of                        (output assertion)
// all proper divisors of num.
```

In general, code that is presented in this text does not include formal verification of the loops. This issue is similar to that of robustness. In an introductory course, a decision must be made on the trade-off between learning new concepts and writing robust programs with formal verification of loops. We encourage the practice, but space and time considerations make it inconvenient to include such documentation at this level. We close this discussion with another example illustrating loop verification.

Consider the problem of finding the greatest common divisor (gcd) of two positive integers. Table 6-13 shows some sample inputs and outputs for this problem.

TABLE 6-13
Several examples of the greatest common divisor (GCD) of two numbers

NUM1	NUM2	GCD(NUM 1, NUM2)
8	12	4
20	10	10
15	32	1
70	40	10

A segment of code to produce the gcd of two positive integers after they have been ordered as small, large is

```java
int trialGcd = small;
boolean gcdFound = false;
while (! gcdFound)
   if ((large % trialGcd == 0) && (small % trialGcd == 0)){
      gcd = trialGcd;
      gcdFound = true;
   }
   else
      trialGcd = trialGcd - 1;
```

Using assertions as previously indicated, this code would appear as

```java
int trialGcd = small;
boolean gcdFound = false;

//      1. small <= large
//      2. trialGcd (small) is the first candidate for gcd
//      3. gcdFound is false

assert small <= large && small == trialGcd && ! gcdFound;

while (! gcdFound)

// trialGcd assumes integer values ranging from small
// to 1. It is decremented by 1 each time through the
// loop. When trialGcd divides both small and large,
// the loop is exited. Exit is guaranteed since 1
// divides both small and large.
```

```
if ((large % trialGcd == 0) && (small % trialGcd == 0)){

// When trialGcd divides both large and small,
// then gcd is assigned that value.

        assert large % trialGcd == 0 && small % trialGcd == 0;

        gcd = trialGcd;
        gcdFound = true;
    }
    else
        trialGcd = trialGcd - 1;

// Output assertion: gcd is the greatest common divisor of small and large.
```

EXERCISE 6.7

1. Write appropriate input assertions and output assertions for each of the following loops.

a.
```
score = reader.nextInt();
while (score != -999){
    numScores = numScores + 1;
    sum = sum + score;
    System.out.print("Enter a score; -999 to quit: ");
    score = reader.nextInt();
}
```
b.
```
count = 0;
power2 = 1;
while (power2 < 100){
    System.out.println(power2);
    power2 = power2 * 2;
    count = count + 1;
}
```

2. Write appropriate loop invariant and loop variant assertions for each of the loops in Question 1 above.

EXERCISE 6.7 Continued

3. Consider the following loop. The user enters a number, guess, and the computer then displays a message indicating whether the guess is correct, too high, or too low. Add appropriate input assertions, output assertions, loop invariant assertions, and loop variant assertions to the following code.

```
correct = false;
count = 0;
while ((count < MAX_TRIES) && (! correct)){
    count = count + 1;
    System.out.print("Enter choice number " + count + ": ");
    guess = reader.nextInt();
    if (guess == choice)
    {
        correct = true;
        System.out.println("Congratulations!");
    }
    else if (guess < choice)
        System.out.println("Your guess is too low");
    else
        System.out.println("Your guess is too high");
}
```

6.8 Graphics and GUIs: Timers and Animations

The shapes, text, and images that we have displayed in graphics applications thus far have been more or less passive objects. The user can move them around a window with a mouse, but none of them know how to move on their own. Now it is time to make these graphics objects active. In this section, we explore the use of timers to construct simple animations.

Extra Challenge

This Graphics and GUIs section gives you the opportunity to explore concepts and programming techniques required to develop modern graphics applications and graphical user interfaces. This material is not required in order to proceed with the other chapters of the book.

The Basic Principles of Animation

As described in Chapter 1, our perception of movement in a motion picture is based on a rapid display of successive frames. In each frame, an object is shown at a different position, but if we are shown 24 frames per second, these changes of position appear as the continuous motion of the object itself.

We already know how to change the position of a graphical object and repaint a panel, so the basic tools for displaying the same object in multiple frames are already available. The speed with which an object appears to change its position depends on the distance it travels between frames and on the number of frames displayed per unit of time. Faster objects can travel a greater distance between frames than slower ones. The realistic depiction of motion also involves many other factors, such as rates of acceleration, the resistance of friction, and some qualities of the objects themselves, such as the "bounciness" of a ball. In addition, computer video artists must worry about such phenomena as the "flicker" caused by the speed of the display medium when painting large, complex images that must appear to move rapidly. In the examples that follow, we ignore most of these details and focus on the simple display of constant motion in two dimensions.

Direction and Velocity of Moving Objects

A moving object has a velocity, which is the distance (in pixels) traveled in a given unit of time, and a direction. An object's direction can be fixed as the angle of its path relative to a base direction. Let's assume that the base direction is due east (to the right of the panel), at 0 degrees. Moving clockwise, south (to the bottom) is 90 degrees, west (to the left) is 180 degrees, north (to the top) is 270 degrees, and 360 degrees returns the direction to due east, as shown in Figure 6-7.

FIGURE 6-7
Representing directions in two dimensions

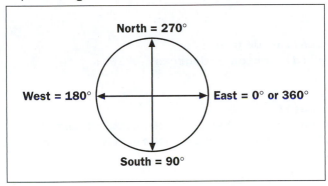

At any given time, we should be able to change a graphical object's velocity and direction. Using good object-oriented style, we ask a graphical object, where possible, to track its own velocity and direction. For example, we can add some instance variables and methods to the `circle` class of Chapter 5 to give it this functionality. Circles have an initial velocity of 0 and an initial direction of 0 degrees (due east). Table 6-14 lists these new methods.

TABLE 6-14
New methods for the circle class

NEW CIRCLE METHOD	WHAT IT DOES
void move()	Changes the position of the circle using its current velocity and direction.
void setDirection(int degrees)	Sets the direction of the circle to the given direction in degrees (the default is 0 degrees for due east).
void setVelocity(int v)	Sets the velocity of the circle to the given velocity (the default is 0 pixels).
void turn(int degrees)	Adds the given amount of degrees to the circle's current direction. If `degrees` is positive, the direction rotates clockwise. If `degrees` is negative, the direction rotates counterclockwise.

The critical new method for movable objects is `move()`. This method moves an object a given distance in a given direction. To implement this method, we must calculate the distances to move in the x and y directions based on the object's current position, its velocity, and its direction. According to basic trigonometry, the x distance is equal to the velocity multiplied by the cosine of the direction angle in radians. The y distance is equal to the velocity multiplied by the sine of the direction angle in radians. We use the methods `Math.radians`, `Math.cos`, and `Math.sin` to compute these values and then cast the results to integers. Here is the code for the new methods:

```java
public void setVelocity(int v){
    velocity = v;
}

public void setDirection(int degrees){
    direction = degrees % 360;
}

public void turn(int degrees){
    direction = (direction + degrees) % 360;
}

public void move(){
    move((int)(velocity * Math.cos(Math.toRadians(direction))),
        (int)(velocity * Math.sin(Math.toRadians(direction))));
}
```

Note that the methods `setDirection` and `turn` use the `%` operator to wrap the direction around if it's greater than 360 degrees (for example, `365 % 360` is the same direction as 5).

Moving a Circle with the Mouse

Our next example program illustrates the use of our new Circle methods. The program displays a filled circle at the center of the panel. When the user presses the mouse, the circle moves 50 pixels in its current direction and then turns 45 degrees. Repeated mouse presses (or "clicks") cause the circle to move in a circular pattern and return to its original position. Here is the code for the panel class:

```java
// Example 6.2: Moves the circle 50 pixels and
// turns it 45 degrees in response to a mouse press

import javax.swing.*;
import java.awt.*;
import java.awt.event.*;

public class ColorPanel extends JPanel{

    private Circle circle;
```

```java
    public ColorPanel(Color backColor, int width, int height){
        setBackground(backColor);
        setPreferredSize(new Dimension(width, height));
        // Circle centered in the panel with radius 25
        circle = new Circle(width / 2, height / 2, 25, Color.red);
        circle.setFilled(true);
        // Move 50 pixels per mouse press
        circle.setVelocity(50);
        addMouseListener(new MoveListener());
    }

    public void paintComponent(Graphics g){
        super.paintComponent(g);
        circle.draw(g);
    }

    private class MoveListener extends MouseAdapter{

        public void mousePressed(MouseEvent e){
            circle.move();
            circle.turn(45);    // Turn 45 degrees
            repaint();
        }
    }
}
```

Timers

A basic algorithm for animating a graphical object can be expressed as follows:

```
Set the initial position of the shape
At regular intervals
   Move the object
   Repaint the panel
```

The first step of the algorithm is accomplished when the panel is instantiated. When the window is displayed, the object is painted in its initial position. The last two steps are accomplished by sending the standard messages to move the object and repaint the panel. But how can this be done automatically at regular intervals? A simple loop will not work. Because execution speeds vary from computer to computer, a simple loop might move the same object faster on one computer than on another.

Java provides a special type of object called a timer to schedule events at regular intervals. When a timer is instantiated, it is given an interval in milliseconds and a listener object similar to those discussed in Chapter 5. When the timer is sent the start message, its clock starts ticking. When each interval of time passes, the listener's actionPerformed method is triggered. In the case of our animation, this method runs the operations to move the object and repaint the panel. Because the timer uses the computer's clock to measure the intervals, they will not vary with the execution speed of the computer.

The timer for animations is an instance of the class `Timer`, which is included in the package `javax.swing`. Assuming that we have the listener class `MoveListener` at our disposal, we can declare, instantiate, and start a timer as follows:

```
javax.swing.Timer projectortimer;
timer  = new javax.swing.Timer(5, new MoveListener());
timer.start();
```

Note that we prefix the `Timer` class with its package name, so as to distinguish this `Timer` from a different class with the same name in the package `java.util`. This practice will allow us eventually to use resources from `java.util` without name conflicts. Our timer is started with an interval of 5 milliseconds. The timer ticks for 5 milliseconds and then fires an event. The `MoveListener` detects this event and runs its `actionPerformed` method. The timer automatically repeats this process until it is stopped or the program quits.

The definition of the class `MoveListener`, like the listener classes for mouse events in Chapter 5, is nested in the panel class. This placement allows the listener's `actionPerformed` method to access the data within the panel. Unlike the earlier listener classes, however, `MoveListener` does not extend an adapter class, but instead implements the `ActionListener` interface. For now, we won't worry about this difference, but just assume that our class includes an `actionPerformed` method. Here is a template for this class:

```
private class MoveListener implements ActionListener{

    public void actionPerformed(ActionEvent e){
        // Code for moving objects goes here
        repaint();
    }
}
```

Like the code for other listener classes, this code requires you to import the package `javax.awt.event`.

Moving a Circle with a Timer

Our next example program automates the movement of the circle in the previous program by using a timer. The `ColorPanel` class still has the same basic structure, but the `MoveListener` class now implements the `ActionListener` interface and packages the code to move the circle in an `actionPerformed` method. After the circle is instantiated, we create a timer with an interval of 125 milliseconds (1/8 of a second). The timer is also passed a new `MoveListener` and then started up. The rest, as they say, is automatic. Here is the code for the modified `ColorPanel` class:

```
// Example 6.3: Moves the circle 50 pixels and
// turns it 45 degrees in response to timer events

import javax.swing.*;
import java.awt.*;
import java.awt.event.*;

public class ColorPanel extends JPanel{
```

```java
    private Circle circle;
    private javax.swing.Timer timer;

    public ColorPanel(Color backColor, int width, int height){
        setBackground(backColor);
        setPreferredSize(new Dimension(width, height));
        // Circle centered in the panel with radius 25
        circle = new Circle(width / 2, height / 2, 25, Color.red);
        circle.setFilled(true);:
        // Move 50 pixels per timer event
        circle.setVelocity(50);
        // Fire timer events every 1/8 second
        timer = new javax.swing.Timer(125, new MoveListener());
        timer.start();
    }

    public void paintComponent(Graphics g){
        super.paintComponent(g);
        circle.draw(g);
    }

    private class MoveListener implements ActionListener{

        public void actionPerformed(ActionEvent e){
            circle.move();
            circle.turn(45);    // Turn 45 degrees
            repaint();
        }
    }
}
```

A Final Example: A Bouncing Circle

Let's incorporate the ideas examined thus far into a program that bounces a circle back and forth horizontally in its panel. At program startup, the circle's left side is flush with the left border of the panel. It moves continuously to the right, until its right side is flush with the panel's right border. At that point, the circle reverses direction and returns to the left border, where it reverses direction again, and so on, indefinitely.

Clearly, the action to move the circle must check to see if the circle has hit a panel boundary and then change the circle's direction if necessary. The circle's default direction is due east (0 degrees). Because the circle is already near the left boundary of the panel at startup, we set its initial direction to due west (180 degrees) so that it hits the left boundary first. Here is the code for the ColorPanel class:

```java
// Example 6.4: A filled circle moves back and forth
// across the panel, appearing to bounce off its edges

import javax.swing.*;
import java.awt.*;
import java.awt.event.*;

public class ColorPanel extends JPanel{
```

```java
    private Circle circle;
    private javax.swing.Timer timer;

    public ColorPanel(Color backColor, int width, int height){
        setBackground(backColor);
        setPreferredSize(new Dimension(width, height));
        // Circle with center point (25, height / 2) and radius 25
        circle = new Circle(25, height / 2, 25, Color.red);
        circle.setFilled(true);:
        // Aim due west to hit left boundary first
        circle.setDirection(180);
        // Move 5 pixels per unit of time
        circle.setVelocity(5);
        // Move every 5 milliseconds
        timer = new javax.swing.Timer(5, new MoveListener());
        timer.start();
    }

    public void paintComponent(Graphics g){
        super.paintComponent(g);
        circle.draw(g);
    }

    private class MoveListener implements ActionListener{

        public void actionPerformed(ActionEvent e){
            int x = circle.getX();
            int radius = circle.getRadius();
            int width = getWidth();
            // Check for boundaries and reverse direction
            // if necessary
            if (x - radius <= 0 || x + radius >= width)
                circle.turn(180);
            circle.move();
            repaint();
        }
    }
}
```

Other Timer Methods

Once it is started, a timer fires events until it is stopped or the program quits. The `Timer` class includes methods for stopping a timer, restarting it, changing its time interval, and so forth. Some of the more commonly used methods are listed in Table 6-15.

TABLE 6-15
Some commonly used `Timer` methods

TIMER METHOD	WHAT IT DOES
`boolean isRunning()`	Returns true if the timer is firing events or false otherwise
`void restart()`	Restarts a timer, causing it to fire the first event after its initial delay
`void setDelay(int delay)`	Sets the timer's delay to the number of milliseconds between events
`void setInitialDelay(int delay)`	Sets the timer's initial delay, which by default is its between-event delay
`void stop()`	Stops the timer, causing it to cease firing events

EXERCISE 6.8

1. Describe how to set up a timer and explain what it does.

2. Describe the factors that affect our perception of the movement of a graphical object.

3. What causes flicker? How can flicker be eliminated?

4. How do the direction and velocity of an object determine where it will be placed after a given unit of time?

Design, Testing, and Debugging Hints

■ Most errors involving selection statements and loops are not syntax errors caught at compile time. Thus, you will detect these errors only after running the program, and perhaps then only with extensive testing.

■ The presence or absence of braces can seriously affect the logic of a selection statement or loop. For example, the following selection statements have a similar look but a very different logic:

```
if (x > 0){
    y = x;
    z = 1 / x;
}
```

```
if (x > 0)
   y = x;
   z = 1 / x;
```

- The first selection statement above guards against division by 0; the second statement only guards against assigning x to y. The following pair of code segments shows a similar problem with a loop:

```
while (x > 0){
   y = x;
   x = x - 1;
}

while (x > 0)
   y = x;
   x = x - 1;
```

- The first loop above terminates because the value of x decreases within the body of the loop; the second loop is infinite because the value of x decreases below the body of the loop.

- When testing programs that use `if` or `if-else` statements, be sure to use test data that force the program to exercise all of the logical branches.

- When testing a program that uses `if` statements, it helps to formulate equivalence classes, boundary conditions, and extreme conditions.

- Use an `if-else` statement rather than two `if` statements when the alternative courses of action are mutually exclusive.

- When testing a loop, be sure to use limit values as well as typical values. For example, if a loop should terminate when the control variable equals 0, run it with the values 0, –1, and 1.

- Be sure to check entry conditions and exit conditions for each loop.

- For a loop with errors, use debugging output statements to verify the values of the control variable on each pass through the loop. Check this value before the loop is initially entered, after each update, and after the loop is exited.

SUMMARY

In this chapter, you learned:

- A complex Boolean expression contains one or more Boolean expressions and the logical operators `&&` (AND), `||` (OR), and `!` (NOT).

- A truth table can determine the value of any complex Boolean expression.

- Java uses short-circuit evaluation of complex Boolean expressions. The evaluation of the operands of `||` stops at the first true value, whereas the evaluation of the operands of `&&` stops at the first false value.

- Nested `if` statements are another way of expressing complex conditions. A nested `if` statement can be translated to an equivalent `if` statement that uses logical operators.

- An extended or multiway `if` statement expresses a choice among several mutually exclusive alternatives.

- Loops can be nested in other loops.

- Equivalence classes, boundary conditions, and extreme conditions are important features used in tests of control structures involving complex conditions.

- Loops can be verified to be correct by using assertions, loop variants, and loop invariants.

VOCABULARY *Review*

Define the following terms:

Arithmetic overflow	Extreme condition	Nested loop
Boundary condition	Input assertion	Output assertion
Combinatorial explosion	Logical operator	Quality assurance
Complete code coverage	Loop invariant	Robust
Equivalence class	Loop variant	Truth table
Extended if statement	Nested if statement	

REVIEW *Questions*

WRITTEN QUESTIONS

Write a brief answer to each of the following questions.

1. List the three logical operators.

2. Construct a truth table for the expression P OR NOT Q.

3. Suppose P is true and Q is false. What is the value of the expression P AND NOT Q?

4. Write an `if` statement that displays whether or not a given number is between a lower bound `min` and an upper bound `max`, inclusive. Use a logical operator in the condition.

5. Rewrite the `if` statement in Question 4 to use a nested `if` statement.

6. Write a nested loop that displays a 10-by-10 square of asterisks.

7. Give an example of an assertion and show how it can be checked with Java's assert statement.

8. Explain the role that variant and invariant assertions play in showing that a loop is correct.

PROJECTS

In keeping with the spirit of this chapter, each program should be robust and should validate the input data. You should try also to formulate the appropriate equivalence classes, boundary conditions, and extreme conditions and use them in testing the programs.

PROJECT 6-1

In a game of guessing numbers, one person says, "I'm thinking of a number between 1 and 100." The other person guesses "50." The first person replies, "No, the number is less." The second person then guesses "25," and so on, until she guesses correctly. Write a program that plays this game. The computer knows the number (a random number between 1 and 100) and the user is the guesser. At the end of the game, the computer displays the number of guesses required by the user to guess the number correctly.

PROJECT 6-2

Rewrite the program of Project 6-1 so that the user knows the number and the computer must guess it.

PROJECT 6-3

Write a program that expects a numeric grade as input and outputs the corresponding letter grade. The program uses the following grading scale:

NUMERIC RANGE	LETTER GRADE
96–100	A+
92–95	A
90–91	A–
86–89	B+
82–85	B
80–81	B–
76–79	C+
72–75	C
70–71	C–
66–69	D+
62–65	D
60–61	D–
0–59	F

PROJECT 6-4

Write a Java method `getLetterGrade` that is based on the grading scale of Project 6-3. This method expects the numeric grade as a parameter and returns a string representing the letter grade. The method header should have the prefix static so it can be called from main. Use this method in a program that inputs a list of grades (ending with –1) and outputs the class average, the class minimum, and the class maximum as letter grades.

PROJECT 6-5

The Euclidean algorithm can be used to find the greatest common divisor (gcd) of two positive integers (n1, n2). You can use this algorithm in the following manner:
  A. Compute the remainder of dividing the larger number by the smaller number.
  B. Replace the larger number with the smaller number and the smaller number with the remainder.
  C. Repeat this process until the smaller number is zero:

The larger number at this point is the gcd of n1 and n2.

Write a program that lets the user enter two integers and then prints each step in the process of using the Euclidean algorithm to find their gcd.

PROJECT 6-6

Review the case study in Chapter 4 in which the Lucky Sevens gambling game program was created. Remove the code that deals with the maximum amount held. Then modify the program so that it runs the simulation 100 times and prints the average number of rolls. (Hint: Put the while loop inside a for statement that loops 100 times. Accumulate the total count and at the end divide by 100.)

PROJECT 6-7

Write a program to print the perimeter and area of rectangles using all combinations of heights and widths running from 1 foot to 10 feet in increments of 1 foot. Print the output in headed, formatted columns.

PROJECT 6-8

Modify the example program of Section 6.8 so that the circle stops moving when the user clicks the mouse. When the user clicks the mouse again, the circle should resume moving. (*Hint:* Define a mouse listener class as shown in Chapter 5.)

PROJECT 6-9

Add another circle to the program of Project 6-8. The second circle should be placed at the right margin of the panel at program startup, exactly opposite the first circle. Both circles should reverse direction when they hit a boundary.

PROJECT 6-10

Use your knowledge of physics to make an interesting change to the program of Project 6-9. Set the initial directions of the two circles to angles other than horizontal (say, 120 degrees for one and 30 degrees for the other). When a circle hits a boundary, it should rebound at the appropriate angle. (Hint: The angle of reflection should equal the angle of incidence.)

CRITICAL*Thinking*

Read the sections of the ACM Code of Ethics that deal with designing and testing reliable computer systems. Prepare a written report to present to your class on the way in which the ACM Code deals with this issue.

IMPROVING THE USER INTERFACE

We do not judge a book by its cover because we are interested in its contents, not its appearance. However, we do judge a software product by its user interface because we have no other way to access its functionality. In this chapter, we explore several ways to improve a program's user interface. First, we present some standard techniques for enhancing terminal-based interfaces, including query-driven input/output (I/O) and menu-driven I/O. This chapter then shows how to format numerical data and examines the output of columns of strings and numbers. The handling of errors in the format of input data is also discussed. Finally, we include a discussion of procedural decomposition and top-down development as methods of organizing a complex task.

7.1 A Thermometer Class

Several examples in this chapter involve converting temperatures between Fahrenheit and Celsius. To support these conversions we first introduce a `Thermometer` class. This class stores the temperature internally in Celsius; however, the temperature can be set and retrieved in either Fahrenheit or Celsius. Here is the code:

```java
public class Thermometer {

    private double degreesCelsius;

    public void setCelsius(double degrees){
        degreesCelsius = degrees;
    }

    public void setFahrenheit(double degrees){
```

```java
public void setFahrenheit(double degrees){
   degreesCelsius = (degrees - 32.0) * 5.0 / 9.0;
}

public double getCelsius(){
   return degreesCelsius;
}

public double getFahrenheit(){
   return degreesCelsius * 9.0 / 5.0 + 32.0;
}
}
```

7.2 Repeating Sets of Inputs

In Chapter 4, we introduced two techniques for handling repeating sets of inputs. We called these count-controlled and sentinel-controlled input. We now present a third technique that we call *query-controlled input*. Before each set of inputs after the first, the program asks the user if there are more inputs. Figure 7-1 shows an example of query-controlled input.

FIGURE 7-1
Interface for a query controlled temperature conversion program

```
Enter degrees Fahrenheit: 32
The equivalent in Celsius is 0.0

Do it again (y/n)? y

Enter degrees Fahrenheit: 212
The equivalent in Celsius is 100.0

Do it again (y/n)?
```

The program is implemented by means of two classes—a class to handle the user interface and the Thermometer class. Following is pseudocode for the interface class:

```
instantiate a thermometer
String doItAgain = "y"
while (doItAgain equals "y" or "Y"){
   read degrees Fahrenheit and set the thermometer
   ask the thermometer for the degrees in Celsius and display
   read doItAgain                    //The user responds with y or n
}
```

The key to this pseudocode is the String variable doItAgain. This variable controls how many times the loop repeats. Initially, the variable equals "y". As soon as the user enters a string other than "y" or "Y", the program terminates. Following is a complete listing of the user interface class:

```
/* Example 7.1: ConvertWithQuery.java
Repeatedly convert from Fahrenheit to Celsius until the user
signals the end.
*/

import java.util.Scanner;

public class ConvertWithQuery {

    public static void main(String [] args){
        Scanner reader = new Scanner(System.in);
        Thermometer thermo = new Thermometer();
        String doItAgain = "y";

        while (doItAgain.equals("y") || doItAgain.equals("Y")){
            System.out.print("\nEnter degrees Fahrenheit: ");
            thermo.setFahrenheit(reader.nextDouble());
            // Consume the trailing newline
            reader.nextLine();
            System.out.println("The equivalent in Celsius is " +
                            thermo.getCelsius());
            System.out.print("\nDo it again (y/n)? ");
            doItAgain = reader.nextLine();
        }
    }
}
```

Note that "Y" and "y" are not equal. Note also that the input of a `double` leaves behind a newline character in the input stream that must be consumed before the next query is read.

_E_XERCISE 7.2

1. Describe the structure of a query-controlled loop that processes repeated sets of inputs.

2. Browse into the String class in Sun's Java API documentation. Explain how the method toLowerCase() could be used to simplify the loop control condition of the query-driven loop in the example program.

7.3 A Menu-Driven Conversion Program

_M_enu-driven programs begin by displaying a list of options from which the user selects one. The program then prompts for additional inputs related to that option and performs the needed computations, after which it displays the menu again. Figure 7-2 shows how this idea can be used to extend the temperature conversion program.

FIGURE 7-2
Interface for a menu-driven version of the temperature conversion program

```
1) Convert from Fahrenheit to Celsius
2) Convert from Celsius to Fahrenheit
3) Quit
Enter your option: 1

Enter degrees Fahrenheit: 212
The equivalent in Celsius is 100

1) Convert from Fahrenheit to Celsius
2) Convert from Celsius to Fahrenheit
3) Quit
Enter your option: 2

Enter degrees Celsius: 0
The equivalent in Fahrenheit is 32

1) Convert from Fahrenheit to Celsius
2) Convert from Celsius to Fahrenheit
3) Quit
Enter your option: 3

Goodbye!
```

Here is a pseudocode design, followed by the program:

```
instantiate a thermometer
menuOption = 4
while (menuOption != 3){
 print menu
 read menuOption
 if (menuOption == 1){
    read fahrenheit and set the thermometer
    ask the thermometer to convert and print the results
 }
 else if (menuOption == 2){
    read celsius and set the thermometer
    ask the thermometer to convert and print the results
 }
 else if (menuOption == 3)
    print "Goodbye!"
 else
    print "Invalid option"
}
```

```java
/* Example 7.2: ConvertWithMenu.java
A menu-driven temperature conversion program that converts from
Fahrenheit to Celsius and vice versa.
*/

import java.util.Scanner;
```

```java
public class ConvertWithMenu {
    public static void main (String [] args) {
        Scanner reader = new Scanner(System.in);
        Thermometer thermo = new Thermometer();
        String menu;            //The multiline menu
        int menuOption;         //The user's menu selection

        //Build the menu string
        menu = "\n1) Convert from Fahrenheit to Celsius"
             + "\n2) Convert from Celsius to Fahrenheit"
             + "\n3) Quit"
             + "\nEnter your option: ";

        //Set up the menu loop
        menuOption = 4;
        while (menuOption != 3){

            //Display the menu and get the user's option
            System.out.print(menu);
            menuOption = reader.nextInt();
            System.out.println("");

            //Determine which menu option has been selected

            if (menuOption == 1){

                //Convert from Fahrenheit to Celsius
                System.out.print("Enter degrees Fahrenheit: ");
                thermo.setFahrenheit(reader.nextDouble());
                System.out.println("The equivalent in Celsius is " +
                                    thermo.getCelsius());

            }else if (menuOption == 2){

                //Convert from Celsius to Fahrenheit
                System.out.print("Enter degrees Celsius: ");
                thermo.setCelsius(reader.nextDouble());
                System.out.println("The equivalent in Fahrenheit is " +
                                    thermo.getFahrenheit());

            }else if (menuOption == 3)

                //User quits, sign off
                System.out.println("Goodbye!");

            else

                //Invalid option
                System.out.println("Invalid option");
        }
    }
}
```

EXERCISE 7.3

1. What role does a menu play in a program?

2. Describe the structure of a menu-driven command loop.

3. Write the code for a menu that gives the user options to specify the size of a pizza, various toppings (mushrooms, peppers, sausage, etc.), place the order, or return to the main menu.

7.4 Formatted Output with `printf` and `format`

The example programs thus far in this book have used the methods `print` and `println` to output data to the terminal. These methods are easy to use and work well in many applications. However, occasionally a program must format data, especially numbers, more carefully. In this section, we examine a couple of methods to accomplish that.

Using printf to Format Numbers

The precision of a floating-point number is the number of digits to the right of the decimal point supported by the programming language. Java supports the type `double` for numbers with many digits of precision. The methods `print` and `println` do not generally display all of these digits, but only enough to convey the necessary information about the number. Sometimes we get too many digits, and other times we get too few. For example, a whole number would be displayed with a single zero to the right of the decimal point, but in financial applications we would want to see dollars and cents displayed with two zeroes. For example, consider the following code segment and its output:

```
double dollars = 25;
double tax = dollars * 0.125;
System.out.println("Income: $" + dollars);
System.out.println("Tax owed: $" + tax);
```

Output:

```
Income: $25.0
Tax owed: $3.125
```

The amount of money on the first line has too few digits to the right of the decimal point, whereas the amount on the second line has too many.

Fortunately, Java 5.0 includes the method `printf` for formatting output. The following code segment modifies the previous one to show these capabilities for floating-point numbers:

```
double dollars = 25;
double tax = dollars * 0.125;
System.out.printf("Income: $%.2f%n", dollars);
System.out.printf("Tax owed: $%.2f%n", tax);
```

The output produced by this code segment is

```
Income: $25.00
Tax owed: $3.13
```

The parameters of the method `printf` consist of a *format string* and one or more data values, according to the following general form:

```
printf(<format string>, <expression-1>, …, <expression-n>)
```

The format string is a combination of literal string information and formatting information. The formatting information consists of one or more *format specifiers*. These codes begin with a '%' character and end with a letter that indicates the format type. In our example code segment, the format specifier `%.2f` says display a number in fixed-point format with exactly two digits to the right of the decimal point. The format specifier `%n` says display an end-of-line character. Table 7-1 lists some commonly used format types.

TABLE 7-1
Commonly used format types

CODE	FORMAT TYPE	EXAMPLE VALUE
d	Decimal integer	34
x	Hexadecimal integer	A6
o	Octal integer	47
f	Fixed floating-point	3.14
e	Exponential floating-point	1.67e+2
g	General floating-point (large numbers in exponential and small numbers in fixed-point)	3.14
s	String	Income:
n	Platform-independent end of line	

The symbol `%n` can be used to embed an end-of-line character in a format string. The symbol `%%` (consecutive percent symbols) produces the literal '%' character. Otherwise, when the compiler encounters a format specifier in a format string, it attempts to match that specifier to an expression following the string. The two must match in type and position. For example, the code

```
int idNum = 758;
double wage = 10.5;
printf("The wage for employee %d is $%.2f per hour.", idNum, wage);
```

matches the code `%d` to the value of the variable `idNum` and the code `%.2f` to the value of the variable `wage` to produce the output

```
The wage for employee 758 is $10.50 per hour.
```

Text Justification and Multiple Columns

Data-processing applications frequently display tables that contain columns of words and numbers. Unless these tables are formatted carefully, they are unreadable. To illustrate, Figure 7-3 shows a table of names, sales, and commissions, with and without formatting. Although both tables contain exactly the same data, only the formatted one is readable. The key feature of a formatted table is that each column has a designated width, and all the values in a column are justified in the same manner—either to the left, right, or center of the column. In the sales table, the names in the first column are left-justified, and the numbers in the other two columns are right-justified.

FIGURE 7-3
A table of sales figures shown with and without formatting

```
              NAME SALES COMMISSION
              Catherine 23415 2341.5
              Ken 321.5 32.15
              Martin 4384.75 438.48
              Tess 3595.74 359.57


      Version 1: Unreadable without formatting


        NAME                SALES     COMMISSION
        Catherine         23415.00       2341.50
        Ken                 321.50         32.15
        Martin             4384.75        438.48
        Tess               3595.74        359.57


        Version 2: Readable with formatting
```

The columns of text in Version 2 are produced by displaying pieces of text that are justified within fields. A field consists of a fixed number of columns within which the characters of a data value can be placed. A data value is left-justified when its display begins in the leftmost column of its field. The value is right-justified when its display ends in the rightmost column of its field. In either case, trailing or leading spaces are used to occupy columns that are not filled by the value. The column of names in Version 2 is left-justified, whereas the two columns of numbers are both right-justified.

The method `printf` includes several *format flags* that support the justification of text as well as other format styles. Some commonly used format flags are listed in Table 7-2

TABLE 7-2
Some commonly used format flags

FLAG	WHAT IT DOES	EXAMPLE VALUE
-	Left justification	34
,	Show decimal separators	20,345,000
0	Show leading zeroes	002.67
^	Convert letters to uppercase	1.56E+3

To output data in formatted columns, we establish the width of each field and then choose the appropriate format flags and format specifiers to use with `printf`. The width of a field that contains a `double` appears before the decimal point in the format specifier `f`. For example, the format specifer `%6.2f` says to use a precision of 2 digits and a field of 6 columns when displaying the floating-point number. One column is reserved for the decimal point and the number is right-justified by default. Thus, the number 4.5 is displayed with three leading spaces. The number 45000.5, on the other hand, exceeds the size of the field and is not right-justified. In general, when the width of the field is less than or equal to the string representation of the number, the string is left-justified. The same rule holds when the field is omitted before the decimal point. You should take care to ensure that the field width for your data is large enough to accommodate them.

The format specifier `%10s` says to use a field of 10 columns to display a string with right justification. However, for the leftmost column of a table, we would like the strings to be left-justified. This is accomplished by using the format flag '–' in the format specifier. Thus, `%-10s` says to use left justification when filling the columns for the string. Table 7-3 shows some examples of format strings and the output results.

TABLE 7-3
Some example format strings and their outputs

VALUES	FORMAT STRING	OUTPUT
34, 56.7	"%d%7.2f"	34 56.70
34, 56.7	"%4d%7.2f"	34 56.70
34, 56.7	"%-4d$%7.2f"	34 $ 56.70
34, 56.7	"%-4d$%.2f"	34 $56.70

Our next program example puts these ideas together to display a formatted table of data contained in two text files. The first file contains the last names of employees. The second file contains their salaries. The program assumes that each file contains the same number of data values and that the position of an employee's name in one file corresponds to the position of her salary in the other file. We also know that no name exceeds 15 letters and no salary exceeds 6 figures. To illustrate the required format for the output, we are given the following example:

```
NAME                        SALARY
Barker                    4,000.00
Lambert                  36,000.00
Osborne                 150,000.00
```

Note that the numbers contain commas in the standard places. Using this information, we present the following design of the program in pseudocode:

```
Open the file of names
Open the file of salaries
Output the formatted header of the table
While there are more names in the file of names
    Read a name from the file of names
    Read a salary from the file of salaries
    Output a formatted line containing the name and salary
```

To format the column of names, we left-justify the header and each name within 16 columns. To format the column of salaries, we right-justify the header within 12 columns and each salary is given 12 columns of width and two columns of precision. In addition, we use a format flag to place commas in the numbers. Here is the code for the program:

```java
// Example 7.3: Display a table of names and salaries

import java.io.*;
import java.util.Scanner;

public class DisplayTable{

    public static void main(String[] args) throws IOException{
        Scanner names = new Scanner(new File("names.txt"));
        Scanner salaries = new Scanner(new File("salaries.txt"));
        System.out.printf("%-16s%12s%n", "NAME", "SALARY");
        while (names.hasNext()){
            String name = names.nextLine();
            double salary = salaries.nextDouble();
            System.out.printf("%-16s%,12.2f%n", name, salary);
        }
    }
}
```

Formatting with String.format

The `String` method `format` can be used to build a formatted string. This method expects the same parameters as `printf` and returns a formatted string. For example, the call `String.format("Income: %,.2f", 2500000)` returns the string `"Income: 2,500,000.00"`.

EXERCISE 7.4

1. Write code segments to output the following formatted strings:

   a. " One space"

   b. " Two spaces"

   c. "Three spaces   "

   d. The value of int variable i, right-justified in a field of six columns

   e. The value of double variable d, right-justified in a field of 10 columns with a precision of 2

2. Write the values returned by the following expressions (include spaces within the strings where relevant):

   a. String.format("%-10s%,10.2f", "Price", 10000.50)

   b. String.format("%6d%7d", 45, 632)

   c. String.format("%5.2f", 34.543)

7.5 Handling Number Format Exceptions during Input

In Sections 4.4 and 6.1, we discussed the idea of programs that respond to errors, particularly when input data are invalid. If data are found to be invalid after input, the program can display an error message and prompt for the data again. Typical errors are input numbers that do not lie within a certain range. However, what happens if the user enters a number in an invalid format? For example, the user might type in the characters "12r8" when she really intends "1258". The datum in that case is not even a number, let alone an invalid one.

Clearly, the implementer of the input methods must detect and do something about number format errors. The `Scanner` methods `nextInt` and `nextDouble` do just that. When format errors are detected, these methods throw an exception that results in halting the program. The bad format is detected, but before the client code can react to the error. It's too late; the program is halted. This behavior may be acceptable during testing and debugging. However, crashing with an arcane error message is the last thing we would want the final release of a program to do.

Fortunately, there is a way to detect and respond to an exception under program control so that the exception does not halt the program. The programmer embeds the call to an input method in a `try-catch` statement. As its name implies, this statement consists of two parts, as shown in the following simplified form:

```
try{
  ,<statements that might throw exceptions>
}catch(Exception e){
    <code to recover from an exception if it's thrown>
}
```

The statements within the `try` clause are executed until one of them throws an exception. If that happens, an exception object is created and sent immediately to the `catch` clause. The code within the `catch` clause is then executed. Alternatively, if no statement throws an exception within the `try` clause, the `catch` clause is skipped. There are actually many specific types of exceptions that could be thrown; our example `try-catch` statement catches all of them. A more detailed discussion of Java exceptions appears in Appendix F.

The next program modifies the query-driven example of Section 7.2 to illustrate the recovery from number format errors. We add a nested input loop that cycles around a `try-catch` statement. The display of the prompt, the input statement, and a `break` statement occur within the `try` clause. If no exception occurs during input, the thermometer is set with the input number and the input loop is broken. Otherwise, when an exception occurs, the `catch` clause immediately displays an error message and consumes the trailing end of line, and the input loop continues. Here is the code:

```
/* Example 7.4: ConvertWithQuery.java
Repeatedly convert from Fahrenheit to Celsius until the user
signals the end. Recovers from a number format error with an
error message.
*/

import java.util.Scanner;
```

```java
public class ConvertWithQuery {
    public static void main(String [] args) {
        Scanner reader = new Scanner(System.in);
        Thermometer thermo = new Thermometer();
        String doItAgain = "y";

        while (doItAgain.equals("y") || doItAgain.equals("Y")){
            // Nested loop until input number is well-formed
            while (true)
                try{
                    // Attempt statements that might throw exceptions
                    System.out.print("\nEnter degrees Fahrenheit: ");
                    thermo.setFahrenheit(reader.nextDouble());
                    break;
                }catch(Exception e){
                    // Code for error recovery
                    System.out.println("Error in number format!");
                    // Consume the trailing newline due to bad input
                    reader.nextLine();
                }
            System.out.println("The equivalent in Celsius is " +
                thermo.getCelsius());
            System.out.print("\nDo it again (y/n)? ");
            // Consume the trailing end of line
            reader.nextLine();
            doItAgain = reader.nextLine();
        }
    }
}
```

As you can see, this version of the program is robust for number format errors. The input loop continues until a properly formatted number is entered.

*E*XERCISE 7.5

1. Assume that a program is trying to read a double value from the keyboard. The user enters the characters "$12.55". Explain what happens next.

2. Explain how a try-catch statement works.

3. Write a code segment that loops until the user has entered a well-formed double value at the keyboard.

7.6 Graphics and GUIs

Because developing GUIs in Java is usually quite complicated, many introductory textbooks either restrict themselves to terminal-based I/O or present a rather limited and distorted version of GUIs. Thus far in this book, we have gradually introduced two limited types of GUIs: those that display and allow the user to interact with graphical images (Chapters 2–6), and those that use

> **Extra Challenge**
>
> This Graphics and GUIs section gives you the opportunity to explore concepts and programming techniques required to develop modern graphics applications and graphical user interfaces. This material is not required in order to proceed with the other chapters of the book.

dialog boxes for numeric and text I/O (Chapter 4). Although dialog box I/O suffices for some simple applications, it really does not reflect the true power of a GUI. A program that uses dialog box I/O forces the user to respond to a rigid sequence of pop-up prompts for data. If more than a single data value must be entered, this process can become quite tedious for the user. Moreover, the user might want to refer back to a datum already entered in the sequence before entering the next value, but the earlier dialog box has already disappeared. This problem only gets worse as the number of data values increases. In contrast, a more realistic and powerful GUI presents the user with entry fields for many of the data values simultaneously. Many different command options are also available, via command buttons or drop-down menus. The user can edit any of the fields until she's satisfied that the right combination of the data is present and then select the appropriate command. The results of the computation can then be displayed in the same window.

In this section, we present several realistic but still fairly simple GUIs of this type. In the process, we show how realistic GUIs also allow a programmer to better organize code to solve problems.

The Model/View/Controller Pattern

We start with a very simple application: the temperature conversion program discussed in Section 7.1. Figure 7-4 shows the user interface for a GUI-based version of this program. To use the program, we enter a temperature in the field labeled **Degrees Fahrenheit** and click the **Convert >>>** button below it. The converted temperature is then displayed in the field labeled **Degrees Celsius**. We can repeat the process as many times as desired and click the window's close icon when finished.

FIGURE 7-4
Interface for the GUI-based temperature conversion program

As you might expect, the GUI version can use the same `Thermometer` class used by all of the other versions of the program in this chapter. We call this class the *data model*, or *model* for short. Its responsibilities are to initialize and manage the data used by the program. A second set of classes is called the *view*. The view consists of a window, buttons, data fields, and labels visible to the user. The view is responsible for displaying a view of the data model and providing the user with visible controls for interaction. A third set of classes is called the *controller*. These controller classes are listeners such as those introduced in Chapters 4 through 6. They are responsible for handling user interaction with the program, usually by responding to events that occur in the view. For example, a listener attached to a button is informed that the user has clicked it. The listener responds by sending a message to the data model and then updates the view with the results.

These three sets of classes make up the *model/view/controller pattern*, which we use to structure all of the GUIs in this section. Last but not least, we use a separate class that sets up these other elements in a `main` method, so as to provide an entry point for running a Java program. We call this type of class, for lack of a better term, the *application*.

Putting Together the Temperature Conversion Program

Our program consists of four programmer-defined classes: `ConvertWithGUI`, `GUIWindow`, `FahrenheitListener`, and `Thermometer`. `ConvertWithGUI` is the application class. It defines a `main` method that instantiates the application's main window, sets some of its attributes, and makes it visible. The code for this class is quite straightforward:

```
/* ConvertWithGUI.java
Application class for a GUI-based temperature conversion
program that coverts from Fahrenheit to Celsius.
*/

import javax.swing.*;

public class ConvertWithGUI{

   // Execution begins in the method main as usual.
   public static void main(String[] args){
      GUIWindow theGUI = new GUIWindow();
      theGUI.setTitle("F to C Converter");
      theGUI.setDefaultCloseOperation(JFrame.EXIT_ON_CLOSE);
      theGUI.pack();
      theGUI.setVisible(true); //Make the window visible
   }
}
```

The main thing to note about this code is that we instantiate a `GUIWindow` instead of a `JFrame` for the main window. We then send to the `GUIWindow` the usual `JFrame` messages to set its attributes. The reason we can do this is that class `GUIWindow` extends `JFrame` (just like `ColorPanel` extends `JPanel` as discussed in previous chapters). Therefore, a `GUIWindow` is just a `JFrame` with some extra behavior.

`GUIWindow` is the main view class. It has the following responsibilities:

1. Instantiate and maintain a reference to the data model, a `Thermometer`.

2. Instantiate and maintain references to the data fields and the command button.

3. Add these widgets to the window's container, under the influence of the appropriate layout.

4. Instantiate and attach a `FarhenheitListener` to the command button.

The class `FahrenheitListener` is a private class defined within `GUIWindow`. This follows the practice established in earlier chapters, in which the code for a listener has access to the data variables of the enclosing view class. Our listener in this case must take input from one data field, use it to reset the thermometer's Fahrenheit value, and reset the other data field with the thermometer's Celsius value. Here is the code for the two new classes, heavily commented to mark the model, view, and controller:

```
/* Example 7.5 GUIWindow.java
The main view for a GUI-based temperature conversion
program that coverts from Fahrenheit to Celsius.
*/
```

```java
import javax.swing.*;
import java.awt.*;
import java.awt.event.*;

public class GUIWindow extends JFrame{

    // >>>>>>> The model <<<<<<<<

    // Declare and instantiate the thermometer
    private Thermometer thermo = new Thermometer();

    // >>>>>>> The view <<<<<<<<

    // Declare and instantiate the widgets.
    private JLabel fahrLabel          = new JLabel("Degrees Fahrenheit");
    private JLabel celsiusLabel       = new JLabel("Degrees Celsius");
    private JTextField fahrField      = new JTextField("32.0");
    private JTextField celsiusField   = new JTextField("0.0");
    private JButton fahrButton        = new JButton("Convert >>>");

    // Constructor
    public GUIWindow(){
        // Set up panels to organize widgets and
        // add them to the window
        JPanel dataPanel = new JPanel(new GridLayout(2, 2, 12, 6));
        dataPanel.add(fahrLabel);
        dataPanel.add(celsiusLabel);
        dataPanel.add(fahrField);
        dataPanel.add(celsiusField);
        JPanel buttonPanel = new JPanel();
        buttonPanel.add(fahrButton);
        Container container = getContentPane();
        container.add(dataPanel, BorderLayout.CENTER);
        container.add(buttonPanel, BorderLayout.SOUTH);
        // Attach a listener to the convert button
        fahrButton.addActionListener(new FahrenheitListener());
    }

    // >>>>>>> The controller <<<<<<<<

    private class FahrenheitListener implements ActionListener{
        public void actionPerformed(ActionEvent e){
            String input = fahrField.getText();        // Obtain input
            double fahr = Double.parseDouble(input);   // Convert to a double
            thermo.setFahrenheit(fahr);                // Reset thermometer
            double celsius = thermo.getCelsius();      // Obtain Celsius
            celsiusField.setText("" + celsius);        // Output result
        }
    }
}
```

The creation of the model and the widgets needs no further comment (although you should browse the Java API for JButton, JTextField, and JLabel if you are curious about setting their attributes, such as the color, text font, and so forth). However, the code in the constructor and the listener call for more detailed explanation.

Although this is a fairly simple GUI with only five widgets, we have to take some care in planning their layout. We decide that a reasonable layout would place the two labels and the two data fields in parallel rows. The single command button would then occupy the third row by itself. Recall that the default layout of a `JFrame` is a `BorderLayout`, but its five regions do not reflect the desired positions of the five widgets. Alternatively, a 2-by-2 `GridLayout` would nicely organize the rows of labels and fields, but what about the button? If we could just get all the data widgets with their grid layout into the center region of the border layout, we could put the button into its south region. The solution is to create a separate panel with a grid layout, add the data widgets to this panel, and then add the panel to the frame's center pane. We also create a new panel for the button because adding it directly to a border layout's region would stretch the button to fill that region. This panel's flow layout causes the button to be centered with its preferred size in the panel. Note finally that the grid layout is created with two extra parameters, which specify the amounts of horizontal and vertical padding around the widgets in pixels.

The code for the `FahrenheitListener` class represents this application's controller. When the **Convert >>>** button is clicked, the listener's `actionPerformed` method is automatically triggered. The first line of code uses the method `getText()` to fetch the string currently in the input field. The method `Double.parseDouble(aString)` then converts this string to a number of type `double`. The number is fed to the thermometer as a Fahrenheit value, and the equivalent Celsius value is then extracted, as in the previous examples. Finally, the method `setText(aString)` is used to output the result to the output field. Note that the number must be converted back to a string before output. Table 7-4 lists some commonly used `JTextField` methods.

TABLE 7-4
Some `JTextField` methods

JTEXTFIELD METHOD	WHAT IT DOES
`String getText()`	Returns the string currently occupying the field
`void setEditable(boolean b)`	The field is read-only by the user if b is `false`. The user can edit the field if b is `true`. The default is `true`.
`void setText(String s)`	Displays the string s in the field

Our first GUI program is simple as far as GUI programs go, but there was quite a lot to learn! However, the basic pattern of model/view/controller helps to organize our code and will be used in most of the GUI examples that remain in this book.

On the other hand, we now have a user interface that's both prettier and easier to use than the corresponding query-driven interface. And we didn't even have to write a loop like we did in the terminal-based version of Section 7.1. This illustrates an important point about GUI-based programs: unlike programs based on terminal I/O or even dialog box I/O, real GUI programs are *event-driven*. This means that when a GUI program opens, it just sits there and waits for events (the user clicking the mouse, typing characters into a field, etc.). You can imagine the JVM running a loop behind the scenes, which halts only when the user clicks the window's close icon. When any other event occurs within this loop, control shifts to the GUI program's method for handling that event, if there is one. When that method finishes, control returns to the JVM's loop. If there are no methods for handling events, they are ignored.

Making Temperature Conversion Go Both Ways

The menu-driven version of the temperature conversion program in Section 7.2 allows the user to convert a Fahrenheit value to a Celsius value or a Celsius value to a Fahrenheit value. This change involved a major restructuring of the query-driven program of Section 7.1, as well as a major change in the user interface. Let's examine the changes in the GUI version to make the conversion go both ways.

The only change to the user interface is the addition of a second button, as shown in Figure 7-5. When the user clicks the **Convert >>>** button, the program uses the Fahrenheit field for input and the Celsius field for output, as before. When the user clicks the new button, **<<< Convert**, the program uses the Celsius field for input and the Fahrenheit field for output.

FIGURE 7-5
A temperature converter that goes both ways

There are only minor changes to the code as well. The GUIWindow class

- Declares and instantiates the second button:

```
private JButton celsiusButton  = new JButton("<<< Convert");
```

- Adds this button to the button panel:

```
buttonPanel.add(celsiusButton);
```

- Creates a listener object and attaches it to the button:

```
celsiusButton.addActionListener(new CelsiusListener());
```

- Defines a separate listener class that converts from Celsius to Fahrenheit:

```
// Example 7.6: Listener to convert Celsius to Fahrenheit
private class CelsiusListener implements ActionListener{
   public void actionPerformed(ActionEvent e){
      String input = celsiusField.getText();        // Obtain input
      double celsius = Double.parseDouble(input);    // Convert to a double
      thermo.setCelsius(celsius);                    // Reset thermometer
      double fahr = thermo.getFahrenheit();          // Obtain Fahrenheit
      fahrField.setText("" + fahr);                  // Output result
   }
}
```

In short, we simply add a new command button and the corresponding controller to take action when the user clicks this button. No matter how many new widgets are added to the GUI, if we maintain the correspondence between a widget and its controller, the basic structure of the program will never change. And still no loop!

Making Temperature Conversion Robust

Section 7.5 discussed a strategy for recovering from format errors in numeric input. A similar technique can be applied to catch input errors with text fields in GUI programs. The methods `Double.parseDouble(aString)` and `Integer.parseInt(aString)` are used to convert strings to numbers of type `double` and `int`, respectively. If either of these methods encounters a number format error, it throws an exception. Let's modify the code that converts from Fahrenheit to Celsius to catch a number format exception and recover from it. The code for `actionPerformed` is now enclosed in a `try-catch` statement. If an exception is thrown, control is shifted to the `catch` clause, which pops up a message dialog box to inform the user. Here is the code for the modified listener:

```java
// Example 7.7: A robust listener for number format errors
private class FahrenheitListener implements ActionListener{
    public void actionPerformed(ActionEvent e){
        try{
            String input = fahrField.getText();        // Obtain input
            double fahr = Double.parseDouble(input);   // Convert to a double
            thermo.setFahrenheit(fahr);                // Reset thermometer
            double celsius = thermo.getCelsius();      // Obtain Celsius
            celsiusField.setText("" + celsius);        // Output result
        }catch(Exception ex){
            JOptionPane.showMessageDialog(GUIWindow.this,
                                "Bad number format",
                                "Temperature Converter",
                                JOptionPane.ERROR_MESSAGE);

        }
    }
}
```

The code for the normal processing of this command is nested in the try clause. If an exception is thrown in the call of `parseDouble`, control is transferred immediately to the `catch` clause, which pops up an error message dialog box.

Note that the first parameter of the method `showMessageDialog` is the expression `GUIWindow.this`, which in this context refers to the current instance of the `GUIWindow` class. This parameter allows the JVM to track the "parent" of the dialog box, that is, the main window from which it was opened. In the examples of earlier chapters, the first parameter had been `null` because no parent window was involved. If we had simply used the parameter `this` instead, the compiler would think that we meant the current instance of `FahrenheitListener`, which is not a GUI component.

Finally, `showMessageDialog` includes two other parameters for the dialog box's title and its type, which displays an error icon, as shown in Figure 7-6.

FIGURE 7-6
Responding to a number format error

(a) Main window   (b) Message box

E XERCISE 7.6

1. Write a code segment that obtains an input from a text field called inputField, converts the input to an integer, and outputs the square root of the integer to a text field called outputField.

2. Assume that an action listener has been added to a button. Which method runs when the user clicks the button?

3. Describe the roles and responsibilities of the model, view, and controller classes in a GUI program.

SUMMARY

In this chapter, you learned:

■ A terminal input/output (I/O) interface can be extended to handle repeated sets of inputs, by using either a query-based pattern or a menu-driven pattern.

■ A graphical user interface (GUI) allows the user to interact with a program by displaying window objects and handling mouse events.

■ In a terminal-based program, the program controls most of the interaction with the user, whereas GUI-based programs are driven by user events.

■ The two primary tasks of a GUI-based program are to arrange the window objects in a window and handle interactions with the user.

VOCABULARY *Review*

> **Define the following terms:**
> Menu-driven progam   Query-controlled input

REVIEW *Questions*

FILL IN THE BLANK

Complete each of the following statements by writing your answer in the blank provided.

1. In contrast to terminal I/O programs, GUI programs are _____ driven.

2. A button allows the user to select a(n) _____.

3. Two types of window objects that support numeric I/O are a(n) _____ and a(n) _____.

4. A window object that supports the I/O of a single line of text is a(n) _____.

5. A separate window that pops up with information is a(n) _____.

PROJECTS

PROJECT 7-1

Newton's method for computing the square root of a number consists of approximating the actual square root by means of a set of transformations. Each transformation starts with a guess at the square root. A better approximation is then (guess + number / guess) / 2. This result becomes the guess for the next approximation. The initial guess is 1. Write a query-driven program that allows the user to enter a number and the number of approximations to compute its square root.

PROJECT 7-2

Modify the program of Project 7-1 so that the user can view the successive approximations. (Hint: Build a formatted string of the approximations during the computation.)

PROJECT 7-3

John has $500 to invest. Sue knows of a mutual fund plan that pays 10 percent interest, compounded quarterly (that is, every 3 months, the principal is multiplied by the 2.5 percent and the result is added to the principal; more generally, the amount of gain each quarter is equal to current balance * (1 + interest rate / 400)). Write a program that will tell John how much money will be in the fund after 20 years. Make the program general; that is, it should take as inputs the interest rate, the initial principal, and the number of years to stay in the fund. The output should be a table whose columns are the year number, the principal at the beginning of the year, the interest earned, and the principal at the end of the year.

PROJECT 7-4

The TidBit Computer Store has a credit plan for computer purchases. There is a 10-percent down payment and an annual interest rate of 12 percent. Monthly payments are 5 percent of the listed purchase price minus the down payment. Write a program that takes the purchase price as input. The program should display a table of the payment schedule for the lifetime of the loan. Use appropriate headers. Each row of the table should contain the following items:

- Month number (beginning with 1)
- Current total balance owed
- Interest owed for that month
- Amount of principal owed for that month
- Payment for that month
- Balance remaining after payment

The amount of interest for a month is equal to balance * rate / 12. The amount of principal for a month is equal to the monthly payment minus the interest owed.

PROJECT 7-5

Modify the final temperature conversion program of Section 7.6 so that it displays the results of each conversion rounded to the nearest hundredth of a degree.

PROJECT 7-6

Write a GUI program that takes a radius as input. The outputs, displayed in separate fields, are the area of a circle, the surface area of a sphere, and the volume of a sphere of this radius.

CRITICAL *Thinking*

A company approaches you about the need for a program and wonders whether to ask for a terminal-based user interface or a graphical user interface. Discuss the issues involved in choosing between these two interfaces from a client's perspective.

CHAPTER 8

INTRODUCTION TO HTML AND APPLETS

8.1 Hypertext, Hypermedia, and the World Wide Web

In 1945, Vannevar Bush, a scientist at MIT, published a prophetic essay, "As We May Think," in the *Atlantic Monthly*. According to Bush, although computers were already wonderful for number crunching, they would soon be used for data storage, data manipulation, and logical reasoning. These predictions came to pass in the 1950s and 1960s, with the advent of such branches of computer science as database management and artificial intelligence.

Bush also raised and attempted to answer the following question: How could we improve the way in which we consult our information sources during research? The traditional researcher used indexing schemes, such as card catalogs, but this method restricts the user to a linear or binary search. By contrast, the human mind uses association to search its own memory bank. For example, when I hear the word "wife," I instantly think of a particular person, namely, my own wife. My mind does not go through a complex search process to retrieve the associated information. Somehow, it just gets it.

Bush proposed to use computer technology to link chunks of information associatively. A *table* or *keyed list* is a data structure that allows a computer to look up an item or entry associated with a given key. An online phone book is an example of such a table, where the keys are owner's names and the entries are their addresses and phone numbers. Now imagine that the entries in such a table also contain embedded keys or links to other entries in other tables. Bush called his imaginary machine a **memex**. Each individual would have a desktop memex, as a virtual extension of his or her memory. The memex would receive chunks of information from a photocopy machine, a keyboard, or a stylus. The information would be stored on microfilm. The user would establish links between chunks of information by means of a few simple keystrokes.

The computer would maintain these *associative links* and also traces of the user's explorations of them. The user could come back to that trail or give it to another user to link into a more general trail. Research would involve following the trails blazed by the masters, not just the examination of their end products.

Hypertext and Hypermedia

By the late 1960s, the technology for realizing Bush's dream became available. In 1967, Theodor Holm Nelson coined the term *hypertext* to refer to Bush's machine. A hypertext is a structure consisting of nodes and the links between them. Each node is a document or chunk of text. Normally, links to other nodes are displayed to the user as embedded, highlighted terms within a given chunk of text. The user moves to a node by using an arrow key or mouse to select an associated term.

Early hypertext systems were

- Douglas Englebart's NLS/Augment (1968)
- Cognetics Corporation's Hyperties (mid-1980s)

In 1987, Apple Computer released Hypercard, one of the first hypermedia platforms. *Hypermedia* is like hypertext, but adds

- GUIs
- Images
- Sound
- Animation
- Applications

For example, a link might appear as an icon or image rather than as highlighted text. The targeted chunk of information might be a full-screen image, a movie, a musical recording, or a computer application such as a database program.

Networks and the World Wide Web

All of the early hypertext systems ran on separate standalone machines, which maintained data storage for the individual user. With the development of the Internet, people began to think of sharing hypertext across a network of communicating machines. Chunks of information, or pages as they are now called, could be stored on many different physical machines around the world. Each page would be linked in a gigantic hypermedia system, the World Wide Web. The Web is now a reality, taken for granted by millions of users.

The Web consists of two kinds of machines:

■ Servers, on which pages of information reside

■ Clients, which run browsers to access information on the servers

In some cases the client and server reside on the same machine.

When you open a browser, you are presented with an initial page of information. Embedded in this page are links to other nodes. When you select a link, the following sequence occurs:

■ The browser sends a message to the node's machine, requesting a transfer of its information.

■ If the request is successful, the information at the node is downloaded to the user's browser.

Because there are different types of computers, a networked hypermedia system requires a uniform means of:

■ Representing information using a machine-independent hypertext markup language

■ Assigning node addresses using machine-independent uniform resource locators (URLs)

■ Transmitting information from site to site using machine-independent network transmission protocols

■ Displaying information with browsers from different vendors, subject to the restriction that all the browsers behave in a similar manner

*E*XERCISE 8.1

1. Describe the basic ideas underlying hypertext.

2. What is the difference between hypertext and hypermedia?

3. What is a URL?

8.2 Overview of the Hypertext Markup Language

The *hypertext markup language* (HTML) was developed as a machine-independent way of representing information in a networked-based hypermedia system. Early word-processing systems such as WordStar bracketed text with codes that specified print formats. For example, the code ^I (control I) indicated italics and ^B indicated bold. To illustrate, the text

```
Bush, Vannevar, ^BAs We May Think^B, ^IAtlantic Monthly^I, July, 1945.
```

would have been printed as

```
Bush, Vannevar, As We May Think, Atlantic Monthly, July, 1945.
```

HTML uses a similar scheme. Codes, called *markup tags*, can indicate the format of textual elements or links to other nodes. Browsers interpret these codes as commands and display the text in the desired format. Figure 8-1 shows the relationship between authors and users of HTML documents.

FIGURE 8-1
The Internet

Author enters HTML pages with embedded tags on a Web server, where they are stored on disk until needed.

User requests pages across the Internet using a Web browser, which then displays pages in format specified by tags.

A Short Example

As a first example of using HTML, we show you how to create the Web page shown in Figure 8-2.

FIGURE 8-2
A simple Web page

The page includes markup tags for

■ A title
■ A heading
■ Two paragraphs of text

The author of the page had to write an HTML document that looks like this:

```
<HTML>
<HEAD>
<TITLE>A Short HTML Document</TITLE>
```

```
</HEAD>
<BODY>
<H1>This is a first heading</H1>
<P>You probably thought that Java applications were fun. Wait until
you get going with HTML and applets!</P>
<P>You will learn to write simple Web pages as platforms
for launching Java programs.</P>
</BODY>
</HTML>
```

When a browser displays the document, the title appears at the top of the browser's window.

There is a blank line between the heading and the first paragraph and between the two paragraphs. The browser uses word wrap to fit the text within the window's boundaries. A typical HTML document consists of multiple HTML pages.

The document must be stored in a file having the extension ".html" on a UNIX system and ".htm" on a Windows system. Pages can be any size, from a few lines to many hundreds of lines. We now turn to a discussion of the tags that define the HTML protocol.

Markup Tags

A markup tag in HTML begins with a left angle bracket (<) and ends with a right angle bracket (>), for example, <title>. Tags are not case sensitive. For instance, the tags <title>, <TITLE>, and< TiTlE> are equivalent, though not equally readable. In this chapter, we use uppercase only to allow you to pick out the tags easily.

Tags usually occur in pairs, for example, <TITLE> and </TITLE>. The opening tag tells the browser where to begin the format, and the closing tag, which includes a slash (/), tells the browser where to end the format.

Tags can include attributes. For example, the tag <P ALIGN=CENTER> tells the browser to align the next paragraph in the center of the window. In this example, ALIGN is the attribute's name and CENTER is the attribute's value. Some commonly used markup tags are listed in Table 8-1.

TABLE 8-1
Basic HTML markup tags

MARKUP TAG	WHAT IT DOES
HTML	Designates an HTML document
HEAD	Designates the head of the document
BODY	Designates the contents of the document
TITLE	Designates the title that appears in the browser's window
P	Designates a paragraph of text
H1, H2, etc.	Designates a heading; there are six levels of headings.
PRE	Designates text to be formatted literally
BR	Indicates a line break
UL	Designates a bulleted (ordered) list
OL	Designates a numbered (ordered) list
LI	Indicates an item within a list

Minimal Document Structure

Every HTML document should have the following minimal structure:

```
<HTML>
<HEAD>
<TITLE> the title goes here </TITLE>
</HEAD>
<BODY>
the text for the document goes here
</BODY>
</HTML>
```

Note the following points:

- The HTML tag informs the browser that it is dealing with an HTML document.

- The HEAD tag identifies the first part of the document.

- The TITLE tag identifies the document's title. The title is displayed at the top of the browser's window and is used during searches for the document. The title is also displayed in bookmark lists (a list of the user's favorite links). We recommend short, descriptive titles.

- The BODY tags enclose the information provided by the HTML document.

- The browser ignores extra white space, such as blank lines and tab characters.

Commenting an HTML Document

Authors often add comments to HTML documents. The browser does not interpret comments or show them to the reader. The form of a comment is

```
<!-- text of comment -->
```

In the following example, we have modified the first example by inserting blank lines and comments to make it more readable. However, a browser will display this page exactly as before.

```
<HTML>
<!-- Authors: Kenneth A. Lambert and Martin Osborne
     Last update: November 30, 2005                -->
<HEAD>
<TITLE>A Short HTML Document</TITLE>
</HEAD>

<BODY>
<H1>This is a first heading</H1>

<P>You probably thought that Java applications were fun. Wait until
you get going with HTML and applets!</P>

<P>You will learn to write simple Web pages as platforms
for launching Java programs.</P>

</BODY>
</HTML>
```

EXERCISE 8.2

1. What does HTML stand for?

2. What is the purpose of HTML tags?

3. Write an HTML code segment that shows the minimal HTML document structure for a Web page.

4. What is an HTML comment? Give an example.

8.3 Simple Text Elements

There are several basic elements for formatting text in a Web page.

Headings

HTML provides six levels of document headings, numbered H1 through H6. The form of a heading is

```
<Hnumber>Text of heading</Hnumber>
```

Headings are displayed in a different font size and style from normal text. The browser inserts a blank line after each heading.

Paragraphs

The end tag </P> may be omitted. The browser then ends the paragraph at the beginning of the next paragraph or heading tag. The browser uses word wrap to fit a paragraph within the borders of the browser's window. Most browsers insert a blank line after the end of each paragraph; however, they ignore blank lines within a paragraph.

The browser recognizes the following alignment attributes:

- LEFT (the default)

- RIGHT

- CENTER

This next example uses headings of several sizes and paragraphs with different alignments:

```
<H1>The first level heading</H1>
<P ALIGN=RIGHT>The first paragraph.</P>
<H2>The second level heading</H2>
<P ALIGN=CENTER>The second paragraph.</P>
<H3>The third level heading</H3>
<P>The third paragraph.</P>
```

The results of this example are shown in Figure 8-3.

FIGURE 8-3
Headings and paragraphs coded with HTML

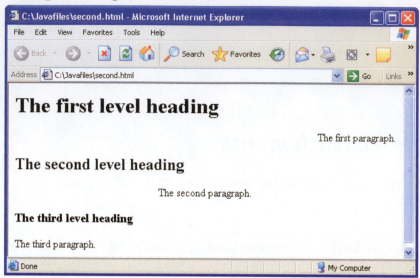

Forced Line Breaks

Occasionally, a Web page author or designer wants to display several lines of text without word wrap. The line break tag, <BR>, is used for this purpose. For example, the following HTML segment would display an address:

```
Department of Computer Science<BR>
Washington and Lee University<BR>
Lexington, VA 24450<BR>
```

Because a line break tag tells the browser where to break a line, no other end tag is required.

Preformatted Text

Suppose you want the browser to display text "as is," with line breaks, extra spaces, and tabs. The <PRE> tag accomplishes this. For example, the following HTML segment displays some Java program code with the indicated indentation and line breaks:

```
<PRE>
    public static void main (String[] args){
    // Lots of code goes here
    }
</PRE>
```

In general, you should not use other markup tags within a chunk of preformatted text.

EXERCISE 8.3

1. When does the HTML programmer need to use forced line breaks?

2. When do we use preformatted text in an HTML document?

3. Write an HTML code segment that shows a level 1 heading and a level 2 heading.

8.4 Character-Level Formatting

In addition to the format of headings and paragraphs, HTML provides some control over the format of characters. Table 8-2 lists some of the commonly used tags and their effects:

TABLE 8-2
Some character format tags

MARKUP TAG	WHAT IT DOES	EXAMPLE HTML	DISPLAYED TEXT
EM	Emphasis, usually italics	<EM>Italics</EM>, for emphasis	*Italics*, for emphasis
STRONG	Strong emphasis, usually bold	<STRONG>Bold</STRONG>, for more emphasis	**Bold**, for more emphasis
CITE	Used for titles of books, etc., usually italics	Plato's <CITE>Republic</CITE>	Plato's *Republic*
B	Bold text	<B>Bold</B> text	**Bold** text
I	Italic text	<I>Italic</I> text	*Italic* text
TT	Typewriter text, a fixed-width font	<TT>Typewriter</TT> text	`Typewriter` text

Escape Sequences

HTML treats <, >, and & as special characters. For example, the characters < and > are treated as the delimiters of an HTML tag. If you want the browser to display these characters rather than interpret them, you must use the escape sequences listed in Table 8-3.

TABLE 8-3
Some escape sequences

CHARACTER	ESCAPE SEQUENCE	EXAMPLE HTML	DISPLAYED TEXT
<	&lt;	The character < begins an HTML markup tag.	The character < begins an HTML markup tag.
>	&gt;	The character > ends an HTML markup tag.	The character > ends an HTML markup tag
&	&amp;	& is an ampersand.	& is an ampersand.

The escape sequences for < and > are easy to remember if you remember that "lt" stands for "less than" and "gt" stands for "greater than."

EXERCISE 8.4

1. What happens if you forget to close the markup tag for italics on a piece of text?

2. What is the purpose of the escape sequences in HTML? Give an example.

8.5 Lists

There are three kinds of lists that can be displayed in a Web page:

- Unordered (bulleted) lists—tag <UL>

- Numbered (ordered) lists—tag <OL>

- Definition (association) lists—tag <DL>

For bulleted and numbered lists, you perform the following steps:

1. Start with the desired list tag (<UL> or <OL>).

2. For each item, enter the <LI> (list item) tag followed by the text of the item. No closing tags are needed for the items.

3. End with the desired list tag.

The markup tags for lists can easily be remembered if you note that "UL" stands for "unordered list," "OL" stands for "ordered list" (i.e., 1, 2, 3, etc.), "DL" stands for "definition list," and "LI" stands for "list item."

An Unordered List Example

The next HTML segment displays a bulleted list of courses that one of the authors taught last year.

```
<UL>
<LI>Fundamentals of Data Structures
<LI>Programming Language Design
<LI>Operating Systems
<LI>Artificial Intelligence
</UL>
```

Figure 8-4 shows the page resulting from this HTML segment.

FIGURE 8-4
An unordered (bulleted) list

A Definition List Example

A *definition list* displays terms and their associated definitions. Several tags are used with these lists:

- The tag <DL> begins the definition list and ends it.

- The tag <DT> precedes each term in a definition list.

- The tag <DD> precedes each definition in a definition list.

The following example uses a definition list to add course numbers to the course list.

```
<DL>

<DT>CSCI111
<DD>Fundamentals of Data Structures

<DT>CSCI312
<DD>Programming Language Design
```

```
<DT>CSCI330
<DD>Operating Systems

<DT>CSCI315
<DD>Artificial Intelligence

</DL>
```

Figure 8-5 shows the page resulting from this HTML segment.

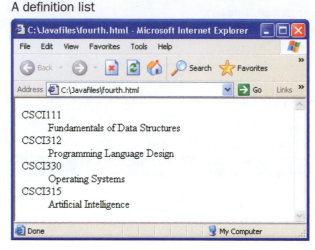

A Nested List Example

Lists can be nested within other lists to any depth, but more than three levels deep can be difficult to read. The following HTML segment nests a numbered list within an unordered one:

```
<UL>
<LI>Fundamentals of Data Structures

<!--The nested, numbered list begins here. -->
<OL>
<LI>Analysis of algorithms
<LI>Collections
<LI>Linked lists
<LI>Stacks
<LI>Queues
<LI>Recursion
<LI>Binary search trees
</OL>
<!--The nested list ends here. -->

<LI>Programming Language Design
<LI>Operating Systems
<LI>Artificial Intelligence
</UL>
```

Figure 8-6 shows the page resulting from this HTML segment.

FIGURE 8-6
A nested list

*E***XERCISE 8.5**

1. List three types of HTML lists and describe their characteristics.

2. Write an HTML code segment that uses a list to display the names of your grandparents and your parents. The list should be organized to show the relationships clearly.

8.6 Linking to Other Documents

Links, also called *hyperlinks* or hypertext references, allow readers to move to other pages in the Web. The markup tag for a link is <A>, which stands for anchor. Placing a link in an HTML document involves the following steps:

1. Identify the target document that will be at the other end of the link. This identifier should be a path name or a URL (see the discussion in the following subsections).

2. Determine the text that labels the link in the browser.

3. Place this information within an anchor, using the following format:

```
<A HREF="target document identifier">text of link</A>
```

For example, the next HTML anchor sets up a link to the file **courses.html** and labels the link "courses last year":

```
<A HREF="courses.html">courses last year</A>
```

Links or anchors can appear within any HTML element. They are often embedded as items in a list or as terms in a paragraph. For example, the following segment displays a link to the file **courses.html** in a sentence that mentions the author's courses:

```
<P>
My <A HREF="courses.html">courses last year</A> were Fundamentals of Data
    Structures, Programming Language Design, Operating Systems, and
    Artificial Intelligence.
</P>
```

When the user browses this page, the link is highlighted in some fashion (i.e., a different color text) and usually underlined, as in Figure 8-7.

FIGURE 8-7
A link to another page

When the user clicks on the link, the browser retrieves and displays the target document, provided that the document has been placed at the appropriate location.

Path Names

Note the path name in the **Address** field in the header portion of Figure 8-7. The path name specifies the path to the file sixth.html on the author's computer. This file contains the page currently being displayed. The path name is said to be an *absolute path name* because it specifies the exact or absolute position of the file in the computer's directory structure.

In HTML anchors, we can use absolute or *relative path names* to specify the location of a target document. A relative path name specifies a document's position relative to that of the currently displayed document. Table 8-4 shows some examples of the relative path name to `MyPage.html`.

TABLE 8-4
Relative path names to MyPage.html

POSITION OF `MYPAGE.HTML` RELATIVE TO CURRENT PAGE	RELATIVE PATH NAME
In the same directory	`MyPage.html`
Below, in a subdirectory called **Sub1**	`/Sub1/MyPage.html`
In the directory immediately above	`../MyPage.html`
In the directory two levels above	`../../MyPage.html`
In a directory Twin1, which is up one and then down one from the current directory	`../Twin1/MyPage.html`

In general, relative path names are easier to use than absolute path names because

- They are shorter and require less figuring out and typing.

- They need not be changed when a group of documents is moved, even to another computer, provided the documents retain their relative positions.

URLs

When a target document resides on another server in the network, a path name no longer suffices to locate the document. Instead, we use a ***uniform resource locator*** (URL) to locate the document on another machine. A URL to another Web site (called a host) has the following format:

```
http://server name/document path name
```

For instance, the URL for author Ken Lambert's home page is

```
<A HREF="http://www.wlu.edu/~lambertk">Ken Lambert</A>
```

Please feel free to visit.

*E*XERCISE 8.6

1. Write the form of the markup tag for links.

2. What is an absolute path name? Give an example.

3. What is a relative path name? Give an example.

4. Write the format of a URL to another Web site.

8.7 *Multimedia*

As a true hypermedia language, HTML supports the presentation of a range of nontextual information such as images, sounds, and movies.

Inline Images

Inline images are graphical images that are displayed when the user opens a page. The form of the markup tag for an inline image is

```
<IMG SRC="ImageLocation">
```

where *ImageLocation* is a URL or path name. Images can be encoded in the GIF or JPEG format and are stored in files with extensions of .gif, .jpg, or .jpeg.

Several parameters can be used with the markup tag of an inline image:

■ Size attributes: These specify the height and width of the image in pixels. For example,

```
<IMG SRC="mypicture.gif" HEIGHT=100 WIDTH=100>
```

■ Alignment attribute: This specifies the position of text relative to the image. By default, text that follows an image starts at the image's lower-right corner. The text moves to the upper right or to the center right of the image when TOP or CENTER are specified. For example,

```
<IMG SRC="mypicture.gif" ALIGN=CENTER>
```

To detach an image from surrounding text, place the image in a separate paragraph. For instance,

```
<P ALIGN=CENTER>

<IMG SRC="mypicture.gif">
</P>
```

External Images

Inline images increase a document's size and slow its transfer across the Internet. For that reason, documents sometimes provide links to *external images*, which are not displayed until the user clicks on a link. The following HTML segment shows two ways of linking to an external image. The first link is a string of text. The second link is a smaller version of the image (sometimes called a thumbnail):

```
<A HREF="mypicture.gif">Sample picture</A>

<A HREF="mypicture.gif"><IMG SRC="mythumbnail.gif"></A>
```

This strategy is also used with other media, such as sound recordings and movies.

Colors and Backgrounds

Browsers normally display black text on a white background with links highlighted in blue. However, an HTML author can easily change the colors of these elements. Background, text, and link colors are controlled by the BGCOLOR, TEXT, and LINK attributes of the <BODY> tag. For example, the following tag sets the background to black, text to white, and links to red:

```
<BODY BGCOLOR="#000000" TEXT="#FFFFFF" LINK="#FF0000">
```

A string of three two-digit hexadecimal numbers specifies a color by indicating the RGB (red, green, blue) components of the color. The first two digits represent the red component, the second the green, and the third the blue. Thus, a total of 224 colors are possible. The string "#000000" indicates black, a total absence of any color, whereas "#FFFFFF" represents white, a total saturation of all colors. Bright red is "#FF0000" and bright green is "#00FF00". There are many useful Web sites that show how to use colors. One good example is http://www.pagetutor.com/pagetutor/makapage/picker/.

Another way to customize a background is to display an image on it. The following tag shows how to use an image as a background:

```
<BODY BACKGROUND="mybackground.jpg">
```

If the image is small, the browser fills the window with the image by a process called *tiling*, which repeatedly displays the image across and down the screen, thus creating a wallpaper-like effect.

Other Media

Table 8-5 shows filename extensions for some typical media used in HTML documents.

TABLE 8-5
Some hypermedia filename extensions

FILE NAME EXTENSION	TYPE OF MEDIUM
.au	AU sound file
.wav	WAV sound file
.mov	QuickTime movie
.mpeg or .mpg	MPEG movie

*E*XERCISE 8.7

1. What is the difference between an inline image and an external image?

2. Write the simplest version of the format of the markup tag for an inline image.

3. Write a markup tag that loads an inline image of the file image.gif, centers the image, and scales its size to 200 pixels × 200 pixels.

4. What are two ways of tagging an external image? Give an example of each.

8.8 Tables

It is often useful to organize information in tables. The page in Figure 8-8 uses a table to display the first two weeks of topics in a data structures course.

FIGURE 8-8
A table

FIGURE 8-8
A table

As you have seen in earlier chapters, tables provide a highly structured way of accessing information. This is true of tables in user interfaces as well.

Tables usually contain the following elements:

- A caption or title, normally at the top of the table.

- A first row containing column headers; each header describes the kind of data contained in the column beneath it.

- Several rows of data; the cells in a row can contain any HTML elements (text, images, links, etc.).

Table 8-6 provides a list of the HTML markup tags used with tables.

TABLE 8-6
Table format tags

TABLE MARKUP TAG	WHAT IT DOES
<TABLE>	Defines a table
<CAPTION>	Defines the title of the table (The default position of the title is at the top of the table, but ALIGN=BOTTOM can also be used.)
<TR>	Defines a row within a table
<TH>	Defines a table header cell
<TD>	Defines a table data cell

The table markup tags accept the attributes shown in Table 8-7.

TABLE 8-7
Table attributes

ATTRIBUTE	TAG	WHAT IT DOES
BORDER	<TABLE>	Display a border
ALIGN (LEFT, CENTER RIGHT)	All	Horizontal alignment of elements in cells
VALIGN (TOP, MIDDLE, BOTTOM)	All except <CAPTION>	Vertical alignment of cells
ROWSPAN=n	<TD>	The number of rows that a cell spans
COLSPAN=n	<TD>	The number of columns that a cell spans
NOWRAP	All except <CAPTION>	Turn off word wrap within a cell

Cell attributes override row attributes, and row attributes override table attributes.

Typical Table Format

The format of a typical table follows. The blank lines between rows increase readability but do not affect the manner in which the table is displayed:

```
<TABLE>
<CAPTION> title of the table </CAPTION>

<TR>
<TH> header of first column </TH>
.
.
<TH> header of last column </TH>
</TR>

<TR>
<TD> contents of first data cell in first row </TD>
.
.
<TD> contents of last data cell in first row </TD>
</TR>
.
.
<TR>
<TD> contents of first data cell in last row </TD>
.
.
<TD> contents of last data cell in last row </TD>
</TR>
</TABLE>
```

A Simple Example

The table shown in Figure 8-8 at the beginning of this section was created using the following HTML code:

```
<TABLE BORDER>

<CAPTION ALIGN=CENTER>
Computer Science 111 - Fundamentals of Data Structures
</CAPTION>

<TR>
<TH>Week #</TH>
<TH>Monday</TH>
<TH>Wednesday</TH>
<TH>Friday</TH>
</TR>

<TR>
<TD ALIGN=CENTER>1</TD> <TD>Introduction</TD>
<TD>Analysis of algorithms</TD> <TD>Analysis of algorithms</TD>
</TR>

<TR>
<TD ALIGN=CENTER>2</TD> <TD>Collection Classes</TD>
<TD>Ordered Collections</TD> <TD>Sorted Collections</TD>
</TR>

</TABLE>
```

*E*XERCISE 8.8

1. Describe how you create a table using the HTML table tags.

2. Write an HTML code segment that displays a 3 × 3 table with cells that are numbered as follows:
   1 2 3
   4 5 6
   7 8 9

8.9 Applets

An *applet* is a Java application that runs in a Web page. Two components are needed to run an applet:

1.   An HTML document that contains an applet markup tag

2.   A byte code file for the applet—that is, a compiled Java applet in a `.class` file

An applet markup tag has the following form:

```
<APPLET CODE="byte code file name" WIDTH=width HEIGHT=height></APPLET>
```

The width and height are the width and height, respectively, of the applet's screen area in pixels.

Applets present a graphical user interface. The examples used in this section are revised versions of GUI applications presented in earlier end-of-chapter sections on graphics and GUIs. You might want to review those sections, particularly in Chapters 6 and 7, before continuing.

Example 1: The Temperature Converter

Let us assume that the Fahrenheit/Celsius temperature converter from Chapter 7 has already been rewritten as a Java applet. It might appear in a Web page as shown in Figure 8-9.

FIGURE 8-9
An applet within a Web page

The applet retains just two classes from the earlier version: `GUIWindow` (the view) and `Thermometer` (the model). Here is the HTML code for the example:

```
<HTML>
<HEAD>
<TITLE>Temperature Converter</TITLE>
</HEAD>

<BODY>
<H1>Temperature Converter</H1>
<UL>
<LI>Enter degrees Fahrenheit or degrees Celsius.
<LI>Click the <STRONG>Convert >>></STRONG> button and the
Celsius equivalent will be displayed.
<LI>Click the <STRONG><<< Convert</STRONG> button and the
Fahrenheit equivalent will be displayed.
</UL>

<APPLET CODE="GUIWindow.class" WIDTH=250 HEIGHT=100>
</APPLET>
```

```
<P>
Applets greatly increase the power of the Web.

</BODY>
</HTML>
```

Note that the Web page loads the byte code for the view class into a rectangular area large enough to accommodate the GUI components. The Web page also displays a title for the applet. Thus, you can think of the Web page as playing the role of the application class, ConvertWithGUI, in the earlier version of the program.

Converting an Application to an Applet

For applications that use a specialized view class for the main window, the conversion to an applet is surprisingly simple. In Section 7.6, the class GUIWindow played this role. We just do two things to this class:

1. Replace the name JFrame with the name JApplet at the beginning of the class definition (extends JApplet).

2. Replace the class's constructor by the method init:

```
public void init(){
    ...
}
```

The following listing comments these changes in just two lines of code in the GUIWindow class:

```
/* GUIWindow.java
The main view for a GUI-based temperature conversion
program that coverts from Fahrenheit to Celsius and back again.
*/

import javax.swing.*;
import java.awt.*;
import java.awt.event.*;

public class GUIWindow extends JApplet{      // First change here!!!

   // >>>>>>> The model <<<<<<<<

   // Declare and intantiate the thermometer
   private Thermometer thermo = new Thermometer();

   // >>>>>>> The view <<<<<<<<

   // Declare and instantiate the window objects.
   private JLabel fahrLabel         = new JLabel("Degrees Fahrenheit");
   private JLabel celsiusLabel      = new JLabel("Degrees Celsius");
   private JTextField fahrField     = new JTextField("32.0");
   private JTextField celsiusField  = new JTextField("0.0");
   private JButton fahrButton       = new JButton("Convert >>>");
   private JButton celsiusButton    = new JButton("<<< Convert");
```

```java
// Constructor
public void init(){                                    // Second change here!!!
    // Set up panels to organize widgets and
    // add them to the window
    JPanel dataPanel = new JPanel(new GridLayout(2, 2, 12, 6));
    dataPanel.add(fahrLabel);
    dataPanel.add(celsiusLabel);
    dataPanel.add(fahrField);
    dataPanel.add(celsiusField);
    JPanel buttonPanel = new JPanel();
    buttonPanel.add(fahrButton);
    buttonPanel.add(celsiusButton);
    Container container = getContentPane();
    container.add(dataPanel, BorderLayout.CENTER);
    container.add(buttonPanel, BorderLayout.SOUTH);
    // Attach a listener to the convert button
    fahrButton.addActionListener(new FahrenheitListener());
    celsiusButton.addActionListener(new CelsiusListener());
}


// >>>>>>> The controller <<<<<<<


private class FahrenheitListener implements ActionListener{
    public void actionPerformed(ActionEvent e){
        try{
            String input = fahrField.getText();        // Obtain input
            double fahr = Double.parseDouble(input);    // Convert to double
            thermo.setFahrenheit(fahr);                 // Reset thermometer
            double celsius = thermo.getCelsius();       // Obtain Celsius
            celsiusField.setText("" + celsius);         // Output result
        }catch(Exception ex){
            JOptionPane.showMessageDialog(null,         // Now null, because we're in an applet
                                "Bad number format",
                                "Temperature Converter",
                                JOptionPane.ERROR_MESSAGE);
        }
    }
}


private class CelsiusListener implements ActionListener{
    public void actionPerformed(ActionEvent e){
        String input = celsiusField.getText();          // Obtain input
        double celsius = Double.parseDouble(input);     // Convert to double
        thermo.setCelsius(celsius);                     // Reset thermometer
        double fahr = thermo.getFahrenheit();           // Obtain Fahrenheit
        fahrField.setText("" + fahr);                   // Output result
    }
}
}
```

Note that the first parameter of the method showMessageDialog is now null. No other changes are necessary. With a few exceptions to be discussed shortly, applets can use all of the view and controller features of standalone applications.

Example 2: Graphics Programs

The structure of the graphics programs introduced in Chapters 2 through 6 is slightly different than that of the temperature conversion program of Chapter 7. The earlier programs consist of a main window class called GUIWindow and one or more specialized panel classes for drawing shapes. In these cases, GUIWindow includes a main method that creates a simple JFrame, to which the panels are added. The `main` method also sets the frame's attributes and displays it. Here is the code for a typical version of this class, which does not vary much from application to application:

```java
// A frame with a specialized panel

import javax.swing.*;
import java.awt.*;

public class GUIWindow{

    public static void main(String[] args){
        JFrame theGUI = new JFrame();
        theGUI.setTitle("GUI Program");
        theGUI.setSize(300, 200);
        theGUI.setDefaultCloseOperation(JFrame.EXIT_ON_CLOSE);
        ColorPanel panel = new ColorPanel(Color.white);
        Container pane = theGUI.getContentPane();
        pane.add(panel);
        theGUI.setVisible(true);
    }
}
```

To convert programs with this structure to applets, we must do several things:

1. `GUIWindow` now extends `JApplet`.

2. Replace `public static void main(String[] args)` with `public void init()`.

3. Do not create a `JFrame`. The operations to set its title, size, close operation, and visibility go away.

We simply create the panel, get the applet's content pane, and add the panel to it. Here is the code for the modified `GUIWindow` class:

```java
// Example 8.2: An applet with a specialized panel
import javax.swing.*;
import java.awt.*;

public class GUIWindow extends JApplet{

    public void init(){
        ColorPanel panel = new ColorPanel(Color.white);
        Container pane = theGUI.getContentPane();
        pane.add(panel);
    }
}
```

As we said earlier, slight variations of this example will convert to applets any of the graphics programs discussed in Chapters 2 through 6.

Using the Applet Viewer

Sun's JDK comes with a tool called an *applet viewer*. This tool allows the programmer to run an applet and view just its GUI, without the surrounding Web page. To use the applet viewer, you must

1. Compile the Java source program as usual.

2. Create an HTML file with at least the minimal applet tag for the applet.

3. At the command line prompt, run the following command:

```
appletviewer <html file name>
```

Figure 8-10 shows the converter applet running within the applet viewer.

FIGURE 8-10
An applet within the applet viewer

Constraints on Applets

There are several major differences between applets and applications:

- To ensure security on the user's machine, applets cannot access files on that machine. Imagine how dangerous it would be to download applets across the Web if the applets could read or trash the files on your computer.

- Applets and the HTML documents that use them should be placed in the same directory. This rule can be violated, but doing so is beyond the scope of this book. Java programs, whether they are standalone applications or applets, frequently utilize classes in addition to those in the standard Java libraries. These classes should usually be in the same directory as the applet.

- The programs in this book use Java 5.0, so only Web browsers that support Java 5.0 can run the applets in this chapter. One such browser is available from www.sun.com.

- The technique for using dialog boxes in applications, as described in Chapter 4, applies to applets, with three qualifications:

    - The parent parameter of the dialog box's constructor should not be the applet, but `null` instead.

    - You might see a warning message at the bottom of the dialog box.

    - The dialog box does not prevent you from returning to the Web page. Once there, you cannot interact with the applet, but you can browse to other pages, quit the browser, and perhaps hang up (or lock up) the computer.

Loading Images into Applets

It is possible to load images into applets. These images must reside on the Web server from which the applet's byte code was sent. The JApplet method getDocumentBase() locates and returns the URL of the applet's Web server. The JApplet method getImage expects this URL and the filename of an image as parameters. The method downloads the image from the Web server and returns an object of the class Image. This object can be converted to an ImageIcon object for further processing by using the ImageIcon(anImage) constructor.

To illustrate, here is the code for the main window class that loaded an image of Smokey the cat in Chapter 5, followed by the corresponding applet:

```java
// Example 5.2: Loading an image from a file (standalone application)

import javax.swing.*;
import java.awt.*;

public class GUIWindow{

   public static void main(String[] args){
      JFrame theGUI = new JFrame();
      theGUI.setTitle("GUI Program");
      theGUI.setSize(300, 300);
      theGUI.setDefaultCloseOperation(JFrame.EXIT_ON_CLOSE);
      ImageIcon image = new ImageIcon("smokey.jpg");
      ColorPanel panel = new ColorPanel(Color.black, image);
      Container pane = theGUI.getContentPane();
      pane.add(panel);
      theGUI.setVisible(true);
   }
}


// Example 8.3: Loading an image from a file (applet)

import javax.swing.*;
import java.awt.*;

public class GUIWindow extends JApplet{

   public void init(){
      // Locate this applet's Web server and load the image
      Image image = getImage(getDocumentBase(), "smokey.jpg");
      // Convert to an image icon for further processing
      ImageIcon imageIcon = new ImageIcon(image);
      ColorPanel panel = new ColorPanel(Color.black, imageIcon);
      Container pane = getContentPane();
      pane.add(panel);
   }
}
```

Passing Parameters to Applets

It is possible to send information from an HTML page to an applet. The information is passed in HTML parameter tags and is retrieved in the applet's code. In the following example, a parameter tag binds the string "5" to the name "numberOfCourses". The parameter tag must appear between the opening and closing applet tag:

```
<APPLET CODE="Courses.class" WIDTH=150 HEIGHT=100>
<PARAM NAME=numberOfCourses VALUE="5">
</APPLET>
```

At any point within the applet, the method getParameter can retrieve the parameter's value, but always as a string:

```
String str = getParameter ("numberOfCourses");
int num = Integer.pasreInt(str);
```

A common location for such code is in the init method.

If there are several parameters, each requires its own tag.

For a fairly complete reference on HTML and Web page design, enter the following URL in your Web browser:

```
http://www.mcli.dist.maricopa.edu/tut/lessons.html
```

*E*XERCISE 8.9

1. Describe the simplest format of an HTML applet tag. Give an example.

2. How is an application converted to an applet?

3. What can an application do that an applet cannot do?

4. Describe the steps required to load an image into an applet.

SUMMARY

In this chapter, you learned:

- The World Wide Web is a hypermedia system that allows users to navigate among and use various resources in a nonlinear manner.

- HTML tags can be used to format text for Web pages. Other markup tags can be used to organize information in lists and tables in a Web page.

- Links to other pages using absolute or relative path names also can be included in HTML elements.

- Web pages also can contain applets or Java applications that are downloaded from a Web server and run in the user's Web browser.

- There are a few simple steps to convert a Java application to an applet. Applets have most of the functionality of applications, including the GUI, but they lack file access to the user's disks.

VOCABULARY *Review*

Define the following terms:

Absolute path name	Hypermedia	Markup tag
Associative link	Hypertext	Memex
Definition list	Hypertext markup language	Relative path name
External image	(HTML)	Uniform resource locator
Hyperlinks	Inline image	(URL)

REVIEW *Questions*

FILL IN THE BLANK

Complete the following sentences by writing the correct word or words in the blanks provided.

1. _____ generalizes hypertext to include images, sound, video, and embedded applications.

2. HTML stands for _____.

3. The three markup tags that any HTML document usually contains are _____, _____, and _____.

4. The _____ markup tag is used to display text in its original format.

5. A(n) _____ markup tag is used to lay out elements in a two-dimensional grid.

6. The _____ method serves a similar role to a constructor for applets.

7. Two program features that are not allowed in applets are _____ and _____.

8. The JDK's _____ allows the programmer to run an applet without a Web browser.

9. URL stands for _____.

10. A(n) _____ path name is used to obtain a resource from a remote server.

PROJECTS

PROJECT 8-1

If you have not done so already, create a home page on your local Web server. Include a title, a brief paragraph that states who you are, and a picture of your favorite pastime.

PROJECT 8-2

Add a list of courses you are currently taking to the home page created for Project 8-1.

PROJECT 8-3

Make each item in the list from Project 8-2 a link to a page that describes that item. Create these pages and test your hypertext thoroughly.

PROJECT 8-4

Add links to each of the pages created in Project 8-3 that return the user to your home page.

PROJECT 8-5

Write an applet that plays the game of guess the number with the user. The applet contains four labeled data fields. One is for the user's input, two are for the lower and upper bounds of the range of numbers to guess, and the fourth is for the program's messages to the user. At startup, the program displays two numbers chosen at random in its two number fields. The program also selects a number at random between these two numbers but keeps it hidden from the user. The user guesses this number by entering a number in the input field and clicking a Guess button. If the user guesses correctly, the program displays a message to that effect and resets its fields to new random numbers for another game. Otherwise, the program displays the message "Too low" or "Too high" and waits for further input.

CRITICAL *Thinking*

Write a short essay that compares the advantages and disadvantages of using Java applications and applets.

THE NEXT STEP WITH JAVA

REVIEW *Questions*

TRUE/FALSE

Circle T if the statement is true or F if it is false.

T F **1.** A mutator method is used to ask an object for the values of its data attributes.

T F **2.** The purpose of a constructor is to change the data type of an object.

T F **3.** Two variables can refer to the same object.

T F **4.** `private` variables are visible within their class and to all clients of that class.

T F **5.** Each method can declare its own private variables, called local variables.

T F **6.** The lifetime of a variable is the region on the program within which it can be used.

T F **7.** An extended `if` statement allows a program to choose among mutually exclusive alternatives.

T F **8.** The logical operator OR is indicated by !.

T F **9.** A `boolean` variable is used to manipulate characters and strings.

T F **10.** It is possible to test all programs to show that they are completely correct.

FILL IN THE BLANK

Complete the following sentences by writing the correct word or words in the blanks provided.

1. The process of creating a new object is called _____.

2. The process of deleting unreferenced objects from memory is called _____.

3. If a variable is declared outside all methods, it is said to be _____.

4. The access modifier that makes methods visible to all clients is _____.

5. Two methods in a program that have the same name but not the same number and types of parameters are said to be _____.

6. When a variable of a reference type is declared but not given a value, its default value is _____.

7. The easiest way to increase numbers by one in a program is to use the _____ operator.

8. The logical operators are _____, _____, and _____.

9. The _____ statement provides a simple way to get out of a loop before all of the statements in the loop process.

10. To determine all the possible values of a Boolean expression, one can use a(n) _____ table.

WRITTEN QUESTIONS

Write your answers to the following questions or problems.

1. Explain the difference between a global variable and a local variable and give an example of each.

2. Assume that x, y, and z are boolean variables. Draw truth tables for the following expressions.
   A. `x && y || z`

   B. `!(x || y || z)`

   C. `x && (y || z)`

3. Define a class called `counter`. A counter contains an integer that initially is 0 but that can be incremented, decremented, or reset to 0. Counter objects should respond to the mutators `increment()`, `decrement()`, and `reset()`, and to the accessor `getValue()`.

4.   What is data encapsulation? Why is it important?

5.   Describe what a class constructor does.

PROJECTS

PROJECT 1

Write a program that takes as inputs the lengths of three sides of a triangle and displays in a message box whether the triangle is scalene, isosceles, or equilateral. Following are some useful facts:

■   In a triangle, the longest side must be less than the sum of the other two sides.

■   A scalene triangle has all sides unequal.

■   An isosceles triangle has two sides equal.

■   An equilateral triangle has all sides equal.

PROJECT 2

In the game of craps, a player provides an initial bankroll and bets from this amount on each roll of the dice. On each roll, the sum of the faces is taken. The outcomes are as follow:

■   If 7 or 11 is rolled, the player wins.

■   If 2, 3, or 12 is rolled, the player loses.

■   Otherwise, the number rolled becomes the player's point. The player rolls the dice repeatedly until the player wins by making point (getting the same number as on the first roll) or loses by crapping out (getting a 7).

Design and implement a craps machine that allows the user to play craps. This machine should be defined as a new class. The interface accepts an amount of money representing an initial bankroll. Before each roll of the dice, the user must make a bet. At the end of the game, the program should display the amount of the user's current bankroll (after adding the gains and deducting the losses).

PROJECT 3

A perfect number is a positive integer such that the sum of the divisors equals the number. Thus, $28 = 1 + 2 + 4 + 7 + 14$ is a perfect number. If the sum of the divisors is less than the number, it is deficient. If the sum exceeds the number, it is abundant. Write a program that takes a positive integer as input and displays whether the number entered is perfect, deficient, or abundant. Your program should define the following two methods:

```
boolean isDivisor (int number, int divisor)

int divisorSum (int number)
```

The method `isDivisor` returns `true` if the `divisor` parameter is a divisor of the `number` parameter and `false` otherwise. The `divisorSum` method uses `isDivisor` to accumulate and return the sum of the proper divisors of the `number` parameter. Be sure to design and test the program incrementally; that is, verify that `isDivisor` works correctly before using it in `divisorSum`.

PROJECT 4

A standard physics experiment is to drop a ball to see how high it bounces. Once the "bounciness" of the ball is determined, the ratio gives a bounciness index. For example, if a ball dropped from a height of 10 feet bounces 6 feet high, the index is 0.6 and the total distance traveled by the ball is 16 feet after one bounce. If the ball continues bouncing, the distance after two bounces would be $(10 + 6) + (6 + 3.6) = 25.6$ feet. Note that the distance traveled for each bounce is the distance to the floor plus 0.6 of that distance as the ball comes back up.

Write a program that takes as inputs the initial height of the ball (in feet), the index of the ball's bounciness, and the number of times the ball is allowed to continue bouncing. The program should output the total distance traveled by the ball. At some point in the process, the distance traveled by the ball after a bounce might become negligible, for example, less than 0.00001 inches. If that stage is reached, terminate the process and output the total distance.

CRITICAL *Thinking*

A number is prime if it has no divisors (other than 1) that are less than or equal to its square root. The number 1 is not prime. Design and implement a method, `isPrime`, that returns `true` if its parameter is a prime number and `false` otherwise. You should use the `isDivisor` method developed in Project U2-3 in the implementation of `isPrime`. Then use these methods in a program that takes as input a number N and displays as output a list of the first N prime numbers.

ARRAYS, RECURSION, AND COMPLEXITY

Unit 3

 Estimated Time for Unit: 19.5 hours

CHAPTER 9

INTRODUCTION TO ARRAYS

OBJECTIVES

Upon completion of this chapter, you should be able to:

- Write programs that handle collections of similar items.

- Declare array variables and instantiate array objects.

- Manipulate arrays with loops, including the enhanced for loop.

- Write methods to manipulate arrays.

- Create parallel arrays and two-dimensional arrays.

Estimated Time: 5 hours

VOCABULARY

Array

Element

Enhanced for loop

Index

Initializer list

Logical size

Multidimensional array

One-dimensional array

Parallel arrays

Physical size

Procedural decomposition

Ragged array

Range-bound error

Structure chart

Subscript

Two-dimensional array

There are situations in which programs need to manipulate many similar items, a task that would be extremely awkward using the language features encountered so far. Earlier we developed a Student class with a name and three test scores. Each test score required a separate instance variable. Imagine how tedious and lengthy the code would have become if a student had 20 scores. Fortunately, there is a way to handle this dilemma. Most programming languages, including Java, provide a data structure called an *array*, which consists of an ordered collection of similar items. An array, as a whole, has a single name, and the items in an array are referred to in terms of their position within the array. This chapter explains the mechanics of declaring arrays and several basic algorithms for manipulating them. Using an array, it is as easy to manipulate a million test scores as it is three.

9.1 Conceptual Overview

To demonstrate the need for arrays, let us consider the data for a `Student` class if there are no arrays, but there are 20 rather than 3 test scores. The declarations for the instance variables look like this:

```
private String name;
private int test1,  test2,  test3,  test4,  test5,
            test6,  test7,  test8,  test9,  test10,
            test11, test12, test13, test14, test15,
            test16, test17, test18, test19, test20;
```

and the computation of the average score looks like this:

```
// Compute and return a student's average
public int getAverage(){
    int average;
    average = (test1 + test2  + test3  + test4  + test5 +
               test6  + test7  + test8  + test9  + test10 +
               test11 + test12 + test13 + test14 + test15 +
               test16 + test17 + test18 + test19 + test20) / 20;
    return average;
}
```

Other methods are affected in a similar manner; however, arrays restore sanity to the situation. The items in an array are called *elements*, and for any particular array, all of the elements must be of the same type. The type can be any primitive or reference type. For instance, we can have an array of test scores, an array of names, or even an array of student objects. Figure 9-1 illustrates these ideas. In the figure, each array contains five elements, or has a *length* of five. The first element in the array `test` is referred to as `test[0]`, the second as `test[1]`, and so on. Here we encounter Java's convention of numbering starting with 0 rather than 1, a convention that is guaranteed to cause us grief whenever we accidentally revert to our lifelong habit of counting from 1. Thus, the elements in an array of length 100 are numbered from 0 to 99. An item's position within an array is called its *index* or *subscript*. In Figure 9-1, the array indexes appear within square brackets (`[ ]`).

FIGURE 9-1
Three arrays, each containing five elements

	Array of five integers called **test**		Array of five strings called **name**		Array of five characters called **grade**	
1st	85	test[0]	"Bill"	name[0]	'B'	grade[0]
2nd	100	test[1]	"Sue"	name[1]	'C'	grade[1]
3rd	75	test[2]	"Grace"	name[2]	'B'	grade[2]
4th	87	test[3]	"Tom"	name[3]	'A'	grade[3]
5th	68	test[4]	"John"	name[4]	'C'	grade[4]

EXERCISE 9.1

1. A program needs many variables to store and process data. How does an array solve this problem?

2. How does the programmer access an item in an array?

3. Mary is using an array of doubles to store an employee's wage amounts for each day of the week (Monday through Friday). Draw a picture of this array with sample items and references to each one.

9.2 Simple Array Manipulations

The mechanics of manipulating arrays are fairly straightforward, as illustrated in the following segments of code. First, we declare and instantiate an array of 500 integer values. (Section 9.4 discusses array declarations in greater detail.) By default, all of the values are initialized to 0:

```
int[] abc = new int[500];
```

Next, we declare some other variables:

```
int i = 3;
int temp;
double avFirstFive;
```

The basic syntax for referring to an array element has the form

```
<array name>[<index>]
```

where `<index>` must be between 0 and the array's length less 1. The subscript operator (`[ ]`) has the same precedence as the method selector (`.`). To illustrate, we assign values to the first five elements:

```
abc[0] = 78;                  // 1st element 78
abc[1] = 66;                  // 2nd element 66
abc[2] = (abc[0] + abc[1]) / 2;   // 3rd element average of first two
abc[i] = 82;                  // 4th element 82 because i is 3
abc[i + 1] = 94;              // 5th element 94 because i + 1 is 4
```

When assigning a value to the 500th element, we must remember that its index is 499, not 500:

```
abc[499] = 76;               // 500th element 76
```

Fortunately, the JVM checks the values of subscripts before using them and throws an `ArrayIndexOutOfBoundsException` if they are out of bounds (less than 0 or greater than the array length less 1). The detection of a *range-bound error* is similar to the JVM's behavior when a program attempts to divide by 0.

In our present example, subscripts must be between 0 and 499. Later in the chapter, we show how to work with arrays of any size and how to write loops that are not tied to a literal value (in this case, 500).

```
abc[-1] = 74;            // NO! NO! NO! Out of bounds
abc[500] = 88;           // NO! NO! NO! Out of bounds
```

To compute the average of the first five elements, we could write

```
avFirstFive = (abc[0] + abc[1] + abc[2] + abc[3] + abc[4])/5;
```

It often happens that we need to interchange elements in an array. To demonstrate, following is code that interchanges any two adjacent elements:

```
// Initializations
. . .
abc[3] = 82;
abc[4] = 95;
i = 3;
. . .


// Interchange adjacent elements
temp = abc[i];                   // temp         now equals 82
abc[i] = abc[i + 1];             // abc[i]       now equals 95
abc[i + 1] = temp;               // abc[i + 1]   now equals 82
```

We frequently need to know an array's length, but we do not have to remember it. The array itself makes this information available by means of a public instance variable called `length`:

```
System.out.println ("The size of abc is: " + abc.length);
```

*E*XERCISE 9.2

1. Assume that the array a contains the five integers 34, 23, 67, 89, and 12. Write the values of the following expressions:

   a. a[1]

   b. a[a.length – 1]

   c. a[2] + a[3]

2. What happens when a program attempts to access an item at an index that is less than 0 or greater than or equal to the array's length?

9.3 Looping Through Arrays

There are many situations in which it is necessary to write a loop that iterates through an array one element at a time. Following are some examples based on the array abc of 500 integers. Later in this section, we show how to work with arrays of any size and how to write loops that are not tied to a literal value (in this case, 500).

Sum the Elements

The following is code that sums the numbers in the array abc. Each time through the loop we add a different element to the sum. On the first iteration we add abc[0] and on the last abc[499].

```
int sum;
sum = 0;
for (int i = 0; i < 500; i++)
   sum += abc[i];
```

Count the Occurrences

We can determine how many times a number x occurs in the array by comparing x to each element and incrementing count every time there is a match:

```
int x;
int count;
x = ...;                         // Assign some value to x
count = 0;
for (int i = 0; i < 500; i++){
   if (abc[i] == x)
      count++;                   // Found another element equal to x
}
```

Determine Presence or Absence

To determine if a particular number is present in the array, we could count the occurrences, but, alternatively, we could save time by breaking out of the loop as soon as the first match is found. The following is code based on this idea. The Boolean variable found indicates the outcome of the search:

```
int x;
boolean found;
x = ...;
found = false;                   // Initially assume x is not present
for (int i = 0; i < 500; i++){
   if (abc[i] == x){
      found = true;
      break;                     // No point in continuing once x is found
   }                             // so break out of the loop
}
if (found)
```

```
      System.out.println("Found");
   else
      System.out.println("Not Found");
```

Determine First Location

As a variation on the preceding example, we now show how to find the first location of x in the array. The variable loc initially equals –1, meaning that we have not found x yet. We then iterate through the array, comparing each element to x. As soon as we find a match, we set loc to the location and break out of the loop. If x is not found, loc remains equal to –1.

```
int x;
int loc;
x = ...;
loc = -1;
for (int i = 0; i < 500; i++){
   if (abc[i] == x){
      loc = i;
      break;
   }
}
if (loc == -1)
   System.out.println("Not Found");
else
   System.out.println("Found at index " + loc);
```

Working with Arrays of Any Size

The examples in this section have assumed that the array contains 500 elements. It is possible and also desirable to write similar code that works with arrays of any size, however. We simply replace the literal 500 with a reference to the array's instance variable length in each of the loops. For example, this code would sum the integers in an array of any size:

```
int sum;
sum = 0;
for (int i = 0; i < abc.length; i++)
   sum += abc[i];
```

*E*XERCISE 9.3

1. Write a loop that prints all of the items in an array a to the terminal screen.

2. Repeat Question 1 but print the items in reverse order.

3. Write a loop that locates the first occurrence of a negative integer in an array a. When the loop is finished, the variable index should contain the index of the negative number or the length of the array if there were no negative numbers in the array.

EXERCISE 9.3 Continued

4. Describe what the following code segments do:

a.

```
for (int i = 0; i < a.length; i++)
    a[i] = Math.abs(a[i]);
```

b.

```
String str = "";
for (int i = 0; i < a.length; i++)
    str += a[i];
```

5. What is the advantage of using the instance variable `length` in a loop with an array?

9.4 Declaring Arrays

Earlier, we declared an array of 500 integers as follows:

```
int[] abc = new int[500];
```

In doing so, we combined two separate statements:

```
int[] abc;              // Declare abc to be a variable that can
                        // reference an array of integers.
abc = new int[500];     // Instantiate an array of 500 integers for abc to
                        // reference.
```

Arrays are objects and must be instantiated before being used. Several array variables can be declared in a single statement like this:

```
int[] abc, xyz;
abc = new int[500];
xyz = new int[10];
```

or like this:

```
int[] abc = new int[500], xyz = new int[10];
```

Array variables are null before they are assigned array objects. Failure to assign an array object can result in a null pointer exception, as shown in the next code segment:

```
int[] abc;
abc[1] = 10;   // run-time error: null pointer exception
```

Because arrays are objects, two variables can refer to the same array, as indicated in Figure 9-2 and the next segment of code:

```
int[] abc, xyz;
abc = new int[5];               // Instantiate an array of five
                                // integers

xyz = abc;                      // xyz and abc refer to the same array
xyz[3] = 100;                   // Changing xyz changes abc as well.
System.out.println (abc[3]);    // 100 is displayed.
```

FIGURE 9-2
Two variables can refer to the same array object

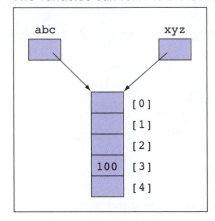

If we want abc and xyz to refer to two separate arrays that happen to contain the same values, we could copy all of the elements from one array to the other, as follows:

```
int[] abc, xyz;             // Declare two array variables
int i;
abc = new int[10];          // Instantiate an array of size 10
for (i = 0; i < 10; i++)    // Initialize the array
    abc[i] = i*i;           // a[0]=0 and a[1]=1 and a[2]=4, etc.

xyz = new int[10];          // Instantiate another array of size 10
for (i = 0; i < 10; i++)    // Initialize the second array
    xyz[i] = abc[i];
```

Also, because arrays are objects, Java's garbage collector sweeps them away when they are no longer referenced:

```
int[] abc, xyz;
abc = new int[10];    // Instantiate an array of 10 integers.
xyz = new int[5];     // Instantiate an array of 5 integers.
xyz = null;           // The array of 5 integers is no longer referenced
                      // so the garbage collector will sweep it away.
```

Arrays can be declared, instantiated, and initialized in one step. The list of numbers between the braces is called an *initializer list*.

```
int[] abc = {1,2,3,4,5}; // abc now references an array of five integers.
```

As mentioned at the outset, arrays can be formed from any collection of similar items. Following then are arrays of doubles, characters, Booleans, strings, and students:

```
double[]   ddd = new double[10];
char[]     ccc = new char[10];
boolean[]  bbb = new boolean[10];
String[]   ggg = new String[10];
Student[]  sss = new Student[10];
String     str;

ddd[5] = 3.14;
ccc[5] = 'Z';
bbb[5] = true;
ggg[5] = "The cat sat on the mat.";
sss[5] = new Student();

sss[5].setName ("Bill");
str = sss[5].getName() + ggg[5].substring(7);
   // str now equals "Bill sat on the mat."
```

There is one more way to declare array variables, but its use can be confusing. Here it is:

```
int aaa[];                  // aaa is an array variable.
```

That does not look confusing, but what about this?

```
int aaa[], bbb, ccc[];   // aaa and ccc are array variables.
                         // bbb is not. This fact might go unnoticed.
```

Instead, it might be better to write:

```
int[] aaa, ccc;          // aaa and ccc are array variables
int bbb;                 // bbb is not. This fact is obvious.
```

Once an array is instantiated, its size cannot be changed, so make sure the array is large enough from the outset.

*E*XERCISE 9.4

1. Declare and instantiate array variables for the following data:

   a. An array of 15 doubles

   b. An array of 20 strings

2. What is an initializer list?

3. Use an initializer list to create the following arrays:

    a. five test scores of 100, 90, 75, 60, and 88

    b. three interest rates of 0.12, 0.05, and 0.15

    c. two strings, your first name and last name

4. Why is it better to use the form `<type>[] <variable>` instead of `<type> <variable>[]` when declaring an array variable?

9.5 Working with Arrays That Are Not Full

When an array is instantiated, the computer automatically fills its cells with default values. For example, each cell in an array of `int` initially contains the value 0. The application then replaces these values with new ones as needed. An application might not use all the cells available in an array, however. For example, one might create an array of 20 `int`s but receive only 5 `int`s from interactive input. This array has a *physical size* of 20 cells but a *logical size* of 5 cells currently used by the application. From the application's perspective, the remaining 15 cells contain garbage. Clearly, the application should only access the first five cells when asked to display the data, so using the array's physical size as an upper bound on a loop will not do. We solve this problem by tracking the array's logical size with a separate integer variable. The following code segment shows the initial state of an array and its logical size:

```
int[] abc = new int[50];
int size = 0;
```

Note that `abc.length` (the physical size) is 50, whereas `size` (the logical size) is 0.

Processing Elements in an Array That Is Not Full

In Section 9.3, we showed how to generalize a loop to process all the data in an array of any size. The loop accesses each cell from position 0 to position `length - 1`, where `length` is the array's instance variable. When the array is not full, one must replace the array's physical length with its logical size in the loop. Following is the code for computing the sum of the integers currently available in the array `abc`:

```
int[] abc = new int[50];
int size = 0;

... code that puts values into some initial portion of the array and sets
    the value of size ...

int sum = 0;
for (int i = 0; i < size; i++)
   sum += abc[i];
```

Adding Elements to an Array

The simplest way to add a data element to an array is to place it after the last available item. One must first check to see if there is a cell available and then remember to increment the array's logical size. The following code shows how to add an integer to the end of array `abc`:

```java
if (size < abc.length){
   abc[size] = anInt;
   size++;
}
```

When `size` equals `abc.length`, the array is full. The `if` statement prevents a range error from occurring. Remember that Java arrays are of fixed size when they are instantiated, so eventually they become full. We examine a way of skirting this limitation of arrays in Chapter 11.

We can also insert an element at an earlier position in the array. This process requires a shifting of other elements and is also presented in Chapter 11.

Removing Elements from an Array

Removing a data element from the end of an array requires no change to the array itself. We simply decrement the logical size, thus preventing the application from accessing the garbage elements beyond that point. (Removing a data element from an arbitrary position is discussed in Chapter 11.)

Arrays and Text Files

We conclude this section with two short programs that use arrays in conjunction with text files. The first program prompts the user for integers and inserts them at the logical end of an array. This process stops when the user enters −1 as input or when the array becomes full. The program then outputs the contents of the array to a text file. Here is the code:

```java
// Example 9.1: Input numbers from the keyboard into an array and
// output the array's numbers to a text file

import java.io.*;
import java.util.Scanner;

public class ArrayToFile{

   public static void main(String[] args) throws IOException {
      // Set up scanner and array
      Scanner reader = new Scanner(System.in);
      int[] array = new int[10];
      int count = 0;

      // Input numbers until full or user enters -1
      while (count < array.length){
         System.out.print("Enter a number (-1 to quit): ");
         int number = reader.nextInt();
         if (number == -1)
            break;
         array[count] = number;
         count++;
      }
```

```
        // Output the numbers to a text file
        PrintWriter writer = new PrintWriter(new File("numbers.txt"));
        for (int i = 0; i < count; i++)
            writer.println(array[i]);
        writer.close();
    }
}
```

The critical variable in this first example is count. This variable tracks the number of numbers input as well as the logical size of the array. The output loop also uses count to test for the logical end of the array.

Our second example program reads numbers from a text file, inserts them into an array, and then displays them in the terminal window. If there is not enough room in the array, an error message is also displayed.

```
// Example 9.2: Input numbers from a file into an array and
// output the array's numbers to the terminal window

import java.io.*;
import java.util.Scanner;

public class FileToArray{

    public static void main(String[] args) throws IOException {
        // Set up scanner and array
        Scanner reader = new Scanner(new File("numbers.txt"));
        int[] array = new int[10];
        int count = 0;

        // Input numbers until full or end of file is reached
        while (count < array.length  && reader.hasNext()){
            int number = reader.nextInt();
            array[count] = number;
            count++;
        }

        // Output the numbers to the terminal window
        for (int i = 0; i < count; i++)
            System.out.println(array[i]);

        // Display error message if not all data are read from file
        if (reader.hasNext())
            System.out.println("Some data lost during input");
    }
}
```

Once again, the critical variable is count, which tracks the number of integers input from the file and the number of integers stored in the array. Arrays that receive data from input are often only partially filled. In extreme cases, an array might not be large enough to hold the number of inputs offered. We examine techniques for dealing with this problem in Chapter 11.

EXERCISE 9.5

1. What happens when the programmer tries to access an array cell whose index is greater than or equal to its logical size?

2. Describe an application that uses an array that might not be full.

9.6 Parallel Arrays

There are situations in which it is convenient to declare what are called *parallel arrays*. Suppose we want to keep a list of people's names and ages. This can be achieved by using two arrays in which corresponding elements are related. For instance

```
String[] name = {"Bill", "Sue", "Shawn", "Mary", "Ann"};
int[]    age  = {20    , 21    , 19      , 24     , 20};
```

Thus, Bill's age is 20 and Mary's is 24. Note that related items have the same index. There are many other uses for parallel arrays, but continuing on with our present example, the following is a segment of code that finds the age of a particular person:

```
String searchName;
int correspondingAge = -1;

searchName = ...;                        // Set this to the desired name
for (int i = 0; i < name.length; i++){   // name.length is the array's size
   if (searchName.equals (name[i])){
      correspondingAge = age[i];
      break;
   }
}

if (correspondingAge == -1)
   System.out.println(searchName + " not found.");
else
   System.out.println("The age is " + correspondingAge);
```

In this example, the parallel arrays are both full and the loops use the instance variable `length`. When the arrays are not full, the code will need an extra variable to track their logical sizes, as discussed earlier.

EXERCISE 9.6

1. What are parallel arrays?

2. Describe an application in which parallel arrays might be used.

3. Declare and instantiate the variables for parallel arrays to track the names, ages, and social security numbers of 50 employees.

4. Assume that the array `names` contains the names of people in a phone book and the parallel array `numbers` contains their phone numbers. Write a code segment that displays each name and number in formatted columns (using the method `printf` introduced in Chapter 7). Names should be left-justified in a width of 20 columns. You may assume that each number is the same length.

5. Write a code segment that creates parallel arrays containing the first 10 nonnegative powers of 2. One array should contain the exponent and the other array should contain 2 raised to that power.

9.7 Two-Dimensional Arrays

The arrays we have been studying so far can represent only simple lists of items and are called *one-dimensional arrays*. For many applications, *multidimensional arrays* are more useful. A table of numbers, for instance, can be implemented as a *two-dimensional array*. Figure 9-3 shows a two-dimensional array with four rows and five columns.

FIGURE 9-3
A two-dimensional array with four rows and five columns

	col 0	col 1	col 2	col 3	col 4
row 0	00	01	02	03	04
row 1	10	11	12	13	14
row 2	20	21	22	23	24
row 3	30	31	32	33	34

Suppose we call the array `table`; then to indicate an element in `table`, we specify its row and column position, remembering that indexes start at 0:

```
x = table[2][3];  // Set x to 23, the value in (row 2, column 3)
```

Sum the Elements

The techniques for manipulating one-dimensional arrays are easily extended to two-dimensional arrays. For instance, the following is code that sums all the numbers in `table`. The outer loop iterates four times and moves down the rows. Each time through the outer loop, the inner loop iterates five times and moves across a different row.

```
int sum = 0;
for (int i = 0; i < 4; i++){      // There are four rows: i = 0,1,2,3
   for (int j = 0; j < 5; j++){ // There are five columns: j = 0,1,2,3,4
      sum += table[i][j];
   }
}
```

This segment of code can be rewritten without using the numbers 4 and 5. The value `table.length` equals the number of rows, and `table[i].length` is the number of columns in row i.

```
int sum = 0;
for (int i = 0; i < table.length; i++){
   for (int j = 0; j < table[i].length; j++){
      sum += table[i][j];
   }
}
```

Sum the Rows

Rather than accumulate all the numbers into a single sum, we now compute the sum of each row separately and place the results in a one-dimensional array called `rowSum`. This array has four elements, one for each row of the table. The elements in `rowSum` are initialized to 0 automatically by virtue of the declaration.

```
int[] rowSum = new int[4];
for (int i = 0; i < table.length; i++){
   for (int j = 0; j < table[i].length; j++){
      rowSum[i] += table[i][j];
   }
}
```

Declare and Instantiate

Declaring and instantiating two-dimensional arrays is accomplished by extending the processes used for one-dimensional arrays:

```
int[][] table;              // The variable table can reference a
                            // two-dimensional array of integers.
table = new int[4][5];      // Instantiate table as an array of size 4,
                            // each of whose elements will reference an array
                            // of 5 integers.
```

Figure 9-4 shows another diagram of `table` that illustrates the perspective revealed in the previous piece of code. The variable `table` references an array of four elements. Each of these elements in turn references an array of five integers. Although the diagram is complex, specifying an element in the resulting two-dimensional array is the same as before, for instance, `table[2][3]`.

FIGURE 9-4
Another way of visualizing a two-dimensional array

Initializer lists can be used with two-dimensional arrays. This requires a list of lists. The number of inner lists determines the number of rows, and the size of each inner list determines the size of the corresponding row. The rows do not have to be the same size, but they are in this example:

```
int[][] table = {{ 0, 1, 2, 3, 4},      // row 0
                 {10,11,12,13,14},      // row 1
                 {20,21,22,23,24},      // row 2
                 {30,31,32,33,34}};     // row 3
```

Variable Length Rows

Occasionally, the rows of a two-dimensional array are not all the same length. We call these *ragged arrays*, and we just mention them in passing. Consider the following improbable declaration:

```
int[][] table;
table    = new int[4][];   // table has 4 rows
table[0] = new int[6];     // row 0 has 6   elements
table[1] = new int[10];    // row 1 has 10  elements
table[2] = new int[100];   // row 2 has 100 elements
table[3] = new int[1];     // row 3 has 1   element
```

Finally, remember that all the elements of a two-dimensional array must be of the same type, whether they are integers, doubles, strings, or whatever.

EXERCISE 9.7

1. What are two-dimensional arrays?

2. Describe an application in which a two-dimensional array might be used.

3. Write a code segment that searches a two-dimensional array for a negative integer. The loop should terminate at the first instance of a negative integer in the array, and the variables `row` and `col` should be set to its position. Otherwise, the variables `row` and `col` should equal the number of rows and columns in the array (we assume that each row has the same number of columns).

4. Describe the contents of the array after the following code segment is run:

```
int [][] matrix = new int[5][5];

for (int row = 0; row < matrix.length; row++)
   for (int col = 0; col < matrix[row].length; col++)
      matrix[row][col] = row * col;
```

9.8 Using the Enhanced for Loop

Most of the loops used with arrays follow common patterns, such as visiting every element from the first position to the last one, or visiting elements until a particular element is found. These loops require the use of an index variable, which is initialized to the first position. They must then test the index for less than the last position to continue. Finally, they must increment the index on each pass. Java 5.0 provides an *enhanced* `for` *loop* that frees the programmer from managing these details. This type of loop visits each element in an array from the first position to the last position. On each pass through the loop, the element at the current position is automatically assigned to a temporary variable. No other loop control information is required.

The syntax of the enhanced `for` loop is much simpler than that of the standard `for` loop:

```
for (<temporary variable declaration> : <array object>)
   <statement>
```

The type of the temporary variable must be compatible with the element type of the array.

To see how the enhanced `for` loop can simplify code, let's modify two earlier examples where we computed the sum of an array of integers and the sum of a two-dimensional array of integers. We place the revised code segments in a short tester program, which should display the results 9 and 27 for the two arrays:

```
// Example 9.3: Testing the enhanced for loop

public class TestForLoop{

   public static void main(String[] args){

      // Sum the elements in a one-dimensional array
      int[] abc = {2, 3, 4};
      int sum = 0;
```

```java
        for (int element : abc)
            sum += element;
        System.out.println("First sum: " + sum);

        // Sum the elements in a two-dimensional array
        int[][] table = {{2, 3, 4}, {2, 3, 4}, {2, 3, 4}};
        sum = 0;
        for (int[]row : table)
            for (int element : row)
                sum += element;
        System.out.println("Second sum: " + sum);
    }
}
```

On each pass through the first loop, the integer at the current position in the array `abc` is automatically assigned to the temporary variable `element`. On each pass through the second loop, the two-dimensional array's current row is assigned to the temporary variable `row`. The nested loop then iterates through this array, assigning each integer at the current column position to another temporary variable `element`.

A `break` statement can also be used when we want to terminate an enhanced `for` loop early. For example, we can revise our earlier example of a search loop as follows:

```java
int x = ...;
boolean found = false;        // Initially assume x is not present
for (int element : abc){
    if (element == x){
        found = true;
        break;                // No point in continuing once x is found
    }                         // so break out of the loop
}
if (found)
    System.out.println("Found");
else
    System.out.println("Not Found");
```

An enhanced `for` loop is clearly simpler to write than a standard `for` loop with an index. The enhanced `for` loop is also less error-prone because Java automates the setup and processing of the loop control information. However, this type of loop *cannot* be used to

- Move through an array in reverse, from the last position to the first position

- Assign elements to positions in an array

- Track the index position of the current element in an array

- Access any element other than the current element on each pass

All of these options require a loop with an index. In general, it's also not a good idea to use an enhanced `for` loop on an array that's not filled. Therefore, if you choose an enhanced `for` loop, be sure that the array is filled, that you're going to visit each element from the first to the last, and that you do not need to assign a value to an element at a given position.

EXERCISE 9.8

1. Assume that array `abc` is filled with strings. Convert the following loops to simpler versions using the enhanced `for` loop:

a.

```
for (int i = 0; i < abc.length; i++)
      System.out.println(abc[i]);
```

b.

```
String target = …;
    boolean found = false;
    for (int i = 0; i < abc.length; i++)
      if (target.equals(abc[i])){
        found = true;
        break;
      }
```

2. List two different problems for which an enhanced `for` loop would not be appropriate.

9.9 Arrays and Methods

When any object is used as a parameter to a method, what actually gets passed is a reference to the object and not the object itself, as illustrated in Figure 9-5. In other words, the actual and formal parameters refer to the same object, and changes the method makes to the object's state are still in effect after the method terminates. In the figure, the method changes the student's name to Bill, and after the method finishes executing the name is still Bill.

FIGURE 9-5
Passing a reference to an object as a parameter

```
...
Student  stuVariable = new Student () ;
doSomethingToStudent (stuVariable);
...
void doSomethingToStudent (Student stuParameter) {
  ...
  stuParameter.setName("Bill");
  ...
}
```

Arrays are objects, so the same rules apply. When an array is passed as a parameter to a method, the method manipulates the array itself and not a copy. Changes made to the array in the method are still in effect after the method has completed its execution. Consequently, passing an array to a method leads to trouble if the method accidentally mishandles the array. A method can also instantiate a new object or a new array and return it using the `return` statement. Following are some illustrations based on examples presented earlier.

Sum the Elements

First, we look at a method that computes the sum of the numbers in an integer array. When the method is written, there is no need to know the array's size. The method works equally well with integer arrays of all sizes, as long as those arrays are full; however, the method cannot be used with arrays of other types, for instance, doubles. Notice that the method makes no changes to the array and therefore is "safe."

```java
int sum (int[] a){
    int result = 0;
    for (int element : a)
        result += element;
    return result;
}
```

Using the method is straightforward:

```java
int[] array1 = {10, 24, 16, 78, -55, 89, 65};
int[] array2 = {4334, 22928, 33291};
...
if (sum(array1) > sum(array2)) ...
```

Search for a Value

The code to search an array for a value is used so frequently in programs that it is worth placing in a method. Following is a method to search an array of integers. The method returns the location of the first array element equal to the search value or −1 if the value is absent:

```java
int search (int[] a, int searchValue){
    for (int i = 0; i < a.length; i++)
        if (a[i] == searchValue)
            return i;
    return -1;
}
```

Sum the Rows

Following is a method that instantiates a new array and returns it. The method computes the sum of each row in a two-dimensional array and returns a one-dimensional array of row sums. The method works even if the rows are not all the same size. We also rely on the fact that Java provides a default value of 0 at each position in the new array.

```java
int[] sumRows (int[][] a){
    int[] rowSum = new int[a.length];
    for (int i = 0; i < a.length; i++){
        for (int j = 0; j < a[i].length; j++){
            rowSum[i] += a[i][j];
        }
    }
    return rowSum;
}
```

Following is code that uses the method. Notice that we do not have to instantiate the array oneD because that task is done in the method sumRows.

```
int[][] twoD = {{1,2,3,4}, {5,6}, {7,8,9}};
int[] oneD;

oneD = sumRows (twoD); // oneD now references the array created and
                       // returned by the method sumRows.
                       // It equals {10, 11, 24}
```

Copy an Array

Earlier, we saw that copying an array must be done with care. Assigning one array variable to another does not do the job. It merely yields two variables referencing the same array. We now examine a method that attempts to solve the problem. The first parameter represents the original array, and the second is the copy. The original is instantiated before the method is called, and the copy is instantiated in the method.

```
void copyOne(int[] original, int[] copy){
   copy = new int[original.length];
   for (int i = 0; i < original.length; i++){
      copy[i] = original[i];
   }
}
```

We now run this method in the following code segment:

```
int[] orig = {1,2,3,4,5};
int[] cp;
...
copyOne (orig, cp);
```

When copyOne terminates, we would like the variable cp to refer to copy. However, that does not happen. Even though the method creates a copy of the original array and assigns it to the array parameter (copy = new int[original.length];), the original variable cp is not changed and does not refer to the array created in the method. We can achieve our goal more successfully by writing a method that returns a copy. We then call the method and assign the returned copy to cp. Following is the code:

```
// First the method
int[] copyTwo (int[] original){
   int[] copy = new int[original.length];
   for (int i = 0; i < original.length; i++){
      copy[i] = original[i];
   }
   return copy;
}

// And here is how we call it.
int[] orig = {1,2,3,4,5};
int[] cp = copyTwo (orig);
```

EXERCISE 9.9

1. What happens when one uses the assignment operator (=) with two array variables?

2. Discuss the issues involved with copying an array.

3. Write a method that returns the average of the numbers in an array of `double`.

4. Write a method `subArray` that expects an array of `int` and two `ints` as parameters. The integers represent the starting position and the ending position of a subarray within the parameter array. The method should return a new array that contains the elements from the starting position to the ending position.

5. Write a method that searches a two-dimensional array for a given integer. This method should return an object of class `Point`, which contains a row and a column. The constructor for `Point` is `Point(anInteger, anInteger)`.

9.10 Arrays of Objects

We examined the use of an array of strings earlier in this chapter. Arrays can hold objects of any type, or more accurately, references to objects. For example, one can declare, instantiate, and fill an array of students (see Chapter 5) as follows:

```
// Declare and reserve 10 cells for student objects
Student[] studentArray = new Student[10];

// Fill array with students
for (int i = 0; i < studentArray.length; i++)
   studentArray[i] = new Student("Student " + i, 70+i, 80+i, 90+i);
```

When an array of objects is instantiated, each cell is `null` by default until reset to a new object. The next code segment prints the average of all students in the `studentArray`. Pay special attention to the technique used to send a message to each object in the array:

```
// Print the average of all students in the array.
int sum = 0;
for (Student s : studentArray)
   sum += s.getAverage();                  // Send message to object in array
System.out.println("The class average is " + sum / studentArray.length);
```

EXERCISE 9.10

1. Write a method `getHighStudent` that expects an array of students as a parameter. The method returns the `Student` object that contains the highest score. You may assume that the `Student` class has a method `getHighScore()`. (*Hint*: The method should declare a local variable of type `Student` to track the student with the highest score. The initial value of this variable should be `null`.)

EXERCISE 9.10 Continued

2. What happens when the following code segment is executed?

```
// Declare and reserve 10 cells for student objects
Student[] studentArray = new Student[10];

// Add 5 students to the array
for (int i = 0; i < 5; i++)
    studentArray[i] = new Student("Student " + i, 70+i, 80+i, 90+i);

// Print the names of the students
for (int i = 0; i < studentArray.length; i++)
    System.out.println(studentArray[i].getName());
```

CASE STUDY: Student Test Scores Again

In Chapter 5 we developed a program for keeping track of student test scores. We now build on that program in two ways:

1. We extend the program so that it allows the user to maintain information on many students.

2. We modify the `student` class so that the grades are stored in an array rather than in separate instance variables.

Both changes illustrate the use of arrays to maintain lists of data.

Request

Modify the student test scores program from Chapter 5 so that it allows the user to maintain information on many students.

Analysis

The user interface for this program should allow the user to enter information for a new student, edit existing information, and navigate through the database of students to access each student's information. The student records are arranged in a linear sequence in the database, so the interface allows the user to navigate through this sequence. In addition, the interface should display the overall class average and the student with the highest score on demand. A menu-driven interface will work well. Here are the menu options:

1. Display the current student

2. Display the class average

3. Display the student with the highest grade

4. Display all of the students

5. Edit the current student

6. Add a new student

7. Move to the first student

8. Move to the last student

9. Move to the next student

10. Move to the previous student

11. Quit the program

Each option runs a command, displays the results, and waits for the user to press the Enter key before returning to the menu. When the menu is displayed, the program also displays the number of students currently in the database and the index position of the current student.

Because the user interface and the data are complex, we use the model/view pattern introduced in Chapter 5 to structure our code. The view class, called `TestScoresView`, is responsible for displaying the menu and handling interactions with the user. The model classes, called `Student` and `TestScoresModel`, are responsible for managing the students' data. A simple "application" class, called `TestScoresApp`, starts the application in a `main` method by instantiating the view and the model.

Our system is in fact complex enough that it would help to diagram the relationships among its classes. Figure 9-6 shows a *UML diagram* that depicts these relationships. UML, which stands for Unified Modeling Language, is a graphical notation developed by software professionals to design and document object-oriented systems. As you can see, the name of each class appears in a box. Various types of connecting lines designate the relationships between the classes. A dashed line ending in a solid arrow indicates that one class simply depends on another. Thus, `TestScoresApp` depends on both `TestScoresView` and `TestScoresModel`. A solid line ending in a diamond indicates that the class nearest the diamond contains and is in part composed of the class at the other end. The numbers that label these lines show the number of instances of the contained class. These numbers can be simple, indicating a fixed number, or a range from one simple number to another, or a star (*), which means zero or more. Thus, `TestScoresView` contains exactly one `TestScoresModel` object, whereas `TestScoresModel` contains any of 0 through 10 `Student` objects.

FIGURE 9-6
A UML diagram of the classes in the student test scores program

Design of the Data Model

We break the design into two parts, one for each set of classes used in the program.

For this program we make two major changes to the `Student` class described in Chapter 5:

1. The three test scores are stored in an array. This provides more flexibility than did the use of a separate instance variable for each test score and allows clients to use the class to deal with a larger number of scores.

2. The `Student` class provides a `validateData` method. Now any application that needs to validate student data can do so easily. For variety, the approach taken to data validation is somewhat different than that used in the `Employee` class of Chapter 6. If the validation code is placed in the user interface class, it would need to be repeated in every user interface that works with student objects, an approach that is wasteful, tedious, and difficult to maintain.

The `TestScoresModel` class represents the database of students. Viewed as a black box, it provides an interface or set of public methods listed in Table 9.1.

TABLE 9-1
Public methods of `TestScoresModel`

METHOD	WHAT IT DOES
`int size()`	Returns the number of students in the database
`int currentPosition()`	Returns the index position of the current student
`Student currentStudent()`	If the database is empty, returns `null`, otherwise returns the current student
`String toString()`	Returns a string containing the string representations of all of the students
`int getClassAverage()`	Returns the average of all of the scores in the database
`Student getHighScore()`	If the database is empty, returns `null`; otherwise, returns the first student with the highest score in the database
`String add(Student s)`	If there is not room for the new student, returns an error message; otherwise, adds `s` to the end of the database, makes the last position current, and returns `null`
`String replace(Student s)`	If the database is empty, returns an error message; otherwise, replaces the student at the current position with `s` and returns `null`
`Student first()`	If the database is empty, returns `null`; otherwise, moves to the first student and returns that student
`Student last()`	If the database is empty, returns `null`; otherwise, moves to the last student and returns that student
`Student next()`	If the database is empty, returns `null`; otherwise, if the current student is the last one, returns that student; otherwise, moves to the next student and returns that student
`Student previous()`	If the database is empty, returns `null`; otherwise, if the current student is the first one, returns that student; otherwise, moves to the previous student and returns that student

Note that we have set up the class's interface to make the management of data as easy as possible for its users (easier, at any rate, than it would be to directly manipulate an array). The following short tester program shows how the database of students might be used:

```
// Case Study 9.1: A tester program for TestScoresModel

public class TestModel{

    public static void main (String[] args){
```

```java
// Create and display an empty model
TestScoresModel model = new TestScoresModel();
System.out.println(model);

// Display the size, current position, and current student
System.out.println(model.size());
System.out.println(model.currentPosition());
System.out.println(model.currentStudent());

// Add and display 3 students
for (int i = 1; i <= 3; i++){
   Student s = new Student("S" + i);
   model.add(s);
}
System.out.println(model);

// Move to the first student and display it
System.out.println(model.first());

// Move to the next and previous and display them
System.out.println(model.next());
System.out.println(model.previous());

// Move to the last and next and display them
System.out.println(model.last());
System.out.println(model.next());

// Display size, current position, and current student
System.out.println(model.size());
System.out.println(model.currentPosition());
System.out.println(model.currentStudent());

// Replace the current student and display the model
int[] grades = {99, 88, 77};
Student newStudent = new Student("Beth", grades);
model.replace(newStudent);
System.out.println(model);

// Add more students and display results
for (int i = 6; i <= 13; i++){
   Student s = new Student("S" + i);
   System.out.println(model.add(s));
}
   }
}
```

The `TestScoresModel` class maintains its data in three instance variables:

- An array of `Student` objects

- The selected index (an `int`)

- The current number of students (an `int`).

The use of a separate class to represent the database of students will allow us to choose among several different data structures for holding the students, without disturbing the view classes. We examine some other options for representing collections of objects in later chapters.

Design of the View and Application Classes

At program startup, the `main` method in the `TestScoresApp` class instantiates a `TestScoresModel` and passes it as a parameter to a new instance of `TestScoresView`. The constructor for `TestScoresView` then starts the main command loop. Here is the code for `TestScoresApp`:

```
// Case Study 9.1: The main application class

public class TestScoresApp{
    public static void main(String[] args){
        TestScoresModel model = new TestScoresModel();
        new TestScoresView(model);
    }
}
```

The `TestScoresView` class maintains a single instance variable for the database, of type `TestScoresModel`. The top-level method of `TestScoresModel` is called `run()`. This method runs the main command loop. Here is the pseudocode for method `run()`:

```
while (true)
    display the count and current index
    display the menu
    prompt for and input a command
    if the command is to quit then
        break
    run the command
    wait for the user to press Enter
```

Because some of these tasks, such as displaying the menu, getting a valid command number from the user, and running a command, are themselves complex, we can decompose them into separate, private helper methods. A refinement of the pseudocode shows how `run()` calls these methods:

```
while (true)
    display the count and current position
    displayMenu()
    command = getCommand("Enter a number [1-11]: ", 1, 11)
    if command == 11
        break
    runCommand(command)
```

`displayMenu()` simply displays the menu options in the terminal window.

`getCommand(aString, anInt, anInt)` expects the prompt and the smallest and largest command numbers as parameters. The method displays the prompt for input and attempts to read a number from the keyboard. If the input is a well-formed number and is within the range of valid command numbers, the method returns this number. Otherwise, the method displays an error message and repeats this process.

`runCommand(anInt)` expects a command number as a parameter. The method performs the appropriate task and waits for the user to press the Enter key. Some of the tasks are simple and require only one line of code, but others, such as adding a new student or editing an existing student, are complex enough to warrant further procedural decomposition.

Figure 9-7 shows a **structure chart** that depicts the relationships among the cooperating methods in the class `TestScoresView`. Needless to say, the single data model object is visible to all of these methods.

FIGURE 9-7

A structure chart for the methods of class `TestScoresView`

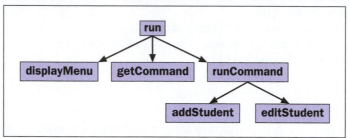

Procedural decomposition is a powerful design tool in situations where a problem calls for one or more complex tasks that operate on the same set of data.

Implementation of the Model

Following is the code for the classes `Student` and `TestScoresModel`. To save space we have kept comments to a minimum; however, we have used descriptive names for variables and methods and hope you will find the code fairly self-documenting. Pay special attention to the constructors in the `Student` class. Note the different options that they give the client for creating a student object and the manner in which chaining them simplifies their code.

```
// Case Study 9.1: Student class

public class Student {

    private String name;
    private int[] tests;

    // Default: name is "" and 3 scores are 0
    public Student(){
        this("");
    }

    // Default: name is nm and 3 scores are 0
    public Student(String nm){
        this(nm, 3);
    }

    // Name is nm and n scores are 0
    public Student(String nm, int n){
```

```java
      name = nm;
      tests = new int[n];
      for (int i = 0; i < tests.length; i++)
         tests[i] = 0;
   }

   // Name is nm and scores are int
   public Student(String nm, int[] t){
      name = nm;
      tests = new int[t.length];
      for (int i = 0; i < tests.length; i++)
         tests[i] = t[i];
   }

   // Builds a copy of s
   public Student(Student s){
      this(s.name, s.tests);
   }

   public void setName (String nm){
      name = nm;
   }

   public String getName (){
      return name;
   }

   public void setScore (int i, int score){
      tests[i - 1] = score;
   }

   public int getScore (int i){
      return tests[i - 1];
   }

   public int getAverage(){
      int sum = 0;
      for (int score : tests)
         sum += score;
      return sum / tests.length;
   }

   public int getHighScore(){
      int highScore = 0;
      for (int score : tests)
         highScore = Math.max (highScore, score);
      return highScore;
   }

   public String toString(){
      String str = "Name:     " + name  + "\n";
      for (int i = 0; i < tests.length; i++)
         str += "test " + i + ":   " + tests[i] + "\n";
      str += "Average: " + getAverage();
```

```java
         return str;
      }

      // Returns null if there are no errors else returns
      // an appropriate error message.
      public String validateData(){
         if (name.equals ("")) return "SORRY: name required";
         for (int score : tests){
            if (score < 0 || score > 100){
               String str = "SORRY: must have "+ 0
                           + " <= test score <= " + 100;
               return str;
            }
         }
         return null;
      }
   }

// Case Study 9.1: TestScoresModel class

public class TestScoresModel{

   private Student[] students;           // Array of students
   private int indexSelectedStudent;     // Position of current student
   private int studentCount;             // Current number of students

   public TestScoresModel(){

      // Initialize the data
      indexSelectedStudent = -1;
      studentCount = 0;
      students = new Student[10];
   }

   // Mutator methods for adding and replacing students

   public String add(Student s){
      if (studentCount == students.length)
         return "SORRY: student list is full";
      else{
         students[studentCount] = s;
         indexSelectedStudent = studentCount;
         studentCount++;
         return null;
      }
   }

   public String replace(Student s){
      if (indexSelectedStudent == -1)
         return "Must add a student first";
      else{
         students[indexSelectedStudent] = s;
         return null;
```

```
      }
}

// Navigation methods

public Student first(){
   Student s = null;
   if (studentCount == 0)
      indexSelectedStudent = -1;
   else{
      indexSelectedStudent = 0;
      s = students[indexSelectedStudent];
   }
   return s;
}

 public Student previous(){
   Student s = null;
   if (studentCount == 0)
      indexSelectedStudent = -1;
   else{
      indexSelectedStudent
          = Math.max (0, indexSelectedStudent - 1);
      s = students[indexSelectedStudent];
   }
   return s;
}

public Student next(){
   Student s = null;
   if (studentCount == 0)
      indexSelectedStudent = -1;
   else{
      indexSelectedStudent
          = Math.min (studentCount - 1, indexSelectedStudent + 1);
      s = students[indexSelectedStudent];
   }
   return s;
}

public Student last(){
   Student s = null;
   if (studentCount == 0)
      indexSelectedStudent = -1;
   else{
      indexSelectedStudent = studentCount - 1;
      s = students[indexSelectedStudent];
   }
   return s;
}

// Accessors to observe data
```

```java
   public Student currentStudent(){
      if (indexSelectedStudent == -1)
         return null;
      else
         return students[indexSelectedStudent];
   }

   public int size(){
      return studentCount;
   }

   public int currentPosition(){
      return indexSelectedStudent;
   }

   public int getClassAverage(){
      if (studentCount == 0)
         return 0;
      int sum = 0;
      for (int i = 0; i < studentCount; i++)
         sum += students[i].getAverage();
      return sum / studentCount;
   }

   public Student getHighScore(){
      if (studentCount == 0)
         return null;
      else{
         Student s = students[0];
         for (int i = 1; i < studentCount; i++)
            if (s.getHighScore() < students[i].getHighScore())
               s = students[i];
         return s;
      }
   }

   public String toString(){
      String result = "";
      for (int i = 0; i < studentCount; i++)
         result = result + students[i] + "\n";
      return result;
   }
}
```

Implementation of the View

We include a skeletal listing of the class `TestScoresView` and leave the completion of its methods as an exercise. Even so, the entire program now compiles and allows the user to enter command numbers at run time. Here is the code:

```java
// Case Study 9.1: TestScoresView class

import java.util.Scanner;
```

```java
public class TestScoresView{

    private TestScoresModel model;

    public TestScoresView(TestScoresModel m){
        model = m;
        run();
    }


    // Menu-driven command loop
    private void run(){
        while (true){
            System.out.println("Number of students: " + model.size());
            System.out.println("Index of current student: " +
                            model.currentPosition());
            displayMenu();
            int command = getCommand("Enter a number [1-11]: ", 1, 11);
            if (command == 11)
                break;
            runCommand(command);
        }
    }

    private void displayMenu(){
    // Exercise: List the menu options
    }

    // Prompts the user for a command number and runs until
    // the user enters a valid command number
    // Parameters: prompt is the string to display
    //             low is the smallest command number
    //             high is the largest command number
    // Returns: a valid command number (>= low && <= high)
    private int getCommand(String prompt, int low, int high){
      // Exercise: recover from all input errors
        Scanner reader = new Scanner(System.in);
        System.out.print(prompt);
        return reader.nextInt();
    }

    // Selects a command to run based on a command number,
    // runs the command, and asks the user to continue by
    // pressing the Enter key
    private void runCommand(int command){
        // Exercise
    }
}
```

9.11 Graphics and GUIs: Changing the View of Student Test Scores

In the preceding case study, we organized the code in two sets of classes called the *model* and the *view*. This strategy split the code fairly equally between managing the interface (getting data from the user and displaying results and error messages) and manipulating a database (including worrying about whether or not an array is full and updating the student count and the index of the selected student). In addition to simplifying the code, this separation of concerns allows us to change the style of the user interface without changing the code for managing the database. To illustrate this point, we now show how to attach a GUI to the same data model.

> **Extra Challenge**
>
> This Graphics and GUIs section gives you the opportunity to explore concepts and programming techniques required to develop modern graphics applications and graphical user interfaces. This material is not required in order to proceed with the other chapters of the book.

Analysis

Figure 9-8 shows a GUI that allows us to view the current student in the database of students. The interface has buttons that support navigation through this database by moving to the first (<<), last (>>), next (>), or previous (<) student. The interface also has buttons that allow the user to add a new student to the end of the database or modify an existing student. The interface displays the index of the current student (**Current Index**) and the current size of the database (**Count**). Table 9-2 explains each of these features in more detail.

FIGURE 9-8
GUI for the student test scores program

TABLE 9-2
Description of buttons

BUTTON	WHAT IT DOES
Add	Creates a new student object with the data displayed and inserts it at the end of the array; the new student becomes the current student. Error-checking makes sure that the array of students is not yet full and that the student data is valid.
Modify	Replaces the current student's data with the data displayed, provided it is valid
<<	Moves to the first student in the database and displays its data
<	Moves to the previous student in the database and displays its data
>	Moves to the next student in the database and displays its data
>>	Moves to the last student in the database and displays its data

Design

The structure of the GUI version of the `TestScoresView` class is similar to that of the `GUIWindow` class for the temperature conversion program discussed in Section 7.6. Here are the main changes to `TestScoresView` from the terminal-based version:

- In addition to the instance variable for the data model, the view class must now contain instance variables for the various widgets, such as labels, text fields, and command buttons.

- The constructor now sets up several panels using the appropriate layouts, adds the widgets to the panels, and instantiates and adds listeners to the command buttons. The constructor can also set the title of the window, set its closing action, and show it (no changes are then necessary in the `main` method of the `TestScoresApp` class).

- The code to handle the individual commands now goes in the listener classes. The best way to do this is to define a separate listener class for each command button. Each listener class then has a fairly simple task, which may involve taking data from text fields, sending messages to the model, and updating the text fields with the results. As usual, the listener classes are defined as private inner classes within the view class.

- In addition to the constructor and listener classes, `TestScoresView` defines two private helper methods to perform the tasks of displaying the model's data in the text fields and creating a new `Student` object from the data in the text fields.

Implementation

The listing that follows is a skeletal version but will compile and display a partially functioning GUI. Its completion is left as an exercise.

```java
// Example 9.4: TestScoresView class (GUI version)

import javax.swing.*;
import java.awt.*;
import java.awt.event.*;


public class TestScoresView extends JFrame{

    // >>>>>>> The model <<<<<<<<

    // Declare the model
    private TestScoresModel model;

    // >>>>>>> The view <<<<<<<<

    // Declare and instantiate the window objects.
    private JButton   addButton       = new JButton("Add");
    private JButton   modifyButton    = new JButton("Modify");
    private JButton   firstButton     = new JButton("<<");
    private JButton   previousButton  = new JButton("<");
    private JButton   nextButton      = new JButton(">");
    private JButton   lastButton      = new JButton(">>");
    private JButton   highScoreButton = new JButton("Highest score");
    private JButton   aveScoreButton  = new JButton("Class Average");
```

```java
private JLabel      nameLabel      = new JLabel("Name");
private JLabel      test1Label     = new JLabel("Test 1");
private JLabel      test2Label     = new JLabel("Test 2");
private JLabel      test3Label     = new JLabel("Test 3");
private JLabel      averageLabel   = new JLabel("Average");
private JLabel      countLabel     = new JLabel("Count");
private JLabel      indexLabel     = new JLabel("Index");
private JTextField  nameField      = new JTextField("");
private JTextField  test1Field     = new JTextField("0");
private JTextField  test2Field     = new JTextField("0");
private JTextField  test3Field     = new JTextField("0");
private JTextField  averageField   = new JTextField("0");
private JTextField  countField     = new JTextField("0");
private JTextField  indexField     = new JTextField("-1");

// Constructor
public TestScoresView(TestScoresModel m){
   model = m;
   // Set attributes of fields
   averageField.setEditable(false);
   countField.setEditable(false);
   indexField.setEditable(false);
   averageField.setBackground(Color.white);
   countField.setBackground(Color.white);
   indexField.setBackground(Color.white);
   // Set up panels to organize widgets and
   // add them to the window
   JPanel northPanel = new JPanel();
   JPanel centerPanel = new JPanel(new GridLayout(5, 4, 10, 5));
   JPanel southPanel = new JPanel();
   Container container = getContentPane();
   container.add(northPanel, BorderLayout.NORTH);
   container.add(centerPanel, BorderLayout.CENTER);
   container.add(southPanel, BorderLayout.SOUTH);
   // Data access buttons
   northPanel.add(addButton);
   northPanel.add(modifyButton);
   northPanel.add(highScoreButton);
   northPanel.add(aveScoreButton);
   // Row 1
   centerPanel.add(nameLabel);
   centerPanel.add(nameField);
   centerPanel.add(countLabel);
   centerPanel.add(countField);
   // Row 2
   centerPanel.add(test1Label);
   centerPanel.add(test1Field);
   centerPanel.add(indexLabel);
   centerPanel.add(indexField);
   // Row 3
   centerPanel.add(test2Label);
   centerPanel.add(test2Field);
   centerPanel.add(new JLabel(""));   // For empty cell in grid
```

```java
      centerPanel.add(new JLabel(""));
      // Row 4
      centerPanel.add(test3Label);
      centerPanel.add(test3Field);
      centerPanel.add(new JLabel(""));
      centerPanel.add(new JLabel(""));
      // Row 5
      centerPanel.add(averageLabel);
      centerPanel.add(averageField);
      centerPanel.add(new JLabel(""));
      centerPanel.add(new JLabel(""));
      // Navigation buttons
      southPanel.add(firstButton);
      southPanel.add(previousButton);
      southPanel.add(nextButton);
      southPanel.add(lastButton);
      // Attach listeners to buttons
      addButton.addActionListener(new AddListener());
      previousButton.addActionListener(new PreviousListener());
      // Other attachments will go here (exercise)
      // Set window attributes
      setTitle("Student Test Scores");
      setDefaultCloseOperation(JFrame.EXIT_ON_CLOSE);
      pack();
      setVisible(true);
   }

   // Updates fields with info from the model
   private void displayInfo(){
      Student s = model.currentStudent();
      if (s == null){  // No current student, so clear fields
         nameField.setText("");
         test1Field.setText("0");
         test2Field.setText("0");
         test3Field.setText("0");
         averageField.setText("0");
         countField.setText("0");
         indexField.setText("-1");
      } else{           // Refresh with student's data
         nameField.setText(s.getName());
         test1Field.setText("" + s.getScore(1));
         test2Field.setText("" + s.getScore(2));
         test3Field.setText("" + s.getScore(3));
         averageField.setText("" + s.getAverage());
         countField.setText("" + model.size());
         indexField.setText("" + model.currentPosition());
      }
   }

   // Creates and returns new Student from field info
   private Student getInfoFromScreen(){
      Student s = new Student(nameField.getText());
      s.setScore(1, Integer.parseInt(test1Field.getText()));
```

```
            s.setScore(2, Integer.parseInt(test2Field.getText()));
            s.setScore(3, Integer.parseInt(test3Field.getText()));
            return s;
    }

    // >>>>>>> The controller <<<<<<<<

    // Responds to a click on the Add button
    private class AddListener implements ActionListener{
        public void actionPerformed(ActionEvent e){
            // Get inputs, validate, and display error and quit if invalid
            Student s = getInfoFromScreen();
            String message = s.validateData();
            if (message != null){
                JOptionPane.showMessageDialog(TestScoresView.this, message);
                return;
            }
            // Attempt to add student and display error or update fields
            message = model.add(s);
            if (message != null)
                JOptionPane.showMessageDialog(TestScoresView.this, message);
            else
                displayInfo();
        }
    }

    // Responds to a click on the < button
    private class PreviousListener implements ActionListener{
        public void actionPerformed(ActionEvent e){
            model.previous();
            displayInfo();
        }
    }

    // Other listeners for modify, highest score, class average, and
    // navigation go here (exercise)
}
```

*E*XERCISE 9.11

1. Write the code for the listener class that displays the class average in the GUI version of the student test scores program.

2. An alternative way to define listeners for command buttons is to define a single listener class and attach a single instance of this class to all of the buttons. The code for the `actionPerformed` method compares each button to the source of the event and takes the appropriate action. The source of the event is obtained by running the method `getSource()` with the `ActionEvent` parameter. Discuss the advantages and disadvantages of this strategy for implementing listeners.

Design, Testing, and Debugging Hints

■ Three things should be done to set up an array:

1. Declare an array variable.

2. Instantiate an array object and assign it to the array variable.

3. Initialize the cells in the array with data, as appropriate.

■ When creating a new array object, try to come up with an accurate estimate of the number of cells for the data. If you underestimate, some data will be lost; if you overestimate, some memory will be wasted.

■ Remember that array variables are `null` until they are assigned array objects.

■ To avoid index out-of-bounds errors, remember that the index of an array cell ranges from 0 (the first position) to the length of the array minus 1.

■ To access the last cell in an array, use the expression `<array>.length - 1`.

■ As a rule of thumb, it is best to avoid having more than one array variable refer to the same array object. When you want to copy the contents of one array to another, do not use the assignment `A = B`; instead, write a copy method and use the assignment `A = arrayCopy(B)`.

■ When an array is not full, take care to track the current number of elements and do not attempt to access a cell that is beyond the last element.

SUMMARY

In this chapter, you learned:

■ Arrays are collections of similar items or elements. The items in arrays are ordered by position. Arrays are useful when a program needs to manipulate many similar items, such as a group of students or a number of test scores.

■ Arrays are objects. Thus, they must be instantiated and they can be referred to by more than one variable.

■ An array can be passed to a method as a parameter and returned as a value.

■ Parallel arrays are useful for organizing information with corresponding elements.

■ Two-dimensional arrays store values in a row-and-column arrangement similar to a table.

■ The enhanced `for` loop is a simplified version of a loop for visiting each element of an array from the first position to the last position.

VOCABULARY *Review*

Define the following terms:

Array	Multidimensional array	Ragged array
Element	One-dimensional array	Range-bound error
Enhanced `for` loop	Parallel arrays	Structure chart
Index	Physical size	Subscript
Initializer list	Procedural decomposition	Two-dimensional array
Logical size		

REVIEW *Questions*

WRITTEN QUESTIONS

Write a brief answer to the following questions.

1. Assume the following declarations are made and indicate which items below are valid subscripted variables.

    ```
    int a[] = new int[10];
    char b[] = new char[6];
    int x = 7, y = 2;
    double z = 0.0;
    ```

    A. `a[0]`

    B. `b[0]`

    C. `c[1.0]`

    D. `b['a']`

    E. `b[a]`

    F. `a[x + y]`

    G. `a[x % y]`

    H. `a[10]`

    I. `c[-1]`

    J. `a[a[4]]`

2. Assume that the array a defined in Question 1 contains the following values.

   ```
   1   4   6   8   9   3   7   10   2   9
   ```

   Indicate if the following are valid subscripts of a and, if so, state the value of the subscript. If invalid, explain why.

   A. `a[2]`

   B. `a[5]`

   C. `a[a[2]]`

   D. `a[4 + 7]`

   E. `a[a[5] + a[2]]`

   F. `a[Math.sqrt(2)]`

3. List the errors in the following array declarations.

   A. `int intArray[] = new double[10];`

   B. `int intArray[] = new int[1.5];`

   C. `double[] doubleArray = new double[-10]`

   D. `int intMatrix[] [] = new int[10];`

4. Write a method `selectRandom` that expects an array of integers as a parameter. The method should return the value of an array element at a randomly selected position.

5. Write code to declare and instantiate a two-dimensional array of integers with five rows and four columns.

6. Write code to initialize the array of Question 5 with randomly generated integers between 1 and 20.

PROJECTS

In some of the following projects, you are asked to write helper methods to process arrays. If you are calling these methods from the `main` method, be sure to begin the helper method's header with the reserved word `static`.

PROJECT 9-1

Write a program that takes 10 integers as input. The program places the even integers into an array called `evenList`, the odd integers into an array called `oddList`, and the negative integers into an array called `negativeList`. The program displays the contents of the three arrays after all of the integers have been entered.

PROJECT 9-2

Write a program that takes 10 floating-point numbers as inputs. The program displays the average of the numbers followed by all of the numbers that are greater than the average. As part of your design, write a method that takes an array of doubles as a parameter and returns the average of the data in the array.

PROJECT 9-3

The mode of a list of numbers is the number listed most often. Write a program that takes 10 numbers as input and displays the mode of these numbers. Your program should use parallel arrays and a method that takes an array of numbers as a parameter and returns the value that appears most often in the array.

PROJECT 9-4

The median of a list of numbers is the value in the middle of the list if the list is arranged in order. Add to the program of Project 9-3 the capability of displaying the median of the list of numbers.

PROJECT 9-5

Modify the program of Project 9-4 so that it displays not only the median and mode of the list of numbers but also a table of the numbers and their associated frequencies.

PROJECT 9-6

Complete the student test scores application from this chapter's case study and test it thoroughly.

PROJECT 9-7

A magic square is a two-dimensional array of positive integers such that the sum of each row, column, and diagonal is the same constant. The following example is a magic square whose constant is 34:

16	3	2	13
5	10	11	8
9	6	7	12
4	15	14	1

Write a program that takes 16 integers as inputs. The program should determine whether or not the square is a magic square and display the result in a text area.

PROJECT 9-8

Pascal's triangle can be used to recognize coefficients of a quantity raised to a power. The rules for forming this triangle of integers are such that each row must start and end with a 1, and each entry in a row is the sum of the two values diagonally above the new entry. Thus, four rows of Pascal's triangle are

```
              1
           1     1
        1     2     1
     1     3     3     1
```

This triangle can be used as a convenient way to get the coefficients of a quantity of two terms raised to a power (binomial coefficients). For example

$$(a+b)^3 = 1 \times a^3 + 3a^2b + 3ab^2 + 1 \times b^3$$

where the coefficients 1, 3, 3, and 1 come from the fourth row of Pascal's triangle.

Write a program that takes the number of rows (up to, say, 10) as input and displays Pascal's triangle for those rows.

PROJECT 9-9

Complete the GUI version of the student test scores program.

PROJECT 9-10

In the game of Penny Pitch, a two-dimensional board of numbers is laid out as follows:

```
1  1  1  1  1

1  2  2  2  1

1  2  3  2  1

1  2  2  2  1

1  1  1  1  1
```

A player tosses five pennies on the board, aiming for the number with the highest value. At the end of the game, the sum total of the tosses is returned. Develop a program that plays this game. The program should display the board and then perform the following steps each time the user presses Enter:

■ Generate two random numbers for the row and column of the toss.

■ Add the number at this position to a running total.

■ Display the board, replacing the numbers with Ps where the pennies land.

(*Hint*: You should use a two-dimensional array of `Square` objects for this problem. Each square contains a number like those shown and a Boolean flag that indicates whether or not a penny has landed on that square.)

CRITICAL *Thinking*

You have been using a method to search for data in arrays like the one described in this chapter, when your friend tells you that it's a poor way to search. She says that you're examining every element in the array to discover that the target element is not there. According to her, a better way is to assume that the elements in the array are in alphabetical order. Start by examining the element at the middle position in the array. If that element matches the target element, you're done. Otherwise, if that element is less than the target element, continue the same kind of search in just the portion of the array to the left of the element just examined. Otherwise, continue the same kind of search in just the portion of the array to the right of the element just examined.

Write an algorithm for this search process, and explain why it is better than the search algorithm discussed in this chapter.

CLASSES CONTINUED

Chapter 5 presented an overview of classes that allowed you to learn to read, modify, and define them. The examples of classes discussed there are simplified versions of what real programmers would see, however. Defining classes is only one aspect of object-oriented programming. The real power of object-oriented programming comes from its capacity to reduce code and to distribute responsibilities for such things as error handling in a software system. This capability can be exploited only when you have an understanding of some related concepts. Following is a brief summary of some of these concepts, which we explore in detail in this chapter:

Static Variables and Methods. When information needs to be shared among all instances of a class, that information can be represented in terms of static variables and it can be accessed by means of static methods.

Interfaces. A Java interface specifies the set of methods available to clients of a class. An interface provides a way of requiring a class to implement a set of methods and a way of informing clients about services regardless of implementation detail. Interfaces thus provide the glue that holds a set of cooperating classes together.

Inheritance. Java organizes classes in a hierarchy. Classes inherit the instance variables and methods of the classes above them in the hierarchy. A class can extend its inherited characteristics by adding instance variables and methods and by overriding inherited methods. Thus, *inheritance* provides a mechanism for reusing code and can greatly reduce the effort required to implement a new class.

Abstract Classes. Some classes in a hierarchy must never be instantiated. They are called *abstract classes*. Their sole purpose is to define features and behavior common to their subclasses.

Polymorphism. Methods in different classes with a similar function are usually given the same name. This is called *polymorphism*. Polymorphism makes classes easier to use because programmers need to memorize fewer method names. In a well-designed class hierarchy, polymorphism is employed as much as possible. A good example of a polymorphic message is `toString`. Every object, no matter which class it belongs to, understands the `toString` message and responds by returning a string that describes the object.

Preconditions and Postconditions. Clients need to know how to use a method correctly and what results to expect if it is so used. Preconditions specify the correct use of a method and postconditions describe what will result if the preconditions are satisfied.

Exceptions for Error Handling. When a method's preconditions are violated, a foolproof way to catch the errors is to throw exceptions, thereby halting program execution at the point of the errors.

Reference Types. The identity of an object and the fact that there can be multiple references to the same object are issues that arise when comparing two objects for equality and when copying an object. There are also subtle rules to master when manipulating objects of different but related types in a hierarchy.

Unfortunately, there is a lot to digest here. But we take you through it one step at a time, and by the end of the chapter you will become a connoisseur of this flavor of programming.

10.1 Class (`static`) *Variables and Methods*

The variables and methods discussed thus far in the book have been instance variables and methods. An instance variable belongs to an object and is allocated storage when the object is created. Each object has its own set of instance variables. An instance method is activated when a message is sent to the object. Java also supports the use of class variables and methods. A *class variable* belongs to a class. Its storage is allocated at program startup and is independent of the number of instances created. A *class method* is activated when a message is sent to the class rather than to an object. The modifier `static` is used to designate class variables and methods. To illustrate, we make some modifications to the `Student` class introduced in Chapter 9.

Counting the Number of Students Instantiated

Suppose we want to count all the student objects instantiated during the execution of an application. To do so, we introduce a variable, which we call `studentCount`. This variable is incremented in the constructor every time a student object is instantiated. Because the variable is independent of any particular student object, it must be a class variable. In addition, we need one method to access the `studentCount` variable. This method, called `getStudentCount`, returns the variable's value on demand. Because `getStudentCount` does not manipulate any particular student object, it must be a class method.

Modifying the `Student` Class

Following are the modifications needed to add the class variable and the the class method in the `Student` class. We are adding the class variable and method to the end of the class template. There is no rule that says they must be placed there, but it is as good a location as any other and is the one usually used in this book.

```java
public class Student {

   private String name;
   ... rest of the instance variables go here ...

   public Student(){
      this("");
    }

   public Student(String nm){
      studentCount++;      // Increment the count when a student is
                           // instantiated
      name = nm;
      tests = new int[3];
      for (int i = 0; i < tests.length; i++)
         tests[i] = 0;
   }

   public Student(String nm, int[] t){
      studentCount++;      // Increment the count when a student is
                           // instantiated
      name = nm;
      tests = new int[t.length];
      for (int i = 0; i < tests.length; i++)
         tests[i] = t[i];
   }

   public Student(Student s){
      this(s.name, s.tests);
   }
   ... rest of the methods without change go here ...

   //-------------- class variables and methods ----------------

   static private int studentCount = 0;

   static public void setStudentCount(int count){
      studentCount = count;
   }

   static public int getStudentCount(){
      return studentCount;
   }
}
```

Following is a code segment that illustrates the new capabilities of the `Student` class:

```
...
s1 = new Student();                                 // Instantiate a student object
...
s2 = new Student();                                 // Instantiate a student object
...
s3 = new Student();                                 // Instantiate a student object
System.out.println(Student.getStudentCount());      // Displays 3
```

Notice that class messages are sent to a class and not to an object. Also, notice that we do not attempt to manipulate the `studentCount` variable directly because, in accordance with the good programming practice of information hiding, we declared the variable to be `private`.

In general, we use a `static` variable in any situation in which all instances share a common data value. We then use `static` methods to provide public access to these data.

Class Constants

By using the modifier `final` in conjunction with `static`, we create a *class constant*. The value of a class constant is assigned when the variable is declared, and it cannot be changed later. To illustrate the use of class constants, we modify the `Student` class again by adding two class constants: `MIN_SCORE` and `MAX_SCORE`. We use these constants in the method `setScore` to hold the score between `MIN_SCORE` and `MAX_SCORE`. It is customary to capitalize the names of class constants. Following are the relevant modifications to the `Student` class:

```
public class Student {

   private String name;

... rest of the instance variables go here ...

... no changes in the methods up to this point ...

   public void setScore (int i, int score){
      // Limit the score to the interval [MIN_SCORE, MAX_SCORE]
      score = Math.max (MIN_SCORE, score);
      score = Math.min (MAX_SCORE, score);

      tests[i - 1] = score;
   }
   ... no changes in the methods here ...

//-------------- static variables and methods ---------------

   static final public int MIN_SCORE = 0;
   static final public int MAX_SCORE = 100;
   ... no changes in the rest of the static stuff ...

}
```

The method `max` in class `Math` returns the maximum of its two parameters and `min` returns their minimum. We declare the two class constants as public because clients might like to access them. Following is a segment of code that illustrates the `Student` class's new features:

```
s = new Student();
s.setScore(1, -20);          // Too small, will be set to MIN_SCORE
s.setScore(2, 150);          // Too large, will be set to MAX_SCORE
s.setScore(3, 55);           // Value is acceptable
System.out.println (s);           // Displays scores of 0, 100, and 55
System.out.println (Student.MIN_SCORE);          // Displays 0
System.out.println (Student.MAX_SCORE);          // Displays 100
```

Rules for Using `static` Variables

There are two simple rules to remember when using `static` variables:

1. Class methods can reference only the `static` variables and never the instance variables.

2. Instance methods can reference `static` and instance variables.

The `Math` Class Revisited

By now you may have guessed that all the methods and variables in the `Math` class are static. `Math.PI` refers to a static constant, whereas `Math.max(MIN_SCORE, score)` activates a static method.

The `Static` Method `Main`

All the application classes presented so far have included the `static` method `main`. Now we can understand more about how `main` works. Consider the following example:

```
import ...;
import ...;

public class MyApp ...{
   ...

   public static void main (String[] args){
      ...
   }
}
```

When the user runs this program by typing

```
java MyApp
```

the Java interpreter sends the message `main` to the class `MyApp`.

EXERCISE 10.1

1. Define a static constant for the default number of test scores in the `Student` class.

2. Describe the manner in which Java allocates memory for instance variables and `static` variables.

3. List two possible situations in which `static` methods might be included in classes.

4. What error occurs in the following code?

```
public class SomeClass{
    private int instVar = 0;
    static public void someMethod(int x){
        classVar = instVar + classVar + x;
    }
    static private int classVar = 0;
    …
}
```

5. Why is it a good idea to define all constants as `public` and `static`?

10.2 *Turtle Graphics*

Java comes with a large array of classes that support graphics operations, many of which are discussed in the optional sections at the end of each chapter of this book. In the next few sections we use `TurtleGraphics`, a nonstandard, open-source Java package, to illustrate various features of object-oriented programming. The implementation of `TurtleGraphics` is discussed in Appendix I.

Turtle graphics were originally developed as part of the children's programming language Logo created by Seymour Papert and his colleagues at MIT in the late 1960s. The name suggests the way in which we can think about the drawing process. Imagine a turtle crawling on a piece of paper with a pen tied to its tail. Commands direct the turtle as it moves across the paper and tell it to lift or lower its tail, turn some number of degrees left or right, and move a specified distance. Whenever the tail is down, the pen drags along the paper leaving a trail. In this manner it is possible to "program" the turtle to draw pictures ranging from the simple to the complex.

Turtle Graphics Messages

In Java, we dispense with the turtle and focus on the pen, which is an instance of the class `StandardPen` (later we will encounter some other not-so-standard pens). Drawing is done in a window. We command a pen by sending it messages such as those shown in Table 10-1.

TABLE 10-1
Pen messages

PEN MESSAGE	WHAT IT DOES
home()	The pen jumps to the center of the graphics window without drawing and points north.
setDirection(degrees)	The pen points in the indicated direction. Due east corresponds to 0 degrees, north to 90 degrees, west to 180 degrees, and south to 270 degrees. Because there are 360 degrees in a circle, setting the direction to 400 degrees would be equivalent to 400 – 360 or 40 degrees and setting it to –30 degrees would be equivalent to 360 – 30 or 330 degrees.
turn(degrees)	The pen adds the indicated degrees to its current direction. Positive degrees correspond to turning counterclockwise. The degrees can be an integer or floating-point number.
down()	The pen lowers itself to the drawing surface.
up()	The pen raises itself from the drawing surface.
move(distance)	The pen moves the specified distance in the current direction. The distance can be an integer or floating-point number and is measured in pixels (picture elements). The size of a pixel depends on the monitor's resolution. For instance, when we say that a monitor's resolution is 800 by 600, we mean that the monitor is 800 pixels wide and 600 pixels high.
setColor(aColor)	Sets the pen's color to aColor.

Initially, a pen is

- In the center of a graphics window (at position [0,0] of a Cartesian coordinate system)
- In the down position
- Pointing north

Drawing a Square with a Pen

The following example is a program that draws a square, 50 pixels per side, in the center of a graphics window:

```
// Example 10.1: Draw a square using Turtle Graphics

import TurtleGraphics.StandardPen;

public class DrawSquare {

    public static void main(String [] args) {

        // Instantiate a pen object
        StandardPen pen = new StandardPen();
```

```
        // Lift the pen, move it to the square's upper-left corner,
        // and lower it again
        pen.up();
        pen.move(25);
        pen.turn(90); pen.move(25);
        pen.down();

        // Draw the square
        pen.turn(90); pen.move(50);
        pen.turn(90); pen.move(50);

        pen.turn(90); pen.move(50);
        pen.turn(90); pen.move(50);
    }
}
```

Figure 10-1 shows the graphics window after the program has completed execution. If the window is resized, the square is automatically redrawn in the center of the window without rerunning the program. The window can be closed in the usual manner.

FIGURE 10-1

A square drawn at the center of a graphics window

Installing Turtle Graphics

Before you can compile and run a program that uses the `TurtleGraphics` package, you must install that package on your hard drive. You can obtain the package at the authors' Web site (see Appendix I for details) or from your instructor. If you're using the command prompt to compile and run Java programs, by far the easiest way to install the package is to copy the `TurtleGraphics` directory that contains the byte codes into your current working directory. When this has been done, your current working directory should contain your `.java` file that imports `TurtleGraphics` and also the `TurtleGraphics` directory. The Java compiler and the JVM should then be able to locate the `TurtleGraphics` package.

If you move to another directory to compile and run a Java program that uses `TurtleGraphics`, you must move the `TurtleGraphics` directory as well. To avoid this annoying maintenance, you can install the file `TurtleGraphics.jar` in the appropriate Java system directories on your hard drive, where it will be accessible no matter where you run the compiler or JVM. This is also the preferred installation alternative when you're running a development environment like BlueJ. See Appendix I for further details on this type of installation.

10.3 Java Interfaces—The Client Perspective

The term *interface* is used in two different ways. On the one hand, an interface is the part of a software system that interacts with human users. On the other, it is a list of a class's public methods. Throughout this chapter we use the term in its latter sense. A class's interface provides the information needed to use a class without revealing anything about its implementation.

When related classes have the same interface, they can be used interchangeably in a program. House painting provides an everyday example. Small delicate brushes are used to paint around windows and doors and large coarse brushes to paint expanses of wall. Yet the different types of brushes are used in the same manner. They are all dipped in paint and wiggled backward and forward on the painting surface. They have, in other words, the same interface. Instructions for how to use one apply to all. Likewise, in a program, code for manipulating a class applies equally to all classes that share the same interface.

We can illustrate these ideas in Java using turtle graphics. The StandardPen used earlier is just one of five classes that conform to the same interface. Two others are WigglePen and RainbowPen. A WigglePen draws wiggly lines, and a RainbowPen draws randomly colored lines. We can think of these as special effects pens; but as pens, they all have the same general behavior and respond to the same messages.

The Pen Interface

Earlier we described the interface for a standard pen by listing its methods in Table 10-1; however, Java provides a more formal mechanism called, not surprisingly, an interface. Following is the code for the Pen interface:

```java
// Pen.java: The behavior common to all types of pens

import java.awt.Color;

public interface Pen{
   public void    down();
   public void    drawString(String text);
   public void    home();
   public void    move(double distance);
   public void    move(double x, double y);
   public void    setColor(Color color);
   public void    setDirection(double direction);
   public void    setWidth(int width);
   public String  toString();
   public void    turn(double degrees);
   public void    up();
}
```

Note that this code is quite simple. It consists of the signatures of the methods followed by semicolons. The interface provides programmers with the information needed to use pens of any type correctly. It is important to realize that an interface is not a class; however, when a class is defined, there is a mechanism, which we see shortly, to specify that the class conforms to the interface.

The Color class, which is defined in the java.awt package, represents colors in Java. The class includes several constants, such as Color.white, Color.black, and Color.blue (the default color of many of the pens), to represent commonly used individual colors.

Drawing with Different Types of Pens

As a short example, we write code to draw a square with three different types of pens:

```
// Example 10.2: Draw squares with three types of pens

import TurtleGraphics.*;

public class TestPens{

    public static void main(String[] args){
        // Declare three variables of the interface type called Pen.
        Pen p1, p2, p3;

        // Instantiate three different types of pens and
        // associate them with the Pen variables.
        p1 = new StandardPen();
        p2 = new WigglePen();
        p3 = new RainbowPen();

        // Draw a square with the standard pen.
        for (int i = 1; i <= 4; i++){
            p1.move(50);
            p1.turn(90);
        }

        // Draw a square with the wiggle pen.
        for (int i = 1; i <= 4; i++){
            p2.move(50);
            p2.turn(90);
        }

        // Draw a square with the rainbow pen.
        for (int i = 1; i <= 4; i++){
            p3.move(50);
            p3.turn(90);
        }
    }
}
```

The three pen variables (p1, p2, and p3) are given the type Pen, which is the name of the interface. Then the variables are associated with specialized types of pen objects. Each object responds to exactly the same messages, those listed in the Pen interface, but with slightly different behaviors. This is an example of polymorphism, which was first mentioned in Chapter 1.

The output from the program is shown in Figure 10-2. Because this book is not printed in full color, some of the detail may be lost. The first square is in blue and has straight sides. The second square, also in blue, has wiggly sides. The third square has straight sides, and each side is in a different randomly chosen color. Note that when the program executes, the windows may appear stacked on top of each other and may have to be separated by dragging them with the mouse.

FIGURE 10-2
A square drawn with three types of pens

Static Helper Methods

The code for drawing squares in the last example suffers from redundancy: it repeats the same `for` loop with three different types of pens. We can factor this common pattern of code into a method where it's written just once. The new method, named `drawSquare`, is then called with each pen as a parameter from the `main` method, as follows:

```
drawSquare(p1);
drawSquare(p2);
drawSquare(p3);
```

Because `drawSquare` is called from the static method `main`, it must also be defined as a static method. The single parameter of the method is of type `Pen` (the interface), so it can accept an actual parameter of any class that implements `Pen`. Here is the code for the method:

```
static private void drawSquare(Pen p){
    // Draw a square with any pen.
    for (int i = 1; i <= 4; i++){
        p.move(50);
        p.turn(90);
    }
}
```

Using Interface Names

In general, when you declare a variable, a formal parameter of a method, or a method's return type, it's a good idea to use an interface name for the type name wherever possible. Thus, code in the last example used `Pen` for the variables' type, instead of `StandardPen` or any of the other pen class names. Using an interface name has two benefits:

1. Methods that use interface types are more general, in that they work with any classes that implement the interface. If we had used `StandardPen` for the parameter of `drawSquare`, that method would only work with one type of pen.

2. It's easier to maintain a program that uses interface types. If you want to modify the program to use a different type of pen, for example, you only have to change the code that instantiates the pen. The code that manipulates the pen does not have to change at all.

*E*XERCISE 10.3

1. State the purpose of a Java interface and explain how it differs from a class.

2. Modify the method `drawSquare` so that it expects parameters for the pen, the coordinates of the square's upper-left corner point, and the length of its side. The method should draw the appropriate square with the pen.

10.4 *Java Interfaces—The Implementation Perspective*

We now show the role interfaces play in the implementation of classes. The implementation of the pen classes in the `TurtleGraphics` package is rather complicated, so a discussion of it is deferred to Appendix I. However, a simpler example is available. Suppose we need to perform some basic manipulations on circles and rectangles. The manipulations include positioning, moving, and stretching these basic geometric shapes. In addition, we want shapes to implement methods that compute their area, draw themselves with a pen, and return descriptions of themselves. Without any concern for implementation details, we can now describe this behavior in an interface called `Shape`, which is shared by circles and rectangles, as shown in the following code:

```java
// Shape.java: Behavior common to all shapes

import TurtleGraphics.Pen;

public interface Shape{
   public double area();
   public void   draw(Pen p);
   public double getXPos();
   public double getYPos();
   public void   move(double xLoc, double yLoc);
   public void   stretchBy(double factor);
   public String toString();
}
```

Classes `Circle` and `Rect`

We implement circles and rectangles in classes we call `Circle` and `Rect`, respectively. We do not use the more obvious name `Rectangle` because Java already includes a class with that name. Working with two classes that have the same name is not impossible, but it does involve complexities we are not ready to discuss. The outline for both implementations look like this:

```java
public class Circle implements Shape{
   ...
}
public class Rect implements Shape{
   ...
}
```

The key feature is the phrase `implements Shape`. The presence of this phrase implies that

- Both classes implement all the methods listed in the `Shape` interface.
- A variable declared as a `Shape` can be associated with an object of either class.

Following is a complete implementation of both classes:

```java
// Circle.java: Implementation of circles

import TurtleGraphics.Pen;

public class Circle implements Shape{

    private double xPos, yPos;
    private double radius;

    public Circle(){
        xPos = 0;
        yPos = 0;
        radius = 1;
    }

    public Circle(double xLoc, double yLoc, double r){
        xPos = xLoc;
        yPos = yLoc;
        radius = r;
    }

    public double area(){
        return Math.PI * radius * radius;
    }

    public void draw(Pen p){
        double side = 2.0 * Math.PI * radius / 120.0;
        p.up();
        p.move (xPos + radius, yPos - side / 2.0);
        p.setDirection (90);
        p.down();
        for (int i = 0; i < 120; i++){
            p.move (side);
            p.turn (3);
        }
    }

    public double getXPos(){
        return xPos;
    }

    public double getYPos(){
        return yPos;
    }
```

```java
    public void move(double xLoc, double yLoc) {
        xPos = xLoc;
        yPos = yLoc;
    }

    public void stretchBy(double factor) {
        radius *= factor;
    }

    public String toString(){
        String str = "CIRCLE\n"
                    + "Radius: " + radius + "\n"
                    + "(X,Y) Position: (" + xPos + "," + yPos + ")\n"
                    + "Area: " + area();
        return str;
    }
}

// Rect.java: Implementation of rectangles

import TurtleGraphics.Pen;

public class Rect implements Shape{

    private double xPos, yPos;
    private double height, width;

    public Rect(){
        xPos = 0;
        yPos = 0;
        height = 1;
        width = 1;
    }

    public Rect(double xLoc, double yLoc, double w, double h){
        xPos = xLoc;
        yPos = yLoc;
        height = h;
        width = w;
    }

    public double area(){
        return height * width;
    }

    public void draw(Pen p){
        p.up();
        p.move (xPos, yPos);
        p.down();
        p.setDirection (0); p.move (width);
        p.turn(-90); p.move(height);
        p.turn(-90); p.move(width);
        p.turn(-90); p.move(height);
    }
```

```java
    public double getXPos(){
        return xPos;
    }

    public double getYPos(){
        return yPos;
    }

    public void move(double xLoc, double yLoc){
        xPos = xLoc;
        yPos = yLoc;
    }

    public void stretchBy(double factor){
        height *= factor;
        width *= factor;
    }

    public String toString(){
        String str = "RECTANGLE\n"
                + "Width & Height: " + width + " & " + height +"\n"
                + "(X,Y) Position: (" + xPos + "," + yPos + ")\n"
                + "Area: " + area();
        return str;
    }
}
```

Testing the Classes

The code for both classes is easy to understand, so we now write a small test program that instantiates a circle and a rectangle and subjects them to a few basic manipulations. Embedded comments explain what is happening, and Figure 10-3 shows the output:

```java
// Example 10.3: Try out some shapes

import TurtleGraphics.*;
import java.awt.Color;
import java.util.Scanner;

public class TestShapes{

    public static void main(String[] args){

        // Declare and instantiate a pen, a circle and a rectangle
        Pen p = new StandardPen();
        Shape s1 = new Circle(20, 20, 20);
        Shape s2 = new Rect(-20, -20, 20, 10);

        // Draw the circle and rectangle
        s1.draw (p);
        s2.draw (p);
```

```
// Display a description of the circle and rectangle
System.out.println(s1);  // toString method called implicitly
System.out.println(s2);  // toString method called implicitly

// Pause until the user is ready to continue
System.out.print("Press <Enter> to continue: ");
Scanner reader = new Scanner(System.in);
reader.nextLine();

// Erase the circle and rectangle and set the pen's color to red
p.setColor(Color.white);
s1.draw(p);
s2.draw(p);
p.setColor(Color.red);

// Move the circle and rectangle, change their size, and redraw
s1.move(30, 30);            s2.move(-30, -30);
s1.stretchBy(2);           s2.stretchBy(2);
s1.draw(p);                s2.draw(p);
    }
}
```

FIGURE 10-3
Output from the `TestShapes` program

Initial Configuration   Command Window   Final Configuration

Final Observations

Before closing this section, we must mention several points:

- An interface contains only methods, never variables.

- The methods in an interface are usually public.

- If more than one class implements an interface, its methods are polymorphic.

- A class can implement methods in addition to those listed in the interface, as we illustrate soon.

- A class can implement more than one interface.

- Interfaces can be organized in an inheritance hierarchy.

EXERCISE 10.4

1. Write an interface named `Account` for bank accounts. Clients should be able to make deposits and withdrawals and check their balances.

2. When the programmer uses the expression `implements <an interface>` in a class definition, what does the compiler expect to see in that definition?

10.5 Code Reuse Through Inheritance

In Java, all classes are part of an immense hierarchy, with the class `Object` at the root. Each class inherits the characteristics (variables and methods) of the classes above it in the hierarchy. A class can add new variables to these inherited characteristics as needed. It also can add new methods and/or modifies inherited methods.

Review of Terminology

To make it easier to talk about inheritance, we begin by reviewing the needed terminology. Figure 10-4 shows part of a class hierarchy, with `Object` as always at the `root` (the top position in an upside-down tree). Below `Object` are its subclasses, but we show only one, which we call `AAA`. Because `AAA` is immediately below `Object`, we say that it extends `Object`. Similarly, `BBB` and `CCC` extend `AAA`. The class immediately above another is called its superclass, so `AAA` is the superclass of `BBB` and `CCC`. A class can have many subclasses, and all classes, except `Object`, have exactly one superclass. The `descendants` of a class consist of its subclasses, plus their subclasses, and so on.

FIGURE 10-4
Part of a class hierarchy

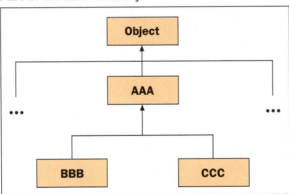

Wheel as a Subclass of Circle

As our first illustration of inheritance, we implement the class `Wheel` as a subclass of `Circle`. A wheel is just a circle with spokes, so much of the code needed to implement `Wheel` is already in `Circle`. We first present the code and a brief test. Comments in the code should make it fairly self-explanatory, but a more detailed explanation follows:

```
import TurtleGraphics.Pen;

public class Wheel extends Circle{
```

```java
private int spokes;      // The number of spokes in the wheel
                         // xPos, yPos, and radius are inherited
                         // from Circle

public Wheel() {
   super();              // Activate the constructor Circle() to
                         // initialize xPos, yPos, and radius.
   spokes = 0;           // Now initialize spokes.
}

public Wheel(double xLoc, double yLoc, double r, int s){
   super(xLoc, yLoc, r);   // Activate the constructor
                           // Circle(double xLoc, double yLoc, double r)
                           // to initialize xPos, yPos, and radius.
   spokes = s;             // Now initialize spokes.
}

public void draw(Pen p){
   // Draw the wheel's rim by calling the draw method in the superclass.
   super.draw(p);

   // Draw the spokes
   for (int i = 1; i <= spokes; i++){
      p.up();
      p.move(xPos, yPos);
      p.setDirection(i * 360.0 / spokes);
      p.down();
      p.move(radius);
   }
}

public void setSpokes (int s){
   spokes = s;
}

public String toString(){
   String str = "WHEEL\n"
                + "Radius: " + radius + "\n"
                + "Spokes: " + spokes + "\n"
                + "(X,Y) Position: (" + xPos + "," + yPos + ")\n"
                + "Area: " + area();
   return str;
}
}
```

Testing the Wheel Class

Following is a test program that draws a circle and a wheel:

```java
// Example 10.4: Draw a circle and a wheel

import TurtleGraphics.*;

public class TestShapes {
```

```
public static void main (String[] args) {
    // Declare and instantiate a pen, a circle and a wheel
    Pen p = new StandardPen();
    Shape s1 = new Circle(20, 20, 20);
    Shape s2 = new Wheel(-20, -20, 20, 6);

    // Draw the circle and wheel
    s1.draw(p);
    s2.draw(p);
}
}
```

Figure 10-5 shows the results of this program.

FIGURE 10-5
A circle and a wheel with the same radius but different positions

Detailed Explanation

We now explain the implementation of `Wheel` in detail.

Class Header

In the class header, we see that `Wheel` extends `Circle`, thereby indicating that it is a subclass of `Circle` and inherits all of `Circle`'s variables and methods. The clause "`implements Shape`" is omitted from the header because `Wheel` inherits this property from `Circle` automatically.

Variables

The variable `spokes`, indicating the number of spokes in a wheel, is the only variable declared in the class. The other variables (`xPos`, `yPos`, and `radius`) are inherited from `Circle`; however, to reference these variables in `Wheel` methods, `Circle` must be modified slightly. In `Circle`, these variables must be declared `protected` instead of `private`. This designation indicates that `Circle`'s descendants can access the variables while still hiding them from all other classes. The change in `Circle` looks like this:

```
protected double xPos, yPos;
protected double radius;
```

Protected Methods

Methods can be designated as `protected` also; however, we will not have any reason to use `protected` methods in this chapter. As with `protected` variables, a `protected` method is accessible to a class's descendants, but not to any other classes in the hierarchy.

Constructors and `super`

Constructors in class `Wheel` explicitly initialize the variable `spokes`; however, constructors in the superclass `Circle` initialize the remaining variables (`xPos`, `yPos`, and `radius`). The keyword `super` is used to activate the desired constructor in `Circle`, and the parameter list used with `super` determines which constructor in `Circle` is called. When used in this way, `super` must be the first statement in `Wheel`'s constructors.

Other Methods and `super`

The keyword `super` also can be used in methods other than constructors, but in a slightly different way. First, it can appear in any place within a method. Second, it takes the form

```
super.<method name> (<parameter list>);
```

Such code activates the named method in the superclass (note that the two methods are polymorphic). In comparison, the code

```
this.<method name> (<parameter list>);     // Long form
                                           //     or
<method name> (<parameter list>);          // Short form
```

activates the named method in the current class. We see an example in the `Wheel` class's `draw` method:

```
// Draw the wheel's rim
super.draw (p);
```

Why Some Methods Are Missing

Not all the `Shape` methods are implemented in `Wheel`. Instead they are inherited unchanged from `Circle`. For instance, if the `move` message is sent to a wheel object, the `move` method in `Circle` is activated.

Why Some Methods Are Modified

Whenever a wheel object must respond differently to a message than a circle object, the corresponding method must be redefined in class `Wheel`. The methods `draw` and `toString` are examples. When convenient, the redefined method can use `super` to activate a method in the superclass.

Why There Are Extra Methods

A subclass often has methods that do not appear in its superclass. The method `setSpokes` is an example. This method provides a more specific piece of behavior than you would find in circles.

What Messages Can Be Sent to a Wheel

Because `Wheel` is a subclass of `Circle`, it automatically implements `Shape`. Therefore, a variable of type `Shape` can be instantiated as a `new` `Wheel` and can receive all `Shape` messages:

```
Shape someShape = new Wheel();
someShape.<any Shape message>;
```

The variable `someShape` cannot be sent the message `setSpokes`, however, even though it is actually a wheel. From the compiler's perspective, `someShape` is limited to receiving messages in the `Shape` interface. There are two ways to circumvent this limitation. The variable `someShape` is either declared as type `Wheel` in the first place, or it is cast to class `Wheel` when it is sent a message unique to class `Wheel`. Following is an example:

```
Wheel v1 = new Wheel();
Shape v2 = new Wheel();

v1.setSpokes (6);            // v1 can be sent all Wheel messages
((Wheel)v2).setSpokes (6);  // v2 must first be cast to class Wheel before
                            // being sent this message
```

Of course, it is a mistake to cast a variable to a type that conflicts with its true identity. Doing so results in a run-time error. For instance:

```
Shape s = new Circle();     // s is a circle

((Wheel)s).setSpokes (6);   // s cannot be cast to class Wheel
```

We cover more examples of casting objects in Chapter 11.

EXERCISE 10.5

1. What is a class hierarchy? Give an example.

2. What syntax is used to get one class to inherit data and behavior from another class?

3. How does the keyword `super` work with constructors?

4. How does the keyword `super` work with methods other than constructors?

5. What is the role of the visibility modifier `protected` in a class hierarchy?

6. Find the error in the following code and suggest a remedy for the problem:
   ```
   Shape s = new Wheel();
   s.setSpokes (5);
   ```

10.6 Inheritance and Abstract Classes

When we examine the Circle and Rect classes, we see duplication of code. Inheritance provides a mechanism for reducing this duplication. To illustrate, we define a new class that is a superclass of Circle and Rect and contains all the variables and methods common to both. We will never have any reason to instantiate this class, so we will make it an *abstract class*, that is, a class that cannot be instantiated. The classes that extend this class and that are instantiated are called *concrete classes*.

It would be nice to call the new class Shape; however, Shape is already the name of our interface. Instead we will call the class AbstractShape. It is convenient, though not necessary, to have this new class implement the Shape interface. Then, the subclasses Circle and Rect no longer need to implement Shape explicitly.

Because AbstractShape is going to implement Shape, it must include all the Shape methods, even those such as area that are completely different in the subclasses and share no code. Methods in AbstractShape such as area for which we cannot write any code are called *abstract methods*, and we indicate that fact by including the word abstract in their headers.

Our extended hierarchy of classes is shown in Figure 10-6.

FIGURE 10-6
The shapes hierarchy

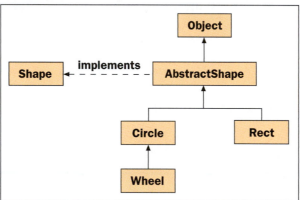

It takes rather a lot of code to implement all these classes; however, the code is straightforward, and the embedded comments explain the tricky parts. Pay particular attention to the attribute final, which is used for the first time in a method definition in class AbstractShape. A *final method* is a method that cannot be overridden by a subclass.

```
// AbstractShape.java: The abstract class for all shapes

import TurtleGraphics.Pen;

// Notice the use of the word "abstract" in the class header.
// This class implements the Shape interface.
// We don't need to say that the class extends Object as that is the
// default.

abstract public class AbstractShape implements Shape{

    // Here we declare variables common to all subclasses.
```

```java
    protected double xPos;
    protected double yPos;

    // Even though this class is never instantiated, it needs constructors
    // to initialize its variables.

    public AbstractShape(){
        xPos = 0;
        yPos = 0;
    }

    public AbstractShape(double xLoc, double yLoc){
        xPos = xLoc;
        yPos = yLoc;
    }


    // There is no code for the next two methods; therefore,
    // they are abstract and terminate with a semicolon.
    // All subclasses must define these methods.

    abstract public double area();

    abstract public void draw(Pen p);

    // These next three methods will never be changed in a subclass;
    // therefore, they are declared final, meaning they
    // cannot be overridden.

    public final double getXPos(){
        return xPos;
    }

    public final double getYPos(){
        return yPos;
    }

    public final void move (double xLoc, double yLoc){
        xPos = xLoc;
        yPos = yLoc;
    }

    // Another abstract method to be defined in subclasses.

    abstract public void stretchBy (double factor);

    // Subclasses will override this method.
    // Notice that the method calls area(). More will be said about
    // this later.

    public String toString(){
        String str = "(X,Y) Position: (" + xPos + "," + yPos + ")\n"
                    + "Area: " + area();
        return str;
    }
}
```

```java
// Circle.java: The class for circles

import TurtleGraphics.Pen;

// This class extends AbstractShape and in the process implements
// the Shape interface.

public class Circle extends AbstractShape{

    protected double radius;

    public Circle(){
        super();                // Activate a constructor in AbstractShape.
        radius = 1;             // Then initialize radius.
    }

    public Circle (double xLoc, double yLoc, double r){
        super (xLoc, yLoc);     // Activate a constructor in AbstractShape.
        radius = r;             // Then initialize radius.
    }

    // The next three methods were abstract in the superclass.
    // Now we define them.

    public double area(){
        return Math.PI * radius * radius;
    }

    public void draw (Pen p){
        double side = 2.0 * Math.PI * radius / 120.0;
        p.up();
        p.move (xPos + radius, yPos - side / 2.0);
        p.setDirection (90);
        p.down();
        for (int i = 0; i < 120; i++){
            p.move (side);
            p.turn (3);
        }
    }

    public void stretchBy (double factor){
        radius *= factor;
    }

    // Notice that the toString method calls the corresponding method in the
    // superclass in order to accomplish its task.

    // In the superclass, the toString method calls area, which will
    // activate the area method in this class and not the area method in the
    // superclass.

    public String toString(){
        String str = "CIRCLE\n"
                    + "Radius: " + radius + "\n"
```

```java
                        + super.toString();
        return str;
    }
}

// Wheel.java: The class for wheels

// We have already explained most of the major points in this class.

import TurtleGraphics.Pen;

public class Wheel extends Circle{

    private int spokes;

    public Wheel(){
        super();
        spokes = 0;
    }

    public Wheel (double xLoc, double yLoc, double r, int s){
        super (xLoc, yLoc, r);
        spokes = s;
    }

    public void draw (Pen p){
        // Draw the wheel's rim
        super.draw (p);

        // Draw the spokes
        for (int i = 1; i <= spokes; i++){
            p.up();
            p.move (xPos, yPos);
            p.setDirection (i * 360.0 / spokes);
            p.down();
            p.move (radius);
        }
    }

    public void setSpokes (int s){
        spokes = s;
    }

    // We could not call super.toString() in this toString method, because
    // doing so would have activated the method in Circle rather than the
    // method we wanted in AbstractShape.

    public String toString(){
        String str = "WHEEL\n"
                    + "Radius: " + radius + "\n"
                    + "Spokes: " + spokes + "\n"
                    + "(X,Y) Position: (" + xPos + "," + yPos + ")\n"
                    + "Area: " + area();
        return str;
```

```java
      }
}

// Rect.java: The class for rectangles

// No additional comments are needed in this class. All the important
// points have already been made.

import TurtleGraphics.Pen;

public class Rect extends AbstractShape {

    private double height, width;

    public Rect() {
        super();
        height = 1;
        width = 1;
    }

    public Rect (double xLoc, double yLoc, double w, double h) {
        super (xLoc, yLoc);
        height = h;
        width = w;
    }

    public double area() {
        return height * width;
    }

    public void draw (Pen p) {
        p.up();
        p.move (xPos, yPos);
        p.down();
        p.setDirection (0); p.move (width);
        p.turn (-90); p.move (height);
        p.turn (-90); p.move (width);
        p.turn (-90); p.move (height);
    }

    public void stretchBy (double factor) {
        height *= factor;
        width *= factor;
    }

    public String toString() {
        String str = "RECTANGLE\n"
                    + "Width & Height: " + width + " & " + height +"\n"
                    + super.toString();
        return str;
    }
}
```

EXERCISE 10.6

1. What is an abstract class? Give an example.

2. Why do we declare abstract methods?

3. What is a final method? Give an example.

4. What is a protected variable? Give an example.

10.7 Some Observations about Interfaces, Inheritance, and Relationships among Classes

We now quickly review some major features of interfaces and inheritance and make a few additional observations.

- A Java interface has a name and consists of a list of method headers.

- One or more classes can implement the same interface.

- If a variable is declared to be of an interface type, then it can be associated with an object from any class that implements the interface.

- If a class implements an interface, then all its subclasses do so implicitly.

- A subclass inherits all the characteristics of its superclass. To this basis, the subclass can add new variables and methods or modify inherited methods.

- Characteristics common to several classes can be collected in a common abstract superclass that is never instantiated.

- An abstract class can contain headers for abstract methods that are implemented in the subclasses.

- A class's constructors and methods can utilize constructors and methods in the superclass.

- Inheritance reduces repetition and promotes the reuse of code.

- Interfaces and inheritance promote the use of polymorphism.

Now let us consider additional observations.

Finding the Right Method

When a message is sent to an object, Java looks for a matching method. The search starts in the object's class and if necessary continues up the class hierarchy.

- Consequently, in the preceding program, when the `move` message is sent to a circle or a rectangle, the `move` method in the `AbstractShape` class is activated. There is no `move` method in either the `Circle` or `Rect` classes.

- On the other hand, when the `stretchBy` message is sent to a circle, Java uses the corresponding method in the `Circle` class.

■ When the `toString` message is sent to a circle, execution begins in the `Circle` class, temporarily transfers to the superclass, and finishes up in the `Circle` class.

```
public String toString() {
   String str = "CIRCLE\n"
              + "Radius: " + radius + "\n"
              + super.toString();           // Transfer to superclass
   return str;
}
```

In the superclass `AbstractShape`, however, something tricky happens:

```
public String toString(){
   String str = "(X,Y) Position: (" + xPos + "," + yPos + ")\n"
              + "Area: " + area();        // Something tricky here
   return str;
}
```

Which `area` method is being called, the one in `AbstractShape` or the one in `Circle`? Actually, this question is not so hard to answer. We must stop to consider which object is involved in all of this. It is a circle object; therefore, the `area` method in the `Circle` class is activated. Nonetheless, it does seem strange that the `toString` method in the superclass activates the `area` method in the subclass.

To be fair, we (the authors) must admit that the last example was specially contrived to be tricky. You may work with Java for a year or more before encountering anything similar.

Implementation, Extension, Overriding, and Finality

You may have noticed that there are four ways in which methods in a subclass can be related to methods in a superclass:

1. *Implementation of an abstract method*: As we have seen, each subclass is forced to implement the abstract methods specified in its superclass. Abstract methods are thus a means of requiring certain behavior in all subclasses.

2. *Extension*: There are two kinds of extension:
   A. The subclass method does not exist in the superclass.
   B. The subclass method invokes the same method in the superclass and also extends the superclass's behavior with its own operations.

3. *Overriding*: In the case of **overriding**, the subclass method does not invoke the superclass method. Instead, the subclass method is intended as a complete replacement of the superclass method.

4. *Finality*: The method in the superclass is complete and cannot be modified by the subclasses. We declare such a method to be `final`.

Working Without Interfaces

Interfaces are a useful and powerful mechanism for organizing code; however, they are not necessary. Without the `Shape` interface, the implementation of `AbstractShape` remains the same except for the header:

```
abstract public class AbstractShape {
```

And defining a variable as `AbstractShape` allows the variable to associate with objects from any shape class:

```
AbstractShape s1, s2, s3;
s1 = new Circle();
s2 = new Rect();
s3 = new Wheel();

s2.<any message in AbstractShape>;
```

Because the `AbstractShape` class contains a list of all the shape methods, we can send any of the shape messages to the variables s1, s2, and s3. Of course, we still cannot send the `setSpokes` message to s3 without first casting s3 to the `Wheel` class.

So should you or shouldn't you use interfaces? This is not really a question of vital importance in an introductory programming class where all the programs are relatively short and simple; however, the prevailing wisdom suggests that we use hierarchies of interfaces to organize behavior and hierarchies of classes to maximize code reuse. Justifying this advice is beyond this book's scope.

Relationships among Classes

Thus far in this book, we have seen that classes can be related to each other in several ways:

1. An object of one class can send a message to an object of another class. For example, a `Circle` object sends a message to a `StandardPen` object to draw that shape. In this case, the sender object's class *depends on* the receiver object's class, and their relationship is called *dependency*.

2. An object of one class can contain objects of another class as structural components. For example, the `TestScoresModel` object described in the case study of Chapter 9 contains `Student` objects. The relationship between a container class and the classes of the objects it contains is called *aggregation* or the *has-a* relationship.

3. An object's class can be a subclass of a more general class. For example, the `Wheel` class is a subclass of `Circle`, which in turn is a subclass of `AbstractShape`. These classes are related by *inheritance*, or the *is-a* relationship.

These three types of relationships among classes are depicted in the UML diagrams in Figure 10-7. Note that the third diagram also shows the relationship between a class (`Abstract-Shape`) and the interface (`Shape`) that it implements.

FIGURE 10-7
Three types of relationships among classes

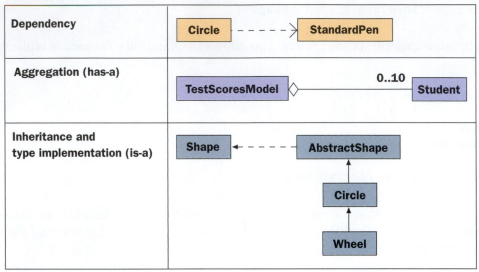

EXERCISE 10.7

1. Describe the process by which the Java Virtual Machine (JVM) locates the right method to execute at run time in the following example:

```
// In the server's code
private int myData;
public String someMethod(int x){
    return myData + super.someMethod(x);
}
// In the client's code
System.out.println(someObject.someMethod(10));
```

2. Give one example, other than those discussed in this chapter, of the relationships of dependency, aggregation, and inheritance among classes.

10.8 Acceptable Classes for Parameters and Return Values

The rules of Java, as enforced by the compiler, state that in any situation in which an object of class BBB is expected, it is always acceptable to substitute an object of a subclass but never of a superclass. The reason is simple. A subclass of BBB inherits all of BBB's methods, whereas no guarantees can be made about the methods in the superclass. The following code segment illustrates these points (the results would be the same if we substituted `Shape` for `AbstractShape` in the first line):

```
AbstractShape s;
Circle c;
Wheel w;

s = new Circle();    // Accepted by the compiler
c = new Circle();    // Accepted by the compiler
w = new Circle();    // Rejected by the compiler
c = new Wheel();     // Accepted by the compiler
```

In the rest of this section, we apply these principles to method parameters and return values. We already know that objects can be passed to and returned from methods. Actually, to speak more precisely, we should say references to objects can be passed to and returned from methods. It is obvious that an object must exist before it is passed to a method, but it is easy to forget that changes made to the object in the method persist after the method stops executing. On the other hand, an object returned by a method is usually created in the method, and it continues to exist after the method stops executing.

Rectangle In, Circle Out

For our first example we write a method that takes a rectangle as an input parameter and returns a circle. The circle has the same area and position as the rectangle. The method makes no changes to the rectangle, and it has to instantiate the circle:

```
static private Circle makeCircleFromRectangle (Rect rectangle){
    double area = rectangle.area();
    double radius = Math.sqrt (area / Math.PI);
    Circle circle = new Circle (rectangle.getXPos(),
                                rectangle.getYPos(),
                                radius);
    return circle;
}
```

Any Shape In, Circle Out

We now modify the previous method so that it accepts any shape as an input parameter—circle, rectangle, or wheel. The fact that all shapes understand the `area` method makes the task easy:

```
static private Circle makeCircleFromAnyShape (Shape shape){
    double area = shape.area();
    double radius = Math.sqrt (area / Math.PI);
    Circle circle = new Circle (shape.getXPos(),
                                shape.getYPos(),
                                radius);
    return circle;
}
```

Any Shape In, Any Shape Out

It is also possible for a method to return an arbitrary rather than a specific shape. The next method has two input parameters. The first parameter is a shape, and the second indicates the type of shape to return:

```java
static private Shape makeOneShapeFromAnother (Shape inShape, String type){
   Shape outShape;                                     // declare outShape
   double area, radius, width, height;
   double x = inShape.getXPos();
   double y = inShape.getYPos();

   area = inShape.area();
   if (type.equals ("circle")){
      radius = Math.sqrt (area / Math.PI);
      outShape = new Circle (x, y, radius);            // assign a circle
   }
   else if (type.equals ("rectangle")){
      width = height = Math.sqrt (area);
      outShape = new Rect (x, y, width, height);       // assign a rectangle
   }
   else{ // it is a wheel
      radius = Math.sqrt (area / Math.PI);
      outShape = new Wheel (x, y, radius, 6);          // assign a wheel
   }
   return outShape;
}
```

The following code is a test of the previous method with the program's output shown in Figure 10-8.

```java
// Example 10.5: Making one shape from another

public class TestShapes {

   public static void main (String[] args){
      Rect rect;
      Shape shape1, shape2, shape3;

      rect = new Rect (1,1,4,6);
      shape1 = makeOneShapeFromAnother (rect, "circle");
      shape2 = makeOneShapeFromAnother (rect, "rectangle");
      shape3 = makeOneShapeFromAnother (rect, "wheel");

      System.out.println ("\nRectangle Area: " + rect.area() +
                          "\nCircle    Area: " + shape1.area() +
                          "\nRectangle Area: " + shape2.area() +
                          "\nWheel     Area: " + shape3.area());
   }

   static private Shape makeOneShapeFromAnother (Shape inShape,
                                                 String type){
```

```
    ... code as shown above ...
    }
}
```

FIGURE 10-8
Areas of various shapes made from a rectangle

```
Rectangle Area: 24.0
Circle    Area: 24.000000000000004
Rectangle Area: 23.999999999999996
Wheel     Area: 24.000000000000004
```

EXERCISE 10.8

1. State the rules for passing a parameter of one class to a method that expects a parameter of another class.

2. Class BB is a subclass of class AA. Method m expects a parameter of type BB. Which of the following method calls is syntactically incorrect?

   a. `m(new AA());`

   b. `m(new BB());`

10.9 Error Handling with Classes

In Chapter 6, we introduced a means of handling possible error conditions in a system that uses classes and objects. In this approach, a class's mutator method returns a boolean value to indicate whether the operation has been successful or an error has occurred and the operation has failed. In addition, the class provides a method that returns a string that states a rule describing the valid use of the mutator method. For example, following is the code for these two methods in an Employee object, followed by its use in some client code:

```java
// In the Employee class
public String getHoursRules(){
    return "between 1 and 60, inclusive";
}

public boolean setHours(int hrs){
    if (!(1 <= hrs && hrs <= 60))
        return false;
    else{
        hours = hrs;
        return true;
    }
}
// In the client that uses an Employee object
// Input the hours worked until valid
System.out.print("Hours worked(" + emp.getHoursRules() + "): ");
while (!emp.setHours(reader.nextInt()));
```

Clearly, this kind of error checking improves the situation in Chapter 5, where our classes simply let errors go undetected. In this section, we introduce a more formal way of describing error conditions in code and another way of detecting and responding to errors.

Preconditions and Postconditions

Before we can implement code for error handling, we must determine what the error conditions for a class are. A systematic way to do this is to state these conditions in the class's interface as *preconditions* and *postconditions*. We can think of preconditions and postconditions as the subject of a conversation between the user and implementer of a method. Following is the general form of the conversation:

Implementer: "Here are the things that you must guarantee to be true before my method is invoked. They are its preconditions."

User: "Fine. And what do you guarantee will be the case if I do that?"

Implementer: "Here are the things that I guarantee to be true when my method finishes execution. They are its postconditions."

A method's preconditions describe what should be true before it is called, and its postconditions describe what will be true after it has finished executing. The preconditions describe the expected values of parameters and instance variables that the method is about to use. Postconditions describe the return value and any changes made to instance variables. Of course, if the caller does not meet the preconditions, then the method probably will not meet the postconditions.

In most programming languages, preconditions and postconditions are conveniently written as comments placed directly above a method's header. Let us add such documentation to a method header for the `Student` method `setScore` from Chapter 9. There are preconditions on each of the method's parameters:

1. The parameter `i`, which represents the position of the score, must be greater than or equal to 1 and less than or equal to the number of scores.

2. The parameter `score` must be greater than or equal to 0 and less than or equal to 100.

The method's postcondition states that the test score at position `i` has been set to `score`. We now return the `boolean` value `true` if the preconditions have been satisfied or `false` otherwise. Following is the code:

```
/*
 * Precondition: 1 <= i <= number of scores
 * Precondition: 0 <= score <= 100
 * Postcondition: test score at position i is set to score
 * Returns: true if the preconditions are satisfied or false otherwise
 */
public boolean setScore(int i, int score){
   if (i < 1 || i > tests.length || score < 0 || score > 100)
      return false;
   tests[i - 1] = score;
   return true;
}
```

Not all methods have pre- and postconditions. For example, the `student` method `getName` simply returns the student's name, so its documentation mentions just the return value.

The writing of pre- and postconditions for each method might seem like a tedious task; however, that's how the developers of Java have done it, as an inspection of Sun's Java documentation reveals. And remember that, like the people at Sun, you are writing code primarily for other people to read.

Exercises 10.9

1. What do preconditions describe? Give an example.

2. What do postconditions describe? Give an example.

10.10 Exceptions

As you have seen in earlier chapters, Java throws an exception to signal a run-time error. There are occasions when you can throw your own exceptions in the classes you write. We now give an overview of how to do this.

Examples of Exceptions

Java provides a hierarchy of exception classes that represent the most commonly occurring exceptions. Following is a list of some of the commonly used exception classes in the package `java.lang`:

```
Exception
    RuntimeException
        ArithmeticException
        IllegalArgumentException
        IllegalStateException
        IndexOutOfBoundsException
            StringIndexOutOfBoundsException
            ArrayIndexOutOfBoundsException
        NullPointerException
        UnsupportedOperationException
```

Java throws an arithmetic exception when a program attempts to divide by 0 and a `null` pointer exception when a program attempts to send a message to a variable that does not reference an object. An array index out-of-bounds exception is thrown when the integer in an array subscript operator is less than 0 or greater than or equal to the array's length. Other types of exceptions, such as illegal state exceptions and illegal argument exceptions, can be used to enforce preconditions on methods. Other packages such as `java.util` define still more types of exceptions. In general, you determine which preconditions you want to enforce and then choose the appropriate type of exception to throw from Java's repertoire.

The syntax of the statement to throw an exception is

```
throw new <exception class>(<a string>);
```

where `<a string>` is the message to be displayed. When you are in doubt about which type of exception to throw, you can fall back on a `RuntimeException`. Following is an example:

```
if (number < 0)
    throw new RuntimeException("Number should be nonnegative");
```

How Exceptions Work

At run time, the computer keeps track of the dynamic context of a program. This context includes a chain of method calls, beginning with the method `main` in the main application class and ending with the currently executing method. When a piece of code in this method throws an exception, the computer examines the code immediately surrounding it for a `try-catch` statement (more on this statement later). If no such statement is found in this context, control returns immediately to the caller of the method. Once again, if no `try-catch` statement is found in that method, control moves up to its caller, and so on, until method `main` is reached. If no `try-catch` statement has been located at any point in this process, the computer halts the program with a trace of the method calls, the type of exception, and its error message, examples of which you have seen in earlier chapters.

Throwing Exceptions to Enforce Preconditions

A more hard-nosed approach to error handling is to have a class throw exceptions to enforce all of its methods' preconditions. Let's adopt that approach for the `Student` method `setScore` discussed earlier. We know the preconditions, so we begin by choosing the appropriate exception classes and describing these in the documentation. We will throw an `IllegalArgumentException` if either parameter violates the preconditions. Because the method either succeeds in setting a score or throws an exception, it returns `void` instead of a `boolean` value. The method header summarizes our error handling:

```
/*
 * Precondition: 1 <= i <= number of scores
 * Precondition: 0 <= score <= 100
 * Postcondition: test score at position i is set to score
 * throws IllegalArgumentException if i < 1 or i > number of scores
 * throws IllegalArgumentException if score < 0 or score > 100
 */
public void setScore (int i, int score){
    if (i < 1 || i > tests.length)
        throw new IllegalArgumentException(
                "i must be >= 1 and <= " + tests.length);
    if (score < MIN_SCORE || score > MAX_SCORE)
        throw new IllegalArgumentException(
                "score must be >= " +
                MIN_SCORE + " and <= " + MAX_SCORE);
    tests[i - 1] = score;
}
```

Catching an Exception

As you can see, the use of exceptions can make a server's code pretty foolproof. However, clients must still check the preconditions of such methods if they do not want these exceptions to halt their programs with run-time errors. There are two ways to do this:

1. Use a simple `if-else` statement to ask the right questions about the parameters before calling a method.

2. Embed the call to the method within a `try-catch` statement.

    The `try-catch` statement allows a client to

■ Attempt the call of a method whose preconditions might be violated.

■ Catch any exceptions that the method might throw and respond to them gracefully.

For example, the following code displays the exception's error message in the terminal window instead of halting the program with the same message and a call trace:

```
int[] scores = {88, 99, 66};
Student s = new Student("Bill", scores);
try{
    s.setScore(4, 85);
}catch(IllegalArgumentException e){
    System.out.println(e);
}
```

When the `setScore` method throws the `IllegalArgumentException`, the computer passes it as a parameter to the `catch` clause, which assumes immediate control and continues execution.

This code catches and handles an exception only of the specified type. Suppose a method can throw two different types of exceptions, such as `IllegalArgumentException` and `IllegalStateException`. To catch either one of these, one can include two catch clauses:

```
try{
    someObject.someMethod(param1, param2);
}catch(IllegalStateException e){
    System.out.println(e);
}catch(IllegalArgumentException e){
    System.out.println(e);
}
```

The computer runs down the list of `catch` clauses until the exception's type matches that of a parameter or no match is found. If no match is found, the exception is passed up the call chain as described earlier.

To guarantee that any exception is caught, you can use the generic `Exception` class, which matches any exception type:

```
try{
    s.setScore(4, 200);
}catch(Exception e){
    System.out.println(e);
}
```

Creating Online Documentation With `javadoc`

As we mentioned in Chapter 5, Sun provides online, browsable documentation of all standard Java classes. This documentation is created with a tool called `javadoc`. You can create similar documentation for your own classes. To do so, you perform the following steps:

1. Edit the `.java` file to include special comment syntax to mark the information that will appear in the document pages. The items marked usually include a summary of the class's purpose, method parameters, method return values, and exceptions thrown by methods.

2. Run the `javadoc` command with the `.java` file to generate the online documentation. `javadoc` generates a set of HMTL files that can be loaded into a Web browser.

The next code listing shows the `Student` class from Chapter 9, updated with static constants and exceptions. We have also inserted comments for `javadoc`. Note the slight difference in syntax from the ordinary Java multiline comments. The symbol `/**` is used instead of `/*` to begin a comment. The comment that describes the purpose of the class should be placed between the class header and the `import` statements (if they exist). The lines that begin with the '`@`' character mark items that receive special formatting in the documentation.

```java
// Case Study 9.1: Student class

/**
Represents a student with a name and several test scores
*/

public class Student{

   /**
   The minimum score (0)
   */
   public static int MIN_SCORE = 0;

   /**
   The maximum score (100)
   */
   public static int MAX_SCORE = 100;

   private String name;
   private int[] tests;

   /**
   Default: name is "" and each of 3 scores is 0
   */
   public Student(){
      this("");
   }

   /**
   Name is nm and each of 3 scores is 0
   @param nm the name of the student
   */
   public Student(String nm){
      this(nm, 3);
   }
```

```java
/**
Name is nm and each of n scores is 0
@param nm the name of the student
@param n the number of scores
*/
public Student(String nm, int n){
    name = nm;
    tests = new int[n];
    for (int i = 0; i < tests.length; i++)
        tests[i] = 0;
}

/**
Name is nm and the scores are taken from array t
@param nm the name of the student
@param t an array of test scores
*/
public Student(String nm, int[] t){
    name = nm;
    tests = new int[t.length];
    for (int i = 0; i < tests.length; i++)
        tests[i] = t[i];
}

/**
Builds a copy of a student
@param s the student to be copied
*/
public Student(Student s){
    this(s.name, s.tests);
}

/**
Changes the student's name
@param nm the new name
*/
public void setName (String nm){
    name = nm;
}

/**
@return the student's name
*/
public String getName (){
    return name;
}

/**
@param i the ith
@param score the ith score
@throws IllegalArgumentException if i < 1 or i > number of scores
@throws IllegalArgumentException if score < MIN_SCORE or score >
MAX_SCORE
*/
public void setScore (int i, int score){
```

```java
      if (i < 1 || i > tests.length)
         throw new IllegalArgumentException(
                  "i must be >= 1 and <= " + tests.length);
      if (score < MIN_SCORE || score > MAX_SCORE)
         throw new IllegalArgumentException(
                  "score must be >= " +
                  MIN_SCORE + " and <= " + MAX_SCORE);
      tests[i - 1] = score;
   }


   /**
   @param i the ith
   @throws IllegalArgumentException if i < 1 or i > number of scores
   @return the student's ith score
   */
   public int getScore (int i){
      if (i < 1 || i >= tests.length)
         throw new IllegalArgumentException(
                  "i must be >= 1 and <= " + tests.length);
      return tests[i - 1];
   }


   /**
   @return the student's average score
   */
   public int getAverage(){
      int sum = 0;
      for (int i = 0; i < tests.length; i++)
         sum += tests[i];
      return sum / tests.length;
   }


   /**
   @return the student's highest score
   */
   public int getHighScore(){
      int highScore;
      highScore = tests[0];
      for (int i = 1; i < tests.length; i++)
         highScore = Math.max (highScore, tests[i]);
      return highScore;
   }


   /**
   @return the student's string representation
   */
   public String toString(){
      String str;
      str = "Name:    " + name  + "\n";
      for (int i = 0; i < tests.length; i++)
         str += "test " + i + ":   " + tests[i] + "\n";
      str += "Average: " + getAverage();
      return str;
   }
```

```
/**
@return null if there are no errors or an appropriate error message
*/
public String validateData(){
    if (name.equals ("")) return "SORRY: name required";
    for (int i = 0; i < tests.length; i++){
        if (tests[i] < 0 || tests[i] > 100){
            String str = "SORRY: must have "+ 0
                        + " <= test score <= " + 100;
            return str;
        }
    }
    return null;
}
}
```

@param, @return, and @throws are the standard tags recognized by javadoc. To process just the Student class, run javadoc as follows:

```
javadoc Student.java
```

Figure 10-9 shows screen shots of two portions of the resulting Web page.

FIGURE 10-9
javadoc Web pages for the Student class

If you have several files to process, you can list them as command-line arguments to javadoc. For example, to process just Student and TestScoresModel from Chapter 9, you can run

```
javadoc Student.java TestScoresModel.java
```

To process all of the source files in the current directory, you can run

```
javadoc *.java
```

EXERCISES 10.10

1. When should a method throw an exception? Give an example.

2. Explain what happens at run time when a method throws an exception.

3. Explain how an exception can be handled under program control.

4. List the three standard tags used to create documentation with `javadoc` and describe their purposes.

10.11 Reference Types, Equality, and Object Identity

In Chapters 2, 5, and 6, we made a distinction between variables of primitive types—which contain numbers, characters, Booleans—and variables of reference types—which contain references or pointers to objects, but never the objects themselves. Thus, it is possible for more than one variable to point to the same object, a situation known as *aliasing*. This occurs when the programmer assigns one object variable to another. It is also possible, of course, for two object variables to refer to distinct objects of the same type.

Comparing Objects for Equality

The possibility of aliasing can lead to unintended results when comparing two object variables for equality. There are two ways to compare objects for equality:

1. Use the equality operator ==.

2. Use the instance method `equals`. This method is defined in the `Object` class and uses the == operator by default. This method is similar to the method `toString`, which was discussed earlier in this book and which, by default, returns the name of the object's class for any object that does not override it. All classes, which are subclasses of `Object`, inherit the method `equals` and use it when it is not overridden in the receiver object's class.

Consider the following code segment, which reads a string from the keyboard, uses both methods to compare this string to a string literal, and outputs the results:

```
String str = reader.nextLine();              // Read string from keyboard.

System.out.println (str == "Java");          // Displays false no matter what
                                             // string was entered.
System.out.println (str.equals ("Java"));    // Displays true if the string
                                             // entered was "Java", and false
                                             // otherwise.
```

Following is the explanation:

- The objects referenced by the variable str and the literal "Java" are two different string objects in memory, even though the characters they contain might be the same. The first string object was created in the keyboard reader during user input; the second string object was created internally within the program.

- The operator == compares the references to the objects, not the contents of the objects. Thus, if the two references do not point to the same object in memory, == returns false. Because the two strings in our example are not the same object in memory, == returns false.

- The method equals returns true, even when two strings are not the same object in memory, if their characters happen to be the same. If at least one pair of characters fails to match, the method equals returns false.

- A corollary of these facts is that the operator != can return true for two strings, even though the method equals also returns true.

- To summarize, == tests for object identity, whereas equals tests for structural similarity as defined by the implementing class.

The operator == also can be used with other objects, such as buttons and menu items. In these cases, too, the operator tests for object identity: a reference to the same object in memory. With window objects, the use of == is appropriate because most of the time we want to compare references. For other objects, however, such as the student objects discussed in Chapter 9, the use of == should be avoided. To test two student objects for equality, we implement the method equals in the Student class. We will consider two students equal if

- They are identical, or

- They are instances of Student and their names are equal.

Following is the code for the method:

```java
// Compare two students for equality
   public boolean equals (Object other){
       if (this == other)                  // Test for identity
          return true;
       if (! (other instanceof Student))   // Test for a Student
          return false;
       Student s = (Student)other;         // Cast to a Student
       return name.equals (s.getName());   // Compare the names
   }
```

Note that the method expects an Object as a parameter. This means that the user can pass an object of any class when the method is called. The method should first compare the receiver object (indicated by the word this) to the parameter object for identity using ==. If the two objects are not identical, the method examines their contents only if the parameter object is in fact an instance of the Student class. Therefore, the method must next do one of two things:

1. Return false if the parameter object is not an instance of Student. The operator instanceof is used to determine the class or interface of an object.

2. If the parameter object is an instance of class Student, cast its class down from Object to Student before accessing the data within it.

Copying Objects

As mentioned in Chapter 5, the attempt to copy an object with a simple assignment statement can cause a problem. The following code creates two references to one student object when the intent is to copy the contents of one student object to another:

```
Student s1, s2;
s1 = new Student("Mary");
s2 = s1;                              // s1 and s2 refer to the same
                                      // object
```

In Chapter 9, we added a constructor for students that expects another object of type `Student` as a parameter. This constructor copies the parameter's data into the instance variables of the new student:

```
Student s1, s2;
s1 = new Student("Mary");
s2 = new Student(s1);                 // s1 and s2 refer to
                                      // different objects
```

When clients of a class might copy objects, there is a more standard way of providing a method that does so. The class implements the Java interface `Cloneable`. This interface authorizes the method `clone`, which is defined in the `Object` class, to construct a field-wise copy of the object. We now can rewrite the foregoing code so that it creates a copy of a student object:

```
Student s1, s2;
s1 = new Student ("Mary");
s2 = s1.clone();                      // s1 and s2 refer to different objects
```

Note that `==` returns `false` and `equals` returns `true` for an object and its clone.

The implementation of the `clone` method returns a new instance of `Student` with the values of the instance variables from the receiver student. Following is the code for method `clone`:

```
// Clone a new student
public Object clone(){
    return new Student(name, tests);
}
```

Many of Java's standard classes, such as `String`, already implement the `Cloneable` interface, so they include a `clone` method. When instance variables of a class are themselves objects that are cloneable, it is a good idea to send them the `clone` message to obtain copies when implementing the `clone` method for that class. This process is called *deep copying* and can help minimize program errors.

Because tests for equality and cloning are fairly standard operations in all implementations, the methods `equals` and `clone` should be added to the Java interface for your classes, if there is one.

EXERCISES 10.11

1. Why should a programmer use the method `equals` instead of the operator == to compare two objects for equality?

2. What are the outputs when the following code segment is run?

```
Student s1 = new Student("Bill");
Student s2 = new Student("Bill");
String name = "Bill";

System.out.println(s1.equals(s2));
System.out.println(s1 == s2);
System.out.println(s1.equals(name));
```

3. What happens when an object is assigned to a variable?

4. How can you obtain a true copy of an object?

10.12 Graphics and GUIs: Drawing Multiple Shapes

The `TurtleGraphics` package used earlier in this chapter automatically refreshes the graphics window with any images that the pen has drawn. In this section, we examine the related problem of how to maintain multiple shapes in graphics programs such as those discussed in Chapters 3 through 6.

> **Extra Challenge**
>
> This Graphics and GUIs section gives you the opportunity to explore concepts and programming techniques required to develop modern graphics applications and graphical user interfaces. This material is not required in order to proceed with the other chapters of the book.

Java's Forgetful Bitmap

As we saw in previous chapters, images and shapes are painted in a GUI component by sending messages to that component's graphics context. This is normally done in the component's `paintComponent` method, which the JVM runs whenever the component's window needs to be refreshed. The method `repaint` also accomplishes a refresh under program control. For example, the programmer can call `repaint` after an image or shape has changed position. This method calls `paintComponent`, which paints the component's background color and redraws all of its shapes and images.

The bitmap of a Java graphics context does not retain the information about images and shapes after they are drawn to a window. This phenomenon is known as a *forgetful bitmap*. That's why the programmer must write a `paintComponent` method and use `repaint` for window refreshes. Actually, the forgetful bitmap is not much of a problem, as long as `paintComponent` knows where to go to find information about the images and shapes to paint. We now consider some simple solutions to this problem.

A Database of Circles

To guarantee that all images and shapes are painted on each refresh, a graphics application must maintain information about them in a database. In this section, we show how to set up and manage a simple database of circles.

In Chapter 5, we designed and implemented a class for representing circles. We then showed how to use this class in a sample application, which draws two circles in a panel. At startup, the panel instantiates the two circles and saves references to them in two instance variables. When the panel needs refreshing, the method `paintComponent` sends the appropriate messages to the two variables to paint the circles. (*A note of caution*: The `Circle` class discussed here is different from the one introduced in Section 10.4, which uses a turtle graphics pen to draw itself.)

When there are more than one or two circles to be accessed, we can store them in an array. The method `paintComponent` traverses the array to paint all of the circles. In addition, we can use the array to perform other functions, such as search for a circle that contains the current mouse coordinates.

Our first example program is a revised version of Example 5.5. This program displays two circles at startup and allows the user to move them around by dragging the mouse. In the new version of the program, an array of 10 circles replaces the two `Circle` instance variables in the `ColorPanel` class. The panel's constructor instantiates the array and fills it with circles of equal size and randomly generated color. `paintComponent` paints all of the circles. The method `mousePressed` in the class `PanelListener` searches the array for a circle that contains the mouse coordinates. If a circle is found, the variable `selectedCircle` is set to that circle. The classes `Circle` and `GUIWindow` remain as they were in Chapter 5. Here is the code for the revised `ColorPanel` class:

```java
// Example 10.6: Displays 10 circles of random color
// Allows the user to drag a circle to another position

import javax.swing.*;
import java.awt.*;
import java.awt.event.*;                //For the mouse events
import java.util.Random;

public class ColorPanel extends JPanel{

    private Circle database[];          // The array of circles
    private Circle selectedCircle;      // Used to track selected shape
    private int x, y;                   // Used to track mouse coordinates

    public ColorPanel(Color backColor){
        setBackground(backColor);
        Random gen = new Random();
        // Create 10 circles of random color
        database = new Circle[10];
        for (int i = 0; i < database.length; i++){
            Color color = new Color(gen.nextInt(256), gen.nextInt(256),
                            gen.nextInt(256));
            Circle c = new Circle(i * 40, 100, 25, color);
            c.setFilled(true);
            database[i] = c;
        }
        selectedCircle = null;
        addMouseListener(new PanelListener());
        addMouseMotionListener(new PanelMotionListener());
    }
```

```java
public void paintComponent(Graphics g){
    super.paintComponent(g);
    for (Circle c: database)        // Draw all the circles
        c.draw(g);
}

private class PanelListener extends MouseAdapter{

    public void mousePressed(MouseEvent e){
        //Select a circle if it contains the mouse coordinates
        x = e.getX();
        y = e.getY();
        // Search for a circle, starting with the last drawn
        for (int i = database.length  - 1; i >= 0; i--)
            if (database[i].containsPoint(x, y)){
                selectedCircle = database[i];
                break;
            }
    }

    public void mouseReleased(MouseEvent e){
        // Deselect the selected circle
        x = e.getX();
        y = e.getY();
        selectedCircle = null;
    }
}

private class PanelMotionListener extends MouseMotionAdapter{

    public void mouseDragged(MouseEvent e){
        // Compute the distance and move the selected circle
        int newX = e.getX();
        int newY = e.getY();
        int dx = newX - x;
        int dy = newY - y;
        if (selectedCircle != null)
            selectedCircle.move(dx, dy);
        x = newX;
        y = newY;
        repaint();
    }
}
}
```

Note that the method `containsPoint` searches the array of circles from right to left, whereas `paintComponent` draws them from left to right. More recently drawn circles will appear on top of other circles when overlap occurs. A search in reverse guarantees that the uppermost circle will be selected when the mouse is clicked in an area of overlap.

A Database of Shapes

The program in example 10.6 maintains a database of circles. More realistic graphics applications might use many other types of shapes as well, such as rectangles, triangles, and more specialized shapes such as houses. A complex shape such as a house might be composed of simpler shapes such as rectangles. If we organize all of these types of shapes in a hierarchy that implements a common interface, we can modify the program of Example 10.6 to draw any kind of shapes. Here is the code for the `Shape` interface:

```java
// Interface for shapes

import java.awt.*;

public interface Shape{

    public void draw(Graphics g);
    public boolean containsPoint(int x, int y);
    public void move(int xAmount, int yAmount);
    public void setFilled(boolean b);
}
```

Let's assume that we have just two types of shapes, called `Circle` and `Rect` (see Section 5.6), that implement `Shape`. The changes to the `ColorPanel` class of Example 10.5 are then quite straightforward. We replace each variable declaration of type `Circle` with a variable declaration of type `Shape` and alter the variable names for readability. For example, the array declaration is changed from

```java
private Circle[] database;
```

to

```java
private Shape[] database;
```

The array can now store any object whose class implements the `Shape` interface. Because any of the methods used with an object in the array, such as `draw`, `containsPoint`, and `move`, work with any shape, we don't have to change any other code. Here is a listing of a revised version of `ColorPanel` that displays several circles and rectangles:

```java
// Example 10.7: Displays 10 shapes of random color
// Allows the user to drag a shape to another position

import javax.swing.*;
import java.awt.*;
import java.awt.event.*;           //For the mouse events
import java.util.Random;

public class ColorPanel extends JPanel{

    private Shape database[];       // The array of shapes
    private Shape selectedShape;    // Used to track selected shape
    private int x, y;               // Used to track mouse coordinates
```

```java
public ColorPanel(Color backColor){
   setBackground(backColor);
   Random gen = new Random();
   // Create 10 shapes of random color
   database = new Shape[10];
   for (int i = 0; i < database.length; i++){
      Color color = new Color(gen.nextInt(256), gen.nextInt(256),
                              gen.nextInt(256));
      // Flip a coin to determine which type of shape to create
      Shape s;
      if (gen.nextInt(2) == 1)
         s = new Circle(i * 40, 50, 25, color);
      else
         s = new Rect(i * 40, 100, 50, 50, color);
      s.setFilled(true);
      database[i] = s;
   }
   selectedShape = null;
   addMouseListener(new PanelListener());
   addMouseMotionListener(new PanelMotionListener());
}

public void paintComponent(Graphics g){
   super.paintComponent(g);
   for (Shape s : database)       // Draw all the shapes
      s.draw(g);
}

private class PanelListener extends MouseAdapter{

   public void mousePressed(MouseEvent e){
      // Select a shape if it contains the mouse coordinates
      x = e.getX();
      y = e.getY();
      // Search for a shape, starting with the last one added
      for (int i = database.length  - 1; i >= 0; i--)
         if (database[i].containsPoint(x, y)){
            selectedShape = database[i];
            break;
         }
   }

   public void mouseReleased(MouseEvent e){
      // Deselect the selected shape
      x = e.getX();
      y = e.getY();
      selectedShape = null;
   }
}

private class PanelMotionListener extends MouseMotionAdapter{

   public void mouseDragged(MouseEvent e){
      //Compute the distance and move the selected shape
      int newX = e.getX();
```

```
            int newY = e.getY();
            int dx = newX - x;
            int dy = newY - y;
            if (selectedShape != null)
                selectedShape.move(dx, dy);
            x = newX;
            y = newY;
            repaint();
        }
    }
}
```

The Model/View Pattern Revisited

We conclude this section with one more refinement of our shape manipulation program. The current version's color panel maintains an array of shapes. This design violates the division of responsibilities between model and view discussed in earlier chapters. The panel should be responsible for displaying shapes but should not have to manage an array of shapes. This problem will only get worse when we start to add and remove shapes based on user inputs.

We can solve the problem by placing all of the shapes in a distinct model object of type ShapeModel. This object is responsible for adding new shapes, selecting a shape, and drawing them. We now present a revised ColorPanel class that uses a ShapeModel with changes marked by comments. The model's implementation is similar to that of the TestScoresModel of Chapter 9 and is left as an exercise:

```java
// Example 10.8: Displays 10 shapes of random color
// Allows the user to drag a shape to another position

import javax.swing.*;
import java.awt.*;
import java.awt.event.*;          // For the mouse events
import java.util.Random;

public class ColorPanel extends JPanel{

    private ShapeModel database;   // Change: just a model
    private Shape selectedShape;   // Used to track selected shape
    private int x, y;              // Used to track mouse coordinates

    public ColorPanel(Color backColor){
        setBackground(backColor);
        Random gen = new Random();
        // Change: create a model for 10 shapes
        database = new ShapeModel(10);
        for (int i = 0; i < 10; i++){
            Color color = new Color(gen.nextInt(256), gen.nextInt(256),
                                    gen.nextInt(256));
            // Flip a coin to determine which type of shape to create
            Shape s;
            if (gen.nextInt(2) == 1)
                s = new Circle(i * 40, 50, 25, color);
            else
```

```
            s = new Rect(i * 40, 100, 50, 50, color);
            s.setFilled(true);
            database.add(s);        // Change: no more array access
        }
        selectedShape = null;
        addMouseListener(new PanelListener());
        addMouseMotionListener(new PanelMotionListener());
    }

    public void paintComponent(Graphics g){
        super.paintComponent(g);
        // Change: draw all the shapes
        database.draw(g);          // Piece of cake!
    }

    private class PanelListener extends MouseAdapter{

        public void mousePressed(MouseEvent e){
            // Select a shape if it contains the mouse coordinates
            x = e.getX();
            y = e.getY();
            // Change: search returns the shape or null
            selectedShape = database.containsPoint(x, y);
        }

        public void mouseReleased(MouseEvent e){
            // Deselect the selected shape
            x = e.getX();
            y = e.getY();
            selectedShape = null;
        }
    }

    private class PanelMotionListener extends MouseMotionAdapter{

        public void mouseDragged(MouseEvent e){
            // Compute the distance and move the selected shape
            int newX = e.getX();
            int newY = e.getY();
            int dx = newX - x;
            int dy = newY - y;
            if (selectedShape != null)
                selectedShape.move(dx, dy);
            x = newX;
            y = newY;
            repaint();
        }
    }
}
```

Note that the model includes the methods add, draw, and containsPoint. These are the only methods needed for this application, but others could be added for more sophisticated applications, as we see in later chapters.

EXERCISE 10.12

1. This chapter presents two different class hierarchies for representing and drawing geometric shapes. One uses turtle graphics to draw the shapes and the other uses Java's standard graphics classes. Discuss the advantages and disadvantages of these two design strategies.

SUMMARY

In this chapter, you learned:

■ Class (`static`) variables provide storage for data that all instances of a class can access but do not have to own separately. Class (`static`) methods are written primarily for class variables.

■ An interface specifies a set of methods that implementing classes must include. An interface gives clients enough information to use a class.

■ Polymorphism and inheritance provide a means of reducing the amount of code that must be written by servers and learned by clients in a system with a large number of cooperating classes. Classes that extend other classes inherit their data and methods. Methods in different classes that have the same name are polymorphic. Abstract classes, which are not instantiated, exist for the sole purpose of organizing related subclasses and containing their common data and methods.

■ Error handling can be distributed among methods and classes by using preconditions, postconditions, and exceptions.

■ Because of the possibility of aliasing, the programmer should provide an `equals` method for comparing two objects for equality and a `clone` method for creating a copy of an object.

VOCABULARY *Review*

Define the following terms:

Abstract class	Concrete class	Interface
Abstract method	Dependency	Overriding
Aggregation	Final method	Postcondition
Class (`static`) method	Inheritance	Precondition
Class (`static`) variable		

REVIEW *Questions*

FILL IN THE BLANK

Complete the following sentences by writing the correct word or words in the blanks provided.

1. Methods and variables that belong to a class rather than an instance are called _____ or _____ variables and methods.

2. The keyword used to invoke a constructor or method in a superclass is called _____.

3. The visibility modifier _____ makes a method or variable visible to subclasses but not to other clients.

4. A(n) _____ class contains common behavior and data for a set of subclasses but is not instantiated.

5. A(n) _____ method consists of just a head and forces all subclasses to implement it.

6. _____ and _____ state the assumptions that are true before a method executes correctly and after it executes correctly.

7. The method _____ is the conventional Java method for comparing two objects for equality, whereas the method _____ is the conventional Java method for copying an object.

PROJECTS

PROJECT 10-1

Design a hierarchy of classes that models the classification of your favorite region of the animal kingdom. Your hierarchy should be at most three classes deep and should employ abstract classes on the first two levels.

PROJECT 10-2

Design a hierarchy of classes that represents the classification of artifacts, such as vehicles.

PROJECT 10-3

Add a method `perimeter` to the `Shape` hierarchy from this chapter. This method should return the circumference of a circle and a wheel and the perimeter of a rectangle.

PROJECT 10-4

Add a `Triangle` class to the `Shape` hierarchy from this chapter. Note the following points:

- A triangle is specified by three vertices or pairs of coordinates. The first pair is the position (xPos, yPos).

- The move method for a triangle, which adds the x and y distances to each of the vertices, must override the move method in the abstract class; therefore, the move method in the abstract class cannot be final.

- The distance between two points $(x1,y1)$ and $(x2,y2)$ is equal to the square root of $((x1 - x2) * (x1 - x2) + (y1 - y2) * (y1 - y2))$.

- The area of a triangle can be computed from its vertices using the formula ½ * the absolute value of $(x1 * y2 - x2 * y1 + x2 * y3 - x3 * y2 + x3 * y1 - x1 * y3)$.

- A triangle is stretched away from its position at $(x\text{Pos},y\text{Pos})$. Thus, the other two vertices are incremented by multiplying their distance from $(x\text{Pos},y\text{Pos})$ by the factors. For example, the new value of $x2$ is equal to $x\text{Pos} + (x2 - x\text{Pos}) *$ factor.

PROJECT 10-5

Design a class hierarchy for bank accounts. The concrete types of accounts are checking accounts, savings accounts, and credit accounts. Common behavior includes deposits, withdrawals, and obtaining a balance. Credit and savings accounts have an interest rate. Credit accounts have a credit line or maximum amount that may be borrowed. Be sure your design includes the appropriate interface, abstract class, and concrete classes.

PROJECT 10-6

Browse Java's class hierarchy on Sun's Web site (see Appendix A). Write an essay that describes the design ideas underlying a class hierarchy that you find interesting among Java's classes.

PROJECT 10-7

Implement the `ShapeModel` class that maintains the shapes used in the drawing program of Section 10.12.

CRITICAL *Thinking*

Jack has written software that uses many similar classes and has written interfaces for them. However, he never writes abstract classes, which he considers too much work. Jill tells him that he needs to use abstract classes where they would be helpful. What can you say to support Jill's advice? Use an example from this chapter.

ARRAYS CONTINUED

In Chapter 9, we examined how to declare array variables, instantiate array objects, and manipulate arrays using the subscript operator, loops, and methods. The current chapter covers more complex operations on arrays, such as searching, sorting, insertions, and removals. Along the way, we examine issues that arise in the use of arrays of objects and we introduce Java's `ArrayList` class. As a prelude to these topics, we begin with a look at some advanced string methods.

11.1 Advanced Operations on Strings

Thus far in this text, we have used strings without manipulating their contents very much. However, most text-processing applications spend time examining the characters in strings, taking them apart, and building new strings. For example, consider the problem of extracting words from a line of text. To obtain the first word, we could copy the string's characters to a new string until we reach the first space character in the string (assuming the delimiter between words is the space) or we reach the length of the string. Following is a code segment that uses this strategy:

```java
// Create a sample string
String str = "Hi there!";

// Variable to hold the first word, set to empty string
String word = "";

// Visit all the characters in the string
for (int i = 0; i < str.length(); i++){

    // Or stop when a space is found
    if (str.charAt(i) == ' ')
        break;

    // Add the non-space character to the word
    word += str.charAt(i);
}
```

As you can see, this code combines the tasks of finding the first space character and building a *substring* of the original string. The problem is solved much more easily by using two separate string methods that are designed for these tasks. The first method, indexOf, expects the target character as a parameter and returns the position of the first instance of that character or −1 if the character is not in the string. The second method, substring, expects two integer parameters indicating the starting and ending positions of the substring. This method returns the substring that runs from the starting position up to but not including the ending position. Here is a short program that uses these methods:

```java
// Example 11.1: Test the methods indexOf and substring

public class TestStringMethods{

    public static void main(String[] args){
        String str = "Hi there!";

        // Search for the position of the first space
        int endPosition = str.indexOf(' ');

        // If there is no space, use the whole string
        if (endPosition == -1)
            endPosition = str.length();

        // Extract the first word
        String word = str.substring(0, endPosition);

        // Output the results
        System.out.println(endPosition);    // Prints 2
        System.out.println(word);           // Prints "Hi"
    }
}
```

Table 11-1 describes some commonly used String methods.

TABLE 11-1
Some commonly used string methods

METHOD	DESCRIPTION
`charAt (anIndex)` returns char	Example: `chr = myStr.charAt(4);` Returns the character at the position `anIndex`. Remember that the first character is at position 0. An exception is thrown (i.e., an error is generated) if `anIndex` is out of range (i.e., does not indicate a valid position within `myStr`).
`compareTo (aString)` returns int	Example: `i = myStr.compareTo("abc");` Compares two strings alphabetically. Returns 0 if `myStr` equals `aString`, a value less than 0 if `myStr` string is alphabetically less than `aString`, and a value greater than 0 if `myStr` string is alphabetically greater than `aString`.
`equals (aString)` returns boolean	Example: `boolean = myStr.equals("abc");` Returns true if `myStr` equals `aString`; else returns false. Because of implementation peculiarities in Java, never test for equality like this: `myStr == aString`

`equalsIgnoreCase`
`(aString)`
returns boolean
	Similar to equals but ignores case during the comparison.

`indexOf (aCharacter)` returns int	Example: `i = myStr.indexOf('z')` Returns the index within `myStr` of the first occurrence of `aCharacter` or −1 if `aCharacter` is absent.

`indexOf (aCharacter,`
`beginIndex)`
returns int
	Example: `i = myStr.indexOf('z', 6);`
	Similar to the preceding method except the search starts at position `beginIndex` rather than at the beginning of `myStr`. An exception is thrown (i.e., an error is generated) if `beginIndex` is out of range (i.e., does not indicate a valid position within `myStr`).

`indexOf (aSubstring)` returns int	Example: `i = myStr.indexOf("abc")` Returns the index within `myStr` of the first occurrence of `aSubstring` or −1 if `aSubstring` is absent.

`indexOf (aSubstring,`
`beginIndex)`
returns int
	Example: `i = myStr.indexOf("abc", 6)`
	Similar to the preceding method except the search starts at position `beginIndex` rather than at the beginning of `myStr`. An exception is thrown (i.e., an error is generated) if `beginIndex` is out of range (i.e., does not indicate a valid position within `myStr`).

`length()` returns int	Example: `i = myStr.length();` Returns the length of `myStr`.

`replace (oldChar,`
`newChar)`
returns String
	Example: `str = myStr.replace('z', 'Z');`
	Returns a new string resulting from replacing all occurrences of `oldChar` in `myStr` with `newChar`. **`myStr`** is not changed.

TABLE 11-1 Continued
Some commonly used string methods

METHOD	DESCRIPTION
substring (beginIndex) returns String	Example: `str = myStr.substring(6);` Returns a new string that is a substring of `myStr`. The substring begins at location `beginIndex` and extends to the end of `myStr`. An exception is thrown (i.e., an error is generated) if `beginIndex` is out of range (i.e., does not indicate a valid position within `myStr`).
substring (beginIndex, endIndex) returns String	Example: `str = myStr.substring(4, 8);` Similar to the preceding method except the substring extends to location `endIndex − 1` rather than to the end of `myStr`.
toLowerCase() returns String	Example: `str = myStr.toLowerCase();` `str` is the same as `myStr` except that all letters have been converted to lowercase. **`myStr` is not changed.**
toUpperCase() returns String	Example: `str = myStr.toUpperCase();` `str` is the same as `myStr` except that all letters have been converted to uppercase. **`myStr` is not changed.**
trim() returns String	Example: `str = myStr.trim();` `str` is the same as `myStr` except that leading and trailing spaces, if any, are absent. **`myStr` is not changed.**

Note that there are no mutator methods for strings. The reason for this is that strings are *immutable objects*. Once a string is created, its length cannot change and one cannot modify any of its characters.

Counting the Words in a Sentence

Our next program illustrates the use of the string methods `length`, `indexOf`, and `substring` to solve a complex problem. The program accepts sentences as inputs from the keyboard. The program displays the number of words in each sentence and the average length of a word. The program assumes that words are separated by at least one blank. Punctuation marks are considered parts of words. The program halts when the user presses just the Enter key. Here is the code followed by a brief discussion:

```java
// Example 11.2: Count the words and compute the average
// word length in a sentence

import java.util.Scanner;

public class SentenceStats{

   public static void main(String[] args){

      Scanner reader = new Scanner(System.in);

      // Keep taking inputs
      while (true){
         System.out.print("Enter a sentence: ");
         String input = reader.nextLine();
```

```java
    // Quit when the user just presses Enter
    if (input.equals(""))
        break;

    // Initialize the counters and indexes
    int wordCount = 0;
    int sentenceLength = 0;
    int beginPosition = 0;
    int endPosition = input.indexOf(' ');

    // Continue until a blank is not seen
    while (endPosition != -1){

        // If at least one nonblank character (a word) was seen
        if (endPosition > beginPosition){
            wordCount++;
            String word = input.substring(beginPosition, endPosition);
            sentenceLength += word.length();
        }

        // Update the indexes to go to the next word
        beginPosition = endPosition + 1;
        endPosition = input.indexOf(' ', beginPosition);
    }

    // If at least one nonblank character was seen
    // at the end of the sentence, consider it a word
    if (beginPosition < input.length()){
        wordCount++;
        String word = input.substring(beginPosition, input.length());
        sentenceLength += word.length();
    }

    // Trap the case where there were no words
    if (wordCount > 0){
        System.out.println("Word count: " + wordCount);
        System.out.println("Sentence length: " + sentenceLength);
        System.out.println("Average word length: " +
                             sentenceLength / wordCount);
    }
        }
    }
}
```

This program contains two loops. The outer loop accepts inputs from the user and runs the nested loop to process each input. The nested loop advances two indexes through an input string. On each pass through this loop, the indexes represent the beginning and ending positions of each word. Initially, the beginning position is 0 and the ending position is the result of running indexOf with a blank character. At this point, there are several cases to consider:

1. indexOf returns −1, meaning that a blank was not found. At this point, the nested loop has moved through the entire input string and there are no more blanks to be seen, or the loop is not entered at all. If the beginning position is less than the length of the input string at

this point (below the loop), the last word needs to be counted and extracted from the input string. The program uses the `substring` method with the length of the input string as the ending position in this case.

2. `indexOf` returns an ending position that is greater than the current beginning position. This means that at least one nonblank character (a word) has been seen before encountering a blank. In this case, the program continues in the nested loop. It increments the word count and extracts the word using `substring` with the current beginning and ending positions. The program then increments the sentence length by the length of the word.

3. `indexOf` returns an ending position that is equal to the current beginning position. This happens if there are any leading blanks in the sentence or there is more than one blank following a word. In this case, the program should not count a word or attempt to extract it from the input string, but just continue in the nested loop. This will have the effect of scanning over the extra blank and ignoring it.

4. In cases 2 and 3, the nested loop continues by updating the beginning and ending positions. The beginning position is incremented to 1 greater than the ending position. Then the ending position is reset to the result of running `indexOf` once more with a blank and the new beginning position. This has the effect of advancing the positions to the beginning and ending positions of the next word, if there is one.

As you can see, counting the words in a sentence using `String` methods is not a simple task. We see a much easier way to do this shortly.

Using a Scanner with a String

Until now, we have used a `Scanner` object to accept the input of integers, floating-point numbers, and lines of text from the keyboard or from text files. Interestingly, a scanner can also be used to read words from the keyboard, a text file, or a string. When used with a file, the `Scanner` method `next()` skips any leading blanks and reads and returns a string containing the next sequence of nonblank characters. The method `next()` has the same behavior when used with a scanner that has been opened on a string. The method `hasNext()` returns `true` if there are still more words in the string to be scanned. The following code segment opens a scanner on a string and uses it to scan and display the words in it:

```
String str = "The rain in Spain falls mainly on the plain.";
Scanner reader = new Scanner(str);
while (reader.hasNext())
    System.out.println(reader.next());
```

The scanner automatically handles the tedious details, such as skipping multiple spaces between words, which made the program of Example 11.2 so complicated. A project at the end of this chapter asks you to simplify this program by using a scanner.

*E*XERCISE 11.1

1. Indicate the outputs of the following code segments:

   a. `String str = "The rain in Spain falls mainly on the plain";`
      `System.out.println(str.indexOf(' '));`

EXERCISE 11.1 Continued

b.
```
String str = "The rain in Spain falls mainly on the plain";
System.out.println(str.indexOf(' ', 4));
```

c.
```
String str = "The rain in Spain falls mainly on the plain";
System.out.println(str.substring(4));
```

d.
```
String str = "The rain in Spain falls mainly on the plain";
System.out.println(str.substring(4, 8));
```

e.
```
String str = "The rain in Spain falls mainly on the plain";
int begin = 0;
while (begin < str.length()){
    int end = str.indexOf(' ', begin);
    if (end == -1)
        end = str.length();
    String word = str.substring(begin, end);
    System.out.println(word);
    begin = end + 1;
}
```

2. Write code segments that perform the following tasks:

a. Replace every blank space character in the string `str` with a newline character (`'\n'`).

b. Find the index of the first instance of the substring `"the"` in the string `str`.

c. Find the index of the first instance of the substring `"the"` after the midpoint of the string `str`.

d. Count the number of instances of the whole word `"the"` in the string `str`.

11.2 Searching

Searching collections of elements for a given target element is a very common operation in software systems. Some examples are the `indexOf` methods for strings discussed earlier. In this section, we examine two typical methods for searching an array of elements—a linear search and a binary search.

Linear Search

In Chapter 9, we developed the code for a method that searches an array of `int` for a given target value. The method returns the index of the first matching value or −1 if the value is not in the array. Following is the code:

```
int search (int[] a, int searchValue){
    for (int i = 0; i < a.length; i++)
        if (a[i] == searchValue)
            return i;
    return -1;
}
```

The method examines each element in sequence, starting with the first one, to determine if a target element is present. The loop breaks if the target is found. The method must examine every element to determine the absence of a target. This method of searching is usually called *linear search*.

Searching an Array of Objects

Suppose we have an array of names that we want to search for a given name. A name is a `String`. We cannot use the search method developed already. But we can use a similar loop in the code for a different search method that expects an array of `String` and a target `String` as parameters. The only change in the loop is that two string elements must be compared with the method `equals` instead of the operator `==`. Following is the code:

```java
int search (String[] a, String searchValue){
   for (int i = 0; i < a.length; i++)
      if (a[i].equals(searchValue))
         return i;
   return -1;
}
```

This method can be generalized to work with any objects, not just strings. We simply substitute `Object` for `String` in the formal parameter list. The method still works for strings, and we can also use it to search an array of `Student` objects for a target student, assuming that the `Student` class includes an appropriate `equals` method. Following is a code segment that uses this single method to search arrays of two different types:

```java
String[]  stringArray = {"Hi", "there", "Martin"};
Student[] studentArray = new Student[5];
Student    stu = new Student("Student 1");

for (int i = 0; i < studentArray.length; i++)
   studentArray[i] = new Student("Student " + (i + 1));

int stringPos = search(stringArray, "Martin");    // Returns 2
int studentPos = search(studentArray, stu);       // Returns 0
```

Binary Search

The method of linear search works well for arrays that are fairly small (a few hundred elements). As the array gets very large (thousands or millions of elements), however, the behavior of the search degrades (more on this in Chapter 12). When we have an array of elements that are in ascending order, such as a list of numbers or names, there is a much better way to proceed. For example, in ordinary life, we do not use a linear search to find a name in a phone book. If we are looking for "Lambert," we open the book at our estimate of the middle page. If we're not on the "La" page, we look before or after, depending on whether we have opened the book at the "M" page or the "K" page. For computation, we can formalize this kind of search technique in an algorithm known as *binary search*. This method is much faster than a linear search for very large arrays.

The basic idea of a binary search is to examine the element at the array's midpoint on each pass through the search loop. If the current element matches the target, we return its position. If the current element is less than the target, then we search the part of the array to the right of the midpoint (containing the positions of the greater items). Otherwise, we search the part of the array to the left of the midpoint (containing the positions of the lesser items). On each pass through the loop, the current leftmost position or the current rightmost position is adjusted to track the portion of the array being searched. Following is a Java method that performs a binary search on an array of integers:

```java
int search (int[] a, int searchValue){
    int left = 0;                       // Establish the initial
    int right = a.length - 1;           // endpoints of the array
    while (left <= right){               // Loop until the endpoints cross
        int midpoint = (left + right) / 2;  // Compute the current midpoint
        if (a[midpoint] == searchValue)     // Target found; return its index
            return midpoint;
        else if (a[midpoint] < searchValue) // Target to right of midpoint
            left = midpoint + 1;
        else                            // Target to left of midpoint
            right = midpoint - 1;
    }
    return -1;                          // Target not found
}
```

Figure 11-1 shows a trace of a binary search for the target value 5 in the array

1 3 5 7 9 11 13 15 17

Note that on each pass through the loop, the number of elements yet to be examined is reduced by half. As we see in Chapter 12, herein lies the advantage of binary search over linear search for very large arrays.

FIGURE 11-1
A trace of a binary search of an array

Comparing Objects and the Comparable Interface

When using binary search with an array of objects, we must compare two objects. But objects do not understand the < and > operators, and we have seen that == is not a wise choice for comparing two objects for equality. However, classes that implement the Comparable interface include the method compareTo, which performs the three different comparisons. Here is the signature of compareTo:

```java
public int compareTo(Object other)
```

The behavior of `compareTo` is summarized in Table 11-2.

TABLE 11-2
The behavior of method `compareTo`

USAGE OF `compareTo`	VALUE RETURNED
`obj1.compareTo(obj2)`	0 if `obj1` is equal to `obj2`, using equals
`obj1.compareTo(obj2)`	A negative integer, if `obj1` is less than `obj2`
`obj1.compareTo(obj2)`	A positive integer, if `obj1` is greater than `obj2`

For example, the `String` class implements the `Comparable` interface; thus, the second output of the following code segment is 0:

```
String str = "Mary";
System.out.println(str.compareTo("Suzanne"));    // Outputs -6
System.out.println(str.compareTo("Mary"));       // Outputs 0
System.out.println(str.compareTo("Bob"));        // Outputs 11
```

The other output integers are system dependent, but the first should be negative, whereas the third should be positive (in the example given, they are –6 and 11, respectively).

Before sending the `compareTo` message to an arbitrary object, that object must be cast to `Comparable`, because `Object` does not implement the `Comparable` interface or include a `compareTo` method. Following is the code for the binary search of an array of objects:

```
int search (Object[] a, Object searchValue){
   int left = 0;
   int right = a.length - 1;
   while (left <= right){
      int midpoint = (left + right) / 2;
      int result = ((Comparable)a[midpoint]).compareTo(searchValue);
      if (result == 0)
         return midpoint;
      else if (result < 0)
         left = midpoint + 1;
      else
         right = midpoint - 1;
   }
   return -1;
}
```

Implementing the Method `compareTo`

As mentioned earlier, objects that are ordered by the relations less than, greater than, or equal to must understand the `compareTo` message. Their class must implement the `Comparable` interface and their interface, if there is one, should also include the method `compareTo`. Suppose, for example, that the `Student` class of Chapter 5, which has no interface, is modified to support comparisons of students' names. Following are the required changes to the code:

```
public class Student implements Comparable{

   <data declarations>
```

```java
public int compareTo(Object other){

    // The parameter must be an instance of Student
    if (! (other instanceof Student))
        throw new IllegalArgumentException("Parameter must be a Student");

    // Obtain the student's name after casting the parameter
    String otherName = ((Student)other).getName();

    // Return the result of comparing the two students' names
    return name.compareTo(otherName);
}

<other methods>
}
```

*E*XERCISE 11.2

1. Why is a linear search called "linear"?

2. Write a linear search method that searches an array of objects for a target object.

3. Which elements are examined during a binary search of the array 34 56 78 85 99 for the target element 100?

4. Jack advises Jill of a modification to linear search that improves its performance when the array is sorted: If the target element is less than the current element, the target cannot be in the array. Modify the linear search method for integers to accomplish this.

5. Describe what the following code segment does:

```java
boolean inOrder = true;
for (int i = 0; i < a.length - 1; i++)
    if (a[i] > a[i + 1]){
        inOrder = false;
        break;
    }
```

11.3 Sorting

We have seen that if the elements in an array are in ascending order, we can write some efficient methods for searching the array. However, when the elements are in random order, we need to rearrange them before we can take advantage of any ordering. This process is called *sorting*.

Suppose we have an array a of five integers that we want to sort from smallest to largest. In Figure 11-2, the values currently in a are as depicted on the left; we want to end up with values as they appear on the right.

FIGURE 11-2
An array before and after sorting

Before Sorting	After Sorting
4	2
5	4
7	5
6	6
2	7

Many sort algorithms have been developed, and in this section we cover a few that are easy to write but not very efficient to run. More sophisticated and more efficient sort algorithms are discussed in Chapter 12.

Selection Sort

The basic idea of a *selection sort* is

For each index position i
    Find the smallest data value in the array from positions i
      through length - 1, where length is the number of data values stored.
    Exchange the smallest value with the value at position i

Table 11-3 shows a trace of the elements of an array after each exchange of elements is made. The items just swapped are marked with asterisks, and the sorted portion is shaded. Notice that in the second and fourth passes, because the current smallest numbers are already in place, we need not exchange anything. Also, after the last exchange, the number at the end of the array is automatically in its proper place.

TABLE 11-3
A trace of the data during a selection sort

UNSORTED ARRAY	AFTER 1ST PASS	AFTER 2ND PASS	AFTER 3RD PASS	AFTER 4TH PASS
4	1*	1	1	1
2	2	2*	2	2
5	5	5	3*	3
1	4*	4	4	4*
3	3	3	5*	5

Before writing the algorithm for this sorting method, note the following:

- If the array is of length n, we need $n - 1$ steps.

- We must be able to find the smallest number.

- We need to exchange appropriate array items.

When the code is written for this sort, note that strict inequality (<) rather than weak inequality (<=) is used when looking for the smallest remaining value. The algorithm to sort by selection is

```
For each i from 0 to n - 1 do
    Find the smallest value among a[i], a[i + 1], . . . a[n - 1]
    and store the index of the smallest value in minIndex
    Exchange the values of a[i] and a[index], if necessary
```

In Chapter 9, we saw a segment of the code we need to find the smallest value of array a. With suitable changes, we will incorporate this segment of code in a method, `findMinimum`, for the selection sort. We also will use a method `swap` to exchange two elements in an array.

Using these two methods, the implementation of a selection sort method is

```java
void selectionSort(int[] a){
    for (int i = 0; i < a.length - 1; i++){
        int minIndex = findMinimum(a, i);
        if (minIndex != i)
            swap(a, i, minIndex);
    }
}
```

The method for finding the minimum value in an array takes two parameters, the array and the position, to start the search. The method returns the index position of the minimum element in the array. Its implementation uses a `for` loop:

```java
int findMinimum(int[] a, int first){
    int minIndex = first;

    for (int i = first + 1; i < a.length; i++)
        if (a[i] < a[minIndex])
            minIndex = i;

    return minIndex;
}
```

The `swap` method exchanges the values of two array cells:

```java
void swap(int[] a, int x, int y){
    int temp = a[x];
    a[x] = a[y];
    a[y] = temp;
}
```

Bubble Sort

Given a list of items stored in an array, a *bubble sort* causes a pass through the array to compare adjacent pairs of items. Whenever two items are out of order with respect to each other, they are swapped. The effect of such a pass through an array of items is traced in Table 11-4. The items just swapped are marked with asterisks, and the sorted portion is shaded. Notice that after such a pass, we are assured that the array will have the item that comes last in order in the final array position. That is, the last item will "sink" to the bottom of the array, and preceding items will gradually "percolate" to the top.

TABLE 11-4
A trace of the data during one pass of a bubble sort

UNSORTED ARRAY	AFTER 1ST SWAP	AFTER 2ND SWAP	AFTER 3RD SWAP	AFTER 4TH SWAP
5	4*	4	4	4
4	5*	2*	2	2
2	2	5*	1*	1
1	1	1	5*	3*
3	3	3	3	5*

The bubble sort algorithm involves a nested loop structure. The outer loop controls the number of (successively smaller) passes through the array. The inner loop controls the pairs of adjacent items being compared. If we ever make a complete pass through the inner loop without having to make an interchange, we can declare the array sorted and avoid all future passes through the array. A pseudocode algorithm for bubble sort is

```
Initialize counter k to zero
Initialize boolean exchangeMade to true
While (k < n - 1) and exchangeMade
   Set exchangeMade to false
   Increment counter k
   For each j from 0 to n - k
      If item in jth position > item in (j + 1)st position
          Swap these items
          Set exchangeMade to true
```

A complete Java method to implement a bubble sort for an array of integers is shown in the following code:

```java
void bubbleSort(int[] a){
   int k = 0;
   boolean exchangeMade = true;
```

```
// Make up to n - 1 passes through array, exit early if no exchanges
// are made on previous pass

while ((k < a.length - 1) && exchangeMade){
    exchangeMade = false;
    k++;
    for (int j = 0; j < a.length - k; j++)
        if (a[j] > a[j + 1]){
            swap(a, j, j + 1);
            exchangeMade = true;
        }
    }
}
```

Insertion Sort

Although it reduces the number of data interchanges, the selection sort apparently will not allow an effective—and automatic—loop exit if the array becomes ordered during an early pass. In this regard, bubble sort is more efficient than selection sort for an array that is nearly ordered from the beginning. Even with just one item out of order, however, bubble sort's early loop exit can fail to reduce the number of comparisons that are made.

The *insertion sort* attempts to take greater advantage of an array's partial ordering. The goal is that on the kth pass through, the kth item among

```
a[0], a[1], ..., a[k]
```

should be inserted into its rightful place among the first k items in the array. Thus, after the kth pass (k starting at 1), the first k items of the array should be in sorted order. This is analogous to the fashion in which many people pick up playing cards and order them in their hands. Holding the first ($k - 1$) cards in order, a person will pick up the kth card and compare it with cards already held until its appropriate spot is found. The following steps will achieve this logic:

```
For each k from 1 to n - 1 (k is the index of array element to insert)
    Set itemToInsert to a[k]
    Set j to k - 1
    (j starts at k - 1 and is decremented until insertion position is found)
     While (insertion position not found) and (not beginning of array)
        If itemToInsert < a[j]
            Move a[j] to index position j + 1
            Decrement j by 1
        Else
            The insertion position has been found
            itemToInsert should be positioned at index j + 1
```

In effect, for each pass, the index j begins at the ($k - 1$)st item and moves that item to position $j + 1$ until we find the insertion point for what was originally the kth item.

An insertion sort for each value of *k* is traced in Table 11-5. In each column of this table, the data items are sorted in order relative to each other above the item with the asterisk; below this item, the data are not affected.

TABLE 11-5
A trace of the data during an insertion sort

UNSORTED ARRAY	AFTER 1ST PASS	AFTER 2ND PASS	AFTER 3RD PASS	AFTER 4TH PASS
2	2	1*	1	1
5 ←	5 (no insertion)	2	2	2
1	1 ←	5	4*	3*
4	4	4 ←	5	4
3	3	3	3 ←	5

To implement the insertion sort algorithm in Java, we use the following code:

```
void insertionSort(int[] a){
   int itemToInsert, j;
   boolean stillLooking;

   // On the kth pass, insert item k into its correct position among
   // the first k entries in array.

   for (int k = 1; k < a.length; k++){
      // Walk backwards through list, looking for slot to insert a[k]
      itemToInsert = a[k];
      j = k - 1;
      stillLooking = true;

      while ((j >= 0) && stillLooking )
         if (itemToInsert  < a[j]) {
            a[j + 1] = a[j];
            j--;
         }else
            stillLooking = false;
         // Upon leaving loop, j + 1 is the index
         // where itemToInsert  belongs
         a[j + 1] = itemToInsert;
   }
}
```

Sorting Arrays of Objects

Any of the sort methods can be modified to sort arrays of objects. We assume that the objects implement the `Comparable` interface and support the method `compareTo`. Then, we simply replace the type of all array parameters with `Object` and make the appropriate use of `compareTo` in which the comparison operators are used. For example, here is the relevant change for the selection sort in the method `findMinimum`:

```java
int findMinimum(Object[] a, int first){
   int minIndex = first;

   for (int i = first + 1; i < a.length(); i++)
      if (((Comparable)a[i]).compareTo(a[minIndex]) < 0)
         minIndex = i;

   return minIndex;
}
```

Testing Sort Algorithms

The sort algorithms developed thus far should be tested. The skeleton of a short tester program follows. The program loads an array with 20 random integers between 0 and 99, displays the array's contents, runs a sort method, and displays the array's contents again. Each sort method and their helper methods should be defined as `private static`.

```java
// Example 11.3: Test sort algorithms

import java.util.Random;

public class TestSortAlgorithms{

   public static void main(String[] args){
      Random gen = new Random();
      int[] a = new int[20];

      //Initialize the array to random numbers between 0 and 99
      for (int i = 0; i < a.length; i++)
         a[i] = gen.nextInt(100);

      printArray(a);
      selectionSort(a);              // Pick one of three to test
      //bubbleSort(a);
      //insertionSort(a);
      printArray(a);
   }

   private static void printArray(int[] a){
      for (int i : a)
         System.out.print(i  + " ");
      System.out.println("");
   }

   // private static sort methods and their helpers go here

}
```

You also should test the methods with an array that is already sorted.

E XERCISE 11.3

1. Draw a diagram that shows the contents of the array 8 7 6 5 4 after each number is moved in a selection sort.

2. Draw a diagram that shows the contents of the array 8 7 6 5 4 after each number is moved in a bubble sort, until the 8 arrives at the end of the array.

3. Describe the behavior of the selection sort, bubble sort, and insertion sort with an array that is already sorted. How many exchanges are made in each sort for an array of size n?

4. Modify the bubble sort method so that it sorts an array of objects.

11.4 Insertions and Removals

In Chapter 9, we discussed how to add or remove an element at the end of an array that is not full. In this section, we show how to perform these operations at arbitrary positions within an array. For simplicity, we make four assumptions:

1. Arrays are of fixed size; thus, when an array becomes full, insertions are not performed.

2. We are working with an array of objects, although we can modify the code to cover arrays of integers, employees, or whatever element type is desired.

3. For successful insertions, 0 <= target index <= logical size. The new element is inserted before the element currently at the target index, or after the last element if the target index equals the logical size.

4. For successful removals, 0 <= target index < logical size.

When an assumption is not satisfied, the operation is not performed and we return `false`; otherwise, the operation is performed and we return `true`.

In the code segments that follow, we use the following data declarations:

```
final int DEFAULT_CAPACITY = 5;
int logicalSize = 0;
Object[] array = new Object[DEFAULT_CAPACITY];
```

As you can see, the array has an initial logical size of 0 and a default physical capacity of 5. For each operation that uses this array, we provide a description of the implementation strategy and an annotated Java code segment. At the end of this section, we ask you to develop some static methods to perform these operations on arrays.

Inserting an Item into an Array at an Arbitrary Position

Inserting an item into an array differs from replacing an item in an array. In the case of a replacement, an item already exists at the given index position and a simple assignment suffices.

Moreover, the logical size of the array does not change. In the case of an insertion, we must do six things:

1. Check for available space before attempting an insertion; if there is no space, return `false`.

2. Check the validity of the target index and return `false` if it is not >= 0 and <= logical size.

3. Shift the items from the logical end of the array to the target index down by one position.

4. Assign the new item to the cell at the target index.

5. Increment the logical size by one.

6. Return true.

Figure 11-3 shows these steps for the insertion of an item at position 1 in an array of four items.

FIGURE 11-3
Inserting an item into an array

Shift down item at *n* - 1	Shift down item at *n* - 2	Shift down item at *i*	Now safe to replace item at position 1	Array after insertion is finished
0 D1	0 D1	0 D1	0 D1	0 D1
1 D2	1 D2	1 D2	1 D2	1 D5
2 D3	2 D3	2 D3	2 D2	2 D2
3 D4	3 D4	3 D3	3 D3	3 D3
4	4 D4	4 D4	4 D4	4 D4

As you can see, the order in which the items are shifted is critical. If we had started at the target index and copied down from there, we would have lost two items. Thus, we must start at the logical end of the array and work back up to the target index, copying each item to the cell of its successor. Following is the Java code for the insertion operation:

```java
// Check for a full array and return false if full
if (logicalSize == array.length)
   return false;

// Check for valid target index and return false if not valid
if (targetIndex < 0 || targetIndex > logicalSize)
   return false;

// Shift items down by one position
for (int i = logicalSize; i > targetIndex; i--)
   array[i] = array[i - 1];

// Add new item, increment logical size, and return true
array[targetIndex] = newItem;
logicalSize++;
return true;
```

Removing an Item from an Array

Removing an item from an array involves the inverse process of inserting an item into the array. Following are the steps in this process:

1. Check the validity of the target index and return `false` if it is not >= 0 and < logical size.

2. Shift the items from the target index to the logical end of the array up by one position.

3. Decrement the logical size by one.

4. Return true.

Figure 11-4 shows these steps for the removal of an item at position 1 in an array of five items.

FIGURE 11-4

Removing an item from an array

As with insertions, the order in which we shift items is critical. For a removal, we begin at the item following the target position and move toward the logical end of the array, copying each item to the cell of its predecessor. Following is the Java code for the removal operation:

```java
// Check for valid target index and return false if not valid
if (targetIndex < 0 || targetIndex >= logicalSize)
    return false;

// Shift items up by one position
for (int i = targetIndex; i < logicalSize - 1; i++)
    array[i] = array[i + 1];

// Decrement logical size and return true
logicalSize--;
return true;
```

Of course, there are other ways to handle potential errors in these operations, as discussed in earlier chapters. Instead of returning a Boolean value, one can return a string indicating the type of error or `null` indicating success. Alternatively, one can throw an exception for each error and return `void`.

A Tester Program for Array Methods

The operations just discussed are so frequently used that it is a good idea to provide methods for them. Ideally, one implements them as `static` methods in a class that serves a utility function similar to Java's `Math` class. In the following code, we specify two of these methods in the context of a tester program. We leave their complete development for you to try in Exercise 11.4, Question 2.

A method to insert a new item at a given index position, `insertItem`, expects the array, its logical size, the target index, and the new item as parameters. `insertItem` returns `true` if the operation is successful and `false` otherwise. This method does not increment the logical size; that responsibility is left to the client, who must check the Boolean value returned to take the appropriate action. A similar method named `removeItem` can be developed for removals.

Following is a short tester program that uses the method described previously:

```java
// Example 11.4: Test insertions and removals

public class TestInsertAndRemove{

    public static void main(String[] args){

        // Create an initial array with 3 positions
        String[] array = new String[3];
        int logicalSize = 0;
        boolean successful = false;

        // Insert strings at positions 0, 1, 1, and 0
        successful = insertItem(array, logicalSize, 0, "Jack");
        if (successful)
            logicalSize++;

        successful = insertItem(array, logicalSize, 1, "Jill");
        if (successful)
            logicalSize++;

        successful = insertItem(array, logicalSize, 1, "sees");
        if (successful)
            logicalSize++;

        successful = insertItem(array, logicalSize, 0, "Before");
        if (successful)
            logicalSize++;

        // Display new logical size and contents
        System.out.println(logicalSize);
        for (int i = 0; i < logicalSize; i++)
            System.out.print(array[i] + " ");
    }

    // Definitions of array methods go here
    private static boolean insertItem(Object[] array, int logicalSize,
                                      int targetIndex, Object newItem){
        // Exercise
    }

    private static boolean removeItem(Object[] array, int logicalSize,
                                      int targetIndex){
        // Exercise
    }

}
```

Although our methods allow clients to perform insertions and removals, clients must still track the logical size of an array and update it. In addition, there is an upper bound on the number of items a client can insert into an array. We will learn how to overcome these limitations of arrays shortly. But first, we must consider some unfinished business with the use of objects in arrays.

EXERCISE 11.4

1. Describe the design strategy for inserting an element at an arbitrary position in an array.

2. Complete the two static methods for insertion and removal of an element at an arbitrary position in an array.

3. Describe what the following code segments do:

   a.

   ```
   if (logicalSize == a.length){
       int[] temp = new int[a.length * 2];
       for (int i = 0; i < a.length; i++)
           temp[i] = a[i];
       a = temp;
   }
   ```

   b.

   ```
   if (a.length >= logicalSize * 4){
       int[] temp = new int[a.length * 2];
       for (int i = 0; i < a.length; i++)
           temp[i] = a[i];
       a = temp;
   }
   ```

11.5 *Working with Arrays of Objects*

The element type of an array can be a primitive type, a reference type (either an abstract or a concrete class), or an interface. The processing of an array of a primitive type, such as array of `int`, is straightforward. Likewise, working with an array of a concrete class, such as `Student`, poses no particular problems. The reason for this is that all of the elements in these arrays, whether integers or students, are of exactly the same type and respond to the same set of operators or messages. When the element type of an array is an interface, an abstract class, or a superclass of one or more other classes, however, the array can actually contain objects of different types, so they might not all respond to a common set of messages. In this section, we deal with the problems that arise with arrays of objects of different types.

Polymorphism, Casting, and `instanceof`

It is quite common to declare and instantiate an array of some interface type, such as the `Shape` interface in Chapter 10. For instance, following is code that reserves 10 cells for shapes:

```
Shape[] shapes = new Shape[10];
```

Now we can store in this array instances of any class that implements `Shape`, such as `Rect`, `Circle`, or `Wheel`, as follows:

```
shapes[0] = new Rect(20, 20, 40, 40);     // Cell 0 refers to a Rect
shapes[1] = new Circle(100, 100, 20);     // Cell 1 refers to a Circle
shapes[2] = new Wheel(200, 200, 20, 6);   // Cell 2 refers to a Wheel
```

As long as we send `Shape` messages to the elements of this array, we can ignore the fact that they are of different concrete classes (that's what polymorphism is all about). For instance, let us now draw all the shapes currently in the array:

```
Pen pen = new StandardPen();
for (int i = 0; i < 3; i++)
    shapes[i].draw(pen);
```

We can also move all the shapes, stretch them, change their colors, or do whatever else is specified in the `Shape` interface quite easily. As soon as we want to do something more specific to a shape, however, such as setting the number of spokes in a wheel, we must resort to some of the tricks mentioned in Chapter 10. Let us assume that we know the position of the wheel object in the array (in our example, it's at position 2). Then, to set its spokes to 5, we perform the following steps:

1. Access the array element with the subscript.

2. Cast the element, which is masquerading as a `Shape`, to a `Wheel`.

3. Send the `setSpokes(5)` message to the result.

    Following is the code:

    ```
    ((Wheel) shapes[2]).setSpokes(5);
    ```

Note the use of parentheses to override the precedence of the method selector, which would otherwise be run before the cast operation. Failure to cast in this code causes a compile-time error.

Now suppose we don't know the position of a wheel in the array of shapes, but we want to set the spokes of each wheel to 5. A loop is a logical choice for this task, but we cannot simply cast each element to a `Wheel` and send it the `setSpokes` message because not all elements are wheels. If we attempt to cast an object to a type that is not its actual type, a `ClassCastException` is thrown. Clearly, in this case, we must first determine that a shape is a wheel before casting, and Java's `instanceof` operator comes to our rescue. Following is a loop that solves the problem:

```
for (int i = 0; i < shapes.length; i++)
    if (shapes[i] instanceof Wheel)
        ((Wheel) shapes[i]).setSpokes(5);
```

Although we have been examining an array of an interface type in this example, the same considerations apply to arrays of abstract classes or of superclasses of one or more other classes. Let us now summarize the use of objects in an array by making two fundamental points:

1. When the element type of an array is a reference type or interface, objects of those types or any subtype (subclass or implementing class) can be directly inserted into the array.

2. After accessing an object in an array, care must be taken to send it the appropriate messages or to cast it down to a type that can receive the appropriate messages.

Arrays of `Object`

The most general type of array is of course an array whose element type is `Object`. This array is the most flexible of any we have seen thus far. Not only can we insert any `Object` into an array of `Object`, but we also can replace any array of `Object` with another array of any reference type (that is, pass one as a parameter or return it as a value of a method). We have already seen examples of general searching and sorting methods that rely on this feature of an array of `Object`. From the implementer's perspective, in the case of a linear search, there is no need to worry about the actual type of the array elements because all objects understand the `equals` message and that is the only message sent to the array elements. In the case of the binary search and the sorting methods, the elements each must be sent the `compareTo` message. Before doing that, the method must cast them to `Comparable` after retrieving them from the array. Therefore, the client must take care to pass an array of comparable objects as a parameter to these methods.

Generally, you should exercise caution after an object is accessed in an array of `Object`. More often than not, casting must occur because `Object` includes so few of the methods that the array element actually supports.

EXERCISE 11.5

1. Assume that the `Student` class used here is as defined in Chapter 9. Describe the errors in the following code segments, or state that they are correct:

a.

```
Object[] a = new Object[10];
a[0] = new Student();
a[1] = "Hi there";
System.out.println(a[1].indexOf("there"));
```

b.

```
Object[] a = new Object[10];
a[0] = new Student();
a[1] = "Hi there";
System.out.println((String)a[1].indexOf("there"));
```

c.

```
Object[] a = new Object[10];
a[0] = new Student();
a[1] = "Hi there";
System.out.println((String[1]).indexOf("there"));
```

d.

```
Object[] a = new Object[10];
a[0] = new Student();
a[1] = "Hi there";
System.out.println((String[0]).indexOf("there"));
```

11.6 The Class java.util.ArrayList

As we have seen, the array is a powerful data structure that has many uses. In earlier sections of this chapter, we developed many complex but useful methods for manipulating arrays. However, arrays are easiest to use when

■ We know how many data elements will be added to them, so we don't run out of cells or waste any cells.

■ We know they are full.

 When these conditions do not hold, clients must

■ Find a way to increase the length of the array when it becomes full or shrink it when many cells become unoccupied.

■ Track the array's logical size with a separate variable.

If necessary, we could develop methods that would increase or decrease the length of an array, but they would add complexity to our code and still not relieve clients of the need to maintain a distinct logical size for each array. Fortunately, clients have a better option in these cases. Like most object-oriented languages, Java provides a wide range of classes for maintaining collections of objects. The collection class most like an array is called ArrayList and is included in the package java.util. In this section, we give an overview of the use of array lists.

What an Array List Is

Like an array, an *array list* is an object that contains a sequence of elements that are ordered by position. Elements in both structures can be accessed and replaced at a given position. However, there are several ways in which an array list is unlike an array:

■ The programmer must use methods rather than the subscript operator [ ] to manipulate elements in an array list.

■ An array list tracks both its logical size (the number of elements that are currently in it) and its physical size (the number of cells available to store elements).

■ When the programmer creates an array list, its logical size is 0. When the programmer inserts elements into an array list, the list automatically updates its logical size and adds cells to accommodate new objects if necessary. The list's logical size is also updated when an element is removed.

■ The positions available for access in an array list range from 0 to its logical size minus 1.

Generic Array Lists and Raw Array Lists

Java 5.0 allows the programmer to use *generic array lists*. A generic array list requires the programmer to specify the element type for the list. This must be done when a list variable is declared and when a list is instantiated. The elements inserted into a generic list must have the same type as its element type or be one of its element type's subtypes.

Earlier versions of Java support only raw array lists. A *raw array list* can contain objects of any reference type. Because raw array lists are considered less safe and less convenient to use than generic array lists, we use generic array lists in this book. For details on raw array lists, you can consult Appendix B.

Declaring and Instantiating an Array List

An array list is an object, so it is instantiated like any other object, as in the following example, which creates an array list of strings:

```
import java.util.ArrayList;

ArrayList<String> list = new ArrayList<String>();
```

Note that the programmer specifies no initial physical length, as is done with arrays. An array list has a default physical length, but the programmer has no need to know what it is. Note also the use of the type specifier `<String>` in both the variable declaration and the use of the constructor. The type specifier restricts the elements in this list to be of type `String`.

Using `ArrayList` Methods

The programmer manipulates an array list by sending it messages. There are methods for examining an array list's logical size, testing it for emptiness (it's never full, at least in theory), insertions, removals, examining or replacing elements at given positions, and searching for a given element, among others. Table 11-6 contains descriptions of these commonly used methods. Note that the type `E` mentioned in some methods is a placeholder for the actual element type used when the list is created.

TABLE 11-6
Some commonly used `ArrayList` methods

ArrayList METHOD	WHAT IT DOES
`ArrayList<E>()`	Constructor builds an empty array list
`boolean isEmpty()`	Returns true if the list contains no elements and false otherwise
`int size()`	Returns the number of elements currently in the list
`E get(int index)`	Returns the element at index
`E set(int index, E obj)`	Replaces the element at index with `obj` and returns the old element
`void add(int index, E obj)`	Inserts `obj` before the element at index or after the last element if index equals the size of the list
`E remove(int index)`	Removes and returns the element at index
`int indexOf(E obj)`	Returns the index of the first instance of `obj` in the list or −1 if `obj` is not in the list

The methods discussed here represent only a small subset of the methods supported by array lists. For details on the other methods, see Appendix B or consult Sun's documentation.

Let us extend the earlier code segment by loading the array list with several strings and then displaying them in the terminal window:

```
import java.util.ArrayList;

ArrayList<String> list = new ArrayList<String>();
```

```
for (int i = 0; i < 5; i++)            // List contains
    list.add(i, "Item" + (i + 1));     // Item1 Item2 Item3 Item4 Item5

for (int i = 0; i < list.size(); i++)       // Display
    System.out.println(list.get(i));        // Item1
                                            // Item2
                                            // Item3
                                            // Item4
                                            // Item5

// Or use an enhanced for loop
for (String str : list)                     // Display
    System.out.println(str);                // Item1
                                            // Item2
                                            // Item3
                                            // Item4
                                            // Item5
```

The next code segment performs some example searches:

```
System.out.println(list.indexOf("Item3"));     // Displays 2
System.out.println(list.indexOf("Martin"));    // Displays -1
```

Our final code segment removes the first element from the list and displays that element and the list's size after each removal, until the list becomes empty:

```
while (! list.isEmpty()){
    String str = list.remove(0);
    System.out.println(str);
    System.out.println("Size: " + list.size());
}
```

Array Lists and Primitive Types

The array list is a powerful data structure. There is one other restriction on its use, however. Unlike an array, an array list can contain only objects, not primitive types. We explore a way of working around this restriction in the next subsection.

Primitive Types and Wrapper Classes

As mentioned earlier, Java distinguishes between primitive data types (numbers, characters, Booleans) and objects (instances of `String`, `Employee`, `Student`, etc.). Arrays can contain either primitive data values or objects, as in

```
int x;                 // An integer variable
int nums[];            // An array of integers
Student student;       // A Student variable
Student students[];    // An array of Students
```

The elements in an array list must all be objects. Thus, the following attempt to declare and create an array list of int fails with a syntax error:

```
ArrayList list<int> list = new ArrayList<int>();   // Invalid (syntax error)
```

A feature called **wrapper classes** allows us to store primitive data types in array lists. A wrapper class is a class that contains a value of a primitive type. Values of the types boolean, char, int, and double can be stored in objects of the wrapper classes Boolean, Character, Integer, and Double, respectively. The following code segment shows how a wrapper class can be manipulated directly:

```
Integer intObj3 = new Integer(3);         // An Integer object containing 3
Integer intObj4 = new Integer(4);         // An integer object containing 4
int x = intObj3.intValue();               // Extracts 3 and saves in x
System.out.println(intObj3);              // Displays 3 using toString()
System.out.println(intObj3.equals(intObj4));      // Displays false
System.out.println(intObj3.compareTo(intObj4));   // Displays a negative
                                                  // number
```

Fortunately, you do not have to bother with these details to use primitive types with array lists. Array lists automatically "box" and "unbox" primitive values when they are used with ArrayList methods. The only requirement is that you use the appropriate wrapper class name as the element type specifier when declaring the array list variable and instantiating the list. The next program example shows some manipulations of a list of integers:

```
// Example 11.5: Test an array list of integers

import java.util.ArrayList;

public class TestArrayList{

   public static void main(String[] args){

      // Create a list of Integers
      ArrayList<Integer> list = new ArrayList<Integer>();

      // Add the ints 1-100 to the list
      for (int i = 1; i <= 100; i++)
         list.add(i);

      // Increment each int in the list
      for (int i = 0; i < list.size(); i++)
         list.set(i, list.get(i) + 1);

      // Display the contents of the list
      for (int i : list)
         System.out.println(i);
   }
}
```

This code works because the methods add and set automatically box an int value into an Integer object, whereas the method get automatically unboxes an Integer object into an int value. Moreover, the enhanced `for` loop at the end of the program also unboxes each `Integer` object into an `int`.

Confusing Arrays and Array Lists

As mentioned earlier, the programmer must send an array list message, whereas the subscript is the only basic array operation. Beginners often confuse the two structures and try to use a subscript with an array list or a method with an array. These two types of errors, both caught by the compiler, are shown in the next code segment:

```java
// Create an array containing 3, 4, and 5
int array[] = {3, 4, 5};

// Create a list and add 2, 3, and 4
ArrayList<Integer> list = new ArrayList<Integer>();
list.add(2); list.add(3); list.add(4);

// Syntax errors: use list methods with the array
for (int i = 0; i < array.size(); i++)
    System.out.println(array.get(i));

// Syntax errors: use subscript and length variable with the list
for (int i = 0; i < list.length; i++)
    System.out.println(list[i]);
```

Should I Use Arrays or Array Lists?

Now that we have seen two options for storing sequences of elements, the array and the array list, it's time to consider the reasons why one might prefer one structure to the other.

Both structures allow the programmer to store and access elements by specifying an integer index position. However, the array list is by far the more powerful and easier to use. There are two reasons why this is so:

1. The array list includes many methods for various tasks, such as insertions, removals, and searches. By contrast, an array provides just a subscript operation. The user of an array must implement any higher-level operations by hand.

2. The array list tracks its own logical size and grows or shrinks automatically with the number of elements contained in it. By contrast, an array always has a fixed physical size that's independent of its logical size. This forces the user of an array to keep track of its logical size and to worry about instantiating an array that is large enough to accommodate the data requirements of a program.

These comparisons might lead us to conclude that we should never use an array in a program when an array list is available. However, arrays are still used to implement higher-level data structures, such as matrices and the array list itself.

There are at least two other situations in which an array might be on at least an equal footing with an array list:

1. We know the exact number of data elements to be inserted in advance, and they are all inserted at startup and are never removed. In this case, the array is always full and is fairly easy to process.

2. The operations on the sequence are more specialized than those provided by an array list, or they consist of simple traversals. In these cases, the programmer really only must choose between using the methods `get` and `set` with an array list and using the subscript with an array (or entirely ignoring them in an enhanced `for` loop).

In any case, because programmers have used arrays ever since the first high-level languages were developed, you will likely see arrays in code at one point or another in your programming experience.

EXERCISE 11.6

1. Write a method `sum` that expects an `ArrayList<Integer>` as a parameter. The method returns an `int` representing the sum of the integers in the array list.

2. Do the sort methods developed earlier for arrays of objects work for arrays of `Integer` objects without modification? Justify your answer.

CASE STUDY: Building a Deck of Cards

In this case study, we show how to build resources that are used in an important class of applications – online card games! (*Note:* the authors do not endorse gambling.) We discuss the analysis, design, and implementation of a deck of cards that can be used in various types of card games. The development of programs for the games themselves is left as exercises.

Request

Develop resources for a deck of cards that can be used in online games.

Analysis

You have probably played some card games, such as Rummy, Crazy Eights, and Hearts. Most computer operating systems include one or more card games for entertaining diversion. Common examples are Freecell and Solitaire on Windows systems. Most card games use a deck of cards with the following attributes:

■ There are 52 cards in a deck.

■ Each card has a suit and a rank.

■ There are four suits: Spades, Hearts, Diamonds, and Clubs.

■ Each suit has a color: black (Spades and Clubs) or red (Hearts and Diamonds).

■ The cards can be ordered from highest to lowest by rank, as follows: King, Queen, Jack, 10, 9,..., 2. An Ace has either the highest or the lowest rank, depending on the game.

■ The cards can also be ordered by suit, as follows: Spades, Hearts, Diamonds, Clubs.

■ A deck has one card of each rank and each suit, which equals 52 (13 * 4) total cards.

■ A card is face up if you can see its suit and rank; otherwise, it is face down.

Cards and a deck can be manipulated in the following ways:

■ Cards can be dealt or transferred from a deck to players.

- A deck can be shuffled, so that the cards can be dealt in random order.

- A card can be turned face up or face down.

- Two cards can be compared for equality, greater than, or less than.

- A card's suit, rank, and color can be examined.

The user interface for this case study consists of several tester programs for the various classes. Modern online card games also typically have flashy graphics that display images of the cards and allow the user to move them around by manipulating a mouse. We defer that aspect to an exercise and for now use a terminal-based interface to develop and illustrate the requirements for our deck of cards.

Classes

The two obvious classes suggested by our discussion of a deck of cards are Deck and Card. A deck contains 0 to 52 cards. It will be convenient to have one other class, called Suit, to represent the suit that each card has. The relationships among these classes are shown in the UML diagram of Figure 11-5.

FIGURE 11-5
The relationships among the classes Deck, Card, and Suit

The interfaces of the Deck and Card classes are listed in Tables 11-7 and 11-8. The Card methods require no comment. Because a deck decreases in size as cards are dealt, we include two Deck methods, size() and isEmpty(), to check on the deck's status. There are two methods for dealing cards. deal() returns a single card or null if the deck is empty. deal(anInt) is used to deal a hand of one or more cards all at once. If the size of the deck is greater than or equal to the integer parameter, this method returns an array of that number of cards. Otherwise, the method returns null. The method shuffle does nothing if the deck is not full. The method reset is used to gather the cards back into the deck to make it full.

The following is a short tester program that creates a deck, shuffles it, deals each card, and displays each card's information:

```java
// Case Study 11.1: Test a deck

public class TestDeck{

    public static void main(String[] args){
        Deck deck = new Deck();
        deck.shuffle();
        int count = 0;
        while (! deck.isEmpty()){
            count++;
            Card card = deck.deal();
```

```
            System.out.println(count + ": " + card);
        }
    }
}
```

TABLE 11-7
The interface for the Deck class

DECK METHOD	WHAT IT DOES
`Deck()`	Constructor; creates a deck of 52 cards, unshuffled
`void reset()`	Restores the deck to its initial state
`void shuffle()`	If the deck is full, shuffles it
`boolean isEmpty()`	Returns `true` if the deck is empty or `false` otherwise
`int size()`	Returns the number of cards in the deck
`Card deal()`	If the deck is not empty, removes and returns a card; otherwise, returns `null`
`Card[] deal(int n)`	If the deck's size is greater than or equal to n, removes and returns n cards in an array; otherwise, returns `null`
`String toString()`	Returns a string representation of the deck

TABLE 11-8
The interface for the Card class

CARD METHOD	WHAT IT DOES
`Card(Suit suit, int rank)`	Constructor; creates a card with the specified suit and rank
`int getRank()`	Returns the card's rank
`Suit getSuit()`	Returns the card's suit
`boolean isFaceUp()`	Returns `true` if the card's face is up or `false` otherwise
`boolean isRed()`	Returns `true` if the card's suit color is red or `false` if it's black
`void turn()`	If the card is face up, makes it face down; or if it's face down, makes it face up
`boolean equals(Object other)`	Comparison for equality by rank
`int compareTo(Object other)`	Comparison for order of rank
`String toString()`	Returns a string representation of the card

From the client's perspective, `Suit` objects should be ordered consecutively like integers but named like strings. The strings "Clubs," "Diamonds", "Hearts," and "Spades" happen to have the appropriate natural ordering, so one might wonder why we would bother to define a new class for this purpose. The reason it is better to do so is that suits should be restricted to four distinct values, whereas there are an infinite number of possible string values. Defining a Suit class also gives us an opportunity to introduce an important design technique that we discuss shortly. The interface of the Suit class includes four static constants and the methods compareTo and toString, as listed in Table 11-9.

TABLE 11-9
The interface for the Suit class

SUIT CONSTANT	WHAT IT DOES
static final Suit spade	The Suit value for all spades
static final Suit heart	The Suit value for all hearts
static final Suit diamond	The Suit value for all diamonds
static final Suit club	The Suit value for all clubs
int compareTo(Object other)	The usual behavior; comparison for order: spade > heart > diamond > club
String toString()	Returns a string representation of the suit

Note that there is no constructor in the interface. The only instances of Suit that ever exist are those named by the constants Suit.spade, Suit.heart, Suit.diamond, and Suit.club.

The next code segment is a short tester program that shows how suits are used.

```
// Case Study 11.1: Test the suits

public class TestSuit{

    public static void main(String[] args){

        Suit s = Suit.spade;
        Suit h = Suit.heart;
        Suit d = Suit.diamond;
        Suit c = Suit.club;

        // Display "spades hearts diamonds clubs"
        System.out.println(s + " " + h + " " + d + " " + c);

        System.out.println(s.equals(s));        // Display true
        System.out.println(s.equals(h));        // Display false
        System.out.println(s.compareTo(s));     // Display 0
        System.out.println(s.compareTo(d));     // Display 2
        System.out.println(d.compareTo(s));     // Display -2
    }
}
```

Our final tester program uses suits to build and manipulate some cards:

```java
// Case Study 11.1: Test some cards

public class TestCard{

    public static void main(String[] args){
        Card queenSpades = new Card(Suit.spade, 12);
        Card jackClubs = new Card(Suit.club, 11);
        Card twoHearts = new Card(Suit.heart, 2);
        Card twoDiamonds = new Card(Suit.diamond, 2);

        // Display "Queen of spades"
        System.out.println(queenSpades);
        // Display true
        System.out.println(twoDiamonds.equals(twoHearts));
        // Display 1
        System.out.println(queenSpades.compareTo(jackClubs));
    }
}
```

Design and Implementation of Card

The design of the Card class calls for little comment. Note just three points in the implementation that follows. First, Card implements the Comparable interface, allowing cards to be used wherever comparisons are made. Secondly, in the method isRed(), suits are compared for equality using == rather than equals. We can get away with this because there is never more than one instance of each of the four suits. Third and finally, the method turn() flips the card by inverting or logically negating the boolean variable faceUp.

```java
// Case Study 11.1: The Card class

public class Card implements Comparable{

    private Suit suit;
    private int rank;
    private boolean faceUp;

    public Card(Suit suit, int rank){
        this.suit = suit;
        this.rank = rank;
        faceUp = false;
    }

    public boolean equals(Object other){
        if (this == other)
            return true;
        else if (! (other instanceof Card))
            return false;
        else{
            Card otherCard = (Card)other;
            return rank == otherCard.rank;
        }
    }
```

```java
    public int compareTo(Object other){
        if (! (other instanceof Card))
            throw new IllegalArgumentException("Parameter must be a Card");
        Card otherCard = (Card)other;
        return rank - otherCard.rank;
    }

    public int getRank(){
        return rank;
    }

    public Suit getSuit(){
        return suit;
    }

    public boolean isFaceUp(){
        return faceUp;
    }

    public boolean isRed(){
        return suit == Suit.heart || suit == Suit.diamond;
    }

    public void turn(){
        faceUp = ! faceUp;
    }

    public String toString(){
        return rankToString() + " of " + suit;
    }

    private String rankToString(){
        if (rank == 1)
            return "Ace";
        else if (rank == 11)
            return "Jack";
        else if (rank == 12)
            return "Queen";
        else if (rank == 13)
            return "King";
        else
            return "" + rank;
    }
}
```

Design and Implementation of Deck

According to the requirements established during analysis, a deck contains from 0 to 52 cards. Thus, an array list of type `card` is an appropriate choice of a data structure to hold the cards. All of the `Deck` methods manage the list of cards for the client. The only method that is complex enough to warrant explicit design is `shuffle()`. A standard way to shuffle real cards is to split the deck and merge the two sets of cards in such a manner that they roughly interleave (the first card of the second half comes after the first card of the first half, and so forth). The development of this algorithm is left as an exercise. Instead, we adopt a simpler method: create a temporary array of 52 positions; remove each card from the list and place it at a random, unoccupied position of the array; and when the list becomes empty, transfer the cards from the array back to the list. Here is the pseudocode for this process:

```
Set array to a new array of 52 cells
While the list is not empty do
    Set card to the last card in the list
    Set index to a random number between 0 and 51
    While array[index] != null
        Set index to a random number between 0 and 51
    Set array[index] to card
For each card in array
    Add the card to the list
```

Note that the nested loop uses random integers to locate an array position that contains null. All of the array's cells are null when the array is instantiated. A null array cell indicates an empty slot in which to insert the next card. Here is a complete listing of the Deck implementation:

```java
// Case Study 11.1: The Deck class

import java.util.*;

public class Deck{

    public static final int MAX_SIZE = 52;

    private ArrayList<Card> cards;

    public Deck(){
        reset();
    }

    public void reset(){
        // Create a new list and add 13 cards from each suit
        cards = new ArrayList<Card>();
        addSuit(Suit.spade);
        addSuit(Suit.heart);
        addSuit(Suit.diamond);
        addSuit(Suit.club);
    }

    // Helper method to add 13 cards from a single suit
    private void addSuit(Suit suit){
        for (int i = 1; i <= 13; i++)
            cards.add(new Card(suit, i));
    }

    public boolean isEmpty(){
        return cards.isEmpty();
    }
```

```
    public int size(){
        return cards.size();
    }

    public Card deal(){
        if (isEmpty())
            return null;
        else
            return cards.remove(cards.size() - 1);
    }

    public Card[] deal(int number){
        if (number > cards.size())
            return null;
        else{
            Card[] hand = new Card[number];
            for (int i = 0; i < hand.length; i++)
                hand[i] = deal();
            return hand;
        }
    }

    public void shuffle(){
        if (cards.size() < MAX_SIZE)
            return;
        Random gen = new Random();
        // Remove cards from the list and place at random positions
        // in an array
        Card[] array = new Card[MAX_SIZE];
        while (cards.size() > 0){
          Card card = cards.remove(cards.size() - 1);
          int i = gen.nextInt(MAX_SIZE);
          while (array[i] != null)
              i = gen.nextInt(MAX_SIZE);
          array[i] = card;
        }
        // Transfer the shuffled cards back to the list
        for (Card card : array)
          cards.add(card);
    }

    public String toString(){
        String result = "";
        for (Card card : cards)
            result += card + "\n";
        return result;
    }
}
```

Design and Implementation of `Suit`

The purpose of the `Suit` class is to provide exactly four distinct instances that represent the suits Spades, Hearts, Diamonds, and Clubs. These objects can be compared for equality and for their relative ordering. As we mentioned earlier, the class's interface includes four static constants for these objects, as well as the methods `compareTo` and `toString`. Equality is determined with the operator ==.

The design of the class is unusual, in that clients cannot instantiate it. However, four instances are indeed created when the static constants are initialized (at program startup). Each instance has an integer that determines its rank in the ordering of suits and a name that is used for its string representation. A private constructor initializes these variables when the instances are created and assigned to the constants. A listing of the `suit` class follows.

```java
// Case Study 11.1: A Suit class

public class Suit implements Comparable{

    static public final Suit spade   = new Suit(4, "spades");
    static public final Suit heart   = new Suit(3, "hearts");
    static public final Suit diamond = new Suit(2, "diamonds");
    static public final Suit club    = new Suit(1, "clubs");

    private int order;
    private String name;

    private Suit(int ord, String nm){
        name = nm;
        order = ord;
    }

    public int compareTo(Object other){
        if (! (other instanceof Suit))
            throw new IllegalArgumentException("Parameter must be a Suit");
        Suit otherSuit = (Suit)other;
        return order - otherSuit.order;
    }

    public String toString(){
        return name;
    }
}
```

11.7 Graphics and GUIs: Menus

In this section, we add drop-down menus to our growing repertoire of GUI features. As the number of commands grows, an application's user interface can become increasingly cluttered with a confusing jumble of command buttons. For example, the student test scores application in Section 9.11 already has eight buttons, but many more commands would be typical in a realistic application. Drop-down menus help to economize on a window's real estate by hiding commands under visible labels that expand only when needed.

Extra Challenge

This Graphics and GUIs section gives you the opportunity to explore concepts and programming techniques required to develop modern graphics applications and graphical user interfaces. This material is not required in order to proceed with the other chapters of the book.

Menu Basics

A drop-down menu system consists of a menu bar, a number of menus, and for each menu, several selections. It is also possible to have submenus, but we ignore these for now. It is easy to add a drop-down menu system to an application. For instance, the student test scores program currently has two rows of buttons, one for data access and another for navigation. We would like to add commands for deleting a student and for transferring the database of students to and from a file. The new commands and the data access commands can be placed under three drop-down menus named **File**, **Edit**, and **Data**. The selections under **File** are the standard **New**, **Open**, and **Save**. The selections under **Edit** are **Add**, **Modify**, and **Delete**. The selections under **Data** are **Highest Score** and **Class Average**. The new user interface is shown in Figure 11-6.

FIGURE 11-6
The new user interface for the student test scores program

We create a menu item object for each menu selection (class `JMenuItem`), a menu object for each menu (class `JMenu`), and the menu bar object in which all of the menu objects will appear (class `JMenuBar`). We then add all of the objects to their appropriate containers. The menus and selections are displayed in the order in which they are added in the code. The following code shows a truncated version of the `TestScoresView` class from Section 9.11, which adds the three menus to the application's window:

```java
// Example 11.6: TestScoresView class (with menus)

import javax.swing.*;
import java.awt.*;
import java.awt.event.*;

public class TestScoresView extends JFrame{

    // >>>>>>> The model <<<<<<<<

    // Declare the model
    private TestScoresModel model;

    // >>>>>>> The view <<<<<<<<

    // Declare and instantiate the menu items
    private JMenuItem newMI     = new JMenuItem("New");
    private JMenuItem openMI     = new JMenuItem("Open");
    private JMenuItem saveMI     = new JMenuItem("Save");
    private JMenuItem addMI     = new JMenuItem("Add");
    private JMenuItem modifyMI     = new JMenuItem("Modify");
    private JMenuItem deleteMI     = new JMenuItem("Delete");
```

```java
    private JMenuItem highScoreMI  = new JMenuItem("Highest Score");
    private JMenuItem aveScoreMI   = new JMenuItem("Class Average");
    // Code for creating the other window objects

    // Constructor
    public TestScoresView(TestScoresModel m){
        model = m;
        // Organize and install the menu system
        JMenu fileMenu =  new JMenu("File");
        fileMenu.add(newMI);
        fileMenu.add(openMI);
        fileMenu.add(saveMI);
        JMenu editMenu =  new JMenu("Edit");
        editMenu.add(addMI);
        editMenu.add(modifyMI);
        editMenu.add(deleteMI);
        JMenu dataMenu =  new JMenu("Data");
        dataMenu.add(highScoreMI);
        dataMenu.add(aveScoreMI);
        JMenuBar bar = new JMenuBar();
        bar.add(fileMenu);
        bar.add(editMenu);
        bar.add(dataMenu);
        setJMenuBar(bar);
        // Code for installing the other window objects
        // Note: The north panel of buttons has been deleted
        // Attach listeners to buttons and menu items
        addMI.addActionListener(new AddListener());
        previousButton.addActionListener(new PreviousListener());
        // Set window attributes
        setTitle("Student Test Scores");
        setDefaultCloseOperation(JFrame.EXIT_ON_CLOSE);
        pack();
        setVisible(true);
    }
    // Code for the rest of the class
}
```

Like buttons, menu items emit action events when selected, so the programmer simply attaches action listeners for the appropriate tasks to the menu items. Therefore, the listener classes in the existing code need no modification whatsoever, although new listeners must be defined for the file operations. The completion of the new version is left as an exercise.

Using Menus in a Graphics Application

Menus also play a critical role in graphics applications. For example, the shape manipulation program of Section 10.12 devotes the entire container region of the window to the panel where the shapes are displayed. If we add commands to change the types of shapes, their colors, and so forth, it will be best to hide these under the relevant menus. We now develop a modified version of this program to illustrate the use of menus.

The most recent version of the program draws several circles and rectangles in random colors at startup. The user can then drag these shapes around the window with the mouse. The user should be able to draw new shapes of either type; specify their color, size, and position; and delete a selected shape. We now update the interface by adding the menus and selections described in Table 11-10.

TABLE 11-10
Menu options for the shape-drawing program

MENU/SELECTION	WHAT IT DOES
Shape/Create	Allows the user to draw shapes of the currently selected type and color
Shape/Move	Allows the user to drag shapes around the window
Shape/Delete	Allows the user to delete selected shapes
Type/Circle	Sets the current type of shape to circle
Type/Rectangle	Sets the current type of shape to rectangle
Color/Black	Sets the current drawing color to black
Color/Blue	Sets the current drawing color to blue
Color/Red	Sets the current drawing color to red
Color/Random	Sets the current drawing color to a random color

As we showed in student test scores example, the new menu system can be immediately installed and viewed in the window class. At program startup, no images are displayed. The new user interface is shown in Figure 11-7.

FIGURE 11-7
The new user interface for the shape drawing program

The listeners attached to the menu items respond by sending messages to the panel. These commands have no immediate visible effects. Instead, each command sets an attribute in the panel to a new value. The attributes come into play later, when the user manipulates the mouse in the drawing area. For example, if the user selects **Color/Red**, all shapes created from that time until a new color is selected will be red, and when the user selects **Type/Circle**, all shapes created will be circles until a subsequent selection is made. If the user does not try to draw a shape, however, nothing changes. The **Shape** menu allows the user to choose which basic type of manipulation to perform. When the user selects **Shape/Create**, a new shape does not suddenly pop into view. The user can draw a shape (of the current type and color) by clicking the mouse and dragging it. The coordinates of the initial click determine the upper-left corner of the new shape if it's a rectangle and the center point if it's a circle. The coordinates of the mouse release determine the new shape's width or radius. Movement works as before, by dragging, whereas a deletion takes effect when the mouse clicks on a shape. To change these attributes, the main window class uses three new methods in the panel class listed in Table 11-11.

TABLE 11-11
New `ColorPanel` Methods

ColorPanel METHOD	WHAT IT DOES
`void setManipType(String type)`	Sets the type of manipulation to type
`void setShapeType (String type)`	Sets the type of shape to type
`void setColor(Color c)`	Sets the color to c

We now structure the application like the student test scores program by using distinct application and view classes. The `main` method moves from the `GUIWindow` class to a new class called `ShapeApp`. `main` now instantiates `GUIWindow` and sends it the appropriate messages. `GUIWindow` now extends `JFrame` and maintains the menu items and the panel as instance variables. A constructor sets up the menu system and attaches its listeners. The listeners are defined as private inner classes in the usual manner. An abbreviated listing of the `GUIWindow` class for the new version of the application follows:

```java
// Example 11.7: Main view class for shape drawing program
// with menus

import javax.swing.*;
import java.awt.*;
import java.awt.event.*;

public class GUIWindow extends JFrame{

    private JMenuItem createMI = new JMenuItem("Create");
    private JMenuItem moveMI   = new JMenuItem("Move");
    private JMenuItem deleteMI = new JMenuItem("Delete");
    private JMenuItem circleMI = new JMenuItem("Circle");
    private JMenuItem rectMI   = new JMenuItem("Rectangle");
    private JMenuItem blackMI  = new JMenuItem("Black");
    private JMenuItem blueMI   = new JMenuItem("Blue");
    private JMenuItem redMI     = new JMenuItem("Red");
    private JMenuItem randomMI = new JMenuItem("Random");
    private ColorPanel panel   = new ColorPanel(Color.white);

    public GUIWindow(){
        Container pane = getContentPane();
        pane.add(panel);
        JMenu shapeMenu = new JMenu("Shape");
        shapeMenu.add(createMI);
        shapeMenu.add(moveMI);
        shapeMenu.add(deleteMI);
        JMenu typeMenu = new JMenu("Type");
        typeMenu.add(circleMI);
        typeMenu.add(rectMI);
```

```java
        JMenu colorMenu = new JMenu("Color");
        colorMenu.add(blackMI);
        colorMenu.add(blueMI);
        colorMenu.add(redMI);
        colorMenu.add(randomMI);
        JMenuBar bar = new JMenuBar();
        bar.add(shapeMenu);
        bar.add(typeMenu);
        bar.add(colorMenu);
        setJMenuBar(bar);
        createMI.addActionListener(new CreateListener());
        moveMI.addActionListener(new MoveListener());
        deleteMI.addActionListener(new DeleteListener());
        circleMI.addActionListener(new CircleListener());
        rectMI.addActionListener(new RectListener());
        redMI.addActionListener(new RedListener());
    }

    private class CreateListener implements ActionListener{
        public void actionPerformed(ActionEvent e){
            panel.setManipType("Create");
        }
    }

    // Other listeners go here (exercise)
}
```

To the `panel` class we add three new instance variables for the current color, type of shape, and type of user manipulation. The values of these variables at startup are `Color.black`, "Circle," and "Create," respectively.

The actions of the mouse listeners depend on the state of the panel's attributes:

■ `mousePressed` saves the current coordinates like it did in the earlier version. If the manipulation type is "Create," that's all it does. If this value is "Move," the model is asked if the coordinates select a shape. If this value is "Delete," `mousePressed` asks the model to delete the selected shape if one is found.

■ `mouseDragged` simply returns if the manipulation type is "Create" or "Delete." If this value is "Move," `mouseDragged` does what it did in the earlier version.

■ `mouseReleased` completes either a movement or a creation of a shape. The action for movement is not different from the earlier version. When a shape is to be created, however, `mouseReleased` must determine its type, color, size, and position, instantiate it appropriately, and add it to the model.

Here is a complete listing of the `ColorPanel` class:

```java
// Example 11.7: displays shapes
// Allows the user to draw shape with a size and position
// Allows the user to drag a shape to another position
// Allows the user to delete a shape
// Uses a distinct data model to maintain the shapes
```

```java
import javax.swing.*;
import java.awt.*;
import java.awt.event.*;        //For the mouse events
import java.util.Random;

public class ColorPanel extends JPanel{

    private ShapeModel database;     // Now just a model
    private Shape selectedShape;     // Used to track selected shape
    private int x, y;                // Used to track mouse coordinates
    private String manipType;        // Type of user manipulation
    private String shapeType;        // Type of shape to create
    private Color color;             // Color for new shapes

    public ColorPanel(Color backColor){
        setBackground(backColor);
        database = new ShapeModel();   // Now can have any number of shapes
        selectedShape = null;
        manipType = "Create";
        shapeType = "Circle";
        color = Color.black;
        addMouseListener(new PanelListener());
        addMouseMotionListener(new PanelMotionListener());
    }

    public void setManipType(String type){
        manipType = type;
    }

    public void setShapeType(String type){
        shapeType = type;
    }

    public void setColor(Color c){
        color = c;
    }

    public void paintComponent(Graphics g){
        super.paintComponent(g);
        // Draw all the shapes
        database.draw(g);
    }

    private class PanelListener extends MouseAdapter{
        public void mousePressed(MouseEvent e){
            x = e.getX();
            y = e.getY();
            // Do nothing if creating
            if (manipType.equals("Create") ) return;
            //Select a shape if it contains the mouse coordinates
            selectedShape = database.containsPoint(x, y);
            if (manipType.equals("Delete") && selectedShape != null){
                // Delete, deselect, and refresh
```

```java
                database.delete(selectedShape);
                selectedShape = null;
                repaint();
            }
        }

        public void mouseReleased(MouseEvent e){
            int newX = e.getX();
            int newY = e.getY();
            if (manipType.equals("Create")){
                // Use the info to create a shape
                int dx = newX - x;
                int dy = newY - y;
                Shape s;
                if (shapeType.equals("Circle"))
                    s = new Circle(x, y, dx, color);
                else
                    s = new Rect(x, y, dx, dy, color);
                s.setFilled(true);
                database.add(s);
                repaint();
            }
            x = newX;
            y = newY;
            //Deselect the selected shape
            selectedShape = null;
        }
    }

    private class PanelMotionListener extends MouseMotionAdapter{
        public void mouseDragged(MouseEvent e){
            // Do nothing if creating or deleting
            if (manipType.equals("Create") || manipType.equals("Delete"))
                return;
            //Compute the distance and move the selected shape
            int newX = e.getX();
            int newY = e.getY();
            int dx = newX - x;
            int dy = newY - y;
            if (selectedShape != null)
                selectedShape.move(dx, dy);
            x = newX;
            y = newY;
            repaint();
        }
    }
}
```

SUMMARY

In this chapter, you learned:

- A linear search is a simple search method that works well for small- and medium-sized arrays.

- A binary search is a clever search method that works well for large arrays but assumes that the elements are sorted.

- Comparisons of objects are accomplished by implementing the `Comparable` interface, which requires the `compareTo` method.

- Selection sort, bubble sort, and insertion sort are simple sort methods that work well for small- and medium-sized arrays.

- Insertions and removals of elements at arbitrary positions are complex operations that require careful design and implementation.

- One can insert objects of any class into an array of `Object`. When they are retrieved from the array, however, objects must be cast down to their classes before sending them most messages.

- The limitation of a fixed-size array can be overcome by using Java's `ArrayList` class. An array list tracks and updates its logical size and provides many useful methods to clients.

- A wrapper class, such as `Integer`, provides a way of packaging a value of a primitive type, such as `int`, in an object so that it can be stored in an array of `Object` or an array list.

VOCABULARY *Review*

Define the following terms:

Array list	Immutable object	Selection sort
Binary search	Insertion sort	Substring
Bubble sort	Linear search	Wrapper class

REVIEW *Questions*

FILL IN THE BLANK

Complete the following sentences by writing the correct word or words in the blanks provided.

1. A search algorithm that examines each element, starting with the first one, is called a(n) _____ search.

2. A search algorithm that examines the element at the list's midpoint on each pass through the loop is called a(n) _____ search.

3. A sort algorithm that exchanges the smallest element with the first one is called a(n) _____ sort.

4. A sort algorithm that percolates the largest element to the end of a list is called a(n) _____ sort.

5. The method _____, which is required by the _____ interface, is used to compare two objects.

6. After retrieving an object from an array of `Object`, one must be careful to use the _____ operator before sending messages to that object.

7. Java's _____ class supports an array object that tracks its own logical size.

8. Java's _____ classes allow values of primitive types to masquerade as objects.

PROJECTS

PROJECT 11-1

Write a program that uses a scanner to report some statistics about words in an input sentence(see Section 11.1). The outputs should be the number of words in the sentence, the average word length, and the length of the sentence.

PROJECT 11-2

Write a program that inputs 10 integers into an array, sorts the array with a selection sort, and displays its contents before and after the sort.

PROJECT 11-3

Write a program that allows the user to search for a given word in a text file. The two inputs are the file's name and the target word. If the target is not found, the program outputs a message to that effect. Otherwise, the program outputs the number of times that this word occurs in the file and the position where it is first encountered (counting from position 0). The program should ignore case when it compares words.

PROJECT 11-4

The package `java.util` includes an `Arrays` class. This class includes several static methods for searching and sorting arrays, among other things. Browse this class in Sun's documentation to get a sense of its interface and method signatures. Then develop your own class, named `MyArrays`, which includes static methods for the linear search, binary search, and selection sort of arrays of objects. Include a short tester program that exercises the methods of `MyArrays`. (*Note*: `MyArrays` includes only methods, no variables.)

PROJECT 11-5

The following paragraph describes a simplified version of the card game of War. For a more complex version, see Hoyle's *Rules of Games* (New York: Signet Books, 2001).

There are two players in the game of War. During the course of a game, each player will have three piles of cards, named an unplayed pile, a war pile, and a winnings pile, respectively. The game moves forward as cards move from the unplayed piles to the war piles and then to the winnings piles. The game ends when a player's unplayed pile has no more cards. At that point, the player with the largest winnings pile wins the game. Here are the detailed rules for moving cards:

1. Each player is dealt 26 cards to her unplayed pile.

2. Repeat steps 3 through 5 until one or both unplayed piles become empty.

3. Each player plays the topmost card from his unplayed pile by placing it face up on his war pile.

4. If the cards have the same rank, repeat step 2.

5. Otherwise, move both war piles to the winnings pile of the player who has the card of a higher rank at the top of her war pile.

6. The player with the largest winnings pile wins.

Write a terminal-based program that uses the resources developed in the Case Study to play this game. The computer should make all of the moves for both players and display the cards played on each move. You should use the appropriate objects to represent the piles of cards.

PROJECT 11-6

Convert the terminal-based program of Project 11-5 to a GUI program. The main window should contain a labeled text field for each player and a single Play button. The cards are dealt at startup, but play does not start until the user clicks Play. The text fields, initially empty, are updated to display the information on the cards played from each hand after each click on Play. When a game ends, a message dialog box pops up to announce the winner. A Reset button allows the user to start a new game at any time.

PROJECT 11-7

After working on Project 11-6, Jack realizes that the game would be a lot more fun if he displayed realistic images of cards. In this project, modify the `Deck` and `Card` classes so that they are capable of displaying images. Write a short GUI tester program that cycles through a deck of cards and displays their images in a single panel.

Free images for decks of cards can be found at many Web sites. A directory containing some images is available from your instructor.

Each card should have an additional instance variable of type `ImageIcon` to hold its image. A new constructor accepts an image's file name as a parameter. The constructor loads the image from the file and sets the card's image variable. The `Card` class also includes a public method `getImage` that return's a card's image.

The `Card` class should have an additional instance variable of type `ImageIcon` to hold its image. A new `Card` constructor accepts an image's file name as a parameter. The constructor loads the image from the file and sets the card's image variable. The `Card` class also includes a public method `getImage` that returns a card's image.

The `Deck` class should have a new constructor that accepts a directory path name as a parameter. When the constructor enters the loop to create new cards, it uses the pathname to build the appropriate file name of each card's image file. You should adopt a scheme for naming these files that supports this process, such as "s1.gif" for the Ace of Spades' file, and so forth. Resulting file names are then passed to the new `Card` constructor mentioned earlier.

The tester program creates a new deck at startup. Its window contains a single panel and two buttons, labeled Deal and Reset. Each time that Deal is clicked, a new card is dealt from the deck and the card's image is displayed in the panel. When no more cards are available, a message dialog box pops up and the panel is cleared. Reset clears the panel and creates a new deck of cards at any time. The window's size should be large enough to accommodate a card's image.

The panel is a specialized version of the `ColorPanel` class used earlier. A new instance variable of type `ImageIcon` is initially `null`. A new public method `setImage(anImageIcon)` sets this variable and repaints the panel. When the panel's image variable is `null`, `paintComponent` just calls itself in the superclass, effectively clearing the panel. Otherwise, `paintComponent` also paints the image.

The window class calls `setImage` with a card's image when it should be displayed in the panel and calls the same method with `null` to clear the panel.

PROJECT 11-8

Use Jack's modified resources from Project 11-7 to develop a GUI-based game of War. (*Hint*: Replace the text fields with card panels.)

PROJECT 11-9

Complete the GUI-based student test scores program developed in Section 11.7. Update the data model so that it can hold any number of students.

PROJECT 11-10

Complete the shape-drawing program developed in Section 11.7. Update the data model so that it can hold any number of shapes.

CRITICAL *Thinking*

Jill is trying to decide whether to use an array or an instance of Java's `ArrayList` class in an application. Explain to her the costs and benefits of using the one data structure or the other.

CHAPTER 12

RECURSION, COMPLEXITY, AND SEARCHING AND SORTING

<table>
<tr><td>

OBJECTIVES

Upon completion of this chapter, you should be able to:

- Design and implement a recursive method to solve a problem.

- Understand the similarities and differences between recursive and iterative solutions of a problem.

- Check and test a recursive method for correctness.

- Understand how a computer executes a recursive method.

- Perform a simple complexity analysis of an algorithm using big-O notation.

- Recognize some typical orders of complexity.

- Understand the behavior of a complex sort algorithm such as the quicksort.

Estimated Time: 4.5 hours

</td><td>

VOCABULARY

Activation record

Big-O notation

Binary search algorithm

Call stack

Complexity analysis

Infinite recursion

Iterative process

Merge sort

Quicksort

Recursive method

Recursive step

Stack

Stack overflow error

Stopping state

Tail-recursive

</td></tr>
</table>

In this chapter, we continue our discussion of sorting and searching and introduce two new topics: recursion and complexity analysis. These topics are intertwined because searching and sorting can involve recursion and complexity analysis. A recursive algorithm is one that refers to itself by name in a manner that appears to be circular. Everyday algorithms, such as a recipe to bake a cake or instructions to change car oil, are not expressed recursively, but recursive algorithms are common in computer science. Complexity analysis is concerned with determining an algorithm's efficiency—that is, how its runtime and memory usage vary as a function of the quantity of data processed. Consider the searching and sorting algorithms presented in Chapter 11. When we test these algorithms on arrays of 10 to 20 elements, they are blindingly fast, but how fast can we expect them to be when the arrays are 100 times larger? Because painting two houses generally takes twice as long as painting one, we might guess that the same linear relationship between size and speed applies equally to sorting algorithms. We would be quite wrong, however, and in this chapter we learn techniques for analyzing algorithms more accurately. It is left to later computer science courses to study this chapter's topics in greater depth.

12.1 *Recursion*

When asked to add the integers from 1 to *n*, we usually think of the process iteratively. We start with 1, add 2, then 3, and so forth until we reach *n*, or expressed differently

```
sum(n) = 1 + 2 + 3 + ... + n, where n >= 1
```

Java's looping constructs make implementing the process easy. There is, however, a completely different way to look at the problem, which at first seems very strange:

```
sum(1) = 1
sum(n) = n + sum(n - 1) if n > 1
```

At first glance, expressing `sum(n)` in terms of `sum(n - 1)` seems to yield a circular definition, but closer examination shows that it does not. Consider, for example, what happens when the definition is applied to the problem of calculating `sum(4)`:

```
sum(4) = 4 + sum(3)
       = 4 + 3 + sum(2)
       = 4 + 3 + 2 + sum(1)
       = 4 + 3 + 2 + 1
```

The fact that `sum(1)` is defined to be 1 without making reference to further invocations of `sum` saves the process from going on forever and the definition from being circular. Functions that are defined in terms of themselves in this way are called *recursive*. The following, for example, are two ways to express the definition of factorial, the first iterative and the second recursive:

1.   factorial(n) = 1 * 2 * 3 * ... * n, where n >= 1

2.   factorial(1) = 1

   factorial(n) = n * factorial(n - 1) if n > 1

In this case, no doubt, the iterative definition is more familiar and thus easier to understand than the recursive one; however, such is not always the case. Consider the definition of Fibonacci numbers first encountered in Chapter 6. The first and second numbers in the Fibonacci sequence are 1. Thereafter, each number is the sum of its two immediate predecessors, as follows:

```
1  1  2  3  5  8  13  21  34  55  89  144  233 ...
```

or

```
fibonacci(1) = 1
fibonacci(2) = 1
fibonacci(n) = fibonacci(n - 1) + fibonacci(n - 2) if n > 2
```

This is a recursive definition, and it is hard to imagine how one could express the definition nonrecursively. Turn back to Chapter 6 to see how difficult it is to write an iterative version of this method.

From these examples, we can see that recursion involves two factors. First, some function `f(n)` is expressed in terms of `f(n - 1)` and perhaps `f(n - 2)` and so on. Second, to prevent the definition from being circular, `f(1)` and perhaps `f(2)` and so on are defined explicitly.

Implementing Recursion

Given a recursive definition of some process, it is usually easy to write a *recursive method* that implements it. A method is said to be recursive if it calls itself. Let us start with a method that computes factorials:

```
int factorial (int n){
//Precondition n >= 1
   if (n == 1)
      return 1;
   else
      return n * factorial (n - 1);
}
```

For comparison, the following is an iterative version of the method. As you can see, it is slightly longer and no easier to understand.

```
int factorial (int n){
   int product = 1;
   for (int i = 2; i <= n; i++)
      product = product * i;
   return product;
}
```

As a second example of recursion, following is a method that calculates Fibonacci numbers:

```
int fibonacci (int n){
   if (n <= 2)
      return 1;
   else
      return fibonacci (n - 1) + fibonacci (n - 2);
}
```

Tracing Recursive Calls

We can better understand recursion if we trace the sequence of recursive calls and returns that occur in a typical situation. Suppose we want to compute the factorial of 4. We call `factorial(4)`, which in turn calls `factorial(3)`, which in turn calls `factorial(2)`, which in turn calls `factorial(1)`, which returns 1 to `factorial(2)`, which returns 2 to `factorial(3)`, which returns 6 to `factorial(4)`, which returns 24, as shown in the following diagram:

```
factorial(4)
          calls factorial(3)
                              calls factorial(2)
                                                  calls factorial(1)
                                                  which returns 1
                              which returns 2 * 1        which is 2
           which returns 3 * 2      which is 6
which returns 4 * 6        which is 24
```

At first, it seems strange to have all these invocations of the `factorial` method, each in a state of suspended animation, waiting for the completion of the ones further down the line.

When the last invocation completes its work, it returns to its predecessor, which completes its work, and so forth up the line, until eventually the original invocation reactivates and finishes the job. Fortunately, we do not have to repeat this dizzying mental exercise every time we use recursion.

Guidelines for Writing Recursive Methods

Just as we must guard against writing infinite loops, so too we must avoid recursions that never come to an end. First, a recursive method must have a well-defined termination or *stopping state*. For the factorial method, this was expressed in the lines

```
// Preconditon: n >= 1
if (n == 1)
    return 1;
```

Second, the *recursive step*, in which the method calls itself, must eventually lead to the stopping state. For the factorial method, the recursive step was expressed in the lines

```
else
    return n * factorial(n - 1);
```

Because each invocation of the factorial method is passed a smaller value, eventually the stopping state must be reached. Had we accidentally written

```
else
    return n * factorial(n + 1);
```

the method would describe an *infinite recursion*. Eventually, the user would notice and terminate the program, or else the Java interpreter would run out of memory, at which point the program would terminate with a *stack overflow error*.

Following is a subtler example of a malformed recursive method:

```
int badMethod (int n){
    if (n == 1)
        return 1;
    else
        return n * badMethod(n - 2);
}
```

This method works fine if n is odd, but when n is even, the method passes through the stopping state and keeps on going. For instance,

```
badMethod(4)
  calls badMethod(2)
    calls badMethod(0)
      calls badMethod(-2)
        calls badMethod(-4)
          calls... badMethod(-6)
            ...
```

Run-time Support for Recursive Methods

Computers provide the following support at run time for method calls:

- A large storage area known as a *call stack* is created at program startup.

- When a method is called, an *activation record* is added to the top of the call stack.

- The activation record contains, among other things, space for the parameters passed to the method, the method's local variables, and the value returned by the method.

- When a method returns, its activation record is removed from the top of the stack.

To understand how a recursive method uses the call stack, we ignore, for the sake of simplicity, all parts of the activation record except for the parameters and the return value. The method factorial has one of each:

```
int factorial (int n){
   if (n <= 1)
      return 1;
   else
      return n * factorial (n - 1);
}
```

Thus, an activation record for this method requires cells for the following items:

- The value of the parameter n

- The return value of factorial

Suppose we call factorial(4). A trace of the state of the call stack during calls to factorial down to factorial(1) is shown in Figure 12-1.

FIGURE 12-1
Activation records on the call stack during recursive calls to factorial

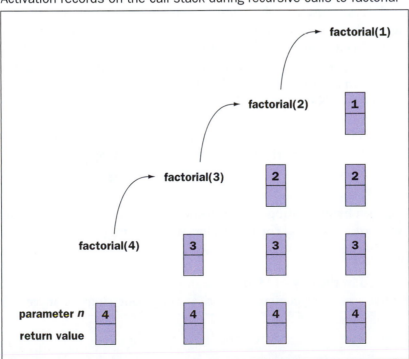

When the recursion unwinds, the return value from each call is multiplied by the parameter n in the record below it, and the top record is removed, as shown in the trace in Figure 12-2.

FIGURE 12-2
Activation records on the call stack during returns from recursive calls to factorial

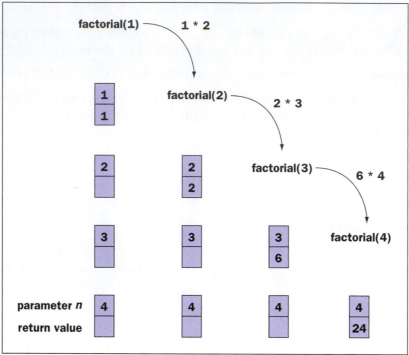

When to Use Recursion

Recursion can always be used in place of iteration, and vice versa. Ignoring the fact that arbitrarily substituting one for the other is pointless and sometimes difficult, the question of which is better to use remains. Recursion involves a method repeatedly calling itself. Executing a method call and the corresponding return statement usually takes longer than incrementing and testing a loop control variable. In addition, a method call ties up some memory that is not freed until the method completes its task. Naïve programmers often state these facts as an argument against ever using recursion. However, there are many situations in which recursion provides the clearest, shortest, and most elegant solution to a programming task—as we soon see. As a beginning programmer, you should not be overly concerned about squeezing the last drop of efficiency out of a computer. Instead, you need to master useful programming techniques, and recursion ranks among the best.

We close this section by presenting two well-known and aesthetically pleasing applications of recursion: the Towers of Hanoi and the Eight Queens problem.

Towers of Hanoi

Many centuries ago in the city of Hanoi, the monks in a certain monastery were continually engaged in what now seems a peculiar enterprise. Sixty-four rings of increasing size had been placed on a vertical wooden peg (Figure 12-3). Beside it were two other pegs, and the monks were attempting to move all the rings from the first to the third peg—subject to two constraints:

- Only one ring could be moved at a time.

- A ring could be moved to any peg, provided it was not placed on top of a smaller ring.

FIGURE 12-3
The Towers of Hanoi

The monks believed that the world would end and humankind would be freed from suffering when the task was finally completed. The fact that the world is still here today and you are enduring the frustrations of writing computer programs seems to indicate the monks were interrupted in their work. They were, but even if they had stuck with it, they would not finish anytime soon. A little experimentation should convince you that for n rings, $2^n - 1$ separate moves are required. At the rate of one move per second, $2^{64} - 1$ moves take about 600 billion years.

It might be more practical to harness the incredible processing power of modern computers to move virtual rings between virtual pegs. We are willing to start you on your way by presenting a recursive algorithm for printing the required moves. In the spirit of moderation, we suggest that you begin by running the program for small values of n. Figure 12-4 shows the result of running the program with three rings. In the output, the rings are numbered from smallest (1) to largest (3). You might try running the program with different numbers of rings to satisfy yourself that the printed output is correct. The number of lines of output corresponds to the formula given earlier.

FIGURE 12-4
Running the TowersOfHanoi program with three rings

The program uses a recursive method called move. The first time this method is called, it is asked to move all *n* rings from peg 1 to peg 3. The method then proceeds by calling itself to move the top *n* – 1 rings to peg 2, prints a message to move the largest ring from peg 1 to peg 3, and finally calls itself again to move the *n* – 1 rings from peg 2 to peg 3. Following is the code:

```
/* Example 12.1: TowersOfHanoi.java
Print the moves required to move the rings in the Towers of Hanoi problem.
1) Enter the number of rings as input.
2) WARNING: Do not run this program with 64 rings.
*/

import java.util.Scanner;

public class TowersOfHanoi {

    public static void main (String [] args) {
    // Obtain the number of rings from the user.
    // Call the recursive move method to move the rings from peg 1 to peg 3
    // with peg 2 available for intermediate usage.
    //   Preconditions  -- number of rings != 64
    //   Postconditions -- the moves are printed in the terminal window

        Scanner reader = new Scanner(System.in);
        System.out.print("Enter the number of rings: ");
        int numberOfRings = reader.nextInt();
        move (numberOfRings, 1, 3, 2);
    }

    private static void move (int n, int i, int j, int k){
    // Print the moves for n rings going from peg i to peg j
    //   Preconditions  -- none
    //   Postconditions -- the moves have been printed
        if (n > 0){                     //Stopping state is n == 0

            // Move the n-1 smaller rings from peg i to peg k
            move (n - 1, i, k, j);

            // Move the largest ring from peg i to peg j
            System.out.println("Move ring " + n + " from peg " + i + " to " +
                                j);

            // Move the n-1 smaller rings from peg k to peg j
            move (n - 1, k, j, i);

            // n rings have now been moved from peg i to peg j
        }
```

```
        }
    }
```

Although you should try this program with different numbers, you should stick with smaller numbers (i.e., <10). Large values of n, even with modern processing speeds, can still take a long time to run and could tie up your computer for some time. Do not attempt to run this program with 64 rings.

Eight Queens Problem

The Eight Queens problem consists of placing eight queens on a chessboard in such a manner that the queens do not threaten each other. A queen can attack any other piece in the same row, column, or diagonal, so there can be at most one queen in each row, column, and diagonal of the board. It is not obvious that there is a solution, but Figure 12-5 shows one.

FIGURE 12-5
A solution of the Eight Queens problem

We now present a program that attempts to solve this problem and others of a similar nature. We call it the ManyQueens program, and it attempts to place *n* queens safely on an *n* × *n* board. The program either prints a solution or a message saying that there is none (Figure 12-6).

FIGURE 12-6
Output of the ManyQueens program for boards of size 2, 4, and 8

```
⎯⎯ Command Prompt                                    _ □ x
C:\Javafiles>java ManyQueens
Enter the board size: 4
Here is a solution for a board of size 4x4
--Q-
Q---
---Q
-Q--

C:\Javafiles>java ManyQueens
Enter the board size: 8
Here is a solution for a board of size 8x8
Q-------
---Q----
-Q------
-----Q--
------Q-
--Q-----
-------Q
----Q---

C:\Javafiles>
```

At the heart of the program is a recursive method called `canPlaceQueen`. Initially, the board is empty, and the first time the method is called, it places a queen at the top of column 1. It then calls itself to place a queen in the first safe square of column 2 and then again to place a queen in the first safe square of column 3 and so forth, until finally it calls itself to place a queen in the first safe square of the last column. If at some step (say, for column 5) the method fails, then it returns and processing resumes in the previous column by looking for the next safe square. If there is one, then the process moves onward to column 5 again or else back to column 3. And so it goes. Either a solution is found or all possibilities are exhausted. The program includes a second method called `attacked`. It determines if a queen placed in row r, column c is threatened by any queens already present in columns 1 to $c - 1$. Following is the code:

```java
/* Example 12.2: ManyQueens.java
Determine the solution to the Many Queens problem for a chessboard
of any size.
1) There is a single input indicating the size of the board.
2) If there is a solution display it, else indicate that there is none.
*/

import java.util.Scanner;

public class ManyQueens {

    public static void main (String [] args) {
    // Process the user's input. Call a recursive function
    // to determine if there is a solution. Print the results.
    //   Preconditions  -- the input is an integer greater
    //                      than or equal to 1
    //   Postconditions -- display a solution or a message stating that there
    //                      is none

        int boardSize;        // The size of the board, for instance, 8 would
                              // indicate an 8x8 board
        boolean[][] board;    // A two-dimensional array representing the board
                              // An entry of false indicates that a square is
                              // unoccupied

        // Initialize the variables
        Scanner reader = new Scanner(System.in);
        System.out.print("Enter the board size: ");
        boardSize = reader.nextInt();
        board = new boolean[boardSize][boardSize];
        for (int row = 0; row < boardSize; row++)
           for (int col = 0; col < boardSize; col++)
              board[row][col] = false;

        // Determine if there is a solution
        if (! canPlaceQueen (0, board))

           // There is no solution
           System.out.println ("Impossible on a board of size " +
                              boardSize + "x" + boardSize);

        else{

           // There is a solution, so print it
           System.out.println ("Here is a solution for a board of size " +
                              boardSize + "x" + boardSize);
           for (int row = 0; row < boardSize; row++){
              for (int col = 0; col < boardSize; col++){
                 if (board[row][col])
                     System.out.print ("Q");
```

```
            else
                System.out.print ("-");
        }
        System.out.println();
    }


}

private static boolean canPlaceQueen (int col, boolean[][] board){
// Mark as true the first unattacked location in column col that
// permits a solution across the remaining columns.
//  Preconditions  -- 0 <= col < board.length
//  Postconditions -- if an entry in col gets marked true
//                    return true else return false

    for (int row = 0; row < board.length; row++){  // Iterate down the column
        if (! attacked (row, col, board)){          // if square is not under attack
            if (col == board.length -1){            // if this is the last column
                board[row][col] = true;             // end recursion, set square true
                return true;                        // recursive ascent true
            }else{                                  // else
                board[row][col] = true;             // trial solution, set square true
                                                    // if recursive descent succeeds
                if (canPlaceQueen (col + 1, board))
                    return true;                    // recursive ascent true
                else                                // else
                    board[row][col] = false;        // trial solution didn't work
            }                                       // end if
        }                                           // end if
    }
    return false;                                   // recursive ascent false
}

private static boolean attacked (int row, int col, boolean[][] board){
// Determine if the square at location (row, col) is under attack.
// from any queen in columns 0 to col - 1
//  Preconditions  -- 0 <= row, col < board.length
//  Postconditions -- returns true if square under attack else false

// Look for horizontal attack
    int i, j, k;
    for (j = 0; j < col; j++){
        if (board[row][j])
            return true;
    }

    // Look for attack from a descending diagonal
    i = row - 1;
    j = col - 1;
    for (k = 0; k <= Math.min(i, j); k++){
        if (board[i][j])
            return true;
        else{
            i--;
            j--;
        }
    }
```

```
// Look for attack from an ascending diagonal
i = row + 1;
j = col - 1;
for (k = 0; k <= Math.min(board.length - i - 1, j); k++){
    if (board[i][j])
        return true;
    else{
        i++;
        j--;
    }
}

return false;
    }
}
```

EXERCISE 12.1

1. What keeps a recursive definition from being circular?

2. What are the two parts of any recursive method?

3. Why is recursion more expensive than iteration?

4. What are the benefits of using recursion?

5. Consider the following definition of the method raise, which raises a given number to a given exponent:

```
int raise(int base, int expo){
    if (expo == 0)
        return 1;
    else
        return base * raise(base, expo - 1);
}
```

Draw a trace of the complete execution of `raise(2, 5)`.

6. Consider the following method:

```
int whatAMethod(int n){
    if (n == 0)
        return 1;
    else
        return whatAMethod(n);
}
```

What happens during the execution of `whatAMethod(3)`?

Programming Skills

RECURSION NEED NOT BE EXPENSIVE

We have seen that the use of recursion has two costs: Extra time and extra memory are required to manage recursive function calls. These costs have led some to argue that recursion should never be used in programs. However, as Guy Steele has shown (in "Debunking the 'Expensive Procedure Call' Myth," *Proceedings of the National Conference of the ACM*, 1977), some systems can run recursive algorithms as if they were iterative ones, with no additional overhead. The key condition is to write a special kind of recursive algorithm called a ***tail-recursive*** algorithm. An algorithm is tail-recursive if no work is done in the algorithm after a recursive call. For example, according to this criterion, the factorial method that we presented earlier is not tail-recursive because a multiplication is performed after each recursive call. We can convert this version of the factorial method to a tail-recursive version by performing the multiplication before each recursive call. To do this, we need an additional parameter that passes the accumulated value of the factorial down on each recursive call. In the last call of the method, this value is returned as the result:

```
int tailRecursiveFactorial (int n, int result){
    if (n == 1)
        return result;
    else
        return tailRecursiveFactorial (n - 1, n * result);
}
```

Note that the multiplication is performed before the recursive call of the method—that is, when the parameters are evaluated. On the initial call to the method, the value of result should be 1:

```
int factorial (int n){
    return tailRecursiveFactorial (n, 1);
}
```

Steele showed that a smart compiler could translate tail-recursive code in a high-level language to a loop in machine language. The machine code treats the method's parameters as variables associated with a loop and generates an ***iterative process*** rather than a recursive one. Thus, there is no linear growth of method calls, and extra stack memory is not required to run tail-recursive methods on these systems.

The catch is that a programmer must be able to convert a recursive method to a tail-recursive method and find a compiler that generates iterative machine code from tail-recursive methods. Unfortunately, some methods are difficult or impossible to convert to tail-recursive versions, and the needed optimizations are not part of most standard compilers. If you find that your Java compiler supports this optimization, you should try converting some methods to tail-recursive versions and see if they run faster than the original versions.

12.2 Complexity Analysis

There is an important question we should ask about every method we write. What is the effect on the method of increasing the quantity of data processed? Does doubling the amount of data double the method's execution time, triple it, quadruple it, or have no effect? This type of examination is called *complexity analysis*. Let us consider some examples.

Sum Methods

First, consider the sum method presented in Chapter 9. This method processes an array whose size can be varied. To determine the method's execution time, beside each statement we place a symbol (t1, t2, etc.) that indicates the time needed to execute the statement. Because we have no way of knowing what these times really are, we can do no better.

```
int sum (int[] a){
    int result = 0;                     // Assignment: time = t1
    for (int i = 0; i < a.length; i++){ // Overhead for going once around the
                                        // loop: time = t2
        result += a[i];                 // Assignment: time = t3
    }
    return result;                      // Return: time = t4
}
```

Adding these times together and remembering that the method goes around the loop n times, where n represents the array's size, yields

```
executionTime
    = t1 + n * (t2 + t3) + t4
    = k1 + n * k2               where k1 and k2 are method-dependent constants
    = n * k2                    for large values of n
```

Thus, the execution time is linearly dependent on the array's length, and as the array's length increases, the contribution of k1 becomes negligible. Consequently, we can say with reasonable accuracy that doubling the length of the array doubles the execution time of the method. Computer scientists express this linear relationship between the array's length and execution time using *big-O notation*:

```
executionTime = O(n).
```

Or phrased slightly differently, the execution time is order of n. Observe that from the perspective of big-O notation, we make no distinction between a method whose execution time is

```
1000000 + 1000000*n
```

and one whose execution time is

```
n / 1000000
```

although from a practical perspective the difference is enormous.

Complexity analysis can also be applied to recursive methods. Following is a recursive version of the sum method. It, too, is O(n).

```
int sum (int[] a, int i){
   if (i >= a.length)             // Comparison: t1
      return 0;                   // Return: t2
   else
      return a[i] + sum (a, i + 1);  // Call and return: t3
}
```

The method is called initially with i = 0. A single activation of the method takes time

```
t1 + t2      if  i >= a.length
```

and

```
t1 + t3      if  i < a.length.
```

The first case occurs once and the second case occurs the a.length times that the method calls itself recursively. Thus, if n equals a.length, then

```
executionTime
    = t1 + t2 + n * (t1 + t3)
    = k1 + n * k2              where k1 and k2 are method-dependent constants
    = O(n)
```

Other O(n) Methods

Several of the array processing methods presented in Chapters 9 and 11 are O(n). Following is a linear search method from Chapter 11:

```
int search (int[] a, int searchValue){
   for (int i = 0; i < a.length; i++)   // Loop overhead: t1
      if (a[i] == searchValue)          // Comparison: t2
         return i;                      // Return point 1: t3
   return location;                     // Return point 2: t4
}
```

The analysis of the linear search method is slightly more complex than that of the sum method. Each time through the loop, a comparison is made. If and when a match is found, the method returns from the loop with the search value's index. If we assume that the search is usually made for values present in the array, then on average, we can expect that half the elements in the array be examined before a match is found. Putting all of this together yields

```
executionTime
    = (n / 2) * (t1 + t2) + t3
    = n * k1 + k2              where k1 and k2 are method-dependent constants.
    = O(n)
```

Now let us look at a method that processes a two-dimensional array:

```java
int[] sumRows (int[][] a){
    int[] rowSum = new int[a.length];            // Instantiation: t1
    for (int row = 0; row < a.length; row++){    // Loop overhead: t2
        for (int col = 0; col < a[row].length; col++){  // Loop overhead: t3
            rowSum[row] += a[row][col];          // Assignment: t4
        }
    }
    return rowSum;                               // Return: t5
}
```

Let n represent the total number of elements in the array and r the number of rows. For the sake of simplicity, we assume that each row has the same number of elements, say, c. The execution time can be written as

```
executionTime
    = t1 + r * (t2 + c * (t3 + t4)) + t5
    = (k1 + n * k2) + (n/c) * t2 + n * (t3 + t4) + t5   where r = n/c
    = (k1 + n * k2) + n * (t2 / c + t3 + t4) + t5
    = k2 + n * k3                              where k1, k2, k3, and k4 are constants
    = O(n)
```

Notice that we have replaced `t1` by `(k1 + n * k2)`. This is based on the perhaps unreasonable assumption that the JVM can allocate a block of memory for the array `rowSum` in constant time `(k1)` followed by the time needed to initialize all entries to zero `(n * k2)`.

An $O(n^2)$ Method

Not all array processing methods are $O(n)$, as an examination of the `bubbleSort` method reveals. Let us first analyze a "dumber" version of this method than the one presented in Chapter 11. This one does not track whether or not an exchange was made in the nested loop, so there is no early exit.

```java
void bubbleSort(int[] a){
    int k = 0;

    // Make n - 1 passes through array

    while (k < a.length() - 1){             // Loop overhead: t1
        k++;
        for (int j = 0; j < a.length() - k; j++)   // Loop overhead: t2
            if (a[j] > a[j + 1])            // Comparison: t3
                swap(a, j, j + 1);          // Assignments: t4
    }
}
```

The outer loop of the sort method executes $n - 1$ times, where n is the length of the array. Each time the inner loop is activated, it iterates a different number of times. On the first activation it iterates $n - 1$ times, on the second $n - 2$, and so on, until on the last activation it iterates once. Thus, the average number of iterations is $n / 2$. On some iterations, elements a[i] and a[j] are interchanged in time t4, and on other iterations they are not. So on the average iteration, let's say time t5 is spent doing an interchange. The execution time of the method can now be expressed as

```
executionTime
    = t1 + (n - 1) * (t1 + (n / 2) * (t2 + t3 + t5))
    = t1 + n * t1 - t1 + (n * n / 2) * (t2 + t3 + t4) -
                        (n / 2) * (t2 + t3 + t4)
    = k1 + n * k2 + n * n * k3
= n * n * k3                          for large values of n
        = O(n²)
```

As discussed in Chapter 11, we can alter this method to track whether or not an exchange was made within the nested loop. If no exchange was made, then the array must be sorted and we can exit the method early. However, because we usually make an exchange on each pass on the average, this trick does not improve the bubble sort's complexity on the average. Nevertheless, it can improve the method's behavior to linear in the best case (a case in which the array is already sorted).

Common Big-O Values

We have already seen several methods that are $O(n)$ and one that is $O(n^2)$. These are just two of the most frequently encountered big-O values. Table 12-1 lists some other common big-O values together with their names.

TABLE 12-1
Names of some common big-O values

BIG-O VALUE	NAME
O(1)	Constant
O(log n)	Logarithmic
O(n)	Linear
O(n log n)	n log n
O(n^2)	Quadratic
O(n^3)	Cubic
O(2^n)	**Exponential**

As an example of $O(1)$, consider a method that returns the sum of the first and last numbers in an array. This method's execution time is independent of the array's length. In other words, it takes constant time. Later in the chapter, we will see examples of methods that are logarithmic and n log n.

The values in Table 12-1 are listed from "best" to "worst." For example, given two methods that perform the same task, but in different ways, we tend to prefer the one that is O(n) over the one that is O(n^2). This statement requires some elaboration. For instance, suppose that the exact run time of two methods is

```
10,000 + 400n        // method 1
```

and

```
10,000 + n²          // method 2
```

For small values of n, method 2 is faster than method 1; however, and this is the important point, for all values of n larger than a certain threshold, method 1 is faster. The threshold in this example is 400. So if you know ahead of time that n will always be less than 400, you are advised to use method 2, but if n will have a large range of values, method 1 is superior.

By the way, from the perspective of complexity analysis, we do not need to distinguish between base 2 and base 10 logarithms because they differ only by a constant factor:

```
log² n = log¹⁰ n * log² 10
```

To get a feeling for how the common big-O values vary with n, consider Table 12-2. We use base 10 logarithms. This table vividly demonstrates that a method might be useful for small values of n but totally worthless for large values. Clearly, methods that take exponential time have limited value, even if it were possible to run them on the world's most powerful computer for billions of years. Unfortunately, there are many important problems for which even the best algorithms take exponential time. You can achieve lasting fame by being the first person to replace one of these exponential time algorithms with one that takes less than exponential time.

TABLE 12-2

How big-O values vary depending on n

n	1	LOG n	n	n LOG n	n^2	n^3	2^n
10	1	1	10	10	100	1,000	1,024
100	1	2	100	200	10,000	1,000,000	≈ 1.3 e30
1,000	1	3	1,000	3,000	1,000,000	1,000,000,000	≈ 1.1 e301

An O(r^n) Method

We have seen two algorithms for computing Fibonacci numbers, one iterative and the other recursive. The iterative algorithm presented in Chapter 6 is O(n). However, the much simpler recursive algorithm presented earlier in this chapter is O(r^n), where $r \approx 1.62$. While O(r^n) is better than O(2^n), it is still exponential. It is beyond the book's scope to prove that the recursive algorithm is O(r^n). Nonetheless, it is easy to demonstrate that the number of recursive calls increases rapidly with n. For instance, Figure 12-7 shows the calls involved when we use the recursive method to compute the sixth Fibonacci number. To keep the diagram reasonably compact, we write `(6)` instead of `fibonacci(6)`.

FIGURE 12-7
Calls needed to compute the sixth Fibonacci number recursively

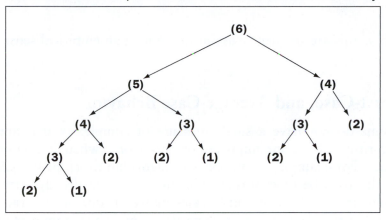

Table 12-3 shows the number of calls as a function of *n*.

TABLE 12-3
Calls needed to compute the *n*th Fibonacci number recursively

n	CALLS NEEDED TO COMPUTE *n*TH FIBONACCI NUMBER
2	1
4	5
8	41
16	1,973
32	4,356,617

The values in Table 12-3 were obtained by running the following program:

```
// Example 12.3: Test fibonacci method

public class Tester{

    private static int count = 0;

    public static void main (String[] args){
        for (int i = 1; i <= 5; i++){
            count = 0;
            int n = (int)Math.pow(2, i);
            int fibn = fibonacci(n);
            System.out.println ("" + n + ":" + count);
        }
    }

    private static int fibonacci (int n){
        count++;
        if (n <= 2)
            return 1;
        else
```

```
            return fibonacci(n - 1) + fibonacci(n - 2);
        }
    }
```

Programs such as this are frequently useful for gaining an empirical sense of an algorithm's efficiency.

Best-Case, Worst-Case, and Average-Case Behavior

Many algorithms do not have a single measure of complexity that applies to all cases. Sometimes an algorithm's behavior improves or gets worse when it encounters a particular arrangement of data. For example, the bubble sort algorithm developed in Chapter 11 can terminate as soon as the array becomes sorted. If the input array is already sorted, the bubble sort requires just N comparisons. In many other cases, however, bubble sort requires N2 comparisons. Clearly, a more detailed analysis may be needed to make programmers aware of these special cases.

A thorough analysis of an algorithm's complexity divides its behavior into three types of cases:

1. *Best case*. Under what circumstances does an algorithm do the least amount of work? What is the algorithm's complexity in this best case?

2. *Worst case*. Under what circumstances does an algorithm do the most amount of work? What is the algorithm's complexity in this worst case?

3. *Average case*. Under what circumstances does an algorithm do a typical amount of work? What is the algorithm's complexity in this typical case?

Let's consider three examples of this kind of analysis for summation, linear search, and bubble sort.

Because the summation algorithm must visit each number in the array, no matter how the numbers are ordered, the algorithm is always linear. Therefore, its best-case, worst-case, and average-case behaviors are $O(n)$.

Linear search is a bit different. The algorithm stops and returns a result as soon as it finds the target element. Clearly, in the best case, this element is at the first position. In the worst case, the target is in the last position. Therefore, the algorithm's best-case behavior is $O(1)$ and its worst-case behavior is $O(n)$. To compute the average-case behavior, we add up all of the comparisons that must be made to locate a target in each position and divide by n. This is $(1 + 2 + \ldots + n) / n$, or $n / 2$. Therefore, by approximation, the average-case behavior of linear search is also $O(n)$.

As we saw in Chapter 11, the "smarter" version of bubble sort can terminate as soon as the array becomes sorted. In the best case, this happens when the input array is already sorted. Therefore, bubble sort's best-case behavior is $O(n)$. However, this case is very rare (1 out of $n!$). In the worst case, even this version of bubble sort will have to bubble each element down to its proper position in the array. The algorithm's worst-case behavior is clearly $O(n^2)$. Bubble sort's average-case behavior is closer to $O(n^2)$ than to $O(n)$, although the demonstration of this fact is a bit more involved than it is for linear search.

As we will see, there are algorithms whose best-case and average-case behaviors are similar, but whose behavior degrades to a worst case. Whether you are choosing an algorithm or developing a new one, it is important to be aware of these distinctions.

EXERCISE 12.2

1. Using big-O notation, state the time complexity of the following recursive methods:

a. `factorial`

b. `raise` (see Exercise 12.1, Question 5)

2. Recursive methods use stack space. Using big-O notation, state the space complexity of the following recursive methods:

a. `factorial`

b. `fibonacci`

3. State the time complexity of the following sort method:

```
void sort(int[] a){
    for (int j = 0; j < a.length - 1; j++){
        int minIndex = j;
        for (int k = j + 1; k < a.length; k++)
            if (a[k] < a[minIndex])
                minIndex = k;
        if (minIndex != j){
            int temp = a[j];
            a[j] = a[minIndex];
            a[minIndex] = temp;
        }
    }
}
```

12.3 Binary Search

Searching is such a common activity that it is important to do it quickly. As mentioned earlier, a linear search starts at the beginning of an array and looks at consecutive elements until either the search value is located or the array's end is encountered. Imagine using this technique to find a number by hand in a list of 10 million entries. It would take an intolerably long time, especially if the elements are strings (recall that all characters in two strings must be compared to ensure equality).

Alternatively, as mentioned in Chapter 11, if we know in advance that the list is in ascending order, we can quickly zero in on the search value or determine that it is absent using the *binary search algorithm*. We shall show that this algorithm is O(log *n*).

We start by looking at the middle of the list. We might be lucky and find the search value immediately. If not, we know whether to continue the search in the first or the second half of the list. Now we reapply the technique repeatedly. At each step, we reduce the search region by a factor of 2. Soon we either must find the search value or narrow the search down to a single element. A list of 1 million entries involves at most 20 steps.

Figure 12-8 is an illustration of the binary search algorithm. We are looking for the number 320. At each step, we highlight the sublist that might still contain 320. Also at each step, all the numbers are invisible except the one in the middle of the sublist, which is the one that we are comparing to 320.

FIGURE 12-8
Binary search algorithm

After only four steps, we have determined that 320 is not in the list. Had the search value been 205, 358, 301, or 314, we would have located it in four or fewer steps. The binary search algorithm is guaranteed to search a list of 15 sorted elements in a maximum of four steps. Incidentally, the list with all the numbers visible looks like Figure 12-9.

FIGURE 12-9
The list for the binary search algorithm with all numbers visible

| 15 | 36 | 87 | 95 | 100 | 110 | 194 | 205 | 297 | 301 | 314 | 358 | 451 | 467 | 486 |

Table 12-4 shows the relationship between a list's length and the maximum number of steps needed to search the list. To obtain the numbers in the second column, add 1 to the larger numbers in the first column and take the logarithm base 2. Hence, a method that implements a binary search is O(log n).

TABLE 12-4
Maximum number of steps needed to binary search lists of various sizes

LENGTH OF LIST	MAXIMUM NUMBER OF STEPS NEEDED
1	1
2 to 3	2
4 to 7	3
8 to 15	4
16 to 31	5
32 to 63	6
64 to 127	7
128 to 255	8
256 to 511	9
512 to 1023	10

TABLE 12-4 Continued
Maximum number of steps needed to binary search lists of various sizes

LENGTH OF LIST	MAXIMUM NUMBER OF STEPS NEEDED
1024 to 2047	11
2^n to $2^{n+1} - 1$	$n + 1$

We now present two versions of the binary search algorithm, one iterative and one recursive, and both O(log n). We will forgo a formal analysis of the complexity. First, the iterative version, as introduced in Chapter 11:

```
// Iterative binary search of an ascending array
int search (int[] a, int target){
    int left = 0;                          // Establish the initial
    int right = a.length - 1;              // endpoints of the array
    while (left <= right){                 // Loop until the endpoints cross
        int midpoint = (left + right) / 2; // Compute the current midpoint
        if (a[midpoint] == target)         // Target found; return its index
            return midpoint;
        else if (a[midpoint] < target)     // Target to right of midpoint
            left = midpoint + 1;
        else                               // Target to left of midpoint
            right = midpoint - 1;
    }
    return -1;                             // Target not found
}
```

Figure 12-10 illustrates an iterative search for 320 in the list of 15 elements. L, M, and R are abbreviations for `left`, `midpoint`, and `right`. At each step, the figure shows how these variables change. Because 320 is absent from the list, eventually (`left > right`) and the method returns –1.

FIGURE 12-10
Steps in an iterative binary search for the number 320

Now for the recursive version of the algorithm:

```java
// Recursive binary search of an ascending array
int search (int[] a, int target, int left, int right){
   if (left > right)
      return -1;
   else{
      int midpoint = (left + right) / 2;
      if (a[midpoint] == target)
         return midpoint;
      else if (a[midpoint] < target)
         return search (a, target, midpoint + 1, right);
      else
         return search (a, target, left, midpoint - 1);
   }
}
```

At heart, the two versions are similar, and they use the variables `left`, `midpoint`, and `right` in the same way. Of course, they differ in that one uses a loop and the other uses recursion. We conclude the discussion by showing how the two methods are called:

```java
int[] a = {15,36,87,95,100,110,194,205,297,301,314,358,451,467,486};
int x = 320;
int location;

location = search (a, x);                    // Iterative version
location = search (a, x, 0, a.length - 1);   // Recursive version
```

EXERCISE 12.3

1. The efficiency of the method `raise` in Question 5 of Exercise 12.1, can be improved by the following changes: If the exponent is even, then raise the base to the exponent divided by 2 and return the square of this number. Otherwise, the exponent is odd, so `raise` the number as before. Rewrite the method `raise` using this strategy.

2. Draw a trace of the complete execution of `raise(2, 10)` as defined in Question 1 in this exercise.

3. What is the time complexity of `raise` in Question 1?

12.4 Quicksort

The sort algorithms presented in Chapter 11 are $O(n^2)$. There are a number of variations on the algorithms, some of which are marginally faster, but they too are $O(n^2)$. In contrast, there are also several better algorithms that are $O(n \log n)$. *Quicksort* is one of the simplest of these. The general idea behind quicksort is this: Break an array into two parts and then move elements around so that all the larger values are in one end and all the smaller values are in the other. Each of the two parts is then subdivided in the same manner, and so on, until the subparts contain only a single value, at which point the array is sorted. To illustrate the process, suppose an unsorted array, called a, looks like Figure 12-11.

FIGURE 12-11
Unsorted array

5	12	3	11	2	7	20	10	8	4	9

Phase 1

1. If the length of the array is less than 2, then it is done.

2. Locate the value in the middle of the array and call it the *pivot*. The pivot is 7 in this example (Figure 12-12).

FIGURE 12-12
Step 2 of quicksort

5	12	3	11	2	<u>7</u>	20	10	8	4	9

3. Tag the elements at the left and right ends of the array as i and j, respectively (Figure 12-13).

FIGURE 12-13
Step 3 of quicksort

4. While a[i] < pivot value, increment i.
   While a[j] > pivot value, decrement j (Figure 12-14).

FIGURE 12-14
Step 4 of quicksort

5. If i > j then
      end the phase
   else
      interchange a[i] and a[j] (Figure 12-15).

FIGURE 12-15
Step 5 of quicksort

6. Increment i and decrement j.
   If i > j then end the phase (Figure 12-16).

FIGURE 12-16
Step 6 of quicksort

5	4	3	11	2	<u>7</u>	20	10	8	12	9
		i					j			

7. Repeat Step 4, that is,
   While a[i] < pivot value, increment i
   While a[j] > pivot value, decrement j (Figure 12-17).

FIGURE 12-17
Step 7 of quicksort

5	4	3	11	2	<u>7</u>	20	10	8	12	9
			i		j					

8. Repeat Step 5, that is,
   If i > j then
     end the phase
   else
     interchange a[i] and a[j] (Figure 12-18).

FIGURE 12-18
Step 8 of quicksort

5	4	3	<u>7</u>	2	11	20	10	8	12	9
			i		j					

9. Repeat Step 6, that is,
   Increment i and decrement j.
   If i > j then end the phase (Figure 12-19).

FIGURE 12-19
Step 9 of quicksort

5	4	3	<u>7</u>	2	11	20	10	8	12	9
				ij						

10. Repeat Step 4, that is,
    While a[i] < pivot value, increment i
    While a[j] > pivot value, decrement j (Figure 12-20).

FIGURE 12-20
Step 10 of quicksort

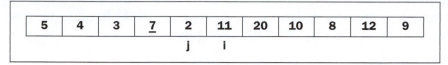

5	4	3	7	2	11	20	10	8	12	9

j   i

11. Repeat Step 5, that is,
    If i > j then
      end the phase
    else
      interchange a[i] and a[j].

12. This ends the phase. Split the array into the two subarrays a[0..j] and a[i..10]. For
    clarity, the left subarray is shaded (Figure 12-21). Notice that all the elements in the left
    subarray are less than or equal to the pivot, and those in the right are greater than or equal
    to the pivot.

FIGURE 12-21
Step 12 of quicksort

5	4	3	7	2	11	20	10	8	12	9

Phase 2 and Onward

Reapply the process to the left and right subarrays, and then divide each subarray in two, and
so on, until the subarrays have lengths of at most 1.

Complexity Analysis

We now present an informal analysis of the quicksort's complexity. During phase 1, i and j
moved toward each other. At each move, either an array element is compared to the pivot or an
interchange takes place. As soon as i and j pass each other, the process stops. Thus, the amount
of work during phase 1 is proportional to n, the array's length.

The amount of work in phase 2 is proportional to the left subarray's length plus the right subarray's length, which together yield n. And when these subarrays are divided, there are four pieces
whose combined length is n, so the combined work is proportional to n yet again. At successive
phases, the array is divided into more pieces, but the total work remains proportional to n.

To complete the analysis, we need to determine how many times the arrays are subdivided.
We make the optimistic assumption that each time the dividing line turns out to be as close to the
center as possible. In practice, this is not usually the case. We already know from our discussion
of the binary search algorithm that when we divide an array in half repeatedly, we arrive at a single element in about $\log_2 n$ steps. Thus, the algorithm is O($n \log n$) in the best case. In the worst
case, the algorithm is O(n^2).

Implementation

The quicksort algorithm can be coded using either an iterative or a recursive approach. The iterative approach also requires a data structure called a *stack*. Because we have described it recursively, we might as well implement it that way too.

```
void quickSort (int[] a, int left, int right){

    if (left >= right) return;

    int i = left;
    int j = right;
    int pivotValue = a[(left + right) / 2];
    while (i < j){
        while (a[i] < pivotValue) i++;
        while (pivotValue < a[j]) j—;
        if (i <= j){
            int temp = a[i];
            a[i] = a[j];
            a[j] = temp;
            i++;
            j--;
        }
    }
    quickSort (a, left, j);
    quickSort (a, i, right);
}
```

EXERCISE 12.4

1. Describe the strategy of quicksort and explain why it can reduce the time complexity of sorting from $O(n^2)$ to $O(n \log n)$.

2. Why is quicksort not $O(n \log n)$ in all cases? Describe the worst-case situation for quicksort.

3. Describe three strategies for selecting a pivot value in quicksort.

4. Jack has a bright idea: When the length of a subarray in quicksort is less than a certain number, say, 50 elements, run an insertion sort to process that subarray. Explain why this is a bright idea.

12.5 Merge Sort

Another algorithm called *merge sort* employs a recursive, divide-and-conquer strategy to break the $O(n^2)$ barrier. Here is an outline of the algorithm:

- Compute the middle position of an array and recursively sort its left and right subarrays (divide and conquer).

- Merge the two sorted subarrays back into a single sorted array.

■ Stop the process when subarrays can no longer be subdivided.

This top-level design strategy can be implemented as three Java methods:

■ mergeSort—the public method called by clients

■ mergeSortHelper—a private helper method that hides the extra parameter required by recursive calls

■ merge—a private method that implements the merging process

The merging process uses an extra array, which we call copyBuffer. To avoid the overhead of allocating and deallocating the copyBuffer each time merge is called, the buffer is allocated once in mergeSort and subsequently passed to mergeSortHelper and merge. Each time mergeSortHelper is called, it needs to know the bounds of the subarray with which it is working. These bounds are provided by two parameters, low and high. Here is the code for mergeSort:

```java
void mergeSort(int[] a){
    // a            array being sorted
    // copyBuffer   temp space needed during merge

    int[] copyBuffer = new int[a.length];
    mergeSortHelper(a, copyBuffer, 0, a.length - 1);
}
```

After checking that it has been passed a subarray of at least two items, mergeSortHelper computes the midpoint of the subarray, recursively sorts the portions below and above the midpoint, and calls merge to merge the results. Here is the code for mergeSortHelper:

```java
void mergeSortHelper(int[] a, int[] copyBuffer,
                     int low, int high){
    // a            array being sorted
    // copyBuffer   temp space needed during merge
    // low, high    bounds of subarray
    // middle       midpoint of subarray

    if (low < high){
        int middle = (low + high) / 2;
        mergeSortHelper(a, copyBuffer, low, middle);
        mergeSortHelper(a, copyBuffer, middle + 1, high);
        merge(a, copyBuffer, low, middle, high);
    }
}
```

Figure 12-22 shows the subarrays generated during recursive calls to `mergeSortHelper`, starting from an array of eight items. Note that in this example the subarrays are evenly subdivided at each stage and there are 2^{k-1} subarrays to be merged at stage k. Had the length of the initial array not been a power of two, then an exactly even subdivision would not have been achieved at each stage and the last stage would not have contained a full complement of subarrays.

FIGURE 12-22
Subarrays generated during calls of `mergeSort`

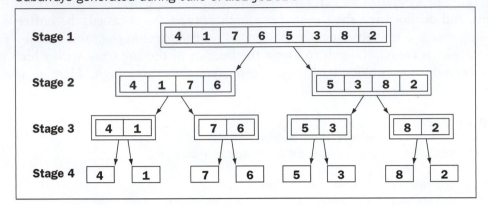

Figure 12-23 traces the process of merging the subarrays generated in the previous figure.

FIGURE 12-23
Merging the subarrays generated during a merge sort

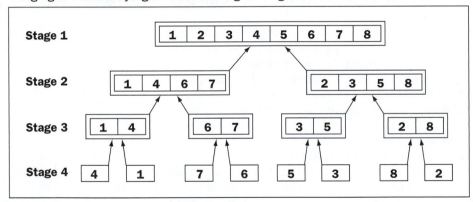

Finally, here is the code for the `merge` method:

```
 1 void merge(int[] a, int[] copyBuffer,
 2            int low, int middle, int high){
 3    // a            array that is being sorted
 4    // copyBuffer   temp space needed during the merge process
 5    // low          beginning of first sorted subarray
 6    // middle       end of first sorted subarray
 7    // middle + 1   beginning of second sorted subarray
 8    // high         end of second sorted subarray
 9
10    // Initialize i1 and i2 to the first items in each subarray
11    int i1 = low, i2 = middle + 1;
12
```

```
13    // Interleave items from the subarrays into the copyBuffer in such a
14    // way that order is maintained.
15    for (int i = low; i <= high; i++){
16       if (i1 > middle)
17          copyBuffer[i] = a[i2++];      // First subarray exhausted
18       else if (i2 > high)
19          copyBuffer[i] = a[i1++];      // Second subarray exhausted
20       else if (a[i1] < a[i2])
21          copyBuffer[i] = a[i1++];      // Item in first subarray is less
22       else
23          copyBuffer[i] = a[i2++];      // Item in second subarray is less
24    }
25
26    for (int i = low; i <= high; i++) // Copy sorted items back into
27       a[i] = copyBuffer[i];            // proper position in a
28 }
```

The `merge` method combines two sorted subarrays into a larger sorted subarray. The first subarray lies between `low` and `middle` and the second between `middle + 1` and `high`. The process consists of three steps:

1. Set up index pointers to the first items in each subarray (line 11). These are at positions `low` and `middle + 1`.

2. Starting with the first item in each subarray, repeatedly compare items. Copy the smaller item from its subarray to the copy buffer and advance to the next item in the subarray. Repeat until all items have been copied from both subarrays. If the end of one subarray is reached before the other's, finish by copying the remaining items from the other subarray (lines 15–24).

3. Copy the portion of `copyBuffer` between `low` and `high` back to the corresponding positions in the array a (lines 26–27).

Complexity Analysis for Merge Sort

The run time of the `merge` method is dominated by the two for statements, each of which loop (`high - low + 1`) times. Consequently, the method's run time is O (`high - low`), and all the merges at a single stage take O(n) time. Because merge sort splits subarrays as evenly as possible at each stage, the number of stages is O(log n), and the maximum run time for merge sort is O(n log n) in all cases.

Merge sort has two space requirements that depend on the array's size. First, O(log n)space is required on the call stack to support recursive calls. Second, O(n) space is used by the copy buffer.

Improving Merge Sort

Merge sort can be improved in three ways. First, the `merge` method can be modified so that the first for statement makes a single comparison on each iteration (see the exercises). Second, there exists a complex process that allows one to merge two subarrays without using a copy buffer and without changing the order of the method. Third, subarrays below a certain size can be sorted using an alternative approach.

Case Study: Comparing Sort Algorithms

For the benefit of those who are unconvinced by mathematical analysis, we now develop a program that compares the speed of our two sort algorithms.

Request

Write a program that allows the user to compare sort algorithms.

Analysis

The program compares bubble sort and quicksort. Because quicksort runs much more quickly than bubble sort, we do not run both sorts on the same array. Instead, we run quicksort on an array that is 100 times longer than the array used with bubble sort. Also, because we have already compared these algorithms by counting their operations, we record run times and compare these instead. The proposed interface is shown in Figure 12-24.

FIGURE 12-24

How run time varies with array length for bubble sort on the left and quicksort on the right

```
C:\Javafiles>java ComparingSortAlgorithms
Enter the array Length [0 to quit]: 1600
            Bubble Sort       QuickSort
Length      1600              160000
Time        20                50

Enter the array Length [0 to quit]: 3200
            Bubble Sort       QuickSort
Length      3200              320000
Time        90                110

Enter the array Length [0 to quit]: 6400
            Bubble Sort       QuickSort
Length      6400              640000
Time        290               211

Enter the array Length [0 to quit]: 0

C:\Javafiles>
```

The user enters the size of the array of integers. The program then performs these actions:

1. Loads two arrays with randomly generated integers ranging from 0 to 100,000. One array is of the size specified by the user, and the other array is 100 times that size.

2. Runs the bubble sort algorithm on the smaller array and the quicksort algorithm on the larger array, and records the running times of each sort in milliseconds.

3. Displays the array sizes and run times for each sort in labeled columns.

Design

The bubble sort and quicksort algorithms have already been presented in this text. There are two other primary tasks to consider:

1. Load an array with randomly generated numbers.

2. Obtain the run time of a sort.

We accomplish the first task by using an instance of the `Random` class to generate the integer assigned to each cell in an array.

We accomplish the second task by using Java's `Date` class, as defined in the package `java.util`. When the program creates a new instance of `Date`, this object contains the current date down to the nearest millisecond, on the computer's clock. Thus, one can record the date at the beginning and end of any process by creating two `Date` objects, as follows:

```
Date d1 = new Date();   // Record the date at the start of a process.
<run any process>
Date d2 = new Date();   // Record the date at the end of a process.
```

To obtain the elapsed time between these two dates, one can use the `Date` instance method `getTime()`. This method returns the number of milliseconds from January 1, 1970, 00:00:00 GMT until the given date. Thus, the elapsed time in milliseconds for the example process can be computed as follows:

```
long elapsedTime = d2.getTime() - d1.getTime();
```

Implementation

To obtain the neatly formatted output shown in Figure 12-24, it is convenient to use the `printf` method as explained in Chapter 7. Following is the code:

```java
// 12.1 Case Study: Compare two sort algorithms

import java.util.*;

public class ComparingSortAlgorithms {

    public static void main(String[] args){
        Random gen = new Random();
        Scanner reader = new Scanner(System.in);
        while(true){
            System.out.print("Enter the array Length [0 to quit]: ");
            int arrayLength = reader.nextInt();
            if (arrayLength <= 0)
                break;
            // Instantiate two arrays,
            // one of this length and the other a 100 times longer.
            int[] a1 = new int[arrayLength];
            int[] a2 = new int[arrayLength * 100];

            // Initialize the first array
            for (int i = 0; i < a1.length; i++)
                a1[i] = gen.nextInt(100001);
            // Random numbers between 0 and 100,000

            // Initialize the second array
            for (int i = 0; i < a2.length; i++)
                a2[i] = gen.nextInt(100001);

            // Time bubble sort
            Date d1 = new Date();
```

```java
            bubbleSort (a1);
            Date d2 = new Date();
            long elapsedTime1 = d2.getTime() - d1.getTime();

            // Time quicksort
            d1 = new Date();
            quickSort (a2, 0, a2.length - 1);
            d2 = new Date();
            long elapsedTime2 = (d2.getTime() - d1.getTime());

            // Display results in pretty format
            System.out.printf("         %12s %14s%n", "Bubble Sort",
                            "QuickSort");
            System.out.printf("Length %8d %16d%n",   arrayLength,   arrayLength
                            * 100);
            System.out.printf("Time    %8d %16d%n%n", elapsedTime1,
    elapsedTime2);
        }
    }

    private static void bubbleSort (int[] a){
        for (int i = 0; i < a.length - 1; i++){
            for (int j = i + 1; j < a.length; j++){
                if (a[i] > a[j]){
                    int temp = a[i];
                    a[i] = a[j];
                    a[j] = temp;
                }
            }
        }
    }

    private static void quickSort (int[] a, int left, int right){
        if (left >= right) return;
        int i = left;
        int j = right;
        int pivotValue = a[(left + right)/2];   // Pivot is at midpoint
        while (i < j){
            while (a[i] < pivotValue) i++;
            while (pivotValue < a[j]) j—;
            if (i <= j){
                int temp = a[i];
                a[i] = a[j];
                a[j] = temp;
                i++;
                j--;
            }
        }
        quickSort (a, left, j);
        quickSort (a, i, right);
    }
}
```

12.6 Graphics and GUIs: Drawing Recursive Patterns

Recursive patterns have played an important role in modern mathematics, art, and the study of nature. In this section, we show how to generate and visualize some recursive patterns that are present in fractals and abstract art. But first we introduce another GUI control, the slider, which is used in our examples.

Sliders

A slider is a GUI control that allows the user to select a value within a range of values. The slider tool appears as a knob that can be dragged from one value to another along a bar. The bar of values can be oriented vertically or horizontally. The slider is usually labeled with ticks that indicate the positions of discrete values (see Figure 12-25). Alternatively, the user can move the knob in either direction along the bar by pressing the keyboard's left or right cursor key.

FIGURE 12-25
A slider control

The following code segment creates a slider with a horizontal alignment, a range of values from 0 to 500, and an initially selected value of 250. It then sets the major tick spacing to 50 and makes the ticks visible.

```java
JSlider slider = new JSlider(SwingConstants.HORIZONTAL, 0, 500, 250);
slider.setMajorTickSpacing(50);
slider.setPaintTicks(true);
```

A slider also responds to the messages `getValue` and `setValue`, which examine and reset its current value, respectively.

When a user moves a slider's knob, the slider emits an event of type `ChangeEvent`. This event can be detected by a listener object that implements the method `stateChanged`. This method is specified in the `ChangeListener` interface. These resources are included in the package `javax.swing.event`. (Until now, all other events and listener resources have come from the package `java.awt.event`.) As usual, the programmer defines a listener class, instantiates it, and attaches this instance to the slider with the method `addChangeListener`.

Armed with this knowledge of sliders, let's modify the temperature conversion program of Section 7.6. In that version of the program, the user enters a Fahrenheit or Celsius value in the appropriate text field and clicks the appropriate button to convert from one type of measure to the other. In the new version, the user manipulates a slider along the Fahrenheit scale and simply observes the appropriate outputs in the two fields. The new user interface is shown in Figure 12-26.

FIGURE 12-26
User interface for the temperature conversion program

Following is the code for the revised view class, with explanatory comments. Note that Fahrenheit values are now integers and Celsius values are displayed with two figures of precision.

```java
// Example 12.4: Revised temperature conversion program
// that uses a slider to change degrees Fahrenheit and degrees Celsius

import javax.swing.*;
import java.awt.*;
import javax.swing.event.*;

public class GUIWindow extends JFrame{

    // >>>>>>> The model <<<<<<<<

    // Declare and intantiate the thermometer
    private Thermometer thermo = new Thermometer();

    // >>>>>>> The view <<<<<<<<

    // Declare and instantiate the window objects.
    private JLabel fahrLabel          = new JLabel("Degrees Fahrenheit");
    private JLabel celsiusLabel       = new JLabel("Degrees Celsius");
    private JTextField fahrField      = new JTextField("32.0");
    private JTextField celsiusField = new JTextField("0.0");
    // Create a slider with horizontal orientation, minimum value of -400,
    // maximum value of 400, and initially selected value of 32
    private JSlider slider = new JSlider(SwingConstants.HORIZONTAL, -400,
                                         400, 32);

    // Constructor
    public GUIWindow(){
        // Set up panels to organize widgets and
        // add them to the window
        JPanel dataPanel = new JPanel(new GridLayout(2, 2, 12, 6));
        dataPanel.add(fahrLabel);
        dataPanel.add(celsiusLabel);
        dataPanel.add(fahrField);
        dataPanel.add(celsiusField);
        // Single input control now is a slider
        slider.setMajorTickSpacing(50);
        slider.setPaintTicks(true);
        JPanel sliderPanel = new JPanel();
        sliderPanel.add(slider);
        Container container = getContentPane();
```

```
    container.add(dataPanel, BorderLayout.CENTER);
    container.add(sliderPanel, BorderLayout.SOUTH);
    // Attach a listener to the slider
    slider.addChangeListener(new SliderListener());
}

// >>>>>>> The controller <<<<<<<

// Single listener responds to slider movement
private class SliderListener implements ChangeListener{
    public void stateChanged(ChangeEvent e){
        int fahr = slider.getValue();              // Obtain slider's value
        fahrField.setText("" + fahr);              // Output Fahrenheit value
        thermo.setFahrenheit(fahr);                // Reset thermometer
        double celsius = thermo.getCelsius();      // Obtain Celsius value
        String str = String.format("%.2f", celsius); // Format to 2 places
        celsiusField.setText(str);                 // Output Celsius value
    }
}
}
```

Recursive Patterns in Abstract Art

Abstract art is a style of painting and sculpture that originated and flourished in Europe and the United States in the mid-20th century. One of its primary features was the use of lines, shapes, and colors to form patterns that made no attempt to represent objects in the physical world. These patterns perhaps expressed an idea, a feeling, or an emotion, but that was left to the viewer's interpretation.

The artist Piet Mondrian (1872–1944) developed a style of abstract painting that exhibited simple recursive patterns. For example, an "idealized" pattern from one of his paintings might look like that shown in Figure 12-27.

FIGURE 12-27

To generate such a pattern with a computer, an algorithm would begin by drawing a rectangle and then repeatedly draw two unequal subdivisions, as shown in Figure 12-28.

FIGURE 12-28
Generating Mondrian-like patterns

As you can see, the algorithm continues this process of subdivision for a number of levels, until an "aesthetically right moment" is reached. In this version, the algorithm appears to divide the current rectangle into portions representing one-third and two-thirds of its area, and it appears to alternate the subdivisions randomly between the horizontal and vertical axes.

Let's develop a simpler version of this algorithm that divides a rectangle along its vertical axis only. The algorithm starts with a given level and the coordinates of a rectangle's upper-left and lower-right corner points. If the level is greater than 0, the rectangle is drawn and the algorithm is run recursively twice to draw the subdivisions. The first recursive call receives the coordinates of one-third of the rectangle to the left and the second call receives the coordinates of the two-thirds of the rectangle to the right. Both calls receive a level that's one less than the current one. Eventually the level becomes 0 and the algorithm just returns. Here is a pseudocode for this algorithm:

```
mondrian(Graphics g, int x1, int y1, int x2, int y2, int level)
   if (level > 0)
      g.drawRect(x1, y1, x2 - x1, y2 - y1)
      mondrian(g, x1, y1, (x2 - x1) / 3 + x1, y2, level - 1)
      mondrian(g, (x2 - x1) / 3 + x1, y1, x2, y2, level - 1)
```

We now develop a graphics program that allows the user to display Mondrian-like patterns of different levels of detail. The user interface consists of a window with a drawing area and a slider (See Figure 12-29).

FIGURE 12-29
User interface for the Mondrian painting program

The slider allows the user to select levels from 0 to 10. Level 1 produces a simple rectangle at the bounds of the panel, level 2 subdivides the single rectangle, level 3 divides these results, and so on. Here is the code for the main graphics window class:

```java
// Example 12.5: Main window for drawing recursive patterns

import javax.swing.*;
import java.awt.*;
import javax.swing.event.*;

public class GUIWindow extends JFrame{

    // Create a slider with horizontal orientation, minimum value of 0,
    // maximum value of 10, and initially selected value of 0
    private JSlider slider = new JSlider(SwingConstants. HORIZONTAL,
                                         0, 10, 0);
    private ColorPanel panel = new ColorPanel(Color.white);
    // Track the current value of the slider for state changes
    private int level = 0;

    public GUIWindow(){
        // Add ticks to the slider and show them
        slider.setMajorTickSpacing(1);
        slider.setPaintTicks(true);
        JPanel sliderPanel = new JPanel();
        sliderPanel.add(slider);
        Container container = getContentPane();
        container.add(panel, BorderLayout.CENTER);
        container.add(sliderPanel, BorderLayout.SOUTH);
        // Attach a listener to the slider
        slider.addChangeListener(new SliderListener());
    }

    // >>>>>>> The controller <<<<<<<<

    private class SliderListener implements ChangeListener{
        public void stateChanged(ChangeEvent e){
            int value = slider.getValue();          // Obtain slider's value
            if (value != level){                    // Check for change in value
                level = value;                      // Reset level if changed
                panel.setLevel(level);              // Draw a new picture
            }
        }
    }
}
```

Note that the GUIWindow class maintains an extra instance variable named level. This variable tracks the current value of the slider. The reason we need this extra variable is that a slider can emit change events even if its value doesn't change. We don't want to set the panel's level and draw a new picture each time a change event occurs but only when the change event results in a change of the slider's value. The method stateChanged handles this restriction by examining and updating level if the slider's value has changed since the last event.

The ColorPanel class implements our recursive algorithm to draw the rectangles and also uses a random number to choose whether to subdivide them along the horizontal or vertical axis.

Further refinements, including the addition of color, are left as exercises. Here is the code for ColorPanel:

```java
// Example 12.5: Panel to draw Mondrian-like paintings

import javax.swing.*;
import java.awt.*;
import java.util.Random;

public class ColorPanel extends JPanel{

    private int level;
    private Random gen;

    public ColorPanel(Color backColor){
        setBackground(backColor);
        setPreferredSize(new Dimension(300, 200));
        level = 0;
        gen = new Random();
    }

    public void setLevel(int newLevel){
        level = newLevel;
        repaint();
    }

    public void paintComponent (Graphics g){
        super.paintComponent(g);
        mondrian(g, 0, 0, getWidth(), getHeight(), level);
    }

    private void mondrian(Graphics g, int x1, int y1, int x2, int y2,
                          int level){
        if (level > 0){
            g.drawRect(x1, y1, x2 - x1, y2 - y1);
            int vertical = gen.nextInt(2) // Decide whether to split vertically
            if (vertical == 0){            // or horizontally.
                mondrian(g, x1, y1, (x2 - x1) / 3 + x1, y2, level - 1);
                mondrian(g, (x2 - x1) / 3 + x1, y1, x2, y2, level - 1);
            }
            else{
                mondrian(g, x1, y1, x2, (y2 - y1) / 3 + y1, level - 1);
                mondrian(g, x1, (y2 - y1) / 3 + y1, x2, y2, level - 1);

            }
        }
    }
}
```

Recursive Patterns in Fractals

Fractals are highly repetitive or recursive patterns. A *fractal object* appears geometric, yet it cannot be described with ordinary Euclidean geometry. Strangely, a fractal curve is not one-dimensional, and a fractal surface is not two-dimensional. Instead, every fractal shape has its own fractal dimension.

An ordinary curve has a precise finite length between any two points. By contrast, a fractal curve has an indefinite length between any two points. The apparent length depends on the level of detail considered. As we zoom in on a segment of a fractal curve, we can see more and more details, and its length appears greater and greater. Consider a coastline. Seen from a distance, it has many wiggles but a discernible length. Now put a piece of the coastline under magnification. It has many similar wiggles, and the discernible length increases. Self-similarity under magnification is the defining characteristic of fractals and is seen in the shapes of mountains, the branching patterns of tree limbs, and many other natural objects.

One example of a fractal curve is a *c-curve*. Figure 12-30 shows c-curves of the first seven degrees. The level-0 c-curve is a simple line segment. The level-1 c-curve replaces the level-0 c-curve with two smaller level-0 c-curves meeting at right angles. The level-2 c-curve does the same thing for each of the two line segments in the level-1 c-curve. This pattern of subdivision can continue indefinitely.

FIGURE 12-30
The first seven degrees of the c-curve

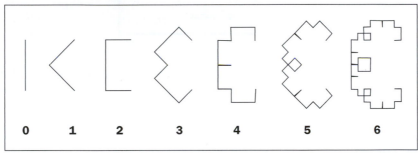

0　　1　　2　　3　　4　　5　　6

Let's develop an algorithm to draw an *n*-level c-curve. The algorithm receives a graphics object, the current level, and the endpoints of a line segment as parameters. At level 0, the algorithm draws a simple line segment. A level *n* c-curve consists of two level *n* − 1 c-curves constructed as follows:

- Let xm be (x1 + x2 + y1 − y2) / 2.

- Let ym be (x2 + y1 + y2 − x1) / 2.

- The first level *n* − 1 c-curve uses the line segment (*x1, y1*), (*xm, ym*), and level *n* − 1, so we recur with these parameters.

- The second level *n* − 1 c-curve uses the line segment (*xm, ym*), (*x2, y2*), and level *n* − 1, so we recur with these parameters.

In effect, as we showed in Figure 12-30, we replace each line segment by two shorter ones that meet at right angles. Here is the pseudocode for the algorithm:

```
cCurve (Graphics g, int x1, int y1, int x2, int y2, int level)
   if (level == 0)
        g.drawLine (x1, y1, x2, y2)
   else
      set xm to (x1 + x2 + y1 - y2) / 2
      set ym to (x2 + y1 + y2 - x1) / 2
      cCurve (g, x1, y1, xm, ym, level - 1)
      cCurve (g, xm, ym, x2, y2, level - 1)
```

The user interface of a program to draw c-curves, as shown in Figure 12-31, is the same one used in the abstract art drawing program. The user adjusts the level by dragging or clicking on the slider. The initial window displays a c-curve of level 0. The endpoints of this line segment are (150, 50) and (150, 150). This line segment is a good starting point for higher-degree curves, all of which fit nicely within the initial window boundaries.

FIGURE 12-31
User interface for the c-curve program

The following code shows the implementation of the class `ColorPanel` for drawing c-curves:

```java
// Example 12.6: Panel to draw c-curves

import javax.swing.*;
import java.awt.*;
import java.util.Random;

public class ColorPanel extends JPanel{

    private int level;

    public ColorPanel(Color backColor){
        setBackground(backColor);
        setPreferredSize(new Dimension(300, 200));
        level = 0;
    }

    public void setLevel(int newLevel){
        level = newLevel;
        repaint();
    }

    public void paintComponent (Graphics g){
        super.paintComponent(g);
        cCurve(g, 150, 50, 150, 150, level);
    }

    private void cCurve (Graphics g, int x1, int y1, int x2, int y2,
                         int level){
        if (level == 0)
            g.drawLine (x1, y1, x2, y2);
```

```
        else{
            int xm = (x1 + x2 + y1 - y2) / 2;
            int ym = (x2 + y1 + y2 - x1) / 2;
            cCurve (g, x1, y1, xm, ym, level - 1);
            cCurve (g, xm, ym, x2, y2, level - 1);
        }
    }
}
```

*E*XERCISE 12.6

1. List how many calls of the `cCurve` method are produced when the initial level is 2, 4, and 8, and give an estimate of the complexity of the algorithm using big-O notation.

2. The `mondrian` method always places the smaller rectangle at the top or the left of a subdivision. Explain how you would modify the method so that it will place the smaller rectangle randomly.

Design, Testing, and Debugging Hints

■ When designing a recursive method, be sure that

1. The method has a well-defined stopping state.

2. The method has a recursive step that changes the size of the data, so that the stopping state will eventually be reached.

■ Recursive methods can be easier to write correctly than the equivalent iterative methods.

■ More efficient code is usually more complex than less efficient code. Thus, it may be harder to write more efficient code correctly than less efficient code. Before trying to make your code more efficient, you should demonstrate through analysis that the proposed improvement is really significant (for example, you will get O($n \log n$) behavior rather than O(n^2) behavior).

SUMMARY

In this chapter, you learned:

■ A recursive method is a method that calls itself to solve a problem.

■ Recursive solutions have one or more base cases or termination conditions that return a simple value or `void`. They also have one or more recursive steps that receive a smaller instance of the problem as a parameter.

■ Some recursive methods also combine the results of earlier calls to produce a complete solution.

■ The run-time behavior of an algorithm can be expressed in terms of big-O notation. This notation shows approximately how the work of the algorithm grows as a function of its problem size.

- There are different orders of complexity, such as constant, linear, quadratic, and exponential.

- Through complexity analysis and clever design, the order of complexity of an algorithm can be reduced to produce a much more efficient algorithm.

- The quicksort is a sort algorithm that uses recursion and can perform much more efficiently than selection sort, bubble sort, or insertion sort.

VOCABULARY *Review*

Define the following terms:		
Activation record	Infinite recursion	Recursive step
Big-O notation	Iterative process	Stack
Binary search algorithm	Merge sort	Stack overflow error
Call stack	Quicksort	Stopping state
Complexity analysis	Recursive method	Tail-recursive

REVIEW *Questions*

FILL IN THE BLANK

Complete the following sentences by writing the correct word or words in the blanks provided.

1. The _____ of a recursive algorithm is the part in which a problem is solved directly, without further recursion.

2. The _____ of a recursive algorithm is the part in which the problem is reduced in size.

3. The memory of a computer is formatted into a large _____ to support recursive method calls.

4. The memory for each recursive method call is organized in a group of cells called a(n) _____.

5. The type of error in a recursive algorithm that causes it to run forever is called a(n) _____.

6. When a recursive method does not stop, a(n) _____ error occurs at run time.

7. The linear, quadratic, and logarithmic orders of complexity are expressed as _____, _____, and _____ using big-O notation.

8. The bubble sort algorithm has a run-time complexity of _____ in the best case and _____ in the worst case.

9. The quicksort algorithm has a run-time complexity of _____ in the best case and _____ in the worst case.

PROJECTS

Some of the projects ask you to implement a method and test it in a `Tester` program. Be sure that the method is defined as a `static` method; otherwise, you will get a syntax error.

PROJECT 12-1

Use a `Tester` program to implement and test a recursive method to compute the greatest common divisor (gcd) of two integers. The recursive definition of `gcd` is

```
gcd(a, b) = b, when a = 0
gcd(a, b) = gcd(b, a % b), when a > 0
```

PROJECT 12-2

Write a recursive method that returns a string with the characters in reverse order and test the method with a `Tester` program. The string and the index position should be parameters. If the position is less than the string's length, recurse with the rest of the string after this position and return the result of appending the character at this position to the result. Otherwise, return the empty string.

PROJECT 12-3

Design, implement, and test a recursive method that expects a positive integer parameter and returns a string representing that integer with commas in the appropriate places. The method might be called as follows:

```
String formattedInt = insertCommas(1000000);  // Returns "1,000,000"
```

(*Hint*: Recurse by repeated division and build the string by concatenating after each recursive call.)

PROJECT 12-4

The phrase "*n* choose *k*" is used to refer to the number of ways in which we can choose *k* objects from a set of *n* objects, where *n* >= *k* >= 0. For example, 52 choose 13 would express the number of possible hands that could be dealt in the game of bridge. Write a program that takes the values of *n* and *k* as inputs and displays as output the value *n* choose *k*. Your program should define a recursive method, `nChooseK(n, k)`, that calculates and returns the result. (*Hint*: We can partition the selections of *k* objects from *n* objects as the groups of *k* objects that come from *n* − 1 objects and the groups of *k* objects that include the *n*th object in addition to the groups of *k* − 1 objects chosen from among *n* − 1 objects.) If you test the program with *n* = 52 and *k* = 13, you should be prepared to wait quite a while for the solution!

PROJECT 12-5

Modify the case study of this chapter so that it counts comparison and exchange operations in both sort algorithms and displays these statistics as well. Run the program with two array sizes and make a prediction on the number of comparisons, exchanges, and run times for a third size.

PROJECT 12-6

Write a tester program to help assess the efficiency of the Towers of Hanoi program. This program should be similar to the one developed for the Fibonacci method.

PROJECT 12-7

Write a tester program to help assess the efficiency of the Many Queens program. This program should be similar to the one developed for the Fibonacci method.

PROJECT 12-8

Modify the program that draws Mondrian-like paintings so that it fills each rectangle with a randomly generated color.

CRITICAL *Thinking*

Jill is trying to decide whether to use a recursive algorithm or an iterative algorithm to solve a problem. Explain to her the costs and benefits of using one method or the other.

ARRAYS, RECURSION, AND COMPLEXITY

REVIEW Questions

TRUE/FALSE

Circle T if the statement is true or F if it is false.

T   F   **1.**   In Java, an array is an ordered collection of methods.

T   F   **2.**   Because arrays are objects, two variables can refer to the same array.

T   F   **3.**   The length of a Java array is fixed at compile time.

T   F   **4.**   One responsibility of the view portion of a program is to instantiate and arrange window objects.

T   F   **5.**   Static variables are associated with a class, not with its instances.

T   F   **6.**   Subclasses can see both public and private names declared in their parent classes.

T   F   **7.**   If you need to use the cast operator, remember that you never cast down, only cast up.

T   F   **8.**   A linear search runs more efficiently than a binary search.

T   F   **9.**   Sorting methods generally cannot perform in better than $O(n^2)$ run time.

T   F   **10.**   Loops are always preferable to recursive methods for solving problems.

FILL IN THE BLANK

Complete the following sentences by writing the correct word or words in the blanks provided.

1.   A(n) _____ is a collection of similar items or elements that are ordered by position.

2.   An item's position within an array is called its _____ or _____.

3.   Two arrays in which the corresponding elements are related are called _____ arrays.

4.   The number of elements currently stored and used within an array is called its _____ size.

5.   Classes that are never instantiated are called _____.

6.   Java organizes classes in a(n) _____.

7.   The toString message, which is understood by every object, no matter which class it belongs to, is a good example of _____.

8. A search method that repeatedly visits the midpoint of an array is called a(n) _____ search.

9. A sorting method that repeatedly moves elements around a pivot element is called a(n) _____.

10. Recursive methods have two parts, the _____ and the _____.

WRITTEN QUESTIONS

Write a brief answer to each of the following questions.

1. Write statements for the following items that declare array variables and assign the appropriate array objects to them.
   A. `intNumbers`, an array of 5 integers

   B. `realNumbers`, an array of 100 real numbers

   C. `bools`, an array of 10 Booleans

   D. `words`, an array of 20 strings

2. Write a `for` loop that initializes an array of 10 integers to the first 10 positive integers.

3. Repeat question 2, but use an initializer list.

4. There are several ways in which methods in a subclass can be related to methods in its superclass. Describe at least two of these.

5. Explain why one would use `static` variables and `static` methods.

PROJECTS

PROJECT 1

Write a program that takes 10 floating-point numbers as inputs. The program then displays the average of the numbers followed by all of the numbers that are greater than the average. As part of your design, write a method that takes an array of doubles as a parameter and returns the average of the data in the array.

PROJECT 2

Write a program to keep statistics for a basketball team consisting of 12 players. Statistics for each player should include shots attempted, shots made, and shooting percentage; free throws attempted, free throws made, and free throw percentage; offensive rebounds and defensive rebounds; assists; turnovers; and total points. Place these data in parallel arrays. Appropriate team totals should be listed as part of the output.

PROJECT 3

Modify the program of Project 2 so that it uses a two-dimensional array instead of the parallel arrays for the statistics.

PROJECT 4

A summation method returns the sum of the numbers from a lower bound to an upper bound. Write a static recursive method for summations and run it with a `tester` program that displays the values of the parameters on each call and the returned value on each call.

PROJECT 5

Write a `static` method that builds a sorted array list from a randomly ordered array list. The method should throw an exception if the parameter's elements are not `Comparable` objects. Test the method in a `tester` program.

CRITICAL *Thinking*

A bank provides several kinds of accounts, among them checking accounts and saving accounts. Design a simple banking system data model that represents these accounts. Be sure to make use of abstract classes, inheritance, polymorphism, and encapsulation. The result of your work should be a set of class summary boxes for the data model of the banking system.

USING ABSTRACT DATA TYPES

OBJECT-ORIENTED ANALYSIS AND DESIGN

In preceding chapters, we learned Java's fundamental mechanisms for working with classes. We have written many programs that use classes, and we have seen how classes are combined to solve problems. We have not, however, addressed the larger question of how to take a significant problem and come up with a system of interacting classes that implement a solution. We will now show you how this is done. We do not expect you to become proficient users of the processes described. Proficiency will come in later courses devoted to software development techniques and not in this course, which emphasizes fundamental programming concepts and Java's core syntax. As you read the chapter, you will see how an experienced programmer chooses classes, develops class hierarchies, and determines the relationships and interactions between classes. Try not to get lost in the details. By the end of the chapter you will have a deeper understanding of how developers think in an object-oriented way about problem solving.

Much of the chapter is organized around a case study based on a computerized adventure game. Case studies throughout this book have presented programming in terms of a software development process consisting of request, analysis, design, and implementation. In this chapter, we explore analysis and design in more detail. There are many methodologies for doing object-oriented analysis and design. These methodologies have two components—a step-by-step process that you follow from request through implementation and various graphical schemes for representing analysis and design decisions. The dominant graphical scheme at this time, and the one we utilize, is called the *Unified Modeling Language (UML)*. Using UML, we show how to think in an object-oriented way about problem solving without becoming enmeshed in too many technical details. Throughout, our emphasis is on building an intuitive understanding of how objects work together to accomplish a task rather than on mastering all the details of the software development process or the formalities of UML.

For an excellent introduction to the Unified Modeling Language see *UML Distilled, Third Edition* (Addison-Wesley, 2003), by Martin Fowler.

13.1 Introduction

To put the chapter in perspective, we begin with a little of the history of analysis and design. In the late 1960s and in the 1970s, the ever-increasing size and complexity of software systems led to what was then a revolution in software development techniques. The first structured programming languages were introduced, previously unstructured languages were enhanced to make them structured, and structured methodologies of analysis and design were discovered and popularized. Industry adopted these techniques as the only rational way to develop systems that were becoming larger and more complex every day. Since then a second revolution has taken place. In the mid-1990s companies began using object-oriented languages and tools to develop most of their new applications. In addition, we have seen the introduction of object-oriented operating systems and object-oriented database systems. Overall, many of the software products and practices of the preceding 40 years have been replaced by a new generation of object-oriented ones.

From a student's perspective, object-oriented methodologies are appealing because they provide a single consistent model and methodology for dealing with the three major phases of software development—analysis, design, and implementation. The models used to illustrate small object-oriented programs are exactly the same as the one used to describe the decomposition of large problems. With object-oriented methodologies, there is no artificial break between programming-in-the-large and programming-in-the-small. The ideas of abstraction, encapsulation, and inheritance that are encountered when first learning an object-oriented language are used again when analyzing and designing large systems.

Analysis and design are at the heart of the software development process, and numerous techniques have been devised for assisting in the task of doing object-oriented analysis and design (OOA&D). These techniques have been grouped in various combinations to form the methodologies that are proclaimed in books and implemented in CASE (computer-aided software engineering) tools. At the moment, the leading graphical notation used in these methodologies is UML. Although the various methodologies have their proponents and detractors, they all share a common goal—to assist in creating and communicating the models that are the major products of analysis and design. Any methodology used iteratively, with intelligence and imagination, leads to ever-increasing insight into what a system ought to do and how it might do it. Thus we attempt to give you an overall feeling for how to decompose a system into classes without becoming overly concerned with the technical details of the particular methodology.

To experience the power and effectiveness of object-oriented analysis and design, we must tackle problems of considerable size and complexity. Unfortunately, most large problems that we could potentially use as examples suffer from one or more of the following defects:

1. We must acquire considerable domain expertise before understanding the problems. *Domain expertise* means knowledge of the field in which the problem occurs. For example, problems in the field of banking require knowledge of accounting and finance, among other fields.

2. The problems involve too many uninteresting and burdensome details.

3. Some dimensions of the problems are too easy, whereas others are too hard.

The first difficulty mentioned is particularly distressing because, without domain expertise, we cannot fully understand proposed solutions and cannot suggest alternatives. To overcome this problem, simplified versions of real problems are sometimes presented in textbooks such as this. In the authors' experience, however, this process of simplification results in problems that are unconvincing because they are overly artificial. Surprisingly, we have found that completely artificial problems—namely games—can be designed that are free of all of the drawbacks mentioned. In this chapter, we use a game of adventure, which we have created as our example.

13.2 Overview of Analysis and Design

The goal of analysis is to model what a system does. The goal of design is to model how it might do it. During analysis fundamental classes, interrelationships, and behavior are determined, and these are added to and refined during design as implementation decisions are made; however, we do not draw a clear line of demarcation between the two phases. Together we treat them as a continuum of activity that moves from the general to the specific, finishing with a description of a system that can be passed to programmers for coding.

Determining the major classes needed in a system is fairly straightforward. The nouns in the description of a problem point the way to an initial list of candidate classes and their attributes. Although classes are eventually organized into hierarchies, it is best not to do this too soon, but to wait until more insight is gained into the workings of a system.

Determining methods is more difficult. Verbs, to some extent, map into methods, but not with the same reliability as nouns into classes and attributes. A better approach to discovering methods is to examine the activities encompassed by a system. Some of these activities are immediately obvious from the description of the problem, and others become apparent when attempts are made at designing the user interface. Examining activities leads to an understanding of the patterns of communications that exist between the classes and thus to knowledge of each class's responsibilities and collaborators. Role-playing and a blackboard are useful props during this process, and the results are recorded using the diagramming conventions of UML. Describing the function and signature of each method completes analysis and design. The process is iterative and implementing prototypes can be very helpful. At any time during the process there can be new insights that lead to changes in work already completed.

Two subtleties of this process must be understood. First and foremost, there is no single correct realization of a system. There are many different combinations of classes, responsibilities, and collaborations that work well together and many more that work badly. Good combinations involve simpler patterns of communications than bad combinations because they are modified more easily and responsibilities are distributed more evenly. An analogy helps us to understand this. Consider a corporation. In one style of management, a company's president looks over every employee's shoulder, telling him what to do and when to do it. But a company operates much more effectively if the employees understand the objectives of the company and their roles in achieving them and are then allowed to make their own decisions, communicating with each other as necessary. Too often beginners tended to create systems that mirror the first style of management.

A second subtlety, and one that is more difficult to grasp, is the difference between the intrinsic attributes of a class and those that are added in order to support a particular pattern of communications. For instance, in a library system, we might discover during analysis that

- Author and title are intrinsic attributes of books.

- It is essential to keep track of which books are checked out to which patrons.

During design, after considering the various activities that involve books and patrons, we must decide how to implement the second requirement. One possibility is to add the nonintrinsic attribute *patron* to *book*, but there are others. The final choice depends on implementation considerations and not on any intrinsic characteristics of books or patrons.

13.3 Request

We are now ready to consider the chapter's extended case study. We begin as usual with a request from a hypothetical customer. We are asked to implement an adventure game whose broad outline is described as follows:

Imagine a world of many places connected to each other by paths (Figure 13-1 shows a corner of such a world). Through this world a heroine wanders, collecting treasures and weapons. Dragons, giants, and other monsters guard the items, so the heroine must defeat these foes in battle before picking up the items. A battle's outcome depends on luck, the relative strength of the contestants, and the power of their weapons. Upon death an entity drops all its items, and the heroine can then pick up these items. As she moves from place to place, the heroine constructs a map of the portion of the world she has seen so far. She also keeps a diary in which she records the actions she performs during the game (moving, picking up things, fighting battles).

FIGURE 13-1
A corner of an adventure world near the entrance to a giant's castle

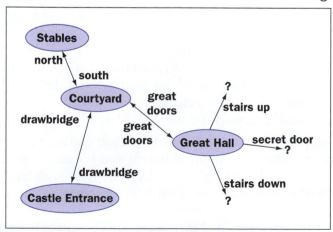

As Figure 13-1 shows, the heroine can pass between the Great Hall and the Courtyard by going through the great doors. From the Courtyard, going north leads to the Stables, and from the Stables, going south returns to the Courtyard. The heroine has not finished exploring the paths from the Great Hall. Stairs lead up and down, and there is a secret door behind a tapestry, but the destination of these paths is currently unknown.

An obvious advantage of this problem is that we are all domain experts from the outset. The world of the game is imaginary and is easy to understand. The game deals with familiar situations and has simple rules. Moving, picking up things, and dropping them are everyday activities. Battles with giants and ogres are less common, fortunately, but easy to picture. Another advantage is that the game is free of the numerous tedious details that dominate real-world problems of similar complexity.

The game can be expanded in many ways, both minor and major. Limiting the heroine's carrying capacity is an example of a minor modification. Adding a store where the heroine can buy and sell weapons and treasures is slightly more difficult. Allowing several users, each controlling a separate heroine, to enter the game world simultaneously leads to a networked-based design and extensive modifications suited to a more advanced computer science course.

13.4 Analysis

Although the description of the game is simple, it involves a surprising number of elements, and the subsequent system is fairly complex. A smaller example would not allow us to illustrate important features of object-oriented systems development; however, the complexity has been carefully chosen to yield an interesting hierarchy of classes. There are numerous associations between the classes, and many of the activities involve several classes simultaneously. Working with this problem, we see that objects are of many different sorts—people, places, things, events, and abstractions in the problem domain. In addition, objects manage computer resources and interfaces. Some objects, such as treasures, are little more than repositories for data and consist of only a few attributes and the methods needed to access them. Other objects, such as the entities, are complex. They implement methods that support the activities of the game (moving from place to place, fighting battles, picking up items), and their internal states are constantly changing.

The initial portion of the analysis is not object-oriented and is the same regardless of the language or methodology used to implement the system. It consists of clarifying the customer's request and designing the interfaces. Once that has been done, we can undertake the object-oriented aspect of the process and determine an appropriate decomposition of the software into a system of cooperating classes.

Use case diagrams, another feature of UML, are frequently used at this stage; however, they are beyond the scope of this book and would add little, if anything, to the present discussion.

Additional Facts Concerning the Game

During our interviews with the customer who requested the software, we learn the following additional details of the game:

- The object of the game is for the heroine, under the user's control, to collect 100 units of treasure as quickly as possible and return to the entrance without losing all of her nine lives.

- Each treasure is worth some number of units.

- At the start of the game, the user does not know how many treasures there are in the world.

- There are many places, but no unreachable ones. There may be places from which there is no return, however, such as the bottom of a deep well.

- Each path connects two places, but some paths are one-way only, such as a wild raft ride down dangerous rapids.

- The heroine passes instantly from place to place by following the paths, and no game actions occur on the paths.

- Every place, path, entity, weapon, and treasure has a name and description.

- Until the heroine follows a path, she does not know where it leads, and once she does know, she adds the destination to her map. Figure 13-1 shows the heroine's map after she has explored just a portion of a giant's castle. In this illustration, the entrance to the world is assumed to start at the entrance to the castle.

- The structure of an adventure world is stored in a text file, and at the beginning of a game, the user selects one of these files. At any time during a game, the user can save the current state of the game and exit.

- At any given moment, an item (treasure or weapon) is either carried by an entity or is lying around in some place. Items are never located on paths.

- The rules of battle are slightly convoluted. When the user enters a place guarded by one or more monsters, she can avoid a battle simply by leaving the place. If the user decides to fight, she/he selects a foe. At that point, the numerical strength of the heroine is multiplied by one plus the numerical force of all her weapons (strength * (1 + force of all weapons)). The resulting number is multiplied by a random number between 1 and 10, representing luck, to give what we call the *battle number*. The same thing is done for the foe with whom she is fighting. The winner is whoever has the larger battle number. If the heroine loses, she forfeits one of her nine lives, and her strength is decremented by one. If she loses her ninth life, the game is over. If there is a draw, there are no changes. If the monster loses, it drops all of its items (weapons and treasures) and dies, and the heroine's strength is incremented by one. The user is able to view all relevant information about the heroine's and monster's states before choosing to fight a battle.

- The entries in the heroine's diary vary depending on the type of event recorded:
  - *Move*—Time, place, path, destination
  - *Pickup*—Time, place, item
  - *Battle*—Time, place, monster, heroine's battle number, monster's battle number

- The time indicates the elapsed time in seconds since the beginning of the game. In addition, the diary indicates the number of lives the heroine has remaining, her strength, and the total force of all her weapons.

The User Interface

The overall requirement is to design an interactive program that allows a user to enter the world we have described and to control the actions of the heroine. The interface must display names and descriptions of all things in the game, as well as the heroine's map and diary. Games of this sort usually involve animated graphics. A graphical user interface is developed in the final section of this chapter. For now, we settle for a menu-driven, terminal-based interface. Some menus for this interface are shown in Figure 13-2.

FIGURE 13-2
Some menus in the user interface for the game

Main Menu	File Menu	Reports Menu	Paths
1: File Menu	1: Open	1: Display Map	1: Drawbridge
2: Reports Menu	2: Save	2: Display Diary	2: South
3: Paths	3: Exit this menu	3: Display Location	3: Great Doors
4: Entities		4: Exit this menu	4: Exit this menu
5: Place Items			
6: Exit this menu			
Entities	Place Items	Purse	
1: Sue	1: Purse	1: Display purse	
2: Aarf	2: Sword	2: Pick up Purse	
3: Hagarth	3: Exit this menu	3: Exit this menu	
4: Exit this menu			

In the following paragraphs, we explain the workings of the user interface.

Overview

There are several menus. The File menu allows us to open and save the game. The Reports menu displays the heroine's map and diary and redisplays the current place's description. For simplicity, the program's three lists are also displayed as menus named Paths, Enitites, and Place Items. The five major menus are listed as items in a main menu displayed at program startup. All menus have an Exit This Menu option.

When the user selects an item from one of the three lists, a submenu appears with options to display information about that item or to run a command associated with it. When the heroine moves to a new location, picks up an item, or fights a battle, other information is displayed. We now explain these features in more detail.

Paths List

This is a list of all the paths leading from the current location. Selecting a path's name displays the path's submenu. Its options are Display and Move. Selecting Display prints the path's description. The path's description says nothing about the path's destination, which is discovered by following the path. The following statement is the description of the secret door:

```
This door looks little used.
```

Selecting Move causes the heroine to move along the path to its destination, and Control exits the submenu.

Entities List

This is a list of all the entities located in the current place. It includes the heroine and her foes. Selecting an entity displays its submenu with options to display, fight, or exit. For instance, Hagarth is described as follows:

Hagarth: A very giant of a giant

Strength: 10

Force of weapons: 20

Value of treasures: 10

Weapon Club: Shaped from a tree trunk Force: 10

Treasure Belt: Gold belt with diamond buckle Value: 10

Weapon Dagger: As large as a small sword Force: 10

Selecting **Fight** in a foe's submenu initiates a battle between the heroine and the foe. Selecting **Fight** in the heroine's submenu has no effect.

Place Items List

This is a list of all the items located in the current place. Select an item to see its submenu with the options Display and Pick Up. Selecting Pick Up causes the heroine to pick up the item.

File/Open Menu Item

This command prompts the user for a filename that is used to open a game file.

File/Save Menu Item

This command prompts the user for a filename that is used to save the current state of the game.

Reports/Map Menu Item

This command displays a map of the portion of the world explored so far (Figure 13-3).

FIGURE 13-3

The map and diary after the heroine has explored a portion of the world near the entrance

Map	Diary
Map of the world seen so far:	Diary of events.
Castle Entrance	TIME EVENT
Drawbridge to Courtyard	7 sec In Castle Entrance PICKUP the Ring.
Courtyard	18 sec MOVE from Castle Entrance and follow Drawbridge to Courtyard.
Drawbridge to ?	42 sec MOVE from Courtyard and follow Great Doors to Great Hall.
South to ?	72 sec In Great Hall BATTLE against Aarf with battle numbers of 660 to 220.
Great Doors to Great Hall	88 sec MOVE from Great Hall and follow Stairs Up to Turret.
Great Hall	92 sec MOVE from Turret and follow Stairs Down to Great Hall.
Great Doors to ?	
Stairs Up to Turret	
Stairs Down to ?	
Secret Door to ?	
Turret	
Stairs Down to Great Hall	

Reports/Diary Menu Item

This command displays a list of all the actions the heroine has performed to date (Figure 13-3).

Report/Current Location Menu Item

This command displays the name and description of the current place.

Format of the Game's Text Files

We now specify the structure of the text file that describes the adventure world. The structure of the file is the same for a new game and for one saved during play. We divide the file into labeled sections, and each section contains multiple lines. Figure 13-4 shows the structure. Clearly, a game file can be created or read using any standard text editor.

FIGURE 13-4
Structure of a game file

```
Time
   elapsedTime
Places
   name, "description"
   etc...
Paths
   name, "description", fromPlaceName, toPlaceName
   etc...
Hero
   name, strength, lives, placeName, "description"
Foes
   name, strength, placeName, "description"
   etc...
Treasures
   name, value, name of place or entity, "description"
   etc...
Weapons
   name, force, name of place or entity, "description"
   etc...
```

In the figure,

- Elapsed time indicates how long the game was in progress when saved. The elapsed time for a new game is zero. When a game is reloaded, time starts at the indicated elapsed time.

- Names of places, entities, and items are assumed to be unique. Names of paths are unique within a place.

- Because descriptions contain punctuation marks, they are enclosed in quotes.

- All paths are treated as if they are one-way only. Thus a two-way path is represented by a matching pair of one-way paths.

- The location of the heroine and foes is indicated by a place name.

- Treasures and weapons are located in a place or are carried by an entity. The name indicates which place an item can be found or which entity is carrying an item.

In Figure 13-4, we do not deal with the problem of how to represent the map and diary, but leave this as an exercise to be attempted later.

Finding the Classes

Developing an accurate description of the problem and designing the interface and file structure is time consuming and difficult, but there is no point in going further until this work is finished. If we make any mistakes, then all our subsequent work is affected adversely, and the longer mistakes go undetected, the more expensive they are to correct.

Assuming that we now understand the user requirements of the game, we are ready to take a first pass at decomposing the system into classes. In general, insights gained later in the process might lead to some changes in this decomposition, but that will not happen here. Our first step is to reread the extended description of the problem and extract the nouns. Some of these nouns represent classes and others represent attributes. We ignore synonyms, that is, different nouns that name the same thing. As mentioned earlier, classes are of many different types—people, places, events, things, and abstractions, plus interface and resource managers. Table 13-1 shows our initial list of classes.

TABLE 13-1
Initial list of classes

CATEGORY	CLASSES
People	Heroine, Foe
Places	GameWorld, Place, Path
Things	Treasure, Weapon
Abstractions	GameMap, Diary
Events	MoveEvent, BattleEvent, PickupEvent
Interface Management	GameView and various support classes
Resource Management	GameFile

We consider GameMap and Diary to be abstractions because we are interested in their content rather than their physical manifestation. The entries in the diary record events. The GameFile class will handle all the details of moving information in and out of the game file.

The problem description also contains many nouns that describe attributes. Examples include names of people, places, and things, strength of people, force of weapons, etc. We return to these attributes in more detail later.

Representing Relationships between Classes

Having identified the major classes, we now consider their interrelationships. Relationships between classes are usually divided into three categories: inheritance, aggregation, and other association. These are described in the following paragraphs.

Inheritance

This is the relationship between a class and its subclasses. It is also called the *is-a relationship*, as in "a circle *is-a* shape."

Aggregation

This is the relationship between a class and its constituent parts, if they also happen to be classes. It is also called the *has-a relationship*, as in "a boat *has-a* rudder."

Other Association

This category encompasses all other relationships and is called the *knows-a relationship*. In a problem description, these relationships might be recognized by verbs such as carries, eats, and rides and phrases such as "is next to."

Figure 13-5 shows how each of these relationships is represented in UML using what are called *class diagrams*.

FIGURE 13-5
How relationships are represented in UML

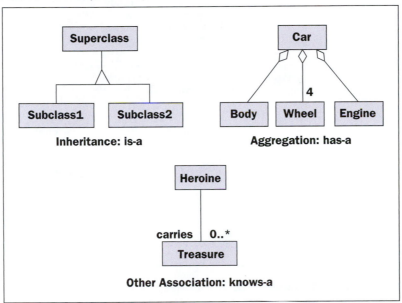

Knows-a associations are sometimes labeled with a word or phrase that describes the relationship. In *has-a* and *knows-a* relationships, the association between classes is assumed to be one-to-one. That is, one object of the first class is associated with one of the second, but UML includes special multiplicity indicators that can be used when this is not the case. These indicators are placed on the line joining two classes. The indicator pertains to the class to which it is closest. Table 13-2 shows a list of the possible indicators (*M* and *N* represent positive integers with $M < N$).

TABLE 13-2
UML multiplicity indicators

MULTIPLICITY INDICATOR	DESCRIPTION
M	Indicates exactly *M*
M..N	Indicates from *M* to *N*
M..*	Indicates *M* or more

Relationships between the Classes in the Game

We now have the tools to represent the relationships between the classes in the game. There are too many classes and relationships to include in a single diagram. We start with Figure 13-6. In this figure, we use the generic word `Entity` to represent the heroine and foes and `Item` to represent treasure and weapons.

FIGURE 13-6
Relationships between the game's principle classes

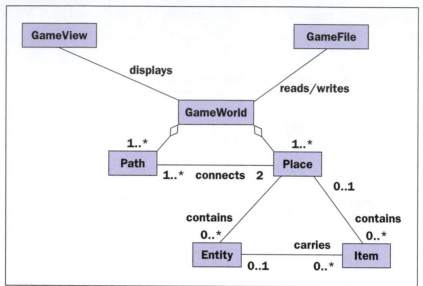

To paraphrase, the diagram says that

The `GameView` displays the `GameWorld`. The `GameFile` transfers the `GameWorld` to and from disk. The `GameWorld` is an aggregate of one or more (1..*) places and paths. Each path connects two places, and each place is connected to at least one other. An entity is located in a place, and an item is either located in a place or carried by an entity. A place contains zero or more (0..*) entities and items, and an entity carries zero or more items.

The introduction of `Entity` and `Item` in Figure 13-6 suggests that we add these classes to our system as abstract superclasses, with `Heroine` and `Foe` as subclasses of `Entity` and `Treasure` and `Weapon` as subclasses of `Item`. But we need not stop there. Many things in the game have a name and description, which suggests introducing the abstract superclass `NamedThing`. Figure 13-7 summarizes these observations. The classes `GameMap` and `Diary` are not part of the hierarchy, but are included in Figure 13-7 because the heroine carries them.

FIGURE 13-7
The NamedThing, Entity, and Item hierarchies

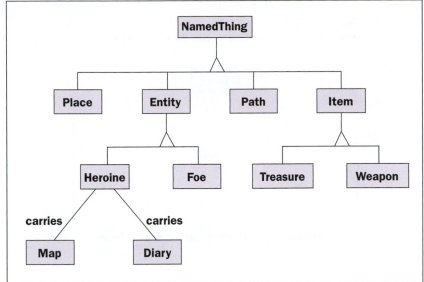

The principal advantage of creating class hierarchies is code sharing. The class NamedThing will include instance variables for name and description and instance methods for accessing them. These variables and methods are then accessible to all the subclasses of NamedThings. However, class hierarchies also have a disadvantage. Classes in a hierarchy become interdependent, and code changes higher up in a hierarchy can adversely affect classes lower in the hierarchy. If the logical relationship between the classes in a hierarchy is weak, these adverse effects are more likely to occur. In the present situation it seems reasonable to think of Heroine and Foe as types of Entity, so we do not expect unfavorable consequences later.

We can develop additional hierarchal relationships between the classes if we are willing to ignore our own advice about there being a logical relationship between the classes. For instance, in Figure 13-6, we see that Entity and Place are both associated with many instances of Item, and in the final implementation of the system both are likely to contain a list of items. Consequently, we could introduce an abstract superclass of Entity and Place called ThingWithItems, but doing so feels like a distortion of the game's inherent structure that would outweigh any benefit from code sharing.

We close this section by examining the relationship between the diary and the events it records. All the events have time and place in common, which suggests an Event class. In addition, each type of event (move, pickup, and battle) has its own unique data requirements, thus yielding the hierarchy shown in Figure 13-8.

FIGURE 13-8
The relationship between the `Diary` and `Event` classes

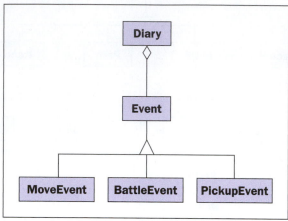

Assigning Responsibilities

Eventually, we must decide all the details concerning how classes interact. We need to determine completely and exactly who sends what messages to whom. As a first step in this process, we assign a set of responsibilities to each class.

We begin by rereading the problem description, looking for any hints indicating the responsibilities of the objects. In general terms, an object is responsible for remembering its internal state (instance variables) and for responding to messages sent to it by other objects (methods). Unfortunately, there are usually numerous different ways of partitioning the responsibilities among objects. But some ways will seem more natural and lead to simpler code than others. Just as nouns help identify classes and their attributes, verbs in a problem's description frequently indicate the methods that classes must implement. Sometimes it takes several iterations to assign responsibilities in what seems like a reasonable manner. Following the advice we gave earlier about distributing responsibilities among the classes rather than allowing any single class to assume a disproportionate role, we arrive at the distribution illustrated in Table 13-3.

TABLE 13-3
Distribution of class responsibilities

CLASS	RESPONSIBILITIES
`GameView`	Provides a terminal user interface to the game; communicates user-initiated commands to the `GameWorld`; obtains file names from the user; tells the `GameFile` to perform input and output operations
`GameWorld`	Knows the state of the game and makes this information available to the interface; responds to user-initiated commands; responds to messages from the `GameFile` during the process of transferring a game to and from a file
`GameFile`	Knows the structure of the text file used to store a game; on input, it reads a file and communicates the content to the `GameWorld`; on output, it asks the `GameWorld` for its contents and stores these contents in a file

TABLE 13-3 Continued
Distribution of class responsibilities

CLASS	RESPONSIBILITIES
NamedThing	Knows its name and description
Item	Same as NamedThing and can be associated with places and entities
Treasure	Same as Item and has a value
Weapon	Same as Item and has a force
Place	Same as NamedThing and can be associated with paths
Path	Same as NamedThing and can be associated with places
Entity	Same as NamedThing and can compute its battle number; knows its strength, the force of its weapons, and the value of its treasures
Heroine	Same as Entity and can move, pick up items, and initiate a battle against a foe; knows how many lives remain; updates her GameMap and Diary
Foe	Same as Entity, can respond to a blow from the heroine and can drop items when defeated
GameMap	Knows where the heroine has been and can display this information in a readable form
Diary	Knows the events initiated by the heroine and can display this information in a readable form
Event	There are three types of events; each entity knows how to record a particular type of event

That concludes our analysis. We now understand the problem thoroughly. We have designed an interface and a suitable file structure for the game. We know the classes, their relationships, and their major responsibilities.

EXERCISE 13.4

1. Does UML provide any support for describing user requirements? If so, what form does this support take?

2. How do we recognize classes and attributes from an informal description of user requirements?

3. Describe in English the meaning of the expression 0..1 from a UML class diagram.

4. Describe in English the meaning of the expression 0..* from a UML class diagram.

5. Explain the difference between aggregation (the *has-a* relationship) and inheritance (the *is-a* relationship) and give one example of each.

EXERCISE 13.4 Continued

6. Give an informal description in English of the relationships expressed by the following class diagram:

7. Draw a class diagram that illustrates the relationships among the classes in the following informal description: A library has many books and patrons and a patron can borrow up to three books.

8. Draw a class diagram that illustrates the relationships among the classes in the following informal description: A bank has many accounts. Accounts can be checking accounts, savings accounts, or credit accounts.

13.5 Interlude: Support Classes for Menu-Driven Programs

To support analysis, programmers frequently develop *prototypes* of a program's user interface. A prototype is a running program that displays enough of the functionality of a finished system to give users and developers a clear idea of its requirements. In this section, we develop a prototype for menu-driven user interfaces that can be used with our game program.

The Support Classes `CommandMenu` and `Command`

In Chapter 7 we discussed the basic structure of a menu-driven user interface. A menu consists of a list of numbered options. The program control for a menu consists of a loop that displays the menu, prompts for and accepts a number from the user, and runs the command associated with that number. For complex systems with many menus and command options, it will help to have some classes that support these features.

There are two primary types of actors in a menu-driven command system: the menu and its individual commands or options. We represent these in the classes `CommandMenu` and `Command`, respectively.

A `Command` object should be able to display itself as an option in a menu and should also be able to run a method when it is selected. Its interface is listed in Table 13-4.

TABLE 13-4
Methods of the `Command` class

METHOD	WHAT IT DOES
`Command(String name)`	Constructor
`boolean run()`	Executes code associated with the command
`String toString()`	Returns the command's name

The programmer uses the `Command` class by defining a specialized subclass with a particular command name and a `run()` method. For example, a command to display the value of π might be created and used as follows:

```
// Define a specialized command as a subclass
private class PIDisplayCommand extends Command{
    private PIDisplayCommand(){
        super("Display PI");
    }

    public boolean run(){
        System.out.println("Pi is " + Math.PI);
        return true;
    }
}
...
// Create and run the command without a menu
Command c = new PIDisplayCommand();
c.run();
```

Each subclass for a specialized command should include a constructor that runs `super` with the command's name and a `run()` method. As we see shortly, when this method returns `true`, the menu's command loop continues. When this method returns `false`, the menu's command loop quits.

A `CommandMenu` object manages a menu-driven command loop. This loop displays the menu's title and a numbered list of options, prompts for and accepts input from the user, and sends the `run()` message to commands when they are selected. The interface for the class `CommandMenu` is listed in Table 13-5.

TABLE 13-5
Methods of the `CommandMenu` class

METHOD	WHAT IT DOES
`CommandMenu(String title, Scanner s)`	Constructor
`void add(Command c)`	Adds a command to the menu
`void clear()`	Removes all commands from the menu
`boolean run()`	Executes the loop for the menu
`String toString()`	Returns the menu's title

The programmer instantiates a CommandMenu with a given title, adds individual Command objects to it, and then sends it the run() message to start its menu-driven loop. For example, the following code segment creates a command menu entitled **Math Constants**, adds an instance of PIDisplayCommand to it, and starts the menu's command loop:

```
CommandMenu menu = new CommandMenu("Math Constants");
menu.add(new PIDisplayCommand());
menu.run();
```

Here is a sample user interaction with this menu (user inputs are in boldface):

```
Math Constants
1: Display PI
2: Exit this menu
Enter a number [1-2]: 1
PI is 3.141592653589793
Math Constants
1: Display PI
2: Exit this menu
Enter a number [1-2]: 3
Try again
Math Constants
1: Display PI
2: Exit this menu
Enter a number [1-2]: 2
```

A command menu automatically numbers its options and adds an **Exit this menu** option before display. The command menu checks user inputs for format and range errors and recovers gracefully.

Because CommandMenu extends Command, it is possible to add command menus as items to other command menus, thus providing support for nested menus. We show this capability in an extended example that concludes this section.

The Implementation of Command and CommandMenu

The code for the classes Command and CommandMenu incorporates the ideas of inheritance and polymorphism introduced in Chapter 10. Because the responsibilities are nicely divided between the two classes, their implementation, which follows, is fairly simple:

```java
// Command.java: Represents a command
// Contains a menu item and requires a run() method

abstract public class Command{

    private String title;

    public Command(String s){
        title = s;
    }

    public String toString(){
        return title;
    }

    abstract public boolean run();
}


// CommandMenu.java: Represents a command menu
// Contains a list of commands and requires a run() method
```

```java
import java.util.ArrayList;
import java.util.Scanner;

public class CommandMenu extends Command{

    private ArrayList<Command> menu;
    private Scanner reader;

    public CommandMenu(String title, Scanner s){
        super(title);
        menu = new ArrayList<Command>();
        reader = s;
    }

    // Adds a command option to the menu
    public void add(Command c){
        menu.add(c);
    }

    // Removes all menu options
    public void clear(){
        menu.clear();
    }

    // Main loop for the menu
    public boolean run(){
        boolean continuing = true;
        while (continuing){
            displayMenu();
            int input = readCommand(1, menu.size() + 1);
            if (input == menu.size() + 1)
                break;
            continuing = menu.get(input - 1).run();
        }
        return true;
    }

    // Displays the menu's title
    // Prepends numbers to items and adds an exit option
    // before displaying them
    private void displayMenu(){
        System.out.println(toString());
        for (int i = 0; i < menu.size(); i++)
            System.out.println((i + 1) + ": " + menu.get(i));
        System.out.println((menu.size() + 1) + ": Exit this menu");
    }

    // Robust input of command numbers
    private int readCommand(int low, int high){
        System.out.print("Enter a number from " + low +
                         " to " + high + ": ");
```

```
        try{
            int input = reader.nextInt();
            if (input < low || input > high){
                System.out.println("The number must be between " +
                                    low + " and " + high);
                return readCommand(low, high);
            }else
                return input;
        }catch(Exception e){
            System.out.println("Input must be a number");
            return readCommand(low, high);
        }
    }
}
```

An Extended Example

To give an idea of the true power of the menu-driven support classes, we present an extended example. The program shows how to set up a main menu with standard About, File, and Edit options. The latter two options refer to nested menus. The Jump to Main option of the Edit menu causes this menu to exit. You'll have to hold your breath when you see the number of private classes in this code, but that's how a realistic menu-driven system is organized. Here is the code:

```
// Example 13.1: Tester program for a menu-driven command interface
// Tests basic menu options and nested menus

import java.util.Scanner;

public class TestMenu{

    public static void main(String[] args){
        new TestMenu();
    }

    public TestMenu(){
        // Create the scanner for all the menus
        Scanner reader = new Scanner(System.in);
        // Create the main menu
        CommandMenu mainMenu = new CommandMenu("Main Menu", reader);
        // Create and add an About option
        Command c0 = new AboutCommand();
        mainMenu.add(c0);
        // Create a File menu, its options, and add them to that menu
        CommandMenu fileMenu = new CommandMenu("File Menu", reader);
        Command c1 = new OpenCommand();
        Command c2 = new SaveCommand();
        fileMenu.add(c1);
        fileMenu.add(c2);
        // Create an Edit menu, its options, and add them to that menu
        CommandMenu editMenu = new CommandMenu("Edit Menu", reader);
        Command c3 = new CutCommand();
        Command c4 = new PasteCommand();
```

```java
        Command c5 = new JumpCommand();
        editMenu.add(c3);
        editMenu.add(c4);
        editMenu.add(c5);
        // Add the File and Edit menus to the main menu
        mainMenu.add(fileMenu);
        mainMenu.add(editMenu);
        // Run the main menu to accept commands
        mainMenu.run();
    }

    // Private classes for the basic menu options

    private class OpenCommand extends Command{

        private OpenCommand(){
            super("Open");
        }

        public boolean run(){
            System.out.println("Running open . . .");
            return true;
        }
    }

    private class SaveCommand extends Command{

        private SaveCommand(){
            super("Save");
        }

        public boolean run(){
            System.out.println("Running save . . .");
            return true;
        }
    }

    private class CutCommand extends Command{

        private CutCommand(){
            super("Cut");
        }

        public boolean run(){
            System.out.println("Running cut . . .");
            return true;
        }
    }
```

```java
private class PasteCommand extends Command{

    private PasteCommand(){
        super("Paste");
    }

    public boolean run(){
        System.out.println("Running paste . . .");
        return true;
    }
}

// This command will exit its caller's menu
private class JumpCommand extends Command{

    private JumpCommand(){
        super("Jump to Main");
    }

    public boolean run(){
        System.out.println("Jumping to Main . . .");
        return false;
    }
}

private class AboutCommand extends Command{

    private AboutCommand(){
        super("About");
    }

    public boolean run(){
        System.out.println("Running about . . .");
        return true;
    }
}
}
```

13.6 Design

Design is more exacting and technically difficult than analysis. It consists of devising the patterns of communication needed to support the game. In UML, this is done using *collaboration diagrams*. We proceed by identifying the game's principal activities and developing a pattern of communication to support each. In the present situation, activities are initiated at the user interface and correspond to selecting menu options and clicking and double-clicking on list items. In what follows, we investigate some typical activities in detail. Other activities are left as exercises for the interested reader.

Activity: Select a Path

We begin with one of the simplest activities. The user clicks on a path. The interface responds by displaying a description of the path. The description does not include information about where the path goes. That can be discovered only by commanding the heroine to move along the path. We present our implementation strategy in three forms. First, we write a narrative that describes the sequences of messages sent. Second, we summarize the narrative in a collaboration diagram. And third, we write pseudocode for the methods revealed in the previous two steps.

The Narrative

Before beginning, we must point out that narratives are often the result of experimentation. When the best solution is not obvious, the designer tries several different patterns of communication and picks the one that is simplest. Following then, is our narrative for the activity of selecting a path:

- When the user selects a path name, the program displays a submenu with options to display the path's description or move on it.

- When the user selects the display option, the program asks the GameWorld to get the path's name and description by sending it the message getPathString(pathName).

- The method getPathString in GameWorld asks the heroine for the current place by sending her the message getPlace. We assume that the GameWorld knows the heroine and the heroine always knows where she is located.

- Once the GameWorld knows the current place, it asks the place to get the path with the indicated name by sending the message getPath(pathName) to the place. We assume that a place has a list of all the paths leading from that place.

- The GameWorld now asks the path retrieved in the previous step for its name description by sending it the message toString. This description is then returned to the helper method in the GameView, where it is displayed in the terminal window.

The Collaboration Diagram

The collaboration diagram in Figure 13-9 shows a graphical representation of the narrative. The diagram is not able to capture all the nuances of the narrative, but it does provide an excellent overview. In the figure, rectangles represent objects of the indicated classes. The colons (:) are required. Arrows are labeled with the names of methods, and numbers indicate the sequence in which the methods are activated.

FIGURE 13-9
Collaboration diagram for the activity of selecting a path

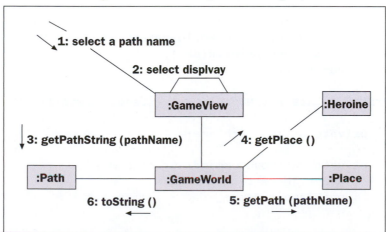

The Pseudocode

The narrative and the collaboration diagram provide an excellent basis for writing pseudocode (shown following) that further clarifies our intentions. As part of the pseudocode, we also list needed instance variables.

```
GameView    private GameWorld gameWorld;
            private CommandMenu paths;        // The menu of path names

            // Displays a description of the current place
            // and updates the paths menu with the info relating to
            // that place
            private void updateAllControls()
               // Update place description
               String str = gameWorld.getPlaceString();
               System.out.println(str);

               // Update the menus of paths, entities, and place items
               updatePaths(paths, gameWorld.getPathNames());
               updateEntities(entities, gameWorld.getEntityNames());
               updatePlaceItems(placesItems, gameWorld.getPlaceItemNames());

            // Resets the paths menu to the paths out of the current place
            private void updatePaths(CommandMenu paths, String[] names)
               paths.clear();
               for (String name : names)
                  CommandMenu menu = new CommandMenu(name, reader);
                  menu.add(new PathDisplayCommand(name));
                  menu.add(new PathMoveCommand(name));
                  paths.add(menu);

            private class PathDisplayCommand extends Command

               private String pathName;

               private PathDisplayCommand(String name)
                  super("Display " + name);
                  pathName = name;

               public boolean run()
                  String str = gameWorld.getPathString(pathName);
                  System.out.println(str);
                  return true;

            private class PathMoveCommand extends Command

               private String pathName;

               private PathMoveCommand(String name)
                  super("Move to " + name);
                  pathName = name;
```

```
                public boolean run()
                    String errorMessage = gameWorld.move(pathName);
                    if (! errorMessage.equals(""))
                        System.out.println(errorMessage);
                        return true;
                    else
                        updateAllControls();
                        return false;

GameWorld   private Heroine heroine;

            public String getPathString(String pathName){
                Place heroineLocation = heroine.getPlace();
                Path selectedPath = heroineLocation.getPath(pathName);
                return selectedPath.toString();

Heroine     private Place place;          // the heroine's location

            public Place getPlace()
                return place;

Place       private List paths;          // list of paths leading from place

            public Path getPath(String pathName)
                Path namedPath = search the list of paths for the named path;
                return namedPath;

Path        public String toString()
                return name + ": " + description;
```

Before we consider the next activity, let us note some important points about the activity just discussed:

- *Changes during implementation*—It is inevitable that the code written during implementation will vary slightly from the plans made during design. In particular, some of a class's internal helper methods may not show up when we are writing the collaboration diagrams and pseudocode. This tends to make the diagrams and pseudocode incomplete rather than incorrect. However, it is always a good idea to update the collaboration diagrams as changes occur. On the other hand, once the system has been implemented, the pseudocode has served its purpose and can be thrown away.

- *The role of the* `GameWorld`—Notice the intermediary role the `GameWorld` plays in the previous scheme. The interface, `GameView`, always communicates with the `GameWorld` rather than directly with the various elements within the world. This level of indirection seems awkward, but it isolates the view from changes in the model and vice versa.

■ *Class summary diagrams*—The additional information gained during the previous process can be added to class summary diagrams. We illustrate with just two (shown following), but in practice we would do the same thing for all the classes.

```
Class:
    GameWorld
Private Instance Variables:
    Heroine heroine
    . . .
Public Methods:
    constructor
    String getPathString
            (String pathName)
    . . .
```

```
Class:
    Heroine
Private Instance Variables:
    Place place
    . . .
Public Methods:
    constructor
    Place getPlace()
    . . .
```

Activity: Pick Up an Item

Picking up an item involves a fairly complex pattern of communications. This time we skip the narrative and present just a collaboration diagram (Figure 13-10) and associated pseudocode. Before presenting either, however, we must have a clear statement of the expected behavior. We assume that the user selects the Pick Up option in a Place Items submenu. If there are any foes in the place or if the heroine has no lives left, then the action fails and a message is displayed in the text area; otherwise, the selected item is moved from the place's list to the heroine's list and the interface is updated.

FIGURE 13-10
Collaboration diagram for the activity of picking up an item

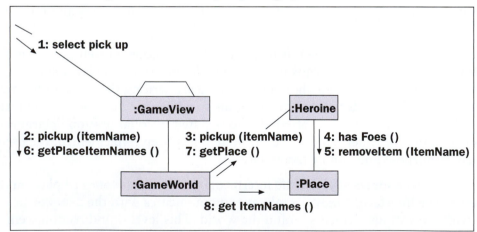

In Figure 13-10, messages 1 through 6 cover removing the item from the place and adding it to the heroine. Messages 7 through 9 update the Place Items menu in the user interface. For the sake of simplicity, we have omitted from the collaboration diagram and the pseudocode the details of updating the heroine's diary.

```
GameView      private GameWorld gameWorld;
              private CommandMenu placesItems; // The menu of place items

                  private class PlaceItemPickupCommand extends Command

                      private String itemName;

                        private PlaceItemPickupCommand(String name)
                           super("Pick up " + name);
                           itemName = name;

                      public boolean run()
                         String errorMessage = gameWorld.pickup(itemName);
                         if (! errorMessage.equals("")){
                            System.out.println(errorMessage);
                            return true;
                         else
                            updatePlaceItems(placesItems,
                                        gameWorld.getPlaceItemNames());
                            return false;

GameWorld     private Heroine heroine;

              public String pickup(String itemName)
                 return heroine.pickup(itemName);

              public String[] getPlaceItemNames()
                 return heroine.getPlace().getItemNames();

Heroine       private Place place;           // the heroine's location
              private List items;            // located in class Entity
              private int lives;             // number of lives remaining

              public String pickup(String itemName)
                 if (lives == 0)
                    return "The heroine is out of lives and cannot pick up.";
                 else if (place.hasFoes())
                    return "Cannot pick up. There are foes present.";
                 else
                    Item item = place.removeItem(itemName);
                    items.add(item);
                    return "";          // No error message.

              // getPlace already presented

Place         private List items;
              private List foes;

              public boolean hasFoes()
                 return false if the foes list is empty else true;

              public Item removeItem (String itemName)
                 remove the named item from the list;
                 return the item;
```

Activity: Move

The move activity is initiated when the user selects the Move option from a Paths submenu. If the heroine has no lives left, she is not able to move. After the move is completed, several aspects of the interface are updated. These updated items are detailed in Table 13-6.

TABLE 13-6
Updated aspects of the interface

INTERFACE ELEMENT	CHANGE MADE
Paths menu	The menu shows the names of all paths leading from the place to which the heroine has moved. We will call this "the new place" for convenience.
Entity menu	The menu shows the names of all entities located in the new place.
Place Items menu	The menu shows the names of all items located in the new place.
Terminal	The terminal displays the name and description of the new place.

In the collaboration diagram (Figure 13-11) and pseudocode (shown following), we update the Entities and the Place Items menus. We omit the messages and classes needed to update the heroine's diary.

FIGURE 13-11
Collaboration diagram for the activity of moving

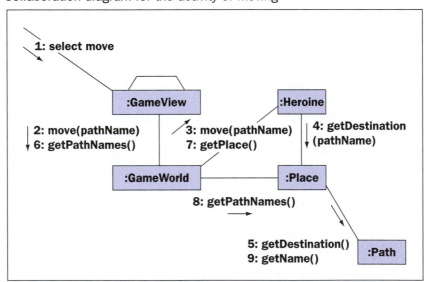

```
GameView    private GameWorld gameWorld;
            private CommandMenu entities, placesItems; // Menus

            // Resets the entities list
            private void updateEntities(CommandMenu entities,
                                        String[] names)
                entities.clear();
```

```
            for (String name : names)
            CommandMenu menu = new CommandMenu(name, reader);
            menu.add(new EntityDisplayCommand(name));
            menu.add(new EntityFightCommand(name));
            entities.add(menu);

         // Resets the entities list
         private void updatePlaceItems(CommandMenu items,
                                       String[] names){
            items.clear();
            for (String name : names)
               CommandMenu menu = new CommandMenu(name, reader);
               menu.add(new PlaceItemDisplayCommand(name));
               menu.add(new PlaceItemPickupCommand(name));
               items.add(menu);
```

GameWorld
```
         private Heroine heroine;

         public String move(String pathName){
            return heroine.move(pathName);
         }

         public String[] getPathNames(){
            return heroine.getPlace().getPathNames();
         }
```

Heroine
```
         private Place place;

         public String move(String pathName){
            if (lives == 0)
               return "The heroine is out of lives and cannot move.";
            else{
               place = place.getDestination(pathName);
               return "";
            }
         }

         // getPlace() presented in a previous subsection
```

Place
```
         private List paths;          // list of paths leading from place

         public Place getDestination(String pathName){
            Path namedPath = search the list of paths for the named path;
            Place destination = namedPath.getDestination();
            return destination;
         }

         public String[] getPathNames(){
            traverse the list of paths;
            ask each path for its name (path.getName());
            build an array of the path names;
            return the array of path names;
         }
```

```
Path        private Place destination;
            private String name;                // located in class NamedThing

            public Place getDestination(){
               return destination;
            }

            public String getName(){            // located in class NamedThing
               return name;
            }
```

These examples demonstrate the overall approach taken during design. By the time we have repeated the process for all the game's activities, we should know exactly how to implement the system.

EXERCISE 13.6

1. Why are analysis and design separate steps in the software development process?

2. Explain how activities are used in the design process.

3. Explain how narratives are used in the design process.

4. Explain how collaboration diagrams are used in the design process.

5. Explain how you write pseudocode using collaboration diagrams.

6. What information goes into a class summary diagram?

13.7 Implementation

It seems strange to start discussing the implementation while the design is incomplete; however, doing so makes a great deal of sense. If we are somehow on the wrong track and our planned design contains unanticipated flaws, we would like to know about the problems sooner rather than later. Therefore, we now propose implementing the system in stages, one activity at a time. If there are flaws, we can correct them before going too far in the wrong direction.

Loading the game from a text file is the first activity we must implement. To circumvent this problem (commonly referred to as a "workaround" in programming jargon), we instead write a method that creates a hard-coded game world. The method, `createHardCodedWorld`, resides in the `GameWorld` class and is called when the user selects menu option **File/Open**. With the hard-coded game world as a basis, we implement the activities of selecting a path and moving. All other aspects of the game are omitted. A listing of this limited code follows, and we encourage you to compare the code carefully with the diagrams presented during analysis and design. Code for the complete system is available from your instructor, and end-of-chapter projects lead you through the design and implementation of the other activities.

```java
// NamedThing.java

abstract public class NamedThing{
   protected String name;
   protected String description;

   public NamedThing(String n, String d){
      name = n;
      description = d;
   }

   public String getName(){
      return name;
   }

   public String toString(){
      return name + ": " + description;
   }
}

// Entity.java

import java.util.ArrayList;

abstract public class Entity extends NamedThing{
   protected int strength;
   protected ArrayList<Item> items;

   public Entity(String nm, String desc, int strngth){
      super(nm, desc);
      strength = strngth;
      items = new ArrayList<Item>();
   }
}

// Heroine.java

public class Heroine extends Entity{
   private Place place;
   private int lives;

   public Heroine(String nm, String desc, int strngth){
      super(nm, desc, strngth);
      lives = 9;
   }

   public Place getPlace(){
      return place;
   }

   public String move(String pathName){
      if (lives == 0)
          return "The heroine is out of lives and cannot move.";
```

```java
      else{
         Place newPlace = place.getDestination(pathName);
         place = newPlace;
         return "";
      }
   }

   public void startAt(Place plc){
      place = plc;
   }
}

// Path.java

public class Path extends NamedThing{
   private Place destination;

   public Path(String nm, String desc, Place dest){
      super(nm, desc);
      destination = dest;
   }

   public Place getDestination(){
      return destination;
   }
}

// Place.java

import java.util.ArrayList;

public class Place extends NamedThing{
   private ArrayList<Path> paths;
   private ArrayList<Item> items;
   private ArrayList<Foe> foes;

   public Place(String n, String d){
      super(n, d);
      paths = new ArrayList<Path>();
      items = new ArrayList<Item>();
      foes = new ArrayList<Foe>();
   }

   public void addPath(Path path){
      paths.add(path);
   }

   public Place getDestination(String pathName){
      Path namedPath = getPath(pathName);
      return namedPath.getDestination();
   }
```

```java
    public Path getPath(String pathName){
        for (Path namedPath : paths)
            if (namedPath.name.equals(pathName))
                return namedPath;
        return null;
    }

    public String[] getPathNames(){
        String[] pathNames = new String[paths.size()];
        for (int i = 0; i < paths.size(); i++)
            pathNames[i] = paths.get(i).getName();
        return pathNames;
    }
}

// GameWorld.java

public class GameWorld{
    private Heroine heroine;

    public void createHardCodedWorld(){
        Place entrance
          = new Place("Castle Entrance",
          "You are standing in front of a drawbridge.");
        Place courtyard
          = new Place("Courtyard",
          "Horses' hooves ring against rough cobbles.");
        Place stables
          = new Place("Stables",
          "Twenty horse stalls line the walls.");
        Place greatHall
          = new Place("Great Hall",
          "You are in a richly furnished hall.");
        Place dungeon
          = new Place("Dungeon",
          "Groans of the oppressed fill the air.");
        Place turret
          = new Place("Turret",
          "You are looking out over the castle's lands.");
        Place well
          = new Place("Well",
          "You have fallen into a deep, slippery well." +
          "\nThere is no way out.");

        heroine
          = new Heroine("Sue",
          "Our strong and worthy heroine, who never says no" +
          "\nto a rousing adventure.", 10);
```

```
    heroine.startAt(entrance);

    entrance.addPath
      (new Path("Drawbridge",
      "Rotting planks and rusting chains do not a good bridge make.",
      courtyard));
    courtyard.addPath
      (new Path("Drawbridge",
      "Rotting planks and rusting chains do not a good bridge make.",
      entrance));

    courtyard.addPath
      (new Path("South",
      "Careful where you step.",
      stables));
    stables.addPath
      (new Path("North",
      "Careful where you step.",
      courtyard));

    courtyard.addPath
      (new Path("Great Doors",
      "Push hard. The doors are immense.",
      greatHall));
    greatHall.addPath
      (new Path("Great Doors",
      "Pull hard. The doors are immense.",
      courtyard));

    greatHall.addPath
      (new Path("Stairs Up",
      "A winding staircase leads up into the darkness.",
       turret));
    turret.addPath
      (new Path("Stairs Down",
      "A winding staircase leads down into the darkness.",
      greatHall));

    greatHall.addPath
      (new Path("Stairs Down",
      "A winding staircase leads down into the darkness.",
      dungeon));
    dungeon.addPath
      (new Path("Stairs Up",
      "A winding staircase leads up into the darkness.",
      greatHall));

    greatHall.addPath
      (new Path("Secret Door",
      "This door looks little used.",
      well));
}
```

```java
    public String[] getPathNames(){
        return heroine.getPlace().getPathNames();
    }

    public String getPathString(String pathName){
        return heroine.getPlace().getPath(pathName).toString();
    }

    public String getPlaceString(){
        if (heroine == null)
            return "You must open a game file first.";
        else
            return heroine.getPlace().toString();
    }

    public String move(String pathName){
        return heroine.move(pathName);
    }
}
// GameView.java: Menu-driven, terminal-based user interface
// for Balbor program
// Start of design version

import java.util.Scanner;

public class GameView{

// ------------ The model
    private GameWorld gameWorld;

// ------------ The view

    // Menus and lists of paths, entities, and place items
    private CommandMenu mainMenu, fileMenu, paths, entities, placesItems;

    // The keyboard for all menus
    private Scanner reader;

    public GameView(){
        // Create the scanner for all the menus
        reader = new Scanner(System.in);

        // Create the main menu
        mainMenu = new CommandMenu("Main Menu", reader);

        // Create a File menu, its option, and add it to that menu
        fileMenu = new CommandMenu("File Menu", reader);
        fileMenu.add(new OpenCommand());

        // Create menus for the lists
        paths       = new CommandMenu("Paths", reader);
        entities    = new CommandMenu("Entities", reader);
        placesItems = new CommandMenu("Place Items", reader);
```

```java
        // Add the file menu and lists to the main menu
        mainMenu.add(fileMenu);
        mainMenu.add(paths);
        mainMenu.add(entities);
        mainMenu.add(placesItems);

        // Instantiate the game world
        gameWorld = new GameWorld();

        // Announce the program and start the main menu
        System.out.println("The Treasures of Balbor");
        mainMenu.run();
    }

    // ------------ The controller

    // Commands for menus

    private class OpenCommand extends Command{

        private OpenCommand(){
            super("Open");
        }

        public boolean run(){
            gameWorld.createHardCodedWorld();
            updateAllControls();
            return false;
        }
    }

    private class PathDisplayCommand extends Command{

        private PathDisplayCommand(String pathName){
            super(pathName);
        }

        public boolean run(){
            String str = gameWorld.getPathString(toString());
            System.out.println(str);
            return true;
        }
    }

    private class PathMoveCommand extends Command{

        private PathMoveCommand(String pathName){
            super(pathName);
        }

        public boolean run(){
            String errorMessage = gameWorld.move(toString());
            if (! errorMessage.equals("")){
                System.out.println(errorMessage);
```

```java
                return true;
            }
            else{
                updateAllControls();
                return false;
            }
        }
    }

    // Helper methods

    // Displays a description of the current place
    // and updates the lists with the info relating to
    // that place
    private void updateAllControls(){
        // Update place description
        String str = gameWorld.getPlaceString();
        System.out.println(str);

        // Update lists
        updatePaths(paths, gameWorld.getPathNames());
        updateList(entities, gameWorld.getEntityNames());
        updateList(placesItems, gameWorld.getPlaceItemNames());
    }

    // Resets the paths list to the paths out of the current place
    private void updatePaths(CommandMenu paths, String[] names){
        paths.clear();
        for (String name : names){
            CommandMenu menu = new CommandMenu(name, reader);
            menu.add(new PathDisplayCommand("Display " + name));
            menu.add(new PathMoveCommand("Move to " + name));
            paths.add(menu);
        }
    }

    // Resets the items in a command menu
    // (used for entities and items lists for now)
    private void updateList(CommandMenu list, String[] names){
        list.clear();
        for (String name : names){
            CommandMenu menu = new CommandMenu(name, reader);
            list.add(menu);
        }
    }
}
```

EXERCISE 13.7

1. Why bother implementing the code for a software system when its design is incomplete?

13.8 Graphics and GUIs: Text Areas, Scrolling List Boxes, and a GUI-Based Adventure Game

The user interface for the adventure game presented in this chapter is not only complex but also counterintuitive. The game has three types of information to present: commands, names of items in a list, and messages that contain detailed textual information about the results of selecting the commands or the item names. The decision to represent the lists of item names as menus results in a simple, consistent pattern of program code but in a user interface that is cumbersome and tedious. Not only must users drill down from a main menu to submenus, but they must select options to either display an item's detailed information or act on it.

> **Extra Challenge**
>
> This Graphics and GUIs section gives you the opportunity to explore concepts and programming techniques required to develop modern graphics applications and graphical user interfaces. This material is not required in order to proceed with the other chapters of the book.

In this section, we show how to create a simpler, more intuitive user interface for the adventure game. This interface places the commands in drop-down menus and the lists of item names in scrolling list boxes. The detailed textual information is displayed in a text area.

Text Areas

A text area is similar to a text field but can display many lines of text. In Java, a text area is an instance of the class `JTextArea`. The principal methods for manipulating a text area are the following:

`String getText()`	which reads a string from a text area
`void setText(aString)`	which clears a text area and prints a string
`void append(aString)`	which appends a string to the end of the text already present in the text area

When the text extends beyond the horizontal and vertical boundaries of a text area, scroll bars can come into play. A scroll bar allows the user to slide the text in two directions so that a hidden part of it becomes visible. The programmer associates scroll bars with a text area by wrapping a `JTextArea` in an instance of the class `JScrollPane`. The `JScrollPane` object is then added to the frame's container.

The following short program shows how to create a text area, add it to a container, and send it messages. The program's main window is shown in Figure 13-12.

FIGURE 13-12
Testing a text area

```
// Example 13.2: Tests a text area
// Reads from, prints to, or clears the text area

import javax.swing.*;
import java.awt.*;
import java.awt.event.*;

public class TestTextArea extends JFrame{

    private JTextArea ta = new JTextArea("");

    public TestTextArea(){
        // Wrap the text area in a scroll pane
        JScrollPane sp = new JScrollPane(ta);
        // Create buttons and add them to the container
        JButton clearBtn = new JButton("Clear");
        JButton printBtn = new JButton("Print");
        JButton readBtn = new JButton("Read");
        JPanel buttonPanel = new JPanel();
        buttonPanel.add(clearBtn);
        buttonPanel.add(printBtn);
        buttonPanel.add(readBtn);
        Container container = getContentPane();
        container.add(buttonPanel, BorderLayout.SOUTH);
        // Add the scroll pane to the container
        container.add(sp, BorderLayout.CENTER);
        clearBtn.addActionListener(new ClearListener());
        readBtn.addActionListener(new ReadListener());
        printBtn.addActionListener(new PrintListener());
    }

    private class ClearListener implements ActionListener{
        public void actionPerformed(ActionEvent e){
```

```
                ta.setText("");
            }
        }

        private class ReadListener implements ActionListener{
            public void actionPerformed(ActionEvent e){
                JOptionPane.showMessageDialog(TestTextArea.this, ta.getText());
            }
        }

        private class PrintListener implements ActionListener{
            public void actionPerformed(ActionEvent e){
                ta.append("This is a long sentence, with many words.  ");
                ta.append("append does not add a newline, so here one is.\n");
            }
        }

        public static void main(String[] args){
            TestTextArea theGUI = new TestTextArea();
            theGUI.setSize(250, 150);
            theGUI.setDefaultCloseOperation(JFrame.EXIT_ON_CLOSE);
            theGUI.setVisible(true);
        }
    }
```

Scrolling Lists

Figure 13-13 illustrates the use of a *scrolling list*. Scrolling lists are instances of the class JList as defined in the package javax.swing. When the user clicks on an entry in a scrolling list, the entry is automatically highlighted, thus giving the user visual feedback. At the same time, a single-click event is triggered. When the user double-clicks on an entry, again it is highlighted, but two events—a single-click event followed by a double-click event—are emitted.

FIGURE 13-13
A user interface containing a scrolling list

Java sets up a scrolling list according to the model/view pattern introduced in Chapter 7. Associated with a scrolling list window object is a *list model*, usually an instance of the class DefaultListModel, which contains the data displayed in the scrolling list. The programmer associates a model with a scrolling list by wrapping the scrolling list around it. The programmer can then send messages to either the scrolling list or its model to accomplish such tasks as selecting an item, or asking which item, if any, has been selected. In addition, a program can add entries to and remove entries from a scrolling list. Table 13-7 describes many of the most useful methods for manipulating a scrolling list and Table 13-8 describes useful methods for its model.

TABLE 13-7
The most useful methods for scrolling lists

JList METHOD	WHAT IT DOES
ListModel getModel()	Returns the model for the list; You should cast the result to a DefaultListModel
int getSelectedIndex()	Returns the position of the selected item
Object getSelectedValue()	Returns the selected item; You should cast the result to a String when using strings
void setSelectedIndex(int index)	Selects the item at the given index
void setSelectedValue(Object obj, boolean shouldScroll)	Selects the given item
void setSelectionMode(int mode)	Sets the mode to allow the user to select either a single item or multiple items

TABLE 13-8
The most useful methods for scrolling lists' models

DefaultListModel METHOD	WHAT IT DOES
add(int index, Object obj)	Inserts an item at the given position
addElement(Object obj)	Adds an item to the end of the list
void clear()	Makes the list empty
Object get(int index)	Returns the item at the given position
Object remove(int index)	Removes the item at the given position
boolean removeElement(Object obj)	Removes the first instance of the given item
Object set(index i, Object obj)	Replaces the item at the given position with the given item
int size()	Returns the number of items in the list
Object[] toArray()	Returns an array of the items

As is the case with a text area, the data displayed in a scrolling list box often extends below or above its visible area. Therefore, the programmer must create a JScrollPane and wrap it around the JList to allow the user to manipulate a scroll bar when necessary. Here is the sequence of the three operations required to set up a typical scrolling list box:

```
DefaultListModel lm = new DefaultListModel();    // Create a list model
JList sl = new JList(lm);                         // Wrap the model in a list
JScrollPane listPane = new JScrollPane(sl);       // Wrap a scroll pane
                                                  // around the list
```

When a user manipulates a scrolling list box, several events are triggered. The two most common types of events are a single-click and a double-click on an item. A single-click automatically selects an item, but a program can respond to this event in other ways, such as by updating information in other window components. A double-click usually results in a more significant action, such as the pop-up of a dialog box.

An easy way to detect and respond to single and double-clicks in a list box is to attach a mouse listener to it. The listener's `mouseClicked` method examines the click count by sending the message `getClickCount()` to its `MouseEvent` parameter. Because clicks can occur in a list box even when it is empty, the method must also detect this situation and do nothing if it occurs. The following code segment shows the pattern for the design of a typical mouse listener for a list box:

```java
// A list mouse listener
private class ListMouseListener extends MouseAdapter{
   public void mouseClicked(MouseEvent e){
      if (listModel.isEmpty())                  // Empty list, so do nothing
         return;
      if (e.getClickCount() == 2)               // A double click
         // Respond to a double click
      else if (e.getClickCount() == 1)          // A single click
         // Respond to a double click
   }
}
```

A Sample Program

The next program illustrates the use of drop-down menus and scrolling lists. Its user interface was shown in Figure 13-13. At startup, the program displays a scrolling list of fruits with the first fruit selected. When the user selects a fruit, its name appears in a text field. When the user selects the menu option **Edit/Delete**, the program removes the selected item from the list and selects the first item. When the user selects the menu option **Edit/Add**, the program adds the text in the field to the end of the scrolling list and selects it. The **Delete** option is disabled when the list becomes empty and enabled when an item is selected. The code's comments explain the use of the relevant methods:

```java
// Example 13.3
// Tests a scrolling list box

import javax.swing.*;
import java.awt.*;
import java.awt.event.*;

public class TuityFruity extends JFrame{

   private JMenuItem addMI = new JMenuItem("Add");
   private JMenuItem deleteMI = new JMenuItem("Delete");
   private JTextField field = new JTextField("");
   private DefaultListModel listModel = new DefaultListModel();
   private JList list = new JList(listModel);
```

```java
public TuityFruity(){
   list.setSelectionMode(ListSelectionModel.SINGLE_SELECTION);
   JScrollPane listPane = new JScrollPane(list);
   // Add initial fruits to the list
   listModel.add(0, "Apple");
   listModel.add(1, "Banana");
   listModel.add(2, "Cherry");
   listModel.add(3, "Orange");
   listModel.add(4, "Peach");
   listModel.add(5, "Pear");
   // Select the first fruit in the list
   list.setSelectedIndex(0);
   field.setText((String)list.getSelectedValue());
   Container container = getContentPane();
   container.add(listPane, BorderLayout.CENTER);
   container.add(field, BorderLayout.SOUTH);
   JMenu menu = new JMenu("Edit");
   menu.add(addMI);
   menu.add(deleteMI);
   JMenuBar bar = new JMenuBar();
   bar.add(menu);
   setJMenuBar(bar);
   addMI.addActionListener(new AddListener());
   deleteMI.addActionListener(new DeleteListener());
   list.addMouseListener(new ListMouseListener());
}

// List mouse listener
private class ListMouseListener extends MouseAdapter{
   public void mouseClicked(MouseEvent e) {
      if (listModel.isEmpty())
         return;
      String name = (String)list.getSelectedValue();
      if (e.getClickCount() == 2)
         JOptionPane.showMessageDialog(TuityFruity.this,
                                       "You double clicked " +
                                       name + ".");
      else if (e.getClickCount() == 1){
         field.setText(name);
         deleteMI.setEnabled(true);
      }
   }
}

private class AddListener implements ActionListener{
   public void actionPerformed(ActionEvent e){
      // Add the user's input to the end of the list,
      // select it, and scroll to it if necessary
      String str = JOptionPane.showInputDialog("Enter a fruit");
      listModel.addElement(str);
      list.setSelectedValue(str, true);
   }
}
```

```
    private class DeleteListener implements ActionListener{
        public void actionPerformed(ActionEvent e){
            // Delete the selected item and select the first
            // item
            listModel.removeElementAt(list.getSelectedIndex());
            if (listModel.size() != 0){
                list.setSelectedIndex(0);
                field.setText((String)list.getSelectedValue());
            }
            else
                deleteMI.setEnabled(false);
        }
    }

    public static void main(String[] args){
        TuityFruity theGUI = new TuityFruity();
        theGUI.setDefaultCloseOperation(JFrame.EXIT_ON_CLOSE);
        theGUI.setSize(300, 150);
        theGUI.setVisible(true);
    }
}
```

A GUI-Based Adventure Game

A GUI-based adventure game displays its three types of information—command options, lists of names, and detailed textual information—in a simple and structured manner, as shown in Figure 13-14. Several command options are now hidden in drop-down menus. The lists of names for places, entities, and items are displayed in three distinct scrolling list boxes. When the user selects a name in a list box, the detailed information for that name is displayed in a text area. A double-click on a name runs a command relevant to that item, such as taking a path, fighting a battle with an entity, or picking up an item. After each action occurs, the elements of the interface are updated appropriately. The user not only sees several related pieces of information at once but has it presented in a highly organized manner.

FIGURE 13-14
The GUI for the adventure game

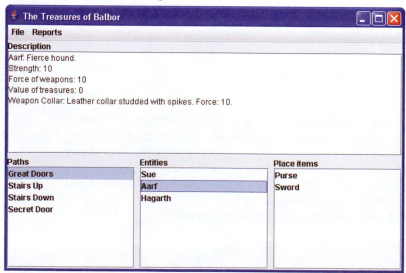

Because we have employed the model/view/controller pattern in the design of the adventure game, replacing its terminal-based interface with a GUI is straightforward. Naturally, the model does not change. The structure of the view class resembles that of the TuityFruity program presented earlier in this section. Instead of a single scrolling list box there are three, instead of a text field there is a text area, and instead of one drop-down menu there are two. All of the menu commands and the responses to list clicks are packaged in listener classes. Here is the code for the view class:

```java
// Example 13.4: GUI version of start of design adventure game

import javax.swing.*;
import java.awt.*;
import java.awt.event.*;

public class GameView extends JFrame {

//---------------------- The model

   private GameWorld gameWorld = new GameWorld();

//---------------------- The view

   // Labels
   private JLabel lbPaths        = new JLabel("Paths");
   private JLabel lbEntities     = new JLabel("Entities");
   private JLabel lbPlaceItems   = new JLabel("Place items");
   private JLabel lbDescription  = new JLabel("Description");

   // List models
   private DefaultListModel modelPaths      = new DefaultListModel();
   private DefaultListModel modelEntities   = new DefaultListModel();
   private DefaultListModel modelPlaceItems = new DefaultListModel();

   // Scrolling lists
   private JList lstPaths      = new JList(modelPaths);
   private JList lstEntities   = new JList(modelEntities);
   private JList lstPlaceItems = new JList(modelPlaceItems);

   // Text area
   private JTextArea taDescription = new JTextArea("");

   // Menu items
   private JMenuItem openMI = new JMenuItem("Open");

   public GameView(){
      // Set up menus
      JMenu fileMenu = new JMenu("File");
      openMI.addActionListener(new OpenListener());
      lstPaths.addMouseListener(new PathsMouseListener());
      fileMenu.add(openMI);
      JMenuBar bar = new JMenuBar();
      bar.add(fileMenu);
```

```java
        setJMenuBar(bar);
        // Set up text area and list boxes
        JPanel textPanel = makeLabeledPanel(taDescription, lbDescription);
        JPanel listPanel = new JPanel(new GridLayout(1, 3, 8, 8));
        listPanel.add(makeLabeledPanel(lstPaths, lbPaths));
        listPanel.add(makeLabeledPanel(lstEntities, lbEntities));
        listPanel.add(makeLabeledPanel(lstPlaceItems, lbPlaceItems));
        Container container = getContentPane();
        container.setLayout(new GridLayout(2, 1, 4, 4));
        container.add(textPanel);
        container.add(listPanel);
        // Set window attributes
        setTitle("The Treasures of Balbor");
        setDefaultCloseOperation(JFrame.EXIT_ON_CLOSE);
        setSize(600, 400);
        setVisible(true);
    }


    // Returns a panel that contains the label above and the widget,
    // wrapped in a scroll pane, below
    private JPanel makeLabeledPanel(Component widget, JLabel label){
        JPanel panel = new JPanel(new BorderLayout());
        JScrollPane pane = new JScrollPane(widget);
        panel.add(label, BorderLayout.NORTH);
        panel.add(pane, BorderLayout.CENTER);
        return panel;
    }


//--------------------- Controller

    // Handles display of info and move on a path
    private class PathsMouseListener extends MouseAdapter{
        public void mouseClicked(MouseEvent e) {
            if (modelPaths.isEmpty())
                return;
            String name = (String)lstPaths.getSelectedValue();
            if (e.getClickCount() == 2){
                String errorMessage = gameWorld.move(name);
                if (! errorMessage.equals(""))
                    taDescription.setText(errorMessage);
                else
                    updateAllControls();
            }
            else if (e.getClickCount() == 1){
                String str = gameWorld.getPathString(name);
                taDescription.setText(str);
            }
        }
    }


    // Opens a game file, initially hard coded
    private class OpenListener implements ActionListener{
        public void actionPerformed(ActionEvent e){
```

```
            gameWorld.createHardCodedWorld();
            updateAllControls();
        }
    }

    //--------------------- Private helper methods

    // Updates the text area and three scrolling lists
    private void updateAllControls(){
        // Update place description
        String str = gameWorld.getPlaceString();
        taDescription.setText(str);
        // Update lists
        updateList(lstPaths, gameWorld.getPathNames());
        updateList(lstEntities, gameWorld.getEntityNames());
        updateList(lstPlaceItems, gameWorld.getPlaceItemNames());
    }

    // Generic method to refresh any scrolling list with names
    private void updateList(JList list, String[] names){
        DefaultListModel listModel = (DefaultListModel)list.getModel();
        listModel.clear();
        for (String name : names)
            listModel.addElement(name);
    }
}
```

EXERCISE 13.8

1. Explain the difference between the JTextArea methods append and setText.

2. Describe the steps required to set up a scrolling list box.

3. Explain how to detect and respond to single-clicks and double-clicks in a scrolling list box.

4. List two advantages of a user interface that presents drop-down menus and scrolling list boxes over a terminal-based, menu-driven user interface.

SUMMARY

In this chapter, you learned:

- The Unified Modeling Language (UML) provides a graphical notation for depicting the relationships among classes and the manner in which objects communicate.

- A class diagram can be constructed from an informal description of user requirements. The three major types of relationships among classes are the *is-a* relationship (inheritance), the *has-a* relationship (aggregation), and the *knows-a* relationship (any other).

■ Classes and their attributes are derived from the nouns in a problem description.

■ A narrative of the communication among objects can be derived from a description of activities in a software system. This communication can then be depicted in collaboration diagrams, from which pseudocode can be derived.

VOCABULARY*Review*

Define the following terms:

Class diagram	*Is-a* relationship	Unified Modeling
Collaboration diagram	*Knows-a* relationship	Language (UML)
Has-a relationship		

REVIEW*Questions*

FILL IN THE BLANK

Complete the following sentences by writing the correct word or words in the blanks provided.

1. The leading graphical notation used in the analysis and design of software is called _____.

2. The _____ provides a graphical description of the relationships among classes.

3. _____ is a relationship in which one class contains one or more other classes.

4. _____ is a relationship in which one class is a parent of one or more other classes.

5. The notation for expressing one or more instances of something is _____.

6. The _____ provides a graphical description of the way in which objects communicate.

7. During design, activity can be expressed informally in a(n) _____.

8. You can pick out the classes and attributes of a software system by looking at the _____ in a problem description.

9. The last step in a design is to express the methods of the software system using _____.

10. The user requirements of a software system can be described with _____.

PROJECTS

What follows are implementation and design projects based on the adventure game. For all of them you should at least develop collaboration diagrams and pseudocode; however, to obtain greater satisfaction, you will probably want to write implementing code. As a starting point for your implementations, you could use the code presented in Section 13.7. If you do all the projects, you will have implemented the complete game. We recommend that you do the projects in the order listed. Except when explicitly requested, ignore maps, diaries, and events. A complete executable version of the game, without source code, is available from your instructor. The program in the first six projects should have a terminal-based user interface. The last project requires the implementation of a graphical user interface.

PROJECT 13-1

Incorporate into the game the activity of selecting an entity's name. Repeat for the activity of selecting an item's name. Both of these options lead to the options of displaying the information associated with the name.

PROJECT 13-2

Incorporate the menu option Reports > Current Location.

PROJECT 13-3

Implement the activity of picking up an item. Remember the heroine cannot pick up an item if a live foe is present.

PROJECT 13-4

Draw collaboration diagrams, write pseudocode, and implement the activity of fighting a battle.

PROJECT 13-5

Incorporate a map into the game. This depends on a new class called `GameMap`. The map itself is stored as a string in the `GameMap` class. You will find the `String` methods `indexOf` and `substring` useful in this endeavor. Before adding a new place name to the map, use `indexOf` to determine if the name is already present. When you travel along a path, you will learn its destination. If you have not been along this path before, on the map the destination shows as a question mark, which should be replaced by the destination name.

PROJECT 13-6

Incorporate the diary and events into the game. Incorporate into the game the `ElapsedTimer` class shown in the following code:

```java
import java.util.Date;

public class ElapsedTimer {
    private int startTime;
    private long clockStart;
```

```java
    public ElapsedTimer(int startTm) {
        startTime = startTm;
        clockStart = (new Date()).getTime();
    }

    public int getTime(){
        long clockNow = (new Date()).getTime();
        return startTime + (int)((clockNow - clockStart) / 1000);
    }
}
```

PROJECT 13-7

Complete the GUI for the game that was begun in Section 13.8.

CRITICAL *Thinking*

Jill is trying to decide whether to use UML to describe the analysis and design of a software system. Explain to her the costs and benefits of using this notation.

LINEAR COLLECTIONS: LISTS

OBJECTIVES

Upon completion of this chapter, you should be able to:

- Distinguish fundamental categories of collections, such as linear, hierarchical, graph, and unordered.

- Understand the basic features of lists and their applications.

- Use the list interface and the major list implementation classes.

- Recognize the difference between index-based operations and content-based operations on lists.

- Use an iterator to perform position-based operations on a list.

- Understand the difference between an iterator and a list iterator.

- Describe the restrictions on the use of list operations and iterator operations.

Estimated Time: 3 hours

VOCABULARY

Abstract data type (ADT)

Abstraction

Backing store

Children

Collection

Content-based operation

Free list

Graph collection

Head

Hierarchical collection

Index-based operation

Iterator

Linear collection

List iterator

Object heap

Parent

Position-based operation

Tail

Type parameter

Type variable

Unordered collection

In the first half of this book, we introduced you to the basic elements of programming and then showed you how to organize a software system in terms of cooperating methods, objects, and classes. In this and the next few chapters, we explore several frequently used classes called *collections*. Although they differ in structure and use, collections all have the same fundamental purpose—they help programmers organize data in programs effectively. In this chapter and the next two chapters, we examine the use of several different types of collections from a client's perspective. Chapters 17 through 19 consider the issues in implementing them. This chapter begins with an overview of collections and then explores the most widely used type, the *list*.

14.1 Overview of Collections

A collection, as the name implies, is a group of items that we want to treat as a conceptual unit. Nearly every nontrivial piece of software involves the use of collections, and although much of what you learn in computer science comes and goes with changes in technology, the basic principles of organizing collections endure. The arrays discussed in Chapters 9 and 11 are the most common and fundamental type of collection. Other important types of collections include strings, stacks, lists, queues, binary search trees, heaps, graphs, maps, sets, and bags. Collections can be *homogeneous*, meaning that all items in the collection must be of the same type, or *heterogeneous*, meaning the items can be of different types. In most languages, arrays are homogeneous, although as we saw in Chapter 11, an array of objects can contain different types of objects. An important distinguishing characteristic of collections is the manner in which they are organized. We now give an overview of four main categories of collections: linear collections, hierarchical collections, graph collections, and unordered collections.

Linear Collections

The items in a *linear collection* are, like people in a line, ordered by position. Each item except the first has a unique predecessor, and each item except the last has a unique successor. As shown in Figure 14-1, D2's predecessor is D1, and its successor is D3.

FIGURE 14-1
A linear collection

Everyday examples of linear collections are grocery lists, stacks of dinner plates, and a line of customers waiting at a bank.

Hierarchical Collections

Data items in *hierarchical collections* are ordered in a structure reminiscent of an upside down tree. Each data item except the one at the top has just one predecessor, its *parent*, but potentially many successors, called its *children*. As shown in Figure 14-2, D3's predecessor (parent) is D1, and its successors (children) are D4, D5, and D6.

FIGURE 14-2
A hierarchical collection

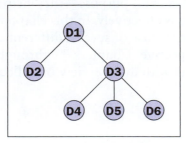

A company's organization tree and a book's table of contents are examples of hierarchical collections.

Graph Collections

A *graph collection*, also called a *graph*, is a collection in which each data item can have many predecessors and many successors. As shown in Figure 14-3, all elements connected to D3 are considered to be both its predecessors and successors.

FIGURE 14-3
A graph collection

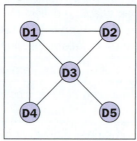

Examples of graphs are maps of airline routes between cities and electrical wiring diagrams for buildings. We do not explore graphs further in this book.

Unordered Collections

As the name implies, items in an *unordered collection* are not in any particular order, and one cannot meaningfully speak of an item's predecessor or successor. Figure 14-4 shows such a structure.

FIGURE 14-4
An unordered collection

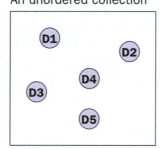

A bag of marbles is an example of an unordered collection. Although one can put marbles into and take marbles out of a bag, once in the bag, the marbles are in no particular order.

Operations on Collections

Collections are typically dynamic rather than static, meaning they can grow or shrink with the needs of a problem. Also, their contents change throughout the course of a program. The actual manipulations that can be performed on a collection vary with the type of collection being used, but generally, the operations fall into several broad categories that are outlined in Table 14-1.

TABLE 14-1
Categories of operations on collections

CATEGORY	DESCRIPTION
Search and retrieval	These operations search a collection for a given target item or for an item at a given position. If the item is found, either it or its position is returned. If the item is not found, a distinguishing value such as `null` or −1 is returned.
Removal	This operation deletes a given item or the item at a given position.
Insertion	This operation adds an item to a collection and usually at a particular position within the collection.
Replacement	Replacement combines removal and insertion into a single operation.
Traversal	This operation visits each item in a collection. Depending on the type of collection, the order in which the items are visited can vary. During a traversal, items can be accessed or modified. Some traversals also permit the insertion or removal of items from the underlying collection.
Test for equality	If items can be tested for equality, then the collections containing them can also be tested for equality. To be equal, two collections must contain equal items at corresponding positions. For unordered collections, of course, the requirement of corresponding positions can be ignored. Some collections, such as strings, also can be tested for their position in a natural ordering using the comparisons less than and greater than.
Determination of size	Every collection contains a finite number of items. This number is the collection's size. Some collections also have a maximum capacity, or number of places available for storing items. An egg carton is a familiar example of a container with a maximum capacity.
Cloning	This operation creates a copy of an existing collection. The copy usually shares the same items as the original, a feat that is impossible in the real world. In the real world, a copy of a bag of marbles could not contain the same marbles as the original bag, given a marble's inability to be in two places at once. The rules of cyberspace are more flexible, however, and there are many situations in which we make these strange copies of collections. What we are copying is the structure of the collection, not the elements it contains. It is possible, however, and sometimes useful to produce a deep copy of a collection in which both the structure and the items are copied.

Abstract Data Types

From the foregoing discussion, we see that a collection consists of data organized in a particular manner together with methods for manipulating the data. Those who use collections in their programs have a rather different perspective on collections than those who are responsible for implementing them in the first place, however.

Users of collections need to know how to declare and use each type of collection. From their perspective, a collection is seen as a means for storing and accessing data in some predetermined manner, without concern for the details of the collection's implementation. From the users' perspective a collection is an *abstraction*, and for this reason, in computer science collections are called *abstract data types* (ADTs).

Developers of collections, on the other hand, are concerned with implementing a collection's behavior in the most efficient manner possible, with the goal of providing the best performance to users of the collections. For each category of collections (linear, hierarchical, etc.), we examine one or more abstract data types and one or more implementations of that type.

The idea of abstraction is not unique to a discussion of collections. It is an important principle in many endeavors both in and out of computer science. For example, when studying the effect of gravity on a falling object, we try to create an experimental situation in which we can ignore incidental details such as the color and taste of the object. (What sort of apple was it that hit Newton on the head?) When studying mathematics, we do not concern ourselves with what the numbers might be used to count, fishhooks or arrowheads, but try to discover abstract and enduring principles of numbers. A house plan is an abstraction of the physical house, and it allows us to focus on structural elements without being overwhelmed by incidental details such as the color of the kitchen cabinets, which is important to the eventual house but not to the house's structural relationships. In computer science, we also use abstraction as a technique for ignoring or hiding details that are, for the moment, inessential, and we often build up a software system layer by layer, each layer being treated as an abstraction by the layers above that utilize it. Without abstraction, we would need to consider all aspects of a software system simultaneously, an impossible task. Of course, the details must be considered eventually, but in a small and manageable context.

In Java, methods are the smallest unit of abstraction, classes and their interfaces are the next in size, and packages are the largest. In this text, we implement abstract data types as classes and their interfaces.

Multiple Implementations

A major concern of the computer scientist is how best to implement different types of collections. There are usually numerous possibilities; however, many of these take so much space or run so slowly that they can be dismissed as pointless. Those that remain tend to be based on four underlying approaches to organizing and accessing memory:

1. Arrays

2. Linear linked structures

3. Other linked structures

4. Hashing into an array

We discuss the first two approaches in Chapter 17, and we encounter the other two later in the book when we study the implementation of hierarchical and unordered collections.

We close this section with a mundane detail. When there is more than one way to implement a collection, programmers define a variable of an interface type and assign to it an object that uses the desired implementation. For instance, `java.util` includes three classes that implement the `List` interface. These classes are `LinkedList`, `ArrayList`, and `Vector`. In the following code snippet, the programmer has chosen the `LinkedList` implementation for a list of strings:

```
List<String> lst = new LinkedList<Sring>();
```

To select a different implementation, the programmer could substitute `ArrayList<String>()` for `LinkedList<String>()` in this code.

Collections and Casting

Like arrays, Java collections can be declared to contain specific types of objects. As we first saw in Chapter 11, these constraints have several consequences:

1. Primitive types, such as int, must be placed in a wrapper object, either by the programmer or automatically, before being added to a collection.

2. Wrapped primitive values are automatically unboxed when accessed in a collection.

3. Although any item coming out of a collection is, from the compiler's perspective, of a specific type, that item might have to be cast to a more specific type before being sent a message.

For examples of casting as used with a collection, you should review Chapter 11, Section 11.5.

*E*XERCISE 14.1

1. Give one example from everyday life of a linear collection, a hierarchical collection, a graph collection, and an unordered collection.

2. For each of the following objects, give the type of collection (linear, hierarchical, graph, or unordered) that would best fit its representation in software:
   a. A recipe
   b. A box of cereal
   c. An outline of a book
   d. A map of the Interstate Highway System

3. What is abstraction? Give an example.

4. An abstract data type consists of an interface and one or more implementing classes. Explain.

5. Why is casting needed when using collections?

14.2 Lists

Overview

A list supports manipulation of items at any point within a linear collection. Some common examples of lists include the following:

- A *recipe*, which is a list of instructions
- A *string*, which is a list of characters
- A *document*, which is a list of words
- A *file*, which is a list of data blocks on disk

In all these examples, order is critically important, and shuffling the items renders the collections meaningless; however, the items in a list are not necessarily sorted. Words in a dictionary and names in a phone book are examples of sorted lists, but the words in this paragraph equally form a list and are unsorted. Although the items in a list are always logically contiguous, they need not be physically contiguous. Array implementations of lists use physical position to represent logical order, but linked implementations do not.

The first item in a list is at its *head*, whereas the last item in a list is at its *tail*. In a list, items retain position relative to each other over time, and additions and deletions affect predecessor/successor relationships only at the point of modification. Figure 14-5 shows how a list changes in response to a succession of operations. The operations are described in Table 14-2.

FIGURE 14-5
The states in the lifetime of a list

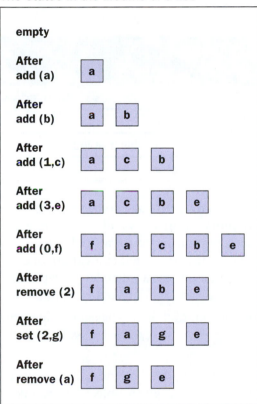

TABLE 14-2
List operations

OPERATION	WHAT IT DOES
add(o)	Adds object o to a list's tail
add(i, o)	Inserts object o at the *i*th index in a list, where the first item is at index 0
remove(o)	Removes the first instance of object o from a list
remove(i)	Removes the object at the *i*th index in a list
set(i, o)	Replaces the object at the *i*th index with object o

Categories of List Operations

Except for the basic operations for determining size, equality of two lists, and cloning, there are no standard operations for lists. For instance, the operation of putting a new item in a list is sometimes called "add" and sometimes "insert." If we look at most textbooks on data structures and at the ADT list provided in Java, however, we can discern several broad categories of operations, which we call index-based operations, content-based operations, and position-based operations.

Index-based operations manipulate items at designated positions within a list. Suppose a list contains n items. Because a list is linearly ordered, we can unambiguously refer to an item in a list via its relative position from the head of the list using an index that runs from 0 to $n-1$. Thus, the head is at index 0 and the tail is at index $n-1$. Table 14-3 shows some fundamental index-based operations.

TABLE 14-3
Index-based operations

INDEX-BASED OPERATION	WHAT IT DOES
add(i, o)	Opens up a slot in the list at index i and inserts object o in this slot
get(i)	Returns the object at index i
remove(i)	Removes and returns the object at index i
set(i, o)	Replaces the object at index i with the object o and returns the original object

When viewed from this perspective, lists are sometimes called *vectors* or *sequences*, and in their use of indexes, they are reminiscent of arrays. However, an array is a concrete data type with a specific and unvarying implementation based on a single block of physical memory, whereas a list is an abstract data type that can be represented in a variety of different ways, among which are array implementations. In addition, a list has a much larger repertoire of basic operations than an array, even though all list operations can be mimicked by suitable sequences of array operations.

Like the array subscript operation, each index-based list operation throws an exception if the specified index is out of range. In the case of Java's list classes, this exception is an `IndexOutOfBoundsException`.

Content-based operations are based not on an index but on the content of a list. Most of these operations search for an object equal to a given object before taking further action. Table 14-4 outlines some basic content-based operations.

TABLE 14-4
Content-based operations

CONTENT-BASED OPERATION	WHAT IT DOES
add(o)	Adds object o at a list's tail
contains(o)	Returns true if a list contains an object equal to object o
indexOf(o)	Returns the index of the first instance of object o in a list
remove(o)	Removes the first instance of object o from a list and returns true if o is removed, else returns false

Position-based operations are performed relative to a currently established position within a list, and in `java.util`, they are provided via an *iterator*. An iterator is an object that allows a client to navigate through a list and perform various operations at the current position. We examine iterators later in this chapter.

The List Interface

Table 14-5 lists the methods in the interface `java.util.List`. The classes `ArrayList`, `LinkedList`, and `Vector` implement this interface. Note that the `List` interface is quite lengthy. The interface includes both the methods discussed thus far and also the methods in the `Collection` interface, which specifies more general methods supported by lists and other collections. We discuss the `Collection` interface in Chapter 16. Figure 14-6 shows the relationships among the two interfaces and the three implementing classes.

FIGURE 14-6
The `list` interface and its implementing classes

TABLE 14-5
The `List` interface

METHOD	DESCRIPTION
`void add(int index, E element)`	Inserts the specified element at the specified position in this list
`boolean add(E element)`	Appends the specified element to the end of this list
`boolean contains(Object element)`	Returns `true` if this list contains the specified element
`E get(int index)`	Returns the element at the specified position in this list
`int indexOf(E element)`	Returns the index in this list of the first occurrence of the specified element or –1 if this list does not contain this element
`int lastIndexOf(E element)`	Returns the index in this list of the last occurrence of the specified element or –1 if this list does not contain this element
`E remove(int index)`	Removes the element at the specified position in this list
`boolean remove(Object element)`	Removes the first occurrence in this list of the specified element

TABLE 14-5 Continued
The List interface

METHOD	DESCRIPTION
`E set(int index, E element)`	Replaces the element at the specified position in this list with the specified element and returns the old element
`boolean isEmpty()`	Returns `true` if this list contains no elements
`int size()`	Returns the number of elements in this list
`boolean addAll(Collection<?> c)`	Appends all of the elements in the specified collection to the end of this list, in the order that they are returned by the specified collection's iterator
`boolean addAll(int index, Collection<?> c)`	Inserts all of the elements in the specified collection into this list at the specified position
`void clear()`	Removes all of the elements from this list
`Object clone()`	Not officially listed here because it is inherited from `Object`
`boolean containsAll (Collection<?> c)`	Returns `true` if this list contains all of the elements of the specified collection
`boolean equals(Object o)`	Compares the specified object with this list for equality
`int hashCode()`	Returns the hash code value for this list (Please ignore this method for now. We discuss hashing in Chapter 18.)
`Iterator<E> iterator()`	Returns an iterator over the elements in this list in proper sequence
`ListIterator<E> listIterator()`	Returns a list iterator of the elements in this list in proper sequence
`ListIterator<E> listIterator(int index)`	Returns a list iterator of the elements in this list in proper sequence, starting at the specified position in this list
`boolean removeAll(Collection<?> c)`	Removes from this list all of the elements that are contained in the specified collection
`boolean retainAll(Collection<?> c)`	Retains only the elements in this list that are contained in the specified collection
`List<E> subList(int fromIndex, int toIndex)`	Returns a view of the portion of this list between the specified `fromIndex`, inclusive, and `toIndex`, exclusive
`Object[] toArray()`	Returns an array containing all of the elements in this list in proper sequence
`<T> T[] toArray(T[] a)`	Returns an array containing all of the elements in this list in proper sequence; the run-time type of the returned array is that of the specified array
`String toString()`	Not officially listed here because it is inherited from `Object`

A Word on Type Parameters and Variables

Recall that lists and other collections are generic, that is, their elements are declared to be of a specific type when a list or collection variable is declared. Thus, the code

```
List<String> list = new ArrayList<String>()
```

creates a list that can contain only strings. You can think of the element type as a *type parameter* that tells the compiler to check for that element type when a collection is used. The corresponding formal parameter is called a *type variable*, which appears in the method signatures of a collection's interface. The symbols E, T, and ? in Table 14-5 are examples of type variables. Java programmers have adopted a conventional use for each of these symbols.

When the symbol E appears in a method signature, the type of the object must be the same as the element type of the collection. Thus, the two add methods expect only objects of the collection's element type as parameters, and the method sublist returns a list of the same element type.

However, some methods, such as contains and remove, allow parameters of type Object. Thus, the user of these methods may pass an object of any class as a parameter. When run with a list of strings, these methods may succeed and find or remove the matching element if the actual parameter happens to be a string. If the actual parameter is not a string but instead some other type of object, no harm is done, but the method obviously does not find or remove an element. Because the methods such as containsAll and removeAll rely on contains and remove in their implementations, their Collection parameter can be of any element type, including Object. The use of the symbol ? instead of E tells the compiler that generic collections of any element type are allowed in these cases.

The type variable T is used to indicate a type that is a supertype of the collection's element type. Thus, an array of Shape can be built from a collection that contains different subtypes of Shape, such as Circle and Rectangle.

Understanding type variables can be tricky, but unfortunately is necessary for understanding the requirements of some collection interfaces.

Some Example List Operations in Action

To make certain that there are no ambiguities in the meaning of the operations shown in Table 14-5, we now present an example that shows a sequence of these operations in action. This sequence is listed in Table 14-6.

TABLE 14-6
The effects of some list operations

LIST OPERATION	STATE OF THE LIST AFTER THE OPERATION	VALUE RETURNED	COMMENT
			Initially, the list is empty.
add(0,a)	a		The list contains the single item a.
add(1,b)	a b		a is the head, b is the tail.
add(1,c)	a c b		c is at index 1.
isEmpty()	a c b	false	The list is not empty.

TABLE 14-6 Continued
The effects of some list operations

LIST OPERATION	STATE OF THE LIST AFTER THE OPERATION	VALUE RETURNED	COMMENT
size()	a c b	3	The list contains three items.
indexOf(b)	a c b	2	The index of b is 2.
indexOf(q)	a c b	-1	q is not in the list.
contains(c)	a c b	true	c is in list.
get(1)	a c b	c	Return c, which is at index 1.
get(3)	a c b	exception	The index is out of range, so throw an exception.
set(2,e)	a c e	b	Replace b at index 2 with e and return b.
remove(0)	c e	a	Remove a at position 0 and return it. c is now at the head of the list.
remove(2)	c e	exception	The index is out of range, so throw an exception.
remove(1)	c	e	Remove and return e.
remove(0)		c	Remove and return c.
isEmpty()		true	The list is empty.
remove(0)		exception	The index is out of range, so throw an exception.
set(0,a)		exception	The index is out of range, so throw an exception.

Linked Lists and Their Operations

Although linked lists are covered in great detail in Chapter 17, we need to describe their behavior and operations so you will know when their use is preferable to array lists. Because the classes LinkedList and ArrayList both implement the List interface, they share the same *logical* behavior. However, the *performance* of these operations can vary greatly depending on which type of implementation is chosen. An array list guarantees constant-time access to an element at any position. Linked lists provide linear-time access to any element other than the first one or the last one. Therefore, most of the list operations generally run faster with array lists than they do with linked lists. However, linked lists also guarantee constant-time insertions and removals at the head and the tail of the list, whereas these operations in array lists can take linear time.

You should use a linked list when elements are accessed, inserted, or removed at the head or the tail only. These operations are so common that the LinkedList class includes them for convenience, as listed in Table 14-7. You should use array lists in almost all other cases.

TABLE 14-7
Extra `LinkedList` methods

METHOD	DESCRIPTION
`void addFirst(E element)`	Inserts the specified element at the head of this list
`void addLast(E element)`	Inserts the specified element at the tail of this list
`E getFirst()`	Returns the element at the head of this list
`E getLast()`	Returns the element at the tail of this list
`E removeFirst()`	Removes and returns the element at the head of this list
`E removeLast()`	Removes and returns the element at the tail of this list

If you must iterate through a linked list, you should use either an enhanced `for` loop or an iterator, which we discuss shortly. If you make the mistake of using `get(anInt)` with a loop index, your code will traverse a linked list in quadratic time!

Applications of Lists

Heap Storage Management

When you studied recursion, you learned one aspect of Java memory management, the call stack. Now we complete that discussion by showing how free space in the *object heap* can be managed using a linked list. Heap management schemes can have a significant impact on an application's overall performance, especially if the application creates and abandons many objects during the course of its execution. Implementers of Java virtual machines (JVMs) are therefore willing to spend a great deal of effort to organize the heap in the most efficient manner possible. Their elaborate solutions are beyond this book's scope, so we present a simplified scheme here.

In our scheme, contiguous blocks of free space on the heap are linked together in a *free list*. When an application instantiates a new object, the JVM searches the free list for the first block large enough to hold the object and returns any excess space to the free list. When the object is no longer needed, the garbage collector returns the object's space to the free list. The scheme, as stated, has two defects. Over time, large blocks on the free list become fragmented into many smaller blocks, and searching the free list for blocks of sufficient size can take $O(n)$ runtime, where n is the number of blocks in the list. To counteract fragmentation, the garbage collector periodically reorganizes the free list by recombining physically adjacent blocks. To reduce search time, multiple free lists can be used. For instance, if an object reference requires 4 bytes, then list 1 could consist of blocks of size 4; list 2, blocks of size 8; list 3, blocks of size 16; list 4, blocks of size 32; and so on. The last list would contain all blocks over some designated size. In this scheme, space is always allocated in units of 4 bytes, and space for a new object is taken from the head of the first nonempty list containing blocks of sufficient size. Allocating space for a new object now takes $O(1)$ time unless the object requires more space than is available in the first block of the last list. At that point, the last list must be searched, giving the operation a maximum runtime of $O(n)$, where n is the size of the last list.

In this discussion, we have completely ignored two difficult problems. The first problem has to do with deciding when to run the garbage collector. Running the garbage collector takes time away from the application, but not running it means the free lists are never replenished. The second problem concerns how the garbage collector identifies objects that are no longer referenced and, consequently, no longer needed. (This problem is not within the scope of this text.)

Organization of Files on a Disk

A computer's file system has three major components—a directory of files, the files themselves, and free space. To understand how these work together to create a file system, we first consider a disk's physical format. Figure 14-7 shows the standard arrangement. The disk's surface is divided into concentric *tracks*, and each track is further subdivided into *sectors*. The numbers of these vary depending on the disk's capacity and physical size; however, all tracks contain the same number of sectors and all sectors contain the same number of bytes. For the sake of this discussion, let us suppose that a sector contains 8 Kbytes of data plus a few additional bytes reserved for a pointer. A sector is the smallest unit of information transferred to and from the disk, regardless of its actual size, and a pair of numbers (t, s) specifies a sector's location on the disk, where t is the track number and s the sector number. Figure 14-7 shows a disk with n tracks. The k sectors in track 0 are labeled from 0 to $k - 1$.

FIGURE 14-7

Tracks and sectors on the surface of a disk

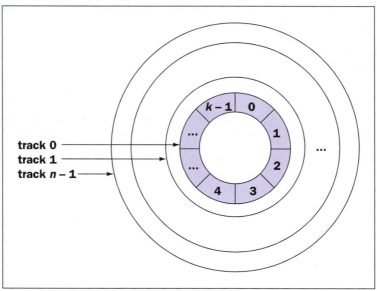

A file system's directory is organized as a hierarchical collection. The directory's internal structure is not a suitable topic for this chapter. However, let us suppose that it occupies the first few tracks on the disk and contains an entry for each file. This entry holds the file's name, creation date, size, and so forth. In addition, it holds the address of the sector containing the first bytes in the file. Depending on its size, a file might be completely contained within a single sector or it might span several sectors. Usually, the last sector is only partially full, and no attempt is made to recover the unused space. The sectors that make up a file do not need to be physically adjacent because each sector except the last one ends with a pointer to the sector containing the next portion of the file. Finally, sectors that are not in use are linked together in a free list. When new files are created, they are allocated space from this list, and when old files are deleted, their space is returned to the list.

Because all sectors are the same size and because space is allocated in sectors, a file system does not experience the same fragmentation problem encountered in Java's object heap. Nonetheless, there is still a difficulty. To transfer data to or from the disk, read/write heads must first be positioned to the correct track, the disk must rotate until the desired sector is under the heads, and then the transfer of data takes place. Of these three steps, the transfer of data takes the least time. Fortunately, data can be transferred to or from several adjacent sectors during a single rotation without the need to reposition the heads. Thus, a disk system's performance is optimized when multisector files are not scattered across the disk. Over time, however, as files of varying sizes are created and destroyed, this sort of scattering becomes frequent, and the file system's performance degrades. As a countermeasure, file systems include a utility, run either automatically or at the explicit request of the user, which reorganizes the file system so that the sectors in each file are contiguous and have the same physical and logical order.

Implementation of Other ADTs

Lists are frequently used to implement other ADTs, such as stacks and queues. There are two ways to do this:

1. Extend the list class, making the new class a subclass of the list class.

2. Use an instance of the list class within the new class and let the list contain the data items.

For example, `java.util` implements a `Stack` class by extending a list class called `Vector`. Extension is not a wise choice in this case, however, because this version of `Stack` inherits the methods from `Vector` that allow users to access items at positions other than the top, thus violating the spirit of the stack ADT. In the case of stacks and queues, a better design decision is to contain a list within the stack or queue. In that case, all of the list operations are available to the implementer, but only the essential stack or queue operations are available to the user. On the other hand, suppose we wanted to implement a sorted list, which is not part of `java.util`. A sorted list has 90 percent of the behavior of a list, including most of the indexed-based, object-based, and positional operations. The only methods that differ are `add`, which inserts an item in its proper place rather than at the end of the list, and mutators for other insertions or replacements, which have extra preconditions to maintain the natural ordering of the objects in the list. Clearly in this case, sorted lists should extend the behavior of lists rather than contain them.

ADTs that use lists inherit their performance characteristics. For example, a stack that uses an array-based list has the performance characteristics of an array-based stack, whereas a stack that uses a link-based list has characteristics of a link-based stack.

The primary advantage of using a list ADT to implement another ADT is that coding becomes easier. Instead of operating on a concrete array or linked structure, the implementer of a stack need only call the appropriate list methods.

In Chapter 16 and Chapter 19 we see other situations in which lists can be used in the implementation of ADTs, although, in the interest of optimizing performance, we do not always do so.

EXERCISE 14.2

1. Describe the difference between index-based and content-based operations on lists.

2. Assume that the list variable list has been assigned a new list object. Draw pictures of the state of the list after each of the following operations:

   a. `for (int i = 1; i <= 4; i++) list.add("" + i);`

   b. `list.remove(2);`

   c. `list.add(1, "5");`

EXERCISE 14.2 Continued

    d. `list.remove("4");`

    e. `list.set(0, "8");`

3. Write code segments to perform the following tasks with the list object named list:

    a. Remove all the objects from the list.

    b. Add the strings "1", "2", and "3" to positions 0, 1, and 2.

    c. Add the string "4" to the end of the list.

    d. Replace the object at position 1 with the string "6".

    e. Insert the string "7" at position 2.

    f. Display the size of the list and all its contents in the terminal window.

4. What is the object heap? Describe how the computer uses a list to manage the object heap.

5. Jill wants to represent a deck of cards for a game-playing program. Is a list a wise choice for this problem? Justify your answer.

6. Explain why the use of `get(anInt)` to traverse an array list takes linear time, whereas it takes quadratic time with a linked list.

14.3 Iterators

As mentioned earlier, an iterator supports position-based operations on a list. An iterator uses the underlying list as a *backing collection*, and the iterator's current position is always in one of three places:

1. Just before the first item

2. Between two adjacent items

3. Just after the last item

Initially, when an iterator is first instantiated, the position is immediately before the first item. From this position the user can either navigate to another position or modify the list in some way. For lists, `java.util` provides two types of iterators, a simple iterator and a list iterator. We now examine both types of iterators.

The Simple Iterator

In Java, a simple iterator is an object that responds to messages specified in the interface `java.util.Iterator`, as summarized in Table 14-8.

TABLE 14-8
The Iterator interface

ITERATOR METHOD	WHAT IT DOES
`boolean hasNext()`	Returns `true` if there are any items following the current position
`E next()`	*Precondition*: `hasNext` returns `true`. Throws a `NoSuchElementException` if `hasNext` returns `false` Returns the next item and advances the position
`void remove()`	*Precondition*: `next` has recently been called. Throws an `IllegalStateException` if the `next` method has not yet been called or if the `remove` method has already been called after the last call to the `next` method Removes the item returned by the most recent call of `next`

You create an iterator object by sending the message `iterator` to a list, as shown in the following code segment:

```
Iterator<String> iter = listOfStrings.iterator();
```

Note that an iterator, like a list, is generic and requires the same element type as the list. The list serves as a **backing store** for the iterator. A backing store is a storage area, usually a collection, where the data elements are maintained. The relationship between these two objects is depicted in Figure 14-8.

FIGURE 14-8
Attaching an interator to a list object

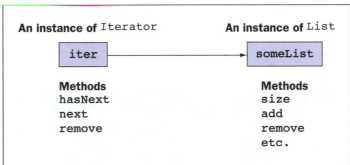

The methods `hasNext` and `next` are for navigating, whereas the method `remove` mutates the underlying list. Note that simple iterators are not restricted to lists but can be used with any other Java collections, although the method `remove` might not be supported by some implementations.

The next code segment demonstrates a traversal of a list to display its contents using an iterator:

```
while (iter.hasNext())
   System.out.println(iter.next());
```

Note that you should avoid doing the following things:

■ Sending a mutator message, such as `add`, to the backing list when an iterator is active

■ Sending the message `remove` to an iterator when another iterator is open on the same backing list

The List Iterator

A *list iterator* responds to messages specified in the interface `java.util.ListIterator`. This interface extends the `Iterator` interface with several methods for navigation and modifying the backing list. Table 14-9 shows the additional navigational methods.

TABLE 14-9
Additional navigation methods

NAVIGATION	ACTION
`hasPrevious()`	Returns `true` if there are any items preceding the current position
`previous()`	Returns the previous item and moves the position backward
`nextIndex()`	Returns the index of the next item or –1 if none
`previousIndex()`	Returns the index of the previous item or –1 if none

Conspicuously absent from this roster of operations are ones for moving directly to either the beginning or end of a list. The authors of `java.util` omitted these operations for reasons best known to themselves. The lack of an operation for returning to the head of a list is not critical because instantiating a new list iterator has the same effect; however, a succession of `next` operations is the only way to move to a list's tail.

Additional mutator operations work at the currently established position in the list (see Table 14-10).

TABLE 14-10
Additional mutator operations

MUTATOR OPERATION	DESCRIPTION
`add(o)`	Inserts object o at the current position (list iterator only)
`set(o)`	Replaces the last item returned by next or previous (list iterator only)

Using a List Iterator

In Table 14-11, we present a sequence of list iterator operations and indicate the state of the underlying list after each operation. Remember that a list iterator's current position is located before the first item, after the last item, or between two items. In the table, the current position is indicated by a comma and by an integer variable called `current position`. Suppose the list contains n items. Then,

■ current position = i if it is located before the item at index i, where $i = 0, 1, 2, \ldots, n - 1$.

■ current position = n if it is located after the last item.

Notice in Table 14-11 that there is always a current position. From the specification for the `ListIterator` interface, we know that `remove` and `set` operate on the last item returned by a successful `next` or `previous` operation, provided there have been no intervening `add` or `remove` operations. In the table, we highlight this last item returned in boldface. If no item is highlighted, then `remove` and `set` are invalid. The highlighted item, when present, can be on either side of the current position indicator—on the left after a `next` operation or on the right after a `previous` operation.

TABLE 14-11
The effects of iterator operations on a list

LIST ITERATOR OPERATION	CURRENT POSITION AFTER THE OPERATION	STATE OF THE LIST AFTER THE OPERATION	VALUE RETURNED	COMMENT
instantiate a new list iterator over a list that contains the items a b c	0	, a b c	a list iterator object	Initially, the list contains a, b, and c, and the current position equals 0. The following operations use this iterator object, and some change the state of the underlying list.
hasNext()	0	, a b c	true	There are items following the current position.
next()	1	a , b c	a	Return a and advance the current position.
next()	2	a b , c	b	Return b and advance the current position.
remove()	1	a , c	void	Remove b, the last item returned by previous or next. Note the location of the current position.
add(b)	2	a b , c	void	Insert b immediately to the left of the current position indicator.

("," indicates the current position and boldface indicates the last item returned)

TABLE 14-11 Continued
The effects of iterator operations on a list

LIST ITERATOR OPERATION	CURRENT POSITION AFTER THE OPERATION	STATE OF THE LIST AFTER THE OPERATION	VALUE RETURNED	COMMENT
next()	3	a b c ,	c	Return c and advance the current position.
next()	3	a b c ,	exception	The current position is at the end of the list; therefore, it is impossible to retrieve a next item.
hasNext()	3	a b c ,	false	The current position is at the end of the list; therefore, there is no next item.
hasPrevious()	3	a b c ,	true	There are items preceding the current position.
previous()	2	a b , **c**	c	Return c and move the current position backward.
remove()	2	a b ,	void	Remove c, the last item returned by previous or next. Note the location of the current position.
previous()	1	a , **b**	b	Return b and move the current position backward.
set(e)	1	a , e	void	Replace b, the last item returned by previous or next. The item e is now considered the last item returned.

("," indicates the current position and boldface indicates the last item returned)

TABLE 14-11 Continued
The effects of iterator operations on a list

LIST ITERATOR OPERATION	CURRENT POSITION AFTER THE OPERATION	STATE OF THE LIST AFTER THE OPERATION	VALUE RETURNED	COMMENT
`add(b)`	2	a b , e	void	Insert b immediately to the left of the current position indicator.
`add(c)`	3	a b c , e	void	Insert c immediately to the left of the current position indicator.
`remove()`	3	a b c , e	exception	add has occurred since the last next or previous.
`previous()`	2	a b , **c** e	c	Return **c** and move the current position backward.
`previous()`	1	a , **b** c e	b	Return **b** and move the current position backward.

("," indicates the current position and boldface indicates the last item returned)

The Enhanced `for` Loop Revisited

In Chapter 9 we introduced the use of the enhanced `for` loop with arrays and in Chapter 11 we showed that this loop can also be used with lists. The enhanced `for` loop is actually syntactic shorthand for a loop that uses an iterator. Thus, instead of the code

```
Iterator<ElementType> iter = list.iterator();
while(iter.hasNext()){
   ElementType e = iter.next();
   // do something with e, other than remove it from iter
}
```

you can use the code

```
for (ElementType e : list)
   // do something with e
```

The enhanced `for` loop is not only simpler to write but it's safer to use: there is no chance of an error in the logic of the loop itself. However, you cannot modify the list (replace, insert, or remove items) with an enhanced `for` loop. For that you need to use a list iterator.

EXERCISE 14.3

1. Assume the iterator `iter` has been opened on a list containing the strings "1", "2", and "3". Describe the effects of the following code segments as they are run in sequence:

   a. `String str = iter.next();`

   b. `iter.remove();`

   c. `str = iter.next();`

   d. `boolean state = iter.hasNext();`

   e. `for (int i = 1; i <= 3; i++) iter.next();`

2. Write code segments to accomplish the following tasks with the list iterator `iter`. You may assume that they are performed in sequence:

   a. Move to the last item and display it.

   b. Move to the first item and display it.

   c. Remove the item at the middle position.

   d. Replace the last item with the string "last".

   e. Insert the string "middle" at the middle position.

3. Describe the position of the object in a list that is accessed by the methods `set` and `remove` of a list iterator.

4. Suppose Jack is running an iterator on a list and he also mutates the list with a list method. Describe the reaction of the computer.

5. Suppose Jill opens two iterators on the same list. Describe what happens when one iterator attempts to remove an item from the list.

SUMMARY

In this chapter, you learned:

- There are several fundamental categories of collections, among which are linear collections, hierarchical collections, graph collections, and unordered collections.

- A list is a linear collection in which elements can be accessed at any position.

- A complete set of list operations includes position-based operations, content-based operations, and index-based operations.

- There is one list interface and several implementations, such as `ArrayList` and `LinkedList`.

- An iterator and a list iterator are two objects that allow clients to perform position-based operations on a list.

VOCABULARY *Review*

Define the following terms:

Abstract data type (ADT)	Graph collection	Object heap
Abstraction	Head	Parent
Backing store	Hierarchical collection	Position-based operation
Children	Index-based operation	Tail
Collection	Iterator	Type parameter
Content-based operation	Linear collection	Type variable
Free list	List iterator	Unordered collection

REVIEW *Questions*

FILL IN THE BLANK

Complete the following sentences by writing the correct word or words in the blanks provided.

1. A(n) _____ collection contains elements that are ordered by position and have unique successors and predecessors.

2. A(n) _____ collection contains elements that are in no particular order.

3. A(n) _____ collection contains elements that have at most one predecessor and zero or more successors.

4. _____ collections are useful for representing airline routes and circuit diagrams.

5. A(n) _____ -based operation uses an integer value to locate an element in a list.

6. A(n) _____ -based operation expects an element as a parameter and accesses this element in a list.

7. The classes _____, _____, and _____ implement the `List` interface in Java.

8. A(n) _____ tracks the current position in a list and allows clients to advance to the next position or remove the element at the current position.

9. A(n) _____ tracks the current position in a list and allows clients to move to the previous position and insert, remove, or replace an element at the current position.

10. The positions of elements in a list are numbered from _____ to the _____.

11. A type _____ is used to specify the element type in a generic collection when a variable is declared.

12. A type _____ is used to specify the element type in the method signatures of a generic collection.

PROJECTS

PROJECT 14-1

Write a program that inserts lines of text from a file into a list and allows the user to view any line of text from the file. The program should present a menu of options that allow the user to enter a filename and to navigate to the first line, the last line, the next line, and the previous line. Be sure to hide the list in a data model class that performs the required tasks.

PROJECT 14-2

Modify the data model of Project 14-1 so that it uses a list iterator for the navigation.

PROJECT 14-3

Write a program that allows the user to perform the following tasks:

- Add a noun to a list of nouns.

- Add a verb to a list of verbs.

- Generate a random sentence from the two lists.

Sentences should be of the form "the <noun> <verb> the <noun> with a <noun>." For example, if the list of nouns contains "girl," "ball," and "bat" and the list of verbs contains "hit," a random sentence is "the girl hit the ball with a bat." Note that some sentences might appear nonsensical although they are grammatically correct.

PROJECT 14-4

Modify the program from Project 14-3 to maintain a history list of the sentences that have been generated. Add a menu option to display all the sentences.

PROJECT 14-5

Modify the program from Project 14-4 to generate only sentences that have not been seen before. The program should generate a candidate sentence and examine its history list for a matching sentence. If a match is not found, this sentence is displayed as usual and added to the history list. If a match is found, the program repeats this process until no match is found or five attempts have been made. After the fifth unsuccessful attempt to generate a unique sentence, the program should ask the user to enter more nouns and/or verbs.

PROJECT 14-6

Modify the program from Project 14-5 so that it allows the user to reject nonsensical sentences. When the user selects the Reject Sentence menu option, the program searches the history list for a sentence that matches the one just generated. If a match is found, the program removes this sentence from the list.

CRITICAL*Thinking*

Jack has been using a simple iterator for processing lists. Jill informs him that an enhanced for loop would make is code simpler and safer. Jack replies, "No way! The enhanced for loop is too limiting." Discuss the merits of his response to Jill.

LINEAR COLLECTIONS: STACKS AND QUEUES

The list collections discussed in Chapter 14 are the most widely used linear collections. There are many applications that call for linear collections with a more restricted set of operations, however. In this chapter, we explore three such restricted linear collections: the *stack*, the *queue*, and a special type of queue called the *priority queue*. We take a client's perspective on these collections and defer a close examination of implementations until Chapters 17 and 19.

15.1 Stacks

Stacks are linear collections in which access is completely restricted to just one end, called the *top*. The classical example is the stack of clean trays found in every cafeteria. Whenever a tray is needed, it is removed from the top of the stack, and whenever clean ones come back from the scullery, they are again placed on the top. No one ever takes some particularly fine tray from the middle of the stack, and it is even possible that trays near the bottom are never used. Stacks are said to adhere to a last-in, first-out protocol (LIFO). The last tray brought back from the scullery is the first one taken by a customer.

The operations for putting items on and removing items from a stack are called *push* and *pop*, respectively. Figure 15-1 shows a stack as it might appear at various stages.

FIGURE 15-1
Some states in the lifetime of a stack

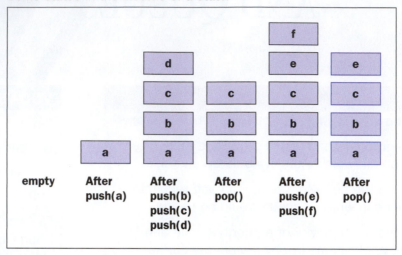

| empty | After push(a) | After push(b) push(c) push(d) | After pop() | After push(e) push(f) | After pop() |

Initially, the stack is empty, and then an item called *a* is pushed. Next, three more items called *b*, *c*, and *d* are pushed, after which the stack is popped, and so forth.

Other everyday examples of stacks include plates and bowls in our kitchen cupboards and PEZ® dispensers. Although we continually add more papers to the top of the piles on our desks, these piles do not quite qualify because we often need to remove a long-lost paper from the middle. With a genuine stack, the item we get next is always the one added most recently.

The Stack Class

The java.util package includes a Stack class that is a subclass of Vector. As we saw in Chapter 14, the Vector class implements the List and Collection interfaces. The relationships between these interfaces and classes are shown in Figure 15-2.

FIGURE 15-2
The Stack class and related resources

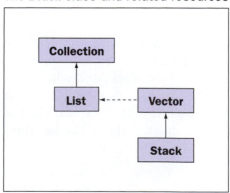

This means that clients can treat stacks as vectors by inserting, replacing, or removing an element at any position, thus violating the spirit of a stack. For now, we ignore this nicety and restrict our attention to the set of methods that *ought* to be used with the Stack class. These methods are listed in Table 15-1.

TABLE 15-1
Methods in the Stack class

METHOD	DESCRIPTION
boolean empty()	Returns true if the stack is empty or false otherwise
E peek()	*Precondition*: The stack is not empty *Throws*: An EmptyStackException if the stack is empty Returns the object at the top of the stack
E pop()	*Precondition*: The stack is not empty *Throws*: An EmptyStackException if the stack is empty Removes and returns the object at the top of the stack
void push(E element)	Adds element to the top of the stack
int size()	Returns the number of objects on the stack

Like vectors, stacks are generic collections, so their element types should be specified when they are created. A simple example illustrates the use of the Stack class. In this example, the strings in a list are transferred to a stack and then displayed. Their display order is the reverse of their order in the list. The last line of code attempts to pop from an empty stack, which throws an EmptyStackException.

```java
// Example 15.1: Tests a stack

import java.util.*;

public class TestStack{

    public static void main(String[] args){
        // Create a list and add some strings
        List<String> lst = new ArrayList<String>();
        for (int i = 0; i <= 5; i++)
            lst.add("String " + i);

        // Create a stack and transfer the strings
        Stack<String> stk = new Stack<String>();
        for (String str : lst)
            stk.push(str);

        // Pop and display objects from the stack
        while (! stk.empty())
            System.out.println(stk.pop());

        // Cause an EmptyStackException
        stk.pop();
    }
}
```

Applications of Stacks

Applications of stacks in computer science are numerous. Following are just a few examples:

- Parsing expressions in context-free programming languages—a problem in compiler design

- Translating infix expressions to postfix form and evaluating postfix expressions—discussed later in this chapter

- Backtracking algorithms—discussed later in this chapter and occurring in problems such as automated theorem proving and game playing

- Managing computer memory in support of method calls—discussed later in this chapter

- Supporting the "undo" feature in text editors, word processors, spreadsheet programs, drawing programs, and similar applications

- Maintaining a history of the links visited by a Web browser

We now discuss three applications of stacks. First, we present algorithms for evaluating arithmetic expressions. These algorithms apply to problems in compiler design, and we use them in one of the chapter's case studies and in one of the projects at the end of this chapter. Second, we describe a general technique for using stacks to solve backtracking problems. The end-of-chapter projects explore applications of the technique. Third, we examine the role of stacks in computer memory management. Not only is this topic interesting in its own right, but it also provides, as we saw in Chapter 11, a foundation for understanding recursion.

Evaluating Arithmetic Expressions

We are so accustomed to evaluating simple arithmetic expressions that we give little conscious thought to the rules involved, and we are surprised by the difficulty of writing an algorithm to do the same thing. It turns out that an indirect approach to the problem works best. First, we transform an expression from its familiar *infix form* to a *postfix form*, and then we evaluate the postfix form. In the infix form, each operator is located between its operands, whereas in the postfix form, an operator immediately follows its operands. Table 15-2 gives several simple examples.

TABLE 15-2
Some infix and postfix expressions

INFIX FORM	POSTFIX FORM	VALUE
34	34	34
34 + 22	34 22 +	56
34 + 22 * 2	34 22 2 * +	78
34 * 22 + 2	34 22 * 2 +	750
(34 + 22) * 2	34 22 + 2 *	112

There are similarities and differences between the two forms. In both, operands appear in the same order; however, the operators do not. The infix form sometimes requires parentheses; the postfix form never does. Infix evaluation involves rules of precedence; postfix evaluation applies operators as soon as they are encountered. For instance, consider the steps in evaluating the infix expression 34 + 22 * 2 and the equivalent postfix expression 34 22 2 * +.

Infix evaluation: 34 + 22 * 2 → 34 + 44 → 78

Postfix evaluation: 34 22 2 * + → 34 44 + → 78

We now present stack-based algorithms for transforming infix expressions to postfix and for evaluating the resulting postfix expressions. In combination, these algorithms allow us to evaluate an infix expression. In presenting the algorithms, we ignore the effects of syntax errors but return to the issue in the case study.

Evaluating Postfix Expressions

Evaluation is the simpler process and consists of three steps:

1. Scan across the expression from left to right.

2. On encountering an operator, apply it to the two preceding operands and replace all three by the result.

3. Continue scanning until reaching the expression's end, at which point only the expression's value remains.

To express this procedure as a computer algorithm, we use a stack of operands. In the algorithm, the term *token* refers to either an operand or an operator:

```
create a new stack
while there are more tokens in the expression
   get the next token
   if the token is an operand
      push the operand onto the stack
   else if the token is an operator
      pop the top two operands from the stack
      use the operator to evaluate the two operands just popped
      push the resulting operand onto the stack
   end if
end while
return the value at the top of the stack
```

The time complexity of the algorithm is $O(n)$, where n is the number of tokens in the expression. Table 15-3 shows a trace of the algorithm as it is applied to the expression 4 5 6 * + 3 –.

TABLE 15-3
Tracing the evaluation of a postfix expression

POSTFIX EXPRESSION: 4 5 6 * + 3 –   **RESULTING VALUE:** 31

PORTION OF POSTFIX EXPRESSION SCANNED SO FAR	OPERAND STACK	COMMENT
		No tokens have been seen yet. The stack is empty.
4	4	Push the operand. 4.
4 5	4 5	Push the operand. 5.
4 5 6	4 5 6	Push the operand. 6.
4 5 6 *	4 30	Replace the top two operands by their product.
4 5 6 * +	34	Replace the top two operands by their sum.
4 5 6 * + 3	34 3	Push the operand. 3.
4 5 6 * + 3 –	31	Replace the top two operands by their difference. Pop the final value.

Transforming Infix to Postfix

We now show how to translate expressions from infix to postfix. For the sake of simplicity, we restrict our attention to expressions involving the operators *, /, +, and -. (Project 15-1 at the end of this chapter adds the exponentiation operator to the set of operators.) As usual, multiplication and division have higher precedence than addition and subtraction, except when parentheses override the default order of evaluation.

In broad terms, the algorithm scans, from left to right, a string containing an infix expression and simultaneously builds a string containing the equivalent postfix expression. Operands are copied from the infix string to the postfix string as soon as they are encountered. Operators must be held back on a stack until operators of greater precedence have been copied to the postfix string ahead of them, however. Following is a more detailed statement of the process:

1. Start with an empty postfix expression and an empty stack, which will hold operators and left parentheses.

2. Scan across the infix expression from left to right.

3. On encountering an operand, append it to the postfix expression.

4. On encountering an operator, pop off the stack all operators that have equal or higher precedence and append them to the postfix expression. Then push the scanned operator onto the stack.

5. On encountering a left parenthesis, push it onto the stack.

6. On encountering a right parenthesis, shift operators from the stack to the postfix expression until meeting the matching left parenthesis, which is discarded.

7. On encountering the end of the infix expression, transfer the remaining operators from the stack to the postfix expression.

Examples in Tables 15-4 and 15-5 illustrate the procedure.

TABLE 15-4
Tracing the conversion of an infix expression to a postfix expression

INFIX EXPRESSION: 4 + 5 * 6 − 3 **EQUIVALENT POSTFIX EXPRESSION:** 4 5 6 * + 3 −

PORTION OF INFIX EXPRESSION SCANNED SO FAR	OPERATOR STACK	POSTFIX EXPRESSION	COMMENT
			No characters have been seen yet. The stack and PE are empty.
4		4	Append 4 to the PE.
4 +	+	4	Push + onto the stack.
4 + 5	+	4 5	Append 5 to the PE.
4 + 5 *	+ *	4 5	Push * onto the stack.
4 + 5 * 6	+ *	4 5 6	Append 6 to the PE.
4 + 5 * 6 −	−	4 5 6 * +	Pop * and +, append them to the PE, and push -.
4 + 5 * 6 − 3	−	4 5 6 * + 3	Append 3 to the PE.
		4 5 6 * + 3 −	Pop the remaining operators off the stack and append them to the PE.

TABLE 15-5
Tracing the conversion of an infix expression with parentheses to a postfix expression

INFIX EXPRESSION: (4 + 5) * (6 − 3) **EQUIVALENT POSTFIX EXPRESSION:** 4 5 + 6 3 − *

PORTION OF INFIX EXPRESSION SCANNED SO FAR	OPERATOR STACK	POSTFIX EXPRESSION	COMMENT
			No characters have been seen yet. The stack and PE are empty.
(	(		Push (onto the stack.
(4	(	4	Append 4 to the PE.
(4 +	(+	4	Push + onto the stack.
(4 + 5	(+	4 5	Append 5 to the PE.

TABLE 15-5 Continued
Tracing the conversion of an infix expression with parentheses to a postfix expression

INFIX EXPRESSION: (4 + 5) * (6 − 3) **EQUIVALENT POSTFIX EXPRESSION:** 4 5 + 6 3 − *

PORTION OF INFIX EXPRESSION SCANNED SO FAR	OPERATOR STACK	POSTFIX EXPRESSION	COMMENT
(4 + 5)	(+	4 5 +	Pop the stack until (is encountered and append operators to the PE.
(4 + 5) *	*	4 5 +	Push * onto the stack.
(4 + 5) * (	* (	4 5 +	Push (onto the stack.
(4 + 5) * (6	* (	4 5 + 6	Append 6 to the PE.
(4 + 5) * (6 -	* (-	4 5 + 6	Push - onto the stack.
(4 + 5) * (6 - 3	* (-	4 5 + 6 3	Append 3 to the PE.
(4 + 5) * (6 - 3)	*	4 5 + 6 3-	Pop stack until (is encountered and append items to the PE.
		4 5 + 6 3 - *	Pop the remaining operators off the stack and append them to the PE.

Backtracking

There are two principal techniques for implementing backtracking algorithms: one uses stacks and the other recursion. Recursion was considered in Chapter 12. We explore the use of stacks for backtracking algorithms in this section. A backtracking algorithm begins in a predefined starting state and then moves from state to state in search of a desired ending state. At any point along the way, when there is a choice between several alternative states, the algorithm picks one, possibly at random, and continues. If the algorithm reaches a state representing an undesirable outcome, it backs up to the last point at which there was an unexplored alternative and tries it. In this way, the algorithm either exhaustively searches all states, or it reaches the desired ending state.

The role of a stack in the process is to remember the alternative states that occur at each juncture. To be more precise:

```
create an empty stack
push the starting state onto the stack
while the stack is not empty
   pop the stack and examine the state
   if the state represents an ending state
      return SUCCESSFUL CONCLUSION
   else if the state has not been visited previously
      mark the state as visited
      push onto the stack all unvisited adjacent states
   end if
end while
return UNSUCCESSFUL CONCLUSION
```

Although short, the algorithm is subtle, and an illustration is needed to elucidate its workings.

Suppose there are just five states, as shown in Figure 15-3, with states 1 and 5 representing the start and end, respectively. Lines between states indicate adjacency. Starting in state 1, the algorithm proceeds to state 4 and then to 3. In state 3, the algorithm recognizes that all adjacent states have been visited and resumes the search in state 2, which leads directly to state 5 and the end. Table 15-6 contains a detailed trace of the algorithm.

FIGURE 15-3
States of the backtracking algorithm

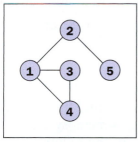

TABLE 15-6
Trace of the backtracking algorithm

NEXT STEP IN ALGORITHM	STACK	CURRENT STATE	VISITED STATES
Push 1.	1		none yet
Pop the stack and note the state.		1	none yet
Mark the state as visited.		1	1
Push unvisited adjacent states.	2 3 4	1	1
Pop stack and note the state.	2 3	4	1
Mark the state as visited.	2 3	4	1 4
Push unvisited adjacent states.	2 3	4	1 4
Pop the stack and note the state.	2 3	3	1 4
Mark the state as visited.	2 3	3	1 4 3
All adjacent states already visited.	2 3	3	1 4 3
Pop the stack and note the state.	2	3	1 4 3
Do nothing, location already visited.	2	3	1 4 3
Pop the stack and note the state.		2	1 4 3
Mark the state as visited.		2	1 4 3 2
Push unvisited adjacent states.	5	2	1 4 3 2
Pop the stack and note the state.		5	1 4 3 2
SUCCESS: This is the ending state.		5	1 4 3 2

Notice in the trace that the algorithm goes directly from state 3 to state 2 without having to back up through states 4 and 1 first. This is a beneficial side effect of using a stack.

It would be interesting to calculate the time complexity of the foregoing algorithm. However, two crucial pieces of information are missing:

1. The complexity of deciding if a state has been visited.

2. The complexity of listing states adjacent to a given state.

If, for the sake of argument, we assume that both of these processes are O(1), then the algorithm as a whole is O(n), where n represents the total number of states.

This discussion has been a little abstract, but at the end of the chapter, Project 15-7 applies backtracking to a maze problem.

Memory Management

During a program's execution, both its code and data occupy computer memory. Although the exact manner in which a computer manages memory depends on the programming language and operating system involved, we can present the following simplified yet reasonably realistic overview. The emphasis must be on the word "simplified" because a detailed discussion is beyond this book's scope.

As you may recall from our earlier discussion, a Java compiler translates a Java program into byte codes. A complex program called the Java virtual machine (JVM) then executes these. The memory, or run-time environment, controlled by the JVM is divided into six regions, as shown on the left side of Figure 15-4.

FIGURE 15-4
The architecture of a run-time environment

Working up from the bottom, these regions contain:

- The Java virtual machine, which executes a Java program. Internal to the JVM are two variables, which we call `locationCounter` and `basePtr`. The `locationCounter` points at the instruction the JVM will execute next. The `basePtr` points at the top activation record's base. More is said about these variables soon.

- Byte codes for all the methods of our program.

- The program's static variables.

- The *call stack*. Every time a method is called, an *activation record* is created and pushed onto the call stack. When a method finishes execution and returns control to the method that called it, the activation record is popped off the stack. The total number of activation records on the stack equals the number of method calls currently in various stages of execution. At the bottom of the stack is the activation record for the method `main`. Above it is the activation record for the method currently called by `main`, and so forth. More will be said about activation records in a moment.

- Unused memory. This region's size grows and shrinks in response to the demands of the call stack and the object heap.

- The object heap. In Java, all objects exist in a region of memory called the *heap*. When an object is instantiated, the JVM must find space for the object on the heap, and when the object is no longer needed, the JVM's garbage collector recovers the space for future use. When low on space, the heap extends further into the region marked *Unused Memory*.

The activation records shown on the right side of the figure contain two types of information. The regions labeled *Local Variables* and *Parameters* hold data needed by the executing method. The remaining regions hold data that allow the JVM to pass control backward from the currently executing method to the method that called it.

When a method is called, the JVM:

1. Creates the method's activation record and pushes it onto the call stack (the activation record's bottom three regions are fixed in size, and the top two vary depending on the number of parameters and local variables used by the method).

2. Saves the `basePtr`'s current value in the region labeled `Prev basePtr` and sets the `basePtr` to the new activation record's base.

3. Saves the `locationCounter`'s current value in the region labeled *Return Address* and sets the `locationCounter` to the first instruction of the called method.

4. Copies the calling parameters into the region labeled *Parameters*.

5. Initializes local variables as required.

6. Starts executing the called method at the location indicated by the `locationCounter`.

While a method is executing, local variables and parameters in the activation record are referenced by adding an offset to the `basePtr`. Thus, no matter where an activation record is located in memory, the local variables and parameters can be accessed correctly provided the `basePtr` has been initialized properly.

Just before returning, a method stores its return value in the location labeled *Return Value*. The value can be a reference to an object, or it can be a primitive data type such as an integer or character. Because the return value always resides at the bottom of the activation record, the calling method knows exactly where to find it.

When a method has finished executing, the JVM:

1. Reestablishes the settings needed by the calling method by restoring the values of the `locationCounter` and the `basePtr` from values stored in the activation record.

2. Pops the activation record from the call stack.

3. Resumes execution of the calling method at the location indicated by the `locationCounter`.

Implementing Stacks

Stacks are linear collections, so the natural choices for implementations are based on arrays and linked structures. The `Stack` class of `java.util` extends `Vector`, which in turn uses an array. We could define a more restricted implementation of a stack by directly using either the `ArrayList` or the `LinkedList` classes discussed in Chapter 14. Let's create a common interface for these implementations called `TrueStack`, to indicate that it includes only methods appropriate for a stack. Here is the code for this interface:

```java
// Example 15.2: Interface for a restricted stack

public interface TrueStack<E>{

    public boolean empty();

    public E peek();

    public E pop();

    public void push(E element);

    public int size();
}
```

Following is the code for the class `TrueArrayStack`, which implements `TrueStack`:

```java
// Example 15.2: ArrayList implementation of a restricted stack

import java.util.*;

public class TrueArrayStack<E> implements TrueStack<E>{

    private List<E> list;

    public TrueArrayStack(){
        list = new ArrayList<E>();
    }

    public boolean empty(){
        return list.isEmpty();
    }
```

```java
   public E peek(){
      if (empty())
         throw new EmptyStackException();
      return list.get(list.size() - 1);
   }

   public E pop(){
      if (empty())
         throw new EmptyStackException();
      return list.remove(list.size() - 1);
   }

   public void push(E element){
      list.add(element);
   }

   public int size(){
      return list.size();
   }
}
```

Note the use of the type variable E to indicate the element type of the stack and its implementing list. A linked implementation using LinkedList is left as an exercise. To test this implementation with the tester program used earlier, we just replace the word Stack with the word TrueArrayStack throughout the class TestStack.

Analyzing the Performance of Stack Implementations

The run-time performance of a stack implementation depends on the run-time performance of the operations on the data structure contained in it. As we have seen, the two options are arrays and linked structures.

Based on our analysis of the list implementations in Chapter 14, a stack that uses an array list or an array can push or pop elements in constant time, with one exception. When the underlying array runs out of room, it must be resized, and this operation takes linear time, as we see in Chapter 17.

On the other hand, elements can always be added to the end or the beginning of a linked structure in constant time. A linked structure requires three times the memory to represent the links and references to the data but no extra memory to represent the data themselves. Thus, where time is of the essence, a linked implementation is usually preferable.

EXERCISE 15.1

1. Assume that a stack s has been created. Draw a picture of the state of the stack after each of the following sequences of operations. You should assume that each sequence follows the previous one from a to c:

a.

```java
for (int i = 1; i <= 5; i++)
   s.push("" + i);
```

EXERCISE 15.1 Continued

b.

```
s.pop();
s.pop();
```

c.

```
s.push("5");
s.push("6");
```

2. Write code segments that accomplish the following tasks with the stack s:

a. Push the strings "hello" and "there" onto the stack.

b. Make the stack be empty.

c. Print the contents of the stack in the terminal window without removing them permanently. (*Hint:* You can use a temporary data structure to accomplish this.)

3. What information is stored in an activation record and how is it used?

4. Why is a stack such a handy data structure when used to evaluate postfix expressions?

5. Explain what happens when a stack overflow error occurs.

6. Why would a programmer prefer a `TrueStack` implementation of a stack over `java.util.Stack`?

15.2 The `StringTokenizer` Class

Before we turn to our first case study, we examine a class that is useful in text analysis applications. Sentences are composed of individual words, or tokens. When you read, you automatically break a sentence into its individual tokens, usually using white-space characters such as blanks, tabs, and newline characters as delimiters. The `java.util` package provides a `StringTokenizer` class that allows you to break a string into individual tokens using either the default delimiters (space, newline, tab, and carriage return) or a programmer-specified delimiter. The process of obtaining tokens from a string tokenizer is called *scanning*. Table 15-7 shows several `StringTokenizer` methods.

TABLE 15-7
Some commonly used `StringTokenizer` methods

METHOD	WHAT IT DOES
`int countTokens()`	Returns the number of tokens in the string tokenizer
`boolean hasMoreTokens()`	Returns `true` if there is still an unscanned token in the string tokenizer
`String nextToken()`	Scans through the string tokenizer, returning the next available token

For example, the following program displays each word of a sentence on a separate line in the terminal output stream:

```java
// Example 15.3: Tests a StringTokenizer

import java.util.StringTokenizer;

public class TestTokenizer{

    public static void main(String[] args){
        String sentence = "Four score and seven years ago, our fathers set "
                        + "forth on this continent a new nation.";

        StringTokenizer tokens = new StringTokenizer(sentence);

        while (tokens.hasMoreTokens())
            System.out.println(tokens.nextToken());
    }
}
```

The program outputs a surprising result. The list of words displayed by `println` include

```
ago,
nation.
```

rather than

```
ago
nation
```

The reason is simple. The delimiters are space, newline, tab, and carriage return. Punctuation marks are treated no differently than letters. To add punctuation marks to the list of delimiters, replace the second line of the `main` method in the preceding code with the following two lines:

```java
String listOfDelimiters = ".,;?! \t\n\r";
StringTokenizer tokens = new StringTokenizer(sentence, listOfDelimiters);
```

EXERCISE 15.2

1. Assume that the `string` variable `str` refers to a string. Write the code to create a string tokenizer that recognizes decimal digits in `str` as delimiter characters.

2. Assume that the `string` variable `str` refers to a string. Write a code segment that uses a string tokenizer to remove the white-space characters in `str`.

3. Generalize the method used in your answer to Question 2 to remove all the instances of any character from a string.

Case Study 1: A Postfix Expression Evaluator

Earlier in this chapter, we developed an algorithm that uses a stack to evaluate postfix expressions. We now place this algorithm in the context of a program.

Request

Write a program that evaluates postfix expressions.

Analysis

The program expects a string as input. If the string represents a syntactically correct postfix expression, the program displays its value. If the string has a syntax error or semantic error, the program outputs an error message. A trace of an interaction with the program is shown in Figure 15-5.

FIGURE 15-5
A sample interaction with the postfix expression evaluation program

A syntactically correct postfix expression consists of the operators +, -, *, and / and numbers, which are strings of digits. All operators and operands must be separated by at least one blank space character or tab character. Table 15-8 lists some syntactically correct and incorrect expressions.

TABLE 15-8
Some syntactically correct and incorrect expressions

CORRECT SYNTAX	INCORRECT SYNTAX
88 77 +	88 77+
88 77 99 + *	88 + 77
22 77 + 99 -	22 77 $ 99 –

An example semantic error is an attempt to divide by 0, as in the expression 77 0 /.

Classes

The program consists of two classes, `EvaluatorView` and `Evaluator`. `EvaluatorView` simply handles the input and output. `Evaluator` implements the algorithm discussed earlier in this chapter.

Design

The view receives a string from the user, sends it to the evaluator for processing, and receives back a string that is either a number or an error message. The evaluator uses a string tokenizer to extract the operators and operands from the input string. These in turn are fed into the algorithm, which is refined to handle malformed expressions appropriately.

The algorithm makes use of the private helper methods `isOperator`, `isOperand`, and `computeValue`. `isOperator` expects a string as a parameter and compares this string to the strings "+", "-", "*", and "/". If a match occurs, the method returns `true`, and if not, the method returns `false`. `isOperand` determines whether its string parameter represents an integer by testing each character with the method `Character.isDigit`. `computeValue` expects the operator and two operand strings as parameters and returns a string representing the result of computing the expression's value. This method returns `null` if the operator is / and the second operand is 0.

Implementation

The view class uses a simple query-based loop. Here is the code:

```java
// Case Study 1: Evaluator of postfix expressions
// View class

import java.util.Scanner;

public class EvaluatorView{

    public static void main (String[] args){
        Scanner reader = new Scanner(System.in);
        Evaluator evaluator = new Evaluator();
        String query = "Y";
        while (query.equalsIgnoreCase("Y")){
            System.out.print("Enter a postfix expression: ");
            String input = reader.nextLine();
            String output = evaluator.run(input);
            System.out.println(output);
            System.out.print("Evaluate another expression[y/n]: ");
            query = reader.nextLine();
        }
    }
}
```

A listing of the model class, `Evaluator`, follows:

```java
// Case Study 1: Evaluator of postfix expressions
// Model class

import java.util.*;
```

```java
public class Evaluator{

    public String run(String input){
        Stack<String> stack = new Stack<String>();
        StringTokenizer tokens = new StringTokenizer(input);
        String operand1 = null, operand2 = null;
        String error = null;
        while (tokens.hasMoreTokens() && error == null){
            String token = tokens.nextToken();
            if (isOperand(token))
                stack.push(token);
            else if (isOperator(token)){
                if (! stack.empty()){
                    operand2 = stack.pop();
                    if (! stack.empty()){
                        operand1 = stack.pop();
                        String result = computeValue(operand1, token, operand2);
                        if (result != null)
                            stack.push(result);
                        else
                            error = "Attempt to divide by 0";
                    }else
                        error = "Malformed expression";
                }else
                    error = "Malformed expression";
            }else
                error = "Malformed expression";
        }
        if (stack.size() != 1)
            error = "Malformed expression";
        if (error != null)
            return error;
        else
            return stack.pop();
    }

    private boolean isOperand(String s){
        for (int i = 0; i < s.length(); i++)
            if (! Character.isDigit(s.charAt(i)))
                return false;
        return true;
    }

    private boolean isOperator(String s){
        return s.equals("+") ||
                s.equals("-") ||
                s.equals("*") ||
                s.equals("/");
    }

    private String computeValue(String op1, String op, String op2){
        int result = 0;
        int intOp1 = Integer.parseInt(op1);
        int intOp2 = Integer.parseInt(op2);
```

```
        if (op.equals("+"))
            result = intOp1 + intOp2;
        else if (op.equals("-"))
            result = intOp1 - intOp2;
        else if (op.equals("*"))
            result = intOp1 * intOp2;
        else if (op.equals("/"))
            if (intOp2 == 0)
                return null;
            else
                result = intOp1 / intOp2;
        return "" + result;
    }
}
```

15.3 Queues and Priority Queues

Like stacks, queues are linear collections. However, insertions in a queue are restricted to one end, called the *rear*, and removals are restricted to the other end, called the *front*. A queue thus supports a first-in, first-out protocol (FIFO). Queues are omnipresent in everyday life and occur in any situation where people or things are lined up for processing on a first-come, first-served basis. Checkout lines in stores, highway tollbooth lines, and airport baggage check-in lines are familiar examples of queues.

Queues have two fundamental operations: *add*, which adds an item to the rear of a queue, and *remove*, which removes an item from the front. (The traditional names of these operations are *enqueue* and *dequeue*, but we use the names adopted by Java in this book.) Figure 15-6 shows a queue as it might appear at various stages in its lifetime. In the figure, the queue's front is on the left and its rear is on the right.

FIGURE 15-6
The states in the lifetime of a queue

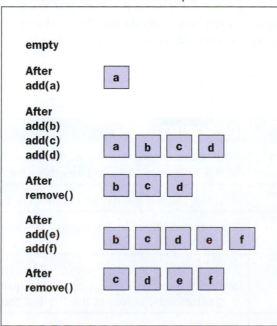

Initially, the queue is empty. Then an item called *a* is added. Next three more items called *b*, *c*, and *d* are added, after which an item is removed, and so forth.

Related to queues is an ADT called a *priority queue*. In a queue, the item removed or served next is always the item that has been waiting the longest. But in some circumstances, this restriction is too rigid, and we would like to combine the idea of waiting with a notion of priority. The result is a priority queue, in which higher priority items are removed before those of lower priority, and items of equal priority are removed in FIFO order. Consider, for example, the manner in which passengers board an aircraft. The first-class passengers line up and board first, and the lower priority coach-class passengers line up and board second. This is not a true priority queue, however, because once the first-class queue has emptied and the coach-class queue starts boarding, late arriving first-class passengers usually go to the end of the second queue. In a true priority queue, they would immediately jump ahead of all the coach-class passengers.

Most examples of queues in computer science involve scheduling access to shared resources, for instance,

- CPU access—Processes are queued for access to a shared CPU.

- Disk access—Processes are queued for access to a shared secondary storage device.

- Printer access—Print jobs are queued for access to a shared printer.

Process scheduling can use either simple queues or priority queues. For example, processes involving keyboard input and screen output are often given higher priority access to the CPU than those that are computationally intensive. The result is that users, who tend to judge a computer's speed by its response time, are given the impression that the computer is fast.

Processes waiting for a shared resource also can be prioritized by their expected duration, with short processes given higher priority than longer ones, again with the intent of improving the apparent response time of a system. Imagine 20 print jobs queued up for access to a printer. If 19 jobs are one page long and one job is 200 pages long, more users will be happy if the short jobs are given higher priority and are printed first.

The Queue Interface and Implementation

The `java.util` package of Java 5.0 includes a `Queue` interface. Like the `List` interface discussed in Chapter 14, the `Queue` interface extends the `Collection` interface, so there are many methods that are available to the user of a queue. The methods that a programmer *ought* to choose are shown in Table 15-9.

TABLE 15-9
The `Queue` interface

METHOD	DESCRIPTION
`boolean add(E element)`	Adds `element` to the rear of the queue and returns `true` if room is available or returns `false` otherwise
`boolean isEmpty()`	Returns `true` if the queue is empty or `false` otherwise
`E peek()`	Returns the object at the front of the queue or `null` if the queue is empty
`E remove()`	*Precondition*: The queue is not empty. *Throws*: An `NoSuchElementException` if the queue is empty. Removes and returns the object at the front of the queue
`int size()`	Returns number of objects in the queue

Table 15-10 gives a short illustration of queue operations in action.

TABLE 15-10
A trace of some Queue operations

OPERATION	STATE OF THE QUEUE AFTER THE OPERATION	VALUE RETURNED	COMMENT
			Initially, the queue is empty.
add(a)	a		The queue contains the single item a.
add(b)	a b		a is at the front of the queue and b is at the rear.
add(c)	a b c		c is added at the rear.
size()	a b c	3	The queue contains three items.
peek()	a b c	a	Return the front item on the queue without removing it.
remove()	b c	a	Remove the front item from the queue and return it. b is now the front item.
remove()	c	b	Remove and return b.
remove()		c	Remove and return c.
size()		0	The queue contains no items.
peek()		exception	Peeking at an empty queue throws an exception.
remove()		exception	Trying to remove an empty queue throws an exception.
add(d)	d		d is the front item.

Applications of Queues

We now look briefly at two applications of queues: one involving computer simulations and the other using round-robin CPU scheduling.

Simulations

Computer simulations are used to study the behavior of real-world systems, especially when it is impractical or dangerous to experiment with these systems directly. For example, a computer simulation could mimic traffic flows on a busy highway. Urban planners could then experiment with factors affecting traffic flows, such as the number and types of vehicles on the highway, the speed limits for different types of vehicles, the number of lanes in the highway, the frequency of tollbooths, and so on. Outputs from such a simulation might include the total number of vehicles able to move between designated points in a designated period and the average duration of a trip. By running the simulation with many combinations of inputs, the planners could determine how best to upgrade sections of the highway subject to the ever-present constraints of time, space, and money.

As a second example, consider the problem faced by the manager of a supermarket when trying to determine the number of checkout clerks to schedule at various times of the day. Some important factors in this situation are

- The frequency with which new customers arrive.

- The number of checkout clerks available.

- The number of items in a customer's shopping cart.

- The period of time considered.

These factors could be inputs to a simulation program, which would then determine the total number of customers processed, the average time each customer waits for service, and the number of customers left standing in line at the end of the simulated time period. By varying the inputs, particularly the frequency of customer arrivals and the number of available checkout clerks, a simulation program could help the manager make effective staffing decisions for busy and slow times of the day. By adding an input that quantifies the efficiency of different checkout equipment, the manager can even decide whether it is cheaper to add more clerks or buy better equipment.

A common characteristic of both examples, and of simulation problems in general, is the moment-by-moment variability of essential factors. Consider the frequency of customer arrivals at checkout stations. If customers arrived at precise intervals, each with exactly the same number of items, it would be easy to determine how many clerks to have on duty. Such regularity does not reflect the reality of a supermarket, however. Sometimes several customers show up at practically the same instant, and at other times no new customers arrive for several minutes. In addition, the number of items varies from customer to customer and, therefore, so does the amount of service required by each customer. All this variability makes it impossible to devise formulas to answer simple questions about the system, such as how customer-waiting time varies with the number of clerks on duty. A simulation program, on the other hand, avoids the need for formulas by imitating the actual situation and collecting pertinent statistics.

Simulation programs use a simple technique to mimic variability. For instance, suppose new customers are expected to arrive on average once every 4 minutes. Then during each minute of simulated time, a program can generate a random number between 0 and 1. If the number is less than .25, the program adds a new customer to a checkout line; otherwise, it does not. More sophisticated schemes based on probability distribution functions produce even more realistic results. Obviously, each time the program runs, the results change slightly, but this only adds to the realism of the simulation.

Now let us discuss the common role played by queues in these examples. Both examples involve service providers and service consumers. In the first example, service providers include tollbooths and traffic lanes, and service consumers are the vehicles waiting at the tollbooths and driving in the traffic lanes. In the second example, clerks provide a service that is consumed by waiting customers. To emulate these conditions in a program, we associate each service provider with a queue of service consumers.

Simulations operate by manipulating these queues. At each tick of an imaginary clock, a simulation adds varying numbers of consumers to the queues and gives consumers at the head of each queue another unit of service. Once a consumer has received the needed quantity of service, it leaves the queue and the next consumer steps forward. During the simulation, the program accumulates statistics such as how many ticks each consumer waited in a queue and the percentage of time each provider is busy. The duration of a tick is chosen to match the problem being simulated. It could represent a millisecond, a minute, or a decade. In the program itself, a tick probably corresponds to one pass through the program's major processing loop.

Object-oriented languages are well suited to implementing simulation programs. For instance, in a supermarket simulation, each customer is an instance of a Customer class. A customer object keeps track of when the customer starts standing in line, when service is first received, and how much service is required. Likewise, a clerk is an instance of a Clerk class, and each clerk object contains a queue of customer objects. A Simulator class coordinates the activities of the customers and clerks. At each clock tick, the simulation object

- Generates new customer objects as appropriate.

- Assigns customers to cashiers.

- Tells each cashier to provide one unit of service to the customer at the head of the queue.

Round-Robin CPU Scheduling

Most modern computers allow multiple processes to share a single CPU. There are various techniques for scheduling these processes. The most common, called *round-robin scheduling*, adds new processes to the end of a *ready queue*, which consists of processes waiting to use the CPU. Each process on the ready queue is removed in turn and given a slice of CPU time. When the time slice runs out, the process is returned to the rear of the queue, as shown in Figure 15-7.

FIGURE 15-7
Scheduling processes for a CPU

Generally, not all processes need the CPU with equal urgency. For instance, user satisfaction with a computer is greatly influenced by the computer's response time to keyboard and mouse inputs; thus, it makes sense to give precedence to processes handling these inputs. Round-robin scheduling adapts to this requirement by using a priority queue and assigning each process an appropriate priority. As a follow-up to this discussion, the chapter's second case study shows how a priority queue can be used to schedule patients in an emergency room.

Implementing the Queue Classes

The `LinkedList` class of `java.util` implements the `Queue` interface. This is a quick and easy implementation to use, as shown in the following short program:

```java
// Example 15.4: Tests a queue that is a LinkedList

import java.util.*;

public class TestQueue{

    public static void main(String[] args){
        // Create a queue and add some strings
        Queue<String> queue = new LinkedList<String>();
        queue.add("First");
        queue.add("Second");
        System.out.println(queue.peek());     // Prints "First"
        System.out.println(queue.remove());   // Prints "First"
    }
}
```

However, like the `Stack` class of `java.util`, this implementation violates the spirit of an ADT, in this case by allowing insertions, removals, and replacements anywhere in the queue (see Figure 15-8 for the relationships among the classes and interfaces).

FIGURE 15-8

The `Queue` interface and related resources

For cases where we need a secure queue that more closely adheres to the definition of the ADT, we can provide linked and array-based implementations. These are designed along the lines of the restricted stack implementations described earlier. The interface `TrueQueue` includes the essential queue methods, as follows:

```java
// Example 15.5: Interface for a restricted queue

public interface TrueQueue<E>{

    public boolean add(E element);

    public boolean isEmpty();

    public E peek();
```

```
        public E remove();

        public int size();
}
```

The class `TrueLinkedQueue` is a linked implementation of `TrueQueue`. This implementation contains a `LinkedList`, as shown in the following listing:

```
// Example 15.5: A restricted queue that contains a LinkedList

import java.util.*;

public class TrueLinkedQueue<E> implements TrueQueue<E>{

    protected LinkedList<E> list;

    public TrueLinkedQueue(){
        list = new LinkedList<E>();
    }

    public boolean add(E element){
        return list.addFirst(element);
    }

    public boolean isEmpty(){
        return list.isEmpty();
    }

    public E peek(){
        if (list.isEmpty())
            return null;
        return list.getFirst();
    }

    public E remove(){
        if (list.isEmpty())
            throw new NoSuchElementException();
        return list.removeLast();
    }

    public int size(){
        return list.size();
    }
}
```

Note that the `list` variable is declared as `protected`. The use of this visibility modifier allows us to create a useful subclass, as we see shortly.

Analyzing the Performance of Queue Implementations

The `LinkedList` class, which implements the `Queue` interface in `java.util`, and our own `TrueLinkedQueue` class are nice implementations of a queue from a performance standpoint. As we have seen, adding elements to one end of a linked list and removing them from the other end are constant-time operations. The only offsetting cost is the additional memory for the links.

A queue implementation based on an `ArrayList` supports constant-time additions or removals but not both. One of these operations must work on the beginning of the list, which causes linear time behavior.

Resources for Priority Queues

As mentioned earlier, a priority queue is a specialized type of queue. When items are added to a priority queue, they are assigned a rank order. When they are removed, items of higher priority are removed before those of lower priority. Items of equal priority are removed in the usual FIFO order.

The `PriorityQueue` class in `java.util` implements the `Queue` interface. Its essential methods are thus the same as those for a common queue listed in Table 15-9. A `PriorityQueue` maintains a natural ordering among its elements to support priority-based access and removals. Thus, a `PriorityQueue` requires that its elements implement the `Comparable` interface. This means, for example, that a `PriorityQueue` can contain strings or integers but not stacks or random number generators. The item with the minimum value in the natural ordering is removed or accessed first.

Here is a short program that illustrates the use of a `PriorityQueue`:

```java
// Example 15.6: Tests a PriorityQueue

import java.util.PriorityQueue;

public class TestPriorityQueue{

   public static void main(String[] args){
      // Create a list and add some strings
      PriorityQueue <String> que = new PriorityQueue<String>();
      for (int i = 1; i <= 5; i++)
         que.add("String" + i);
      // Add one more to show prioritization
      que.add("String" + 0);

      // Remove and display objects from the queue
      while (! que.isEmpty())
         System.out.println(que.remove());

      // Cause an NoSuchElementException
      que.remove();
   }
}
```

In this book, we discuss two implementations of a priority queue. The `PriorityQueue` class uses a heap-based implementation. We examine heaps in Chapter 19. Unfortunately, this implementation does not guarantee FIFO access to elements that have the same priority. A second implementation, which we consider shortly, not only maintains a natural ordering of elements but also guarantees a FIFO ordering in cases where the elements have the same priority.

A Sorted List Implementation of a Priority Queue

A sorted list is a list of comparable elements that are maintained in a natural order. A priority queue's list should be arranged so that the minimum element is always accessed at or removed from just one end of the list. The elements are inserted in their proper places in the ordering. A linked list will work well if we remove the minimum element from either the head or the tail of the list. If an element is greater than or equal to a given element, the new element can be inserted at the position before the given element. This will guarantee a FIFO ordering in cases of tied priorities. But this means that the elements must be in descending order in the list, and elements will always be peeked at or removed from the tail position. Figure 15-9 shows a logical view of the ordering of some elements in this implementation.

FIGURE 15-9
A priority queue's sorted list

The only operation that needs development is add. This operation searches for the element's proper place in the list and then inserts it there. The search begins at the head of the list and proceeds until the new element is greater than or equal to an element in the list. The new element is then inserted at that position. If the search runs off the tail of the list, the new element is the new minimum and it goes at the tail. Here is a pseudocode algorithm for the add operation:

```
Set position to 0
While position < size and new element < element at position do
    Increment position
Insert the new element at position
```

The new priority queue class is called TrueLinkedPriorityQueue. Like the TrueLinkedQueue class discussed earlier, the new class implements the TrueQueue interface and contains a linked list. In fact, the implementation of every method except for add is exactly the same in the two classes. Therefore, TrueLinkedPriorityQueue is a perfect candidate for becoming a subclass of TrueLinkedQueue. Figure 15-10 shows the relationships between the classes and the interface. A listing of the new class follows.

FIGURE 15-10
The true priority queue class hierarchy

```
// Example 15.7: A restricted implementation of a priority queue based
// on a true linked queue

// Variable inherited from TrueLinkedQueue: list (a LinkedList)
// Methods inherited from TrueLinkedQueue: isEmpty, peek, remove, and size

import java.util.*;

public class TrueLinkedPriorityQueue<E extends Comparable<E>>
        extends TrueLinkedQueue<E>{

    public TrueLinkedPriorityQueue(){
        super();
    }

    public boolean add(E element){
        int position = 0;
        while (position < list.size() &&
                element.compareTo(list.get(position)) < 0)
            position++;
        list.add(position, element);
        return true;
    }
}
```

There are several important points to note about this implementation:

1. In the heading of the class, the element type for `TrueLinkedPriorityQueue` is not merely the variable `E` but the expression `E extends Comparable<E>`. This means that any element type used in the collection must also implement the `Comparable` interface. (`extends` in this context can mean either `extends` or `implements`.)

2. The element type of the superclass, `TrueLinkedQueue`, is still specified by the simple variable `E`. This means that it can contain any type of elements, although in this case it will actually contain any elements that implement `Comparable`.

3. Because the element type of `TrueLinkedPriorityQueue` has been restricted to a `Comparable`, the code for the method `add` does not have to cast the element to `Comparable` before sending that element the `compareTo` message.

4. The expression `Comparable<E>` in the class heading indicates a *generic comparable*, a topic to which we now turn.

Using the `Comparable` Interface with Generic Collections

The version of the method `compareTo` used in the class `TrueLinkedPriorityQueue` is different in two ways from the one we used with arrays of objects in Chapter 11:

1. The receiver object (the left operand of the comparison) is not cast to `Comparable` because it already is a `Comparable`.

2. The parameter object must be of the collection's element type (also a `Comparable`).

Because we are using `compareTo` in the context of a generic collection whose element type is known at compile time, the signature of the method should also be generic. As a consequence, any element type that is used in the collection must implement the generic version of the `Comparable` interface. Here is the code for the generic `Comparable` interface:

```java
public interface Comparable<T>{
    public int compareTo(T element);
}
```

Element types that are candidates for inclusion in generic collections with a natural ordering should use syntax such as

```java
public class ElementClass implements Comparable<ElementClass>{

    public int compareTo(ElementClass other){
        // code that does the comparison, with no casting of other needed
    }
}
```

Several classes, such as `String` and the numeric wrapper classes, already implement the generic `Comparable`.

Of course, it is still possible to develop collection classes that use the "raw" `Comparable` interface that we saw in Chapter 11. But the generic version is preferred because it is safer (with compile-time type checking) and easier to use.

*E*XERCISE 15.3

1. Assume that a queue q has been created. Draw a picture of the state of the queue after each of the following sequences of operations. You should assume that each sequence follows the other from a to c:

   a.

   ```java
   for (int i = 1; i <= 5; i++)
       q.add("" + i);
   ```

   b.

   ```java
   q.remove();
   q.remove();
   ```

   c.

   ```java
   q.add("5");
   q.add("6");
   ```

2. Write code segments that accomplish the following tasks with the queue q:
   a. Add the strings "hello" and "there" onto the queue.
   b. Make the queue be empty.
   c. Print the contents of the queue in the terminal window without removing them permanently. (*Hint:* You can use a temporary data structure to accomplish this.)

3. Name three processes in the real world that can be simulated using queues.

EXERCISE 15.3 Continued

4. Assume that a priority queue `q` has been created with three priorities. Draw a picture of the state of the queue after each of the following sequences of operations. You should assume that each sequence follows the other from a to c:

   a.
   ```
   for (int i = 1; i <= 3; i++)
       q.add("" + i);
   ```

   b.
   ```
   q.remove();
   q.remove();
   ```

   c.
   ```
   q.add("5");
   q.add("6");
   ```

5. Write code segments that accomplish the following tasks with the priority queue `q`:
   a. Add the strings "hello" and "there" onto the queue with priority 1.
   b. Make the queue be empty.

6. Jack says he can't print the items in a priority queue without permanently removing them. Jill says he can. Who is right and why?

7. For each of the following applications, state which data structure would be appropriate—stack, queue, or priority queue.
   a. Tracking a line of customers at a supermarket
   b. Tracking the information for a series of method calls on a computer
   c. Scheduling patients in a hospital emergency room

8. The heading for the `Student` class is `public class Student implements Comparable`. Modify this heading so that it uses the generic `Comparable`.

Case Study 2: An Emergency Room Scheduler

Request

Write a program that allows a supervisor to schedule treatments for patients coming into a hospital's emergency room. Because some patients are in more critical condition than others, they are not treated on a strictly first-come, first-served basis but are assigned a priority when admitted. Patients with a high priority receive attention before those with a lower priority.

Analysis

Patients come into the emergency room in one of three conditions (in order of priority):

1. Critical
2. Serious
3. Fair

When the user selects the Schedule option, the program allows the user to enter a patient's name and condition and the patient is placed in line for treatment according to the severity of his condition. When the user selects the Treat Next Patient option, the program removes and displays the patient first in line with the most serious condition. When the user selects the Treat All Patients option, the program removes and displays all patients in order from patient to serve first to patient to serve last.

Each command button produces an appropriate message in the output area. Table 15-11 lists the interface's responses to the commands.

TABLE 15-11
The commands of the emergency room program

COMMAND	RESPONSE
Schedule	<patient name> is added to the <condition> list.
Treat Next Patient	<patient name> is being treated.
Treat All Patients	<patient name> is being treated.
	...
	<patient name> is being treated.

An interaction with the terminal-based interface is shown in Figure 15-11.

FIGURE 15-11
The user interface for the emergency room program

Classes

The application consists of an application class, called ERApp, a view class, called ERView, and a set of model classes. As usual, the application class defines the main method and instantiates the view class. The view interacts with the user and sends messages to the model. The class ERModel maintains a priority queue of patients. The class Patient represents patients and the class Condition represents the three possible conditions. The relationships among the classes are shown in Figure 15-12.

FIGURE 15-12
The classes in the ER scheduling system

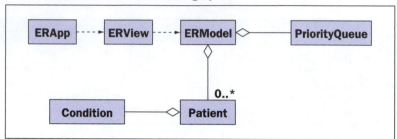

Design and Implementation

The Condition class is similar to the Suit class developed for playing cards in Chapter 11. There are only three distinct instances, named by the static variables Condition.critical, Condition.serious, and Condition.fair. They are ranked in decreasing order. Conditions can be compared and viewed as strings.

The Patient class maintains a patient's name and condition. Patients can be compared (according to their conditions) and viewed as strings.

The implementations of the Condition and Patient classes use the generic Comparable interface. Here is the code for the two classes:

```java
// Case Study 15.2: The Condition class
// Implements generic Comparable

public class Condition implements Comparable<Condition>{

    static public final Condition critical = new Condition(1, "critical");
    static public final Condition serious = new Condition(2, "serious");
    static public final Condition fair    = new Condition(3, "fair");

    private int order;
    private String name;

    private Condition(int ord, String nm){
        name = nm;
        order = ord;
    }

    public int compareTo(Condition other){
        return order - other.order;
    }
```

```java
    public String toString(){
        return name;
    }
}

// Case Study 15.2: The Patient class

public class Patient implements Comparable<Patient>{

    private String name;
    private Condition condition;

    public Patient(String n, Condition c){
        name = n;
        condition = c;
    }

    public int compareTo(Patient other){
        return condition.compareTo(other.condition);
    }

    public String toString(){
        return name + " / " + condition;
    }
}
```

The class ERView uses a typical menu-driven loop. We structure the code using several helper methods. Here is a complete listing:

```java
// Case Study 15.2: The ERView class

import java.util.Scanner;

public class ERView{

    private ERModel model = new ERModel();

    public ERView(){
        Scanner reader = new Scanner(System.in);
        int command = 1;
        String menu = "1. Schedule a patient\n" +
                      "2. Treat the next patient\n" +
                      "3. Treat all patients\n" +
                      "4. Exit the program\n";
        while (command != 4){
            command = getCommand(1, 4, menu);
            if (command == 1)
                schedule();
            else if (command == 2)
                treatNext();
            else if (command == 3)
                treatAll();
        }
    }
```

```java
private void schedule(){
   Scanner reader = new Scanner(System.in);
   System.out.print("Enter the patient's name: ");
   String name = reader.nextLine();
   Condition condition = getCondition();
   model.schedule(new Patient(name, condition));
   System.out.println(name + " is added to the " +
                        condition + " list\n");
}

private void treatNext(){
   Patient patient = model.treatNext();
   if (patient == null)
      System.out.println("No patients available to treat");
   else
      System.out.println(patient + " is being treated");
}

private void treatAll(){
   Patient patient = model.treatNext();
   if (patient == null){
      System.out.println("No patients available to treat");
      return;
   }
   while (patient != null){
      System.out.println(patient + " is being treated");
      patient = model.treatNext();
   }
}

private Condition getCondition(){
   String menu = "CONDITION\n" +
                 "1. Critical\n" +
                 "2. Serious\n" +
                 "3. Fair\n";
   int i = getCommand(1, 3, menu);
   if (i == 1)
      return Condition.critical;
   else if (i == 2)
      return Condition.serious;
   else
      return Condition.fair;
}

private int getCommand(int low, int high, String menu){
   Scanner reader = new Scanner(System.in);
   int number = 0;
   System.out.print(menu);
   System.out.print("Enter a number [" + low + "-" +
                                     high + "]: ");
   try{
      number = reader.nextInt();
      if (number < low || number > high){
         System.out.println("Number must be >= " + low +
                            " and <= " + high);
```

```
            return getCommand(low, high, menu);
         }
         else
            return number;
      }catch(Exception e){
         System.out.println("You must enter a number");
         return getCommand(low, high, menu);
      }
   }
}
```

The class `ERModel` uses a priority queue to schedule the patients. Its implementation is left as a programming project.

15.4 Graphics and GUIs: Check Boxes and Radio Buttons

To our growing list of GUI controls we now add check boxes and radio button groups. Before diving into the details, we present a simple demonstration interface. Figure 15-13 shows a user interface from a demo program and contains, among other GUI components, the following features:

- Two check boxes labeled Driver and Passenger, with the Driver box currently checked.

- A radio button group containing buttons labeled Married, Single, and Divorced, with the Single radio button selected.

FIGURE 15-13
Some sample check boxes and radio buttons

Following is a listing of the demo program, which we discuss in the next two subsections:

```
// Example 15.8: Test check boxes and radio buttons

import javax.swing.*;
import java.awt.*;
import java.awt.event.*;
```

```java
public class CheckBoxTester extends JFrame{

    private JLabel checkLabel = new JLabel("Check Box State");
    private JLabel radioLabel = new JLabel("Radio Button State");

    private JTextField checkField = new JTextField("");
    private JTextField radioField = new JTextField("");

    private JCheckBox cbDriver    = new JCheckBox("Driver");
    private JCheckBox cbPassenger = new JCheckBox("Passenger");

    private JRadioButton  rbMarried  = new JRadioButton("Married");
    private JRadioButton  rbSingle   = new JRadioButton("Single");
    private JRadioButton  rbDivorced = new JRadioButton("Divorced");

    private JButton getStateBTN = new JButton("Get states");

    public CheckBoxTester(){
        // Mark the default check box and radio button
        cbDriver.setSelected (true);
        rbSingle.setSelected (true);

        // Add the radio buttons to a button group
        ButtonGroup bgMaritalStatus = new ButtonGroup();
        bgMaritalStatus.add(rbMarried);
        bgMaritalStatus.add(rbSingle);
        bgMaritalStatus.add(rbDivorced);

        // Attach listener to the command button
        getStateBTN.addActionListener(new GetStateListener());

        // Add the controls to the container
        JPanel crbPanel = new JPanel(new GridLayout(5, 1));
        crbPanel.add(cbDriver);
        crbPanel.add(cbPassenger);
        crbPanel.add(rbMarried);
        crbPanel.add(rbSingle);
        crbPanel.add(rbDivorced);
        JPanel dataPanel = new JPanel(new GridLayout(4, 1));
        dataPanel.add(checkLabel);
        dataPanel.add(checkField);
        dataPanel.add(radioLabel);
        dataPanel.add(radioField);
        JPanel buttonPanel = new JPanel();
        buttonPanel.add(getStateBTN);
        Container container = getContentPane();
        container.add(crbPanel, BorderLayout.WEST);
        container.add(dataPanel, BorderLayout.EAST);
        container.add(buttonPanel, BorderLayout.SOUTH);
    }

    private class GetStateListener implements ActionListener{
        public void actionPerformed(ActionEvent e){
```

```java
            String cbStr = "", rbStr = "";
            if (cbDriver.isSelected())
                cbStr = "Driver";
            if (cbPassenger.isSelected())
                cbStr = cbStr + "Passenger";
            checkField.setText(cbStr);
            if (rbMarried.isSelected())
                rbStr = "Married";
            else if (rbDivorced.isSelected())
                rbStr = "Divorced";
            else if (rbSingle.isSelected())
                rbStr = "Single";
            radioField.setText(rbStr);
        }
    }

    public static void main(String[] args){
        CheckBoxTester theGUI = new CheckBoxTester();
        theGUI.setDefaultCloseOperation(JFrame.EXIT_ON_CLOSE);
        theGUI.setSize(300, 200);
        theGUI.setVisible(true);
    }
}
```

Check Boxes

Check boxes are instantiated and added to a container in a now familiar manner. For instance

```java
cbDriver = new JCheckBox("Driver");
cbrPanel.add(cbDriver);
```

Table 15-12 shows two frequently used methods: `setSelected` and `isSelected`.

TABLE 15-12
Check box and radio button methods

NAME OF METHOD	WHAT IT DOES
setSelected (aBoolean)	If aBoolean is true, then mark the check box or radio button; else clear the check box or radio button.
isSelected()returns boolean	Return true if marked; else return false.

Unlike radio buttons, more than one check box can be selected simultaneously, so the `isSelected` method can return `true` for more than one check box at any given time. The code for `actionPerformed` in the demo program illustrates the different logic for testing the states of check boxes and radio buttons:

```java
public void actionPerformed(ActionEvent e){
    String cbStr = "", rbStr = "";
    if (cbDriver.isSelected())
        cbStr = "Driver";
```

```
   if (cbPassenger.isSelected())
       cbStr = cbStr + "Passenger";
   checkField.setText(cbStr);
   if (rbMarried.isSelected())
       rbStr = "Married";
   else if (rbDivorced.isSelected())
       rbStr = "Divorced";
   else if (rbSingle.isSelected())
       rbStr = "Single";
   radioField.setText(rbStr);
}
```

Radio Buttons

Radio buttons behave as a group, insofar as selecting one automatically deselects the others. To use radio buttons, one must instantiate a `ButtonGroup` and several radio buttons and then add each radio button to the group. In the demo program, radio buttons are instantiated as follows:

```
rbMarried  = new JRadioButton("Married");
rbSingle   = new JRadioButton("Single");
rbDivorced = new JRadioButton("Divorced");
```

The code to select a default radio button and to associate the radio buttons in a button group goes in the constructor method:

```
// Mark the default check box and radio button
cbDriver.setSelected(true);
rbSingle.setSelected(true);

// Add the radio buttons to a button group
ButtonGroup bgMaritalStatus = new ButtonGroup();
bgMaritalStatus.add(rbMarried);
bgMaritalStatus.add(rbSingle);
bgMaritalStatus.add(rbDivorced);
```

Later, when the program needs to know which radio button has been selected, it sends the `isSelected()` message to each radio button until one of them returns `true`.

SUMMARY

In this chapter, you learned:

- A stack is a linear collection that enforces a last-in, first-out order of elements.

- Operations on stacks are pushed for insertion and popped for removal of elements. Elements are accessed at just one end of a stack called the top.

- A queue is a linear collection that enforces a first-in, first-out order of elements.

- Operations on queues are add for insertion and remove for removal of elements. Elements are added at one end of the queue called the rear and removed at the other end called the front.

- A priority queue is a linear collection that enforces a first-in, first-out order of elements when they have equal priority and orders them by priority otherwise.

VOCABULARY *Review*

Define the following terms:

Front	Priority queue	Round-robin scheduling
Generic comparable	Push	Stack
Infix form	Queue	Token
Pop	Rear	Top
Postfix form		

REVIEW *Questions*

FILL IN THE BLANK

Complete the following sentences by writing the correct word or words in the blanks provided.

1. The order in which elements are accessed in a stack is called _____ order.

2. The order in which elements are accessed in a queue is called _____ order.

3. The operation to insert an element into a stack is called _____.

4. The operation to remove an element from a stack is called _____.

5. Elements are inserted into a queue at one end called the _____.

6. Elements are removed from a queue at one end called the _____.

7. The process of returning to a previous state in a computation or a search is called _____.

8. The modeling of a process that uses a queue to schedule events is called _____.

9. A(n) _____ orders elements according to a ranking scheme.

10. A recursive process is supported using a(n) _____.

PROJECTS

PROJECT 15-1

Complete the first case study program and test it. Then add the operator ^ to the language of postfix expressions. This operator represents exponentiation. Thus, for example, the expression 2 3 ^ should evaluate to 8. Test your program with this new operator.

PROJECT 15-2

A palindrome is a sentence that reads the same forward and backward. For example, "ABLE WAS I ERE I SAW ELBA" is a palindrome attributed to Napoleon. Write a program that tests its inputs for palindromes. (*Hint*: Use a string tokenizer and a stack.)

PROJECT 15-3

Like the class `TrueArrayStack`, the class `TrueLinkedStack` implements the `TrueStack` interface discussed in Section 15.1. However, this class uses a linked list, which allows it to add or remove elements in constant time. Implement and test the class `TrueLinkedStack`.

PROJECT 15-4

Jack complains to Jill, the designer of the true linked priority queue, that the method `add` runs in quadratic time. Think about why this is so, and write and test an alternative implementation of the method that runs in linear time. (*Hint*: Review the discussion of `ListIterator` in Chapter 14.)

PROJECT 15-5

Complete the case study involving the emergency room scheduler.

PROJECT 15-6

Replace the terminal-based view class for the emergency room scheduler with a GUI-based view class. ERView should display a labeled text field for the patient's name, radio buttons for the conditions, a text area for output, and three command buttons for the user's options, as shown in Figure 15-14.

FIGURE 15-14
GUI for the ER scheduler

PROJECT 15-7

Write a program that solves a maze problem. In this particular version of the problem, a hiker must find a path to the top of a mountain. Assume that the hiker leaves a parking lot, marked P, and explores the maze until she reaches the top of a mountain, marked T. Figure 15-15 shows what this particular maze looks like.

FIGURE 15-15
A maze problem

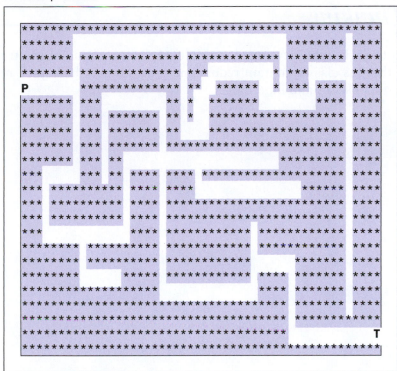

Java source code for the program's GUI can be obtained from your instructor together with executable code for the program as a whole. You should run the program a few times before writing your own solution. The interface allows the user to enter a picture of the maze as a grid of characters. The character * marks a barrier, and P and T mark the parking lot and mountain top, respectively. A blank space marks a step along a path. The interface includes a Set maze button, and when the user selects it, the view should send a message to the model with the contents of the grid as a string parameter. When the user then selects the Solve button, the model attempts to find a path through the maze and returns "solved" or "unsolved" to the view depending on the outcome. In the model, begin by representing the maze as a matrix of characters (P, T, *, or space), and during the search mark each visited cell with a dot. Redisplay the grid at the end with the dots included. The following is the backtracking algorithm that is at the core of the solution:

```
Instantiate a stack
Locate the character 'P' in the matrix and replace it with a ' '
Push its location onto the stack
While the stack is not empty
    Pop a location, loc, off the stack
    Store a dot in the matrix at position loc
    For each cell of the matrix adjacent to loc
```

```
            If the cell contains a 'T'
                Return true
            If the cell contains a ' '
                Push its location onto the stack
        EndFor
    Endwhile
    Return false
```

CRITICAL *Thinking*

Jill complains to Jack, who developed multiple implementations of the true stack and true queue interfaces, that his classes contain redundant code. Discuss how Jack might improve his code by using abstract classes and inheritance.

CHAPTER 16

UNORDERED COLLECTIONS: SETS AND MAPS

OBJECTIVES

Upon completion of this chapter, you should be able to:

- Understand the basic features of sets and their applications.
- Use the set interface and the set implementation class.
- Understand the differences between a set and a sorted set.
- Understand the basic features of maps and their applications.
- Use the map interface and the map implementation class.
- Understand the differences between a map and a sorted map.
- Understand the general features of collections.
- Use the collection interface.

Estimated Time: 3.5 hours

VOCABULARY

Association

Association list

Comparator

Dictionary

Generic method

Hashing

Key

Keyed list

Map

Set

Sorted map

Sorted set

Value

The collection ADTs we have covered thus far are all ordered. That is, each item in an ordered collection has a position at which the client can locate it. Another category contains the unordered collections. From the client's perspective, the items in an unordered collection are in no particular positions. Thus, none of the operations on an unordered collection are position-based. Clients can insert, retrieve, or remove objects from unordered collections, but they cannot access the *i*th item, the next item, or the previous item. Some examples of unordered collections are sets and maps. This chapter gives a client's view of these collections. Implementation strategies are examined in Chapter 18.

16.1 Sets

The concept of a set should be familiar from mathematics. A *set* is a collection of items that, from the client's perspective, are unique. That is, there are no duplicate items in a set. There are many operations on sets in mathematics. Some of the most typical are

- Test for the empty set.

- Return the number of items in the set.

- Add an item to the set.

- Remove an item from the set.

- Test for set membership (whether or not a given item is in the set).

- Return the *union* of two sets. The union of two sets A and B is a set that contains all of the items in A and all of the items in B.

- Return the *intersection* of two sets. The intersection of the two sets A and B is the set of items in A that are also items in B.

- Return the *difference* of two sets. The difference of two sets A and B is the set of items in A that are not also items in B.

- Test a set to determine whether or not another set is its *subset*. The set B is a subset of set A if and only if B is an empty set or all of the items in B are also in A.

To describe the contents of a set, we use the notation {<item1> . . . <item-n>} and assume that the items are in no particular order. Table 16-1 shows the results of some operations on example sets.

TABLE 16-1
Results of some typical set operations

SETS A AND B	A.UNION(B)	A.INTERSECTION(B)	A.DIFFERENCE(B)	A.SUBSET(B)
{12 5 17 6} {42 17 6}	(12 5 42 17 6}	{17 6}	{12 5}	false
{21 76 10 3 9} {}	{21 76 10 3 9}	{}	{21 76 10 3 9}	true
{87} {22 87 23}	{22 87 23}	{87}	{}	false
{22 87 23} {87}	{22 87 23}	{87}	{22 23}	true

The `java.util.Set` Interface

The most commonly used methods in the `Set` interface are listed in Table 16-2.

TABLE 16-2
Commonly used methods in the `Set` interface

METHOD	WHAT IT DOES
`boolean add(Object obj)`	If the object is not already in the set, then adds the object to the set, increasing the set's size by one, and returns `true`; otherwise, returns `false`
`boolean contains(Object obj)`	Returns `true` if the object is in the set, else `false`
`boolean isEmpty()`	Returns `true` if the set contains no objects, else `false`
`Iterator<E> iterator()`	Returns an iterator on the set
`boolean remove(Object obj)`	If the object is in the set, removes it and returns `true`; otherwise, returns `false`
`int size()`	Returns the number of objects currently in the set

Note that sets support a generic `iterator` method. You might have been wondering how you can examine all the items in a set after they have been added, in view of the fact that there is no index-based access as with lists. You use an iterator, which supports the visiting of items in an unspecified order.

Applications of Sets

Aside from their role in mathematics, sets have many applications in the area of data processing. For example, in the field of database management, the answer to a query that contains the conjunction of two keys could be constructed from the intersection of the sets of items containing these keys.

Implementing Classes

The implementing classes for sets in `java.util` are called `HashSet` and `TreeSet`. We examine `TreeSet` in the next section. The name `HashSet` derives from the technique by which the set's items are accessed, called *hashing*. We examine this concept in detail in Chapter 18. The following code segment is a trivial illustration of the use of a `HashSet` of strings:

```java
Set<String> s = new HashSet<String>();

s.add("Bill");
s.add("Mary");
s.add("Jose");
s.add("Bill");                          // Duplicate element

System.out.println(s.size());           // Prints 3
System.out.println(s.contains("Jose")); // Prints true
```

Now suppose we want to print the names in this set. By creating an iterator on the set, we can retrieve the names one by one and print them:

```
Iterator<String> iter = s.iterator();

while (iter.hasNext()){
    String name = iter.next();
    System.out.println(name);
}
```

An enhanced `for` loop works just as well and is simpler and foolproof:

```
for (String name : s)
    System.out.println(name);
```

As another example, let us define a `static` method that creates the intersection of two sets. The intersection of two sets is a new set containing only the items the two sets have in common. Following is the code:

```
public static <E> Set<E> intersection(Set<E> a, Set<E> b){
    Set<E> result = new HashSet<E>();
    for (E element : a)
        if (b.contains(element))
            result.add(element);
    return result;
}
```

Note the use of the notation `<E>` following the terms `public static` in the method's header. This notation indicates that the method is generic and uses the type variable `E`. The syntax of a *generic method* is

```
modifiers <type-variables> return-type method-name(parameters)
```

As we see shortly, when a generic method uses more than one type variable, they appear in a list within the angle brackets.

EXERCISE 16.1

1. In what way does a set differ from a list?

2. Assume that the set `s` contains the string "3". Describe the sequence of sets resulting from the following operations:

a. `s.add("4");`

b. `s.add("4");`

c. `s.add("5");`

d. `s.remove("3");`

EXERCISE 16.1 Continued

3. How do you visit all the items in a set?

4. Write a generic method for the set difference operation.

5. Write a generic method for the subset operation.

6. Suppose you want to work with a set of integers. How will you go about adding integers to the set and accessing them in the set?

16.2 Sorted Sets

Sets are unordered collections; however, there is sufficient need for a sorted version that Java includes the interface `SortedSet` and the implementation `TreeSet`. The interface `SortedSet` extends the interface `Set`, so sorted sets have the same behavior as unsorted sets as well as some additional behavior. The iterator on a sorted set accesses its items in a sorted order, but there is a catch: All the items in a sorted set must implement the generic `Comparable` interface.

Consider, for example, the problem of sorting a list of unique items. We could use one of the sort methods from Chapter 11 or Chapter 12, rewritten, of course, to manipulate a list. But another way to proceed is to transfer the items from the list to a *sorted set* and then transfer the items back to the list. A precondition is that the list contains unique, comparable items. Following is the code:

```
// Produce a sorted list of unique strings

List<String> list = new ArrayList<String>();

// . . . add any strings, including duplicates, to the list . . .

SortedSet<String> set = new TreeSet<String>();

for (String str : list)              // Copy the strings to the sorted set
    set.add(str);

list.clear();
for (String str : set)              // Copy the strings back to the list
    list.add(str);
```

The `java.util.SortedSet` Interface

The `SortedSet` interface extends the `Set` interface with the methods listed in Table 16-3.

TABLE 16-3
The `SortedSet` interface

METHOD	WHAT IT DOES
`Comparator<E> comparator()`	Returns the comparator associated with this sorted set, or `null` if it uses its elements' natural ordering
`Object first()`	Returns the first (lowest) element currently in this sorted set
`SortedSet<E> headSet(E toElement)`	Returns a view of the portion of this sorted set whose elements are strictly less than `toElement`
`Object last()`	Returns the last (highest) element currently in this sorted set
`SortedSet<E> subSet(E fromElement,` `                E toElement)`	Returns a view of the portion of this sorted set whose elements range from `fromElement`, inclusive, to `toElement`, exclusive
`SortedSet<E> tailSet(E fromElement)`	Returns a view of the portion of this sorted set whose elements are greater than or equal to `fromElement`

The following code segment uses a sorted set to display the contents of a set of strings in alphabetical order:

```java
// Create a set of strings and add some to it

Set<String> set1 = new HashSet<String>();

// . . . add strings to the set . . .

// Copy the strings to a sorted set

Set<String> set2 = new TreeSet<String>();

for (String str : set1)
   set2.add(str);

// Print the strings in the sorted set

for (String str : set2)
   System.out.println(str);
```

The Performance of the Set Implementations

The class `HashSet` provides constant-time access, insertions, and removals of elements. These operations are logarithmic for `TreeSet`. We see why this is the case in Chapters 18 and 19. Thus, you should use a `HashSet` unless the elements must be accessed in a sorted order.

Using Comparators and the `Comparator` Interface

Table 16-3 includes a method `comparator`, which returns a `Comparator` object for a set if it happens to be using one. A *comparator* allows the programmer to create a set that sorts its elements in an order other than their natural one.

The default `TreeSet` constructor creates a set whose elements are ordered according to the `compareTo` method of the element type. A second constructor expects a `Comparator` object as a parameter. A set created in this fashion uses the comparator's `compare` method to order the set's elements. This method is specified in `java.util`'s `Comparator` interface as follows:

```java
public interface Comparator<T>{
    public int compare(T obj1, T obj2);
}
```

The method `compare` has similar behavior to the method `compareTo`, returning a negative number, 0, or a positive number if a given field of `obj1` is less than, equal to, or greater than the same field of `obj2`, respectively.

Now suppose we want to create two sets of the same students, one naturally ordered according to the students' names and the other ordered by their IDs. The first step is to define a special class that implements `Comparator` for comparing the IDs, as follows:

```java
public class CompareByID implements Comparator<Student>{
    public int compare(Student obj1, Student obj2){
        return obj1.getID().compareTo(obj2.getID());
    }
}
```

The next step is to instantiate the two sets, one with and the other without an instance of the comparator:

```java
// This set maintains the default natural ordering of students, by name
Set<Student> setByName = new TreeSet<Student>();

// This set uses the comparator to order the students by ID
Set<Student> setByID = new TreeSet<Student>(new CompareByID<Student>());

// Run any operations on the two sets
```

EXERCISE 16.2

1. Why must the items added to a sorted set be comparable?

2. Explain how one can use a comparator to impose an order on a set's elements that is different from their natural order.

16.3 Example Application: Word Frequencies

Assume that someone wants to display a table of the frequencies of the words in a segment of text. The table should have two columns. The first column is a sorted list of the unique words. The second column is a list containing the corresponding frequencies of the words in the first column. Figure 16-1 shows a sample text file and the corresponding table of words and frequencies.

FIGURE 16-1
The input and output of a word frequency program

One could implement an algorithm to solve this problem using arrays or lists. But such an algorithm is very complicated. A simpler algorithm uses a list and a sorted set as follows:

1. Transfer all of the words from the text to the list.

2. Create a sorted set of words from this list.

3. Print the words in the sorted set and use these words to look up the associated frequencies in the list and print these frequencies.

Following is the pseudocode:

```
Create a list called wordList

While there are more words in the file
    Read the next word and convert it to uppercase
    Add the word to wordList

Create a sorted set called wordSet from wordList

For each word in wordSet
    Print the word
    Print the number of occurrences of that word in wordList
    Print a newline
```

Following is a further refinement of our algorithm that is closer to Java code:

```java
List<String> wordList = new ArrayList<String>();

While there are more words in the file
    String word = read the next word
    wordList.add(word.toUppercase());

SortedSet<String> wordSet = new TreeSet<String>();
for (String word : wordList)
    wordSet.add(word);

for (String word : wordSet){
    int frequency = occurrencesOf(wordlist, word);
    System.out.printf("%-20s%5d%n", word, frequency);
}
```

This code relies on the helper method `occurrencesOf`, which returns the number of occurrences of a given object in a list. Here is a listing of the complete program:

```java
// Example 16.1: Displays a file's words and their frequencies

import java.io.*;
import java.util.*;

public class WordFrequencies{

    public static void main(String[] args) throws IOException{
        Scanner reader = new Scanner(System.in);
        String query = "y";
        while (query.equalsIgnoreCase("y")){
            // Read the words from a file into a list
            System.out.print("Enter a file name: ");
            String fileName = reader.nextLine();
            Scanner fileReader = new Scanner(new File(fileName));
            List<String> wordList = new ArrayList<String>();
            while (fileReader.hasNext()){
                String word = fileReader.next();
                wordList.add(word.toUpperCase());
```

```
        }
        // Copy the words from the list to a sorted set
        SortedSet<String> wordSet = new TreeSet<String>();
        for (String word : wordList)
            wordSet.add(word);
        // Print each unique word and its frequency in columns
        for (String word : wordSet){
            int frequency = occurrencesOf(wordList, word);
            System.out.printf("%-30s%5d%n", word, frequency);
        }

        System.out.print("Analyze another file?[y/n]: ");
        query = reader.nextLine();
    }

}

private static int occurrencesOf(List<String> list, String word){
    int total = 0;
    for (String s : list)
        if (s.equals(word))
            total++;
    return total;
}
}
```

16.4 Maps

A *map*, sometimes also referred to as a *table*, is a collection in which each item, or *value*, is associated with a unique *key*. Users add, remove, and retrieve items from a map by specifying their keys. A map is occasionally referred to as a *keyed list*, *dictionary*, or an *association list*. The package `java.util` defines several classes, `Dictionary`, `Hashtable`, and `Map`, which all represent maps. Another way to think of a map is as a collection of unique items called *entries* or *associations*. Each entry contains a key and a value (the item).

Table 16-4 shows the data in two maps. The first map is keyed by strings, and the second map is keyed by integers.

TABLE 16-4
A map keyed by strings and a map keyed by integers

MAP 1		MAP 2	
KEY	**VALUE**	**KEY**	**VALUE**
"occupation"	"teacher"	80	"Mary"
"hair color"	"brown"	39	"Joe"
"height"	72	21	"Sam"
"age"	72	95	"Renee"
"name"	"Bill"	40	"Lily"

Note the following points about the two example maps:

■ The keys are in no particular order.

■ The keys are unique. That is, the keys for a given map form a set.

■ The values need not be unique. That is, the same value can be associated with more than one key.

There are many operations that one could perform on maps. At a bare minimum, a client should be able to:

■ Test a map for emptiness.

■ Determine a map's size.

■ Insert a value at a given key.

■ Remove a given key (also removing the associated value).

■ Retrieve a value at a given key.

■ Determine whether or not a map contains a key.

■ Determine whether or not a map contains a value.

■ Examine all of the keys.

■ Examine all of the values.

Maps have a wide range of applications. For example, interpreters and compilers of programming languages make use of symbol tables. Each key in a symbol table corresponds to an identifier in a program. The value associated with a key contains the attributes of the identifier—a name, a data type, and other information. Perhaps the most prevalent application of maps is in database management.

The `java.util.Map` Interface

Table 16-5 lists and describes the most frequently used `Map` methods. In this table, the object associated with a key is called its *value*. A map uses two type variables, named K and V, to refer to the map's key type and value type, respectively.

TABLE 16-5
The most frequently used `Map` methods

METHOD	WHAT IT DOES
`boolean containsKey(Object key)`	Returns `true` if the map contains the indicated key or `false` otherwise
`boolean containsValue (Object value)`	Returns `true` if the map contains at least one instance of the indicated value or `false` otherwise
`V get(Object key)`	Returns the value associated with the indicated key if the key is in the map or `null` otherwise
`boolean isEmpty()`	Returns `true` if the map is empty or `false` otherwise
`Set<K> keySet()`	Returns a set view of the keys in the map
`V put(K key, V value)`	If the key is already in the map, replaces the previous value with the new value and returns the previous value; otherwise, adds the key and the associated value to the map and returns `null`
`V remove(Object key)`	If the key is in the map, removes the key value pair from the map and returns the value; otherwise, returns `null`
`int size()`	Returns the number of key value pairs currently in the map
`Collection<V> values()`	Returns a collection view of the values in the map

Note that the methods `keySet` and `values` allow the client to examine all of a map's keys and values, respectively. We discuss the `Collection` type and the idea of a collection view later in this chapter. For now, suffice it to say that one can open an iterator on a collection view. The following code segment, which associates strings with integers in a map, shows how easy it is to visit all the keys and values in the map with iterators:

```
Map<String, Integer> map = new HashMap<String, Integer>();

// . . . add a bunch of keys and values to the map

// Obtain the views of the map's keys and values.
Set<String> s = map.keySet();
Collection<Integer> c = map.values();

// Open iterators on these views and display their contents
Iterator<String> keys = s.iterator();
while (keys.hasNext())
    System.out.println(keys.next());
```

```
Iterator<Integer> values = c.iterator();
while (values.hasNext())
    System.out.println(values.next());
```

Note that a generic map needs two type parameters when it is declared and instantiated. The first type is the key type and the second type is the value type. Occasionally, you will see nested type parameters when used with maps or other generic collections. For example, suppose we need a map of sets of strings, keyed by strings. The next code segment declares and instantiates such a map:

```
Map<String, Set<String>> map = new HashMap<String, Set<String>>();
```

Implementing Class

`java.util` provides two implementations of the `Map` interface called `HashMap` and `TreeMap`. In the following example code segment, we set up a `HashMap` whose keys are student IDs and whose values are the associated `Student` objects:

```
// Declare and instantiate a map
Map<String, Student> studentMap = new HashMap<String, Student>();

for (int i = 1; i <= 4; i++){
    Student stu = new Student();       // Instantiate a new student
    stu.setId("s" + i);                // Set the student's attributes
    stu.setName . . .                  // . . .
    stu.setScore . . .                 // . . .
    studentMap.put("s" + i, stu);      // Add the student to the map using
                                       // the student's ID as the key
}
```

Notice the following points about this code:

■ We have added an attribute called ID to the `Student` class. Unlike a name, which might be duplicated, an ID is unique.

■ A student ID is both one of its attributes and its key. It is common practice to choose an object's key from among its attributes.

An object is retrieved from a map using the `get` method, as illustrated in this statement that retrieves and displays the student whose key is `s1`:

```
System.out.println(studentMap.get("s1"));
```

EXERCISE 16.4

1. How do maps differ from sets?

2. What happens when a key is used for inserting a value in a map and that key is already present?

3. State two applications in which a map would be an appropriate data structure.

16.5 Sorted Maps

Sorted maps are to maps as sorted sets are to sets. That is, a sorted map has all the features of a map but in addition allows the client to visit the keys in sorted order. The method `keySet` now returns a sorted set, which can return an iterator that supports a traversal of the map's keys in sorted order. Needless to say, the keys of a sorted map must be comparable.

The `java.util.SortedMap` Interface

The interface for `SortedMap` is similar to the interface for `SortedSet`. It extends the `Map` interface with the methods listed in Table 16-6.

TABLE 16-6
The `SortedMap` interface

METHOD	DESCRIPTION
`Comparator<K> comparator()`	Returns the comparator associated with this sorted map, or `null` if it uses its keys' natural ordering
`K firstKey()`	Returns the first (lowest) key currently in this sorted map
`SortedSet<K> headMap(K toKey)`	Returns a view of the portion of this sorted map whose keys are strictly less than `toKey`
`K lastKey()`	Returns the last (highest) element currently in this sorted map
`SortedMap<K,V> subMap(K fromKey, K toKey)`	Returns a view of the portion of this sorted map whose keys range from `fromKey`, inclusive, to `toKey`, exclusive
`SortedMap<K,V> tailMap(K fromKey)`	Returns a view of the portion of this sorted map whose keys are greater than or equal to `fromKey`

Implementing Class and Application

`java.util` includes the class `TreeMap` to implement a sorted map. An excellent application for a sorted map is any database application in which the records are accessed by content (such as a name) and must be maintained in sorted order. For example, the student list of Chapters 9 and 11 can be represented as a sorted map if the `Student` objects can be ordered by ID number.

The Performance of the Map Implementations

The performance of the classes `HashMap` and `TreeMap` parallel the performance of the classes `HashSet` and `TreeSet` discussed earlier. Thus, you should use a `HashMap` unless the keys must be accessed in sorted order.

*E*XERCISE 16.5

1. Write a code segment that displays the keys and values of a sorted map in two columns.

Case Study: The Therapist

To illustrate the use of maps, we offer an amusing program that will allow you to earn a fortune as a nondirective psychotherapist.

Request

Write a program that emulates a nondirective psychotherapist. The practitioner of this kind of therapy is essentially a good listener who responds to a patient's statements by rephrasing them or indirectly asking for more information.

Analysis

Figure 16-2 shows the system's interface as it changes throughout a sequence of exchanges with the user. When the user enters a statement, the program responds in one of two ways:

1. With a randomly chosen hedge, such as "Please tell me more."

2. By changing some keywords in the user's input string and appending this string to a randomly chosen qualifier; Thus, to "My teacher always plays favorites," the program might reply with "Why do you say that your teacher always plays favorites?"

FIGURE 16-2
A sequence of interactions between a user and the therapist program

```
C:\Javafiles>java TherapistApp
Good day. What is your problem?

Enter your response here: my teacher always plays favorites

Many of my patients tell me the same thing

Enter your response here: she always calls on the girls in class

Why do you say that she always calls on the girls in class

Enter your response here:
```

The program consists of three classes: `TherapistApp`, `TherapistView` and `Therapist`. A `TherapistView` object runs a sentinel-driven loop, passes user inputs to a `Therapist` object, and displays that object's reply. A `Therapist` object does the actual work of constructing a reply from the user's statement.

Design of the `TherapistView` Class

The `TherapistView` class creates a new `Therapist` object at program startup, displays a prompt, and waits for user input. The following is pseudocode for the main loop:

```
output a greeting to the patient
while true
    prompt for and input a string from the patient
    ask the therapist object for its reply to this string
    display the therapist's reply to the patient
```

As you can see, this process appears to go on forever. Our therapist may not be an expert, but there is no charge for its services. However, if the patient has to quit to do something else, she can do so by pressing Ctrl+C.

Design of the Therapist Class

The Therapist class stores hedges and qualifiers in two sets and stores keywords and their replacements in a map. These collections are initialized when a therapist object is instantiated. The principal method in the Therapist class is called reply. The structure chart in Figure 16-3 shows the relationship between the reply method and its subordinate methods.

FIGURE 16-3
Structure chart for the reply method

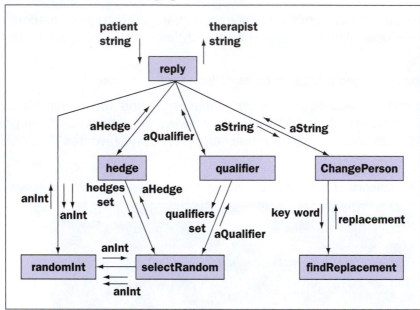

Following is pseudocode for the methods in the structure chart:

```
String reply(String patientString){
    pick a random number between 1 and 3
    if the number is 1
        call the hedge method to return a randomly chosen hedge
    else{
        call the qualifier method to randomly choose a qualifying phrase
        call the changePerson method to change persons in the patient's string
        return the concatenation of these two strings
    }
}
```

```
String hedge(Set set){
    randomly select a number between 0 and the size of the hedges set - 1
    use that number to return the string from the hedges set
}

String qualifier(Set set){
    randomly select a number between 0 and the size of the qualifiers set - 1
    use that number to return the string from the qualifiers set
}

String changePerson(String patientString){
    open a string tokenizer on the patientString (see Chapter 15)
    create an empty result string
    while the tokenizer has more tokens
        get the next token
        find the replacement word for that token
        append the replacement word to the result string
    }
    return the result string
}

String findReplacement(String word){
    if the word is a key in the replacements map
        return the value stored at that key
    else
        return the word
}

String selectRandom(Set set){
    generate a random number between 0 and one less than the set's size
    use this number to locate a string in the set
    return the string
}

int randomInt(int low, int high){
    use Math.random to generate a random double 0 <= x < 1
    map x to an integer low <= i <= high
    return i
}
```

We are now ready to present the Java code for the classes.

Implementation of the `TherapistView` Class

```java
// Case Study: View for the therapist program

import java.util.Scanner;

public class TherapistView{

    private Therapist therapist = new Therapist();

    public TherapistView(){
        Scanner reader = new Scanner(System.in);
        System.out.println("Good day. What is your problem?");
        while (true){
            System.out.print("\nEnter your response here: ");
            String patientString = reader.nextLine();
            String therapistString = therapist.reply(patientString);
            System.out.println("\n" + therapistString);
        }
    }
}
```

Implementation of the `Therapist` Class

```java
/* Case Study: Therapist.java
1) This class emulates a nondirective psychotherapist.
2) The major method, reply, accepts user statements and generates
   a nondirective reply.
*/

import java.util.*;

public class Therapist{

    private Set<String> hedgeSet;                    // The set of hedges
    private Set<String>  qualifierSet;               // The set of qualifiers
    private Map<String, String>   replacementMap;    // The map of
                                                     // replacement words

    public Therapist(){
        hedgeSet = new HashSet<String>();
        hedgeSet.add("Please tell me more");
        hedgeSet.add("Many of my patients tell me the same thing");
        hedgeSet.add("It is getting late, maybe we had better quit");

        qualifierSet = new HashSet<String>();
        qualifierSet.add("Why do you say that ");
        qualifierSet.add("You seem to think that ");
        qualifierSet.add("So, you are concerned that ");

        replacementMap = new HashMap<String, String>();
        replacementMap.put("i", "you");
        replacementMap.put("me", "you");
```

```
        replacementMap.put("my", "your");
        replacementMap.put("am", "are");
}

public String reply(String patientString){
// Replies to the patient's statement with either a hedge or
// a string consisting of a qualifier concatenated to
// a transformed version of the patient's statement.
//  Preconditions  -- none
//  Postconditions -- returns a reply

    String reply = "";                    // The therapist's reply
    int choice = randomInt(1, 3);         // Generate a random number
                                          // between 1 and 3

    // If the patient says nothing, then encourage him.
    if (patientString.trim().equals(""))
        return "Take your time. Some things are difficult to talk about.";

    // Else reply with a hedge or a qualified response
    if(choice == 1)
        reply = hedge(hedgeSet);                  // Hedge 1/3 of the time
    else if (choice == 2 || choice == 3)
        reply = qualifier(qualifierSet) +    // Build a qualified response
                changePerson(patientString);// 2/3 of the time
    return reply;
}

private String hedge(Set<String> hedgeSet){
// Selects a hedge at random
//  Preconditions  -- the hedge set has been initialized
//  Postconditions -- returns a randomly selected hedge

    return selectRandom(hedgeSet);
}

private String qualifier(Set<String> qualifierSet){
// Selects a qualifier at random
//  Preconditions  -- the qualifier set has been initialized
//  Postconditions -- returns a randomly selected qualifier

    return selectRandom(qualifierSet);
}

private String changePerson(String str){
// Returns a string created by swapping i, me, etc. for you, your, etc.
// in the string str
//  Preconditions  -- none
//  Postconditions -- returns the created string

  // Tokenize str
    StringTokenizer tokens = new StringTokenizer(str, " \n.,!;?");
    String result = "";                         // Create a response string
```

```java
        // Build the response from replacements of the tokens
        while (tokens.hasMoreTokens()){
            String keyWord = tokens.nextToken();
            String replacement = findReplacement(keyWord);
            result = result + replacement + " ";
        }
        return result;
    }

    private String findReplacement(String keyWord){
    // Returns the value associated with the keyword or the keyword itself
    // if the keyword is not in the map.
    //   Preconditions  -- the replacement map has been initialized
    //   Postconditions -- returns the replacement

        keyWord = keyWord.toLowerCase();
        if (replacementMap.containsKey(keyWord))
            return (String) replacementMap.get(keyWord);
        else
            return keyWord;
    }

    private String selectRandom(Set<String> set){
    // Selects an entry at random from the set
    //   Preconditions  -- the set is not empty
    //   Postconditions -- returns the random entry

        int index = randomInt(0, set.size() - 1);
        Iterator<String> iter = set.iterator();
        for (int i = 0; i < index; i++)
            iter.next();
        return iter.next();
    }

    private int randomInt(int low, int high){
    // Generate a random number between low and high
    //   Preconditions  -- low <= high
    //   Postconditions -- returns the random number

        return (int) (low + Math.random() * (high - low  + 1));
    }
}
```

16.6 The Glue that Holds Collections Together

Thus far in this book, we have considered the ways in which different categories of collections vary. Now it is time to ask about the ways in which they are similar. All collections contain objects, have a definite size at any given time, and can grow or shrink in size. Are there any operations that all collections have in common? These operations, if they exist, would serve as a kind of glue that holds collections together, allowing them to interact in very powerful ways.

Addition, Removal, and Membership

Each type of collection we have examined thus far supports some form of addition and removal of elements. Some collections have more than one way to do this; for example, lists have index-based and object-based versions of additions and removals, and position-based versions via a list iterator. It seems that every collection allows at least object-based additions and removals. Indeed, the object-based methods add and remove for lists and sets have the same signature. These collections also support a method to test an object for membership in the collection, namely, contains. Maps include variants of these operations for keys and values, whereas stacks and queues support only additions and removals with more specific names such as pop and dequeue. Clearly any list of general collection operations will have some of these basic operations among them or will use them to implement others.

Iterators

Items can be transferred from a set to a list by using an iterator. An iterator also can be used to transfer items in the other direction, from a list to a set, although other list operations exist to accomplish this as well. The Map method keySet, which returns a set of a map's keys, allows one to open an iterator on a map. It is a critical fact that iterators work the same way, whether they are used with lists, sets, or maps. Indeed, as we see in Chapter 17, we can provide iterators for any collections that work in the same manner. Thus, iterators belong in the list of common collection operations.

Other Operations

One common operation on any collection removes all its elements, thus producing an empty collection. The implementation code for this method, called clear(), can be the same for any collection if we use an iterator that supports the method remove. We simply iterate through the elements and use the Iterator method remove all the way. This method is in fact implemented in this manner for lists and sets.

Programmers often must construct operations that involve more than one collection. We saw examples earlier in this chapter of the set operations union, intersection, and difference, which the Set collection does not include but which we can implement quite easily. Other, more general tasks that apply to any pair of collections cry out for standard methods. Consider the following four:

- Add all the elements of one collection to another collection.

- Remove all the elements of one collection from another collection.

- Retain only the elements of one collection in another collection.

- Determine whether or not one collection contains all the elements in another collection.

It would be quite simple to implement all of these operations for any pair of collections, including two collections of different types, with just an iterator and the methods add, remove, and contains.

The `java.util.Collection` Interface

Several of the common collection operations discussed thus far are included in the `java.util.Collection` interface. Both the `List` and the `Set` interfaces extend this interface, so these operations are available to lists and sets. Figure 16-4 shows the relationships among the collection interfaces in `java.util`. Note that the `Map` interface does not extend `Collection`. Table 16-7 describes the `Collection` methods.

FIGURE 16-4
The interface hierarchies of the collections in `java.util`

TABLE 16-7
The `Collection` interface

COLLECTION METHOD	DESCRIPTION
`boolean add(Object o)`	Ensures that this collection contains the specified element (optional operation)
`boolean addAll(Collection<? extends E> c)`	Adds all of the elements in the specified collection to this collection (optional operation)
`void clear()`	Removes all of the elements from this collection (optional operation)
`boolean contains(Object o)`	Returns `true` if this collection contains the specified element
`boolean containsAll(Collection<?> c)`	Returns `true` if this collection contains all of the elements in the specified collection
`boolean isEmpty()`	Returns `true` if this collection contains no elements
`Iterator<E> iterator()`	Returns an iterator over the elements in this collection
`boolean remove(Object o)`	Removes a single instance of the specified element from this collection, if it is present (optional operation)
`boolean removeAll(Collection<?> c)`	Removes all this collection's elements that are also contained in the specified collection (optional operation)
`boolean retainAll(Collection<?> c)`	Retains only the elements in this collection that are contained in the specified collection (optional operation)
`int size()`	Returns the number of elements in this collection

TABLE 16-7 Continued
The `Collection` interface

COLLECTION METHOD	DESCRIPTION
`Object[] toArray()`	Returns an array containing all of the elements in this collection
`<T> T[] toArray(T[] a)`	Returns an array containing all of the elements in this collection whose run-time type is that of the specified array

Some of the operations in Table 16-7, such as `removeAll`, are listed as optional. This means that the implementing classes must include these methods but need not support them. In practical terms, if a given method is not supported, the calls to this method in a client's code will compile but these calls will throw an `UnsupportedOperationException` at runtime.

Several operations expect a parameter of type `Collection`. This means that one can pass for this parameter an object of any class that implements the `Collection` interface. That would be all of the list and set classes in `java.util`.

Finally, the list and set classes include constructors that expect a parameter of type `Collection`. These constructors provide a simple way of converting one type of collection to another.

Some Examples of the Use of General Collection Operations

The following code segments show some examples of the power of the collection methods.

Set union

```
Set<String> unionSet = new HashSet<String>(set1).addAll(set2);
```

Set intersection

```
Set<String> intersectionSet = new HashSet<String>(set1).retainAll(set2);
```

Set difference

```
Set<String> differenceSet = new HashSet<String>(set1).removeAll(set2);
```

Sort a list, removing duplicates

```
List<String> sortedList = new ArrayList<String>(
                          new SortedSet<String>(unsortedList));
```

The `Collections` Class

Given the wide array of operations on collections, the programmer can write new methods for almost any occasion. For example, as we saw in Chapter 11, you can write methods for searching and sorting lists using several different algorithms. Other useful methods, such as searching for a minimum or maximum value, also can be written easily. Several of these operations are so common that `java.util` implements them in a set of static methods, primarily for use with lists. These methods are included in the `Collections` class.

For example, you can sort and search a list of strings as follows:

```
Collections.sort(list);                 // Assume list contains only strings
Collections.binarySearch(list, "Mary"); // See if "Mary" is in list
```

Table 16-8 describes some commonly used `Collections` methods, followed by an explanation of the extraordinary syntax.

TABLE 16-8
Some `Collections` methods

COLLECTIONS METHOD AND DESCRIPTION

`static <T> int`
 	
`binarySearch(List<? extends Comparable<? super T>> list, T key)`
 	
Searches the specified list for the specified object using the binary search algorithm

`static <T extends Object & Comparable<? super T>> T`
 	
`max(Collection<? extends T> coll)`
 	
Returns the maximum element of the given collection, according to the natural ordering of its elements

`static <T extends Object & Comparable<? super T>> T`
 	
`min(Collection<? extends T> coll)`
 	
Returns the minimum element of the given collection, according to the natural ordering of its elements

`static void reverse(List<?> list)` Reverses the order of the elements in the specified list; this method runs in linear time
`static void shuffle(List<?> list)` Randomly permutes the specified list using a default source of randomness
`static <T extends Comparable<? super T>> void sort(List<T> list)` Sorts the specified list into ascending order, according to the natural ordering of its elements

Each of the method signatures starts with the modifier `static`. This of course means that the user of the method sends a message to the `Collections` class, not to an instance of any class. The method headings for `shuffle` and `reverse` have the simplest syntax. They allow `List` parameters of any element type, as specified by the wildcard symbol `?`. In the case of `shuffle`, this is actually shorthand for the syntax `static <T> void shuffle(List<T>)`.

The syntax becomes more alarming in the headings of the other methods. Let's start with `sort`. This method expects a `List` with an element type parameter `T`. However, the method is generic not just for any element type `T`, but for an element type `T` that is restricted by implementing the generic `Comparable` interface. This restriction is expressed not in the formal parameter, but in the type parameter information between the modifier `static` and the return type `void`. Moreover, we find there not just the familiar `<T extends Comparable<T>>` but instead the more daunting `<T extends Comparable<? super T>>`. This means not just a type `T` that implements

Comparable but also any supertype of T that implements Comparable. For example, we might have a list of bank accounts, wherein there are not only checking accounts but also savings accounts. If the two specific types of accounts are subclasses of a common bank account class that implements Comparable, then we can apply this sort method to that list.

The notation used with the methods min and max allows one to use these methods with collections of any objects that extend type T and also implement the generic Comparable.

Fortunately, you don't have to memorize this syntax or even thoroughly understand it to use these methods!

EXERCISE 16.6

1. State three properties that all collections have.

SUMMARY

In this chapter, you learned:

- A set is an unordered collection of unique objects.

- The objects in a sorted set can be visited in a natural order by using an iterator.

- A map associates a set of keys with values; the values can be accessed, inserted, or removed by using their keys.

- The keys in a sorted map can be visited in their natural order by using the methods keySet and iterator.

- Java organizes sets and lists in a hierarchy of collections. Both types of collections implement the Collection interface, which includes general methods for operating on collections. Java provides an extra set of static methods for manipulating collections in the Collections class. Among these are methods for a binary search, a sort, and a shuffle.

VOCABULARY *Review*

Define the following terms:

Association	Hashing	Set
Association list	Key	Sorted map
Comparator	Keyed list	Sorted set
Dictionary	Map	Value
Generic method		

REVIEW *Questions*

FILL IN THE BLANK

Complete the following sentences by writing the correct word or words in the blanks provided.

1. The items in an unordered collection have no particular _____.

2. The set of items that two other sets have in common is called their _____.

3. The set of items that two other sets have altogether is called their _____.

4. The set of items in the first set that are not present in the second set is called their _____.

5. You visit all the items in a set using a(n) _____.

6. A map contains associations of _____ and _____.

7. To insert, remove, or access a value in a map, one uses the value's _____.

8. A(n) _____ map is a type of map in which you can visit items in sorted order.

9. The _____ methods work with either lists or sets.

10. The _____ class provides a set of static methods for tasks such as sorting and searching lists.

PROJECTS

PROJECT 16-1

Define and test a `sets` class. This class should include generic static methods for common operations on sets, such as union, intersection, difference, and subset.

PROJECT 16-2

Write a complete program that computes the frequencies of words in a text file. The input is a text file. The output is a table, in formatted columns, of the unique words and their associated frequencies in the input file. Use a sorted map in your program.

PROJECT 16-3

Add a history set to the case study in this chapter. The history set keeps track of the user's unique inputs. At regular intervals, the therapist should reply to a randomly chosen item from the history set, using the prefix "Earlier you said that."

PROJECT 16-4

Add a map of keywords and their associated responses to the case study of this chapter. Each keyword should have more than one possible response. For example, the set of responses for the keyword "mother" might be "Your mother keeps coming up in our conversation" and "Tell me more about your parents." At regular intervals, the program should examine the user's input for one of these keywords. If a match is found, the program replies with one of the associated responses chosen at random.

PROJECT 16-5

A phone book application allows a user to add entries, remove them, and view them. An entry consists of a name and a phone number. The interface should be similar to the adventure game case study in Chapter 13, with the names in a scrolling list and the entry for a selected name in a text area. Input dialog boxes allow the user to add a new entry. The model class should use a sorted map to store the entries, keyed by name. Write a program that implements this application.

CRITICAL*Thinking*

java.util does not include the Map classes in its hierarchy of collections. Discuss the advantages and disadvantages of this design decision. Propose a way of including maps in the collections hierarchy.

USING ABSTRACT DATA TYPES

REVIEW *Questions*

TRUE/FALSE

Circle T if the statement is true or F if the statement is false.

T   F   **1.** UML provides graphical notation for describing the results of analysis and design but not user requirements.

T   F   **2.** Collaboration diagrams belong to the design phase of the software development process.

T   F   **3.** The elements in a linear collection are ordered by position.

T   F   **4.** Unordered collections are useful for representing sequences of elements.

T   F   **5.** A stack is a first-in, first-out collection.

T   F   **6.** A queue is useful for scheduling resources on a first-come, first-served basis.

T   F   **7.** The values in a map are accessed by content rather than position.

T   F   **8.** All iterators support the methods `next`, `hasNext`, and `remove`.

T   F   **9.** The values in a sorted map cannot be visited in any particular order.

T   F   **10.** The different categories of collection have almost nothing in common.

FILL IN THE BLANK

Complete the following sentences by writing the correct word or words in the blanks provided.

1. Lists, stack, and queues are examples of _____ collections.

2. Sets and maps are examples of _____ collections.

3. An object that is capable of visiting all the items in a collection is called a(n) _____.

4. A class diagram is the UML notation used during the _____ phase of the software development process.

5. In UML, the symbols 0..* and 1..* mean _____ and _____ respectively.

6. The keys in a map form a(n) _____.

7. The set of elements that two sets have in common is called their _____.

8. The elements in a stack are accessed in _____ order.

9. The collection that allows the client to attach priorities to elements is called the _____.

10. All collections support the method _____ which returns the number of elements.

WRITTEN QUESTIONS

Write a brief answer to each of the following questions or problems.

1. Write the code that transfers the elements from the list `list1` to the list `list2`. The elements in `list2` should be in the reverse order from their original positions in `list1`.

2. Write the code that transfers the elements from a stack `s` to a queue `q`.

3. Write the code that displays all of the elements in a set `s` in the terminal window.

4. Jack has chosen to use a stack to represent a line of customers waiting at a bank teller's window. Discuss the wisdom of this choice and propose and justify a better one.

5. Jill is working on a library application in which each book has a unique ISBN or ID number. Suggest and justify your choice of an appropriate collection for storing books.

PROJECTS

PROJECT U4-1

Write a program that inputs an unknown number of names into a list. The user terminates the inputs by entering an empty string (by pressing Enter). The program should sort the list alphabetically and output its contents to the terminal window.

PROJECT U4-2

Add to the program in Project U4-1 the capability of deleting duplicate names from the list. Use a set to accomplish this task.

PROJECT U4-3

Modify the program in Project U4-2 so that it allows the user to enter a password associated with each name. These pairs of data should be stored in a map and the output should be in two columns—one for the names and the other for the passwords.

PROJECT U4-4

The `Collection` classes (lists and sets) include a constructor that expects a parameter of type `Collection` and copies the elements from this collection to the new collection. Add these constructors to the `TrueArrayStack` and `TrueLinkedQueue` classes of Chapter 15 and test them.

CRITICAL *Thinking*

A bag is like a set except that duplicate elements are allowed. Describe the interface for this new collection. Include any methods that seem appropriate.

IMPLEMENTING ABSTRACT DATA TYPES

Unit 5

 Estimated Time for Unit: 10.5 hours

IMPLEMENTING LISTS

This chapter presents several different implementations of lists and compares their performance characteristics. These implementations fall into two categories: array-based structures and link-based structures. The link-based implementations are in turn of two types: *singly linked structures* and *doubly linked structures*. A variety of other linked structures are used in the implementation of collection classes, and the study of singly and doubly linked structures provides a good foundation for their study. We close the chapter with a brief discussion of the implementation of iterators.

17.1 Interfaces, Multiple Implementations, and Prototypes

A class has two aspects: its interface as seen by clients and its internal implementation. The interface is defined by the class's public methods. The internal implementation depends on the class's choice of instance variables and the coding details of its methods. From a client's perspective, it is important that a class's interface provide useful services in a clear, concise, and stable manner. The third characteristic, stability, is critical because changing a class's interface necessitates recoding its clients. On the other hand, changing a class's internal implementation does not disturb the class's clients and may in fact be highly beneficial if it results in greater computing efficiency.

Before the first object-oriented language appeared, computer scientists realized the advantages of separating a resource's interface from its underlying implementation. They called this concept an abstract data type (ADT). Early programming languages lacked mechanisms to support the easy development of ADTs, so they were used only with difficulty and less frequently than warranted. Now, however, with the widespread acceptance of object-oriented languages, the use of ADTs has become pervasive and automatic.

The `List` interface introduced in Chapter 14 is a good example of an ADT. Although we did not examine list implementations in Chapter 14, we did mention that Java provides two—namely `ArrayList` and `LinkedList`. In this chapter, we develop some simplified versions of list implementations and in the process clarify the distinction between interfaces and implementations.

As we saw in Chapter 14, a list ADT is a linear collection of objects ordered by position. At any given moment, each object in a list except the first has a unique predecessor, and each object except the last has a unique successor. Java's list classes provide three types of access to the items they contain:

1. *Indexed-based access.* Methods such as `get`, `set`, `add`, and `remove` expect an integer index as a parameter. This value specifies the position, counting from 0, at which the access, replacement, insertion, or removal occurs.

2. *Object-based access.* Methods such as `contains`, `indexOf`, and `remove` expect an object as a parameter and search the list for the given object. Actually, there are two versions of `remove`, one that is index based and the other object based.

3. *Position-based access.* Through the use of a list iterator, position-based methods support moving to the first, last, next, or previous item in a list. Each of these methods establishes a current position in the list, and we can then access, replace, insert, or remove the item at this current position.

Java's `List` interface includes the index-based and object-based operations, and Java's `ListIterator` interface supports the position-based operations.

Before writing large complex systems, computer scientists sometimes implement a ***prototype***. A prototype is a simplified version of a system that includes only the most essential features of the real thing. By experimenting with a prototype, computer scientists are able to explore a system's core issues in a simplified context, free from distracting details. With that idea in mind, in the rest of this chapter, we define and implement several prototypes for lists. The prototypes are sufficiently complex to allow us to explore the trade-offs between different implementations, yet simple enough to keep the classes small. We define all our prototypes in terms of interfaces, and we then implement these interfaces in several different ways. Table 17-1 gives an overview.

TABLE 17-1

An overview of this chapter's interfaces and implementations

INTERFACE	IMPLEMENTATION	DESCRIPTION
IndexedList	FSAIndexedList	Fixed-size array indexed list
	SLIndexedList	Singly linked indexed list
PositionalList	FSAPositionalList	Fixed-size array positional list
	DLPositionalList	Doubly linked positional list

EXERCISE 17.1

1. What is an abstract data type? Give two examples.

2. Describe the difference between index-based access and position-based access to items in a list.

3. What is a prototype?

17.2 The `IndexedList` Interface

Our first prototype consists of a subset of the index-based methods in Java's `List` interface plus a few others that are described in Table 17-2. Note that no type variables appear in the interface. For simplicity, our prototypes are not generic, though they can contain any objects. Thus, their element type is specified as `Object` and they behave in the manner of "raw" collections mentioned in Chapter 11. Also, if a method's preconditions are not satisfied, it throws an exception.

TABLE 17-2
Public methods in the `IndexedList` interface

METHOD	PRECONDITIONS	POSTCONDITIONS
`void add(int index,` `       Object obj)`	The list is not full and `0 <= index <= size`	Inserts `obj` at position `index` and increases the size by one
`Object get(int index)`	`0 <= index < size`	Returns the object at position `index`
`boolean isEmpty()`	None	Returns `true` if the list is empty and `false` otherwise
`boolean isFull()`	None	Returns `true` if the list is full and `false` otherwise
`Object remove(int index)`	`0 <= index < size`	Removes and returns that object at position `index`
`void set(int index,` `       Object obj)`	`0 <= index < size`	Replaces the object at position `index` with `obj`
`int size()`	None	Returns the number of objects in the list
`String toString()`	None	Returns the concatenation of the string representations of the items in the list

As mentioned in earlier chapters, an interface contains method headers, and each implementation is obliged to define all the corresponding methods. An interface can also include comments that state the preconditions and postconditions for each method. Following is the code for the IndexedList interface:

```java
// File: IndexedList.java
// Interface for the indexed list prototype

public interface IndexedList{

    public void add(int index, Object obj);
    // Preconditions:  The list is not full and
    //                     0 <= index <= size
    // Postconditions: Inserts obj at position index and
    //                 increases the size by one.

    public Object get(int index);
    // Preconditions:  0 <= index < size
    // Postconditions: Returns the object at position index.

    public boolean isEmpty();
    // Postconditions: Returns true if the list is empty or false otherwise.

    public boolean isFull();
    // Postconditions: Returns true if the list is full or false otherwise.

    public Object remove(int index);
    // Preconditions:  0 <= index < size
    // Postconditions: Removes and returns the object at position index.

    public void set(int index, Object obj);
    // Preconditions:  0 <= index < size
    // Postconditions: Replaces the object at position index with obj.

    public int size();
    // Postconditions: Returns the number of objects in the list

    public String toString();
    // Postconditions: Returns the concatenation of the string
    //                 representations of the items in the list.
}
```

EXERCISE 17.2

1. What is the purpose of an interface?

2. What are the preconditions of an index-based operation?

17.3 The Fixed-Size Array Implementation of Indexed Lists

It is easy to implement an indexed list using an array. Figure 17-1 shows an array implementation of the list (D1, D2, D3). The array contains three data items and has two cells unoccupied. In an array implementation of a list, it is crucial to keep track of both the list's size (three in this case) and the array's length (five in this case). We track the list's size in an integer variable that is initially set to 0. Once the list's size equals the array's length, the list is full and no more items can be added. Consequently, clients should always check to see if a list is full before adding items to a fixed-size array-based implementation. Alternatively, it is possible to move a list into a larger array once the existing array becomes full. When a list is instantiated, it must in turn instantiate its underlying array using some predefined length, such as 10.

FIGURE 17-1
An array of implementation of a list

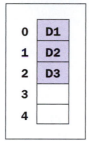

The next code segment shows part of our FSAIndexedList class. We have completed only the constructor. Completion of the other methods is left as Project 17-1. All the needed techniques were presented in Chapter 11.

```java
// File: FSAIndexedList.java

import java.io.*;                              // Needed for serialization

public class FSAIndexedList implements IndexedList, Serializable{

    private static int DEFAULT_CAPACITY = 10;     // Array's length

    private Object[] items;                        // The array of objects
    private int listSize;                          // The list size

    public FSAIndexedList(){
        items = new Object[DEFAULT_CAPACITY];
        listSize = 0;
    }
```

```java
public void add(int index, Object obj){
   if (isFull())
      throw new RuntimeException("The list is full");
   if (index < 0 || index > listSize)
      throw new RuntimeException
      ("Index = " + index + " is out of list bounds");
   // Project 17-1
}

public boolean isEmpty(){. . .}

public boolean isFull(){. . .}

public Object get(int index){. . .}

public Object remove(int index){. . .}

public void set(int index, Object obj){. . .}

public int size(){. . .}

public String toString(){. . .}
}
```

Note that the class `FSAIndexedList` implements two interfaces: `IndexedList` and `Serializable`. The latter interface is required so that lists can be stored easily on disk (see Appendix H). Note also that the `add` method contains code to test for its preconditions. When a precondition is violated, the implementation throws an exception (see Chapter 10 and Appendix F for details on exceptions).

EXERCISE 17.3

1. The size of a list might not be the same as the length of the array that implements it. Describe the problems that this fact poses for the users and implementers of a list.

2. Why does a list class implement the `Serializable` interface?

3. Describe the use of exceptions in a list implementation.

4. Complete the code for the `FSAIndexedList` method `get`.

17.4 The Singly Linked Implementation of Indexed Lists

Linked structures provide a frequently used mechanism for implementing lists. As the name implies, a linked structure consists of objects linked to other objects. The fundamental building block of such a structure is called a *node*. A node has two parts: an object and references, or *pointers*, to other nodes. Of the many different linking schemes, the singly linked structure (or singly linked list) is the simplest. In a singly linked structure, each node contains an object and a pointer to a successor node. The structure as a whole is accessed via a variable called `head` that points to the first node. Figure 17-2 shows a singly linked structure containing the objects D1, D2, and D3. The last node in a singly linked structure has no successor, which is indicated by a backslash or *null pointer*.

FIGURE 17-2
A singly linked structure

Coding with Nodes

In Java, the nodes in a singly linked structure are instances of a `Node` class, which we define as follows:

```java
public class Node {

    public Object value;    // Object stored in this node
    public Node   next;     // Reference to the next node

    public Node(){
        value = null;
        next = null;
    }

    public Node(Object value, Node next){
        this.value = value;
        this.next = next;
    }
}
```

To keep the discussion that follows as simple as possible, we declare the attributes as `public`. Later, we change them to `private`. We now present some code segments that illustrate how to use the `Node` class in a singly linked structure.

Building a Linked Structure

First, we build a singly linked structure containing the following three strings:

```
Throw
the
ball

// Build a singly linked representation of the list
// ("Throw", "the", "ball")

// Declare some Node variables
Node head, node0, node1, node2;    // We count from 0 as usual
```

```
// Instantiate the nodes
node0 = new Node();
node1 = new Node();
node2 = new Node();

// Put an object in each node and link the nodes together
head = node0;

node0.value = "Throw";
node0.next  = node1;

node1.value = "the";
node1.next  = node2;

node2.value = "ball";
```

Figure 17-3 shows the result of this effort.

FIGURE 17-3

Singly linked representation of the list ("Throw", "the", "ball")

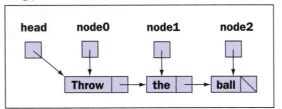

Building the Linked List Again

We can achieve the same result more concisely as illustrated in this next code segment:

```
// More concise code for building the list
// ("Throw", "the", "ball")

// Declare some Node variables
Node head, node0, node1, node2;

// Initialize and link the nodes
node2 = new Node ("ball" , null);          // Warning: a node must be created
node1 = new Node ("the"  , node2);         // before it is used in a link.
node0 = new Node ("Throw", node1);
head  = node0;
```

Building the Linked List for the Last Time

We can even build the list without declaring the variables node0, node1, and node2:

```
// Most concise code for building the list
// ("Throw", "the", "ball")

// Declare the head variable
Node head;
```

```java
// Initialize and link the nodes
head = new Node ("ball" , null);
head = new Node ("the"  , head);
head = new Node ("Throw", head);
```

Traversing a Linked List

Now suppose that we know only the head of the list and are asked to print the third word. To do this, we have to traverse the list and follow the pointers as we go.

```java
// Print the string in node 2

Node pointer;

pointer = head;                    // Now pointing at node 0
pointer = pointer.next;            // Now pointing at node 1
pointer = pointer.next;            // Now pointing at node 2

System.out.println (pointer.value);    // Print the string in node 2
```

To generalize the preceding code, we print the string in node *i*:

```java
// Print the string node i, i = 0, 1, 2, . . .

int  index, i = 2;

pointer = head;                    // Start at the beginning of the list
for (index = 0; index < i; index++)    // Traverse the list
      pointer = pointer.next;

System.out.println (pointer.value);    //Print the string in node i
```

Searching a Linked List

We illustrate the basic technique for searching a linked list by looking for the word "cat" and printing "found" or "not found" depending on the outcome:

```java
// Search a list for the word "cat" and print "found" or "not found"
// depending on the outcome.

Node pointer;
String str;

for (pointer = head; pointer != null; pointer = pointer.next){
   str = (String)(pointer.value);
   if (str.equals("cat")
      break;
}
if (pointer == null)
   System.out.println ("not found");
else
   System.out.println ("found");
```

Null Pointer Exceptions

A common error occurs when writing code to manipulate linked structures. It is the null pointer exception, first introduced in Chapter 5. This exception occurs when the code treats `null` as if it were an object. For instance, consider the following code fragment:

```
Node node0;
. . .
node0.value = "Throw";      // This will generate a null pointer exception if
                            // node0 does not refer to an object.
```

If `node0` is used with the dot operator before it has been associated with an object, then a null pointer exception is thrown. There are three ways to deal with this situation. First, we can use the `try-catch` mechanism to handle the exception immediately or at a higher level:

```
// Handling the exception immediately.
Node node0;
. . .
try{
   node0.value = "Throw";
}catch (NullPointerException e){
   . . . some corrective action goes here . . .
}




// Handling the exception at a higher level
. . .
try{
   . . . call a method that works with nodes and that might throw
        a null pointer exception . . .
}catch (NullPointerException e){
   . . . some corrective action goes here . . .
}
```

Second, we can detect the problem before it occurs:

```
Node node0;
. . .
if (node0 != null){
   node0.value = "Throw";
}else{
   . . . some corrective action goes here . . .
}
```

Third, we can ignore the exception, in which case the JVM prints an error message in the terminal window.

The `SLIndexedList` Class

We now have sufficient background to understand the singly linked implementation of the `IndexedList` prototype. Following is an outline of the class. For now most of the methods are empty, but in the subsections that follow, we fill them in. Notice that the Node class is defined inside the SLIndexedList class. Thus, it is called a *private inner class*. There are several advantages to using a private inner class. First, it is accessible only to code within the enclosing class. Second, even though its attributes and methods are private, they are visible to the enclosing class. Third, if two classes give their inner classes the same name, there is no naming conflict.

```java
// File: SLIndexedList.java

import java.io.*;                       // Needed for serialization

public class SLIndexedList implements IndexedList, Serializable{

   private Node head;                   // Pointer to first node
   private int listSize;                // The list size
   private Node nodeAtIndex;            // The node at index position or null if
                                        // past the end of the list.
   private Node nodeBefore;             // The node before index position or null
                                        // if before the beginning of the list.

   public SLIndexedList(){
      head = null;
      listSize = 0;
   }

   public void add(int index, Object obj){. . .}

   public boolean isEmpty(){
      return listSize == 0;
   }

   public boolean isFull(){
      return false;
   }

   public Object get(int index){. . .}

   public Object remove(int index){. . .}

   public void set(int index, Object obj){. . .}

   public int size(){
      return listSize;
   }

   public String toString(){
      String str = "";
      for (Node node = head; node != null; node = node.next)
          str += node.value + " ";
      return str;
   }
```

```
    private void locateNode(int index){. . .}

    // ---------------- Private inner class for Node ----------------

    private class Node {

        private Object value;     // Object stored in this node
        private Node    next;     // Reference to the next node

        private Node(){
            value = null;
            next = null;
        }

        private Node(Object value, Node next){
            this.value = value;
            this.next = next;
        }
    }
}
```

The `locateNode` Method

To locate node i ($i = 0, 1, 2, ...$) in a linked list, we must start at the head node and visit each successive node until we reach node i. This traversal process is used in the methods `get`, `set`, `add`, and `remove`, so to save time, we write a private helper method, `locateNode`, to implement the process. This helper method takes an index i as a parameter and sets the variable `nodeAtIndex` to node i. In addition, it also sets the variable `nodeBefore` to node i - 1. The latter variable is used by the methods `add` and `remove`. Figure 17-4 shows the outcome of calling `locateNode(2)`. If the index equals the list size, the method sets `nodeBefore` to the last node and `nodeAtIndex` to `null`.

FIGURE 17-4
The outcome of calling locateNode(2)

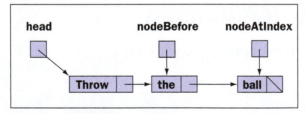

Following is the code for `locateNode`:

```
    private void locateNode(int index){
    // Obtain pointers to the node at index and its predecessor
    // Preconditions    0 <= index <= listSize
    // Postconditions   nodeAtIndex points to the node at position index
    //                  or null if there is none
    //                  nodeBefore points at the predecessor or null
    //                  if there is none
        nodeBefore = null;
        nodeAtIndex = head;
```

```
        for (int i = 1; i < listSize && i <= index; i++){
            nodeBefore = nodeAtIndex;
            nodeAtIndex = nodeAtIndex.next;
        }
        if (index == listSize){
            nodeBefore = nodeAtIndex;
            nodeAtIndex = null;
        }
    }
```

The get and set Methods

The methods get and set use locateNode to access the node at a given index position. The get method then retrieves the value in the node, whereas the set method changes the value. Following is the code for get. The set method is left as part of Project 17-2.

```
    public Object get(int index){
        if (index < 0 || index >= listSize)
            throw new RuntimeException
            ("Index = " + index + " is out of list bounds");

        locateNode(index);
        return nodeAtIndex.value;
    }
```

The remove Method

The remove method locates an indicated node, deletes it from the linked list, and returns the value stored in the node. A node is deleted by adjusting pointers. There are two cases to consider.

1. To delete the first node, set the head pointer to the first node's next pointer (Figure 17-5).

FIGURE 17-5
Removing the first node from a linked list

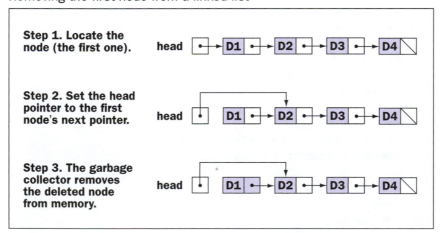

2. To delete any other node, locate it. Then set the predecessor's next pointer to the deleted node's next pointer. (Figure 17-6).

FIGURE 17-6
Removing any node other than the first from a linked list

In the second case, if the deleted node is the last one, then the predecessor's `next` pointer is set to `null`. Following is the code for the `remove` method:

```
public Object remove(int index){
    if (index < 0 || index >= listSize)        // Check precondition
        throw new RuntimeException
        ("Index = " + index + " is out of list bounds");

    Object removedObj = null;

    if (index == 0){                           // Case 1: item is first one
        removedObj = head.value;
        head = head.next;
    }else{
        locateNode(index);
        nodeBefore.next = nodeAtIndex.next;
        removedObj = nodeAtIndex.value;
    }

    listSize--;
    return removedObj;
}
```

The add Method

The add method must deal with the following situations:

Case 1: If the index is 0, the new node becomes the first node in the list. To accomplish this, the new node's next pointer is set to the old head pointer, and the head pointer is then set to the new node. Figure 17-7 shows a node with the object D2 being inserted at the beginning of a list.

FIGURE 17-7
Adding a new node at the beginning of a linked list

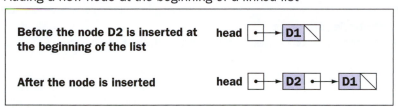

Case 2: If the index is greater than 0, the new node is inserted between the node at position index – 1 and the node at position index or after the last node if the index equals the list size. To accomplish this, we locate the node at position index. We then aim the new node's next pointer at the node at position index and the predecessor's next pointer at the new node. Figure 17-8 shows a node containing the object D3 being inserted at position 1 in a list.

FIGURE 17-8
Adding a new node to a linked list at position 1

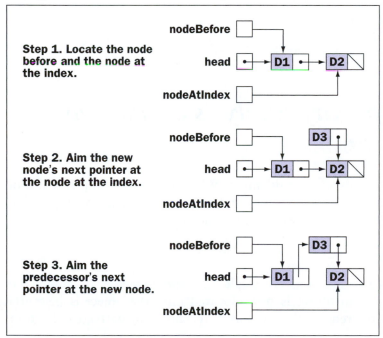

Following is the code for the add method:

```
public void add(int index, Object obj){
    if (index < 0 || index > listSize)          // Check precondition
        throw new RuntimeException
        ("Index = " + index + " is out of list bounds");

    if (index == 0)                             // Case 1: Head of list
        head = new Node(obj, head);
    else{                                       // Case 2: Other positions
        locateNode(index);
        nodeBefore.next = new Node(obj, nodeAtIndex);
    }
    listSize++;
}
```

*E*XERCISE 17.4

1. What is a node?

2. What is the null pointer exception?

3. Draw a diagram of the linked structure that is formed by running the following code, which uses the Node class defined in this section:

```
Node node = null;
for (int i = 1; i <= 5; i++)
    node = new Node("" + i, node);
```

17.5 Complexity Analysis of Indexed List Implementations

Users of indexed lists face a dilemma. Which of the two implementations should they use? An understanding of the memory usage and run-time efficiency of the implementations provides an answer. We begin with an analysis of the memory usage.

Memory Usage

Java maintains a region of memory called *dynamic memory* from which it allocates space for objects. Memory for an object is not allocated until the object is instantiated, and when the object is no longer referenced, the memory is reclaimed by garbage collection.

When an FSAIndexedList is instantiated, a single block of *contiguous memory* is allocated for the list's underlying array. If the array is too small, then it fills up, and if it is too large, there is much unused space. In the first instance, an application may fail because at some point it can no longer add items to a list, and in the second instance, it may hog so much memory that the computer's overall performance is degraded. The space occupied by the array depends on two factors: the array's length and the size of each entry. As the array contains references to objects and not the actual objects themselves, each entry is exactly the same size, or 4 bytes on most computers. The total space occupied by a list equals the space needed by the objects plus $4n$ bytes, where n represents the array's length.

With an `SLIndexedList`, memory is allocated one node at a time and is recovered each time a node is removed. Each node contains two references: one to an object in the list and the other to the next node in the linked structure. Consequently, the total space occupied by a list equals the space needed by the objects plus $8m$ bytes, where m represents the list's length.

We can now compare the memory usage of the two implementations. When the underlying array is less than half full, the array implementation occupies more memory than the corresponding linked implementation. Beyond the halfway point, the array implementation holds the advantage. Consequently, if we can accurately predict the maximum size of our list and if we do not expect the list's size to vary greatly, then an array implementation makes better use of memory. At other times, the linked implementation has the advantage.

Run-Time Efficiency

There are several factors that affect the run-time efficiency of the two implementations. First, consider the problem of accessing an item at a particular position within a list. The entries in an array are in adjacent memory locations, which make it possible to access an entry in constant time. Figure 17-9 shows an array in which each entry is 4 bytes long. The array's *base address* (i.e., the address of the array's first byte) is at location 100, and each successive entry starts 4 bytes past the beginning of the previous one. When we write code that refers to array element `a[i]`, the following computation is performed:

```
Address of array entry i = base address + 4 * i
```

The quantity `4 * i` is called the *offset* and equals the difference between the base address and the location of the desired entry. Once the computation has been completed, the array element is immediately accessible. Because the address computation is performed in constant time, accessing array elements is an O(1) operation.

FIGURE 17-9
Memory map for an array with base address 100 and entry size of 4 bytes

In contrast, the nodes in a linked structure are not necessarily in physically adjacent memory locations. This implies that a node cannot be accessed by adding an offset to a base address; instead, it is located by following a trail of pointers, beginning at the first node. Thus, the time taken to access a node is linearly dependent on its position within the linked structure or O(n).

From this discussion we conclude that the `get` and `set` methods are O(1) for an array implementation and O(n) for a linked implementation.

Next consider the problem of adding an item to a list. In an array implementation, insertion is preceded by shifting all the array entries at and below the insertion point down one slot. This is an O(n) operation and is followed by the O(1) operation of storing a new reference in the array at the insertion point. Thus, the operation is O(n) overall. For a linked list, locating the insertion point requires a traversal and is an O(n) operation. This is followed by instantiating a new node and tying it into the linked structure, which is an O(1) operation. Thus, the operation is O(n) overall.

A similar analysis shows that removing an item from a list is O(n) for both implementations. The `toString` method involves traversing the list from beginning to end and is an O(n) operation for both implementations, whereas the remaining operations (`isEmpty`, `isFull`, and `size`) are obviously O(1). Table 17-3 summarizes these findings.

TABLE 17-3
The run times of the indexed list implementations

METHOD LIST	COMPLEXITY FIXED-SIZE ARRAY (FSAIndexedList)	SINGLY LINKED (SLIndexedList)
`boolean isEmpty()`	O(1)	O(1)
`boolean isFull()`	O(1)	O(1)
`int size()`	O(1)	O(1)
`void add(int i, Object o)`	O(n)	O(n)
`Object get(int i)`	O(1)	O(n)
`Object remove(int i)`	O(n)	O(n)
`Object set(int i, Object o)`	O(1)	O(n)
`String toString()`	O(n)	O(n)

In conclusion, we see that the fixed-size array implementation provides better run-time performance than the singly linked implementation; however, in situations in which we cannot predict a list's maximum size, the array implementation incurs the risk of either running out of space or wasting it. This drawback is overcome by using dynamic rather than fixed-size arrays. When a dynamic array fills, it is replaced by a larger array, and when it shrinks beyond a certain point, it is replaced by a smaller array. Each time this happens, the entries are copied from the old to the new array. Although this approach solves the memory problem, it reintroduces a performance problem. Copying entries between arrays is an O(n) operation, but it is experienced only occasionally. In fact, we can show that, on average, this operation can remain O(1), provided dynamic arrays grow and shrink by a factor of 2.

EXERCISE 17.5

1. How are arrays represented in memory, and what effect does this representation have on the performance of array processing?

2. How are linked structures represented in memory, and what effect does this representation have on the performance of linked structure processing?

17.6 Positional Lists

A *positional list* has a more complex interface than an indexed list, and in contrast to an indexed list, it does not provide direct access to an item based on an index. Instead, a client moves a pointer called the *current position indicator* forward or backward through the list until a desired position is reached. Other operations can then replace, insert, or remove an item relative to the current position. Table 17-4 gives an overview of the methods organized by category. In the rest of this section, we explain these methods and their use more fully. We call our interface `PositionalList`, and it is similar to Java's standard `ListIterator` interface.

TABLE 17-4
Overview of the `PositionalList` interface

METHOD CATEGORIES	METHOD NAMES
Move	moveToHead, moveToTail, next, previous
Check position	hasNext, hasPrevious
Modify content	add, remove, set
Other	isEmpty, isFull, size, toString

Navigating

The current position indicator is part of the state of a positional list, and provided the list is not empty, it always has a value. To navigate in a positional list, a client

- Moves to the head or the tail of the list using the methods `moveToHead` and `moveToTail`.

- Determines if either end of the list has been reached using the methods `hasNext` and `hasPrevious`.

- Moves to the next or previous item in the list using the methods `next` and `previous`.

To illustrate, consider Table 17-5, which shows the effect of navigating in a list of three items. In the table, an arrow represents the current position indicator.

TABLE 17-5
Navigation in a list of three items

ACTION	hasNext	hasPrevious	EFFECT
moveToHead	true	false	D1 D2 D3
next	true	true	D1 D2 D3
next	true	true	D1 D2 D3
next	false	true	D1 D2 D3

The following is a code segment that traverses a positional list from beginning to end:

```
list.moveToHead();
while (list.hasNext()){
    Object item = list.next();
    <do something with the item>
}
```

Alternatively, we can traverse a list in the opposite direction:

```
list.moveToTail();
while (list.hasPrevious()){
    Object item = list.previous();
    <do something with the item>
}
```

An exception is thrown if `next` or `previous` is called when `hasNext` or `hasPrevious` is false, respectively.

Adding an Object

The `add` method expects an object as a parameter, and provided the list is not full, it does one of the following:

- If the list is empty, it adds the object to the list and places the current position indicator immediately after the object.

- Otherwise, it inserts the object immediately before the current position indicator.

The following code segment adds the numbers from 1 to 5 to a positional list:

```
for (int i = 1; i <= 5; i++)
    list.add(new Integer(i));      // list contains 1 2 3 4 5
```

Removing an Object

The `remove` method deletes the current object if there is one. The current object is the object returned by the most recent `next` or `previous` operation, provided there have been no intervening `add`, `remove`, `moveToHead`, `moveToTail`, or `toString` operations. The following code segment removes the second object from a list of at least two objects:

```
list.moveToHead();
list.next();
list.next();
list.remove();
```

The `remove` method locates the current position indicator in the space vacated by the removed object.

Setting an Object

The `set` method replaces the current object with the object specified in the method's parameter. The replacement then becomes the current object, and the current position indicator does not change. Following is an example that sets the second object in a list:

```
list.moveToHead();
list.next();
list.next();
list.set(anObject);
```

The Interface

Having established a clear picture of how positional lists work, we now present the interface. Table 17-6 describes the methods. If a method's preconditions are not satisfied, it throws an exception.

TABLE 17-6
The methods in the `PositionalList` interface

METHOD	PRECONDITIONS	POSTCONDITIONS
A default constructor	None	An empty positional list is instantiated. The current position is not defined.
A constructor that takes an `IndexedList` as a parameter	The size of the indexed list is not greater than the maximum capacity of a positional list.	A positional list is instantiated and contains the same objects as are in the `IndexedList`. The current position immediately precedes the first object.
void add(Object obj)	The list is not full.	Inserts `obj` at the current position in a nonempty list or simply adds it to an empty list. The current position indicator is located after the object just inserted.
boolean hasNext()	None	Returns `true` if the current position indicator is followed by an `object` and `false` otherwise.

TABLE 17-6 Continued
The methods in the `PositionalList` interface

METHOD	PRECONDITIONS	POSTCONDITIONS
`boolean hasPrevious()`	None	Returns `true` if the current position indicator is preceded by an object and `false` otherwise
`boolean isEmpty()`	None	Returns `true` if the list is empty and `false` otherwise
`boolean isFull()`	None	Returns `true` if the list is full and `false` otherwise
`void moveToHead()`	None	Moves the current position indicator immediately before the first object if there is one
`void moveToTail()`	None	Moves the current position indicator immediately after the last object if there is one
`Object next()`	`hasNext` returns true.	Returns the object after the current position indicator and then moves the indicator after the object.
`Object previous()`	`hasPrevious` returns true.	Returns the object before the current position indicator and then moves the indicator before the object.
`Object remove()`	There is a current object.	Removes the current object.
`void set(Object obj)`	There is a current object.	Replaces the current object with `obj`.
`int size()`	None	Returns the number of objects in the list
`String toString()`	None	Returns a string that is the concatenation of the string representations of the objects in the list

Following is the Java code for the interface:

```
// File: PositionalList.java
// Interface for the positional list prototype

/* At all times a current position indicator (cpi) is associated with
   the list.
   In a nonempty list the indicator is one of the following:
     Before the first item
     Between two items
     After the last item
   In an empty list the indicator exists without any items.
*/
```

```java
public interface PositionalList {

    public void add(Object obj);
    // Preconditions:  The list is not full
    // Postconditions: obj is inserted immediately before the cpi

    public boolean hasNext();
    // Postconditions: Returns true if there is an object after the
    //                 cpi and false otherwise

    public boolean hasPrevious();
    // Postconditions: Returns true if there is an object before the
    //                 cpi and false otherwise

    public boolean isEmpty();
    // Postconditions: Returns true if the list contains no items
    //                 and false otherwise

    public boolean isFull();
    // Postconditions: Returns true if the list cannot take another item
    //                 and false otherwise

    public void moveToHead();
    // Postconditions: Moves the cpi before the first object if
    //                 the list is not empty

    public void  moveToTail();
    // Postconditions: Moves the cpi after the last object if
    //                 the list is not empty

    public Object next();
    // Preconditions:  hasNext returns true
    // Postconditions: Returns the object following the cpi
    //                 and moves the cpi after that object.

    public Object previous();
    // Preconditions:  hasPrevious returns true
    // Postconditions: Returns the object preceding the cpi
    //                 and moves the cpi before that object

    public Object remove();
    // Preconditions:  None of add, remove, moveToHead, moveToTail, toString
    //                 have been called since the last successful call
    //                 to next or previous
    // Postconditions: Removes the object encountered by the most
    //                 recent next or previous
    //                 The cpi retains its position relative to the items
    //                 that are left in the list

    public void set(Object obj);
    // Preconditions:  None of add, remove, moveToHead, moveToTail, toString
    //                 have been called since the last successful call to
    //                 next or previous
```

```
// Postconditions: Replaces the object returned by the most
//                  recent next or previous

public int size();
// Postconditions: Returns the number of items in the list

public String toString();
// Postconditions: Returns a string representation of the list by
//                  concatenating the string representations of the
//                  individual items in the list
}
```

EXERCISE 17.6

1. How do you navigate through a positional list?

2. Assume that the positional list `list` has been instantiated and that the objects a, b, and c have been added to it. Write code segments that accomplish the following tasks:

a. Remove item b.

b. Add item d after the last item in the list.

c. Replace item a with item e.

17.7 Fixed-Size Array Implementation of Positional Lists

There are two primary problems to solve when implementing a positional list:

1. Keeping track of the interacting preconditions and postconditions of all the operations

2. Keeping track of the current position and current object

In the fixed-size array implementation, we solve these problems by means of the instance variables `curPos` and `lastItemPos`. As the name suggests, `curPos` is the current position indicator. It equals i if the current position is immediately before the item at index position i in the list ($i = 0, 1, 2, ...$), and it equals the list size if the current position is after the last item. The variable `lastItemPos` equals the index of the last item returned by `next` or `previous` or -1 if there has been an intervening `add`, `remove`, `moveToHead`, `moveToTail`, or `toString` operation. It also equals -1 initially. Thus, when `lastItemPos` equals -1, the methods `remove` and `set` are blocked because we know their preconditions are not satisfied. Following is a code segment of the fixed-size array implementation of a positional list:

```
import java.io.*;              // Needed for serialization

public class FSAPositionalList implements PositionalList,
                                          Serializable{
```

```
    private static int DEFAULT_CAPACITY = 10;      // Maximum list size

    private Object[] items;          // The array of objects
    private int listSize;            // The list size

    private int curPos;
        // Current position indicator
        // Equals i if immediately before the item at index i
        // Equals listSize if after the last item

    private int lastItemPos;
        // Equals index of last item returned by next or previous
        // Equals -1 initially and after add, remove, moveToHead,
        // and moveToTail

    // Constructors

    public FSAPositionalList(){
        items = new Object[DEFAULT_CAPACITY];
        listSize = 0;
        curPos = 0;
        lastItemPos = -1;   // Block remove and set until after a successful
                            // next or previous
    }

    public FSAPositionalList(IndexedList list){
        // Project 17-3
    }

    // Methods that indicate the state of the list

    public boolean isEmpty(){
        return listSize == 0;
    }

    public boolean isFull(){
        return listSize == items.length;
    }

    public boolean hasNext(){
        return curPos < listSize;
    }

    public boolean hasPrevious(){
        return curPos > 0;
    }

    public int size(){
        return listSize;
    }
```

```java
// Methods that move the current position indicator

public void moveToHead(){
   curPos = 0;
   lastItemPos = -1;      // Block remove and set until after a successful
                          // next or previous
}

public void  moveToTail(){
   curPos = listSize;
   lastItemPos = -1;      // Block remove and set until after a successful
                          // next or previous
}

// Methods that retrieve items

public Object next(){
   if (!hasNext())
      throw new RuntimeException
      ("There are no more elements in the list");

   lastItemPos = curPos;  // Remember the index of the last item returned
   curPos++;              // Advance the current position
   return items[lastItemPos];
}

public Object previous(){
   if (!hasPrevious())
      throw new RuntimeException
      ("There are no more elements in the list");

   lastItemPos = curPos -1;

                                     // Remember the index of the last item
                                     // returned
   curPos--;                         // Move the current position backward
   return items[lastItemPos];
}

// Methods that modify the list's contents

public void add(Object obj){
   // Exercise
}

public Object remove(){
   // Exercise
}

public void set(Object obj){
   if (lastItemPos == -1)
      throw new RuntimeException (
                "There is no established item to set.");

   items[lastItemPos] = obj;
}
```

```
// Method that returns a string representation of the list.

public String toString(){
    String str = "";
    for (int i = 0; i < listSize; i++)
        str += items[i] + " ";
    return str;
}
}
```

EXERCISE 17.7

1. Write the code segment for the `FSAPositionalList` constructor method that expects an `IndexedList` as a parameter.

17.8 Doubly Linked Implementation of Positional Lists

We never use a singly linked structure to implement a positional list because it provides no convenient mechanism for moving one node to the left—that is, to a node's predecessor. In a singly linked list, moving left requires repositioning to the head of the list and then traversing right. The cost of doing this is O(*n*). In a doubly linked list, it is equally easy to move left and right. Both are O(1) operations. Figure 17-10 shows a doubly linked structure with three nodes.

FIGURE 17-10
A doubly linked structure with three nodes

It turns out that the code needed to manipulate a doubly linked list is simplified if one extra node is added at the head of the list. This node is called a ***sentinel node***, and it points forward to the first node and backward to the last node. The head pointer now points to the sentinel node. The last node points forward to the sentinel node. The resulting structure is called a ***circular linked list***. The sentinel node does not contain a list item, and when the list is empty, the sentinel remains. Figure 17-11 shows an empty circular linked list and a circular linked list containing three items.

FIGURE 17-11
Two circular doubly linked lists with sentinel nodes

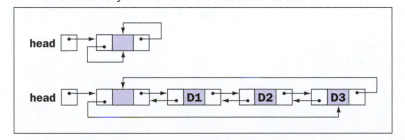

The basic building block of a doubly linked list is a node with two pointers: next, which points right; and previous, which points left. We define the node in a private inner class called Node. As in the array implementation, we rely heavily on the variables curPos and lastItemPos; however, they now represent two-way nodes rather than integers. The following is a code segment of the class DLPositionalList. The missing parts are left as Project 17-4.

```java
import java.io.*;                    // Needed for serialization

public class DLPositionalList implements PositionalList,
                                         Serializable{

   private Node head;
         // Sentinel head node

   private Node curPos;
         // Current position indicator
         // Points at the node that would be returned by next
         // The current position is considered to be immediately
         // before this node
         // If curPos == head then at end of list
         // If curPos.previous == head then at beginning of list

   private Node lastItemPos;
         // Points at the last item returned by next or previous
         // Equals null initially and after add, remove, moveToHead,
         // moveToTail, and toString

   private int listSize;
         // The number of items in the list

   // Constructor

   public DLPositionalList(){
      head = new Node(null, null, null);
      head.next = head;
      head.previous = head;
      curPos = head.next;
      lastItemPos = null;
      listSize = 0;
   }

   public DLPositionalList (IndexedList list){
      // Project 17-4
   }

   // Methods that indicate the state of the list

   public boolean isEmpty(){
      return listSize == 0;
   }
```

```java
public boolean isFull(){
   return false;
}

public boolean hasNext(){
   return curPos != head;
}

public boolean hasPrevious(){
   return curPos.previous != head;
}

public int size(){
   return listSize;
}

// Methods that move the current position indicator

public void moveToHead(){
   curPos = head.next;
   lastItemPos = null;       // Block remove and set until after a
                             // successful next or previous

}

public void  moveToTail(){
   curPos = head;
   lastItemPos = null;     // Block remove and set until after a
                           // successful next or previous

}

// Methods that retrieve items

public Object next(){      // Returns the next item
   if (!hasNext())
      throw new RuntimeException
      ("There are no more elements in the list");

   lastItemPos = curPos;  // Remember the index of the last item returned
   curPos = curPos.next;  // Advance the current position
   return lastItemPos.value;
}

public Object previous(){     // Returns the previous item
   if (!hasPrevious())
      throw new RuntimeException
      ("There are no more elements in the list");

   lastItemPos = curPos.previous;  // Remember the index of the last item
                                   // returned
   curPos = curPos.previous;       // Move the current position backward
   return lastItemPos.value;
}
```

```java
// Methods that modify the list's contents

public void add(Object obj){
    // To be discussed
}

public Object remove(){
    // Project 17-4
}

public void set(Object obj){
    if (lastItemPos == null)
        throw new RuntimeException (
                    "There is no established item to set.");

    lastItemPos.value = obj;
}

// Method that returns a string representation of the list.

public String toString(){
    String str = "";
    for (Node node = head.next; node != head; node = node.next)
        str += node.value + " ";
    return str;
}

// ---------------- Private inner class for Node ----------------

private class Node implements Serializable {
    private Object value;       // Value stored in this node
    private Node    next;       // Reference to next node
    private Node    previous;   // Reference to previous node

    private Node(){
        value = null;
        previous = null;
        next = null;
    }

    private Node(Object value){
        this.value = value;
        previous = null;
        next = null;
    }

    private Node(Object value, Node previous, Node next){
        this.value = value;
        this.previous = previous;
        this.next = next;
    }
}
}
```

The add Method

Figure 17-12 shows the steps required to insert a node into a doubly linked list. The new node is inserted immediately before the one pointed to by curPos.

FIGURE 17-12

Steps required to insert a node into a doubly linked list

The same steps are required even when there are no data nodes already in the list. In that case, the header node is both the successor and the predecessor of the new node. Following is the code for the add method:

```java
public void add(Object obj){
    // Create new node for object obj (steps 2 and 3 in Figure 17-12)
    Node newNode = new Node(obj, curPos.previous, curPos);

    // Link the new node into the list (steps 4 and 5 in Figure 17-12)
    curPos.previous.next = newNode;
    curPos.previous = newNode;
```

```
              // curPos does not change

        listSize++;
        lastItemPos = null;    // Block remove and set until after a successful
                               // next or previous
      }
```

The add method is remarkably simple; however, without a sentinel node, the code would be considerably more complex.

EXERCISE 17.8

1. What advantages does a doubly linked list have over a singly linked list?

2. What advantages does a circular linked list with a sentinel node have over a plain linked list?

17.9 Complexity Analysis of Positional Lists

The memory requirements of positional and indexed lists are similar. The only difference is that the nodes in doubly linked lists utilize two pointers rather than one. Table 17-7 summarizes the run times of the positional list implementations. The unfilled slots are left to be completed in Exercise 17.9. Because an item is added, removed, or replaced at the current position indicator, no search is required to locate the position.

TABLE 17-7
The run times of the positional list implementations

METHOD LIST	COMPLEXITY FIXED-SIZE ARRAY	DOUBLY LINKED
	(FSAPositionalList)	(DLPositionalList)
boolean isEmpty()	O(1)	O(1)
boolean isFull()	O(1)	O(1)
int size()	O(1)	O(1)
boolean hasNext()	O(1)	O(1)
boolean hasPrevious()	O(1)	O(1)
void moveToHead()	O(1)	O(1)
void moveToTail()	O(1)	
Object next()	O(1)	O(1)
Object previous()	O(1)	O(1)
void add(Object o)		
void remove(Object o)		
void set(Object o)		

EXERCISE 17.9

1. Complete the analysis in Table 17-7 by filling in the correct value in the blank cells.

17.10 *Iterators*

To a certain extent, the behavior of an iterator is similar to that of a positional list. All iterators maintain a current position pointer to an element in the backing collection. Simple iterators allow the client to move this pointer to the next element and to ask whether there are more elements after the pointer. These iterators may also allow the client to remove the item just visited. List iterators extend this behavior by allowing movement to previous elements and by allowing insertions and replacements of elements as well.

The implementation of an iterator is complicated by two factors:

1. Messages can also be sent to the backing collection. If a mutator message such as add or remove is sent, the state of the backing collection can become inconsistent with the position of the iterator. Thus, an iterator must have a way of tracking mutations to the backing collection and throwing exceptions after they have occurred.

2. More than one iterator can be open on the same backing collection. If an iterator supports mutations to the backing collection, the collection's state can become inconsistent with the positions of the other iterators. Thus, an iterator must also have a way of tracking the mutations that other iterators make and disallowing these as well.

In general, it is most convenient to implement an iterator as a private inner class within the collection class. In the case of a simple iterator, this class implements the Iterator interface, whereas a list iterator implements the ListIterator interface. To track and validate mutations to the backing collection, a private integer instance variable called modCount is declared in the enclosing collection class and is incremented each time a mutator message is sent to the collection. When an iterator is instantiated, it records this count in its own instance variable called expectedModCount. Whenever the iterator receives a message, it compares these two values and throws an exception if they are not equal (meaning that someone sent a mutator message to the backing collection before the current message was sent to the iterator). Whenever the iterator performs a mutation on the backing collection, the two values are incremented to keep them consistent for that iterator. Other iterators, which have their own expectedModCount, can then also detect any inconsistency. The implementation of a simple iterator is left as the task of Project 17-5.

SUMMARY

In this chapter, you learned:

- Implementations of linear collections can be achieved by using arrays or linked structures.

- There are two types of linked structures used to implement linear collections: singly linked structures and doubly linked structures. A singly linked structure allows clients to move in one direction only, whereas a doubly linked structure allows clients to move in both directions.

- There are various trade-offs between arrays and linked structures. Index-based access is faster with arrays than with linked structures. Linked structures can provide a more economical use of memory than arrays.

- The run-time and memory aspects of arrays and linked structures depend on their underlying representation in computer memory. Arrays are represented with blocks of adjacent memory cells, whereas linked structures contain references to potentially nonadjacent chunks of memory.

VOCABULARY *Review*

Define the following terms:

Base address	Linked structure	Positional list
Circular linked list	Node	Private inner class
Contiguous memory	Null pointer	Prototype
Current position indicator	Offset	Sentinel node
Doubly linked structure	Pointer	Singly linked structure
Dynamic memory		

REVIEW *Questions*

FILL IN THE BLANK

Complete the following sentences by writing the correct word or words in the blanks provided.

1. The array implementation of an indexed-based list provides access to an element at a specified position in _____ time.

2. The linked implementation of an indexed-based list provides access to an element at a specified position in _____ time.

3. A singly linked structure contains a sequence of _____, each of which contains a data element and a link to the next _____.

4. The end of a singly linked structure is detected by testing for _____.

5. A linked implementation of a positional list uses a(n) _____ linked structure.

6. The operations of an iterator most closely resemble those of a(n) _____ list.

7. An iterator should disallow _____ messages to be sent to its backing collection.

8. A(n) _____ linked structure would be a wise choice for a stack implementation.

9. A(n) _____ linked structure would be a wise choice for a queue implementation.

10. Iterators are implemented using a(n) _____ class.

PROJECTS

PROJECT 17-1

Complete the class `FSAIndexedList` and test it with an appropriate tester program.

PROJECT 17-2

Complete the class `SLIndexedList` and test it with the tester program from Project 17-1.

PROJECT 17-3

Complete the class `FSAPositionalList` and test it with an appropriate tester program.

PROJECT 17-4

Complete the class `DLPositionalList` and test it with an appropriate tester program.

PROJECT 17-5

Add an `iterator` method to the interface `IndexedList`. Then implement this method in the class `FSAIndexedList` using the techniques described in this chapter. Test your iterator with an appropriate tester program.

CRITICAL*Thinking*

Jack decides to implement an iterator for stacks. Jill uses his code and complains that his iterator should not support a remove method. Discuss the issues involved in this disagreement.

CHAPTER 18

IMPLEMENTING SETS AND MAPS

OBJECTIVES

Upon completion of this chapter, you should be able to:

- Explain why a list implementation of sets and maps is simple but inefficient.

- Develop hash functions to implement sets and maps.

- Understand different strategies for resolving collisions during hashing.

- Understand why a hashing implementation of sets and maps can be very efficient.

Estimated Time: 3.5 hours

VOCABULARY

Bucket

Chaining

Chains

Clustering

Collision

Density ratio

Hash code

Hash function

Linear collision
    processing

Load factor

Quadratic collision
    processing

Most clients who use sets and maps want to build higher-level, more application-specific operations with the primitives provided. These operations likely employ many insertions and retrievals. Thus, the paramount consideration from the implementer's perspective is the speed of insertion and retrieval in sets and maps.

Unordered collections can be implemented using several of the collections already presented. For example, one might use a list to implement a set. This is not a wise choice, however, because a list supports only linear searches and insertions.

Another consideration is that we want sets and maps to contain any objects, not just comparable objects. This implies that we cannot use sorted collections, whose items must be comparable, to implement general unordered collections. It seems that this restriction does not bode well for the implementation of more efficient (better than linear) searches and insertions, which, so far as we have seen, require a special ordering of the data. However, we can overcome this restriction and obtain optimal performance by using a new access technique called *hashing*. Hashing can potentially achieve O(1) efficiency for insertion and retrieval operations. In this chapter, we examine both implementation strategies.

18.1 The Set and Map Prototypes

As we did for linear collections in Chapter 17, here we work with prototypes of sets and maps rather than full versions, so we can examine the essential features of the different implementations. As in Chapter 17, our prototypes are nongeneric collections whose elements are of type `Object`. The set prototype's interface is called `SetPT`, and its methods appear in Table 18-1.

TABLE 18-1
The `SetPT` interface

METHOD	WHAT IT DOES
`boolean add(Object obj)`	If the object is not already in the set, then adds the object to the set, increasing the set's size by one, and returns `true`; otherwise, returns `false`
`void clear()`	Makes the set empty
`boolean contains(Object obj)`	Returns `true` if the object is in the set, else `false`
`boolean isEmpty()`	Returns `true` if the set contains no objects, else `false`
`Iterator iterator()`	Returns an iterator on the set
`boolean remove(Object obj)`	If the object is in the set, removes it and returns `true`; otherwise, returns `false`
`int size()`	Returns the number of objects currently in the set

The map prototype's interface is called `MapPT`, and its methods appear in Table 18-2.

TABLE 18-2
The `MapPT` interface

METHOD	WHAT IT DOES
`boolean containsKey(Object key)`	Returns `true` if the map contains the indicated key or `false` otherwise
`void clear()`	Makes the map empty
`boolean containsValue(Object value)`	Returns `true` if the map contains at least one instance of the indicated value or `false` otherwise
`Object get(Object key)`	Returns the value associated with the indicated key if the key is in the map or `null` otherwise
`boolean isEmpty()`	Returns `true` if the map is empty or `false` otherwise
`SetPT keySet()`	Returns a set view of the keys in the map
`Object put(Object key, Object value)`	If the key is already in the map, replaces the previous value with the new value and returns the previous value; otherwise, adds the key and the associated value to the map and returns `null`
`Object remove(Object key)`	If the key is in the map, removes the key value pair from the map and returns the value; otherwise, returns `null`
`int size()`	Returns the number of key value pairs currently in the map
`Collection values()`	Returns a collection view of the values in the map

The implementations of sets are `ListSetPT` and `HashSetPT`, whereas the implementations of maps are `ListMapPT` and `HashMapPT`. The relationships among these resources are diagrammed in Figure 18-1.

FIGURE 18-1
The prototypes for sets and maps

18.2 *List Implementations of Sets and Maps*

Sets

The list implementation of sets is fairly simple. A set contains a list. Because we do not have to worry about ordering the elements, they can be added at the head of the list, which is an O(1) operation with a linked list. Thus, we choose an instance of class `LinkedList` to contain the set's elements. Most of the `ListSetPT` methods simply call the corresponding `List` methods to accomplish their tasks. The only exception is the `ListSetPT` method `add`, which must prevent a duplicate object from being inserted into the set. Following is the code for the method `add`:

```
// In the class ListSetPT

public boolean add(Object obj){
   if (list.contains(obj))
      return false;
   else{
      list.addFirst(obj);
      return true;
   }
}
```

Maps

Unlike set elements, the entries in a map consist of two parts: a key and a value. Because insertions, accesses, and removals are based on a key rather than an entire entry, the methods in a list implementation of maps cannot simply consist of calls to the corresponding list methods. The `ListMapPT` class deals with this problem by maintaining parallel lists of keys and values. The methods `get`, `put`, and `remove` all rely on a single pattern involving these lists:

```
Find the index of the key in the list of keys
If the index is -1
   Do what is needed when the key does not exist
Else
   Manipulate the element at the index in the list of values
```

If we use instances of `ArrayList` for the lists, then accessing a value in the list of values, once we have located the key in the list of keys, is O(1). The following code employs this pattern in the `ListMapPT` method `get`:

```
public Object get(Object key){
   int index = keysList.indexOf(key);
   if (index == -1)
      return null;
   else
      return valuesList.get(index);
}
```

Complexity Analysis of the List Implementations of Sets and Maps

The list implementation of sets requires very little programmer effort but unfortunately does not perform well. A quick inspection of the major accessing methods shows that every one of them is linear.

The list implementation of maps does not behave any better than that of sets. All of the methods that must access a key in the list of keys are linear. Clearly, we should hope for faster implementations. There are some, as we shall see in the next section with hashing.

*E*XERCISE 18.2

1. Why is a list a poor choice for implementing an unordered collection?

18.3 Overview of Hashing

Hash Functions

Hashing is a technique of storing and retrieving data in which each item is associated with a *hash code*. This code is based on some property of the item and can be computed in constant time by a function known as a *hash function*. The same hash function is run when an item is inserted, retrieved, or removed, so these operations are potentially O(1). How can this be? Suppose we use the item's hash code to locate the item's index in an array. The expression for this is

```
hashCode % array.length;
```

and it runs in constant time.

There are various ways to generate hash codes, but Java already includes a method, `hashCode()`, for any object. This method returns a large number that may be negative, so the expression for locating an item's index in an array becomes

```
Math.abs(item.hashCode() % array.length)
```

The following short tester program allows the user to input the array's length and the number of items to store and displays the items, their hash codes, and their array index positions:

```java
// Example 18.1

import java.util.Scanner;

public class TestHashing{
    public static void main(String [] args){
        Scanner reader = new Scanner(System.in);
        String query = "y";
        while (query.equalsIgnoreCase("y")){
```

```
System.out.print("Enter the size of the array: ");
int arrayLength = reader.nextInt();
System.out.print("Enter the number of items: ");
int numberOfItems = reader.nextInt();

System.out.println(" Item     hash code   array index");

for (int i = 0; i < numberOfItems; i ++){
    String str = "Item " + i;
    int code = str.hashCode();
    int index = Math.abs(code % arrayLength);
    System.out.println(str + " " + code + " " + index);
}
reader.nextLine();
System.out.print("Run again?[y/n]");
query = reader.nextLine();
    }
  }
}
```

Figure 18-2 shows the results of two runs of this program. The first run locates distinct index positions for 10 items in an array of length 20. The second run increases the number of items to 15. In this case, distinct positions are found for each item except items 9 and 10, which share position 8. Clearly, this situation, which is called a *collision*, is not a good thing.

FIGURE 18-2
Computing hash codes and indexes

Unfortunately, the collision does not go away when we increase the size of the array. Also, there will be more collisions as the number of items approaches the array's length. In the following section, we examine several methods for resolving collisions.

Linear Collision Processing

For insertions, the simplest way to resolve a collision is to search the array, starting from the collision spot, for the first available empty position—referred to as *linear collision processing*.

When a search reaches the last position of the array, the search wraps around to continue from the first position. If we assume the array does not become full and that an array cell is `null` when unoccupied, the code for insertions is as follows:

```
// Get an initial hash code
int index = item.hashCode() % array.length;

// Stop searching when an empty cell is encountered
while (array[index] != null)

    // Increment the index and wrap around to first position if necessary
    index = (index + 1) % array.length;

// An empty cell is found, so store the item
array[index] = item;
```

Retrievals and removals work in a similar manner, except that we search for an item that matches the target item.

Linear collision processing is prone to a problem known as *clustering*. This situation occurs when the items that cause a collision are relocated to the same region (a cluster) within the array. This placement usually leads to other collisions with other relocated items. During the course of an application, several clusters may develop and coalesce into larger clusters, making the problem worse.

Quadratic Collision Processing

One way to avoid the clustering associated with linear collision processing is to advance the search for an empty position a considerable distance from the collision point. *Quadratic collision processing* accomplishes this by incrementing the current index by the square of a constant on each attempt. If the attempt fails, we increment the constant and try again. Put another way, if we begin with an initial hash code k and a constant c, the formula used on each pass is $k + c^2$.

Following is the code for insertions, updated to use quadratic collision processing:

```
// Set the initial hash code, index, and constant
int hashCode = item.hashCode() % array.length;
int constant = 2;
int index = hashCode % array.length;

// Stop searching when an empty cell is encountered
while (array[index] != null){

    // Increment the index and wrap around to first position if necessary
    index = (hashCode + constant * constant) % array.length;
    constant++;
}

// An empty cell is found, so store the item
array[index] = item;
```

Chaining

In a collision processing strategy known as *chaining*, the items are stored in an array of linked lists, or *chains*. Each item's hash code locates the *bucket*, or index, of the chain in which the item already resides or is to be inserted. The retrieval and removal operations each perform the following steps:

1. Compute the item's hash code or index in the array.

2. Search the linked list at that index for the item.

If the item is found, it can be returned or removed. Figure 18-3 shows an array of linked lists with five buckets and eight items.

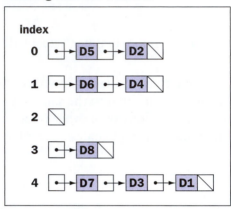

FIGURE 18-3
Hashing with five buckets

The hash code of each item is the index of its linked list in the array. For example, the items D7, D3, and D1 have the hash code 4.

To insert an item into this structure, we perform the following steps:

1. Compute the item's hash code or index in the array.

2. If the array cell is empty, create a node with the item and assign the node to the cell.

3. Otherwise, a collision occurs. The existing item is the head of a linked list or chain of items at that position. Insert the new item at the head of this list.

Borrowing the `Node` class discussed in Chapter 17, following is the code for inserting an item using chaining:

```java
// Get the hash code
int index = item.hashCode() % array.length;

// Access a bucket and store the item at the head of its linked list
array[index] = new Node(item, array[index]);
```

Load Factors

To understand the complexity analysis of the various hashing methods, you need to become acquainted with the concept of a *load factor* or *density ratio*. An array's load factor is the result of dividing the number of items by the array's capacity. For example, let E be 30 items and let A be 100 array cells. Then the load factor of the structure, E/A, is 30/100 or 0.3. Without realizing it, we first encountered load factors in our comparison of array and linked-based implementations of lists (Chapter 17), where we claimed that arrays less than half full waste more memory than the corresponding linked structures. In the context of hashing, as the load factor increases, so does the likelihood of collisions.

Complexity Analysis

Linear Collision Processing

As we have seen, the complexity of linear collision processing depends on the load factor as well as the tendency of relocated items to cluster. In the worst case, when the method must traverse the entire array before locating an item's position, the behavior is linear. One study of the linear method (Donald E. Knuth, *The Art of Computer Programming*, Volume 3, *Searching and Sorting*, Menlo Park, CA: Addison-Wesley, 1973) showed that its average behavior in searching for an item that cannot be found is

```
(1/2) [1 + 1/(1 - D)²]
```

where D is the density ratio or load factor.

Quadratic Collision Processing

Because the quadratic method tends to mitigate clustering, we can expect its average performance to be better than that of the linear method. According to Knuth (cited earlier), the average search complexity for the quadratic method is

```
1 - logₑ(1 - D) - (D / 2)
```

for the successful case and

```
1 / (1 - D) - D - logₑ(1 - D)
```

for the unsuccessful case.

Chaining

Analysis shows that the process of locating an item using this strategy consists of two parts:

1. Computing the index
2. Searching a linked list when collisions occur

The first part has constant time behavior. The second part has linear behavior. The amount of work is O(n) in the worst case. In this case, all of the items are in one chain, which is a linked list. However, if the lists are evenly distributed throughout the array and the array is fairly large, the second part can be close to constant as well. In the best case, each array cell is occupied by a chain of length 1, so the performance is exactly O(1). Random insertion of items tends to result in an even distribution. As the load factor increases past 1, however, the lengths of the chains also increase, resulting in degraded performance. Unlike the other methods, chaining need not resize the array.

Other trade-offs and optimizations of various hashing strategies are the subject of later courses in computer science.

EXERCISE 18.3

1. Explain how hashing can provide constant-time access to a data structure.

2. What causes collisions?

3. How does the linear method of resolving collisions work?

4. What causes clustering?

5. How does the quadratic method of resolving collisions work, and how does it mitigate clustering?

6. Compute the load factors for the following situations:
   a. An array of length 30 with 10 items
   b. An array of length 30 with 30 items
   c. An array of length 30 with 100 items

7. Explain how chaining works.

18.4 Hashing Implementation of Maps

Our prototype map class uses the bucket/chaining method described earlier. Thus, the implementation must maintain an array and represent entries in such a manner as to allow chaining. To manage the array, we declare three instance variables: `table` (the array), `size` (the number of entries in the map), and `capacity` (the number of cells in the array). To represent an entry, we define the private inner class `Entry`. The attributes of an entry are similar to those of the node classes of earlier chapters: a key, a value, and a pointer to the next entry in a chain. The value of `capacity` is by default a constant, which we define as 3 to ensure frequent collisions.

Because the same technique is used to locate the position of an entry for insertions, retrievals, and removals, we implement it in one method, `containsKey`. From the client's perspective, this method just searches for a given key and returns `true` or `false`. From the implementer's perspective, this method also sets the values of some instance variables to information that can be used during insertions, retrievals, and removals. Table 18-3 gives the variables and their roles in the implementation.

TABLE 18-3
The variables used for accessing entries in the class HashMapPT

TEMPORARY INSTANCE VARIABLE	PURPOSE
Entry foundEntry	Contains the entry just located or is undefined otherwise
Entry priorEntry	Contains the entry prior to the one just located or is undefined otherwise
int index	Contains the index of the chain in which the entry was just located or is undefined otherwise

We now examine how `containsKey` locates an entry's position and sets these variables. Following is the pseudocode for this process:

```
containsKey(key)
Set index to the hash code of the key (using the method described earlier)
Set priorEntry to null
Set foundEntry to table[index]
while (foundEntry != null)
   if (foundEntry.key equals key)
      return true
   else
      Set priorEntry to foundEntry
      Set foundEntry to foundEntry.next
return false;
```

As you can see, the algorithm uses `index`, `foundEntry`, and `priorEntry` during the search. If the algorithm hashes to an empty array cell, then no entry was found, but `index` contains the bucket for a subsequent insertion of its first entry. If the algorithm hashes to a nonempty array cell, then the algorithm loops down the chain of entries until it finds a matching entry or runs off the chain. In either case, the algorithm leaves `foundEntry` and `priorEntry` set to the appropriate values for a subsequent retrieval, insertion, or removal of the entry.

The method `get` just calls `containsKey` and returns the value contained in `foundEntry` if the key was found or returns `null` otherwise:

```
get(key)
if containsKey(key)
   return foundEntry.value
else
   return null
```

The method `put` calls `containsKey` to determine whether or not an entry exists at the target key's position. If the entry is found, `put` replaces its value with the new value and returns the old value. Otherwise, `put`

1. Creates a new entry whose next pointer is the entry at the head of the chain.

2. Sets the head of the chain to the new entry.

3. Increments the size.

4. Returns `null`.

Following is the pseudocode for `put`:

```
put(key, value)
if (!containsKey (key))
    Entry newEntry = new Entry (key, value, table[index])
    table[index] = newEntry
    size++
    return null
else
    Object returnValue = foundEntry.value
    foundEntry.value = value
    return returnValue
```

The strategy of the method `remove` is similar, although `remove` uses the variable `priorEntry` when the entry to be removed comes after the head of the chain. Following is the partially completed code of the class `HashMapPT`:

```
// Example 18.2: HashMapPT

import java.util.Collection;

public class HashMapPT implements MapPT{

    private static final int DEFAULT_CAPACITY = 3;
                                    // Purposely set to a small value in order
                                    // to ensure collisions

    // Temporary variables
    private Entry foundEntry;     // entry just located
                                  // undefined if not found
    private Entry priorEntry;     // entry prior to one just located
                                  // undefined if not found
    private int    index;         // index of chain in which entry located
                                  // undefined if not found

    // Instance variables
    private int    capacity;      // size of table[]
    private Entry table[];        // the table of collision lists
    private int    size;          // number of entries in the map

    public HashMapPT(){
        capacity = DEFAULT_CAPACITY;
        clear();
    }

    public void clear(){
        size = 0;
        table = new Entry[capacity];
    }
```

```java
public boolean containsKey (Object key){
    index = Math.abs(key.hashCode()) % capacity;
    priorEntry = null;
    foundEntry = table[index];
    while (foundEntry != null){
        if (foundEntry.key.equals (key))
            return true;
        else{
            priorEntry = foundEntry;
            foundEntry = foundEntry.next;
        }
    }
    return false;
}

public boolean containsValue (Object value){
    for (int i = 0; i < table.length; i++){
        for (Entry entry = table[i]; entry != null; entry = entry.next)
            if (entry.value.equals (value))
                return true;
    }
    return false;
}

public Object get(Object key){
    if (containsKey (key))
        return foundEntry.value;
    else
        return null;
}

public boolean isEmpty(){
    return size == 0;
}

public SetPT keySet(){
    // Exercise 18.4, Question 1
    return null;
}

public Object put(Object key, Object value){
    if (!containsKey (key)){
        Entry newEntry = new Entry (key, value, table[index]);
        table[index] = newEntry;
        size++;
        return null;
    }else{
        Object returnValue = foundEntry.value;
        foundEntry.value = value;
        return returnValue;
    }
}
```

```java
public Object remove(Object key){
   if (!containsKey (key))
      return null;
   else{
      if (priorEntry == null)
         table[index] = foundEntry.next;
      else
         priorEntry.next = foundEntry.next;
      size--;
      return foundEntry.value;
   }
}

public int size(){
   return size;
}

public String toString(){
   String rowStr;
   String str = "HashMapPT: capacity = " +  capacity
               + " load factor = " + ((double)size() / capacity);
   for (int i = 0; i < table.length; i++){
      rowStr = "";
      for (Entry entry = table[i]; entry != null; entry = entry.next)
         rowStr += entry + " ";
      if (rowStr != "")
         str += "\nRow " + i + ": " + rowStr;
   }
   return str;
}

public Collection values(){
   // Exercise 18.4, Question 2
   return null;
}

private class Entry {

   private Object key;      // Key for this entry
   private Object value;    // Value for this entry
   private Entry  next;     // Reference to next entry

   private Entry(){
      this(null, null, null);
   }

   private Entry(Object key, Object value, Entry next){
      this.key = key;
      this.value = value;
      this.next = next;
   }
```

```
        public String toString(){
            return "(" + key + ", " + value + ")";
        }
    }
}
```

Note that the method `toString` returns not only the string representations of each key/value pair but also the current capacity and load factor of the map. This information allows the client to examine the complexity of the map at run time.

EXERCISE 18.4

1. Add the method `keySet` to the class `HashMapPT`. This method should create and return an instance of class `HashSetPT` that contains the keys in the map. (You won't be able to compile or run this code until you implement `HashSetPT`—see the next section.)

2. Add the method `values` to the class `HashMapPT`. This method should create and return an object of class `LinkedList` that contains the values in the map.

3. The `put` method can be modified to take advantage of the map's knowledge of the current load factor. Describe a strategy for implementing this change in `put`.

4. Implement a `HashMapPT` constructor that allows the client to specify the capacity of the array.

18.5 Hashing Implementation of Sets

The design of the class `HashSetPT` is quite similar to the design of the class `HashMapPT`. Because we use the same hashing strategy, the instance variables are the same. Each object of class `Entry` now consists of just an item and a pointer to the next entry in the chain.

The design of the methods for `HashSetPT` is also virtually the same as the corresponding methods in `HashMapPT`. Following are the differences:

1. The method `contains` searches for an item in an entry instead of a key.

2. The method `add` inserts an item only if it is not already present in the set.

3. The methods `add` and `remove` return a boolean value to indicate the success or failure of an addition or removal.

4. There is a single `iterator` method instead of two methods that return keys and values.

Following is a partial implementation of the class `HashSetPT`, omitting the iterator and the code that is the same as in `HashMapPT`:

```
// Example 18.3: HashSetPT

public class HashSetPT implements SetPT{

    // Same data as in HashMapPT
```

```java
public HashSetPT(){
   capacity = DEFAULT_CAPACITY;
   clear();
}

public boolean add(Object item){
   if (!contains (item)){
      Entry newEntry = new Entry (item, table[index]);
      table[index] = newEntry;
      size++;
      return true;
   }else
      return false;
}

public void clear(){
   size = 0;
   table = new Entry[capacity];
}

public boolean contains(Object item){
   index = Math.abs(item.hashCode()) % capacity;
   priorEntry = null;
   foundEntry = table[index];
   while (foundEntry != null){
      if (foundEntry.item.equals (item))
         return true;
      else{
         priorEntry = foundEntry;
         foundEntry = foundEntry.next;
      }
   }
   return false;
}

public boolean isEmpty(){
    size == 0;
}

public Iterator iterator(){
// Project 18-5 - must create an inner class as well
}

public boolean remove(Object item){
   if (!contains (item))
      return false;
   else{
      if (priorEntry == null)
         table[index] = foundEntry.next;
      else
         priorEntry.next = foundEntry.next;
      size--;
      return true;
```

```
        }
    }

    public int size(){
        return size;
    }

    public String toString(){
        String rowStr;
        String str = "HashSetPT: capacity = " +  capacity
                    + " load factor = " + ((double)size() / capacity);
        for (int i = 0; i < table.length; i++){
            rowStr = "";
            for (Entry entry = table[i]; entry != null; entry = entry.next)
                rowStr += entry + " ";
            if (rowStr != "")
                str += "\nRow " + i + ": " + rowStr;
        }
        return str;
    }

    private class Entry {

        private Object item;       // Item for this entry
        private Entry  next;       // Reference to next entry

        private Entry(){
            this(null, null);
        }

        private Entry(Object item, Entry next){
            this.item = item;
            this.next = next;
        }

        public String toString(){
            return "" + item;
        }
    }
}
```

*E*XERCISE 18.5

1. How does the implementation of `HashSetPT` differ from the implementation of `HashMapPT`?

2. Describe a design strategy for the iterator for the class `HashSetPT`. You can assume that the Iterator method `remove` is not supported.

3. Write a constructor method for `HashSetPT` that expects a `Collection` as a parameter. The constructor should transfer the items from the collection to the new set.

SUMMARY

In this chapter, you learned:

- The implementations of maps and sets, which use a list, are easy to write but provide inefficient (linear) access to items.

- Hashing can provide constant-time access to items in sets and maps. A hashing strategy uses a hash function to locate the index position of an item in an array.

- When using hashing, the position of a new item can collide with the position of an item already in an array. Several techniques exist to resolve collisions. Among these are linear collision processing, quadratic collision processing, and chaining.

- Chaining employs an array of buckets, which are linked structures that contain the items.

- The run-time and memory aspects of hashing methods involve the load factor of the array. When the load factor (logical size / physical size) approaches 1, the likelihood of collisions, and thus of extra processing, increases.

VOCABULARY *Review*

Define the following terms:

Bucket	Collision	Linear collision processing
Chaining	Density ratio	Load factor
Chains	Hash code	Quadratic collision
Clustering	Hash function	processing

REVIEW *Questions*

FILL IN THE BLANK

Complete the following sentences by writing the correct word or words in the blanks provided.

1. The list-based implementations of sets and maps access items in _____ time.

2. The hashing implementations of sets and maps can access items in _____ time.

3. The code used to locate an item's position in a hashing technique is called a(n) _____, whereas the function that generates this code is called a(n) _____.

4. A(n) _____ occurs when two items hash to the same index position.

5. The linear method of resolving collisions can produce an undesirable effect known as_____.

6. The _____ method of resolving collisions increments the item's code by the square of an increasing constant.

7. The _____ represents the ratio of the capacity of the array to the number of items.

8. The behavior of hashing strategies can be _____ in the worst case.

9. The chaining strategy of removing collisions uses structures called _____.

10. The `HashMapPT` method `keySet` returns an object of type _____.

PROJECTS

PROJECT 18-1

Modify the program for generating hash codes and index positions (`TestHashing` in Section 18.3) to count and display the number and positions of the collisions that occur on each run. Use an array of integers to track this information. The data will hash to positions in this array. At the beginning of each run, input the number of items and the load factor of the hash table. Then instantiate the array and set each cell to 0. Each time a position is hit, increment the integer stored there by 1. Display just the indexes and contents of the array and the total number of collisions at the end of each run. Use this version of the program to experiment with various load factors, say, 0.33, 0.5, 0.75, and 1. Define `static` helper methods to generate a hash code and to print the results. Track the total collisions in a `static` variable.

PROJECT 18-2

Modify the program from Project 18-1 to implement the linear method of resolving collisions. Experiment with arrays of sufficient capacity to observe any clusters that develop. Track and display the number of comparisons required to resolve collisions as well. Test this method with load factors of 0.33, 0.5, 0.75, and 1, then compare the results to those of Project 18-1.

PROJECT 18-3

Modify the program from Project 18-2 to use the quadratic method of resolving collisions. Use the same test data as in Project 18-2.

PROJECT 18-4

Add a new method of computing the hash code to the program from Project 18-3. This method returns a random integer between 0 and the largest integer allowed by Java. Accumulate results for this method using the same test runs as in earlier projects and compare them with the other results.

PROJECT 18-5

Complete the implementation of the iterator for the class `HashSetPT`. This iterator does not have to support the method `remove`.

CRITICAL *Thinking*

Another method of resolving collisions is known as *rehashing*. That is, when a collision occurs using one hash function, code can be written to try to find an empty position using a different hash function. Discuss the costs and benefits of this method.

CHAPTER 19

IMPLEMENTING TREES AND PRIORITY QUEUES

<table>
<tr><td>

OBJECTIVES

Upon completion of this chapter, you should be able to:

- Use the appropriate terminology to describe trees.

- Distinguish different types of hierarchical collections, such as general trees, binary trees, binary search trees, and heaps.

- Understand the basic tree traversals.

- Use binary search trees to implement sorted sets and sorted maps.

- Use heaps to implement priority queues.

Estimated Time: 3.5 hours

</td><td>

VOCABULARY

Binary search tree

Binary tree

Expression tree

General tree

Heap

Heap property

Interior node

Leaf

Left subtree

Parse tree

Right subtree

Root

</td></tr>
</table>

A third major category of collections, which we called "hierarchical" in Chapter 14, consists of various types of tree structures. As with lists, these collections have no standard set of operations and most programming languages do not include them as standard classes. Their primary use is in implementing other collections, such as sorted sets and sorted maps in Java and similar types of collections that require efficient searching and that, like priority queues, must impose some priority order on their elements. In this chapter we examine the basic properties of trees that make them useful data structures and explore their role in implementing several types of collections.

19.1 An Overview of Trees

Trees are characterized by the fact that each item can have multiple successors and all items, except a privileged item called the *root*, have exactly one predecessor.

For example, consider Figure 19-1, which is the *parse tree* for the following sentence: "The girl hit the ball with a bat." A parse tree describes the syntactic structure of a sentence in terms of its component parts, such as noun phrases and verb phrases. In this and in all diagrams of trees, the items are called *nodes*. Trees are drawn with the root at the top. Immediately below a node and connected to it by lines are its successors, or *children*. A node without children (in italics in the figure) is called a *leaf*. Immediately above a node is its predecessor, or *parent*. Thus, the root node "Sentence" has two children but no parent. In contrast, the leaf node "ball" has a parent but no children. Any node, such as "Noun phrase," that has children is called an *interior node*.

FIGURE 19-1

Parse tree for a sentence

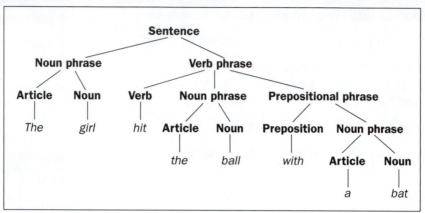

A book's table of contents is another familiar example of a hierarchical collection or tree. In addition, trees are used to organize a computer's file system, as we are reminded every time we view the files on our hard drive.

Talking About Trees

We have already introduced some terminology associated with trees, but there is more. The terminology is a peculiar mix of biological, genealogical, and geometric terms. Table 19-1 provides a quick summary of these terms.

TABLE 19-1
A summary of terms used to describe trees

TERM	DEFINITION
Node	An item stored in a tree
Root	The topmost node in a tree; It is the only node without a predecessor or parent.
Child	A successor of a node; A node can have more than one child, and its children are viewed as organized in left-to-right order. The leftmost child is called the first child, and the rightmost is the last child.
Parent	The predecessor of a node; A node can have only one parent.
Siblings	The children of a common parent
Edge/Branch	The line that connects a parent to its child
Descendant	A node's descendants include its children, its children's children, and so on, down to the leaves.
Ancestor	A node's ancestors include its parent, its parent's parent, and so on, up to the root.
Path	The sequence of edges that connect a node and one of its descendants
Path length	The number of edges in a path
Leaf	A node that has no children
Interior node	A node that has at least one child
Depth or level	The depth or level of a node equals the length of the path connecting it to the root. Thus, the root depth or level of the root is 0. Its children are at level 1, and so on.
Height	The height of a tree equals the length of the longest path in the tree, or put differently, the maximum level number among leaves in the tree.
Subtree	The tree formed by considering a node and all its descendants; We exclude the root when forming subtrees.

Figure 19-2 shows a tree and some of its properties.

FIGURE 19-2
A tree and some of its properties.

	PROPERTY	VALUE
	Number of nodes	10
	Height	3
	Root node	H
	Leaves	A,C,J,L,M,N
	Interior nodes	H,B,F,E
	Nodes at level 2	A,C,J,E
	Ancestors of E	F,H
	Descendants of F	J,E,L,M,N
	Nodes in right subtree of F	E,L,M,N

Level 0: H
Level 1: B, F
Level 2: A, C, J, E
Level 3: L, M, N

General Trees and Binary Trees

The trees we have been discussing are sometimes called *general trees* to distinguish them from a special category called *binary trees*. In a binary tree, each node has at most two children, referred to as the *left child* and the *right child*. In a binary tree, when a node has only one child, we distinguish it as being a left child or a right child. Thus, the two trees shown in Figure 19-3 are not the same when considered as binary trees, although they are the same when considered as general trees.

FIGURE 19-3
Two unequal binary trees that have equal sets of nodes

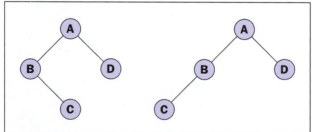

Recursive Definitions of Trees

Although at this point you probably have a clear understanding of what a tree is, we now give a more formal definition. As is often the case, one cannot understand the formal definition without an intuitive grasp of the concept being defined; the formal definition is important, however, because it provides an unambiguous and precise basis for further discussion. Furthermore, because recursive processing of trees is common, we offer recursive definitions of them.

Recursive Definition of a General Tree

A general tree is either empty or consists of a finite set of nodes T. One node r is distinguished from all others and is called the *root*. In addition, the set $T - \{r\}$ is partitioned into disjoint subsets, each of which is a general tree.

Recursive Definition of a Binary Tree

A binary tree is either empty or consists of a root plus a **left subtree** and a **right subtree**, each of which are binary trees.

From now on in this chapter, we restrict our attention to various types of binary trees.

Complete Binary Trees

Trees in nature come in various shapes and sizes, and so do trees as data structures. Some trees are thin, almost linear, whereas others are bushy. The notion of a *complete binary tree* gives a formal cast to the "bushiness" of binary trees. A binary tree is complete if each level except the last has a complete complement of nodes and if the nodes on the last level are filled in from the left (see Figure 19-4). Complete or nearly complete binary trees are considered desirable because they support efficient searching, insertions, and removals.

FIGURE 19-4
Different types of binary trees

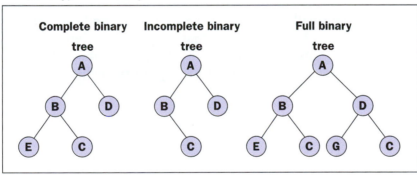

Full Binary Trees

A *full binary tree* contains the maximum number of nodes for its height. Each node in a full binary tree is either an interior node with two nonempty children or a leaf. The number of leaves in a full binary tree is one greater than the number of interior nodes. A full binary tree has the minimum height necessary to accommodate a given number of nodes. Such a tree is *fully balanced*. A fully balanced tree of height d can accommodate up to $2^d - 1$ nodes. In a fully balanced binary tree, there can be up to $2n$ nodes in level n. The height of a fully balanced tree of n nodes is $\log_2 n$. Figure 19-4 shows some examples of trees that have the various properties mentioned. The examples are a complete but not full binary tree, a binary tree that is not complete, and a full binary tree.

Heaps

A *heap* is a binary tree in which the item in each node is less than or equal to the items in both of its children. This constraint on the order of the nodes is called the **heap property**. You should not confuse this kind of heap with the heap that a computer uses to manage dynamic memory. Figure 19-5 shows two examples of heaps.

FIGURE 19-5
Examples of heaps

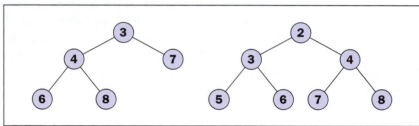

As the figure shows, the smallest item is in the root node, and the largest items are in the leaves. Note that the shape of a heap is close to that of a complete binary tree, according to the definition given earlier. The arrangement of data in a heap supports an efficient sorting method called the *heap sort*. Heaps are also used to implement priority queues.

Expression Trees

In Chapter 15, we showed how to use a stack to convert infix expressions to postfix form. We also showed in Chapter 15 how to use a stack to evaluate postfix expressions. Yet another way to process expressions is to build a data structure called a *parse tree* during parsing. For a language of expressions, this structure is also called an ***expression tree***. Figure 19-6 shows several expression trees that result from parsing infix expressions.

FIGURE 19-6
Some expression trees

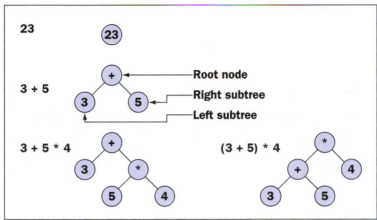

Note that an expression tree consists of either a number or an operator whose operands are its left and right subtrees.

Binary Search Trees

You will remember our use of call trees to trace the execution of recursive methods in Chapter 12. The call tree for a binary search of a typical sorted array is shown in Figure 19-7. The items visited for comparison are shaded.

FIGURE 19-7
A call tree for the binary search of an array

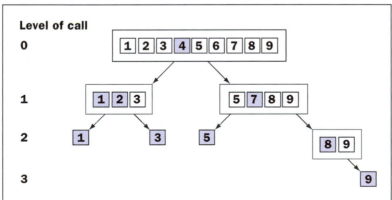

As the figure shows, it requires at most four comparisons to search the entire array of eight items. Because the array is sorted, the search algorithm can reduce the search space by one-half after each comparison.

Now, let us transfer the items that are shaded in the call tree for the binary search to an explicit binary tree structure, as shown in Figure 19-8.

FIGURE 19-8
A binary search tree

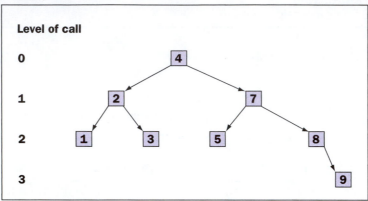

This tree is a **binary search tree**. Note that each node in the tree is greater than or equal to its left child and less than or equal to its right child.

Now, consider the following recursive search process using this tree:

```
If the tree is empty
    Return false
Else if the item in the root equals the target
    Return true
Else if the item in the root is greater than the target
    Return the result of searching the root's left subtree
Else
    Return the result of searching the root's right subtree
```

Like the binary search of a sorted array, the search of a binary search tree potentially can throw away one-half of the search space after each comparison. We say "potentially" because the efficiency of the search depends in part on the shape of the tree. Figure 19-9 shows three binary search trees that contain the same items but have different shapes.

FIGURE 19-9
Three binary tree shapes with the same data

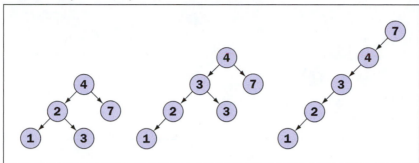

The trees degrade in their support for efficient search from left to right. The leftmost tree is complete, and it is said to be balanced. As such, it supports the most efficient searches. The right-most tree looks just like a one-way linked list and as such supports only a linear search. Thus, everything depends on how the data come into the tree. In particular, data coming into the tree in close to sorted order produce a tree whose shape is not optimal for searching.

EXERCISE 19.1

1. What are the leaf nodes and the interior nodes in the following tree?

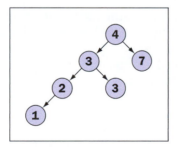

2. Which of the following trees are complete or full?

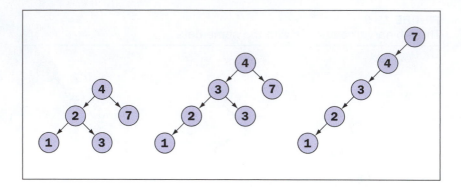

3. What is a heap?

4. What is an expression tree?

19.2 Binary Tree Traversals

In earlier chapters, we saw how to traverse the items in collections using iterators. There are four types of traversals for binary trees: preorder, inorder, postorder, and level order. Each type of traversal follows a particular path and direction as it visits the nodes in the tree.

Preorder Traversal

The preorder traversal algorithm visits the root node, traverses the left subtree, and traverses the right subtree. The path traveled by a preorder traversal is illustrated in Figure 19-10.

FIGURE 19-10
A preorder traversal

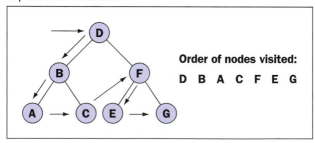

Inorder Traversal

The inorder traversal algorithm traverses the left subtree, visits the root node, and traverses the right subtree. This process has the effect of moving as far to the left in the tree as possible before visiting a node. The path traveled by an inorder traversal is illustrated in Figure 19-11.

FIGURE 19-11
An inorder traversal

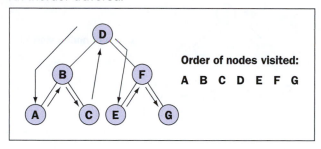

Order of nodes visited:

A B C D E F G

Postorder Traversal

The postorder traversal algorithm traverses the left subtree, traverses the right subtree, and visits the root node. The path traveled by a postorder traversal is illustrated in Figure 19-12:

FIGURE 19-12
A postorder traversal

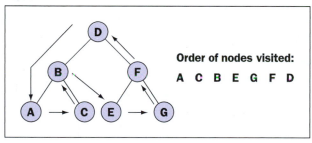

Order of nodes visited:

A C B E G F D

Level-Order Traversal

Beginning with level 0, the level-order traversal algorithm visits the nodes at each level in left-to-right order. The path traveled by a level-order traversal is illustrated in Figure 19-13.

FIGURE 19-13
A level-order traversal

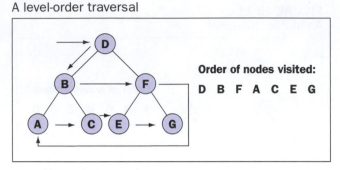

The preorder, inorder, and postorder traversals of an expression tree can be used to generate representations of the expression in prefix, infix, and postfix forms, respectively.

*E*XERCISE 19.2

1. List the items resulting from the different types of traversals of the tree shown here.

   a. A preorder traversal

   b. An inorder traversal

   c. A postorder traversal

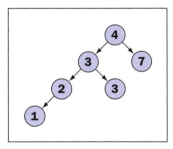

2. What would be an appropriate application of a preorder traversal?

19.3 A Linked Implementation of Binary Trees

Two common implementations of binary trees use an array and a linked structure, respectively. We examine an array implementation in section 19.4. In this section, we explore a linked implementation of a binary search tree. As usual, we develop a prototype interface and a prototype implementation class.

The Binary Search Tree Interface

The interface for a binary search tree should include methods needed to implement sorted sets and sorted maps. Therefore, the element type of any binary search tree should implement `Comparable`. In addition, a search tree should support the different types of traversals mentioned in the previous section. These methods, which are coded in the Java interface `BSTPT` (Binary Search Tree ProtoType), are described in Table 19-2. Note that the interface is generic for the element type `E`.

TABLE 19-2
The methods of the BSTPT interface

METHOD	WHAT IT DOES
`E add(E obj)`	If the element is not already in the tree, then adds the element to the tree, increasing the tree's size by one, and returns `null`; otherwise, replaces the old element with the new one and returns the old element
`E contains(E obj)`	Returns the node's value if the element is in the tree, else `null`
`boolean isEmpty()`	Returns `true` if the tree contains no elements, else `false`
`Iterator<E> iterator()`	Returns an iterator on the tree; The iterator allows the client to visit the elements in alphabetical order. The tree is not used as a backing store, so the method `remove` has no effect.
`List<E> inorderTraverse()`	Returns a list that contains the results of an inorder traversal of the tree
`List<E> levelorderTraverse()`	Returns a list that contains the results of a level-order traversal of the tree
`List<E> postorderTraverse()`	Returns a list that contains the results of a postorder traversal of the tree
`List<E> preorderTraverse()`	Returns a list that contains the results of a preorder traversal of the tree
`E remove(E obj)`	If the element is in the tree, removes it and returns the node's value; otherwise, returns `null`

TABLE 19-2 Continued
The methods of the BSTPT interface

METHOD	WHAT IT DOES
`int size()`	Returns the number of elements in the tree
`String toString()`	Returns a string containing the string representations of the elements in a format that shows the tree structure

In the code that follows, the element type `E` of `BSTPT` is restricted to one that implements `Comparable`, using the notation `<E extends Comparable<E>>` introduced in Chapter 15. The `BSPST` interface also extends the `Iterable` interface. The `Iterable` interface requires its implementing classes to include an `iterator` method. Collections that implement the `Iterable` interface can be traversed with an enhanced `for` loop.

```java
// Example 19.1: The interface for binary search tree prototypes

import java.util.List;

public interface BSTPT<E extends Comparable<E>> extends Iterable<E>{

    public E add(E element);
    public E contains(E element);
    public boolean isEmpty();
    public E remove(E element);
    public int size();
    public String toString();
    public List<E> inorderTraverse();
    public List<E> levelorderTraverse();
    public List<E> postorderTraverse();
    public List<E> preorderTraverse();
}
```

The class diagram in Figure 19-14 summarizes the relationships among the binary search tree resources.

FIGURE 19-14
The interfaces and classes used in the binary search tree prototype

The Class `LinkedBSTPT`

The linked implementation of a binary search tree has an external pointer to the tree's root node. Each node contains a data element and links to the node's left subtree and right subtree. The following code segment shows the data declarations and constructor for the class `LinkedBSTPT`:

```java
// Example 19.1 (continued): The linked implementation of the
// binary search tree prototype

import java.util.*;

public class LinkedBSTPT <E extends Comparable<E>> implements BSTPT<E>{
   private Node<E> root;
   private int size;

   public LinkedBSTPT(){
      root = null;
      size = 0;
   }

   private class Node<E>{

      private E value;
      private Node<E> left, right;

      private Node(E v){
         this(null, v, null);
      }

      private Node(Node<E> l, E v, Node<E> r){
         left = l;
         value = v;
         right = r;
      }
   }
}
```

Note that the class `LinkedBSPST` implements the `BSPST` interface. In this context, `BSPST` is generic for the element type `E`. `LinkedBSPST` restricts this element type to one that implements `Comparable`. We now develop several operations for this implementation.

Inserting an Item into a Binary Search Tree

The `add` method inserts an object in its proper place in the binary search tree. Because we will be using a binary search tree to implement sorted sets and sorted maps, this method also replaces a duplicate item with a new item and returns the old item.

In general, an item's proper place will be either the root node (if the tree is already empty) or in a leaf node to the left of the item's natural successor or to the right of the item's natural predecessor, as determined by using the method `compareTo`. Thus, all items must implement the `Comparable` interface. The `add` method uses a loop to advance a temporary pointer until the correct position is found. Following is the code for method `add`:

```java
public E add(E element){
    Node<E> newNode = new Node<E>(element);

    // Tree is empty, so the new item goes at the root
    if (root == null){
        root = newNode;
        size++;
        return null;
    }

    // Search for the new item's spot or until a duplicate item is found
    else{
        Node<E> probe = root;
        while (probe != null){
            int relation = element.compareTo(probe.value);

            // A duplicate is found, so replace it and return it
            if (relation == 0){
                E oldValue = probe.value;
                probe.value = element;
                return oldValue;
            }

            // The new item is less, so go left until its spot is found
            else if (relation < 0)
                if (probe.left != null)
                    probe = probe.left;
                else{
                    probe.left = newNode;
                    size++;
                    return null;
                }

            // The new item is greater, so go right until its spot is found
            else if (probe.right != null)
                probe = probe.right;
            else{
                probe.right = newNode;
                size++;
                return null;
            }
        }
        return null;    // Never reached
    }
}
```

Searching a Binary Search Tree

The `contains` method returns the node's value if an object is in the tree or `null` otherwise. We can use a recursive strategy that takes advantage of the recursive structure of the tree nodes. Following is a pseudocode algorithm for this process, where `tree` is a node:

```
if tree is null
    return null
else if the object equals the root item
    return the root item
else if the object is less than the root item
    return the result of searching the left subtree
else
    return the result of searching the right subtree
```

Because the recursive search method requires an extra parameter for the node, we cannot include it as a public method. Instead, we define it as a private helper method that is called from the public `contains` method. Following is the code for the two methods:

```java
public E contains(E element){
    return contains(root, element);
}

private E contains(Node<E> tree, E element){
    if (tree == null)
        return null;
    else{
        int relation = element.compareTo(tree.value);
        if (relation == 0)
            return tree.value;
        else if (relation < 0)
            return contains(tree.left, element);
        else
            return contains(tree.right, element);
    }
}
```

Traversals and the Iterator

As mentioned earlier, there are four ways to traverse the items in a tree. Each type of traversal can use a recursive strategy and can be implemented using a pair of methods as we did with the search operation. Each traversal builds and returns a list of items accumulated.

Inorder Traversal

The inorder traversal uses the following two methods:

1. The private method `inorderTraverse` expects an empty list and a tree's root node as parameters and adds the items from an inorder traversal to the list.

2. The public method `inorderTraverse` returns a list of items accumulated from an inorder traversal of the tree.

Following is the code for these methods:

```
public List<E> inorderTraverse(){
   List<E> list = new ArrayList<E>();
   inorderTraverse(root, list);
   return list;
}

private void inorderTraverse(Node<E> tree, List<E> list){
   if (tree != null){
      inorderTraverse(tree.left, list);
      list.add(tree.value);
      inorderTraverse(tree.right, list);
   }
}
```

Level-Order Traversal

The algorithm for a level-order traversal starts with level 0 and visits each node from left to right at that level. The algorithm then repeats this process for the next level and so on, until all the nodes have been visited. Clearly, we need some way of constraining the recursive process to march across a tree at each level. A convenient way is to schedule the nodes to be visited on a queue. In the present example, the top-level public method `levelorderTraverse` creates a queue and a list, the queue for scheduling and the list to return to the client. The method places the root node at the front of the scheduling queue and passes the two collections to the helper method `levelorderTraverse`:

```
public List<E> levelorderTraverse(){
   List<E> list = new ArrayList<E>();          // List to accumulate
                                               // values
   Queue<E> levelsQu = new LinkedList<E>();    // Scheduling queue

   if (!isEmpty()){
      levelsQu.add(root);
      levelorderTraverse(levelsQu, list);
   }
   return list;
}
```

The recursive pattern for a level-order traversal removes a node for processing from the queue and then adds the left and right subtrees to the queue before the recursive call. Following is the pseudocode for the pattern:

```
If the levels queue is not empty
    Remove the node from the levels queue and add
        its value to the values list
    If the node's left subtree is not null
        Add the left subtree to the levels queue
    If the node's right subtree is not null
        Add the right subtree to the levels queue
    Call levelorderTraverse with the levels queue and the list
```

The order in which the subtrees are enqueued determines the order in which the process moves across each level of the tree. At any given time, the scheduling queue contains the nodes remaining to be visited on one and only one level.

The complete implementation of these and the remaining traversals is left as Project 19-5.

Iterator

Clients using a binary search tree to implement sorted sets and maps would prefer to have an iterator method that allows them to visit items in alphabetical order. The `iterator` method for a binary search tree simply returns an iterator on the list that results from an inorder traversal. Note that the iterator's `remove` method will have no effect on the tree because the iterator's backing store is the list, not the tree. Following is the code for the iterator:

```java
public Iterator<E> iterator(){
    return inorderTraverse().iterator();
}
```

Because the `LinkedBSPST` class implements the `Iterable` interface, the programmer can use an enhanced `for` loop to perform an inorder traversal of a binary search tree.

toString

The `toString` method can be implemented with any of the traversals. Because it is used primarily in testing and debugging, it will be useful to return a string that displays the tree's structure as well as its elements. A convenient way to do this for text-only display is to "rotate" the tree 90 degrees counterclockwise and display vertical bars between the interior nodes. The following code builds the appropriate string by first recursing with the right subtree, then visiting an item, and finally recursing with the left subtree.

```java
public String toString(){
    return toString(root, 0);
}
```

```java
private String toString(Node<E> tree, int level){
    String str = "";
    if (tree != null){
        str += toString(tree.right, level + 1);
        for (int i = 1; i <= level; i++)
            str = str + "| ";
        str += tree.value.toString() + "\n";
        str += toString(tree.left, level + 1);
    }
    return str;
}
```

A Tester Program

The following program tests all of the methods. The output of this program is shown in Figure 19-15.

```java
// Example 19.1 (continued): A tester program for the binary search tree prototype

import java.util.*;

public class TestBST{

    public static void main(String[] args){

        BSTPT<String> tree = new LinkedBSTPT<String>();

        System.out.println("Adding D B A C F E G");
        tree.add("D");
        tree.add("B");
        tree.add("A");
        tree.add("C");
        tree.add("F");
        tree.add("E");
        tree.add("G");

        System.out.println("ToString:\n" + tree);

        System.out.print("Iterator (inorder traversal): ");
        Iterator<String> iter = tree.iterator();
        while (iter.hasNext())
            System.out.print(iter.next() + " ");

        // Use a for loop instead
        System.out.print("\nfor loop (inorder traversal): ");
        for (String s : tree)
            System.out.print(s + " ");
```

```
            System.out.print("\nPreorder traversal: ");
            List<String> list = tree.preorderTraverse();
            printList(list);

            System.out.print("\nPostorder traversal: ");
            list = tree.postorderTraverse();
            printList(list);

            System.out.print("\nLevel order traversal: ");
            list = tree.levelorderTraverse();
            printList(list);

            System.out.print("\nRemovals: ");
            for (char ch = 'A'; ch <= 'G'; ch++)
                System.out.print(tree.remove("" + ch) + " ");
        }

    private static <E> void printList(List<E> list){
        for (E element : list)
            System.out.print(element + " ");
    }
}
```

FIGURE 19-15
The output of the binary search tree tester program

```
Adding D B A C F E G
ToString:
| | G
|   F
| | E
D
| | C
|   B
| | A

Iterator (inorder traversal): A B C D E F G
for loop (inorder traversal): A B C D E F G
Preorder traversal: D B A C F E G
Postorder traversal: A C B E G F D
Level order traversal: D B F A C E G
Removals: A B C D E F G
```

Removing an Item from a Binary Search Tree

You will recall that removing an item from an array causes a shift of items to fill the hole. Removing an item from a linked list requires rearranging a few pointers. Removing an item from a binary search tree can require both. Following is an outline of the strategy for this process:

1. Save a pointer to the root node.

2. Attempt to locate the node to be removed, its parent, and its parent's pointer to this node.

3. If the item is not in the tree, return `false`.

4. Otherwise, if the node has a left child and a right child, replace the node's value with the largest value in the left subtree and delete that value's node from the left subtree.

5. Otherwise, set the parent's pointer to the node to the node's only child.

6. Reset the root node to the saved pointer.

7. Decrement the size and return `true`.

Step 4 in this process is fairly complex, so it can be factored out into a helper method, which takes the node to be deleted as a parameter. The outline for this method follows (we refer to the node containing the item to be removed as the top node):

1. Search the top node's left subtree for the node containing the largest item. This will be in the rightmost node of the subtree. Be sure to track the parent of the current node during the search.

2. Replace the top node's value with the item.

3. If the top node's left child contained the largest item (e.g., that node had no right subtree, so the parent pointer still refers to the top node), set the top node's left child pointer to its left child's left child pointer.

4. Otherwise, set the parent node's right child pointer to that right child's left child pointer.

The coding of these two methods is left as Project 19-1.

Complexity Analysis of Binary Search Trees

As you might expect, binary search trees are set up with the intent of replicating the O(log$n$) behavior for the binary search of a sorted array. Unfortunately, as mentioned earlier, this intent is not always realized. Optimal behavior depends on the shape of the tree. A bushy tree, one that is close to complete in the technical sense defined earlier, supports close to logarithmic searches. In the worst case, when the items are inserted in alphabetical order (either ascending or descending), the tree's shape becomes linear, as does its search behavior. Insertions in random order actually result in a tree with reasonable search behavior.

The run time of insertions is also highly dependent on the shape of the tree. Recall that an insertion involves a search for the item's spot. Thus, the run time of an insertion into a bushy tree is likely to be close to logarithmic.

Removals also require a search for the target item, with behavior similar to that of the other operations.

*E*XERCISE 19.3

1. Write a pseudocode algorithm for a preorder traversal of a binary search tree.

2. Write a constructor for a binary search tree that expects a collection as a parameter and transfers the items from the collection to the tree.

3. Describe how insertions can have a negative effect on subsequent searches of a binary search tree.

19.4 An Array Implementation of Binary Trees

An array-based implementation of a binary tree is also possible, but is difficult to define and practical only in some special situations. Mapping stacks, queues, and lists to arrays is straightforward because all are linear and support the same notion of adjacency, each element having an obvious predecessor and successor. But given a node in a tree, what would be its immediate predecessor in an array? Is it the parent or a left sibling? What is its immediate successor? Is it a child or a right sibling? Trees are hierarchical and resist being flattened. Nevertheless, for complete binary trees, there is an elegant and efficient array-based representation.

Consider the complete binary tree in Figure 19-16.

FIGURE 19-16
A complete binary tree

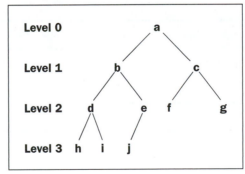

In an array-based implementation, the elements are stored by level, as shown in Figure 19-17.

FIGURE 19-17
An array representation of a complete binary tree

Given an arbitrary item at position i in the array, it is easy to determine the location of related items, as shown in the Table 19-3.

TABLE 19-3
The locations of given items in an array representation of a complete binary tree

ITEM	LOCATION
Parent	$(i - 1) / 2$
Left sibling, if there is one	$i - 1$
Right sibling, if there is one	$i + 1$
Left child, if there is one	$i * 2 + 1$
Right child, if there is one	$i * 2 + 2$

Thus, for item d at location 3 we get the results shown in Table 19-4.

TABLE 19-4
The relatives of a given item in an array representation of a complete binary tree

ITEM	LOCATION
Parent	b at 1
Left sibling, if there is one	Not applicable
Right sibling, if there is one	e at 4
Left child, if there is one	h at 7
Right child, if there is one	i at 8

One might naturally ask why the array representation does not work for incomplete binary trees. The reason is not hard to see. In an incomplete binary tree, some levels are not filled above others. But the calculation of a node's relatives in an array is based on being able to multiply or divide its index by 2, which cannot be done when levels are not filled in a top-down manner.

Needless to say, the array representation is pretty rare and is used mainly to implement a heap, which is discussed in the next section.

EXERCISE 19.4

1. Give the formulas for locating a node's parent, a node's left child, and a node's right child in an array representation of a binary tree.

2. What are the constraints on a binary tree that is contained in an array?

19.5 *Implementing Heaps*

We will use a heap to implement a priority queue, so the heap interface should recognize messages to return its size, add an item, remove an item, and peek at an item (see Table 19-5).

TABLE 19-5
The methods in the interface `HeapPT`

METHOD	WHAT IT DOES
`boolean add(E obj)`	Inserts the element in its proper place in the heap, increasing the heap's size by one, and returns `true`
`Iterator<E> iterator()`	Returns an iterator on the heap; This iterator visits the items from the minimum to the maximum and its `remove` method has no effect.
`E peek()`	Precondition: The heap is not empty. Returns the element at the top of the heap
`E pop()`	Precondition: The heap is not empty. Removes and returns the topmost element in the heap
`int size()`	Returns the number of elements in the heap

The two most critical heap operations are `add` and `pop`. The method `add` expects a comparable element as a parameter and inserts the element into its proper place in the heap. That place is generally at a level above an element that is larger and below an element that is smaller. Duplicate elements are placed below previously entered ones. The method `pop` deletes the topmost node in the heap, returns the element contained there, and maintains the heap property. The `peek` operation returns but does not remove the topmost element in a heap. Here is the code for the interface `HeapPT`:

```
// Example 19.2: The interface for the heap prototype

public interface HeapPT<E extends Comparable<E>> extends Iterable<E>{

    public boolean add(E element);
    public E peek();
    public E pop();
    public int size();
}
```

Implementing add and pop

The methods `add` (insertion) and `pop` (removal), which are used throughout the heap implementation, are defined in the class `ArrayHeapPT`. In the array-based implementation, both methods need to maintain the structure of the heap within the array (we actually use an `ArrayList` but refer to the structure as an array in the following discussion). This structure is similar to the array representation of a binary tree discussed earlier, with the constraint that each node is less than either of its children.

Let us consider insertion first. The goal is to find the new element's proper place in the heap and insert it there. Following is our strategy for insertions:

1. Begin by inserting the element at the bottom of the heap. In the array implementation, this will be in the position after the last element currently in the array.

2. Then, enter a loop that "walks" the new element up the heap, while the new element's value is less than that of its parent. Each time this relationship is true, we swap the new element with its parent. When this process stops (either the new element is greater than or equal to its parent or we have reached the top node), the new element is in its proper place.

Recall that the position of an element's parent in the array is computed by subtracting 1 from the element's position and dividing the result by 2. The top of the heap is at position 0 in the array. In the implementation the instance variable `heap` refers to an instance of `ArrayList`. Following is the code for the method `add`:

```
public boolean add (E element){
    int curPos, parent;

    heap.add(element);
    curPos = heap.size() - 1;
    while (curPos > 0){
        parent = (curPos - 1) / 2;
        E parentItem = heap.get(parent);
        if (parentItem.compareTo(item) <= 0)
            return true;
        else{
            heap.set(curPos, heap.get(parent));
            heap.set(parent, item);
            curPos = parent;
        }
    }
    return true;
}
```

A quick analysis of this method reveals that at most $\log_2 n$ comparisons must be made to walk up the tree from the bottom, so the `add` operation is $O(\log n)$. The method occasionally triggers a doubling in the size of the underlying array. When this occurs, the operation is $O(n)$, but amortized over all additions, the operation is $O(1)$ per addition.

The goal of a removal is to return the element in the root node after deleting this node and adjusting the positions of other nodes so as to maintain the heap property. Following is our strategy for removals:

1. Begin by saving pointers to the top element and the bottom element in the heap and by moving the element from the bottom of the heap to the top.

2. Walk down the heap from the top, moving the smallest child up one level, until the bottom of the heap is reached.

Following is the code for the method pop:

```
public E pop(){
    if (size() == 0)
        throw new NoSuchElementException
            ("Trying to remove from an empty heap");

    int curPos, leftChild, rightChild, maxChild, lastIndex;
    E topItem = heap.get(0);
    E bottomItem = heap.remove(heap.size() - 1);
    if (heap.size() == 0)
        return bottomItem;

    heap.set(0, bottomItem);
    lastIndex = heap.size() - 1;
    curPos = 0;
    while (true){
        leftChild = 2 * curPos + 1 ;
        rightChild = 2 * curPos + 2;
        if (leftChild > lastIndex) break;
        if (rightChild > lastIndex)
            maxChild = leftChild;
        else{
            E leftItem  = heap.get(leftChild);
            E rightItem = heap.get(rightChild);
            if (leftItem.compareTo(rightItem) < 0)
                maxChild = leftChild;
            else
                maxChild = rightChild;
        }
        E maxItem = heap.get(maxChild);
        if (bottomItem.compareTo(maxItem) <= 0)
            break;
        else{
            heap.set(curPos, heap.get(maxChild));
            heap.set(maxChild, bottomItem);
            curPos = maxChild;
        }
    }
    return topItem;
}
```

Once again, analysis shows that the number of comparisons required for a removal is at most $\log_2 n$, so the pop operation is $O(\log n)$. The method pop occasionally triggers a halving in the size of the underlying array. When it occurs, this operation is $O(n)$, but amortized over all removals, the operation is $O(1)$ per removal.

*E*XERCISE 19.5

1. How do the runtimes of the heap operations differ from their counterparts in binary search trees?

2. What is the advantage of using an array list over an array to implement a heap?

3. Write a toString() method for ArrayHeapPT that shows the structure of the heap, using a similar algorithm to the one employed in the toString() method for LinkedBSTPT.

4. Write a method heapSort to sort a list using a heap. This method should be defined as a public static method in the ArrayHeapPT class. The method should expect a list of comparable elements as a parameter and return void.

5. What is the runtime and memory complexity of the heap sort described in Exercise 4?

19.6 Using a Heap to Implement a Priority Queue

You may recall the discussion of priority queues in Chapter 15, where we implemented a true priority queue ADT with a sorted linked list. Another common implementation of priority queues uses a heap. The class java.util.PriorityQueue is such an implementation. Items with the highest priority (the lexically smallest items) are located near the top of the heap. The following code segment shows the class HeapPriorityQueue, which is based on the heap prototype developed in the previous section and the TrueQueue interface discussed in Chapter 15:

```java
// Example 19.3: The heap implementation of a priority queue

import java.util.*;

public class HeapPriorityQueue<E extends Comparable<E>> implements TrueQueue<E>{

    private HeapPT<E> heap;       // A heap of items

    public HeapPriorityQueue(){
        heap = new ArrayHeapPT<E>();
    }

    public boolean add(E element){
        heap.add(element);
        return true;
    }
```

```java
   public boolean isEmpty(){
      return size() == 0;
   }

   public Iterator<E> iterator(){
      return heap.iterator();
   }

   public E peek(){
      if (size() == 0)
         return null;
      return heap.peek();
   }

   public E remove(){
      if (size() == 0)
        throw new NoSuchElementException();
      return heap.pop();
   }

   public int size(){
      return heap.size();
   }
}
```

SUMMARY

In this chapter, you learned:

- There are various types of trees or hierarchical collections, such as general trees, binary trees, binary search trees, and heaps.

- The terminology used to describe hierarchical collections is borrowed from biology, genealogy, and geology.

- The four different types of tree traversals are the preorder traversal, the inorder traversal, the postorder traversal, and the level-order traversal.

- A binary search tree preserves a natural ordering among its items and can support operations that run in logarithmic time. Binary search trees are useful for implementing sorted sets and sorted maps.

- A heap is useful for ordering items according to priority. A heap also guarantees logarithmic insertions and removals. Heaps are useful for implementing priority queues.

- Binary search trees typically have a linked implementation, whereas heaps typically have an array representation.

VOCABULARY *Review*

> **Define the following terms:**
>
> | | | |
> |---|---|---|
> | Binary search tree | Heap | Left subtree |
> | Binary tree | Heap property | Parse tree |
> | Expression tree | Interior node | Right subtree |
> | General tree | Leaf | Root |

REVIEW *Questions*

FILL IN THE BLANK

Complete the following sentences by writing the correct word or words in the blanks provided.

1. The node with no predecessor in a tree is called its _____ node.

2. A node in a binary tree has at most _____ children.

3. To visit the items in a binary search tree in alphabetical order, we use a(n) _____ traversal.

4. The number of levels in a full binary tree is _____ times the number of items.

5. Each item in a heap is generally _____ than its parent and _____ than either of its children.

6. The worst-case behavior of the search and insertion operations on a binary search tree is _____.

7. A tree node with no children is called a(n) _____ node.

8. A tree node with at least one child is called a(n) _____ node.

9. A binary search tree that supports optimal searches is called a(n) _____ tree.

10. Each node in a(n) _____ tree can have zero or more children.

11. To be used in an enhanced `for` loop, a collection must implement the _____ interface.

PROJECTS

PROJECT 19-1

Write and test a `remove` method for the binary search tree.

PROJECT 19-2

Write the implementation of a sorted set class using a binary search tree. Your solution should consist of an interface, `SortedSetPT`, an implementing class, `TreeSetPT`, and a tester program. Both of these are generic for elements that implement `Comparable`. You should decide which methods should be included in the sorted set's interface. A programmer should be able to traverse the elements in a sorted set with an enhanced `for` loop.

PROJECT 19-3

Write the implementation of a sorted map class using a binary search tree. Your solution should consist of an interface, `SortedMapPT`, an implementing class, `TreeMapPT`, and a tester program. You should decide which methods should be included in the sorted map's interface. Also, you should include a private inner class called `MapEntryPT` to contain a key and the associated value. This class should implement the `Comparable` interface and include a `compareTo` method. The binary search tree should receive instances of this class. The methods `get`, `put`, and `removeKey` should create a map entry that contains the key for processing by the tree. When the tree returns an element, it will be an entry, so the map methods should extract the appropriate parts to return to the client. Remember that maps are generic for the key and the value types.

PROJECT 19-4

Modify the emergency room scheduler case study program from Chapter 15 so that it uses a heap-based priority queue.

PROJECT 19-5

Add the remaining traversal methods to the binary search tree class. Each of these methods should return a list of items accumulated during the traversal.

PROJECT 19-6

Define a class for representing expression trees. Interior nodes should contain operators (strings) and leaf nodes should contain integers (instances of class `Integer`). A `toString` method should return the result of an inorder traversal. Test this class with a tester program.

PROJECT 19-7

Write a program that evaluates expression trees and also generates expressions from them in infix, prefix, and postfix forms. The evaluation algorithm should traverse a tree and return its value. The other traversals should return strings. All of these operations should be methods included in the `ExpressionTree` class.

CRITICAL*Thinking*

Jack thinks that binary search trees could be used to implement sorted lists. Jill disagrees, claiming that some list operations would be difficult or impossible to support. Discuss the issues in this debate.

IMPLEMENTING ABSTRACT DATA TYPES

REVIEW *Questions*

TRUE/FALSE

Circle T if the statement is true or F if the statement is false.

T   F   **1.** The linked implementation of a list allows the size of a list to grow indefinitely, whereas an array implementation does not.

T   F   **2.** Insertions into a linked list are generally faster than insertions into an array list.

T   F   **3.** A singly linked structure is a wise choice for implementing a positional list.

T   F   **4.** A doubly linked structure is a wise choice for implementing a queue.

T   F   **5.** Hashing guarantees constant-time access.

T   F   **6.** A list is a wise choice for implementing a set.

T   F   **7.** A node in a general tree can have zero or more children but at most one parent.

T   F   **8.** A node in a heap is generally smaller than either of its two children.

T   F   **9.** A complete binary tree has a complete set of nodes at each level.

T   F   **10.** All access operations in a binary search tree are logarithmic in the worst case.

FILL IN THE BLANK

Complete the following sentences by writing the correct word or words in the blanks provided.

1. A circular linked list often has a(n) _____ node.

2. The appropriate linked structure for a stack implementation is a(n) _____ linked structure.

3. The hierarchical structure used to implement a priority queue is a(n) _____.

4. The _____ method of hashing resolves collisions by simply searching the array for the next available slot.

5. The _____ method of hashing resolves collisions by taking the square of an incremental distance until an empty slot is found.

6. The _____ method of hashing resolves collisions by associating a linked structure with each slot in the array.

7. A tree node that has no children is called a(n) _____.

8. A(n) _____ traversal returns a binary search tree's items in alphabetical order.

9. A heap most often uses a(n) _____ implementation of a tree.

10. The number of levels in a full binary tree is equal to _____ the number of nodes.

WRITTEN QUESTIONS

Write a brief answer to the following questions or problems.

1. Discuss the issues involved in using a linked structure to implement a queue.

2. In the context of hashing, what are collisions and how can they be resolved?

3. Write the pseudocode algorithm for an inorder traversal of a binary search tree. You can assume that its root node is named `tree`.

4. Jill proposes to use an array to implement a binary search tree. Discuss the costs and benefits of this proposal.

5. Describe how a heap can be used to sort a list of items.

CRITICAL *Thinking*

The stack and queue ADTs have many implementations. Discuss the ways in which the code could be simplified by creating abstract classes for stacks and queues.

Java Resources

Java Documentation and the J2SE

Sun Microsystems maintains an excellent Web site where programmers can find complete documentation for the Java API (Application Programming Interface) and download a free J2SE (Java 2 Standard Edition). The following sections discuss some of the items that you can access on the Web. *Note*: The terms *SDK* (Software Development Kit), *JDK* (Java Development Kit), and *JRE* (Java Runtime Environment) may also appear on Sun's Web site. *J2SE* is an umbrella term that encompasses all of these terms. The term *JRE* (Java Runtime Environment) refers to the JVM (Java Virtual Machine), a small plug-in that can be downloaded just to run Java programs or to update your Web browser. To develop Java programs, you should download the full SDK or JDK that contains both the Java compiler and the JRE.

Sun's Top-Level Java Page (http://www.sun.com/)

This page contains news about events in the Java world and links to documentation, Java-related products, program examples, and free downloads of J2SE.

Products and API (http://java.sun.com/products/)

This page allows you to select the version of J2SE that matches your computer and to begin the download process. You also can download the documentation if you do not want to access it on the Web.

Package Index (http://java.sun.com/j2se/1.5.0/docs/api/)

This page has links to all of the packages in J2SE 1.5.0.

We suggest that you bookmark all of these links and use the last one on a daily basis. You might even bookmark the links to the most commonly used packages, such as `java.lang`, `java.util`, and `javax.swing`. When you visit a package, you can browse all of the classes in that package. When you visit a class, you can browse all of the variables and methods defined in that class. There are numerous cross-references to superclasses and related classes in a given package. You also can download the J2SE documentation for quicker browsing on your hard drive.

Be sure to select J2SE 1.5. Various features of Java, such as the `scanner` class, the enhanced `for` loop, and generic collections, are not supported in version 1.4 and earlier. Note that at the time of this writing, the most current version of J2SE was J2SE 1.5_05. After downloading, you install the J2SE on your computer by running the installation program. You should print the Readme file for further reference. If you are working on a PC with Windows XP, the installation will leave two J2SE system directories in the c:\Program Files\Java directory.

Using the DOS Command Prompt and Other IDEs

Before you use the J2SE, make sure that your Java source program (.java) files are in the current directory (this can be any directory on your computer). You can define more than one class in a source file, but the usual procedure is to have one source file for each class. Each source file should begin with the same name as the class that it contains and should end with .java. Remember that Java class names and filenames are case sensitive. If you want to run an applet, the appropriate HTML file also should be in this directory.

Most commercial and free IDEs automatically locate the J2SE system files on your computer. If you use the DOS command prompt to compile and run Java programs, run the following command at the beginning of each working session:

path=c:\Program Files\Java\jdk1.5.0_04\bin

This command allows Windows XP to locate the `javac`, `java`, `javadoc`, and `appletviewer` commands in the system directory.

Using the Basic J2SE Tools

You can then do the following at the system command prompt:

- *Compile a program.* The basic syntax is `javac <filename>`, where `<filename>` is a Java source filename (ending in .java). Java locates and compiles all of the files required by your program. Any syntax error messages are displayed in the command window, and a byte code (.class) file is generated for each class defined in your program. The command `javac *.java` is a quick way to compile a program that consists of several source files.

- *Run an application.* The basic syntax is `java <filename>`, where `<filename>` is the name of the class that defines the `main` method of your program. Note that the .class extension must be omitted. Run-time error messages are displayed in the command window.

- *Run an applet.* The basic syntax is `appletviewer <filename>`, where `<filename>` is the name of an HTML file that links to your applet.

Java Language Elements

This appendix covers some extra features of Java that are useful. We make no attempt to provide a complete description of Java. For a full reference, consult the documentation at Sun's Web site.

Reserved Words

The words shown in bold are not discussed in this book. For a discussion of them, see the references on Sun's Web site.

abstract	do	if	**operator**	switch
boolean	double	implements	**outer**	**synchronized**
break	else	import	package	this
byte	extends	**inner**	private	throw
case	final	instanceof	protected	throws
catch	**finally**	int	public	**transient**
char	float	interface	**rest**	try
class	for	long	return	**var**
const	**future**	**native**	short	void
continue	**generic**	new	static	**volatile**
default	**goto**	null	super	while

Data Types

Java supports two data types: primitive types and reference types. Primitive types represent numbers, characters, and Boolean values. The numeric data types are listed in Table B-1.

TABLE B-1
Java's primitive data types

TYPE	STORAGE REQUIREMENTS	RANGE
byte	1 byte	−128 to 127
short	2 bytes	−32,768 to 32,767
int	4 bytes	−2,147,483,648 to 2,147,483,647
long	8 bytes	−9,223,372,036,854,775,808L to 9,223,372,036,854,775,807L
float	4 bytes	−3.40282347E+38F to 3.40282347E+38F
double	8 bytes	−1.79769313486231570E+308 to 1.79769313486231570E+308

Type char represents the Unicode character set, consisting of 65,536 values. These values include those of the traditional ASCII set and other international characters. A table listing the ASCII character set appears in Appendix D.

Character literals are enclosed in single quotation marks (for example, 'a'). Table B-2 lists some commonly used escape sequences for nonprinting characters.

TABLE B-2
Some escape sequences

ESCAPE SEQUENCE	MEANING
\b	backspace
\t	tab
\n	newline
\"	double quotation mark
\'	single quotation mark
\\	backslash

The type boolean represents the Boolean values true and false. boolean is the type of all expressions that serve as conditions of if statements and loops.

Reference types represent objects, such as strings, arrays, other built-in Java objects, and user-defined objects.

Casting Numeric Types

The numeric types from least to most inclusive are

```
byte   short   int   long   float   double
```

The cast operator converts a more inclusive type to a less inclusive one. The form of the operator is

```
(<less inclusive type name>) <more inclusive value>
```

For instance, following is a sequence of assignment statements in which we begin with a double, cast to an int, and finally cast to a char:

```
double d;
int i;
char c;

d = 65.57;
i = (int) d;           // i contains 65, due to truncation.
c = (char) i;          // c contains 'A'.
writer.println(c);     // Displays 'A'.
```

As we notice in this example, the cast operation can destroy information. In general, the fractional part of a `double` or `float` is thrown away when cast to `byte`, `short`, `int`, or `long`. In addition, if the number being cast is outside the range of the target type, unexpected values can result. Thus,

```
(int)8.88e+009    becomes    290065408
```

The cast operator also can be used within expressions. Normally, when an operator involves mixed data types, the less inclusive type is automatically converted to the more inclusive before the operation is performed. For instance

```
2 / 1.5             becomes    2.0 / 1.5
2 + 1.5             becomes    2.0 + 1.5
aByte  / aLong      becomes    aLong   / aLong
aFloat - anInt      becomes    aFloat  - aFloat
aFloat % aDouble    becomes    aDouble % aDouble
```

We could present other examples in a similar vein. Sometimes, though, we want to override this automatic conversion and, for instance, to treat

```
aFloat / anInt    as    anInt / anInt
```

This can be achieved by using the cast operation again, as illustrated next:

```
(int)aFloat * anInt          becomes    anInt  * anInt
aByte        / (byte)aLong   becomes    aByte  / aByte
aFloat       + (float)aDouble becomes   aFloat + aFloat
```

In these expressions, the unary cast operator has higher precedence than the binary arithmetic operators.

Type-Safe Enumerations

Occasionally a program uses a variable that has a special range of values. In many cases where there are only two possible values, the variable can be a Boolean, with the values `true` or `false`. For example, a window is either visible or not, and the variable `visible` is of type `boolean`, where `true` means on and `false` means off.

```
boolean visible = false;    // Visibility is initially off
```

For a variable that has a finite range of more than two values, the programmer can define named integer constants, such as MARRIED, SINGLE, and DIVORCED, for the values. However, because the variable `maritalStatus` is of type `int`, *any* integer besides the named constants can be assigned to it, thus opening the door to semantic errors.

```
final int MARRIED = 0;
final int SINGLE = 1;
final int DIVORCED = 2;

int maritalStatus = SINGLE;    // Initially we're all single
maritalStatus = MARRIED;       // Get married
maritalStatus = 15;            // Error: meaning not defined in the domain
```

Java 5.0 includes a data type known as a *type-safe enumeration* to solve this problem. An enumeration is a named type that has one or more named values. The type allows no other values. For example, the enumerated type MartialStatus with the values MARRIED, SINGLE, and DIVORCED is defined and used in the following code segment:

```java
// Define the new type
public enum MaritalStatus = {MARRIED, SINGLE, DIVORCED}

// Declare and manipulate a variable
private MaritalStatus myStatus = SINGLE;
myStatus = MARRIED;
myStatus = 15;                         // Syntax error: incompatible type
System.out.println(myStatus);          // Displays "MARRIED"
```

If a new type is defined as public within a class, the type name and its values can be accessed by programmers by using the usual selector notation. If the previous code segment is nested in the class TaxReturn, then a programmer can run code such as the following:

```java
// Declare and initialize a MartialStatus variable
TaxReturn.MaritalStatus myStatus = TaxReturn.MaritalStatus.MARRIED;
```

Control Statements

Compound Statement

A compound statement consists of a list of zero or more declarations and statements enclosed within braces, {}. A semicolon must terminate each statement, except for the compound statement itself. Following is the form:

```
{
    <declaration or statement-1>
    .
    .
    <declaration or statement-n>
}
```

do-while Statement

do-while statements have the following form:

```
do
    <statement>
while (<boolean expression>)
```

SWITCH Statement

The switch statement handles a selection among cases, where each case is a constant of a primitive type. Following is an example:

```java
switch (ch){
    case 'a':
    case 'A': doSomething1();
```

```
                    break;
        case 'b':
        case 'B': doSomething2();
                    break;
        case 'c': doSomething3();
                    break;
        default:  doSomething4();
    }
```

The `break` statements are optional in this example, but they are required if the case lists are to be considered mutually exclusive. The `default` statement is also optional but highly recommended.

Math Class Methods

The `Math` class includes many static methods that allow clients to perform trigonometric functions and so forth. For example, the code

```
System.out.println(Math.sqrt(2));
```

outputs the square root of 2. Table B-3 lists most of these methods.

TABLE B-3
Math class methods

Math Class METHOD	DESCRIPTION
`double abs(double a)`	Returns the absolute value of a `double` value; Similar methods exist for `float`, `int`, and `long`.
`double acos(double a)`	Returns the arc cosine of an angle, in the range of 0.0 through pi
`double asin(double a)`	Returns the arc sine of an angle, in the range of –pi/2 through pi/2
`double atan(double a)`	Converts rectangular coordinates (b, a) to polar (r, theta)
`double atan2(double a, double b)`	Converts rectangular coordinates (b, a) to polar (r, theta)
`double ceil(double a)`	Returns the smallest (closest to negative infinity) `double` value that is not less than the argument and is equal to a mathematical integer
`double cos(double a)`	Returns the trigonometric cosine of an angle
`double exp(double a)`	Returns the exponential number e (i.e., 2.718...) raised to the power of a `double` value
`double floor(double a)`	Returns the largest (closest to positive infinity) `double` value that is not greater than the argument and is equal to a mathematical integer
`double log(double a)`	Returns the natural logarithm (base e) of a `double` value
`double max(double a, double b)`	Returns the greater of two `double` values; Similar methods exist for `float`, `int`, and `long`.

Math Class METHOD	DESCRIPTION
`double min(double a, double b)`	Returns the smaller of two double values; Similar methods exist for `float`, `int`, and `long`.
`double pow(double a, double b)`	Returns the value of the first argument raised to the power of the second argument
`double random()`	Returns a `double` value with a positive sign, greater than or equal to 0.0 and less than 1.0
`double rint(double a)`	Returns the double value that is closest in value to a and is equal to a mathematical integer
`long round(double a)`	Returns the closest `long` to the argument
`double sin(double a)`	Returns the trigonometric sine of an angle
`double sqrt(double a)`	Returns the correctly rounded positive square root of a `double` value
`double tan(double a)`	Returns the trigonometric tangent of an angle
`double toDegrees(double angrad)`	Converts an angle measured in radians to the equivalent angle measured in degrees
`double toRadians(double angdeg)`	Converts an angle measured in degrees to the equivalent angle measured in radians

The Character and Integer Classes

The `Character` and `Integer` classes allow `char` and `int` values to masquerade as objects when included in collections. These classes also include several static methods that are useful in processing numeric data. For example, `Character` methods exist for converting between single digits and the numbers they represent, and `Integer` methods exist for the conversion of strings of digits to numbers. Tables B-4 and B-5 list some of these methods.

TABLE B-4
Some Character class methods

Character METHOD	DESCRIPTION
`int digit(char ch, int radix)`	Returns the numeric value of the character `ch` in the specified radix
`char forDigit(int digit, int radix)`	Determines the character representation for a specific digit in the specified radix
`int getNumericValue(char ch)`	Returns the Unicode numeric value of the character as a nonnegative integer
`boolean isDigit(char ch)`	Determines if the specified character is a digit
`boolean isLetter(char ch)`	Determines if the specified character is a letter
`boolean isLowerCase(char ch)`	Determines if the specified character is a lowercase character
`boolean isUpperCase(char ch)`	Determines if the specified character is an uppercase character
`boolean isWhiteSpace(char ch)`	Determines if the specified character is white space according to Java
`char toLowerCase(char ch)`	The given character is mapped to its lowercase equivalent; if the character has no lowercase equivalent, the character itself is returned.
`char toUpperCase(char ch)`	Converts the character argument to uppercase

TABLE B-5
Some Integer class methods

Integer METHOD	DESCRIPTION
`int parseInt(String s)`	Parses the string argument as a signed decimal integer
`int parseInt(String s, int radix)`	Parses the string argument as a signed integer in the radix specified by the second argument
`String toString(int i)`	Returns a new `String` object representing the specified integer
`String toString(int i, int radix)`	Creates a string representation of the first argument in the radix specified by the second argument
`Integer valueOf(String s)`	Returns a new `Integer` object initialized to the value of the specified `String`
`Integer valueOf(String s, int radix)`	Returns a new `Integer` object initialized to the value of the specified `String`

The Class `java.util.Arrays`

Common operations on arrays include searching, sorting, comparing two arrays for equality, and filling an array's cells with a default value. The class `java.util.Arrays` includes many static methods that perform these functions. Most of them are overloaded for arrays of different element types, including all the primitive types and the class `Object`. Table B-6 lists one example of each type of operation; we refer the reader to Sun's documentation for descriptions of the others.

TABLE B-6
Some `Arrays` methods

Arrays METHOD	DESCRIPTION
`static int binarySearch(int[]a, int key)`	Searches the array a for the integer key using the binary search algorithm
`static Boolean equals(int[] a, int[] a2)`	Returns true if the two specified arrays of ints are *equal* to one another
`static void fill(int[] a, int val)`	Assigns the specified int value to each element of the specified array of ints
`static void sort(int[] a)`	Sorts the specified array of ints into ascending numerical order

The Class `java.util.ArrayList`

The package `java.util` includes several list classes, each of which implements the `List` interface. The class `ArrayList` provides the basic behavior of an array (including random access of elements) but also allows clients to add or remove elements. An array list tracks the number of elements currently available and also allows the client to set an initial capacity or trim the capacity to the number of elements. Table B-7 describes the `ArrayList` methods. Note that this is the "raw" version of `ArrayList`, which accepts any objects as elements.

TABLE B-7
The `ArrayList` methods

ArrayList METHOD	DESCRIPTION
`ArrayList()`	Constructs an empty list
`ArrayList(Collection c)`	Constructs a list containing the elements of the specified collection, in the order they are returned by the collection's iterator
`ArrayList(int initialCapacity)`	Constructs an empty list with the specified initial capacity
`void add(int index, Object element)`	Inserts the specified element at the specified position in this list
`boolean add(Object o)`	Appends the specified element to the end of this list
`boolean addAll(Collection c)`	Appends all of the elements in the specified `Collection` to the end of this list, in the order that they are returned by the specified `Collection`'s `Iterator`

TABLE B-7 Continued
The ArrayList methods

ArrayList METHOD	DESCRIPTION
boolean addAll(int index, Collection c)	Inserts all of the elements in the specified Collection into this list, starting at the specified position
void clear()	Removes all of the elements from this list
Object clone()	Returns a shallow copy of this ArrayList instance
boolean contains(Object elem)	Returns true if this list contains the specified element
void ensureCapacity(int minCapacity)	Increases the capacity of this ArrayList instance, if necessary, to ensure that it can hold at least the number of elements specified by the minimum capacity argument
Object get(int index)	Returns the element at the specified position in this list
int indexOf(Object elem)	Searches for the first occurence of the given argument, testing for equality using the equals method
boolean isEmpty()	Tests if this list has no elements
int lastIndexOf(Object elem)	Returns the index of the last occurrence of the specified object in this list
Object remove(int index)	Removes the element at the specified position in this list
protected void removeRange(int fromIndex, int toIndex)	Removes from this list all of the elements whose index is between fromIndex, inclusive and toIndex, exclusive
Object set(int index, Object element)	Replaces the element at the specified position in this list with the specified element
int size()	Returns the number of elements in this list
Object[] toArray()	Returns an array containing all of the elements in this list in the correct order
Object[] toArray(Object[] a)	Returns an array containing all of the elements in this list in the correct order
void trimToSize()	Trims the capacity of this ArrayList instance to be the list's current size

Three-Dimensional Arrays

Java does not limit the number of dimensions for arrays. Following is the declaration and initialization of a three-dimensional array:

```
int[][][] threeD = {{{ 1, 2, 3}, { 4, 5, 6}},
                     {{ 7, 8, 9}, {10,11,12}},
                     {{13,14,15}, {16,17,18}}};
```

The array's elements fill a box whose dimensions are 3 by 2 by 3. To refer to an element, we indicate its position in the box, remembering as usual to start counting at 0. Thus, element 8 is at position (1,0,1) and is referred to as follows:

```
threeD[1][0][1]
```

Operator Precedence

Table C-1 shows the operator precedence. The operators shown in bold are not discussed in this book. For a discussion of them, see the references on Sun's Web site.

TABLE C-1
Operator precedence

OPERATOR	FUNCTION	ASSOCIATION
()	Parentheses	Left to right
[]	Array subscript	
.	Object member selection	
++	Increment	Right to left
--	Decrement	
+	Unary plus	
-	Unary minus	
!	Boolean negation	
~	**Bitwise negation**	
(*type*)	Type cast	
*	Multiplication	Left to right
/	Division	
%	Modulus	
+	Addition or concatenation	Left to right
-	Subtraction	
<<	**Bitwise shift left**	**Left to right**
>>	**Bitwise shift right**	
>>>	**Bitwise shift right, sign extension**	

TABLE C-1 Continued
Operator precedence

OPERATOR	FUNCTION	ASSOCIATION
<	Less than	Left to right
<=	Less than or equal to	
>	Greater than	
>=	Greater than or equal to	
instanceOf	Class membership	
==	Equal to	Left to right
!=	Not equal to	
&	**Boolean AND (complete)**	**Left to right**
&	**Bitwise AND**	
^	**Boolean exclusive OR**	**Left to right**
^	**Bitwise exclusive OR**	
|	**Boolean OR (complete)**	**Left to right**
|	**Bitwise OR**	
&&	Boolean AND (partial)	Left to right
||	Boolean OR (partial)	Left to right
?:	**Ternary conditional**	**Right to left**
=	Assign	Right to left
+=	Add and assign	
-=	Subtract and assign	
*=	Multiply and assign	
/=	Divide and assign	
%=	Modulo and assign	
<<=	**Shift left and assign**	
>>=	**Shift right, sign extension, and assign**	
>>>=	**Shift right, no sign extension, and assign**	
&=	**Boolean or bitwise AND and assign**	
|=	**Boolean or bitwise OR and assign**	
^=	**Boolean or bitwise exclusive OR and assign**	

APPENDIX D

ASCII Character Set

Table D-1 shows the ordering of the ASCII character set. The digits in the left column represent the leftmost digits of the ASCII code, and the digits in the top row are the rightmost digits. Thus, the ASCII code of the character R at row 8, column 2, is 82. The printable characters range from ASCII 33 to ASCII 126. The values from ASCII 0 to ASCII 32 and ASCII 127 are associated with white-space characters, such as the horizontal tab (HT), or nonprinting control characters, such as the escape key (ESC).

TABLE D-1
Ordering of the ASCII character set

	0	1	2	3	4	5	6	7	8	9
0	NUL	SOH	STX	ETX	EOT	ENQ	ACK	BEL	BS	HT
1	LF	VT	FF	CR	SO	SI	DLE	DC1	DC2	DC3
2	DC4	NAK	SYN	ETB	CAN	EM	SUB	ESC	FS	GS
3	RS	US	SP	!	"	#	$	%	&	`
4	(	)	*	+	,	-	.	/	0	1
5	2	3	4	5	6	7	8	9	:	;
6	<	=	>	?	@	A	B	C	D	E
7	F	G	H	I	J	K	L	M	N	O
8	P	Q	R	S	T	U	V	W	X	Y
9	Z	[	\	]	^	_	`	a	b	c
10	d	e	f	g	h	i	j	k	l	m
11	n	o	p	q	r	s	t	u	v	w
12	x	y	z	{	|	}	~	DEL		

APPENDIX E

Number Systems

When we make change at the store, we use the decimal (base 10) number system. The digits in this system are the characters 0 through 9. Computers represent all information in the binary (base 2) system. The digits in this system are just the characters 0 and 1. Because binary numbers can be very long strings of 1s and 0s, programmers also use the octal (base 8) and hexadecimal (base 16) number systems, usually for low-level programming in assembly language. The octal digits range from 0 to 7, and the hexadecimal digits include the decimal digits and the letters A through F. These letters represent the numbers 10 through 15, respectively.

To identify the system being used, one can attach the base as a subscript to the number. For example, the following numbers represent the quantity 414 in the binary, octal, decimal, and hexadecimal systems:

```
414 in binary notation            110011110₂
414 in octal notation             636₈
414 in decimal notation           414₁₀
414 in hexadecimal notation       19E₁₆
```

Note that as the size of the base grows, either the number of digits or the digit in the largest position might be smaller.

Each number system uses positional notation to represent a number. The digit at each position in a number has a positional value. The positional value of a digit is determined by raising the base of the system to the power specified by the position. For an n-digit number, the positions (and exponents) are numbered 0 through $n - 1$, starting with the rightmost digit and moving to the left. For example, as Figure E-1 illustrates, the positional values of a three-digit decimal number are 100 (10^2), 10 (10^1), and 1 (10^0), moving from left to right in the number. The positional values of a three-digit binary number are 4 (2^2), 2 (2^1), and 1 (2^0).

FIGURE E-1
Positional values of base 10 and base 2 numbers

base 10				base 2			
positional values	100	10	1	positional values	4	2	1
positions		2	1	0	positions	2	1	0

The quantity represented by a number in any system is determined by multiplying each digit (as a decimal number) by its positional value and adding the results. The following examples show how this is done for numbers in several systems:

```
414 base 10 =
```

$$4 * 10^2 + 1 * 10^1 + 4 * 10^0 =$$

```
4 * 100 + 1 * 10 + 4 * 1 =

400      + 10      + 4 = 414
```

```
110011110 base 2 =
```

$$1 * 2^8 + 1 * 2^7 + 0 * 2^6 + 0 * 2^5 + 1 * 2^4 + 1 * 2^3 + 1 * 2^2 + 1 * 2^1 + 0 * 2^0 =$$

```
1 * 256 + 1 * 128 + 0 * 64 + 0 * 32 + 1 * 16 + 1 * 8 + 1 * 4 + 1 * 2 + 0 * 1 =

256     + 128     + 0      + 0      + 16     + 8     + 4     + 2     + 0 = 414
```

```
636 base 8 =
```

$$6 * 8^2 + 3 * 8^1 + 6 * 8^0 =$$

```
6 * 64 + 3 * 8 + 6 * 1 =

384    + 24    + 6 = 414
```

```
19E base 16 =
```

$$1 * 16^2 + 9 * 16^1 + E * 16^0 =$$

```
1 * 256 + 9 * 16 + 14 * 1

256     + 144    + 14 = 414
```

Each of these examples appears to convert from the number in the given base to the corresponding decimal number. To convert a decimal number to a number in a given base, we use division and remainder rather than multiplication and addition. The process works as follows:

1. Find the largest power of the given base that divides into the decimal number.

2. The quotient becomes the digit at that power's position in the new number.

3. Repeat steps 1 and 2 with the remainder until the remainder is less than the number.

4. If the last remainder is greater than 0, the remainder becomes the last digit in the new number.

5. If you must skip a power of the base when performing step 3, then put a 0 in that power's position in the new number.

To illustrate, let us convert the decimal number 327 to the equivalent binary number.

The highest power of 2 by which 327 is divisible is 256 or 2^8. Thus, we'll have a nine-digit binary number, with 1 in position 8:

The remainder of the first division is 71. The highest power of 2 by which 71 is divisible is 64 (2^6). Thus, we have skipped 128 (2^7), so we write 0 in position 7 and 1 in position 6:

The remainder of the second division is 7. Thus, as you can see, we skip 3 more powers of 2 (32, 16, and 8) on the next division in order to use 4. So, we place 0s at positions 5, 4, and 3, and 1 at position 2 in the new number:

The remainder of the third division is 3. This is divisible by the next power of 2, which is 2, so we put 1 at position 1 in the new number. The remainder of the last division, 1, goes in position 0:

One reason that programmers prefer to use octal or hexadecimal notation instead of binary notation is that octal and hexadecimal are more expressive (one can say more with less). Another reason is that it is very easy to convert an octal number or a hexadecimal number to the corresponding binary number. To convert octal to binary, you assume that each digit in the octal number represents three digits in the corresponding binary number. You then start with the rightmost octal digit and write down the corresponding binary digits, padding these to the left with 0s to the count of 3, if necessary. You proceed in this manner until all of the octal digits have been converted. The following examples show such conversions:

The conversion of hexadecimal numbers to binary numbers works in a similar way, except that each hexadecimal digit translates to four binary digits.

Java Exception Handling

Java divides run-time errors into two broad categories: errors and exceptions. Errors are serious run-time problems that usually should not be handled by the programmer. For example, if a method gets stuck in an infinite recursion, Java will throw a StackOverflowError. Java defines a separate class for each type of error. You can browse through these in Sun's Web site, as described in Appendix A, starting with the class Error in the package java.lang.

Exceptions come in two varieties: those that Java requires the programmer to handle, such as IOException, and those that the programmer may or may not handle, such as ArithmeticException and ArrayIndexOutOfBoundsException. To explore Java's Exception class hierarchy on Sun's Web site, select the desired package in the package index and scroll to the bottom of the page. Most of the exception classes are defined in java.lang, but several important ones also are defined in java.io and java.util.

The following code segments show how you might handle exceptions in the cases of division and array subscripting:

```java
// Catch an attempt to divide by zero

try{
   quotient = dividend / divisor;
   System.out.println("Successful division");
}
catch (ArithmeticException e){
   System.out.println("Error1: " + e.toString());
}
```

```java
// Catch an attempt to use an array index that is out of range

try{
   a[x] = 0;
   System.out.println("Successful subscripting");
}
catch (ArrayIndexOutOfBoundsException e){
   System.out.println("Error2: " + e.toString());
}
```

When Java detects an error and throws an exception, control is immediately transferred from the offending instruction in the try statement to the catch statement. Thus, the output of the first message would be skipped if an exception occurs in either of the preceding code segments. If the try statement completes successfully, the catch statement is not executed.

A `try` statement can be followed by more than one `catch` statement. For example, the following code segment combines the exception handling of the previous two segments:

```java
// Catch an attempt to divide by zero and to use an array index
// that is out of bounds

try{
    quotient = dividend / divisor;
    System.out.println("Successful division");
    a[x] = quotient;
    System.out.println("Successful subscripting");
 }
catch (ArithmeticException e){
    System.out.println("Error1: " + e.toString());
}
catch (ArrayIndexOutOfBoundsException e){
    System.out.println("Error2: " + e.toString());
}
```

The same two exceptions are possible in this example, but Java will get to throw only one of them. When this occurs, control shifts to the first `catch` statement following the `try` statement. If the class of the exception thrown is the same as or is a subclass of the class of that `catch` statement's parameter, then the code for the `catch` statement executes. Otherwise, Java compares the exception thrown to the parameter of the next `catch` statement and so on.

It is possible (and often desirable) to define new kinds of exceptions that can be thrown by methods in user-defined classes. The complete rules for doing this are beyond the scope of this book but can be found on Sun's Web site.

Java Packages and `jar` Files

Using and Developing Packages

A Java package is a name that stands for a set of related classes. For example, the package `java.io` stands for all of the Java file stream classes. Exceptions and interfaces also can be parts of a package.

The package `java.lang` contains many commonly used classes, such as `Math` and `String`. This package is implicitly imported into every Java program file, so no `import` statement is required. To use any other package, such as `java.io`, in a program file, the programmer must explicitly import the package with an `import` statement.

Programs can import all of the classes in a given package, using the form:

```
import <package name>.*;
```

It is also possible to import selected classes from a given package and omit others. For example, the following line imports just the `ArrayList` class from the `java.util` package and omits the others:

```
import java.util.ArrayList;
```

This statement has the effect of making the `ArrayList` class visible to the program file, but leaves the rest of the classes in the `java.util` package invisible.

Occasionally, a program uses classes that have the same name but are defined in different packages. For example, the `List` class in `java.awt` implements a scrolling list box (similar to `javax.swing.JList`), whereas the `List` interface in `java.util` specifies operations for Java's list collections. To avoid ambiguity in these programs, you must prefix the class name with its package wherever the class name is used. Following is an example:

```
import java.util.*;
import java.awt.*;

   .
   .

   // Instantiate a scrolling list box to display the data
   java.awt.List listView = new java.awt.List();

   .
   .

   // Instantiate an array list to contain the data
   java.util.List<String> listModel = new ArrayList<String>();
```

To define and compile a package, perform the following steps:

1. Create three directories on your disk. Name the first directory `testbed` and the second directory `sources`. The third directory should have the name of the package you are defining, such as `mypackage`. The `sources` and `mypackage` directories should be contained as subdirectories in the `testbed` directory.

2. Place a tester program (say, `Tester.java`) for your package in the `testbed` directory.

3. Open a DOS window and move to the `mypackage` directory.

4. Place the Java source files (`.java` extension) for your package in the `mypackage` directory. Each source file in the package should have the line:

```
package mypackage;
```

at the beginning of the file.

5. Compile the Java files using the DOS command `javac *.java`. If all goes well, the byte code files (`.class` extension) should be in the `mypackage` directory.

6. Move up to the `testbed` directory and compile the tester program.

7. Run the tester program using the DOS command `java Tester`. If all goes well, your package is ready for release. Before distributing your package, move the source (`.java`) files to the `sources` directory. A package should have just `.class` files.

Go back to Step 5 each time you need to modify a source file in the package.

Using and Developing `jar` Files

A `jar` file contains a collection of Java byte codes and possibly other resources, such as images. `jar` files provide a convenient way to distribute libraries of program code and standalone Java applications. Because they are compressed, `jar` files can also significantly reduce the file size of program code.

All of the Java applications developed in this book consist of one or more byte code files. To run an application, you open a command prompt window and run the `java` command with the byte code file that contains the program's `main` method. Alternatively, if a program's byte codes are bundled in an executable `jar` file, you can launch the program just by double-clicking on the `jar` file's icon.

To create an executable `jar` file, you must perform the following steps:

1. Open a text editor and create a text file named `manifest.tmp`. This file should contain a line of code that specifies the name of the class that contains the `main` method of your Java application. For example, if your main class is named `MyApplication`, the line of code in the file should be:

```
Main-Class: MyApplication
```

Save the file in the directory that contains your byte code files.

2. At the command prompt run the jar command with the tags cfm, the name of the jar file, name of the manifest file, and the names of the byte code files as command line arguments. For example, the following command will generate an executable jar file named MyApplication.jar from all of the byte code files in the current directory, using the manifest file manifest.tmp:

```
jar cfm MyApplication.jar manifest.tmp *.class
```

3. Test the resulting jar file by launching it.

A program library usually consists of one for more Java packages. You can use a library by placing the directories that contain the packages in your current working directory. However, this necessitates moving these directories every time you change to another working directory. A far better way to use (and distribute) a program library is to bundle its packages in a jar file. The jar file can then be placed in Java's system directory, where it is accessible from any working directory or from most commercial and free IDEs.

To create a jar file for a program library, you must perform the following steps:

1. Place the package directory for the library in your current working directory. If there is more than one package in the library, they should already be organized in a hierarchy of subdirectories or as several directories at the same level. Note that the directories should contain just byte code files (files with a .class extension).

2. At the command prompt run the jar command with the tag cvf, the name of the jar file, and the top-level package directory name. For example, if the package name is TurtleGraphics, you would run the command line:

```
jar cvf TurtleGraphics.jar TurtleGraphics
```

3. To test the resulting jar file, copy it to the appropriate places in Java's system directory. On a PC running Windows XP, these two directories are:

```
c:\Program Files\Java\jdk1.5.0_05\jre\lib\ext
c:\Program Files\Java\jre1.5.0_05\lib\ext
```

On a Macintosh, this directory is Macintosh Hard Drive/Library/Java/Extensions. Compile and run a Java program that uses the library, after making sure that the library does not exist in the program's current working directory.

APPENDIX H

Files

Data stored in variables is temporary, existing for the lifetime of an application at most. Data that must last longer is saved in files on secondary storage devices, such as magnetic disks, optical disks (CDs and DVDs), and magnetic tapes. When needed again later, the data is read from the files back into variables. Dealing directly with directory structures and file layouts on disk is a complex process, so operating systems provide a layer of software to hide the messy details. In addition, Java has built a hierarchy of classes on top of this layer to give it an object-oriented interface. When working with files, a program deals with these Java classes, which in turn manage the actual transfer of data between memory and secondary storage.

Java supports two types of file access: sequential and random. If we imagine a file as a long sequence of contiguous bytes, then *random access* allows a program to retrieve a byte or group of bytes from anywhere in a file. *Sequential access* forces a program to retrieve bytes sequentially starting from the beginning of a file. Thus, to retrieve the 100th byte, a program must first retrieve the preceding 99. The text files processed in examples in this book are sequential access files.

At the lowest level, Java views the data in files as a stream of bytes. A stream of bytes from which data is read is called an *input stream*, and a stream of bytes to which data is written is called an *output stream*. Java provides classes for connecting to and manipulating data in a stream. The classes are defined in the package `java.io` and are organized in a large complex hierarchy. The classes `Scanner` (from `java.util`) and `PrintWriter` (from `java.io`) are used for text file input/output (I/O) and insulate the programmer from the details of Java's file streams. However, processing other types of files requires the knowledge of several other types of file streams, to which we now turn.

The Classes `FileInputStream`, and `FileOutputStream`

The basic classes for file I/O at the byte level are `FileInputStream` and `FileOutputStream`. When the programmer creates a `Scanner` to read from a text file, the scanner is instantiated as follows:

```
Scanner reader = new Scanner(new File(filename));
```

The scanner in turn wraps a `FileInputStream` around the `File` object as follows:

```
FileInputStream stream = new FileInputStream(aFile);
```

The scanner can then read bytes from this stream and use them to construct whatever tokens (strings, ints, doubles) the client requests.

Likewise, when a `PrintWriter` is created with an output file name, using the notation `new PrintWriter(new File(filename))`, the `PrintWriter` creates a `FileOutputStream` as follows:

```
FileOutputStream stream = new FileOutputStream(aFile);
```

The print writer can then write bytes from its output data to this stream.

The details of opening these streams are hidden from programmers who process text files with a `Scanner` and a `PrintWriter`. However, similar operations must be performed when programmers process other types of files. For convenience, both `FileInputStream` and `FileOutputStream` have a second constructor that accepts a file name as a parameter and wraps a `File` object around it.

Binary Files, Data Input Streams, and Data Output Streams

When the `print` and `println` methods write a number to a `PrintWriter`, they transform the number to its humanly readable character string representations. If the number needs to be read later by another program, the `Scanner` method `nextInt` or `nextDouble` first reads the string representing the number from the text file and then converts it back to the appropriate numeric data type.

Some applications simply need to store data in files without any need to represent it in human readable form. Java provides support for this type of application in the form of *binary file I/O*. A primitive type or string written to a `DataOutputStream` is represented in binary format that may not be humanly readable but can be read back into a program using a `DataInputStream`. Table H-1 lists several useful methods in these two classes.

TABLE H-1

Methods in the classes `DataInputStream` and `DataOutputStream`

METHOD	WHAT IT DOES
`char readChar()`	Reads a `char` from a `DataInputStream`
`double readDouble()`	Reads a `double` from a `DataInputStream`
`int readInt()`	Reads an `int` from a `DataInputStream`
`String readUTF()`	Reads a `String` from a `DataInputStream`
`void writeChar (char ch)`	Writes a `char` to a `DataOutputStream`
`void writeDouble (double d)`	Writes a `double` to a `DataOutputStream`
`void writeInt (int i)`	Writes an `int` to a `DataOutputStream`
`void writeUTF (String s)`	Writes a `String` to a `DataOutputStream`

A program reading from a data input stream must know the order and types of data expected at each moment. To illustrate, we present a sample program that

- Generates a user-specified number of random integers (the number is entered as a parameter in the command line)

- Writes these integers to a data output stream

- Reads them back in from a data input stream

- Outputs the integers to the terminal window

```java
/* Example H1: TestDataStreams.java
1) Write randomly generated integers to a data output stream. A command
line parameter specifies the number of integers to generate.
2) Read them back in using a data input stream and display them in
   the terminal window.
*/

import java.io.*;
import java.util.Random;

public class TestDataStreams{

    public static void main (String[] args){
```

```java
// Obtain the number of ints from the command line parameters.
int number = Integer.parseInt(args[0]);

// Generate random ints and write them to a data output stream.
Random gen = new Random();
try{
    FileOutputStream foStream = new FileOutputStream("ints.dat");
    DataOutputStream doStream = new DataOutputStream(foStream);
    int i;
    for (i = 0; i < number; i++)
        doStream.writeInt(gen.nextInt(number + 1));
    doStream.close();
}catch(IOException e){
    System.err.println("Error during output: " + e.toString());
}

// Read the ints from a data input stream and display them in
// a terminal window.
try{
    FileInputStream fiStream = new FileInputStream("ints.dat");
    DataInputStream diStream = new DataInputStream(fiStream);
    while (true){
        int i = diStream.readInt();
        System.out.println(i);
    }
}catch(EOFException e){
    System.out.println("\nAll done.");
}catch(IOException e){

    System.err.println("Error in input" + e.toString());
}
    }
}
```

A data input stream is processed within an exception-driven loop. Using the expression `while (true)`, the loop continues until an `EOFException` occurs. This exception is not viewed as an error but rather as a good reason to exit the loop. The `catch` statement in this example prints a reassuring message.

Now that we have seen two different ways to handle file input and output, it is natural to ask when to use each one. Here are two rules of thumb:

1. It is appropriate to use a print writer for output and a scanner for input when the file must be viewed or created with a text editor or when the order and types of data are unknown.

2. It is appropriate to use a data input stream for input and a data output stream for output when the file need not be viewed or created with a text editor and when the order and types of data are known.

Serialization and Object Streams

Until now we have focused on reading and writing primitive data types and strings. Java also provides methods for reading and writing complete objects. This makes it easy to save a program's state before closing it and to restore the state when the program is run again. Objects that are saved between executions of a program are said to be *persistent*, and the process of writing them to and reading them from a file is called *serialization*. To use serialization, a programmer must do two things:

1. Make classes `serializable`. (We will explain how this is done momentarily.)

2. Write objects using an `ObjectOutputStream` and read them later using an `ObjectInputStream`.

For example, consider the version of the student test scores program presented in Chapter 10. This program was written using a model/view pattern in which the model encapsulates the program's data requirements and the view manages the user interface. The data model in turn consists of the two classes `Student` and `TestScoresModel`. To serialize these classes, we import the package `java.io` and add the qualifier `implements Serializable` to each class's definition. The changes are commented in the following code:

```java
import java.io.*;        // Change here

public class TestScoresModel implements Serializable{  // Change here

   // Instance variables
   private Student[] students = new Student[10];
   private int       indexSelectedStudent;
   private int       studentCount;

   . . .

}




import java.io.*;        // Change here

public class Student implements Serializable{          // Change here

   // Instance variables
   private String name;
   private int[] tests = new int[3];

   . . .

}
```

The view class for the program maintains a reference to an object called model that is of type TestScoresModel. Saving and restoring the program's data involves nothing more than serializing this single object, which we do in the methods saveModel and loadModel. These methods are activated when the user selects the corresponding options from the menu.

```java
import java.io.*;
. . .

public class TestScoresView{
    . . .

    private TestScoresModel model;
    . . .

    public TestScoresView(TestScoresModel tm){
        model = tm;
    . . .
    }


    // Controller code


    . . .

    private void saveModel(){
        String outputFileName;
        . . . use a terminal prompt or file dialog to ask the user for the name
              of the output file
        try{
            FileOutputStream foStream = new FileOutputStream(outputFileName);
            ObjectOutputStream ooStream = new ObjectOutputStream(foStream);
            ooStream.writeObject(model);
            foStream.flush();
            foStream.close();
        }catch (IOException e){
            System.out.println("Error during output: " + e.toString());
        }
    }

    private void loadModel(){
        String inputFileName;
        . . . use a terminal prompt or file dialog to ask the user for the name
              of the input file
        try{
            FileInputStream fiStream = new FileInputStream(inputFileName);
            ObjectInputStream oiStream = new ObjectInputStream(fiStream);
            model = (TestScoresModel) oiStream.readObject();
            fiStream.close();
        }catch (Exception e){
            System.out.println("Error during input: " + e.toString());
        }
    }


    . . .
}
```

In this code, the method `writeObject` outputs the model object to the object output stream, which in turn triggers automatic serialization of the array of students and each individual student in the array. Likewise, the method `readObject` inputs the model object and all its constituent parts from the object input stream. Note that

- The method `readObject` returns an `Object`, which is cast to a `StudentTestScoresModel` before it is stored in the variable.

- The methods `readObject` and `writeObject` can throw several different types of exceptions. To catch all of these in a single `catch` clause, we use the generic `Exception` object as a parameter.

The methods `readObject` and `writeObject` can be used with objects of any type, such as strings, arrays, or user-defined objects. When reading an object, the programmer must be aware of its type and its position in the input stream and must cast and store it in the appropriate type of variable. As you can see, object streams and serialization are powerful and convenient tools for managing persistence.

Random Access Files

The types of files thus far discussed are sequential access files. Their data is accessed by reading or writing one value after another, starting with the value at the beginning of the file. By contrast, a random access file allows the programmer to read or write a datum at an arbitrary position in the file. The programmer specifies a position in the file with a special *seek* operation and then reads or writes a datum at that position. Thus, a random access file has the logical behavior of an array and supports much faster access than a sequential access file. The catch, however, is that the programmer must be able to specify the position of a datum in terms of the number of bytes between it and the beginning of the file. To do that, the programmer must also know the type of each datum and the number of bytes required to store it. We give an example of how this is done for a file of integers shortly.

The class `RandomAccessFile` supports random access file processing in Java. The most convenient constructor expects a file name and a *mode* as parameters. The modes "rw" and "r" specify read/write and read-only access, respectively. We use "rw" for output files and "r" for input files in our example.

Like the data I/O streams discussed earlier, `RandomAccessFile` includes several type-specific methods for input and output. For example, `readInt()` reads the four bytes at the current position in the file and returns the integer represented in those bytes. Conversely, `writeInt(anInt)` converts its parameter to four bytes and writes these to the current position in the file.

Before each input or output operation, the method seek(aLong) must be called to locate the position of the datum in the file. The position of the first datum is always 0. The position of the second datum is equal to the byte length of the first datum plus 0. In general, the position of the *i*th datum after the first one is equal to the position of the datum at position *i* − 1 plus that datum's byte length. The byte lengths of the various primitive types are listed in Table B-1. If we are dealing with a file of a single type of data, such as integers, then calculating the position of each datum can be reduced to a simple expression such as i * 4. The position of a datum is usually called its *offset*, to indicate the number of bytes between it and the beginning position in the file.

Other useful RandomAccessFile methods include length(), which returns the length of the file in bytes, and getFilePointer(), which returns the offset of the current position in bytes.

Our program example tests random access files by doing three things:

1. Create a random access file and save three integers from an array to this file.

2. Open the file for input and read the data at each position in sequence. Each datum and its position are displayed.

3. Open the file for input and read the integer at the file's middle position. The number of integers, the datum, and its position are displayed.

Here is the code:

```java
// Example H2: Test random access files

import java.io.*;

public class TestRandomFile{

    private int[] testArray = {23, 46, 67};

    public static void main(String[] args){
        TestRandomFile app = new TestRandomFile();
    }

    public TestRandomFile(){
        arrayToFile(testArray);
        sequentialTraverse();
        testInput();
    }
```

```java
// Write the numbers from the array to the file
public void arrayToFile(int[] array){
    try{
        RandomAccessFile output = new RandomAccessFile("test", "rw");
        for (int i = 0; i < array.length; i++){
            output.seek(i * 4);
            output.writeInt(array[i]);
        }
        output.close();
    }catch(Exception e){}
}

// Read the number at the midpoint of the file
public void testInput(){
    try{
        RandomAccessFile input = new RandomAccessFile("test", "r");
        int numberOfInts = (int)(input.length() / 4);
        // Get number of ints
        int midpoint = numberOfInts / 2 * 4;
        // Get position of middle int
        input.seek(midpoint);
        // Move directly to midpoint
        int item = input.readInt();
        // read the int
        System.out.println("Number of ints = " + numberOfInts);
        System.out.println("Midpoint       = " + midpoint);
        System.out.println("Middle int     = " + item);
        input.close();
    }catch(Exception e){}
}

// Sequential traversal using indices
void sequentialTraverse(){
    try{
        RandomAccessFile input = new RandomAccessFile("test", "r");
        long numberOfItems = input.length() / 4;
        for (long i = 0; i <= numberOfItems; i++){
            input.seek(i * 4);
            System.out.println(i + ": " + input.readInt());
        }
        input.close();
    }catch(Exception e){}
}
}
```

More detailed information on random access files can be found in Sun's documentation.

File Dialog Boxes

Throughout this book, filenames have been hard-coded into the programs or have been entered from the keyboard. Problems can arise if the specified file does not exist or if the user cannot remember a file's name. These problems are minimized if a file dialog box is used. The user can then browse through the computer's directory structure to find a desired filename or can back out by canceling the dialog box. Figure H-1 shows typical input file and output file dialog boxes as supported by Swing's `JFileChooser` class. Table H-2 lists important `JFileChooser` methods.

FIGURE H-1
Typical file dialog boxes

TABLE H-2
Important `JFileChooser` methods

METHOD	WHAT IT DOES
`JFileChooser()`	Constructor that creates a file dialog box that is attached to the user's home directory
`JFileChooser(String directoryPathName)`	Constructor that creates a file dialog box that is attached to the specified directory
`int showOpenDialog(JFrame parent)`	Opens a file dialog box for an input file and returns the `JFileChooser` constant APPROVE_OPTION if the user has selected a file or the constant or CANCEL_OPTION if the user has canceled
`int showSaveDialog(JFrame parent)`	Opens a file dialog box for an output file and returns the `JFileChooser` constant APPROVE_OPTION if the user has selected a file or the constant or CANCEL_OPTION if the user has canceled
`File getSelectedFile()`	Returns the selected file

The following program displays file dialog boxes for input and output files. After the dialog boxes close, the code displays the filename if the user did not cancel the dialog box; otherwise, the code displays a message saying the dialog box was canceled. At instantiation, the dialog box is attached to the directory c:\Javafiles (on a PC). The program is entirely GUI-based, using a standard File menu with Open and Save options.

```java
// Example H3: Testing file dialog boxes

import javax.swing.*;
import java.awt.event.*;
import java.io.*;

public class TestFileDialog extends JFrame{

   private void openFile(){
      JFileChooser chooser = new JFileChooser("c:\\Javafiles");
      int result = chooser.showOpenDialog(this);
      if (result == JFileChooser.CANCEL_OPTION)
        JOptionPane.showMessageDialog(this,
                                      "The dialog was cancelled.");
      else
         try{
            File file = chooser.getSelectedFile();
            JOptionPane.showMessageDialog(this, "File name: " +
                                          file.getName());
         }catch(Exception e){
            JOptionPane.showMessageDialog(this,
                                          "Error opening input file " +
                                          e.toString());

         }
   }

   private void saveFile(){
      JFileChooser chooser = new JFileChooser("c:\\Javafiles");
      int result = chooser.showSaveDialog(this);
      if (result == JFileChooser.CANCEL_OPTION)
        JOptionPane.showMessageDialog(this,
                                      "The dialog was cancelled.");
      else
         try{
            File file = chooser.getSelectedFile();
            JOptionPane.showMessageDialog(this,"File name: " +
                                          file.getName());
         }catch(Exception e){
            JOptionPane.showMessageDialog(this,
                                          "Error opening input file " +
                                          e.toString());

         }
   }
```

```java
private class OpenListener implements ActionListener{
   public void actionPerformed(ActionEvent e){
      openFile();
   }
}

private class SaveListener implements ActionListener{
   public void actionPerformed(ActionEvent e){
      saveFile();
   }
}

public TestFileDialog(){
   JMenu menu = new JMenu("File");
   JMenuItem openMI = new JMenuItem("Open");
   JMenuItem saveMI = new JMenuItem("Save");
   menu.add(openMI);
   menu.add(saveMI);
   JMenuBar bar = new JMenuBar();
   bar.add(menu);
   setJMenuBar(bar);
   openMI.addActionListener(new OpenListener());
   saveMI.addActionListener(new SaveListener());
}

public static void main(String[] args){
   TestFileDialog theGUI = new TestFileDialog();
   theGUI.setSize(100, 100);
   theGUI.setDefaultCloseOperation(JFrame.EXIT_ON_CLOSE);
   theGUI.setVisible(true);
}
}
```

The TurtleGraphics Package

This appendix provides a quick reference to an open-source package that supports turtle graphics. This package is called `TurtleGraphics`. Methods that are part of `AWT` and `Swing` are so noted. For more details, byte code, source code, a tutorial, and a related package, `BreezySwing`, that uses only Swing components, see the Web site at http://www.wlu.edu/~lambertk/hsjava/.

Programs that use `TurtleGraphics` should import the package as follows:

```
import TurtleGraphics.*;
```

The package provides classes and methods for manipulating a pen in a graphics window. The pen or turtle is an invisible device, initially positioned at the center of a sketchpad. This center point, also called home, is at the origin of a Cartesian coordinate system. The programmer draws images with the pen by sending it messages. There are several types of pens, as listed in Table I-1. All implement the `Pen` interface, as described in the following section.

TABLE I-1
The `Pen` classes

Pen CLASS	FEATURES
StandardPen	Draws with a straight line in the pen's current color
BackwardPen	Moves in the opposite direction of a standard pen
RainbowPen	Draws with a straight line in randomly generated colors
WigglePen	Draws with a wiggly line in the pen's current color
WiggleRainbowPen	Draws with a wiggly line in randomly generated colors

The `Pen` Interface

The `Pen` interface specifies the methods that all of the types of pens support. A pen is initially positioned at the home position (the origin or center of the sketchpad), faces due north, and is placed down on the sketchpad's surface. A non-rainbow pen's default color is blue. When placed down and moved, the pen draws; when picked up and moved, the pen simply moves without drawing. Following are the methods:

void home()

Action: The pen jumps to the center of the graphics window without drawing and points north.

Example: `pen.home();`

void setDirection(double degrees)

Action: The pen points in the indicated direction. Due east corresponds to 0 degrees, north to 90 degrees, west to 180 degrees, and south to 270 degrees. Because there are 360 degrees in a circle, setting the direction to 400 would be equivalent to 400 – 360 or 40 and setting it to –30 would be equivalent to 360 – 30 or 330.

Example: `pen.setDirection(90);    // Make the pen point due north`

void turn(double degrees)

Action: The pen adds the indicated degrees to its current direction. Positive degrees correspond to turning counterclockwise. The degrees can be an integer or floating-point number.

Example: `pen.turn(-45); // Rotate the pen 45 degrees clockwise`

void down()

Action: The pen lowers itself to the drawing surface.

Example: `pen.down();`

void up()

Action: The pen raises itself from the drawing surface.

Example: `pen.up();`

void move(double distance)

Action: The pen moves the specified distance in the current direction. The distance can be an integer or floating-point number and is measured in pixels (picture elements). The size of a pixel depends on the monitor's resolution. For instance, when we say that a monitor's resolution is 800 by 600, we mean that the monitor is 800 pixels wide and 600 pixels high.

Example: `pen.move(100);`

void move(double x, double y)

Action: The pen moves to the position (x, y).

Example: `pen.move(50, 50);`

void drawString(String string)

Action: The string is drawn at the pen's position.

Example: `pen.drawString("Here is the turtle!");`

void setColor(Color color)

Action: The pen's color is set to the specified color.

Example: `pen.setColor(Color.red);`

void setWidth(int width)

Action: The pen's width is set to the specified width.

Example: `pen.setWidth(8);`

Pens, Sketchpads, and Sketchpad Windows

Three classes cooperate to implement a turtle graphics program. They are one of the pen classes mentioned earlier, the `SketchPad` class, and the `SketchPadWindow` class. `SketchPadWindow`, a subclass of `JFrame`, provides the application window for turtle graphics. `SketchPad`, a subclass of `JPanel`, provides the drawing area within a sketchpad window. Associated with each sketchpad is a pen. Thus, the programmer can manipulate several pens in a single sketchpad window by creating several sketchpads and adding them to the window. In the remaining sections of this appendix, we describe three ways to create turtle graphics applications using these classes.

Method 1: Create Just a Pen

The simplest way to create a turtle graphics program is to instantiate a pen and start sending it messages. The framework automatically associates a pen with a sketchpad, places this panel in a window that is 150 pixels by 150 pixels, and opens the window. Following is an example code segment:

```
import TurtleGraphics.*;

public class TestTurtleGraphics{
   public static void main(String [] args) {
      Pen pen = new StandardPen();
      pen.move(100, 100);
   }
}
```

The constructors for `WigglePen` and `WiggleRainbowPen` require the user to specify the number of wiggles and a wiggle angle as parameters. The following code creates a `WigglePen` with 10 wiggles and a wiggle angle of 45:

```
Pen pen = new WigglePen(10, 45);
```

The user can manipulate a sketchpad window like any other window. Any images that the pen has drawn will automatically be refreshed. Note, however, that the programmer has no control over the window and there is only a single drawing area with one pen.

Method 2: Create a Sketchpad Window with a Pen

To give the programmer control over a pen's window, you can create it before associating it with a pen. The process consists of two steps:

1. Instantiate a `SketchPadWindow`. Its width and height can be passed as optional parameters, or you get a default size of 150 by 150.

2. Instantiate a pen with the `SketchPadWindow` as a parameter. The window is opened at this point.

Following is an example code segment:

```
import TurtleGraphics.*;

public class TestTurtleGraphics{
    public static void main(String [] args) {
        SketchPadWindow win = new SketchPadWindow(400, 400);
        Pen pen = new StandardPen(win);
        pen.move(100, 100);
    }
}
```

Method 3: Create a Sketchpad and a Pen

To give the programmer control over a pen's sketchpad or drawing area; to work with multiple drawing areas and pens in a single window; or to associate a sketchpad with any application window, an applet, or a dialog box; you can create a sketchpad before associating it with a pen. The process consists of three steps:

1. Instantiate a `SketchPad`.

2. Instantiate a pen with the `SketchPad` as a parameter.

3. Add the `SketchPad` to the window. You can use the `add` method if you are implementing an application, dialog box, or applet with `JFrame`, `JDialog`, or `JApplet`. Alternatively, you can instantiate a `SketchPadWindow` with the `SketchPad` as a parameter.

The following code segment shows the first option of Step 3. The program creates two sketchpads, sets their background colors, associates them with different types of pens, adds them to an application window, and draws similar images in them.

```
import TurtleGraphics.*;
import javax.swing.*;
import java.awt.*;

public class TestTurtleGraphics extends JFrame{

    private SketchPad leftPad, rightPad;
    private Pen leftPen, rightPen;

    public TestTurtleGraphics(){
        leftPad = new SketchPad();
        rightPad = new SketchPad();
        leftPad.setBackground(Color.pink);
        rightPad.setBackground(Color.yellow);
        leftPen = new StandardPen(leftPad);
        rightPen = new WigglePen(rightPad, 10, 45);
        Container container = getContentPane();
        container.setLayout(new GridLayout(1,2));
        container.add(BorderLayout.WEST, leftPad);
        container.add(BorderLayout.EAST, rightPad);
    }
```

```
    public static void main(String [] args) {
        TestTurtleGraphics theGUI = new TestTurtleGraphics();
        theGUI.setSize(200, 200);
        theGUI.setDefaultCloseOperation(JFrame.EXIT_ON_CLOSE);
        theGUI.setVisible(true);
        theGUI.leftPen.move(100, 100);
        theGUI.rightPen.move(100, 100);
    }
}
```

AP Correlations

This textbook covers all of the required features of Java for the AP A exam, as well as other features potentially relevant to the first course in programming but not tested. Table J-1 provides a reference to these features in the book.

TABLE J-1
AP exam features covered in this text

TESTED IN A, AB EXAM	TESTED IN AB EXAM ONLY	POTENTIALLY RELEVANT TO CS1/ CS2 COURSE BUT NOT TESTED
`int, double, boolean` (p. 60, 112, 203)		`short, long, byte, char, float` (p. B-1)
+ , -, *, /, %, ++, — (p. 64, 106)		
=, +=, -=, *=, /=, %= (p. 106)		
==, !=, <, <=, >, >= (p. 114)		
&&, II, ! and short-circuit evaluation (p. 202, 205)		
`(int), (double)` (p. 67)		Other numeric casts such as `(char)` or `(float)` (p. B-3)
String concatenation (p. 68)		
Escape sequences \" \\ \n inside strings (p. 69)		Other escape sequences (\' \t \unnnn) (p. B-2)
`System.out.print,` `System.out.println` (p. 44)		System.in, Stream input/output, GUI input/output, parsing input, formatted output (p. 252–258)
		`public static void main(String args)` (p. 355)
1-dimensional arrays, 2-dimensional rectangular arrays (p. 305, 318)		arrays with 3 or more dimensions, ragged arrays (p. B-10)
`if, if/else, while,` `for, enhanced for, return` (p. 113, 116, 120, 321)		`do/while, switch, break` (p. B-4)
Modify existing classes (p. 155)	Design classes (p. 507)	

TABLE J-1 Continued
AP exam features covered in this text

TESTED IN A, AB EXAM	TESTED IN AB EXAM ONLY	POTENTIALLY RELEVANT TO CS1/CS2 COURSE BUT NOT TESTED
public classes, private instance variables, public or private methods or constants (p. 163)		protected or package visibility (p. 369)
final local variables, static final class variables (p. 355)		final instance variables, methods or classes (p. 352)
static methods (p. 352)		static non-final variables (p. 352)
null, this, super (p. 161, 167, 370) this.method(args),	super.method(args) (p. 370)	this.var, this(args) (p. 370)
Constructors and initialization of static variables (p. 352)		default initialization of instance variables, initialization blocks (p. 313)
Understand inheritance hierarchies, modifying subclass implementations and implementations of interfaces (p. 367)	Design and implement subclasses (p. 507)	
Understand the concepts of abstract classes and interfaces (p. 372)	Design and implement abstract classes and interfaces (p. 507, 594)	
Understand equals, == and != comparison of objects (p. 405)	Comparable.compareTo (p. 610)	clone, implementation of equals (p. 406, 414–416)
Conversion to supertypes and (Subtype) casts (p. 371)		instanceof (p. 427)
Procedural decomposition		
		Inner classes (p. 190)
Package concept, import x.y.z; (p. 73)		import x.y.z, defining packages, class path (p. G-1)
Exception concept, common exceptions, throwing standard unchecked exceptions (p. 182, 385)		
String, Math, Random, Object, ArrayList (generic version) (p. 68, 107, 108, 405, 430)	Comparable, List, Set, Map, Queue, Stack, PriorityQueue, Iterator, ListIterator, LinkedList, HashSet, TreeSet, HashMap, TreeMap (generic versions) (p. 557, 572, 583, 601, 608, 610, 625)	
	Sorting methods in Arrays & Collections (p. 648, B-8)	

GLOSSARY

A

absolute path name A string that specifies the location of a resource, such as an HTML file, on a Web server.

abstract Simplified or partial, hiding detail.

abstract class A class that defines attributes and methods for subclasses but is never instantiated.

abstract data type (ADT) A class of objects, a defined set of properties of those objects, and a set of operations for processing the objects.

abstract method A method that is specified but not implemented in an abstract class. The subclasses must implement this method.

Abstract Windowing Toolkit (AWT) A Java package that contains the definitions of classes used to set up graphical user interfaces.

abstraction A simplified view of a task or data structure that ignores complex detail.

accessor A method used to examine an attribute of an object without changing it.

accumulator A variable used for the purpose of summing successive values of some other variable.

activation record An area of computer memory that keeps track of a method call's parameters, local values, return value, and the caller's return address. *See also* **run-time stack**.

actual parameter A variable or expression contained in a method call and passed to that method. *See also* **formal parameter**.

adapter class A Java class that allows another class to implement an interface class without implementing all of its methods. *See also* **interface**.

address An integer value that the computer can use to reference a location. Often called address of a memory location.

aggregation A relationship between two classes in which instances of one class are contained in an instance of the other class.

algorithm A finite sequence of effective statements that, when applied to a problem, will solve it.

alias A situation in which two or more names in a program can refer to the same memory location. An alias can cause subtle side effects.

analysis The phase of the software life cycle in which the programmer describes what the program will do.

applet A Java program that can be downloaded and run on a Web browser.

application software Programs that allow human users to accomplish specialized tasks, such as word processing or database management.

argument A value or expression passed in a method call.

arithmetic expression A sequence of operands and operators that computes a value.

arithmetic/logic unit (ALU) The part of the central processing unit that performs arithmetic operations and evaluates expressions.

arithmetic overflow A situation that arises when the computer's memory cannot represent the number resulting from an arithmetic operation.

array A data structure whose elements are accessed by means of index positions.

array index The relative position of the components of an array.

array list A class that represents a linear sequence of zero or more elements and supports many types of operations, including constant-time access by index position.

ASCII character set The American Standard Code for Information Interchange ordering for a character set (see Appendix D).

assembly language   A computer language that allows the programmer to express operations and memory addresses with mnemonic symbols.

assertion   Special comments used with if statements and loops that state what you expect to happen and when certain conditions will hold.

assignment operator   The symbol =, which is used to store a value in a variable.

assignment statement   A method of putting values into memory locations.

association   A pair of items consisting of a key and a value.

association list   A list in which each value is associated with a unique key.

associative link   A means of recognizing and accessing items in a network structure, such as the World Wide Web.

attribute   A property that a computational object models, such as the balance in a bank account.

B

backing store   A storage area, usually a collection, that holds the data accessed by an iterator.

base address   The memory address of the first cell in an array.

behavior   The set of actions that a class of objects supports.

big-O notation   A formal notation used to express the amount of work done by an algorithm or the amount of memory used by an algorithm.

binary digit   A digit, either 0 or 1, in the binary number system. Program instructions are stored in memory using a sequence of binary digits. *See also* **bit**.

binary search   The process of examining a middle value of a sorted array to see which half contains the value in question and halving until the value is located.

binary search tree   A binary tree in which each node's left child is less than that node and each node's right child is greater than that node.

binary tree   A tree in which each node has at most two children.

binary search algorithm   A method of searching a collection of items with a natural ordering that allows the search to discard ½ of the elements on each pass.

bit   A binary digit.

bitmap   A data structure used to represent the values and positions of points on a computer screen or image.

block   An area of program text, enclosed in Java by the symbols {}, that contains statements and data declarations.

Boolean expression   An expression whose value is either true or false. *See also* **compound Boolean expression** *and* **simple Boolean expression**.

border layout   A Java layout class that allows the programmer to place window objects in five areas (north, south, west, east, and center) of a window. Border layout is the default layout for Java applications.

bottom-up implementation   A method of coding a program that starts with lower-level modules and a test driver module.

boundary condition   A value at which two equivalence classes meet.

boxing   The process whereby the Java virtual machine automatically wraps values of primitive types in objects so they can be stored in collections.

bubble sort   A sorting algorithm that swaps consecutive elements that are out of order to bubble the elements to the top or bottom on each pass.

bucket   The location in an array to which an item is hashed using the chaining method of collision processing. A bucket also holds a linked list of items.

buffer   A block of memory into which data are placed for transmission to a program, usually with file or string processing.

button object   A window object that allows the user to select an action by clicking a mouse.

byte   A sequence of bits used to encode a character in memory. *See also* **word**.

byte code   The kind of object code generated by a Java compiler and interpreted by a Java virtual machine. Byte code is platform independent.

C

call   Any reference to a method by an executable statement. Also referred to as **invoke**.

call stack The trace of method calls that appears when Java throws an exception during program execution.

cancellation error A condition in which data are lost because of differences in the precision of the operands.

cast An operator that is used to convert a value of one type to a value of a different type (e.g., `double` to `int`).

c-curve A fractal shape that resembles the letter C.

central processing unit (CPU) A major hardware component that consists of the arithmetic/logic unit and the control unit.

chaining A strategy of resolving collisions in which the items that hash to the same location are stored in a linked structure.

chains The linked structures used in the chaining method of resolving collisions.

character set The list of characters available for data and program statements.

check box A window object that allows the user to check a labeled box.

children Elements that directly succeed a given element in a hierarchical collection.

circular linked list A linked structure in which the next pointer of the last node is aimed at the first node.

class A description of the attributes and behavior of a set of computational objects.

class constant A constant that is visible to all instances of a class and, if public, is accessed by specifying the class name. For example, `Math.PI` is a class constant.

class diagram A graphical notation that describes the relationships among the classes in a software system.

class (static) method A method that is invoked when a message is sent to a class. For example, `Math.sqrt` is a class method. *See also* **message**.

class (static) variable A variable that is visible to all instances of a class and, if public, is accessed by specifying the class name.

client A computational object that receives a service from another computational object.

client/server relationship A means of describing the organization of computing resources in which one resource provides a service to another resource.

clustering A phenomenon in which several items are placed in adjacent array locations during hashing.

coding The process of writing executable statements that are part of a program to solve a problem. *See also* **implementation**.

cohesive method A method designed to accomplish a single task.

collaboration diagram A graphical notation that describes the manner in which objects communicate in a software system.

collection A group of data elements that can be treated as one thing. A collection tracks a number of elements, which can be added or removed.

collision A situation that takes place when two items hash to the same array location.

combinatorial explosion A multiplicative growth.

comments Nonexecutable statements used to make a program more readable.

comparator An object whose purpose is to compare elements in a sorted collection.

compatible type Expressions that have the same base type. A formal parameter and an actual parameter must be of compatible type, and the operands of an assignment statement must be of compatible type.

compilation error An error detected when the program is being compiled. *See also* **design error, runtime error,** *and* **syntax error**.

compiler A computer program that automatically converts instructions in a high-level language to machine language.

complete code coverage A set of tests in which every line in a program is executed at least once.

complexity analysis The process of deriving a formula that expresses the rate of growth of work or memory as a function of the size of the data or problem that it solves. *See also* **big-O notation**.

component An object that supports the display of an image, such as a button, menu item, or window, in a graphical user interface.

compound assignment An assignment operation that performs a designated operation, such as addition, before storing the result in a variable.

compound Boolean expression Refers to the complete expression when logical connectives and negation are used to generate Boolean values. *See also* **Boolean expression** *and* **simple Boolean expression**.

compound statement A statement that uses the symbols { and } to group several statements and data declarations as a unit. *See also* **block**.

concatenation An operation in which the contents of one data structure are placed after the contents of another data structure.

concrete class A class that can be instantiated. *See also* **abstract class**.

conditional statement *See* **selection statement**.

conjunction The connection of two Boolean expressions using the logical operator && (AND), returning false if at least one of the expressions is false or true if they are both true.

constant A symbol whose value cannot be changed.

constructor A method that is run when an object is instantiated, usually to initialize that object's instance variables.

contained class A class that is used to define a data object within another class.

container A Java class that allows the programmer to group window objects for placement in a window.

content-based operation An operation that involves a search for a given element irrespective of its position in a collection.

contiguous memory Computer memory that is organized so that the data are accessible in adjacent cells.

control statement A type of statement that chooses alternative courses of action based on the truth or falsity of a given condition. *See also* **if-else statement** *and* **while loop**.

control structure A structure that controls the flow of execution of program statements.

control unit The part of the central processing unit that controls the operation of the rest of the computer.

coordinate system A grid that allows a programmer to specify positions of points in a plane or of pixels on a computer screen.

counter A variable used to count the number of times some process is completed.

count-controlled loop A loop that stops when a counter variable reaches a specified limit.

current position indicator The pointer in a positional list that locates the item about to be accessed with a next or a previous operation.

D

data The particular characters that are used to represent information in a form suitable for storage, processing, and communication.

data flow diagram A graphical depiction of the communication between program components that share data.

data input stream A Java class that supports the input of data from a binary file.

data output stream A Java class that supports the output of data to a binary file.

data type A formal description of the set of values that a variable can have.

data validation The process of examining data prior to its use in a program.

debugging The process of eliminating errors, or "bugs," from a program.

decrement To decrease the value of a variable.

default constructor A method that Java provides for creating objects of a class. The programmer can override this method to do extra things.

definition list An HTML structure that allows an author to display a keyed list on a Web page.

density ratio A measure of the degree to which an array is filling with items, computed by dividing the number of items by the array's capacity.

dependency A relationship between two classes in which an instance of one class uses an instance of the other class to perform a task.

design The phase of the software life cycle in which the programmer describes how the program will accomplish its tasks.

design error An error such that a program runs, but unexpected results are produced. Also referred to as a logic error. *See also* **compilation error, runtime error,** *and* **syntax error.**

dialog box A type of window that pops up to display information or receive it from the user.

dictionary A data structure that allows the programmer to access items by specifying key values.

DOS development environment A set of software tools that allows you to edit, compile, run, and debug programs using the DOS operating system.

double A Java data type used to represent numbers with a decimal point, e.g., a real number or a floating-point number.

doubly linked structure A linked structure in which each node has a pointer to the previous node and a pointer to the next node.

do-while loop A post-test loop examining a Boolean expression after causing a statement to be executed. *See also* **for loop, loops,** *and* **while loop.**

driver A method used to test other methods.

dynamic memory Memory allocated under program control from the heap and accessed by means of pointers. *See also* **heap** *and* **pointer.**

dynamic structure A data structure that may expand or contract during execution of a program. *See also* **dynamic memory.**

E

element A value that is stored in an array or a collection.

empty link *See* **null value.**

empty statement A semicolon used to indicate that no action is to be taken. Also referred to as a **null statement.**

encapsulation The process of hiding and restricting access to the implementation details of a data structure.

end-of-file marker A special marker inserted by the machine to indicate the end of the data file.

end-of-line character A special character ('\n') used to indicate the end of a line of characters in a string or a file stream.

enhanced for loop A special type of for loop that traverses an array or array list from beginning to end, binding a local variable to each element in the array or list.

enumeration A user-defined type that consists of a set of symbols.

entry-controlled loop *See* **pretest loop.**

equivalence class All the sets of test data that exercise a program in the same manner.

error *See* **compilation error, design error, logic error, run-time error,** *and* **syntax error.**

event An occurrence, such as a button click or a mouse motion, that can be detected and processed by a program.

event-driven loop A process, usually hidden in the operating system, that waits for an event, notifies a program that an event has occurred, and returns to wait for more events.

exception An abnormal state or error that occurs during runtime and is signaled by the operating system.

exception-driven loop The use of exceptions to implement a normal loop, usually for file input.

execute To carry out the instructions of a program.

exit-controlled loop *See* **post-test loop.**

explicit type conversion The use of an operation by a programmer to convert the type of a data object.

exponential form *See* **floating-point.**

expression tree A tree in which each leaf node contains a number and each interior node contains an operator.

extended if statement Nested selection in which additional if-else statements are used in the else option. *See also* **nested if statement.**

external image An image displayed when the user clicks a link on a Web page.

external pointer A special pointer that allows users to access the nodes in a linked list.

extreme condition Data at the limits of validity.

F

Fibonacci numbers   A series of numbers generated by taking the sum of the previous two numbers in the series. The series begins with the numbers 1 and 2.

field width   The number of columns used for the output of text. *See also* **formatting**.

file   A data structure that resides on a secondary storage medium.

file input stream   A Java class used to connect a program to a file for input.

file output stream   A Java class used to connect a program to a file for output.

final method   A method that cannot be implemented by a subclass.

fixed-point   A method of writing real numbers in which the decimal is placed where it belongs in the number. *See also* **floating-point**.

floating-point   A method for writing numbers in scientific notation to accommodate numbers that may have very large or very small values. *See also* **fixed-point**.

flow layout   A Java layout class that allows the user to place window objects in wrap-around rows in a window. Flow layout is the default layout for applets.

flowchart   A diagram that displays the flow of control of a program. *See also* **control structure**.

flushing   The process of clearing an output buffer before closing an output file stream.

font   The kind of typeface used for text, such as Courier and Times Roman.

for loop   A structured loop consisting of an initializer expression, a termination expression, an update expression, and a statement.

forgetful bitmap problem   A problem that occurs when an image is lost when the user resizes or minimizes a window.

formal parameter   A name, introduced in a method definition, that is replaced by an actual parameter when the method is called.

formal specification   The set of preconditions and postconditions of a method.

formatting   Designating the desired field width when displaying text. *See also* **field width**.

fractal geometry   A theory of shapes that are reflected in various phenomena, such as coastlines, water flow, and price fluctuations.

fractal object   A type of mathematical object that maintains self-sameness when viewed at greater levels of detail.

frame   A Java class that defines the window for an application. *See also* **application software**.

free list   An area of memory used to allocate storage for objects.

front   The end of a queue from which elements are removed.

G

garbage collection   The automatic process of reclaiming memory when the data of a program no longer need it.

general tree   A tree in which each node can have zero or more children.

generic array list   A type of array list that allows the programmer to declare the element type that is expected when the list is created.

generic comparable   An interface that elements in a generic sorted collection must implement.

generic method   A method that has a single implementation but also has type variables that allow it to be used with data of different actual types.

global identifier   A name that can be used by all of the methods of a class.

global variable   *See* **global identifier**.

graph collection   A collection whose elements may have zero or more predecessors and successors.

graphical user interface (GUI)   A means of communication between human beings and computers that uses a pointing device for input and a bitmapped screen for output. The bitmap displays images of windows and window objects such as buttons, text fields, and pull-down menus. The user interacts with the interface by using the mouse to directly manipulate the window objects. *See also* **window object**.

graphics context   In Java, an object associated with a component where the images for that component are drawn.

grid layout   A Java layout class that allows the user to place window objects in a two-dimensional grid in the window.

H

hacking   The use of clever techniques to write a program, often for the purpose of gaining access to protected resources on networks.

hardware   The computing machine and its support devices.

has-a **relationship**   A relationship between two classes in which one class contains an instance of the other class.

hash code   A number that is used to determine the location of an item in an array.

hash function   A method of generating a hash code in constant time.

hashing   A method by which the position of an item in a collection is related to the item's content and can be determined in constant time.

head   The first element in a list.

heap   A tree in which each node is less than or equal to either of its children. An area of computer memory in which storage for dynamic data is available.

heap property   The relationship that characterizes nodes and their children in a heap (e.g., each node is less than or equal to either of its children).

heap underflow   A condition in which memory leakage causes dynamic memory to become unavailable.

helper method   A method used within the implementation of a class but not used by clients of that class.

hierarchical collection   A collection whose elements may have zero or more successors but at most one predecessor.

high-level language   Any programming language that uses words and symbols to make it relatively easy to read and write a program. *See also* **assembly language** *and* **machine language.**

hyperlinks   An item in a hypertext document that allows the user to navigate to another document.

hypermedia   A data structure that allows the user to access different kinds of information (text, images, sound, video, applications) by traversing links.

hypertext   A data structure that allows the user to access different chunks of text by traversing links.

hypertext markup language (HTML)   A programming language that allows the user to create pages for the World Wide Web.

I

identifiers   Words that must be created according to a well-defined set of rules but can have any meaning subject to these rules.

identity   The property of an object that it is the same thing at different points in time, even though the values of its attributes might change.

`if-else` **statement**   A selection statement that allows a program to perform alternative actions based on a condition.

immutable object   An object whose internal data or state cannot be changed.

implementation   The phase of the software life cycle in which the program is coded in a programming language.

increment   The process of increasing a number by 1.

index   *See* **array index.**

index-based operation   An operation that accesses an element by specifying its position in a collection. For lists, the position is specified as an integer ranging from 0 to the size of the collection minus 1.

infinite loop   A loop in which the controlling condition is not changed in such a manner to allow the loop to terminate.

infinite recursion   The state of a running program that occurs when a recursive method cannot reach a stopping state.

infix form   The form of an expression in which the operator is surrounded by its operands.

information hiding   A condition in which the user of a module does not know the details of how it is implemented, and the implementer of a module does not know the details of how it is used.

inheritance The process by which a subclass can reuse attributes and behavior defined in a superclass. *See also* **subclass** *and* **superclass**.

initializer list A means of expressing a set of data that can be assigned to the cells of an array in one statement.

inline image An image that is loaded when the user accesses a Web page.

input Data obtained by a program during its execution.

input assertion A precondition for a loop.

input device A device that provides information to the computer. Typical input devices are a mouse, keyboard, disk drive, microphone, and network port. *See also* **I/O device** *and* **output device**.

input stream A data object that allows a program to input data from a file or the keyboard.

insertion sort A sorting algorithm that locates an insertion point and takes advantage of partial orderings in an array.

instance A computational object bearing the attributes and behavior specified by a class.

instance method A method that is called when a message is sent to an instance of a class. *See also* **message**.

instance variable Storage for data in an instance of a class.

instantiation The process of creating a new object or instance of a class.

integer arithmetic operations Operations allowed on data of type `int`. These include the operations of addition, subtraction, multiplication, division, and modulus to produce integer answers.

integer overflow A condition in which an integer value is too large to be stored in the computer's memory.

integrated development environment (IDE) A set of software tools that allows you to edit, compile, run, and debug programs within one user interface.

interface A formal statement of how communication occurs between the user of a module (class or method) and its implementer.

interface A Java file that simply specifies the methods to be implemented by another class. A class that implements several interfaces can thus adopt the behavior of several classes.

interior node A node that has at least one child.

invariant expression An assertion that is true before the loop and after each iteration of the loop.

invoke *See* **call**.

I/O device Any device that allows information to be transmitted to or from a computer. *See also* **input device** *and* **output device**.

***is-a* relationship** A relationship between two classes in which one class is a subclass of the other class.

iteration *See* **loops**.

iterative process A running program that executes a loop.

iterator An object that allows clients to navigate a collection by tracking a current position indicator. Basic operations are visiting the next element, testing for the presence of a next element, and removing the element just visited.

J

Java virtual machine (JVM) A program that interprets Java byte codes and executes them.

just-in-time compilation (JIT) A feature of some Java virtual machines that first translates byte codes to the machine's code before executing them.

justification The process of aligning text to the left, the center, or the right within a given number of columns.

K

key An item that is associated with a value and is used to locate this value in a collection.

keyed list A data structure that allows the programmer to access items by using key values.

keywords *See* **reserved words**.

***knows-a* relationship** A relationship between two classes in which one class neither has the other class nor is the other class but instead carries it or displays it or eats it or some other such thing.

L

label object A window object that displays text, usually to describe the roles of other window objects.

leaf A node without children.

left subtree The node and its descendants to the left of a given node in a binary tree.

library A collection of methods and data organized to perform a set of related tasks. *See also* **class** *and* **package**.

lifetime The time during which a data object or method call exists.

linear An increase of work or memory in direct proportion to the size of a problem.

linear collection A collection whose elements have at most one predecessor and at most one successor.

linear collision processing A strategy of resolving collisions that searches the array for the next available empty slot for an item.

linear search *See* **sequential search**.

linked structure A structure in which each item is linked to the next one by means of a pointer. *See also* **recursive data structure**.

list iterator An object that extends an iterator to allow insertions, replacements, and removals of elements from a list.

listener A Java class that detects and responds to events.

literal An element of a language that evaluates to itself, such as 34 or "hi there."

load factor A measure of the degree to which an array is filling with items, computed by dividing the number of items by the array's capacity.

loader A system software tool that places program instructions and data into the appropriate memory locations before program start-up.

local identifier A name whose value is visible only within a method or a nested block.

local variable *See* **local identifier**.

logarithmic An increase of work in proportion to the number of times that the problem size can be divided by 2.

logic error *See* **design error**.

logical operator Either of the logical connective operators && (and), || (or), or ! (negation).

logical size The number of data items actually available in a data structure at a given time. *See also* **physical size**.

logical structure The organization of the components in a data structure, independent of their organization in computer memory.

long A Java data type used to represent large integers.

loop A type of statement that repeatedly executes a set of statements.

loop invariant An assertion that expresses a relationship between variables that remains constant throughout all iterations of the loop.

loop variant An assertion whose truth changes between the first and final execution of the loop.

loop verification The process of guaranteeing that a loop performs its intended task.

loops Program statements that cause a process to be repeated. *See also* **do-while** loop, **for** loop, *and* **while** loop.

low-level language *See* **assembly language**.

M

machine language The language used directly by the computer in all its calculations and processing.

main (primary) memory The high-speed internal memory of a computer, also referred to as random access memory (RAM). *See also* **memory** *and* **secondary memory**.

main unit A computer's main unit contains the central processing unit (CPU) and the main (primary) memory; it is hooked to one or more **input devices** and one or more **output devices**.

mainframe Large computers typically used by major companies and universities. *See also* **microcomputer** *and* **minicomputer**.

mantissa/exponent notation A notation used to express floating-point numbers.

map An unordered collection in which each value is associated with a unique key.

markup tag A syntactic form in the hypertext markup language used to create different elements displayed on a Web page.

mathematical induction A method of proving that parts of programs are correct by reasoning from a base case and an induction hypothesis to a general conclusion.

matrix   A two-dimensional array that provides range checking and can be resized.

megabyte   Shorthand for 1 million bytes.

memex   A hypothetical machine proposed by Vannevar Bush that would allow users to store and retrieve information via associative links.

memory   The ordered sequence of storage cells that can be accessed by address. Instructions and variables of an executing program are temporarily held here. *See also* **main memory** *and* **secondary memory**.

memory location   A storage cell that can be accessed by address. *See also* **memory**.

menu-driven program   A program that allows the user to repeatedly select a command from a list of command options.

menu item   A window object that displays as an option on a pull-down menu or pop-up menu.

merge   The process of combining lists. Typically refers to files or arrays.

merge sort   An *n*log*n* sort algorithm that uses a divide-and-conquer strategy.

message   A symbol used by a client to ask an object to perform a service. *See also* **method**.

message box   A window object used to display text to a user, allowing the user to close the box by clicking a button.

method   A chunk of code that can be treated as a unit and invoked by name. A method is called when a message is sent to an object. *See also* **class method** *and* **instance method**.

method heading   The portion of a method implementation containing the function's name, parameter declarations, and return type.

microcomputer   A computer capable of fitting on a laptop or desktop, generally used by one person at a time. *See also* **mainframe** *and* **minicomputer**.

minicomputer   A small version of a mainframe computer. It usually is used by several people at once. *See also* **mainframe** *and* **microcomputer**.

mixed-mode   Expressions containing data of different types; the values of these expressions will be of either type, depending on the rules for evaluating them.

modal   A state in which the computer user cannot exit without explicitly signaling the computer, usually with an "Accept" or "Cancel" option.

model/view/controller pattern   A design plan in which the roles and responsibilities of the system are cleanly divided among data management (model), user interface display (view), and user event handling (controller) tasks.

modem   A device that connects a computer to a telephone system to transmit data.

module   An independent unit that is part of a larger development. Can be a method or a class (set of methods and related data).

module specifications   In the case of a method, a description of data received, information returned, and task performed by a module. In the case of a class, a description of the attributes and behavior.

multidimensional array   An array whose elements are accessed by specifying more than one index.

mutator   A method used to change the value of an attribute of an object.

mutually comparable   A property of two items such that they can be related by less than, greater than, or equal to.

N

negation   The use of the logical operator ! (not) with a Boolean expression, returning true if the expression is false, and false if the expression is true.

nested `if` statement   A selection statement used within another selection statement. *See also* **extended `if` statement**.

nested loop   A loop as one of the statements in the body of another loop.

nested selection   Any combination of selection statements within selection statements. *See also* **selection statement**.

network   A collection of resources that are linked together for communication.

node   A component of a linked structure, consisting of a data item and one or more pointers to other nodes.

null pointer   A special value that indicates the end of a linked structure or an empty linked structure.

null statement *See* **empty statement.**

null value A special value that indicates that no object can be accessed.

O

object A collection of data and operations, in which the data can be accessed and modified only by means of the operations.

object code *See* **object program.**

object heap An area of memory used to allocate storage for objects.

object-oriented programming The construction of software systems that use objects.

object program The machine code version of the source program.

off-by-one error Usually seen with loops, this error shows up as a result that is one less or one greater than the expected value.

offset The quantity added to the base address of an array to locate the address of an array cell.

one-dimensional array An array in which each data item is accessed by specifying a single index.

one-way list A list that supports navigation in one direction only.

operating system A large program that allows the user to communicate with the hardware and performs various management tasks.

option panes Window objects that provide standard services, such as prompting for input values, yes/no queries, and message boxes.

ordinal data type A data type ordered in some association with the integers; each integer is the ordinal of an associated value of the data type.

origin The point (0,0) in a coordinate system.

output Information that is produced by a program.

output assertion A postcondition for a loop.

output device A device that allows you to see the results of a program. Typically, it is a monitor, printer, speaker, or network port. *See also* **input device** *and* **I/O device.**

output stream A data object that allows a program to output data to a file or the terminal screen.

overflow In arithmetic operations, a value may be too large for the computer's memory location. A meaningless value may be assigned or an error message may result. *See also* **underflow.**

overloading The process of using the same operator symbol or identifier to refer to many different functions. *See also* **polymorphism.**

overriding The process of reimplementing a method already implemented in a superclass.

P

package A group of related classes in a named directory.

panel A window object whose purpose is to contain other window objects.

parallel arrays Arrays of the same length but with different component data types.

parameter *See* **argument.**

parameter list A list of parameters. An actual parameter list is contained in a method call. A formal parameter list is contained in a method heading.

parent The immediate superclass of a class; A given node's predecessor in a tree.

parse tree A tree that contains the structure of a sentence.

peripheral memory *See* **memory** *and* **secondary memory.**

persistence The property of a data model that allows it to survive various runs of an application. *See also* **serialization.**

physical size The number of memory units available for storing data items in a data structure. *See also* **logical size.**

pivot A data item around which an array is subdivided during the quicksort.

pixel A picture element or dot of color used to display images on a computer screen.

pointer A reference to an object that allows you to access it.

polymorphism The property of one operator symbol or method identifier having many meanings. *See also* **overloading.**

pop The operation that removes an element from a stack.

portable Able to be transferred to different applications or computers without changes.

positional list A list in which a client navigates by moving a current position indicator.

position-based operation An operation performed with respect to a current position indicator in a collection.

postcondition A statement of what is true after a certain action is taken.

postfix form The form of an expression in which the operator follows its operands.

post-test loop A loop in which the control condition is tested after the loop is executed. A do-while loop is a post-test loop. Also referred to as an **exit-controlled loop**.

precondition A statement of what is true before a certain action is taken.

prefix form The form of an expression in which the operator precedes its operands.

pretest condition A condition that controls whether or not the body of the loop is executed before going through the loop.

pretest loop A loop in which the control condition is tested before the loop is executed. A while loop is a pretest loop. Also referred to as an **entrance-controlled loop**.

primary memory See **main memory** and **memory**.

priming input statement An input statement that must be executed before a loop control condition is tested.

primitive data type A data type such as char, int, double, or boolean whose values are stored directly in variables of that type. Primitive data types are always passed by value when they are parameters in Java and copied during assignment statements.

print stream A Java class that sends text output to the terminal window.

priority queue A collection in which the items are ordered according to priority.

private inner class A class that is defined as a helper class within another class.

private method A method that is accessible only within the scope of a class definition.

private variable A variable that is accessible only within the scope of a class definition.

procedural programming A style of programming that decomposes a program into a set of methods or procedures.

program A set of instructions that tells the machine (the hardware) what to do.

program proof An analysis of a program that attempts to verify the correctness of program results.

program walk-through The process of carefully following, using pencil and paper, steps the computer uses to solve the problem given in a program. It is also referred to as a **trace**.

programming language Formal language that computer scientists use to give instructions to the computer.

protected variable A variable that is accessible only within the scope of a class definition, within the class definition of a subclass, or within the class's package.

prototype A trimmed-down version of a class or software system that still functions and allows the programmer to study its essential features.

pseudocode A stylized half-English, half-code language written in English but suggesting Java code.

public method A method that is accessible to any program component that uses the class.

public variable A variable that is accessible to any program component that uses the class.

pull-down menu A window object that allows the user to pull down and select from a list of menu items. See also **menu item**.

push The operation that adds an element to a stack.

Q

quadratic An increase of work or memory in proportion to the square of the size of the problem.

quadratic collision processing A strategy of resolving collisions that searches the array for the next available empty slot for an item, using the square of an incrementally increasing distance to leapfrog potential clusters.

quality assurance The ongoing process of making sure that a software product is developed to the highest standards possible subject to the ever-present constraints of time and money.

query-controlled input A style of taking multiple user inputs and asking the user if she wants to continue after each one.

queue A data structure that allows the programmer to insert items only at one end and remove them from the other end.

quicksort A sorting technique that moves elements around a pivot and recursively sorts the elements to the left and the right of the pivot.

R

ragged array A two-dimensional array in which each row may have a different length.

random access data structure A data structure in which the time to access a data item does not depend on its position in the structure.

range-bound error The situation that occurs when an attempt is made to use an array index value that is less than 0 or greater than or equal to the size of the array.

rear The end of a queue to which elements are added.

recursion The process of a subprogram calling itself. A clearly defined stopping state must exist. Any recursive subprogram can be rewritten using **iteration**.

recursive data structure A data structure that has either a simple form or a form that is composed of other instances of the same data structure. *See also* **linked structure**.

recursive method A method that calls itself.

recursive step A step in the recursive process that solves a similar problem of smaller size and eventually leads to a termination of the process.

recursive subprogram *See* **recursion**.

reference type A data type such as array, String, or any other Java class, whose instances are not stored directly in variables of that type. References or pointers to these objects are stored instead. References to objects are passed when they are parameters in Java, and only the references, not the objects, are copied during assignment statements.

refreshable image An image that is redisplayed when the user resizes or minimizes a window.

relational operator An operator used for comparison of data items of the same type.

relative path name A string that specifies the location of a resource without mentioning the Web server.

repetition *See* **loops**.

representational error A condition in which the precision of data is reduced because of the order in which operations are performed.

reserved words Words that have predefined meanings that cannot be changed. A list of reserved words for Java is in Appendix B.

return type The type of value returned by a method.

right subtree The node and its descendants to the right of a given node in a binary tree.

robust The state in which a program is protected against most possible crashes from bad data and unexpected values.

root The node in a tree that has no predecessor.

round-off error A condition in which a portion of a real number is lost because of the way it is stored in the computer's memory.

round-robin scheduling The use of a queue to rotate processes for access to a resource.

run-time error An error detected when, after compilation is completed, an error message results instead of the correct output. *See also* **compilation error, design error, exception,** *and* **syntax error**.

run-time stack An area of computer memory reserved for local variables and parameters of method calls.

S

scanning The process of picking words or tokens out of a stream of characters.

scope of identifier The largest block in which the identifier is available.

screen coordinate system A coordinate system used by most programming languages in which the origin is in the upper-left corner of the screen, window, or panel, and the *y* values increase toward the bottom of the drawing area.

secondary memory An auxiliary device for memory, usually a disk or magnetic tape. *See also* **main memory** *and* **memory**.

selection The process by which a method or a variable of an instance or a class is accessed.

selection sort A sorting algorithm that sorts the components of an array in either ascending or descending order. This process puts the smallest or largest element in the top position and repeats the process on the remaining array components. *See also* **quicksort**.

selection statement A control statement that selects some particular logical path based on the value of an expression. Also referred to as a **conditional statement**.

self-documenting code Code that is written using descriptive identifiers.

semantics The rules for interpreting the meaning of a program in a language.

sentinel node A special node in a linked structure that contains no data but instead marks the beginning or end of the structure.

sentinel value A special value that indicates the end of a set of data or of a process.

sequential access A situation in which access to a data item depends on its position in the data structure.

sequential search The process of searching a list by examining the first component and then examining successive components in the order in which they occur. Also referred to as a **linear search**.

sequential traversal The process of visiting each data item in an array or a linked list from beginning to end.

serialization A mechanism that maintains the persistence of objects in a data model. *See also* **persistence**.

server A computational object that provides a service to another computational object.

set An unordered collection of unique items.

short A Java data type used to represent small integers.

short-circuit evaluation The process by which a compound Boolean expression halts evaluation and returns the value of the first subexpression that evaluates to true, in the case of ||, or false, in the case of &&.

side effect A change in a variable that is the result of some action taken in a program, usually from within a method.

simple Boolean expression An expression in which two numbers or variable values are compared using a single relational operator. *See also* **Boolean expression** and **compound Boolean expression**.

singly linked structure A collection of items in which each item except the last has a link or reference to the next item in the structure.

software Programs that make the machine (the hardware) do something, such as word processing, database management, or games.

software development life cycle (SDLC) The process of development, maintenance, and demise of a software system. Phases include analysis, design, coding, testing/verification, maintenance, and obsolescence.

software engineering The process of developing and maintaining large software systems.

software reuse The process of building and maintaining software systems out of existing software components.

sorted collection A collection whose elements are arranged in sorted order.

sorted map A type of map that allows clients to visit its keys in sorted order.

sorted set A type of set that allows clients to visit its items in sorted order.

source code The program text as viewed by the human who creates or reads it, prior to compilation.

source program A program written by a programmer.

stack A dynamic data structure in which access can be made from only one end. Referred to as a LIFO (last-in, first-out) structure.

stack overflow error A situation that occurs when the computer runs out of memory to allocate for its call stack. This situation usually arises during an infinite recursion.

stand-alone program A Java program that runs directly on a computer without the aid of a Web browser.

state The set of all the values of the variables of a program at any point during its execution.

statement An individual instruction in a program.

statement block (synonym compound statement) A form by which a sequence of statements and data declarations can be treated as a unit.

stepwise refinement The process of repeatedly subdividing tasks into subtasks until each subtask is easily accomplished. *See also* **structured programming** *and* **top-down implementation**.

stopping state The well-defined termination of a recursive process.

stream A channel in which data are passed from sender to receiver.

string An abbreviated name for a string literal.

string literal One or more characters, enclosed in double quotation marks, used as a constant in a program.

string tokenizer A Java class that allows the programmer to access text in a string one word at a time.

structure chart A graphical method of indicating the relationship between modules when designing the solution to a problem.

structured programming Programming that parallels a solution to a problem achieved by top-down implementation. *See also* **stepwise refinement** *and* **top-down implementation**.

stub programming The process of using incomplete functions to test data transmission among the functions.

subclass A class that inherits attributes and behavior from another class.

subscript *See* **array index**.

substring A string that represents a segment of another string.

superclass The class from which a subclass inherits attributes and behavior. *See also* **inheritance** *and* **subclass**.

Swing Toolkit A set of Java classes used to create programs with graphical user interfaces.

syntax The rules for constructing well-formed programs in a language.

syntax error An error in spelling, punctuation, or placement of certain key symbols in a program. *See also* **compilation error, design error,** *and* **runtime error**.

system software The programs that allow users to write and execute other programs, including operating systems such as Windows and MacOS.

T

tail The last element in a list.

tail-recursive The property that a recursive algorithm has of performing no work after each recursive step. *See also* **recursion**.

task-controlled loop A type of loop that terminates when it is finished performing some task.

terminal I/O interface A user interface that allows the user to enter input from a keyboard and view output as text in a window.

text area object A window object that provides a scrollable region within which the user can view or enter several lines of text.

text field object A window object in which the user can view or enter a single line of text.

text files Files that contain characters and are readable and writable by text editors.

token An individual word or symbol.

top The end of a stack where elements are added or removed.

top-down implementation A method for coding by which the programmer starts with a top-level task and implements subtasks. Each subtask is then subdivided into smaller subtasks. This process is repeated until each remaining subtask is easily coded. *See also* **stepwise refinement** and **structured programming**.

trace *See* **program walk-through**.

truth table A means of listing all of the possible values of a Boolean expression.

turtle graphics A set of methods that manipulate a pen in a graphics window.

two-dimensional array An array in which each data item is accessed by specifying a pair of indices.

type *See* **data type**.

type parameter The type of element used in a generic collection, which the programmer must supply when a variable of that collection type is declared and an object of that type is instantiated.

type promotion The process of converting a less inclusive data type, such as `int`, to a more inclusive data type, such as `double`.

type variable A symbol that specifies an element type in the definition of a generic type.

U

ubiquitous computing A situation in which computational resources are accessible to people no matter where they are.

unboxing The process whereby the Java virtual machine automatically unwraps values of primitive types from objects when they are retrieved from collections.

underflow A value that is too small to be represented by a computer; it is automatically replaced by its negation. *See also* **overflow**.

unicode A character set that uses 16 bits to represent over 65,000 possible characters. These include the ASCII character set as well as symbols and ideograms in many international languages. *See also* **ASCII character set**.

Unified Modeling Language (UML) A graphical notation for describing a software system in various phases of development.

uniform resource locator (URL) The address of a page on the World Wide Web.

unordered collection A collection whose elements are in no particular order from the client's perspective.

user-defined class A new data type introduced and defined by the programmer.

user-defined method A new function introduced and defined by the programmer.

user-friendly Describes an interactive program with clear, easy-to-follow messages for the user.

V

value An item that is associated with a key and is located by a key in a collection.

variable A memory location, referenced by an identifier, whose value can be changed during execution of a program.

vector A one-dimensional array that supports resizing, insertions, and removals.

virtual machine A software tool that behaves like a high-level computer.

virus A program that can enter a computer and perhaps destroy information.

visibility modifier A symbol (`public`, `protected`, or `private`) that specifies the kind of access that clients have to a server's data and methods.

void method A method that returns no value.

W

waterfall model A series of steps in which a software system trickles down from analysis to design to implementation. *See also* **software development life cycle**.

while loop A pretest loop that examines a Boolean expression before causing a statement to be executed.

window A rectangular area of a computer screen that can contain window objects. Windows typically can be resized, minimized, maximized, zoomed, or closed. *See also* **frame**.

window object A computational object that displays an image, such as a button or a text field, in a window and supports interaction with the user.

word A unit of memory consisting of one or more bytes. Words can be addressed.

wrapper class A class designed to contain a primitive data type so that the primitive type can behave like a reference type. *See also* **primitive data type** *and* **reference type**.